READING MASTER

READING
MASTER

KB056931

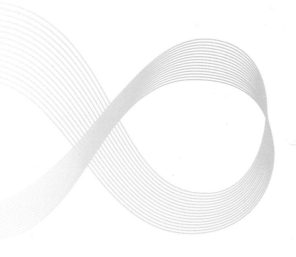

수능 실전

WRITERS

박선하
백기창
서정환
여기상
이혜은
조금희

STAFF

발행인 정선욱
퍼블리싱 총괄 남형주
개발 김태원 김한길 박하영 양소현 송경미
기획·디자인·마케팅 조비호 김정인 강윤정
유통·제작 서준성 신성철

Reading Master 수능 실전   202405 제3판 1쇄   202407 제3판 2쇄

펴낸곳 이투스에듀(주) 서울시 서초구 남부순환로 2547
고객센터 1599-3225
등록번호 제2007-000035호
ISBN 979-11-389-2555-6 [53740]

• 이 책은 저작권법에 따라 보호받는 저작물이므로 무단전재와 무단복제를 금합니다.
• 잘못 만들어진 책은 구입처에서 교환해 드립니다.

학습 목표별 수능 영어 독해의 체계적 완성

READING MASTER

Reading Master 수능 유형

수능과 내신 대비가 가능한 고등 입문 유형 학습서

수능 독해의 각 유형별 특징 및 해결 전략을 학습하고 이를 풍부한 연습 문제에 적용해보면서 전략적인 수능 대비가 가능하도록 하였습니다. 또한 앞에서 학습한 지문을 변형하여 주요 내신 출제 패턴을 학습하고 연습 문제에 적용해보면서 내신 대비까지 가능하도록 하였습니다.

Reading Master 수능 실전

2~3등급을 목표로 하는 학생들의 실전서

수능 실전 감각을 기를 수 있도록 모든 유형을 골고루 배치한 하프 모의고사 15회를 수록하여 회별로 균형 있게 다양한 유형의 독해 학습이 가능하도록 하였습니다. 또한 고난도 유형의 문제만 집중 연습할 수 있는 고난도 모의고사 5회를 수록하여 심층적인 독해 학습을 통해 고난도 문항 대비까지 가능하도록 하였습니다.

Reading Master 수능 고난도

상위권을 위한 검증된 고퀄리티의 고난도 실전서

실제 성적 데이터를 통해 검증된 고난도 우수 문항을 선별하여 회별 12문항씩 고난도 모의고사 15회를 수록하였습니다. 오답률이 높은 고난도 문항을 풀며 상위권 학생들의 집중적인 고난도 학습이 가능하도록 하였습니다. 또한 앞에서 학습한 지문을 유형을 바꾸어 출제한 REVIEW 모의고사 5회를 수록하여 복습과 테스트가 동시에 가능하도록 하였습니다.

FEATURES

PART I 하프 모의고사

하프 모의고사

수능 영어 독해의 모든 유형을 난이도를 고려하여 회별 14문항씩 15회를 수록하였습니다.

주어진 시간 안에 문제를 풀며 실제 수능 문제를 푸는 것 같은 실전 감각을 기를 수 있도록 하였습니다.

GRAMMAR REVIEW

각 회별 지문에 나온 문장을 그대로 활용하여 만든 드릴식 문법 문제를 수록하였습니다. 수능/내신에 자주 출제되는 필수 문법을 점검하면서 회별 학습을 마무리할 수 있습니다.

부록

WORDS LIST

하프 모의고사와 고난도 모의고사의 어휘를 회별로 모아 정리하여 어휘 학습의 편의성을 높였습니다.

WORDS REVIEW

각 회별 암기한 어휘를 테스트하면서 복습할 수 있도록 하였습니다.

PART II 고난도 모의고사

고난도 모의고사

수능 영어 독해 심화 학습이 가능하도록 어려운 유형
만 선별하여 회별 8문항씩 5회를 수록하였습니다.
고난도 유형의 문제를 집중적으로 풀어보며 수능 독
해에 대한 적응력과 자신감이 높아질 수 있도록 하였
습니다.

정답 및 해설

지문 해석, 해설, 매력적 오답, TEXT FLOW, 구문 등을 제시하여 학습자가 스스로
학습하기에 어려움이 없도록 상세한 풀이를 제공하였습니다.

매력적 오답

매력적 오답을 분석하여 학생들이 함정에 빠지지 않고 정답을 찾을 수 있도록 하였
습니다.

TEXT FLOW

지문의 논리적 흐름을 이해할 수 있도록 지문 구조를 분석하여 요약 정리한 TEXT
FLOW를 수록하였습니다.

CONTENTS

PART I 하프 모의고사

PART II 고난도 모의고사

부록

PART

하프
모의고사

01 다음 글의 목적으로 가장 적절한 것은?

Dear Joan, Jane, and Beth:

It is with some difficulty that I write this letter, but I think it is important. I saw Harriet and her husband Hank in the grocery store yesterday. We all know that she has been ailing for some time, but it is now obvious that she is seriously ill. Hank confirms it, but says her spirits are good and in most every way she is the Harriet we have known and loved for so long. I think this is the time to demonstrate how strong our friendship is. I would like to gather a small group of friends to visit her at home. We can arrange with Hank for the right time, and bring some treats. I hope we can try to put something together for next week. I will be in touch soon.

Sincerely,
Monica

① 부부 동반 모임의 일자를 변경하려고
② 아픈 친구를 문병하자는 제안을 하려고
③ 유능한 간병인을 구할 수 있는지 문의하려고
④ 병원 자원봉사에 참여해 준 것에 감사하려고
⑤ 식료품을 공동 구매할 의향이 있는지 확인하려고

02 다음 글에서 필자가 주장하는 바로 가장 적절한 것은?

Imagine you are swimming in a tropical ocean in the middle of a storm. You are being thrown around haphazardly by the waves and wind. So you decide to dive down several miles into the ocean. As you swim beyond the rough surface waters, past fish and seaweed, deeper and deeper, you reach still and peaceful waters. The water is warm and you are no longer being thrown around. The deeper you dive, the quieter and calmer the waters around you become. Even as the storm rages at the surface above, deep down below where you remain, it is still and calm. Just like the tranquility at the bottom of the ocean, the spirit residing in your physical body is untouchable by the storm of events around you. You can endure any stressful or difficult situation, while remaining calm within yourself, because your spirit resides in an untouchable place within you. That is what you should do.

*haphazardly: 아무렇게나   **rage: (폭풍우가) 사납게 몰아치다
***tranquility: 평온함

① 고난도 삶의 일부이므로 이겨내려고 하기보다는 받아들여라.
② 평상시의 충분한 휴식을 통해 고난에 대한 면역력을 길러 두라.
③ 고난도 자기 정신을 성장시키므로 항상 낙관적 태도를 유지 하라.
④ 고난에 자기 정신이 무너지지 않도록 평소에 신체 단련에 힘 쓰라.
⑤ 자기 정신의 무사함을 믿고 내적 평온을 유지하며 고난을 견 뎌내라.

03 밑줄 친 has no place for passports가 다음 글에서 의미하는 바로 가장 적절한 것은?

Citizens must have unique privileges of participation in government: voting and holding public office. Otherwise there would be no point to the distinction between citizens and aliens. Citizens may also have special rights to the benefits of residence: rights to enter the country when abroad, for example, which aliens, who may be refused a visa, do not have. Government has special responsibilities of care and concern for citizens and other residents. A nation's economic policy may be designed primarily to favor its own residents, and it may distribute welfare and other benefits to them that it does not distribute to people living in other countries. In all this, a nation may — and to some degree must — discriminate in favor of its own citizens and therefore against those not its own. But the deliberate infliction of injury is different, and government has no right or authority deliberately to injure foreigners for reasons or in circumstances in which it would not be permitted to injure its own citizens. This is emphatically true when the injury is grave. The domain of human rights has no place for passports.

*emphatically: 단연코

① focuses on simplifying complicated procedures
② is closely related to a nation's economic prosperity
③ allows every citizen to visit the places they want to go
④ is grounded on treating everyone without discrimination
⑤ guarantees unique privileges of participation in government

04 다음 글의 주제로 가장 적절한 것은?

When perspective was first used in art during the early Renaissance, it was a revolution in the human conception of space. For the first time, "man's" gaze turned from the heavens above to the "landscape" beyond. Perspective places the individual, for the first time, as the center of his world. We see the picture through the eyes of the beholder. It is through man's eyes, and not God's grace, that we view the world beyond. And everything in the field of view becomes the object of man's attention. Perspective brings human beings into a new spatial realm of subject-object relationships. It is the beginning point for what the sociologist Max Weber would later describe as the "disenchantment of the world."

① how perspective was originally invented
② perspective in art as a typical optical illusion
③ the early Renaissance's artists and their works
④ a strong desire for God that was expressed in art
⑤ the significance of the introduction of perspective in art

05 다음 도표의 내용과 일치하지 <u>않는</u> 것은?

Most In-Demand Programming Languages (2021-2022)

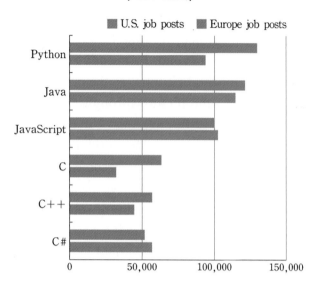

■ U.S. job posts　■ Europe job posts

The above graph shows the most sought-after programming languages by number of job postings in the U.S. and Europe from 2021 to 2022. ① In the U.S., the demand for Python programmers was the highest during this period, with about 130,000 job postings. ② In Europe, however, Java was the most sought-after language, with more than 110,000 job postings, immediately followed by JavaScript and Python. ③ In the U.S., the demand for C# programmers was the smallest, with less than 50,000 job postings. ④ In Europe, the number of job postings for both C and C++ programmers was below 50,000. ⑤ On the other hand, the number of job postings for C# programmers in Europe was over 50,000.

06 다음 글의 밑줄 친 부분 중, 어법상 <u>틀린</u> 것은?

To foster innovation in your organization, you need to attract and recruit people who will be innovative. It may seem ①<u>that</u> you need to develop techniques and instruments to identify innovative people and then hire them. However, ②<u>it</u> is not that simple. True, some people are more naturally innovative than others, but the interplay between the person and his or her environment ultimately ③<u>determine</u> the level of innovativeness. Even a person who has a proven ability to be innovative would find innovating on an ongoing basis ④<u>difficult</u>, if not impossible, if put in a culture and situation that do not foster creativity. The culture could stifle his or her innovation, either because the culture is so comfortable for him or her that new approaches do not come to mind, or ⑤<u>because</u> the culture is so foreign and uncomfortable that it disrupts that person's ability to work and contribute.

*stifle: 억누르다

07 다음 빈칸에 들어갈 말로 가장 적절한 것은?

To become the best at leading, or at anything, you have to challenge yourself, take on stretch assignments, step outside your comfort zone, experiment with new ways of doing things, make mistakes, and learn from failure. These are all just a natural part of the process when you're learning to become the best leader you can be. That's all well and good; however, you're not likely to do these things if there's no one there to teach you, coach you on how to improve, cheer you on and cheer you up, catch you when you fall, and comfort you when you hit the wall. Learning to lead requires getting help from others. _____ is a necessary condition for growth and development, particularly when that learning is challenging. "The single most important thing you can do to ensure your future success," according to the Gallup organization's study of more than 27 million employees worldwide, "is to find someone who has an interest in your development."

① Social support
② Internal conflict
③ Repeated failure
④ Behavior change
⑤ Rational decision

08 다음 빈칸에 들어갈 말로 가장 적절한 것은?

You have probably seen those ads comparing incandescent light bulbs with compact fluorescent light bulbs, the latter of which are being promoted as environmentally sound. If you are a global warming skeptic, or if you base your purchases on more common criteria such as your personal interests, the ads slant toward selling you on _____. In just one example among many, a 60-watt conventional bulb costs $0.75 and lasts one thousand hours, compared to a 14-watt compact fluorescent lamp that costs $2.00 and lasts ten thousand hours. You get the same amount of light from both. The total cost to operate each bulb for ten thousand hours, including the bulb replacement cost, is $59 for the incandescent bulb and $12 for the compact fluorescent lamp. Which one should you buy?

① the long-term cost savings
② the tendency of loss-hating
③ the natural appeal of the new
④ the availability of each device
⑤ the rise of the prices of the device

09 다음 글에서 전체 흐름과 관계 없는 문장은?

Sometimes our intuitions help us develop scientific understandings of the world, and sometimes they hinder them. Most importantly, folk theories are not a reliable means of constructing the boundaries of a phenomenon and should not be attributed explanatory validity. ① For instance, evolutionary biological science tells us that the differences among animal species are not accurately portrayed as taxonomic differences in kind but as differences in degree as measured by genetic proximity. ② Further, species may be more similar than they appear. ③ For example, male capuchinos (birds) can look and sound very different across species, despite being almost identical genetically. ④ Folk knowledge has been the basis for the wide range of activities that sustain a society and its environment in different parts of the world for many centuries. ⑤ Therefore, folk theories do not always provide a useful and accurate conceptual foundation from which to develop scientific theories about how the material world, including religion, works.

*attribute: (성질 등이) 있다고 생각하다
**taxonomic: 분류학상의   ***proximity: 근접성

10 주어진 글 다음에 이어질 글의 순서로 가장 적절한 것은?

Without carbon, physical life is impossible. No other element displays the rich chemical behavior needed to form the range of complex molecular structures life requires.

(A) One of the wonders of Earth is that it is sufficiently carbon-rich and carbon-poor. It carries enough carbon for life but not so much as to interfere with life's atmospheric needs, such as the appropriate pressure and density for efficient operation of lungs and a temperature range (and variability) that supports a wide diversity of active, advanced species.

(B) Too much carbon translates into too much carbon dioxide, carbon monoxide, and methane. In large quantities, these gases are poisonous. In modest quantities, their greenhouse properties keep the planet sufficiently warm for life. In larger quantities, they can heat a planet's surface beyond what physical life can tolerate.

(C) Given that physical life must be carbon-based, why would God make a universe with so little carbon? Researchers have found that the quantity of carbon must be carefully balanced between just enough and not too much because carbon, though essential for life, can also be destructive to life.

① (A) – (C) – (B)   ② (B) – (A) – (C)
③ (B) – (C) – (A)   ④ (C) – (A) – (B)
⑤ (C) – (B) – (A)

11 글의 흐름으로 보아, 주어진 문장이 들어가기에 가장 적절한 곳은?

> The most authoritative source, the *Aircraft Year Book*, compiled the figures from newspaper clippings.

In the early twentieth century, flights in America were almost wholly unregulated. The country had no system of licensing and no requirements for training. (①) Anyone could buy a plane, in any condition, and legally take up paying passengers. (②) The United States was so slack about flying that it didn't even keep track of the number of airplane crashes and fatalities. (③) The authors of that annual report were in no doubt that the absence of regulations was holding back progress and causing needless deaths. (④) They estimated that more than 300 people had been killed and 500 injured since airplanes were first made available. (⑤) They also made it clear that many accidents would have been prevented had there been a law regulating the operation of commercial aircraft.

*slack: 느슨한

12 다음 글의 내용을 한 문장으로 요약하고자 한다. 빈칸 (A), (B)에 들어갈 말로 가장 적절한 것은?

Many people once thought that if a particular area of the adult brain was damaged, the nerve cells could not form new connections or regenerate, and the functions controlled by that area of the brain would be permanently lost. However, new research on animals and humans has overturned this mistaken old view. Today, scientists are certain that the brain continually adjusts and reorganizes. In fact, while studying monkeys, they found that the neuronal connections in many brain regions appear to be organized differently each time they are examined. Existing neural pathways that are inactive or used for other purposes show the ability to take over and carry out functions lost to degeneration, and there is evidence that reorganization in the adult brain can even involve the formation of new neural connections.

⬇

> Contrary to ___(A)___ belief, the adult brain has the ability to dynamically ___(B)___ itself by forming new neural connections.

	(A)		(B)
①	modern	.....	reorganize
②	modern	.....	control
③	conventional	.....	reorganize
④	conventional	.....	control
⑤	conventional	.....	detect

[13-14] 다음 글을 읽고, 물음에 답하시오.

Emotions influence cognitive processing and decision making, but they do not always produce the optimal result. Emotions may well deserve part of their reputation for irrationality, but then again people who lack emotions seem to have (a)considerable trouble negotiating their way through human social life. The bottom line must be that emotions do more good than harm, even if the results are far from perfect. If emotions mainly disrupted thinking, then people who were relatively immune to emotions would be wiser and more rational. This view was (b)denied by the character Mr. Spock on the old "Star Trek" television shows. Spock was from a different planet and race, and although he was similar to human beings in most respects, he did not have emotions. He never tired of explaining to his earthling colleagues that decisions should be made on the basis of reason and logic rather than on emotions, and in the show he was one of the most rational and reliable characters.

Yet human reality is quite (c)different. Researchers such as Antonio Damasio have studied people who have suffered brain injuries or other problems that prevent them from having emotions. They are not superbly wise, calm, and rational beings like Mr. Spock. Instead, they (d)show poor and unpredictable judgment and are prone to engage in highly impulsive behavior patterns that mess up their lives badly. Emotions remain important aids to rational thought. To live in human society today, it is important to have the entire system functioning properly. Having no emotions to help guide your behavior would be just as (e)disastrous as acting solely on the basis of emotions.

*earthling: (공상 과학 소설에서) 지구인

13 윗글의 제목으로 가장 적절한 것은?

① Superiority of Reasoning over Emotions
② Humans' Inevitable Tendency to Make Errors
③ Emotions Are Indispensable to Rational Thinking
④ Negative Outcomes of Highly Impulsive Behaviors
⑤ Different Functions Between Reasoning and Emotion

14 밑줄 친 (a)~(e) 중에서 문맥상 낱말의 쓰임이 적절하지 않은 것은?

① (a)   ② (b)   ③ (c)   ④ (d)   ⑤ (e)

지문의 문장으로 점검하는 수능 빈출 주요문법!

빈칸에 주어진 단어를 올바른 형태로 쓰거나, 네모 안에서 알맞은 것을 고르시오.

1 It is with some difficulty what / that I write this letter, but I think it is important. 01번

2 The water is warm and you are no longer ____(be)____ thrown around. 02번

3 It is the beginning point for what / that the sociologist Max Weber would later describe as the "disenchantment of the world." 04번

4 In the U.S., the demand for Python programmers was / were the highest during this period, with about 130,000 job postings. 05번

5 The culture could stifle his or her innovation, either because the culture is so comfortable for him or her that / which new approaches do not come to mind, or because the culture is so foreign and uncomfortable that it disrupts that person's ability to work and contribute. 06번

6 Folk knowledge has been the basis for the wide range of activities that sustain / sustains a society and its environment in different parts of the world for many centuries. 09번

7 Researchers have found that the quantity of carbon must be carefully balanced between just enough and not too much because carbon, though / despite essential for life, can also be destructive to life. 10번

8 They estimated that more than 300 people had been killed and 500 injured since airplanes were first made available / availably . 11번

9 Many people once thought that if a particular area of the adult brain was damaged, the nerve cells could not form new connections or regenerate, and the functions ____(control)____ by that area of the brain would be permanently lost. 12번

10 Researchers such as Antonio Damasio have studied people who have suffered brain injuries or other problems that prevent them / themselves from having emotions. 13-14번

01 다음 글에 드러난 'I'의 심경으로 가장 적절한 것은?

I went to Bruges for a day. I walked for a day with my mouth open. I looked in at the Groeninge Museum and visited the famous Béguinage, its courtyard lawns swimming in daffodils, but mostly I just walked the streets, agog at such a concentration of perfection. Even the size of the place was perfect — big enough to be a city, to have bookstores and interesting restaurants, but compact enough to feel contained and friendly. You could walk every street within its encircling canal in a day or so. I did just that and never once saw a street I wouldn't want to live on, a view I wouldn't wish to call my own. It was hard to accept that it was real — that people came home to these houses every night and shopped in these shops and walked their dogs on these streets and went through life thinking that this is the way of the world.

① jealous and guilty
② scared and nervous
③ impressed and admiring
④ grateful and sympathetic
⑤ disappointed and annoyed

02 다음 글의 요지로 가장 적절한 것은?

Even if people are kind and generous in one context, it does not necessarily translate to every situation. This is known as 'moral self-licensing', where individuals who behave in a moral way in one situation can later display behaviours that are inconsistent in another. Past good deeds can liberate individuals to engage in behaviours that are immoral, unethical, or otherwise problematic; behaviours that they would otherwise avoid for fear of feeling or appearing immoral. Someone who volunteers to help at their church fundraiser to help the poor may later decide not to donate to another charity. When asked to write either about their positive or negative moral traits, those that describe themselves as more generous donate less to a charity, whereas those who reflect on how bad they are, donate more.

① 사람들은 도덕적 행동을 과시하여 과거의 잘못을 만회하려 한다.
② 누군가의 도덕적 행위는 상대방 행위의 도덕성에 따라 결정된다.
③ 사람들은 도덕적 행동을 한 후에 자유롭게 비도덕적 행동을 한다.
④ 긍정적인 도덕적 특성은 도덕적 행동을 유발할 가능성이 더 높다.
⑤ 사람들의 도덕적 행위는 사회적 기대가 아니라 자기 신념에 기인한다.

03 다음 글의 제목으로 가장 적절한 것은?

When judgment is passed by the people who surround us, it is imprinted in our minds — the neurons in our brains do their work, establishing connections even when the tiniest of data is entered through our senses. If it is an isolated judgment, or is passed by a person outside our immediate circle, the trace it leaves is pale and weak and would not affect our overall behavior now, or in the future. But if it comes repeatedly from someone we are close to, and is confirmed by others as well, it would be deeply imprinted in our minds and would become a label. Whether a label would turn into a belief or not depends mostly on time — on how long we have been subjected to its influence — its emotional charge that affects us, and our resistance to it. Believe it or not, under the influence of labels attached to us, which have become a part of our idea of who we are, we form the qualities of our character, and they in turn, determine the success or failure of all our endeavors.

① Save Your Judgment for People You're Not Close To
② A Positive Self-Image: The Key to Success in Life
③ Others' Judgment: Reflected in Our Identity
④ Our Senses: Often Failing to Capture What Is Real
⑤ Listen to Judgments from Others Only They're Repeated

04 Beowulf에 관한 다음 글의 내용과 일치하지 <u>않는</u> 것은?

Beowulf is an Old English epic poem consisting of 3,182 long lines. It is possibly the oldest surviving long poem in Old English and is commonly cited as one of the most important works of Old English literature. The epic is half rooted in Norse legend and half in sixth-century Danish history. It was written in England some time between the eighth and the early eleventh centuries. The author was an anonymous Anglo-Saxon poet. The full poem survives in the manuscript known as the Nowell Codex, located in the British Library. For years, scholars treated the epic more like a historical and linguistic source than a literary masterpiece. One of the first to argue that readers should value the gory and fantastic elements of *Beowulf* was the Oxford professor J.R.R. Tolkien, author of *The Lord of Rings*. In a 1936 lecture called "The Monsters and the Critics," he called the unknown author of *Beowulf* a great poet but not an overly imaginative historian.

*gory: 유혈과 폭력이 난무하는

① 고대 영어로 쓰인 남아 있는 서사시로는 가장 오래되었다.
② 노르웨이 신화와 6세기 덴마크 역사에 뿌리를 두고 있다.
③ 현재 대영 도서관에 시 전체가 수록된 원고가 있다.
④ 수년간 학자들에 의해 역사적이고 언어적인 자료로 취급받았다.
⑤ J.R.R. Tolkien에 의해 내용이 잔인하고 폭력적이라고 비판받았다.

05 다음 글의 밑줄 친 부분 중, 문맥상 낱말의 쓰임이 적절하지 않은 것은?

The theory of evolution is attributed to Charles Darwin, but it was not Darwin who ①initiated the study of evolution. King Solomon stated, "There is nothing new under the sun," a philosophical statement alluding to the observation that the world is in a ②constant state of flux. At any given time, we see the current situation around us, but we also follow changes that take place in our lifetime, and we are ③aware of changes occurring over periods of time that we are unable to observe directly. The evidence regarding changes that took place in the past often ④forbids us to infer what caused those changes. That applies both to the physical world, such as rocks, flora and fauna, and to society, including modes of behavior, fashion, literature, medical practices, and technology. The changes take place according to their own mechanism. Sometimes it is ⑤clear to us what survives, what is modified, and what becomes extinct, but it is not always easy to identify the mechanism.

*allude: 언급하다 **flora and fauna: 동식물

06 다음 빈칸에 들어갈 말로 가장 적절한 것은?

The liar doesn't want to own his words. When a person is making a truthful statement, he emphasizes the pronouns, *I*, *we*, and *us* as much as or more than the rest of the sentence. Instead of saying, "Yes, I am," a person who is lying may respond with a simple *yes*. In this view, it is not surprising that computers _____. It analyzes text, looking for a pattern of objectively-observed predictors of deception. A computer can quickly examine text to look for an abnormally low number of first-person pronouns. While humans can be deceived by a number of visual stimuli, computers detect only the given cues, which can be relied on as truthful. Many studies show that our ability to distinguish truth from fiction is no better than chance, because we rely on our subconscious mind, so called 'gut feelings.'

① ignore linguistic cues of lying
② often arrive at a hasty judgment
③ provide us with partial evidence
④ are better at detecting lies than us
⑤ can deal with the sudden deviations

07 다음 빈칸에 들어갈 말로 가장 적절한 것은?

We so want to be lovely that we can sometimes convince ourselves that we really did do what our friends think we did and that we really did have the right motives that they attribute to us. A boss can fool herself into thinking her jokes have gotten funnier when she became the boss; I can easily come to believe my class really is fabulous even after the exam is graded and the students are quiet, and my friend at the foundation handing out millions of dollars in grants can really believe that his control of the budget has nothing to do with why people keep asking if he has lost weight. ("You look fabulous!") Strategic flattery can succeed because _____. Once you realize the importance people place on being loved and lovely, you become a little better at detecting strategic flattery. And you're less likely, perhaps, to indulge in it yourself.

① it is partly based on the positive attributes we have
② the flatterer's intention is not easily detected by others
③ we want to believe the compliments we receive are real
④ the reward it offers is so much bigger than its tiny cost
⑤ we take it for granted that higher positions bring more privileges

08 다음 글에서 전체 흐름과 관계 없는 문장은?

Science is a web of interlinking theories containing observations, explanations, models, and hypotheses, some highly confirmed, some more tentative. ① It is not possible to introduce a new idea in science that would not have dependency relationships of various sorts with the existing body of scientific knowledge. ② Part of what it means to be trained in science is to acquire an understanding of one's specialized area of this web. ③ Science sometimes crosses the line, but for the most part it is a valuable answer to our prayers for more food for the poor and cures for diseases. ④ This involves developing a good sense of where the open questions are, what parts are most secure, and what parts might be open to refinement, revision, or even rejection. ⑤ Developing good judgment about these interconnections, and the weight of evidence for each, allows one to assess the prior probability of a claim, whether it be ordinary or revolutionary, and so adjust one's degree of skepticism accordingly.

*tentative: 잠정적인 **skepticism: 회의(론)

09 주어진 글 다음에 이어질 글의 순서로 가장 적절한 것은?

Children are all too ready to try to please their parents, and so they do try hard.

(A) That is why people persist for many years, sometimes for a whole lifetime, in trying to please someone who is not capable of being pleased. Or in trying to obtain love from somebody who is unwilling or incapable of giving it. Or in trying to 'save' somebody who is determined not to be saved.

(B) As a consequence, they are often precociously able and responsible. But that power is built on a foundation of inner powerlessness to obtain the love and care they themselves need to grow up.

(C) They then bring that 'powerless-power' into adult life. They are on the unconscious lookout for another chance to use it, to achieve in adult life what they could never achieve in childhood.

*precociously: 조숙하게

① (A) – (C) – (B)   ② (B) – (A) – (C)
③ (B) – (C) – (A)   ④ (C) – (A) – (B)
⑤ (C) – (B) – (A)

10 주어진 글 다음에 이어질 글의 순서로 가장 적절한 것은?

Traditionally, we've viewed cancer as the body's dragon; it has no redeeming value whatsoever.

(A) That's one of the great hopes of doctors: to find the mechanisms that kill cancer cells, or prevent them from growing in the first place. To us, that's one of the most important reasons why we should learn about cancer.

(B) But more recently, we've learned that it can be a teacher, too. Any doctor who studies, researches, and treats cancer gets an up-close look at how the body is supposed to work and how it responds when it doesn't.

(C) By learning a little about the wonders of the human body and what happens when your body malfunctions, you can learn better ways to make it work better. Actually, cancer doesn't always kill. But you can give yourself a hand with smart prevention strategies and early detection.

① (A) – (C) – (B)   ② (B) – (A) – (C)
③ (B) – (C) – (A)   ④ (C) – (A) – (B)
⑤ (C) – (B) – (A)

11 글의 흐름으로 보아, 주어진 문장이 들어가기에 가장 적절한 곳은?

This is not to say that one must be perpetually open-minded for, as the philosopher Bertrand Russell pointed out, that would be a mind that is vacant.

One effect of Thomas Kuhn's influential historical and philosophical research on the structure of scientific revolutions is that scientists love the idea of being involved in a paradigm shift. (①) Scientists, therefore, feel a mixture of frustration and excitement if an experiment, or some new observation, goes against expectations. (②) While the most likely explanation is that one made a mistake in a procedure or calculation, there is always the chance that it represents an opening through which new light will be shown. (③) A general skeptical attitude allows one to be open to this possibility. (④) However, scientists need to be ready to question even long-held assumptions in the field if the evidence begins to go against them. (⑤) One should develop the habits of mind that allow for a properly balanced and calibrated judgment.

*perpetually: 영구히 **skeptical: 회의적인
***calibrate: 조정하다

[12~14] 다음 글을 읽고, 물음에 답하시오.

(A)

In August 2008, I noticed a stray ginger cat coming into my garden. (a)He had discovered that I sometimes threw scraps out for the birds. I started to put food out for him, but he was really wild and I couldn't get near him. Nevertheless, he kept coming most evenings for food.

(B)

After nurturing and giving him many months of encouragement, (b)he finally conquered his fears and allowed me to touch him. From that point we never looked back; he is now a much loved and extremely affectionate member of the family.

(C)

Then, in late November, I discovered that back in February, (c)he had escaped from a vet clinic 2 kilometers away. After trapping and returning him to the clinic to be reunited with his owner, I assumed I'd seen the last of him. But 12 days later, he was back in the garden — I couldn't believe my eyes.

(D)

Later, I found out that the cat had become so wild that the owner could not cope with him. So (d)he had let him go. The cat had voted with his paws, and made the 2-kilometer journey back to where (e)he wanted to be. After all that effort, what could I do but accept him?

14 윗글의 a stray ginger cat에 관한 내용으로 적절하지 **않은** 것은?

① 필자의 정원에 들어오는 황갈색 고양이였다.
② 처음에는 필자를 경계했다.
③ 2킬로미터 떨어진 동물병원에서 탈출했다.
④ 원래 주인에게 학대를 받은 적이 있다.
⑤ 원래의 주인을 떠나 필자에게 돌아왔다.

12 주어진 글 (A)에 이어질 내용을 순서에 맞게 배열한 것으로 가장 적절한 것은?

① (B) – (D) – (C)   ② (C) – (B) – (D)
③ (C) – (D) – (B)   ④ (D) – (B) – (C)
⑤ (D) – (C) – (B)

13 밑줄 친 (a)~(e) 중에서 가리키는 대상이 나머지 넷과 **다른** 것은?

① (a)   ② (b)   ③ (c)   ④ (d)   ⑤ (e)

GRAMMAR REVIEW

지문의 문장으로 점검하는 수능 빈출 주요문법!

빈칸에 주어진 단어를 올바른 형태로 쓰거나, 네모 안에서 알맞은 것을 고르시오.

1 When ____(ask)____ to write either about their positive or negative moral traits, those that describe themselves as more generous donate less to a charity, whereas those who reflect on how bad they are, donate more. 02번

2 The neurons in our brains do their work, ____(establish)____ connections even when the tiniest of data is entered through our senses. 03번

3 It is possibly the oldest surviving long poem in Old English and is commonly ____(cite)____ as one of the most important works of Old English literature. 04번

4 The theory of evolution is attributed to Charles Darwin, but it / that was not Darwin who initiated the study of evolution. 05번

5 We so want to be lovely that / because we can sometimes convince ourselves that we really did do what our friends think we did and that we really did have the right motives that they attribute to us. 07번

6 Part of what / which it means to be trained in science is to acquire an understanding of one's specialized area of this web. 08번

7 Or in trying to 'save' somebody who is determined not to save / be saved . 09번

8 Any doctor who studies, researches, and treats cancer gets an up-close look at how the body is supposed to work and how it responds when it isn't / doesn't . 10번

9 However, scientists need to be ready to question even long-held assumptions in the field if the evidence begins to go against it / them . 11번

10 Later, I found out that the cat ____(become)____ so wild that the owner could not cope with him. 12-14번

01 다음 글의 목적으로 가장 적절한 것은?

Dear Participants,

　Thank you to everyone who has registered for the Langley Community Art Contest! We are thrilled by the enthusiastic response and look forward to seeing your creative entries. This email is to inform you of an important change to the contest criteria. After careful consideration and feedback from the local art community, we have made minor adjustments to the original contest criteria to better reflect the diverse talents and artistic expressions of our participants. Originally, only unexhibited artwork was accepted. Now, previously exhibited work is also welcome, as long as it hasn't won a major award. The changed criteria are now available on our website at www.LCAC.net. We encourage you to review them carefully and make any necessary adjustments to your entries. We appreciate your understanding and continued participation in the Langley Community Art Contest.

Sincerely,
Timothy Jones

① 공모전 출품작 저작권 규정을 설명하려고
② 자선 경매 행사에 미술품 기부를 요청하려고
③ 미술 대회의 변경된 출품 기준을 안내하려고
④ 미술관 투어 시 관람 규칙을 지킬 것을 당부하려고
⑤ 미술 작품 전시 행사에 참여할 예술가들을 모집하려고

02 다음 글에서 필자가 주장하는 바로 가장 적절한 것은?

　When a company encourages its employees to innovate but then punishes them when their new approach fails, it sends a mixed signal. Punishing failure deters people from taking risks and trying new ideas. Even worse, it can reduce the ability to learn from failures, as people would try to hide them. A culture that accepts mistakes and encourages discussing and learning from them results in more risk-taking and more failures but ultimately more successes. Cultivate a company culture that allows for exploration and encourages even the wildest of ideas, and it just might pay off. Admittedly, it's easier said than done. It can be challenging to create an environment in which high-performing, achievement-driven, competitive individuals can thrive but also feel comfortable sharing and publicly analyzing their mistakes. But remember, a culture in which everyone feels like they can readily admit failures naturally extends to a reduced fear of making them in the first place. In such an environment, daring innovation would flourish.

① 기업 혁신의 방향성을 모든 사원에게 투명하게 공유하라.
② 기업이 마주하게 되는 위기를 혁신을 위한 기회로 삼아라.
③ 성공과 실패에 있어 구성원들의 기여도를 명확하게 파악하라.
④ 조직 구성원의 특성을 고려한 다양한 종류의 유인책을 제시하라.
⑤ 혁신을 위한 과감한 시도를 장려하고 실패에 수용적인 회사 문화를 조성하라.

03 밑줄 친 the ironic process가 다음 글에서 의미하는 바로 가장 적절한 것은?

Research in cognitive psychology, combined with experience with psychotherapy and the practice of meditation, teaches us very clearly that we cannot get rid of thoughts just by wishing. In fact, if we try to stop thinking of something specific deliberately, we curiously achieve the exact opposite effect; we think about this very same topic obsessively. As Fyodor Dostoyevsky said in *Winter Notes on Summer Impressions*, "Try to pose for yourself this task: not to think of a polar bear, and you will see that the cursed thing will come to mind every minute." This intuition was later supported by beautiful research, pioneered by the late Dan Wegner, with the phenomenon that was later dubbed "the ironic process." Trying to stop a thought is not some fancy experimental task reserved for a lab setting but rather an everyday necessity for all of us. From suppression of thoughts and feelings, as has been described by Freud and others, to trying to avoid thinking about various traumas, and trying to stay in control by not worrying too much, not thinking is a constant challenge.

*dub: 이름을 붙이다

① Necessity can arise from the most traumatic circumstances.
② The pursuit of something can be more fulfilling than its acquisition.
③ Attempts to suppress thoughts lead to their increased occurrence.
④ The most prepared people often face the most unexpected situations.
⑤ People with high empathy tend to neglect their own emotional needs.

04 다음 글의 주제로 가장 적절한 것은?

The use of technology to alter living organisms for human use is almost as old as the human race. When the first humans started farming, they soon found that some seeds and crops were better than others in producing more food. Humans saved those seeds, planted them on fertile land, and killed the competitors. This was a great opportunity for the plants to spread their genes. Humans also began to notice that when some animals were tamed, many uses were found not only for the meat of these animals, but also for their hides, hooves, horns, and other body parts. For example, early humans discovered that some kinds of sheep could be bred for their wool and they tried to keep the chosen sheep over other kinds of sheep. Those species prospered with humans and spread their genes easily with their help.

① the natural selection for the superior
② advantages the early crops had over others
③ the criteria for selecting plants for farming
④ reasons agriculture began in Europe and Asia
⑤ human's mediation in the competition of species

05 Sherburne National Wildlife Refuge Youth Photography Contest에 관한 다음 안내문의 내용과 일치하지 <u>않는</u> 것은?

Sherburne National Wildlife Refuge Youth Photography Contest

Rules
- Kindergarten through 12th grade
- Captured during daylight hours, in areas open to the public
- Taken and edited by participants

Categories
- Big pictures: Landscape, Wildlife, Recreation
- Closer Look: Magnified view of plants, insects, wildlife

Submissions
- 8″ x 10″, printed on photo paper
- Mailed by 5 p.m. on Friday, October 8
- Send digital copy to sherburne@fws.gov

Prizes
- 1st Place Overall: $30 / The photo will be displayed at the Oak Savanna Learning Center.
- Per Category: 1st: $20 / 2nd: $15 / 3rd: $10
The winners will be announced at our award ceremony on November 17.

For more information, please visit our website.

① 낮 시간대에 촬영된 사진을 제출해야 한다.
② 식물, 곤충, 야생 동물의 확대 사진 부문이 있다.
③ 출품작은 10월 8일 오후 5시까지 우편으로 보내야 한다.
④ 종합 1위 수상자는 30달러의 상금을 받는다.
⑤ 수상자는 시상식 전에 개별적으로 공지된다.

06 다음 글의 밑줄 친 부분 중, 어법상 틀린 것은?

Think of our own 'Arabic' numerals: 0, 1, 2, 3, 4, 5, 6, 7, 8 and 9. They come in fact from India, ① where their use developed in the first few centuries of the Christian era. A decimal system for whole numbers ② seems to have been known to the Indian astrologer Aryabhatta (476 AD). This system reached Mesopotamia around 670 where the Nestorian bishop Severus Sebokht praised it as being superior to ③ that used by the Greeks. Within a hundred years after the death of the Prophet Muhammad (632 AD), the founder of Islam, Muslim influence ④ extended over northern Africa, much of Spain, and eastwards as far as the borders of China. As a result of this expansion, Muslims began to acquire foreign learning, and by the time of the Caliph al-Mansur, Indian and Persian astronomical texts were translated into Arabic — much of this new knowledge was in turn ⑤ bringing to Muslim Spain.

*whole number: 〈수학〉 정수

07 다음 빈칸에 들어갈 말로 가장 적절한 것은?

One use remains to astronomy: it continues to play a crucial role in our discovery of the _____. It was the problem of the motion of the planets that led Newton to the discovery of his laws of motion and gravitation. The fact that atoms emit and absorb light at only certain wavelengths, which in the twentieth century led to the development of quantum mechanics, was discovered in the early nineteenth century in observations of the spectrum of the Sun. Later in the nineteenth century, these solar observations revealed the existence of new elements, such as helium, that were previously unknown on Earth. Early in the twentieth century, Einstein's General Theory of Relativity was tested astronomically, at first by comparison of his theory's predictions with the observed motion of the planet Mercury, and then through the successful prediction of the deflection of starlight by the gravitational field of the Sun.

*quantum mechanics: 양자 역학 **deflection: 굴절

① laws of nature
② loneliness of Earth
③ universal narratives
④ limitation of intelligence
⑤ science's practical usage

08 다음 빈칸에 들어갈 말로 가장 적절한 것은?

Worker bees are females that lack the ability to produce a fertilized egg. A worker bee's existence is _____, which is one of the profound mysteries that govern a hive. During her brief life, she performs many diverse roles: nurse, producer of wax, builder of honeycomb, housekeeper, forager, water carrier, guard, and warrior. She passes from one of these roles to another, depending on age and experience. A bee is like a worker in industry who is rewarded for her experience and length of service with successive raises and promotions, until the employee is considered a cost rather than an asset. For the bee, indignity rarely accompanies old age. Efficiency and hive demands and not personal status or job assignment determine her roles throughout life and into death.

① dependent on its nurturing
② supported by social networks
③ composed of three main phases
④ subject to the queen bee's orders
⑤ regulated by a biological timetable

09 다음 글에서 전체 흐름과 관계 <u>없는</u> 문장은?

In an ancient epic called *The Odyssey*, Homer tells the story of a man named Odysseus and his wife Penelope. Odysseus and Penelope are very much in love. One day, Odysseus is called away to the Trojan War. ① Because he is gone for a long time, everyone assumes he is dead, and they demand that Penelope remarry. ② Men come from far and wide, each one claiming to be just as good as Odysseus but Penelope rejects every one of them. ③ *The Odyssey* is believed to be the work of the Greek poet Homer, who also composed *The Iliad*, an epic poem about legendary or historical heroes. ④ Soon a mysterious stranger comes along who really is just as good as Odysseus at everything. ⑤ Fortunately for Penelope, the man turns out to be the long lost Odysseus himself, in disguise.

10 주어진 글 다음에 이어질 글의 순서로 가장 적절한 것은?

According to great man theory, someone born a leader will always be a leader, while those born without certain genetic traits will never become leaders. This theory was widely accepted until the nineteenth century and used to justify the differences in status between royals and the common people.

(A) According to this idea, the leader emerges not as a result of genetic traits, but rather is someone who is in the right place at the right time. This person relies on their followers and the situation to maintain their leadership position.

(B) Consider Mahatma Gandhi, Winston Churchill, and Martin Luther King Jr. Do they possess identical traits? Of course not; they are different from each other in many respects. Certainly, some common traits exist, but very few that we could consider obligatory for leadership. This has led to the development of new leadership theories, one of which is situational leadership theory.

(C) In the past, being born into a royal or aristocratic family defined you as having "blue blood," that is, being genetically equipped for a leadership role. In keeping with this theory, one should assume that all major leaders possess an identical list of traits. However, no such list actually exists.

*aristocratic: 귀족의 **blue blood: 명문가 출신

① (A) – (C) – (B)　　　② (B) – (A) – (C)
③ (B) – (C) – (A)　　　④ (C) – (A) – (B)
⑤ (C) – (B) – (A)

11 글의 흐름으로 보아, 주어진 문장이 들어가기에 가장 적절한 곳은?

> But when Abrams checked on the experiment, he found something unbelievable.

Some animals, such as salamanders and sea stars, can regrow a body part if they lose one. (①) That's what biologist Michael Abrams expected to happen when he removed two of eight arms from a young moon jellyfish. (②) Instead of regrowing limbs, the jellyfish had rearranged its remaining arms so they were spaced an equal distance around the body. (③) For a young moon jellyfish, or an adult, being symmetrical is crucial for movement and feeding. (④) For Abrams' test animal to achieve that, muscles contracted in its body, which pushed and pulled the remaining arms until they were once again evenly spaced. (⑤) The scientists had stumbled upon a phenomenon completely new to science, which they call "symmetrization."

*salamander: 도롱뇽 **moon jellyfish: 무럼해파리

12 다음 글의 내용을 한 문장으로 요약하고자 한다. 빈칸 (A), (B)에 들어갈 말로 가장 적절한 것은?

In 1956, an old tanker carried a load of odd-looking metal boxes; they were containers. This technology helped transform the world of commerce in dramatic ways. Before the invention of containers, goods were handled by workers. Each product needed specific packages, boxes, and workers. In contrast, containers were standardized metal boxes that could be carried and handled by machines. Thanks to containers, merchants could use a highly automated system for moving goods with a minimum cost and complication. Both ports and the economy were dramatically reshaped. Before 1956, the local markets were mostly supplied by small local industries. Today it is difficult to find a strictly local market. With containers, people gained access to a wide range of consumer goods produced at extremely low prices as far away as China, Singapore or Vietnam.

> The invention and use of containers increased ____(A)____ in transportation and at the same time ____(B)____ the economy.

	(A)		(B)
①	costs	······	globalized
②	costs	······	depressed
③	safety	······	depressed
④	efficiency	······	globalized
⑤	efficiency	······	fixed

[13-14] 다음 글을 읽고, 물음에 답하시오.

Temporal order is the order events occur in time. An event at two o'clock precedes an event at three o'clock. It is true that a cause cannot occur (a)after its effect in time. Rain today doesn't help crops last month, and a homerun next Saturday won't win last week's game. It is also true that not all causes precede their effects; some are (b)simultaneous with their effects. For instance, a baseball's hitting a window causes it to break, but the hitting and the breaking occur at the same time. However, it is sometimes tempting to think that because one event precedes another, the first event causes the second, especially if those events are (c)paired often enough.

Consider classic superstitions: walking under a ladder or letting a black cat cross your path gives you bad luck; wearing your lucky socks will help your team win; not forwarding those emails about love or friendship will give you bad luck. These superstitions often arise out of our desire to (d)control reality. If you win a game, you might begin looking for some cause that you can use to help you win the next game. "It just so happens that I wore my red socks today; that might be the reason we won!" If you win the next game wearing the same socks, you might be (e)hesitant to think that the superstition is confirmed and that wearing your red socks causes you to play better.

13 윗글의 제목으로 가장 적절한 것은?

① How Mistaking Temporal Order with Causality Creates Superstitions
② The Future Is Unwritten: Breaking Free from Superstitions
③ Correlation vs. Causation: Understanding the Difference
④ Factors Distorting the Mind's Perception of Time
⑤ Why Superstitions Offer Emotional Stability

14 밑줄 친 (a)~(e) 중에서 문맥상 낱말의 쓰임이 적절하지 않은 것은?

① (a)　　② (b)　　③ (c)　　④ (d)　　⑤ (e)

GRAMMAR REVIEW

지문의 문장으로 점검하는 수능 빈출 주요문법!

빈칸에 주어진 단어를 올바른 형태로 쓰거나, 네모 안에서 알맞은 것을 고르시오.

1 We are thrilled by the enthusiastic response and look / looks forward to seeing your creative entries. 01번

2 From suppression of thoughts and feelings, as has been described by Freud and others, to trying to avoid thinking about various traumas, and ___(try)___ to stay in control by not worrying too much, not thinking is a constant challenge. 03번

3 When the first humans started farming, they soon found that some seeds and crops were better than others in ___(produce)___ more food. 04번

4 As a result of this expansion, Muslims beginning / began to acquire foreign learning, and by the time of the Caliph al-Mansur, Indian and Persian astronomical texts were translated into Arabic — much of this new knowledge was in turn brought to Muslim Spain. 06번

5 Efficiency and hive demands and not personal status or job assignment determine / determining her roles throughout life and into death. 08번

6 Because he is gone for a long time, everyone assumes he is dead, and they demand that Penelope remarry / remarries . 09번

7 This has led to the development of new leadership theories, one of them / which is situational leadership theory. 10번

8 That's what biologist Michael Abrams expected ___(happen)___ when he removed two of eight arms from a young moon jellyfish. 11번

9 Thanks to containers, merchants could use a highly ___(automate)___ system for moving goods with a minimum cost and complication. 12번

10 However, it is sometimes tempted / tempting to think that because one event precedes another, the first event causes the second, especially if those events are paired often enough. 13-14번

01 다음 글에 드러난 Dave의 심경 변화로 가장 적절한 것은?

Late at night Dave had gone down to the beach to see if everything was all right with his boat. As he came back up the small path leading to his cabin, he suddenly heard a banging noise. A chill ran down his spine. Slowly, he walked towards it and pointed his flashlight in that direction. The light fell onto a bear in front of the cabin, carefully searching the garbage can for remainders of food. He went to his car, started it and slowly drove towards the animal. The headlights were focused on the bear, which seemed not to be bothered in the least. Then Dave honked his horn until the bear finally ran away. After the animal disappeared into the darkness, Dave exhaled deeply. After he managed to go in the cabin and lock the door, he slumped onto the floor.

① shocked → proud
② curious → confident
③ satisfied → annoyed
④ frightened → relieved
⑤ confused → sympathetic

02 다음 글의 요지로 가장 적절한 것은?

Not realizing that others want to be intrinsically motivated — that they want to do something interesting and meaningful with people they enjoy — can stand in the way of our relationships with family, friends, and colleagues. When a parent undervalues a child's quest for intrinsic motivation in school, assuming she cares for high grades rather than having a meaningful, life-changing experience, it can undermine their relationship. And at work, when employers underestimate employees' intrinsic motivation while employees underestimate employers' intrinsic motivation, the interaction across the organizational hierarchy suffers. One study found that job candidates underemphasize intrinsic motivation in job interviews. The reason: although candidates want to be intrinsically motivated, they underestimate how much recruiters care about, and therefore are impressed by, expressions of intrinsic motivation. Thinking that employers are looking for someone who wants to climb the ladder, candidates don't mention how meaningful the job might feel.

*intrinsically: 내재적으로 **hierarchy: 위계

① 직원 채용 시 성취동기가 높은 구직자를 선발해야 한다.
② 외적인 보상은 업무 관련 내재적 동기를 저하시킬 수 있다.
③ 상호 신뢰에 기반한 관계는 효과적인 동기부여를 가능하게 한다.
④ 도전적인 과제를 부여하면 학생들의 내재적 동기를 유발할 수 있다.
⑤ 타인의 내재적 동기를 과소평가하는 것은 인간관계에 부정적 영향을 미칠 수 있다.

03 다음 글의 제목으로 가장 적절한 것은?

Over the last couple of decades it has been agreed that inflammation in the body plays an important role in the accumulation of blocked arteries. To prove this, Richard Watt and his team analyzed data from over 11,000 adults who took part in the Scottish Healthy Survey. The results showed that their oral health behaviors were generally good, with 62% of participants saying they visit the dentist every six months, and 71% reporting that they brush their teeth twice a day. Once the data were adjusted for established heart disease risk factors such as social class, obesity, smoking and family history of heart disease, the authors found that individuals who reported less frequent toothbrushing had a 70% higher risk of heart disease compared to individuals who brushed their teeth twice a day, although the overall risk remained quite low.

① A Clean Mouth: A Way to a Healthy Heart
② Myths Surrounding Frequent Toothbrushing
③ How Brushing Your Teeth Releases Tension
④ Oral Health: An Indicator of One's Economic Status
⑤ Bacteria: Your Supporter That Strengthens the Heart

04 다음 도표의 내용과 일치하지 <u>않는</u> 것은?

Healthcare Workers' Perceptions of Adequate Staffing Levels and Work Pace for Patient Safety in Seven Countries (2021)

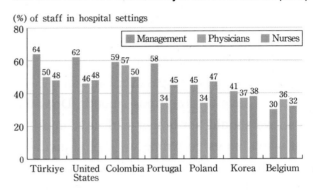

The graph above shows the perceptions of hospital healthcare workers in seven countries about adequate staffing levels and work pace for patient safety in 2021, categorized into three job roles (management, physicians, nurses). ① In six of the seven countries, the percentage of management staff who responded that staffing levels and work pace were adequate was higher than that of physicians. ② Among the countries in the graph, Colombia had the highest proportion of nurses who reported that staffing levels and work pace were adequate, and Belgium had the lowest. ③ In Türkiye, the United States, and Colombia, over 40% of physicians reported that staffing levels and work pace were adequate for patient safety. ④ In Portugal, Poland, and Korea, a larger percentage of nurses than physicians responded that staffing levels and work pace were adequate. ⑤ Among the seven countries, the percentage of physicians who said staffing levels and work pace were adequate was the lowest in Belgium, at just over 35%.

05 다음 글의 밑줄 친 부분 중, 문맥상 낱말의 쓰임이 적절하지 <u>않은</u> 것은?

To complain that things ought to be different when they can never realistically be so is a waste of emotional energy, an infantile unwillingness to deal with the imperfection of the world. Such acceptance need not be passive. For example, the course of love ①<u>rarely</u> runs smooth. Does that mean we should not bother with love at all, or that when things go wrong we should just walk away, and shrug, 'I knew it!'? Of course not. The ②<u>mature</u> thing is to work with the imperfection. The same is true of political reform. We don't give up on it, nor do we accept the inevitability that it will all end in tears. Rather, we work in full knowledge of the ③<u>limits</u> of politics, knowing that good governance will never be perfect governance, and nor will it cure all the ills of the world. This can be ④<u>easy</u> to do, because many drawn to politics are by instinct idealists, who fear that to be anything else will be to give up and sell out. This is a fear based on a simplistic black-and-white view of the world, which is itself a source of the kind of moral distortion which leads to ⑤<u>wrong</u> complaint.

*infantile: 유아적인

06 다음 빈칸에 들어갈 말로 가장 적절한 것은?

As might be true in any big family, the Galloanserae clan has some gorgeous and some plain-looking members. Interestingly, the most colorful Galloanserae males may not be _____, according to a recent study. "There have been lots of theories that the ornaments, the beautiful colors and big tails, are owned by the most fit males," says evolutionary biologist Judith Mank. "We were testing that theory." Mank and her colleagues analyzed genetic materials from six species of birds, both gorgeous and plain. In the gorgeous-looking birds they found a rapidly evolving genome marked by mild gene mutations, which can cause inferior characteristics; in the plain-looking ones they didn't find that. When females mate with gorgeous-looking males, those genetic flaws are passed on. That may affect the species' prospects in the future.

*Galloanserae: 닭기러기류
**genome: 게놈(생물의 기능을 유지하기 위한 최소한의 염색체 세트)

① blending in the background
② showing their interest in females
③ excluding the inferior competitors
④ passing on the best genes to offspring
⑤ distinguishing their colors from others

07 다음 빈칸에 들어갈 말로 가장 적절한 것은?

We have a physical body, we are dependent on social relations with others, and we need to find a meaning with our lives. This mix of physical nature, social relations and meaning is possible to understand primarily because _____. Place becomes an active agent in the forming of our 'self.' There is a reciprocal (or dialectic) relation between 'self' and place. We start life as kids in our parents' home and a hometown which influences the formation of our 'self' in the first instance. But then we may move to another place to study or start traveling in the world. We have our 'roots,' but the development of our 'self' is influenced through new experiences in new places. To some extent we also influence the places we come to, particularly the social life around us, friends and lovers, definitely the 'meaning' of others and sometimes even the physical structures. If we get involved as a farmer, a housebuilder or politician, this is definitely the case.

*dialectic: 변증법적

① we all need a safe place to live
② public spaces are becoming safer
③ it involves activities in place and space
④ social relations transform a neutral place into home
⑤ the distinction between place and space is fundamental

08 다음 글에서 전체 흐름과 관계 <u>없는</u> 문장은?

The first clue that something is amiss in the world of elephants is the lack of older group members. In a species whose wild longevity is easily 50 or 60 years, poachers slaughtering the animals for their tusks has driven the median age of the African elephant down to 35.9 years. ① The animals that manage to survive poaching are likely to be orphans, belonging to shattered family units that no longer have a matriarchal leader. ② These leaderless groups tend to gather, perhaps turning to their instinct of ganging up to defend themselves against primitive humans. ③ In ages past, these aggregations were temporary, and elephants dispersed when the danger was gone. ④ While some populations of the African elephant are secure and expanding, primarily in southern Africa, numbers are continuing to fall in other areas, particularly in central Africa and parts of East Africa. ⑤ In modern-day Africa, however, where elephants are under continual stress, the groups no longer break up.

*amiss: 잘못된 **matriarchal: 모계 중심의

09 주어진 글 다음에 이어질 글의 순서로 가장 적절한 것은?

If we want to rein in the power of our belief biases, and our blind trust in our own intuition, we have to be aware of the psychological phenomenon of belief perseverance. Once we have decided that we believe something, we will tend to keep on believing it, even in the face of disconfirming evidence.

(A) They gave both groups two sets of research findings: one set that supported the claim that the death penalty deters crime and the other set refuting that position. The subjects ended up being more impressed with the studies that supported their original beliefs.

(B) Thus, instead of leading to a more mindful consideration of the issue, the mix of studies on both sides showed that the pro- and anti-death-penalty groups strengthened their original convictions.

(C) In 1979, the psychologist Charles Lord and his colleagues provided a classic study illustrating how difficult it is to change beliefs. They studied people with opposing views on capital punishment.

① (A) – (C) – (B)   ② (B) – (A) – (C)
③ (B) – (C) – (A)   ④ (C) – (A) – (B)
⑤ (C) – (B) – (A)

10 글의 흐름으로 보아, 주어진 문장이 들어가기에 가장 적절한 곳은?

Still, golfers couldn't shorten their swings, and balls were too easily sailing out into the surrounding water.

When pro golfer Jack Nicklaus was hired in the 1980s to design a golf course on Grand Cayman Island, he faced a difficult challenge. (①) The island, a mere six miles wide and twenty-two miles long, was too small to accommodate a full-size course. (②) In his first attempt to deal with the problem, Nicklaus and his team cleverly designed a nine-hole course that could be played twice from different tees. (③) At this point, instead of continuing to focus on the size of the course, Nicklaus reframed the problem: *What if golf balls didn't travel as far?* (④) After heavy testing and research, Nicklaus and the MacGregor Golf Company developed the limited-flight "Cayman ball," which drives half the distance of a regular golf ball with the same amount of swing. (⑤) Small island hotels and backyard duffers everywhere rejoiced.

*tee: 티(골프공을 올려놓는 작은 받침) **duffer: 서투른 사람

11 글의 흐름으로 보아, 주어진 문장이 들어가기에 가장 적절한 곳은?

> This disbelief can be increased and converted into the recognition that we are, in fact, dreaming.

In most dreams, we are convinced that we are awake. (①) But, sometimes, dream events are so incredible as to make us wonder. (②) By lucid dreaming, we thus mean the reacquisition during dreaming of an important aspect of waking consciousness that is usually lost, mainly the accurate recognition of the state that we are in. (③) When we are awake, we know it and we can check on our knowledge very easily. (④) We are able to make voluntary movements; we are able to control our thoughts; we are able, if we are sceptical, even to pinch ourselves and see that we feel things and are behaving in relation to external stimuli. (⑤) In dreaming, we normally lose this self-reflective awareness; we are unaware of the state that we are in; we are unable to control our thoughts; and we are unable to make critical judgements.

*lucid dreaming: 자각몽(自覺夢)

[12-14] 다음 글을 읽고, 물음에 답하시오.

(A)

On a beautiful spring afternoon, there was a softball game between rivals Central Washington University and Western Oregon University. Western's Sara Tucholsky had never hit a home run — not even in batting practice. Then, in the second inning she smashed the ball over the center field fence. With two players on base, it would be a three-run shot. Thrilled, Tucholsky sprinted toward first base. But as she watched the ball clear the fence, she missed first base. When she stopped quickly to go back and touch it, something in (a)her knee gave out. She fell to the ground.

(B)

At each base, they paused to let Tucholsky touch the bag with (b)her uninjured leg. At second base, Holtman said, "I wonder what this must look like to other people." The three players burst out laughing. The other people in the stadium weren't laughing, though. They were crying. The Western Oregon team, the coaches, and members of the crowd were shedding tears at seeing such a moving act of sportsmanship.

(C)

That's when Mallory Holtman stepped in. Holtman played first base for the other team. She was also Central Washington's all-time home run leader. She knew that if (c)her team lost the game, their playoff hopes would probably be gone. But after listening to the coach and umpire for a while, she asked a question. *Can we do it? Is the other team allowed to carry* (d)*her around the bases?* The umpires said there was nothing in the rule book against it. So Holtman and Central's shortstop, Liz Wallace, walked over and helped Tucholsky up. Carrying her, they resumed the home run walk.

＊shortstop: 유격수(2루와 3루 사이를 지키는 내야수)

(D)

In terrible pain, Tucholsky crawled through the dirt back to first base. The Western Coach rushed onto the field. The umpires told the coach it was against the rules for Tucholsky's Western teammates to help her around the bases. The coach *could* substitute a runner for (e)her. But then the hit would be judged a single. The only home run of Tucholsky's four-year career would be erased. The coach didn't know what to do.

12 주어진 글 (A)에 이어질 내용을 순서에 맞게 배열한 것으로 가장 적절한 것은?

① (B) – (D) – (C) ② (C) – (B) – (D)
③ (C) – (D) – (B) ④ (D) – (B) – (C)
⑤ (D) – (C) – (B)

13 밑줄 친 (a)~(e) 중에서 가리키는 대상이 나머지 넷과 다른 것은?

① (a) ② (b) ③ (c) ④ (d) ⑤ (e)

14 윗글의 Sara Tucholsky에 관한 내용으로 적절하지 않은 것은?

① 2회에 홈런을 쳤다.
② 갑작스러운 무릎 이상으로 땅바닥에 쓰러졌다.
③ 2루에 도착했을 때 아파서 눈물을 터뜨렸다.
④ 상대팀 선수들의 부축을 받아 홈까지 걸었다.
⑤ 극심한 고통에도 불구하고 기어서 1루로 돌아갔다.

GRAMMAR REVIEW

지문의 문장으로 점검하는 수능 빈출 주요문법!

빈칸에 주어진 단어를 올바른 형태로 쓰거나, 네모 안에서 알맞은 것을 고르시오.

1   ___(Think)___ that employers are looking for someone who wants to climb the ladder, candidates don't mention how meaningful the job might feel. 02번

2   The results showed that their oral health behaviors were generally good, with 62% of participants ___(say)___ they visit the dentist every six months, and 71% ___(report)___ that they brush their teeth twice a day. 03번

3   The graph above shows the perceptions of hospital healthcare workers in seven countries about adequate staffing levels and work pace for patient safety in 2021, ___(categorize)___ into three job roles (management, physicians, nurses). 04번

4   We don't give up on it, nor do / does we accept the inevitability that it will all end in tears. 05번

5   "There have been lots of theories that / which the ornaments, the beautiful colors and big tails, are owned by the most fit males," says evolutionary biologist Judith Mank. 06번

6   We start life as kids in our parents' home and a hometown which / where influences the formation of our 'self' in the first instance. 07번

7   These leaderless groups tend to gather, perhaps turning to their instinct of ganging up to defend them / themselves against primitive humans. 08번

8   They gave both groups two sets of research findings: one set that supported the claim that the death penalty deters crime and the other set ___(refute)___ that position. 09번

9   After heavy testing and research, Nicklaus and the MacGregor Golf Company developed the limited-flight "Cayman ball," it / which drives half the distance of a regular golf ball with the same amount of swing. 10번

10   We are able to make voluntary movements; we are able to control our thoughts; we are able, if we are sceptical, even to pinch ourselves and see that / what we feel things and are behaving in relation to external stimuli. 11번

01 다음 글의 목적으로 가장 적절한 것은?

Dear Mr. Sniper,

In spite of the global economic recession, we've kept the prices of our products static until now, but it seems we can no longer do so. Due to an unexpected price increase from our manufacturer in Italy, we are forced to raise the dealer's prices of all our imported pigskin leather women's shoes (all sizes and all colors) by 4.7%, effective September 1. Orders entered *before* that date will be invoiced at our old price levels. We sincerely regret the need for increased prices. However, we know you will understand that this across-the-board increase, which is caused by inflation as well as higher production and labor costs, is beyond our control. We do appreciate your business and look forward to a continuing association with your company.

Sincerely,
Sylvia Trager

① 제품 개발 연구의 필요성을 설명하려고
② 경기 침체에 따른 거래 중단을 알리려고
③ 제품 가격 인상에 대한 양해를 구하려고
④ 경기 침체에서 벗어날 방안을 제시하려고
⑤ 생산비 절감 방안에 대한 의견을 구하려고

02 다음 글에서 필자가 주장하는 바로 가장 적절한 것은?

Consider the thought *Someday we will die*. Most of us agree that this is a true thought, but getting caught up in it might not help you. Perhaps you'll end up thinking about how dangerous life is, and in order to avoid dangerous things you won't want to leave the house. Or perhaps you'll reason that since you're going to die anyway, you might as well live life to the fullest and do and eat whatever you want. Either response is not likely to move you toward your values. So rather than debating with yourself about whether the thought you're having is true or not, ask if the thought will move you toward or away from your values. If it moves you toward them, then great. Follow it! If it moves you away from them, then thank those who gave it to you very much for sharing and move toward your values anyway.

① 낙관적인 태도로만 일관하지 말고 항상 최악의 사태에 대비하라.
② 건강 관리에 해로운 생활 습관이 있는지 평소의 생활을 잘 살펴보라.
③ 사소한 것에 관해서라도 자기 생각을 공유해 주는 이들에게 감사하라.
④ 생각의 진실 여부에 신경 쓰지 말고 자신의 가치에 다가가는 데 힘쓰라.
⑤ 실내에 있는 시간이 너무 많지 않도록 외출하는 기회를 자주 마련하라.

03 밑줄 친 "with every funeral."이 다음 글에서 의미하는 바로 가장 적절한 것은?

One of the pleasures of actually doing science is proving someone wrong — even yourself at an earlier time. How do scientists even know for sure when they know something? When is something known to their satisfaction? When is the fact final? In reality, only false science worships "facts," thinks of them as permanent and claims to be able to know everything and predict with exact accuracy. Indeed, when new evidence forces scientists to modify their theories, it is considered a triumph, not a defeat. Max Planck, the brilliant physicist who led the revolution in physics now known as quantum mechanics, was asked how often science changed. He replied: "with every funeral." As new young scientists come to maturity, unrestricted by the ideas and "facts" of the previous generation, conception and comprehension are free to change in ways both revolutionary and incremental. Real science is a revision in progress, always. It proceeds in fits and starts of ignorance.

*quantum mechanics: 양자 역학 **incremental: 점진적인
***in fits and starts: 있다가 없다가

① science triumphs over ignorance in the end
② scientific changes are not only radical but gradual
③ science sometimes returns to its earlier approaches
④ scientific theories are always in the process of revision
⑤ science evolves when old insights yield to new ones

04 다음 글의 주제로 가장 적절한 것은?

People choose to speak one language over another for social, economic, and political factors; this causes language shift. Language shift refers to speakers turning away from their heritage language and adopting another language, either by force or voluntarily. Giving up a heritage language eventually leads to its extinction. Class, status, ethnicity, and outside influences, such as media and education, affect language and influence language shifts. For instance, in Mexico, Spanish is most closely identified with literacy and academia and ultimately with higher socio-economic class. In a colonization situation, the smaller culture invariably must accommodate the dominant culture, and this is when language shift will most likely take place. Although there are 68 officially recognized indigenous languages in Mexico, and 364 distinct dialects, only six percent of the population speaks any one of them; all others speak Spanish.

① definition of language shift and its example
② the reasons so many dialects exist in the world
③ close relationship between language and thought
④ difficulties in shifting from one language to another
⑤ the importance of preventing minor languages from disappearing

05 Khan Academy에 관한 다음 글의 내용과 일치하지 않는 것은?

Khan Academy is a nonprofit educational organization created in 2006 by educator Salman Khan to provide "a free, world-class education for anyone, anywhere." The organization produces micro lectures in the form of YouTube videos. In addition to micro lectures, the organization's website features exercises and tools for educators. It is funded by donations. It has significant backing from the Bill & Melinda Gates Foundation, Ann and John Doerr, the Brazil-based Lemann Foundation, and Google. Salman Khan earned three degrees from MIT and started working as a hedge fund manager. To help his sister, relatives, and friends with math, he made video tutorials and distributed them on YouTube. The project grew almost instantly, and Khan quit his job to focus on those tutorials.

① 2006년에 설립된 비영리 교육 기관이다.
② 학습자들에게는 강의, 교육자들에게는 연습 문제와 교수 도구를 제공한다.
③ Bill & Melinda Gates 재단을 포함한 여러 단체의 기부금으로 운영된다.
④ 설립자인 Salman Khan이 주변 사람들을 돕기 위해 만든 동영상이 시초가 되었다.
⑤ 설립자인 Salman Khan은 아직까지 헤지 펀드 매니저로 일하고 있다.

06 다음 글의 밑줄 친 부분 중, 어법상 틀린 것은?

Contemporary theories of aging cannot account for why people ① age. One theory, the wear and tear theory, ② maintains that the body simply wears out over time. Some theories deal with the changes within the cells themselves, while still others state that aging is programmed, and that the aging process is regulated by an aging clock ③ located in the hypothalamus. The gene theory maintains that there are certain genes ④ which contribute to bodily dysfunctions, and that these genes appear to become activated as persons grow older. Further, there is the cellular garbage theory that claims that there are certain deposits ⑤ accumulate in cells to create dysfunctions that lead to aging and, ultimately, death.

*hypothalamus: 시상하부

07 다음 빈칸에 들어갈 말로 가장 적절한 것은?

Anything worth having takes time. "What we obtain too easily, we esteem too lightly," Thomas Paine wrote. But in addition to hard work and the occasional long wait or detour through the wilderness, a key ingredient is _____. For example, thousands have tried to conquer Mount Everest. Of those who make the attempt, only one in seven make it to the top. One of the greatest factors in success versus failure is the climbers' ability to see where they are headed. When storms blow in and obscure the top of the mountain, the climbers grow discouraged and despondent and consider retreat. But when storm air clears and the climbers see the peak again, the journey becomes easier, commitment renews, and faith is strengthened. Suddenly, getting there feels possible.

① vision
② patience
③ creativity
④ generosity
⑤ cooperation

08 다음 빈칸에 들어갈 말로 가장 적절한 것은?

Giorgio Vasari, the art historian, tells us that when Michelangelo painted the Sistine Chapel, he built a scaffold almost to the ceiling and painted for twenty months. As Vasari writes, "The work was executed in great discomfort, as Michelangelo had to stand with his head thrown back, and he so injured his eyesight that for several months he could only read and look at designs in that posture." This may have been a case of his brain _____, to see only in the odd position that it had adapted itself to. Vasari's claim might seem incredible, but studies show that when people wear prism inversion glasses, which turn the world upside down, they find that, after a short while, their perceptual centers "flip," so that they perceive the world right side up and even read books held upside down. Taking the glasses off, they see the world as though it were upside down, until they readapt, as Michelangelo did.

*scaffold: (건축) 비계

① lacking creativity
② changing its circuits
③ predicting the future
④ escaping from reality
⑤ feeling uncomfortable

09 다음 글에서 전체 흐름과 관계 <u>없는</u> 문장은?

The thinking error of labeling involves summarizing your feelings about yourself, a situation, or another person with a negative label. ① Most often people with social anxiety apply negative labels to themselves, not other people. ② These labels cause problems because they shift your attention from something specific that you might be unhappy with (something you said or did) to a total negative judgment about your personality or character. ③ What defines your personality or character is not your failure, but how you get back and overcome that failure. ④ This is the difference between saying to yourself that you made some mistakes on the project versus calling yourself an *incompetent oaf.* ⑤ Not only does the label make you feel bad, it can make you feel stuck and hopeless about changing anything.

*oaf: 멍청이

10 주어진 글 다음에 이어질 글의 순서로 가장 적절한 것은?

Social media such as Twitter, YouTube, and Facebook are truly *social*, spreading word of mouth through public messages and through messages visible only to friends.

(A) These social exchanges through several ways can themselves spark word of mouth and get more consumers involved in the conversation and the brand or product. When a product or brand is popular on Twitter, for example, many users will click to see what others are tweeting about.

(B) In turn, other consumers may keep the conversation going by reposting or retweeting the original message, echoing it in their own words, recording a video response, or in other ways.

(C) Similarly, when a YouTube video attracts so many views that it lands on the YouTube home page, that additional exposure is responsible for more views.

① (A) – (C) – (B)　　　② (B) – (A) – (C)
③ (B) – (C) – (A)　　　④ (C) – (A) – (B)
⑤ (C) – (B) – (A)

11 글의 흐름으로 보아, 주어진 문장이 들어가기에 가장 적절한 곳은?

As the crew learned more about meditation, they became more united, their strokes got smoother, and there was less resistance.

In preparing for the World Rowing Championships, the coach of a leading crew team invited a meditation instructor. (①) He wanted the instructor to teach concentration, relaxation and stress management techniques to his crew. (②) He believed that such training would enhance their rowing effectiveness and improve their sense of unity. (③) In spite of these benefits, the irony was that their performance decreased steadily and they went slower. (④) Surprisingly, it turned out that the team's players were more interested in being in harmony than in winning. (⑤) They realized that winning is not the only goal and found the way to enjoy games together.

12 다음 글의 내용을 한 문장으로 요약하고자 한다. 빈칸 (A), (B)에 들어갈 말로 가장 적절한 것은?

Since about the mid-1990s, statistics have shown that the yearly rate of increase for the crops is decreasing. Also there is evidence that productivity increases in other areas have slowed. For example, one of the staple food crops in many developing countries is a tropical root known as cassava. Since 1970, the amount of land devoted to the production of cassava has increased about 43 percent, while the amount of production increased by only 20 percent during that time. This is an indication that poorer quality land is being put into production. Since the population exploded in many areas, new farmers had no choice but to farm on marginal land. As a result, more water and fertilizer is put into farming only to produce less food per acre. This has tremendous implications not only for feeding people but also for the impact on the environment.

*cassava: 카사바(고구마처럼 생긴, 열대 지방의 주식)

Due to the population increase, more _____(A)_____ is used for agriculture, dropping the _____(B)_____ of farming.

	(A)		(B)
①	subsidies	......	incentives
②	subsidies	......	productivity
③	barren land	......	complexity
④	barren land	......	productivity
⑤	ground water	......	incentives

[13~14] 다음 글을 읽고, 물음에 답하시오.

It is not just bike lanes that require equitable investments, but the means to access them. Nice Ride, Minneapolis's bike share system, was one of the first such programs in the United States. When it launched in 2010, stations were distributed in the most densely (a) populated parts of the city so that a relatively small system of sixty-five stations and seven hundred bikes could be located close together to serve many people taking short trips. Although effective for proving the success of a pilot, the rollout left North Minneapolis without (b) adequate bike share stations.

Initially, no bike share stations at all were installed in North Minneapolis. Although Nice Ride received additional funds the following year, through a Minneapolis Department of Health grant, to install eleven stations, residents read this (c) oversight as a signal of marginalization. It formed the association that bike sharing was not for communities of color even when the fastest growth in bicycling was among the Latinx, Black, and Asian American populations of the city. This story is not (d) unique to Minneapolis. While public bike sharing has expanded across the United States, it is not always distributed evenly. Research suggests that communities of color are often (e) overrepresented among bike share users. Lack of bike share stations is only one factor in limiting these groups. Cost, lack of payment options, and unfamiliarity are other barriers.

*pilot: 시범적인 프로그램 **rollout: (신제품 따위의) 첫 공개

13 윗글의 제목으로 가장 적절한 것은?

① Share Your Bike for a Better Future World!
② Racial Discrimination Colors Public Bike Sharing Too!
③ Is Bike Sharing Really a Green Means of City Commuting?
④ Some Races Favor Certain Modes of Transportation
⑤ Where Should Bike Sharing Stations Be Installed in a City?

14 밑줄 친 (a)~(e) 중에서 문맥상 낱말의 쓰임이 적절하지 않은 것은?

① (a)　　② (b)　　③ (c)　　④ (d)　　⑤ (e)

GRAMMAR REVIEW

지문의 문장으로 점검하는 수능 빈출 주요문법!

빈칸에 주어진 단어를 올바른 형태로 쓰거나, 네모 안에서 알맞은 것을 고르시오.

1 Perhaps you'll end up thinking about how dangerous | life is / is life |, and in order to avoid dangerous things you won't want to leave the house. 02번

2 In reality, only false science worships "facts," thinks of them as permanent and claims to be able to know everything and | predict / predicts | with exact accuracy. 03번

3 Further, there is the cellular garbage theory that claims that there are certain deposits accumulated in cells | creates / to create | dysfunctions that lead to aging and, ultimately, death. 06번

4 When storms blow in and obscure the top of the mountain, the climbers grow ___(discourage)___ and despondent and consider retreat. 07번

5 This may have been a case of his brain ___(change)___ its circuits, to see only in the odd position that it had adapted itself to. 08번

6 Most often people with social anxiety | apply / applies | negative labels to themselves, not other people. 09번

7 Similarly, when a YouTube video attracts so many views | that / which | it lands on the YouTube home page, that additional exposure is responsible for more views. 10번

8 He believed | what / that | such training would enhance their rowing effectiveness and improve their sense of unity. 11번

9 As a result, more water and fertilizer is put into farming only ___(produce)___ less food per acre. 12번

10 Lack of bike share stations | is / are | only one factor in limiting these groups. 13-14번

01 다음 글에 드러난 Ginny의 심경 변화로 가장 적절한 것은?

The examiner climbed into the passenger seat and instructed Ginny to pull away from the curb. She wiped her sweaty palms on her thighs, and then carefully checked her mirrors. She saw her mother waving at her in the rearview mirror. The examiner spoke curtly, saying little more than, "Turn left ... turn right ... stop here," as he made notes on his clipboard. Parallel parking worried Ginny the most. By the time they got to parallel parking, Ginny was sweating like an ice cube on a hot stove. The examiner chose a spot with two empty spaces to test her parking skills, and she managed to park the car into it. "Very good, Ms. Ginny," the examiner said when the car arrived back at the licensing office. "You passed with flying colors." Ginny almost hugged him. Instead, she jumped out of the car and ran to her mother. "I passed! Mom, I passed!"

*curb: (도로 가의) 연석

① jealous   → regretful
② nervous   → delighted
③ frustrated   → grateful
④ curious   → embarrassed
⑤ disappointed   → satisfied

02 다음 글의 요지로 가장 적절한 것은?

On the journey of growing up, there are times when we find ourselves on the edge of the unknown, unsure of what lies ahead. When faced with this unfamiliar territory, our minds can sometimes react in ways that don't seem to make much sense. Imagine the night before a big event; even though you've prepared as best you can, there's still a lingering anxiety about what might happen. This anxiety can lead to decisions that may not seem logical, such as staying up all night or avoiding the situation altogether. Similarly, when it comes to making decisions about our future or trying new things, the fear of making a mistake can hold us back, causing us to stick with what we know rather than take risks. It's like trying to solve a puzzle with missing pieces — our brains like things to be clear and predictable, and when they are not, we may act in ways that seem irrational. In sum, fear of the unknown can paralyze us and prevent us from acting rationally.

*lingering: 좀체 사라지지 않는

① 인간은 두려움을 극복하면서 정신적으로 성숙해진다.
② 미지의 것에 대한 두려움은 비합리적인 행동을 초래한다.
③ 미지의 것을 탐구하면 이전에 없었던 창의성이 생성된다.
④ 인간의 뇌는 복잡하고 변화무쌍하며 무작위적인 시스템이다.
⑤ 실수에 대한 두려움 때문에 인간은 비판에 민감해질 수 있다.

03 다음 글의 제목으로 가장 적절한 것은?

One cellular phone has an average of 6.8 milligrams of gold. That means 1,000 cellular phones contain around 6.8 grams of gold. Lighter and smaller is the gold standard of high-tech electronic devices. Most cell phones use gold in their circuit boards, as it is high in connectivity. The amount used is not negligible. While only 5 grams of gold can usually be extracted from 1 ton of ore, 1 ton of mobile phones yields 150 grams of gold, 30 times the amount from ore. Currently, the world is in a resource war, with mineral prices rising daily. We should now turn our eyes to urban mining. Korea's diffusion rate of cellular phones is very high, and we are a nation where many people change their cellular phones yearly to follow trends. If there were a sincere campaign to collect cell phones sitting in people's drawers, we would be able to collect a great amount of resources, gold.

① Korea: A Country Lacking in Resources
② A New Gold Rush Toward Cellular Phones
③ A Cellular Phone Deprives You of Your Personality
④ A Cellular Phone as an Integration of All Functions
⑤ More Cellular Phones Mean More Wasting Resources

04 Sunrise Summer Tennis Lessons에 관한 다음 안내문의 내용과 일치하는 것은?

Sunrise Summer Tennis Lessons

Are you planning to take tennis lessons this summer? Just call the Welcome Center at 377-8803 to schedule them.

Lessons
- Private Tennis Lessons
- Small Group Tennis Lessons (2-3 players)

Per Person Hourly Rates
- Private Lessons: $60 for non-members, $40 for members
- Small Group lessons:
  • 2 participants: $40 for non-members, $25 for members
  • 3 participants: $30 for non-members, $20 for members

Tennis Courts
• Members may make reservations up to 48 hours in advance.
• A twenty-four-hour notice should be given for cancellations.
• A 15-minute grace period will be allowed for all reserved courts.
• Non-members may play, if courts are available (No Reservations).

For more information, please visit our website www.sunrisesummertennis.com.

＊grace period: 유예 기간

① 회원의 개인 강습비는 시간당 60달러이다.
② 참가자가 3명일 경우 비회원의 강습비는 시간당 35달러이다.
③ 회원은 최대 48시간 전까지 코트를 예약할 수 있다.
④ 코트 예약 취소는 강습 시작 전에 아무때나 할 수 있다.
⑤ 비회원은 예약을 해야 코트에서 경기를 할 수 있다.

05 다음 글의 밑줄 친 부분 중, 문맥상 낱말의 쓰임이 적절하지 않은 것은?

The incentive structure generated by markets is a lot like that accompanying the check-out at a busy retail store or driving on the freeway. Like the ① number of people in a lane, profits and losses provide market participants with information about the advantages and disadvantages of different economic activities. Losses indicate that an economic activity is busy, and, as a result, producers are unable to ② cover their costs. In such a case, successful market participants will shift their resources away from such activities toward other, more ③ valuable uses. Conversely, profits are indicative of a ④ crowded lane, the opportunity to experience gain if one shifts into an activity in which the price is high relative to the per-unit cost. As producers and resource suppliers shift away from activities characterized by crowdedness and into those characterized by the opportunity for profit, they ⑤ enlarge the flow of economic activity.

06 다음 빈칸에 들어갈 말로 가장 적절한 것은?

When it comes to the news, having perspective involves an ability _____. With perspective in mind, we soon realize that — contrary to what the news suggests — hardly anything is totally novel, few things are truly amazing and very little is absolutely terrible. The revolution will not mean the end of history; it will just change a lot of things in many different, small, and complicated ways. The economic prospects are bad, but we have experienced drops many times over the last century. Even the worst scenarios only predict that we will return to a standard of living we had a few decades ago, when life was still possible. A bad flu may disrupt international travel and defeat known drugs for a while, but research laboratories will eventually understand and contain it. The floods look dramatic, but in the end they will affect only a part of the population.

① to compare present events with the events in the past
② to empathize with others who are experiencing tragedies
③ to look for the experts who know the solution of the crisis
④ to trust the power of technology that has saved the humanity
⑤ to distinguish proven facts from opinions of certain groups

07 다음 빈칸에 들어갈 말로 가장 적절한 것은?

A 1970s filmmaking team was working on an idea that involved a menacing alien. Dan O'Bannon and Ron Shusett worked together on the story and, like most moviemakers, needed a way to pitch it to studios. They pitched the movie using three simple words: "*Jaws* in Space." The movie *Jaws*, directed by Steven Spielberg, hit the theaters in 1975 and was a huge hit. Millions saw the movie, and even those who did not knew the story. O'Bannon and Shusett, by invoking the *Jaws* name, set the stage for their idea. Apparently, it worked. Their idea became the Oscar-winning movie *Alien*, directed by Sir Ridley Scott and starring Sigourney Weaver. Since its release in 1979, it has made more than $100 million worldwide. Anyone who has seen *Alien* can see that "*Jaws* in Space" was a useful introduction to the big idea of the movie. Why did it work? Because O'Bannon and Shusett were able to _____. The studio representatives had likely seen *Jaws* and could use this knowledge to imagine the big idea behind *Alien*.

*pitch: 홍보하다 **invoke: 들먹이다

① have great interest in meeting real aliens in space
② put good, popular, and famous actors in their new movie
③ apply their science knowledge to novel and unfamiliar situations
④ connect their idea to something their audience already understood
⑤ come up with a creative idea that had not occurred to many people

08 다음 글에서 전체 흐름과 관계 <u>없는</u> 문장은?

Although the power of technology today is unprecedented, the tipping point occurred over 2.5 million years ago. ① The dawn of the technological era is signaled archaeologically by the first chipped stone artifact — a tool or weapon plausibly used for killing big game. ② After that point, for animals confronted by humans, the characteristics that would ordinarily convey fitness could increasingly become a liability. ③ The process of natural selection and survival of the fittest was undermined. ④ Natural selection led species to develop adaptive traits for survival in various environments. ⑤ Intelligent humans with weapons could kill whichever animals they liked, fit or unfit, young or old, large or small, and the animals, trapped by the biology of inheritance, had no effective response.

*tipping point: 티핑 포인트(균형을 깨뜨리는 극적인 변화의 시작점)
**plausibly: 그럴듯하게 ***liability: 불리한 것

09 주어진 글 다음에 이어질 글의 순서로 가장 적절한 것은?

Bhutan, located to the far east of the Himalayas, is a small kingdom with a population of about 700,000 people and the GDP per capita of around $2,000. The television was first introduced in 1999, and the Internet debuted in 2000.

(A) The reason why Bhutanese feel such a great level of happiness has something to do with the county's policy of GNH (Gross National Happiness), an idea that was introduced by former King Jigme Singye Wangchuck in 1972.

(B) Despite its relatively small economy and population and its lack of technological advancements, Bhutan was selected as the eighth happiest country in the world.

(C) Instead of pursuing economic development at all costs, he put forth a policy to protect the environment and equally divided wealth. More importance was placed on internal satisfaction than money.

① (A) – (C) – (B)　　② (B) – (A) – (C)
③ (B) – (C) – (A)　　④ (C) – (A) – (B)
⑤ (C) – (B) – (A)

10 주어진 글 다음에 이어질 글의 순서로 가장 적절한 것은?

In the 20th century, physicists, including Werner Heisenberg and Albert Einstein, began to question the possibility of a universal, objective "truth." They observed that different experiments designed to address the same question yielded different results depending on how the question was asked.

(A) That is, scientists shape the outcome to some extent by their interaction with the phenomenon. Even scientific interpretations are based on preexisting perspectives and grounded in particular cultures of inquiry with rules for what to observe and how to make sense of it.

(B) For example, when light was hypothesized to be composed of waves, the experiments produced a pattern that suggested it was waves. But when light was hypothesized to be made up of particles, the tests revealed a pattern of particles.

(C) Was it possible that light was both wave and particle, both energy and matter, at the same time? Heisenberg concluded that the experimental process itself interacts with reality, that there is no completely objective stance from which to view truth.

① (A) – (C) – (B)　　② (B) – (A) – (C)
③ (B) – (C) – (A)　　④ (C) – (A) – (B)
⑤ (C) – (B) – (A)

11 글의 흐름으로 보아, 주어진 문장이 들어가기에 가장 적절한 곳은?

The military campaigns produced individuals who were close to death and were consequently sent home to die with their families.

Homesickness has long been sentimentalized to the point at which the only legitimate sufferers were children away from their parents for the first time. (①) Yet in 1688 Johannes Hofer wrote that homesickness or nostalgia was a medical condition. (②) The *nostos* of returning home, and the *algos* of pain or longing were understood as the pain a sick person feels because he wishes to return to his native land, and fears never to see it again. (③) For Hofer, it was a condition that belonged to an era in which the great nations were always at war. (④) At that time, soldiers might spend years at a time in foreign lands, suspecting that they might never again set foot in their native countries. (⑤) As soon as they came in sight of their cities or countries, however, they made a remarkable recovery.

[12-14] 다음 글을 읽고, 물음에 답하시오.

(A)

Edgar Jackson is famous for his classic story "Message of the Maples," which contains an enduring message for every one. The basis for the story came from Jackson's struggle to overcome a huge wall of adversity in his life. Prior to writing the story, Jackson had a stroke and lost his speech. When (a)he recovered, he moved to a farm in Corinth, Vermont, where he met a writer named Edward Zieglar.

(B)

Jackson noted that people are like those maples. Some people encounter problems, adjust to those problems by incorporating them into their lives, and then continue on, growing tall and triumphant in the process. Others allow their difficulties to twist, distort and ruin their lives. The difference between trees and people is that people can choose how they will grow. Jackson never said a word about (b)his own stroke or the painful process he had undergone, but Zieglar could fully understand his message. After all, (c)he was a maple who grew out of adversity.

(C)

The owner waited until the trees were sturdy, and then he ran barbed wire from one tree to the next. While Jackson was walking from tree to tree with Zieglar, (d)he pointed out how different maples had responded to the barbed wire wrapped around their sensitive skin. Some trees had incorporated the wires into their trunks, and grew strong and upright despite the barbed wire. But some of the trees never adjusted to the intrusion of the barbed wire, and they grew twisted and deformed.

*barbed wire: 가시철조망

(D)

Zieglar was a writer for *Readers' Digest*, and he had read many of Jackson's books. As a writer himself, he had gained great respect for Jackson. He was experiencing a number of serious personal problems, and he went to Jackson for help. Jackson talked with Zieglar for a while, and then invited him out into his pasture. They walked over to a three-acre pasture that was encircled by maple trees planted by the former owner. Jackson pointed to the trees and explained that the former owner had planted them so that (e)he wouldn't have to set posts for a fence.

12 주어진 글 (A)에 이어질 내용을 순서에 맞게 배열한 것으로 가장 적절한 것은?

① (B) – (D) – (C)　　② (C) – (B) – (D)
③ (C) – (D) – (B)　　④ (D) – (B) – (C)
⑤ (D) – (C) – (B)

13 밑줄 친 (a)~(e) 중에서 가리키는 대상이 나머지 넷과 다른 것은?

① (a)　② (b)　③ (c)　④ (d)　⑤ (e)

14 윗글의 Jackson에 관한 내용으로 적절하지 <u>않은</u> 것은?

① 뇌졸중을 겪었다가 회복되었다.
② Vermont로 옮긴 후 Zieglar를 만났다.
③ 자신의 뇌졸중에 관해 Zielgar에게 설명해 주었다.
④ 자신을 존경하는 Zielgar의 방문을 받았다.
⑤ 단풍나무들로 둘러싸인 목초지로 Zielgar를 데려갔다.

빈칸에 주어진 단어를 올바른 형태로 쓰거나, 네모 안에서 알맞은 것을 고르시오.

1 The examiner climbed into the passenger seat and instructed Ginny to pull / pulling away from the curb. 01번

2 It's like trying to solve a puzzle with missing pieces — our brains like things to be clear and predictable, and when they do / are not, we may act in ways that seem irrational. 02번

3 Currently, the world is in a resource war, with mineral prices ____(rise)____ daily. 03번

4 As producers and resource suppliers shift away from activities characterized by crowdedness and into that / those characterized by the opportunity for profit, they enlarge the flow of economic activity. 05번

5 With perspective in mind, we soon realize that — contrary to what / which the news suggests — hardly anything is totally novel, few things are truly amazing and very little is absolutely terrible. 06번

6 The movie *Jaws*, directed by Steven Spielberg, hit the theaters in 1975 and was a huge hit. Millions saw the movie, and even those who did not know / knew the story. 07번

7 The dawn of the technological era is signaled archaeologically by the first chipped stone artifact — a tool or weapon plausibly ____(use)____ for killing big game. 08번

8 Even scientific interpretations are based on preexisting perspectives and grounded in particular cultures of inquiry with rules for what to observe and how to make sense of it / them . 10번

9 Homesickness has long been sentimentalized to the point which / at which the only legitimate sufferers were children away from their parents for the first time. 11번

10 When he recovered, he moved to a farm in Corinth, Vermont, which / where he met a writer named Edward Zieglar. 12-14번

01 다음 글의 목적으로 가장 적절한 것은?

Calcium is essential for building and maintaining bone, yet surveys indicate up to 50 percent of Asian women may consume less than the recommended daily amount. Dairy foods are an easy way to get it: one tub of low-fat yogurt and 300 ml of high-calcium milk daily will give you most of the recommended amount. However, it is very hard to get too much calcium. Most adults can safely consume up to 2,000 mg a day, but larger amounts can lead to problems including elevated calcium levels in the blood, impaired kidney function and decreased absorption of other minerals. But according to a recent study, high calcium levels lower the risk of bowel cancer. So it is highly recommended to get enough calcium every day.

① 새롭게 개발된 비타민을 홍보하려고
② 새로운 칼슘 섭취 방법을 제안하려고
③ 과다한 약물 복용의 위험성을 경고하려고
④ 칼슘이 일으킬 수 있는 질병을 설명하려고
⑤ 매일 충분한 칼슘을 섭취할 것을 권장하려고

02 다음 글에서 필자가 주장하는 바로 가장 적절한 것은?

Statistics and figures are a vital part of the reporter's job these days, whether in the form of a balance sheet or a sheaf of statistics. Many reporters seem to take pride in saying, 'Oh, I'm no good at maths' as though it were a lifestyle choice, such as being vegetarian or wearing a beard. Obviously if they were a talented mathematician they would be working as an accountant or a mathematician or a statistician. They are working as a reporter because their skills lie elsewhere. But just as we would expect a statistician or accountant to be able to pull together a readable report about their statistics or balance sheets, and might sneer if they couldn't, so it is reasonable to expect an intelligent reporter to be able to understand and read a basic balance sheet and understand the basics of statistics.

*balance sheet: 대차 대조표 **sheaf: 묶음 ***sneer: 비웃다

① 기자는 수치 정보와 통계 자료를 이해할 수 있는 기본 소양을 갖추어야 한다.
② 대중이 경제 상황을 이해할 수 있도록 쉬운 용어로 기사를 작성해야 한다.
③ 기업은 사회적 책임과 신뢰를 위해 회계 자료의 투명성을 유지해야 한다.
④ 기자는 보도 전에 통계 정보의 출처와 정확성을 면밀히 검증해야 한다.
⑤ 언론인은 경제적 이해 관계로부터 철저한 독립성을 유지해야 한다.

03 밑줄 친 <u>similar chickens</u>가 다음 글에서 의미하는 바로 가장 적절한 것은?

A culture that places a greater emphasis on the derivative and collaborative nature of scientific advances, along with a reduced emphasis on rewarding hypercompetitive behavior and the cult of the "rock star" investigator, would improve science. The evolutionary biologist David Sloan Wilson has recounted an attempt to improve the productivity of egg-laying hens by Purdue researcher William Muir. The approach of selecting the most productive individual hens from each group to breed the next generation was compared with selecting the most productive groups of hens. Unexpectedly, the latter approach was most successful because the individuals within successful groups had learned to function cooperatively, and the happier hens laid more eggs. Productivity plummeted when the star performers were grouped together, and all but three hens in this group were dead by the end of the experiment. After a lecture describing these results, a professor in the audience exclaimed, "That describes my department! I have names for those three chickens!" Unfortunately, many of us know <u>similar chickens</u> in our own departments.

*derivative: 파생적인 **cult: 추종 ***plummet: 급락하다

① scholars who are uninterested in gaining academic fame
② scientists who manipulate data to achieve a desired outcome
③ researchers who prioritize individual achievement over teamwork
④ academics who are more focused on theory than practical application
⑤ investigators who lack novel ideas and only build on existing research

04 다음 글의 주제로 가장 적절한 것은?

In modern society, the destiny of an individual is deeply influenced by the bigness and complexity of contemporary life. For example, a rationalized form of organization called bureaucracy eventually replaced charismatic leadership and tradition. Based on rules, regulations and hierarchy of authority, bureaucracy functions according to universal rules designed to treat people impersonally. Technically, bureaucracy is the most efficient means of controlling work related to large numbers of people. However, bureaucracy often creates problems of its own, particularly in connection with its tendency to end up as a mindless application of impersonal rules. So, some argue that bureaucracy is actually out of control. They claim that bureaucratic authority is undemocratic and the blind adherence to rules may inhibit the exact actions necessary to achieve organizational goals.

① the basic principles of bureaucracy
② the ideal and limitations of bureaucracy
③ innovative aspects in bureaucratic organizations
④ the necessity of an impartial application of laws
⑤ the tendency for humans to obey authority figures

05 다음 도표의 내용과 일치하지 <u>않는</u> 것은?

Share of Electricity Generated from Wind in the UK in 2010 and 2019

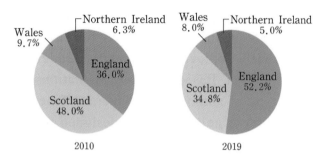

The above two pie charts show the share of wind-generated electricity in four countries in the UK in 2010 and in 2019. ① In 2010, Scotland had the largest share of wind-generated electricity of the four UK countries. ② However, in 2019, England was the largest supplier of wind-generated electricity in the UK. ③ Both in 2010 and in 2019, Scotland accounted for over 40 percent of the total wind-generated electricity in the UK. ④ From 2010 to 2019, the shares of wind-generated electricity in both Northern Ireland and Wales slightly fell. ⑤ Northern Ireland showed the lowest share of wind-generated electricity among the four countries both in 2010 and in 2019, with less than 7 percent in each of those years.

06 다음 글의 밑줄 친 부분 중, 어법상 <u>틀린</u> 것은?

Like scientists, literate human beings are made, not born. Like science, the ability to read is, most assuredly, *not* a maturationally natural cognitive skill. Is there any intellectual skill, other than science, ① that requires more practice? Learning to read and write calls not merely for years of hard work and tutelage but for the availability of materials to ② write on and to read. The extensive availability of both printed materials and systems of schooling continued over many years of a child's life is a uniquely modern phenomenon, which to this day is ③ confined primarily to the wealthiest half of the world's nations. The principal reason that science has been so rare in human history is that the unnatural cognitive accomplishment ④ on which it depends, literacy, has itself been so rare in human history. Most cultures did not develop a system of writing and only a fraction of those that even adopted one ⑤ having produced a substantial corpus.

*tutelage: 교육 **corpus: 언어 자료

07 다음 빈칸에 들어갈 말로 가장 적절한 것은?

There is a reason why modern audiences are likely to sidestep opportunities for high-minded consumption: because they are _____. Modern work demands a punishing amount from its participants. We typically return from our jobs in a state of depletion. In such a state, the products and services for which we will be in the mood have to be of a very particular cast. We may be too brutalised to care much about the suffering of others, or to think empathetically of unfortunates in faraway tea plantations or cotton fields. We may have endured too much boredom to stay patient with arguments that are intelligently reticent and studiously subtle. We may be too anxious to have the strength to explore the more sincere sections of our own minds. We may hate ourselves a bit too much to want to eat and drink only what is good for us. Our lives may be too lacking in meaning to concentrate only on what is meaningful. To counterbalance what has happened at work, we may instinctively move towards what is excessively sweet, salty, distracting, easy, colourful, explosive, and sentimental.

*brutalise: 무정하게 만들다 **reticent: 조심하는
***studiously: 학구적으로

① idealistic
② exhausted
③ hypocritical
④ materialistic
⑤ overambitious

08 다음 빈칸에 들어갈 말로 가장 적절한 것은?

The character you choose to narrate your novel will affect the overall voice, tone, and style of your work. It will also affect how the story gets told, what events are emphasized or de-emphasized, and how the events are filtered, through the character, to your reader. For instance, how might *To Kill a Mockingbird* have changed if it hadn't been narrated by Scout, a child at the time of the novel's main events? Scout is both innocent and nonjudgmental, which clearly comes to bear on the narrating of the events itself. What about the recent novel *The Lovely Bones*? This novel is narrated by Susie Salmon, who announces from the novel's first sentence that she's already dead and narrating from the great beyond. The novel would have been an entirely different entity altogether had a different character narrated it. One of the reasons readers are drawn in a novel so quickly, I imagine, is because of

_____.

① the author's popularity
② the story's authenticity
③ other readers' responses
④ famous critics' comments
⑤ the point of view of the story

09 다음 글에서 전체 흐름과 관계 없는 문장은?

Transmission by voice and hearing is the most basic definition of a folk song. ①The absence of written texts and the need to hear and remember affect folk songs in several ways. ②Simplicity is the major quality, as it aids in remembering the words, tune, and basic meaning of the song. ③As in any folk song, the meaning is sacrificed for the sake of rhyming. ④The latter is important, for if one forgets part of a verse, knowing the basic message may allow recovery of the missing part or the creation of an appropriate substitute. ⑤Memory aids in the form of rhyme, repeated choruses, or musical reminders are common to folk songs.

10 주어진 글 다음에 이어질 글의 순서로 가장 적절한 것은?

The most powerful learning comes from experiencing failures as well as successes. It is also nearly impossible to learn anything without doing it yourself, by experimenting along the way, and by recovering from the inevitable failures.

(A) Although I could pass a written test on the material, it wasn't until I was in the lab, dissecting nerves under a microscope and manually turning the dials on the oscilloscope, that I fully understood the concepts.

(B) Likewise, you can read as many books on leadership as you want, but until you experience the challenges that face real leaders, you will never be prepared to take charge.

(C) Everytime I think about what learning through experiencing is, I'm reminded of my time as a graduate student in neuroscience. I had taken several courses in which we "learned" the principles of neurophysiology.

＊oscilloscope: 역전류 검출관(전류 변화를 화면으로 보여 주는 장치)

① (A) – (C) – (B)   ② (B) – (A) – (C)
③ (B) – (C) – (A)   ④ (C) – (A) – (B)
⑤ (C) – (B) – (A)

11 글의 흐름으로 보아, 주어진 문장이 들어가기에 가장 적절한 곳은?

However, early digital cameras failed on one crucial feedback dimension.

Digital cameras generally provide better feedback to their users than film cameras. (①) After each shot, the photographer can see a small version of the image just captured. (②) This eliminates all kinds of errors that were common in the film era, from failing to load the film properly, to forgetting to remove the lens cap, and to cutting off the head of the central figure of the picture. (③) When a picture was taken, there was no audible cue to indicate that the image had been captured. (④) Modern models now include a very satisfying but completely fake 'shutter click' sound when a picture has been taken. (⑤) Most cell phones these days include a fake dial tone, for similar reasons.

12 다음 글의 내용을 한 문장으로 요약하고자 한다. 빈칸 (A), (B)에 들어갈 말로 가장 적절한 것은?

In a study, four- and five-year-olds watched an episode of the family-hour program *Adam-12*. The episode dealt with students being truant from school and getting into trouble. One group of students watched the show with a teacher who made neutral comments such as "Let's sit here and watch a TV show." A second group watched with the same teacher, but the teacher highlighted important information and explained what was going on in the show with comments such as "Oh, no! That boy is in trouble. He did not go to school when he was supposed to. That is bad." Children in the second group learned more specific details of the program, increased their knowledge of truancy, and increased their positive attitudes in the direction of the teacher's comments. The differences between the two groups were still evident one week later, indicating that the discussion enhanced retention as well as immediate learning.

*truant: 무단결석하는

⬇

By ___(A)___ what was happening in a TV show, the teacher ___(B)___ not only students' learning and positive attitudes but also their memory.

	(A)		(B)
①	imitating	⋯⋯	promoted
②	predicting	⋯⋯	undermined
③	predicting	⋯⋯	promoted
④	interpreting	⋯⋯	undermined
⑤	interpreting	⋯⋯	promoted

[13~14] 다음 글을 읽고, 물음에 답하시오.

Much of the literature on strategy makes a fundamental assumption that strategy making is a rational process. Managers take strategic decisions based on (a) full knowledge of their own organization and its environment. Those decisions are made rationally by considering the evidence and working out the best possible solution.

Studies of managers in action, however, have cast (b) doubt on whether strategy is actually done this way. In a series of articles in *Harvard Business Review* in the 1970s and in a later series of books, the Canadian academic Henry Mintzberg suggested that most managers actually spend very (c) much of their time engaged in formal planning and strategy making. The day-to-day pressures of work mean that managers are constantly having to respond to events and people around them. Decisions are often required (d) quickly, before there is time to collect all the facts and analyze them in detail. Opportunities have to be grasped before they disappear. In these situations, strategy tends to be made 'on the wing', with decisions taken more or less (e) intuitively based on the information that is immediately available. Mintzberg believes that very few managers actually make strategy in a formal and rational way. Instead, strategy 'emerges' in an informal and *ad hoc* way as a result of a series of decisions that are taken in various parts of the organization.

* ad hoc: 임시방편적인

13 윗글의 제목으로 가장 적절한 것은?

① How Personality Traits Affect Management Styles
② Decision Making in Business: The Sooner, the Better
③ Various Management Strategies for Spotting Business Opportunities
④ Rethinking Long-Term Business Planning in the Age of Uncertainty
⑤ The Myth of Rational Strategizing: How Managers Really Make Strategies

14 밑줄 친 (a)~(e) 중에서 문맥상 낱말의 쓰임이 적절하지 않은 것은?

① (a)　　② (b)　　③ (c)　　④ (d)　　⑤ (e)

GRAMMAR REVIEW

정답 및 해설 42쪽

지문의 문장으로 점검하는 수능 빈출 주요문법!

빈칸에 주어진 단어를 올바른 형태로 쓰거나, 네모 안에서 알맞은 것을 고르시오.

1 The approach of selecting the most productive individual hens from each group to breed the next generation being / was compared with selecting the most productive groups of hens. `03번`

2 Based on rules, regulations and hierarchy of authority, bureaucracy functions according to universal rules ___(design)___ to treat people impersonally. `04번`

3 The extensive availability of both / either printed materials and systems of schooling continued over many years of a child's life is a uniquely modern phenomenon, which to this day is confined primarily to the wealthiest half of the world's nations. `06번`

4 We may be too brutalised to care much about the suffering of others, or to think / thinking empathetically of unfortunates in faraway tea plantations or cotton fields. `07번`

5 This novel is narrated by Susie Salmon, who announces from the novel's first sentence that / which she's already dead and narrating from the great beyond. `08번`

6 Simplicity is the major quality, as it aids in ___(remember)___ the words, tune, and basic meaning of the song. `09번`

7 I had taken several courses which / in which we "learned" the principles of neurophysiology. `10번`

8 Modern models now include a very ___(satisfy)___ but completely fake 'shutter click' sound when a picture has been taken. `11번`

9 A second group watched with the same teacher, but the teacher highlighted important information and ___(explain)___ what was going on in the show with comments such as "Oh, no! That boy is in trouble. He did not go to school when he was supposed to. That is bad." `12번`

10 In these situations, strategy tends to be made 'on the wing', with decisions taken / taking more or less intuitively based on the information that is immediately available. `13-14번`

01 다음 글에 드러난 'I'의 심경 변화로 가장 적절한 것은?

Then it was time for the grand finale, the solo dance, the opportunity to go to nationals .... It was all coming down to this moment. "Our final category is Solo Dance! In third place, Ruby Taylor!" *Third? She's a dancer who considers second place a crushing defeat.* Sure enough, she headed to the stage with a sour face. "Did I actually beat her? Did I get second?" I whispered to myself, shaking like a leaf. "In second place, Malia Scott!" *What? Number two is my usual spot. Did I not rank at all? Or ... or ...* I held my breath. *Say Kate Baker, say Kate Baker ...* "And our number one solo dance is ... Kate Baker!" *Oh. My. Gosh. I did it! I did it! I WON!!* I ran to the stage like crazy. There, I saw my mom and dad in the crowd waving at me wildly. I felt great about what I did. I'd proven I was ready to compete on a national stage. *NATIONALS. New York City, HERE I COME!*

① nervous   →   proud
② jealous   →   ashamed
③ annoyed   →   grateful
④ relieved   →   frightened
⑤ expectant   →   disappointed

02 다음 글의 요지로 가장 적절한 것은?

Newspapers have no place in the modern media landscape as they are not environmentally friendly. They are a waste of paper when there are many other efficient ways in which news can be spread. For example, a single annual subscription to *The New York Times* roughly generates 520 pounds of waste, which equates to approximately 4.25 trees being cut down per reader per year. When you take into account all the other publications that are printed throughout the world, this equates to a lot of wastage of increasingly scarce natural resources which could be avoided. Using digital tools to distribute news is more efficient as you only use resources when the content is actually required rather than the print media method in which the product is printed even when it may not be necessarily purchased and consumed.

① 환경 보호를 위해 재생지 사용을 확대해야 한다.
② 신문지 재활용을 확대하기 위한 대책 마련이 필요하다.
③ 대중매체가 앞장서서 환경 보호 운동을 이끌어야 한다.
④ 인쇄된 신문보다는 디지털 신문이 환경적으로 바람직하다.
⑤ 디지털 뉴스의 범람으로 뉴스를 보는 비판적인 시각이 요구된다.

03 다음 글의 제목으로 가장 적절한 것은?

Some gardeners don't need watches at work. They just look at their flowers. Telling time by the flowers dates back to the 1700s. Scientists of that time already knew that certain kinds of flowers opened and closed at definite times of the day. This fascinated a Swedish scientist Carolus Linnaeus. He studied the schedules of flowers around him. Then he figured out how a gardener could plant a flower bed that would keep time all day long. Linnaeus made a list of flowers that would open or close at certain times of the day. He chose local flowers that would "perform" on time, even on cloudy or cold days. Years later, an artist drew his version of Linnaeus' idea as a clock face. Each of the 12 daylight hours shows a kind of flower that opens or closes at that time of day.

① Flowers Classified by Linnaeus
② Flowers as a Clock That Tells Time
③ Linnaeus's Scientific Achievements
④ Gardeners Communicating with Flowers
⑤ Conditions to Nurture Flowers Successfully

04 Avicenna에 관한 다음 글의 내용과 일치하는 것은?

Avicenna, also known as Ibn-Sina, was born in the Samanid Empire in Persia. From an early age, Avicenna displayed extraordinary intelligence and memory. By the age of ten, he had memorized the entire Quran. However, this was not enough for Avicenna. He wanted to learn more about the world to enable him to make sense of it. Avicenna was already showing great interest in the sciences and philosophy. He was so good at learning that by the time he was fourteen years old, he knew more than his teachers. By sixteen, he began studying medicine. He learned medical theory and then started his own experimentation, discovering new methods of treatment. Soon, sick people started to flock to his house for treatment. His fame spread as he often treated them for free, and he could deliver "miracle" cures that other physicians could not. To cure people, Avicenna was, of course, relying solely on science, physics and chemistry rather than on anything supernatural. By eighteen, he had achieved full status as a qualified physician.

① 10살 때부터 코란을 암기하기 시작했다.
② 과학과 철학에는 큰 관심이 없었다.
③ 14살에 의대에서 의학을 공부했다.
④ 아픈 사람들을 무료로 자주 치료해 주었다.
⑤ 환자 치료를 위해 초자연적인 것에도 의존했다.

05 다음 글의 밑줄 친 부분 중, 문맥상 낱말의 쓰임이 적절하지 <u>않은</u> 것은?

Global commerce is becoming more dense and sped up. No single firm can effectively compete as an autonomous agent working ① <u>solely</u> through a market-exchange mechanism. Today, going it alone is a prescription for ② <u>extinction</u>. Only by pooling resources and sharing risks and revenue streams in ③ <u>network-based</u> relationships can firms survive. This means ④ <u>gaining</u> some autonomy in return for entrepreneurial advantages and security that come with networked arrangements. While competition still exists among firms — markets aren't disappearing any time soon — ⑤ <u>cooperation</u> in the form of outsourcing, co-sourcing, gain-sharing, and shared saving agreements are increasingly becoming the norm.

06 다음 빈칸에 들어갈 말로 가장 적절한 것은?

When people receive new information that is contrary to what they already believe, they become uncomfortable. The distress, great or small, causes them to seek release from the tension and anxiety. If little of consequence is attached to the issue, it is simple enough to adapt our vision of reality to include the new perspective and the tension is released. On the other hand, if one has a personal investment in the matter in question, one will search for other information that supports the original view or that discredits the new information. The more heavily one is invested, emotionally or financially, in the original perspective, the more effort goes into maintaining it. If millions of dollars or a lifetime of work are invested, it is possible for the people involved to _____ so that they hear the opposite of what is expressed, or simply, to block it out of consciousness entirely.

① change the original perspective
② turn new information inside out
③ understand and accept the change
④ sacrifice themselves without hesitation
⑤ increase their investment in something new

07 다음 빈칸에 들어갈 말로 가장 적절한 것은?

There are two major ways to limit the effects of invasive species. The first is to prevent new invasions, and the second is to minimize their impact once they have colonized a region. Initial invasions can be held in check by using quarantine techniques, but these techniques are hampered by our inability to predict which species might become invasive. In addition, countries such as the United States and Australia apply an "innocent until proven guilty" approach to incoming species, mostly to avoid limits on trade. In other words, all species _____. A major problem with this approach is that once we know a species is harmful, it is often too late to control its spread.

*quarantine: 격리

① are let in until we know they are harmful
② have similar evolutionary processes and traits
③ are believed to be innocent when they are in herds
④ have a right to be protected from invasive species
⑤ are vulnerable in that they are born with imperfection

08 다음 글에서 전체 흐름과 관계 <u>없는</u> 문장은?

One of the most important changes to occur during the productivist era was the increased pressure on farmers to alter their behaviour towards the natural environment (nature). ① Farmers have always been sensitive to the conservation of the environment, although this has tended to be narrowly defined in terms of such features as the management of soil, farm woodland and moorland. ② But the logic of the industrialization of agriculture placed pressure on farmers to take an exploitative rather than conservative behaviour towards their natural resource base. ③ The conservation of all natural resources is an integral part of our commitment to sustainable development. ④ For example, intervention by the state reduced the risks associated with agricultural specialization, and protected prices for farm products: besides which, new farming technology was output-increasing as well as cost-reducing. ⑤ In sum, financial expediency tended to override best farming practice in relation to conservation of the natural environment.

*moorland: 황무지 **expediency: 편의

09 주어진 글 다음에 이어질 글의 순서로 가장 적절한 것은?

Canadian Sarah Harmer was leading her team in the cross-country team spirit ski race when her right ski pole snapped. She was hopeless. On an uphill slope, several skiers passed her.

(A) However, he didn't understand all the attention. "The Olympic spirit is the way we try to follow," he told a newspaper. "If you win but don't help somebody when you should have, what's the use of winning?"

(B) It was not until after the race that Harmer learned that her benefactor was Asle Fagestroem, the coach of the Norwegian team, which came in fourth. He became an immediate hero in Canada.

(C) Then something marvelous happened. A man stepped forward from the side of the course and handed Harmer another pole. She got back in the race, made up for the lost time and in the end, Canada captured the silver medal.

① (A) – (C) – (B)   ② (B) – (A) – (C)
③ (B) – (C) – (A)   ④ (C) – (A) – (B)
⑤ (C) – (B) – (A)

10 글의 흐름으로 보아, 주어진 문장이 들어가기에 가장 적절한 곳은?

Any infant raised in any environment can learn the language to which they are exposed.

There does appear to be evidence that we have windows of opportunity and are preconfigured to attend to certain information from the environment. (①) For example, human language development is usually trumpeted as one of the best examples of a brain-based ability that is both uniquely human and biologically anchored. (②) In *The Language Instinct*, Steven Pinker points out that just about every child, irrespective of where they are raised, learns to speak a language almost effortlessly at roughly the same time, whereas their pet hamster raised in the same household does not. (③) It doesn't matter how much you talk to your pet, you won't get them answering you back. (④) The only sensible explanation for this is that the human brain is pre-programmed to learn a language, whereas pet hamsters' brains are not. (⑤) This proves that there is a built-in, uniquely human capacity to learn language, which must be genetically encoded, but that the actual language acquired is determined by the environment.

*preconfigure: 미리 설정하다 **trumpet: 자랑스럽게 알리다

11 글의 흐름으로 보아, 주어진 문장이 들어가기에 가장 적절한 곳은?

> But they were even more amazed when they deciphered the writing on the dog's collar.

The destruction of Pompeii on August 24, 79 A.D. by volcanic eruption was so sudden that people had only a moment's warning and could not escape. (①) But of the 2,000 skeletons found almost nineteen centuries later, none told a story so heartbreaking as that of the form of a dog stretched protectively over that of a child. (②) Hot ash had rained down upon the city, entombing all. (③) Uncovering the ancient dog and child bodies, the excavators were moved by the silent tableau of faithfulness to the last breath. (④) The finely etched inscription on it told how the dog had saved the child's father, Severinus, three times — once from drowning, once from thieves during an ambush, and once from a wolf. (⑤) The dog's dying action was to give his body in the brave but futile protection of the child he loved.

*decipher: 해독하다 **tableau: 장면

[12-14] 다음 글을 읽고, 물음에 답하시오.

(A)

Mr. Watson, a child psychologist, was doing a study on child development. Having personally interviewed more than one hundred children, now he was down to the last three children. He buzzed for his secretary and asked her to bring in the first of the three children. A few minutes later the secretary came back with a little boy named Tom. Mr. Watson asked him the series of questions and noted his answers on his clipboard. Wrapping up his set of questions, (a)he asked the boy, "What do you want to be, Tom?" The young child responded right away," I want to be a doctor."

(B)

The boy's answer really took Mr. Watson by surprise, and (b)he failed to comprehend why the boy thought that being blind could somehow help him to be more successful in life; so he asked, "Why do you think that?" The little boy turned to the direction of the psychologist's voice and responded, "Because unlike everyone else, I am incapable of seeing my obstacles." The doctor was stunned and next to that boy's name, he wrote the word: GENIUS.

(C)

Mr. Watson asked him the reason, and he responded, "Doctors make lots of money. I want to be rich." Next to his name, the psychologist wrote the word: *AVERAGE*. Then, (c)he asked the secretary to bring in the next child. This time the secretary brought in a little girl named Sarah. Mr. Watson asked her all of the same questions, and when he asked her what she wanted to be, she responded, "I want to be a ballerina." When he asked her why, she replied, "Ballerinas are beautiful. I want to be beautiful." Next to that girl's name, he also wrote the word: *AVERAGE*.

(D)

When the last child named Rick came in, Mr. Watson immediately noticed that this boy was blind. (d)He asked the blind boy the same questions. When he asked him what he wanted to be, the little boy thought about it for a second and then said, "I don't know yet, but I know I am going to be successful." Mr. Watson asked him how (e)he could be so sure that he was going to be successful. To that, the little boy responded, "That's because I am blind."

12 주어진 글 (A)에 이어질 내용을 순서에 맞게 배열한 것으로 가장 적절한 것은?

① (B) – (D) – (C)   ② (C) – (B) – (D)
③ (C) – (D) – (B)   ④ (D) – (B) – (C)
⑤ (D) – (C) – (B)

13 밑줄 친 (a)~(e) 중에서 가리키는 대상이 나머지 넷과 <u>다른</u> 것은?

① (a)   ② (b)   ③ (c)   ④ (d)   ⑤ (e)

14 윗글의 Mr. Watson에 관한 내용으로 적절하지 <u>않은</u> 것은?

① 100명이 넘는 아이들을 인터뷰했다.
② 자신의 장애에 대한 Rick의 태도에 감동했다.
③ Tom의 이름 옆에 '보통'이라고 썼다.
④ 마지막 세 아이에게 모두 같은 질문을 했다.
⑤ Rick의 눈이 멀었다는 것을 처음에는 몰랐다.

GRAMMAR REVIEW

지문의 문장으로 점검하는 수능 빈출 주요문법!

빈칸에 주어진 단어를 올바른 형태로 쓰거나, 네모 안에서 알맞은 것을 고르시오.

1 There, I saw my mom and dad in the crowd waving / waved at me wildly. 01번

2 They are a waste of paper when there are many other efficient ways which / in which news can be spread. 02번

3 Each of the 12 daylight hours show / shows a kind of flower that opens or closes at that time of day. 03번

4 He learned medical theory and then started his own experimentation, _____ (discover) new methods of treatment. 04번

5 No single firm can _____ (effective) compete as an autonomous agent working solely through a market-exchange mechanism. 05번

6 A major problem with this approach is that / what once we know a species is harmful, it is often too late to control its spread. 07번

7 Farmers have always been sensitive to the conservation of the environment, although this has tended to be narrowly _____ (define) in terms of such features as the management of soil, farm woodland and moorland. 08번

8 A man stepped forward from the side of the course and _____ (hand) Harmer another pole. 09번

9 The only sensible explanation for this is that the human brain is pre-programmed to learn a language, whereas pet hamsters' brains do / are not. 10번

10 The boy's answer really took Mr. Watson by surprise, and he failed to comprehend why the boy thought that _____ (be) blind could somehow help him to be more successful in life; so he asked, "Why do you think that?" 12-14번

01 다음 글의 목적으로 가장 적절한 것은?

Dear Parents,

Did you know that our school has a paper recycling program called the Paper Retriever? You can recycle all of your newspapers, magazines, shopping catalogs, office and school papers and mail every day right here in our green and yellow bin. This is an easy way for you to help us raise money for projects like playgrounds, landscaping, books, and other school needs. By recycling paper, not only do you save energy, but our school earns money for every pound of paper you help us collect. Please put all of your magazines, mail, newspapers and office papers in the green and yellow bin in our parking lot, but do not include cardboard or phone books. Thank you for your continued support of this important fundraising effort.

Sincerely,
Tom Duffy
Vice President of Green High School

① 교내 환경 정화의 필요성을 주장하려고
② 교내 에너지 절약을 위한 조치를 설명하려고
③ 종이 재활용을 통한 모금 운동 참여를 독려하려고
④ 올바른 재활용 쓰레기 분리수거 방법을 안내하려고
⑤ 재활용 쓰레기 수거함 설치를 위한 공사를 안내하려고

02 다음 글에서 필자가 주장하는 바로 가장 적절한 것은?

Rewards need to be reconsidered in an innovation biome. Creating a billion dollars of incremental value at a startup generates great wealth for the entrepreneurs who are the forces behind it. Creating a billion dollars of incremental value within a large corporation may bring about a handsome reward, but it is nowhere near the same level as at a startup. Clearly, the two settings have many differences and risk profiles, but if corporations don't want to lose their greatest value creators, the rewards system needs to be realigned so that internal innovators and entrepreneurs share far more in the benefits they helped create. The rewards for success need to match the value created, and a promotion or a generous annual bonus simply does not incentivize extreme value creation. Why not pay someone $20 million or more if they have developed a billion dollars of incremental value? This is an issue the leadership of an organization must tackle if there is a desire to create a new generation of value.

*biome: 생태계 **incremental: 점증적인

① 건강한 경제 생태계를 위해 대기업이 협력 신생 기업과 이익을 나눠야 한다.
② 이익 분배에 대한 논의에 직원 의견을 반영하도록 보상 체계가 조정돼야 한다.
③ 큰 가치를 창출하려면 신생 기업도 창출한 가치에 맞는 보상을 지급해야 한다.
④ 기업 지도부는 새로운 가치 창출이 가능한 사업 영역을 찾아서 발굴해야 한다.
⑤ 물질적 보상과 함께 합리적인 승진 체계를 구비한 종합적 인력 관리가 필요하다.

03 밑줄 친 the salt of science가 다음 글에서 의미하는 바로 가장 적절한 것은?

In recommending a skeptical or critical attitude toward something, one often says that it should be taken "with a grain of salt." The expression goes back to the ancient Greeks, specifically to Pliny the Elder's *Naturalis Historia*, in which he describes a traditional recipe for an antidote. Take a couple of dried walnuts, a couple of figs, twenty rue leaves and pound them together, adding the proverbial grain of salt. Take a dose of this mixture, and one will be "proof against all poisons for the day." The figurative meaning developed later, such as applied to certain biblical claims by Scriptural commentators when skepticism was warranted to avoid error. A pinch of skeptical salt helps one avoid taking in dangerous, false claims. Skeptical tests are the proof against such poisons. To test something and to taste something are similar, in that the basic appeal is to the evidence of experience. In this sense, skepticism is <u>the salt of science</u>.

*skeptical: 회의적인 **antidote: 해독제 ***Scriptural: 성경의

① the misunderstanding about the possibility of objective truth
② the result of the application of scientific knowledge
③ the cause of common errors in scientific research
④ the defense against the blind acceptance of information
⑤ the balance in the pursuit of scientific and religious truth

04 다음 글의 주제로 가장 적절한 것은?

Boys and girls do have different interests, abilities, and personalities. But what boy or girl, or man or woman, wouldn't be more successful with a fuller deck of cognitive and emotional skills? Studies of gifted teenagers confirm that intelligence and academic excellence are associated more with cross-gender abilities and less with stereotypical gender roles. There can be no doubt that success in our world increasingly requires a mixture of male and female strengths — speaking, reading, writing, maths, spatial ability, mechanical dexterity, and physical skills, along with equal measures of empathy and ambition, diplomacy and assertiveness. The earlier we can step in and tweak kids' growing neurons and synapses, the better our chances of raising both boys and girls with well-balanced sets of skills.

*neuron: 뉴런(신경 단위) **synapse: 시냅스(신경 세포의 자극 전달부)

① dangers of stereotypical gender roles
② how to make your child emotionally mature
③ effects of having cross-gender abilities on success
④ differences between boys' and girls' learning patterns
⑤ relationship between intelligence and academic excellence

05 Decal's Gymnastics Summer Camp에 관한 다음 안내문의 내용과 일치하지 <u>않는</u> 것은?

Decal's Gymnastics Summer Camp

This camp will include gymnastics skills, team building games, and strength and conditioning activities. All activities will focus on a different theme for each week.

Pre-registration for our gymnastics camp is required and a $20 non-refundable deposit per camp week is required at time of registration. Camp tuition balance will be charged to the credit card provided and due August 1 for all camp weeks.

*Weekly camp fee: $170.00 (including the $20 deposit)
*Ages: 3 to 12 (Campers will be divided into appropriate age groups.)
*Schedule: All summer camps will be Monday through Friday from 9 a.m. to 1 p.m.
*Parents must provide lunches, drinks and healthy snacks for their children.

① 모든 캠프 활동은 매주 다른 주제에 초점을 맞춘다.
② 캠프에 등록할 때 내는 보증금 20달러는 캠프 취소 시 환불된다.
③ 캠프 참가자들은 각각의 연령대별로 적절하게 나누어진다.
④ 평일 오전 9시부터 오후 1시까지 진행된다.
⑤ 점심, 음료, 간식은 캠프 참가 아동의 부모가 따로 준비해야 한다.

06 다음 글의 밑줄 친 부분 중, 어법상 <u>틀린</u> 것은?

There's little dispute among archaeologists that farming made it possible for settlements, and ultimately for civilizations, ① <u>to thrive</u> over time. But there's also evidence ② <u>that</u> many settlements predated farming. There were religious sites with temples and permanent dwellings ③ <u>established</u> long before the first cultivated crops appeared. Places such as Pikimachay in western Peru and Gobekli Tepe in eastern Turkey ④ <u>were</u> located, circa 10,000 BC, near fishable rivers or in regions where the food supply was easy pickings. Wild sources of grains, fruits, and protein were abundant and reliable — until they ⑤ <u>didn't</u>. A drought or blight may have come along, or the populations outgrew the wild food supply, and the settlers had to find ways to make do with whatever edible plants remained.

*circa: 대략 ~쯤 **blight: 마름병

07 다음 빈칸에 들어갈 말로 가장 적절한 것은?

A conductor is one of the few people whose authority is exercised in public. Although you would think that the highly visible nature of the role might make it easier to understand than the work of someone behind the scenes, the opposite seems to be the case. It is clearly the _____ of the conductor that creates the confusion. Conductors are more hands on than most leaders. The complication is that the language conductors use is figurative, and their mode of communication can appear questionable to an audience that is probably not meant to see it at work at all. It's hard for the public in a concert hall to avoid observing the physicality of a conductor, but their gestures are no more a means to an end than is an instrumentalist's fingering. I'm not sure it should matter to the listener what a conductor looks like — yet everything about the visual mechanics of a live orchestral concert seems to suggest that it does.

① sight　　　　　　② career
③ capacity　　　　 ④ leadership
⑤ personality

08 다음 빈칸에 들어갈 말로 가장 적절한 것은?

Sport is _____. For example, golfers tend to "waggle" their clubs a consistent number of times before striking the ball and tennis players like to bounce the ball a standard number of times before serving. These preferred action sequences are called "pre-performance routines" (PPRs) and involve task-relevant thoughts and actions which athletes engage in systematically prior to their performance of specific sport skills. Usually, PPRs are evident prior to the execution of self-paced actions such as serving in tennis, free-throwing in basketball, and putting in golf. Such routines are used extensively by athletes, and recommended by coaches and psychologists, as a form of mental preparation both to improve focusing skills and to enhance competitive performance.

① a goal-directed activity
② a highly ritualized activity
③ a fairly universal language
④ a kind of relief, an escape thing
⑤ a legacy passed down through ages

09 다음 글에서 전체 흐름과 관계 <u>없는</u> 문장은?

To solve the problem of who to learn from, we can start by looking at who performs well. Alex is an excellent cook; Renee is great at maintaining good social relationships; it makes sense to learn from them. ① But even when we have narrowed down the problem in this way, we're left with many potential actions to imitate. ② How do we work out exactly how and why Alex was able to cook such a great dish? ③ Our intuitions help us rule out some factors — it probably wasn't his hairdo — but there remain many possibilities, ranging from the most obvious, such as the ingredients or the cooking time, to the least, such as the specific type of onions used or how the rice was stirred. ④ A good cook respects — in all senses of the word — food: where it comes from, how it's traditionally used, how it got to him or her, and how to best prepare it. ⑤ As we find out when we try replicating a cook's recipe, the determinants of success can sometimes be quite opaque.

*opaque: 불분명한

10 주어진 글 다음에 이어질 글의 순서로 가장 적절한 것은?

Too many teachers plan as though what a child will learn or needs to learn is dependent on the previous learning experiences they have had in school.

(A) When it is of good quality it can make learning more systematic, but schools should never be so presumptuous as to act as though they are the only conveyors of knowledge.

(B) But this is to ignore the profound impact of children's learning away from the school environment. Children come from homes, from families, from communities that are rich in experiences that touch on every aspect of school learning. School learning is the icing on the cake.

(C) When teachers plan to introduce something new they should always ask, "What do these children in this class already know?"; "What might some of the children be able to teach each other — and me — about this aspect of their experience?"

① (A) – (C) – (B)   ② (B) – (A) – (C)
③ (B) – (C) – (A)   ④ (C) – (A) – (B)
⑤ (C) – (B) – (A)

11 글의 흐름으로 보아, 주어진 문장이 들어가기에 가장 적절한 곳은?

In some countries, such as Sweden and France, the creation of state-funded child care facilities compensated for these developments by helping teach, supervise, and discipline children.

The socialization function of the family was more pronounced a century ago, partly because adult family members were more readily available for child care than they are today. (①) As industry grew across America, families left farming for city work in factories and offices. (②) Especially after the 1950s, many women had to work outside the home for a wage. (③) Fathers did not compensate by spending more time with their children. (④) In fact, because divorce rates have increased and many fathers have less contact with their children after divorce, children probably see less of their fathers on average now than they did a century ago. (⑤) In the United States, however, child care became a big social problem, leading in some cases to child neglect and abuse.

12 다음 글의 내용을 한 문장으로 요약하고자 한다. 빈칸 (A), (B)에 들어갈 말로 가장 적절한 것은?

In the past, broadcasters did research, assessed customer interest, developed content for the market, and devised a schedule. In those days, the audience was forced to watch what broadcasters provided. But these days the tide has turned. In the on-demand interactive environment, the customer has choice. Yes, the customer may still tune in for a scheduled event, such as a football game, newscast, or the first showing of a weekly sitcom — but the "tune-in" may not occur when the "tune" is played. For the most part, rather than tuning in to a broadcast, the customer will access a multimedia database of programming. As a result, the role of broadcasters shifts from scheduling for the viewers to offering a good database for them to watch and enjoy.

⬇

In the past, broadcasters had the ___(A)___ position in the relationships with the audience, while today they mainly play a part as ___(B)___.

	(A)		(B)
①	neutral	······	content providers
②	dominant	······	profit makers
③	dominant	······	content providers
④	subordinate	······	information monitors
⑤	subordinate	······	profit makers

[13-14] 다음 글을 읽고, 물음에 답하시오.

To use a military analogy, battles are fought in particular geographic locations, with particular equipment, to beat particular rivals. Increasingly, business strategies need to be formulated with that level of precision. The driver of (a) categorization will in all likelihood be the outcomes that particular customers seek ("jobs to be done") and the alternative ways those outcomes might be met. This is vital, because the most substantial threats to a given advantage are likely to arise from a peripheral or nonobvious location.

This further raises the issue that a firm may not have a (b) single approach that holds for all the arenas in which it participates. Instead, the approach may be adapted to the (c) general arena and competitors it is facing. For example, consider the strategy of language-teaching firm Berlitz. As Marcos Justus, their former Brazilian president, told me, in Brazil, competition for the mass market was fierce, but competition for customers in the (d) upper income brackets was less so. There, a strategy of focusing on the upper classes and positioning the brand as an elite product made sense. In the United States, where the majority of customers are somewhere in the middle, a (e) different positioning featuring convenience and flexibility made sense. These are two different strategies, responding to the demands of the two different arenas. Both of these strategies, however, drive Berlitz's evolution toward the cultural consultancy it aspires to become.

*peripheral: 주변부의 **consultancy: 자문 회사

13 윗글의 제목으로 가장 적절한 것은?

① Life Is Not a Battle; It Is a Series of Negotiations
② Diversify Your Strategies for Every Different Arena
③ Meet Every Challenge with Confidence and Courage
④ Think of the World as One Great Arena for Success
⑤ Knowledge of Oneself: A Powerful Weapon for Battle

14 밑줄 친 (a)~(e) 중에서 문맥상 낱말의 쓰임이 적절하지 않은 것은?

① (a)   ② (b)   ③ (c)   ④ (d)   ⑤ (e)

GRAMMAR REVIEW

지문의 문장으로 점검하는 수능 빈출 주요문법!

빈칸에 주어진 단어를 올바른 형태로 쓰거나, 네모 안에서 알맞은 것을 고르시오.

1 Did you know that our school has a paper recycling program ____(call)____ the Paper Retriever? 01번

2 Create / Creating a billion dollars of incremental value within a large corporation may bring about a handsome reward, but it is nowhere near the same level as at a startup. 02번

3 Take / Taking a dose of this mixture, and one will be "proof against all poisons for the day." 03번

4 Studies of ____(gift)____ teenagers confirm that intelligence and academic excellence are associated more with cross-gender abilities and less with stereotypical gender roles. 04번

5 There's little dispute among archaeologists what / that farming made it possible for settlements, and ultimately for civilizations, to thrive over time. 06번

6 A conductor is one of the few people who / whose authority is exercised in public. 07번

7 Usually, PPRs are evident prior to the execution of self-paced actions such as serving in tennis, free-throwing in basketball, and ____(putt)____ in golf. 08번

8 But there remain / remains many possibilities, ranging from the most obvious, such as the ingredients or the cooking time, to the least, such as the specific type of onions used or how the rice was stirred. 09번

9 Children come from homes, from families, from communities that are rich in experiences where / that touch on every aspect of school learning. 10번

10 The socialization function of the family was more pronounced a century ago, partly because adult family members were more readily available for child care than they are / do today.
11번

01 다음 글에 드러난 'I'의 심경 변화로 가장 적절한 것은?

Did you see the passenger at gate 26? The fellow was looking at the ticket agent with puppy eyes. That was me. A front from the north blasted the Midwest, freezing O'Hare Airport in Chicago and blowing a thousand itineraries to the wind, including mine. I was asking if I could take the final flight of the day to San Antonio. I was pouring what little charm I had on the kind but tired ticket agent. I had a job interview the next day and she held my future in her hands. "Are there any seats left?" I was winking, but she didn't notice. She just looked at the screen and sighed, "I'm afraid..." Afraid of what? I waited for her to complete her sentence. "I'm afraid there are no more seats in coach. We are going to have to bump you up to first class. Do you mind if we do that?" I almost cried out, "Do you mind if I hug you?" I boarded the plane and nestled down in a wide seat with extra leg room.

*front: 〈기후〉 전선(前線)

① grateful → curious
② anxious → delighted
③ relieved → frightened
④ annoyed → sympathetic
⑤ anticipant → disappointed

02 다음 글의 요지로 가장 적절한 것은?

When we carefully examine the genetics of the simplest kinds of animals and their ancestors, we can learn something crucial about ourselves. Down at the base of the tree of animal life, deep in the ancestral roots, it becomes impossible to tell the difference between our kin and the forerunners of mushrooms. Animals and fungi merge, forming a stout 1-billion-year-old limb that combines the two. Evidence for this union comes from comparing animal and fungal DNA. This molecular phylogenetic work has been widespread for detecting evolutionary relatedness for thirty years. As methods have tightened and data sets have expanded, the case for the affinity between animals and fungi has strengthened. So, beyond the illogic of claiming transcendence over mushrooms that we see on a lawn, we are related to them. We are more similar to fungi than we are to plants or to any of the other major groupings of life.

*phylogenetic: 계통 발생(론)의

① 생물 진화의 증거를 DNA에서 찾을 수 있다.
② 유전학상 가까운 생물에게서 높은 친밀감을 느낀다.
③ DNA의 유사성에 있어 동물과 식물의 차이는 크지 않다.
④ 진화 생물학상 인간은 균류와 매우 가까운 계통에 속한다.
⑤ 다양한 생물에 대한 분석은 인간 본성에 대한 통찰력을 높인다.

03 다음 글의 제목으로 가장 적절한 것은?

Becoming comfortable with life as it is involves honoring where you came from. Not necessarily liking it, mind you, but coming to seeing how it shaped you, and making adult choices based not in ignorance and denial but in courage and awareness of your past. You see, when we try to ignore the lingering effects our starter kit has on our lives, we end up walking around in a world of illusion. We may think that we're not very bright or that we don't matter or that we don't fit in, but it's not true. Once we can let go of those illusions and face how we became who we are, we can develop the capacity to be all right within ourselves, to recognize that no matter where we came from or what happens, we'll be all right.

① Respect Yourself, Protect Yourself
② Think Positive, Things Will Go Right
③ How to Forgive and Move on: Teach Yourself
④ Understanding Your Past: The Way to Find Your True Self
⑤ Hoping for Something Better: Refusing to Settle for Life as Usual

04 다음 도표의 내용과 일치하지 <u>않는</u> 것은?

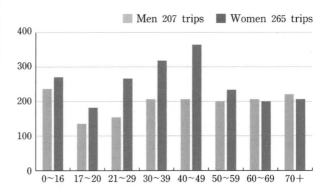

Walking Trips Per Person, by Age and Gender, England, 2020

The above graph shows the number of walking trips per person by age and gender in England in 2020. ①On average, women made more walking trips per person than men — 265 trips for women compared to 207 trips for men. ②Only men in the two oldest age groups made more walking trips per person than their female counterparts. ③The number of walking trips for men stayed around 200 for most of the age groups, and it was the highest for those aged 70 and over. ④For women, on the other hand, those aged 40 to 49 made the highest number of walking trips per person across all the age groups. ⑤Both men and women aged 17 to 20 made the fewest number of walking trips per person.

05 (A), (B), (C)의 각 네모 안에서 문맥에 맞는 낱말로 가장 적절한 것은?

Animals belong in their natural habitats in the wild. It is a breach of their natural rights to take them by force into (A) captivity / liberation for our own purposes. They are prevented from gathering their own food, developing their own social orders and generally behaving in ways that are natural to them. No matter how hard we may try to (B) destroy / replicate their surroundings in a zoo, we will never achieve the full result. Predators need to hunt and taking from them their ability to do so by (C) taming / liberating them is beyond cruel. A 2008 study by the journal *Science* found that Asian elephants in European zoos had a median lifespan of just 18.9 years compared to 41.7 years for wild elephants in an Asian logging camp. Excessive human involvement in the food cycle has disrupted it considerably. Let nature take its course.

*breach: 침해

	(A)		(B)		(C)
①	captivity	......	destroy	......	taming
②	captivity	......	replicate	......	taming
③	captivity	......	replicate	......	liberating
④	liberation	......	destroy	......	taming
⑤	liberation	......	replicate	......	liberating

06 다음 빈칸에 들어갈 말로 가장 적절한 것은?

It seems that it is only when bodies of knowledge have reached a certain level of sophistication that we can begin to think about how they connect with each other. We can understand the meaning of the whole picture only when we understand the meaning of the parts. _____. In the western world, the early twentieth century was the right time. The domain of social science had come into being as a result of the growing sense of outrage felt by a few responsible people about the miserable living conditions of the majority of the population. The hold of religious beliefs, especially those that promised people the prospect of a reward for their sufferings after death, was beginning to lose their grip. There was a growing feeling that we could improve the human condition in this life through our own efforts without having to wait for divine intervention.

① Imperfection is beauty
② Fortune favors the bold
③ Analysis precedes synthesis
④ Two wrongs don't make a right
⑤ You can't see the forest for the trees

07 다음 빈칸에 들어갈 말로 가장 적절한 것은?

We don't associate any single color with funny. It's all about the context. So, too, with the elements of your presentation. A field biologist for The Nature Conservancy once showed up to a presentation wearing a suit and tie when everyone in the audience was dressed casually. If you know anything about field biologists, then you know they spend a lot of time crouched in forests or up to their knees in mud. On the job they wear jeans or chinos or shorts a lot. So the field biologist making this presentation in the seminar room of a prep school found himself in the unusual position of being overdressed. He looked down at his tie and looked up at the audience and returned his gaze to his tie and lifted his eyes again to his audience and said, "Those of you who know me may be a little surprised to learn something my mother has always been proud of: I clean up well." Everyone in his audience laughed. In the context of his presentation, _____.

*crouch: 웅크리다

① his appearance didn't matter
② a sense of humor was innate
③ his outfit didn't suit him at all
④ a plain suit and tie were funny
⑤ the key to success was sincerity

08 다음 글에서 전체 흐름과 관계 없는 문장은?

The Middle East possesses geographical conditions not seen in any other part of the world. ① On the positive side, by virtue of its situation between Europe and Asia, the region can surely be a center of global trade and cultural exchange. ② That, after all, was its vocation a millennium ago, and it is the role that the United Arab Emirates has been successfully recreating as the Middle East's trading and tourist center. ③ The majority of job contracts in the United Arab Emirates are short-term, with the emirate nations not allowing for citizenship or the ownership of land or property. ④ Being in the "middle" has also exposed the region to centuries of interference and meddling by neighboring countries and distant powers. ⑤ It is a region that is particularly difficult to defend militarily because it is vulnerable to attack from so many directions.

09 주어진 글 다음에 이어질 글의 순서로 가장 적절한 것은?

People tend to form attachments and relationships with artifacts, and respond to them in ways that are essentially social.

(A) She left the valuable antique cello on the hotel balcony in the snow, and she "forgot" it several times in the back of cabs. Then when her life started to look up, she held the cello and apologized to it.

(B) The concert cellist Jacqueline du Pré was depicted in a memoir as treating her cello unkindly when she felt the demands of her musical career were limiting her life.

(C) For example, many people talk to their cars, give them names, pat their dashboards encouragingly, and curse at them when they fail. They may form human-like attachments to tools that are an essential part of their work and creative processes.

① (A) – (C) – (B)   ② (B) – (A) – (C)
③ (B) – (C) – (A)   ④ (C) – (A) – (B)
⑤ (C) – (B) – (A)

10 주어진 글 다음에 이어질 글의 순서로 가장 적절한 것은?

The vast majority of people would say that they are not against people with disabilities, and that may be true.

(A) Disablism is also exhibited in the widespread use of separate and unequal entrances to public buildings for the disabled. A non-disablist environment would allow elderly people, mothers with small children and others temporarily or permanently impaired equal access to shopping centres and other public institutions or spaces.

(B) However, the majority still do not consider people with disabilities as equal, and cannot appreciate the obstacles that exist in society preventing disabled people from living "normal" lives. For example, some people use parking spaces set aside for people with disabilities with the result that disabled drivers may have to turn back home.

(C) Disablism spreads throughout all layers of society. Conscious disablism on economic grounds is widespread (e.g., discrimination in hiring), but it is the unconscious disablism, resulting from ignorance or a general lack of understanding. This may show in an "attitude of apartheid", that is, the societal view that inclusive planning is not of high importance since people with mobility impairments have their own separate buildings and institutions, and means of transport.

*disablism: 장애인 차별주의 **apartheid: 차별 정책
***impairment: 장애

① (A) – (C) – (B)   ② (B) – (A) – (C)
③ (B) – (C) – (A)   ④ (C) – (A) – (B)
⑤ (C) – (B) – (A)

11 글의 흐름으로 보아, 주어진 문장이 들어가기에 가장 적절한 곳은?

On the other hand, sometimes this association may be a real clue to causation.

In science we often try to figure out if something or event causes another thing or event, usually because we have noticed that the first thing is often followed by the second thing. The important question that has to be asked is whether the first thing is both *sufficient* and *necessary* to cause the second thing. Sufficient *and* necessary. (①) Often, quite often, you can show only one or the other. (②) Nature is inexplicably stingy when it comes to causes versus correlations. (③) Correlations are the weak stepchildren of causes — and they play tricks on you all the time. (④) Because two things happen close to each other in time does not necessarily mean that one is a cause of the other, or for that matter that they owe anything at all to each other. (⑤) This is where necessity and sufficiency come in.

*inexplicably: 설명할 수 없을 정도로 **stingy: 인색한

[12~14] 다음 글을 읽고, 물음에 답하시오.

(A)

A little country school was heated by a coal stove. A little boy had the job of coming to school early each day to start the fire and warm the room before his teacher and his classmates arrived. One morning, they arrived to find the school in flames. They dragged the unconscious little boy out of the flaming building. (a) He had major burns over the lower half of his body and was taken to a nearby hospital.

(B)

One day his mother wheeled him out into the yard. This day, instead of sitting in his wheelchair, he threw himself to the ground. He pulled himself across the grass, dragging his legs behind him. He worked his way to the fence. With great effort, (b) he raised himself up on the fence. Then, he began dragging himself along the fence, resolving that he would walk. He started to do this every day until he wore a smooth path all around the yard beside the fence.

(C)

Ultimately through his iron persistence and his resolute determination, (c) he did develop the ability to stand up, then to walk by himself, and then to run. He began to walk to school, then to run to school, to run for the sheer joy of running. Later in college he made the track team. Still later this determined young man who was not expected to survive, who would surely never walk, who could never hope to run, Glenn Cunningham ran the world's fastest mile!

(D)

From his bed the little boy faintly heard the doctor talking to his mother. (d)He told his mother that her son would surely die, for the terrible fire had devastated the lower half of his body. But the brave boy didn't want to die. He made up his mind that he would survive. To the amazement of the physician, he did survive. When the mortal danger was past, he again heard the doctor and his mother speaking quietly. His mother was told that (e)her son was doomed to be a lifetime cripple with no use at all of his lower limbs. Once more the brave boy made up his mind. He would walk.

12 주어진 글 (A)에 이어질 내용을 순서에 맞게 배열한 것으로 가장 적절한 것은?

① (B) – (D) – (C)   ② (C) – (B) – (D)
③ (C) – (D) – (B)   ④ (D) – (B) – (C)
⑤ (D) – (C) – (B)

13 밑줄 친 (a)~(e) 중에서 가리키는 대상이 나머지 넷과 다른 것은?

① (a)   ② (b)   ③ (c)   ④ (d)   ⑤ (e)

14 윗글의 Glenn Cunningham에 관한 내용으로 적절하지 않은 것은?

① 학교에 일찍 와서 난롯불을 피우는 일을 맡았다.
② 하반신에 큰 화상을 입는 사고를 겪었다.
③ 길이 생겨날 때까지 울타리를 따라 자신의 몸을 끌고 다녔다.
④ 대학에서 육상부가 되었다.
⑤ 노력하면 걷게 될 것이라는 의사의 말을 듣고 희망을 얻었다.

빈칸에 주어진 단어를 올바른 형태로 쓰거나, 네모 안에서 알맞은 것을 고르시오.

1   This molecular phylogenetic work is / has been widespread for detecting evolutionary relatedness for thirty years. 02번

2   Becoming comfortable with life as it is ___(involve)___ honoring where you came from. 03번

3   For women, on the other hand, that / those aged 40 to 49 made the highest number of walking trips per person across all the age groups. 04번

4   Predators need to hunt and taking from them their ability to do so by taming them is / are beyond cruel. 05번

5   There was a growing feeling that / which we could improve the human condition in this life through our own efforts without having to wait for divine intervention. 06번

6   A field biologist for The Nature Conservancy once showed up to a presentation ___(wear)___ a suit and tie when everyone in the audience was dressed casually. 07번

7   They may form human-like attachments to tools what / that are an essential part of their work and creative processes. 09번

8   This may show in an "attitude of apartheid", that is, the societal view that / which inclusive planning is not of high importance since people with mobility impairments have their own separate buildings and institutions, and means of transport. 10번

9   The important question that has to ask / be asked is whether the first thing is both *sufficient* and *necessary* to cause the second thing. 11번

10 He told his mother that her son would surely die, for the terrible fire ___(devastate)___ the lower half of his body. 12-14번

01 다음 글의 목적으로 가장 적절한 것은?

Dear Ms. Carter,

Thank you for inviting us to sponsor the Maperville Community Job Fair. We appreciate the fair's mission to stimulate the local economy and applaud your efforts to support such a worthy cause. Unfortunately, due to the current economic climate, many companies, including ours, are re-evaluating their charitable giving programs. As a result, we have already committed our budget for charitable contributions this year and will not be able to sponsor the job fair. We understand the importance of the Maperville Community Job Fair and would be happy to consider your request again at the end of February next year. We sincerely wish you the best of luck in your fundraising efforts.

Sincerely,
Claire Adams

① 채용 박람회 후원 요청을 거절하려고
② 채용 박람회 예산 삭감에 대해 항의하려고
③ 직원 채용 계획이 변경되었음을 공지하려고
④ 지역 일자리 창출을 위한 정책을 제안하려고
⑤ 채용 박람회 부스 운영 방법에 대해 문의하려고

02 다음 글에서 필자가 주장하는 바로 가장 적절한 것은?

Showing appreciation for the things others do for you has a profound effect on how you're perceived. Keep in mind that everything someone does for you has an opportunity cost. That means if someone takes time out of his or her day to attend to you, there's something they haven't done for themselves or for someone else. It's easy to fool yourself into thinking your request is small. But when someone is busy, there are no small requests. They have to stop what they're doing, focus on your request, and take the time to respond. With that in mind, there is never a time when you should not thank someone for doing something for you. In fact, assume a thank-you note is in order, and look at situations when you don't send one as the exception.

① 주변에서 일어나는 일에 관심을 가져야 한다.
② 가끔 나 자신을 돌아보는 시간을 가져야 한다.
③ 다른 사람의 호의에 항상 감사를 표해야 한다.
④ 다른 사람들의 부탁은 가능한 한 들어주어야 한다.
⑤ 규칙에는 예외가 있을 수 있다는 사실을 기억해야 한다.

03 밑줄 친 the opposite direction이 다음 글에서 의미하는 바로 가장 적절한 것은?

No debate in the development literature has persisted as long and with such intensity as that related to government intervention in economic activity. In the last half century alone, views and actual policies have changed considerably. In the 1950s and 1960s, it was believed that markets failed widely and government intervention was necessary to speed up the process of economic transformation and the rate of economic growth. Most developing countries, including those in the Middle East and North Africa, adopted import substitution strategies in conjunction with high levels of protection, central planning, public ownership, and nonuniform policies across sectors and activities. In the 1970s and 1980s, it became increasingly evident that governments fail too, and in many cases they fail even more than markets. So, the pendulum swung in the opposite direction. Promarket reforms were adopted, especially in the 1980s, frequently with the support of the World Bank and the IMF. The Washington Consensus emphasized macroeconomic stability, trade and price liberalization, privatization, and competition as key ingredients for rapid economic growth.

*pendulum: 추(錘) **The Washington Consensus: 워싱턴 합의 (개발도상국 대상 경제 정책 제안)

① managing the economy through strict central planning
② limiting the influence of international trade organizations
③ prioritizing economic fairness over rapid economic growth
④ encouraging developing countries to deal with market failures
⑤ embracing market-driven policies with less government intervention

04 다음 글의 주제로 가장 적절한 것은?

Imagine a life without words! Most of us would not give up words for anything. Every day we utter thousands of words. Communicating our joys, fears, opinions, fantasies, wishes, requests, demands, feelings — and the occasional threat or insult — is a very important aspect of being human. The air is always thick with our verbal emissions. There are so many things we want to tell the world. Some of them are important, some of them are not. But we talk anyway — even when we know that what we are saying is totally unimportant. We love chitchat and find silent encounters awkward, or even oppressive. A life without words would be a horrendous privation.

① the value of being silent
② successful speaking techniques
③ ways of expressing our opinions
④ the importance of words for expression
⑤ individual differences in choosing words

05 Montague Russell Page에 관한 다음 글의 내용과 일치하지 <u>않는</u> 것은?

Montague Russell Page was born in Lincolnshire, the second son of three children of Harold Ethelbert Page. From 1927 to 1932 he studied art in Paris and took some small gardening jobs in France. Between 1934 and 1938 he contributed articles to the periodical *Landscape and Gardening*. From 1935 to 1939 he worked in partnership with Geoffrey Jellicoe. Page and Jellicoe designed the landscape and building for the 'Caveman Restaurant' at Cheddar Gorge on the Longleat estate in Somerset. Page went on to design gardens in Europe and the USA. His works include the National Capitol Columns in Washington's United States National Arboretum. In 1962, Page's autobiography, *The Education of a Gardener*, was published and he died on January 4, 1985 in London.

① 세 아이 중 둘째 아들로 태어났다.
② 파리에서 미술을 공부했다.
③ Geoffrey Jellicoe와 동업했다.
④ 유럽과 미국에서 정원을 디자인했다.
⑤ 사후에 자서전이 출간되었다.

06 (A), (B), (C)의 각 네모 안에서 어법에 맞는 표현으로 가장 적절한 것은?

When Neil Armstrong stepped onto the moon he uttered a memorable sentence: "That's one small step for a man, one giant leap for mankind." If he had landed on the moon in the mid-1990s, no doubt he would (A) say / have said a much more politically correct sentence: "That's one small step for a person, one giant leap for humankind." Less poetic but (B) certain / certainly more literally representative of the whole of the human race! Certain language can help to reinforce stereotypes on gender roles in society. For example, "A director must be committed to the well-being of his company," but "A nurse is expected to show her devotion by working long hours." The use of such words (C) show / shows the tendency to associate certain jobs with men or women.

	(A)		(B)		(C)
①	say	⋯⋯	certain	⋯⋯	show
②	say	⋯⋯	certainly	⋯⋯	shows
③	have said	⋯⋯	certain	⋯⋯	show
④	have said	⋯⋯	certainly	⋯⋯	shows
⑤	have said	⋯⋯	certain	⋯⋯	shows

07 다음 빈칸에 들어갈 말로 가장 적절한 것은?

If you walk into a room that smells of freshly baked bread, you quickly detect the rather pleasant aroma. However, stay in the room for a few minutes, and the smell will seem to disappear. In fact, the only way to reawaken it is to walk out of the room and come back in again. Exactly the same concept applies to many areas of our lives, including happiness. Everyone has something to be happy about. Perhaps they have a loving partner, good health, interesting hobbies, caring parents, a roof over their heads, clean water to drink, or enough food to eat. As time passes, however, they get used to what they have and just like the smell of fresh bread, these wonderful assets vanish from their consciousness. As the old cliché goes, you don't know what you've got till it's _____.

① gone   ② used
③ known   ④ visible
⑤ enough

08 다음 빈칸에 들어갈 말로 가장 적절한 것은?

Here's a drug-free way to ease moderate pain: simply _____. In a recent study, researchers briefly applied somewhat painful pulses of heat to the palms of 52 women. When the volunteers were instructed to breathe at roughly half their normal rates, their ratings of pain intensity and unpleasantness dropped by as much as 30 percent. Slow breathing seems to slow the body's stress reactions, such as a faster heart rate and higher blood pressure, says study leader Alex Zautra, at Arizona State University. This may help explain why other studies have found some meditation techniques can reduce pain. To get the benefit, count the number of breaths you take in a minute, then sit quietly while gradually slowing the rate.

① tap your palm
② slow your breathing
③ monitor your heart rate
④ tell others your symptoms
⑤ study how to reduce stress

09 다음 글에서 전체 흐름과 관계 <u>없는</u> 문장은?

Sailors have an expression about the weather: they say, the weather is a great bluffer. ①I guess the same is true of our human society — things can look dark, then a break shows in the clouds, and all is changed, sometimes rather suddenly. ②Clouds form when moist, warm rising air cools and expands in the atmosphere. ③It is quite obvious that the human race has made a queer mess of life on this planet. ④But as a people, we probably harbor seeds of goodness that have lain for a long time waiting to sprout when the conditions are right. ⑤Man's curiosity, his relentlessness, his inventiveness, his ingenuity have led him into deep trouble. We can only hope that these same traits will enable him to claw his way out.

10 주어진 글 다음에 이어질 글의 순서로 가장 적절한 것은?

In India, elephants are used for manual labor. But what is to be done with them when they are not working? How does one restrain them?

(A) Finally, the elephants gave up and the fight was over. And now the interesting part. From that moment on, they strongly believed that there was absolutely no hope of getting rid of the rope.

(B) They accepted the "fact" that it limited them. And with this imprinted belief in place, their handlers were able to tie them with extremely small ropes. And even as adults, weighing 8,000 pounds and more, they never attempted to break free because they "knew" they had no chance of doing so. The elephants' limits were not real, but only existed in their minds.

(C) Their handlers came up with the idea of "programming" them while they were still very young by setting self-imposed limits in their thinking. How did it work? When the elephants were still small, weighing around 150 pounds, they were tied with a very heavy rope. All day long, they tried to get rid of it, whined, tugged at it, and some even tried to chew it. But they couldn't break free.

*whine: 끙끙거리다 **tug at: ~을 세게 잡아당기다

① (A) – (C) – (B) 　② (B) – (A) – (C)
③ (B) – (C) – (A) 　④ (C) – (A) – (B)
⑤ (C) – (B) – (A)

11 글의 흐름으로 보아, 주어진 문장이 들어가기에 가장 적절한 곳은?

Some researchers wanted to find out whether trained musicians can do better in discriminating this emotional information found in human voice, compared to nonmusicians.

If you've ever cried because you were yelled at, you know: words convey emotions. (①) You can find out what somebody is feeling by detecting how they are saying something. (②) In one study, English-speaking musicians and nonmusicians heard various emotions expressed in Tagalog, a Philippine language that was foreign to them. (③) They were asked to identify any emotion they heard. How good were they at detecting the emotional information in what was being said, even though they could not understand the words? (④) The results were dramatic. Trained musicians were champs, while nonmusicians were surprisingly bad at it. (⑤) Musicians were especially good at discerning sadness and fear.

12 다음 글의 내용을 한 문장으로 요약하고자 한다. 빈칸 (A), (B)에 들어갈 말로 가장 적절한 것은?

The model of finding a place in the economy that needs skilled labor, training people to meet that need, and ranking them for employment according to their performance on set criteria will not only miss the moving target of a rapidly developing economy but also, because of knowledge monoculture, produce worse outcomes. Humans do not think or create alone, so cultivating many people all trained to the best standard will simply result in teams of people with overlapping and redundant skill sets instead of the diverse cognitive toolsets necessary for innovation. This affects testing and training policy. Measurement of skill on any single metric or even a range of metrics (say, by testing people and hiring those who test the best) will create teams of people who all tested well — who all overlap. These "best" teams — best precisely because they have all excelled at the same standard — will substantially underperform teams that include members with diverse cognitive toolsets, even if those toolsets are considered less valuable for a given task at hand.

⬇

People all trained to meet the highest standard will have ___(A)___ abilities, so forming a team of people with various cognitive toolsets will ___(B)___ innovation.

	(A)		(B)
①	diverse	······	interfere with
②	advanced	······	contribute to
③	unique	······	result in
④	similar	······	contribute to
⑤	limited	······	interfere with

[13~14] 다음 글을 읽고, 물음에 답하시오.

Importantly, listening has the potential to influence what is or is not offered in the first place. In other words, we cannot necessarily assume the (a) existence of a discrete message that either will or will not be heard and therefore included (and ultimately considered). Just as our own preferences and perspectives may change as a result of listening to others, the very perspective we offer may be influenced by practices of (b) listening themselves.

Research in communications, for example, has found that the quality of an audience's listening can (c) shape the speaker's message. Specifically, experiments in autobiographical storytelling show that "narrators change stories for inattentive listeners" by "changing the content they narrate, offering different interpretive content, and altering story structure." In my own classes, I have (d) adjusted a lecture when confronted with what appeared to be a tired or uninterested group of students. And in our own everyday conversations and personal interactions, we often find ourselves more eager to share a story or opinion if we believe someone is really listening. This (e) passive relationship between speaking and listening has important implications for inclusion, as listening can affect the very content of what people share in deliberation.

13 윗글의 제목으로 가장 적절한 것은?

① Listen Up! Your Heart Is Speaking
② Learning to Listen, Listening to Learn
③ Listening Well: The Art of Empathic Understanding
④ The Art of Speaking: How to Speak So People Really Listen
⑤ Listen Carefully, You Can Change What Others Say

14 밑줄 친 (a)~(e) 중에서 문맥상 낱말의 쓰임이 적절하지 않은 것은?

① (a)　　② (b)　　③ (c)　　④ (d)　　⑤ (e)

GRAMMAR REVIEW

지문의 문장으로 점검하는 수능 빈출 주요문법!

빈칸에 주어진 단어를 올바른 형태로 쓰거나, 네모 안에서 알맞은 것을 고르시오.

1 We appreciate the fair's mission to stimulate the local economy and applaud / applauds your efforts to support such a worthy cause. 01번

2 They have to stop what they're doing, focus on your request, and take / taking the time to respond. 02번

3 Most developing countries, including those in the Middle East and North Africa, adopted / adopting import substitution strategies in conjunction with high levels of protection, central planning, public ownership, and nonuniform policies across sectors and activities. 03번

4 Communicating our joys, fears, opinions, fantasies, wishes, requests, demands, feelings — and the occasional threat or insult — is / are a very important aspect of being human. 04번

5 If you walk into a room where / that smells of freshly baked bread, you quickly detect the rather pleasant aroma. 07번

6 To get the benefit, count the number of breaths you take in a minute, then sit quietly while gradually slowed / slowing the rate. 08번

7 From that moment on, they strongly believed that / what there was absolutely no hope of getting rid of the rope. 10번

8 In one study, English-speaking musicians and nonmusicians heard various emotions _____ (express) in Tagalog, a Philippine language that was foreign to them. 11번

9 These "best" teams — best precisely because they have all excelled at the same standard — will substantially underperform teams how / that include members with diverse cognitive toolsets, even if those toolsets are considered less valuable for a given task at hand. 12번

10 In my own classes, I have adjusted a lecture when confronted / confronting with what appeared to be a tired or uninterested group of students. 13-14번

01 다음 글에 드러난 Kate의 심경 변화로 가장 적절한 것은?

Kate clutched her old soccer ball, her stomach full of butterflies. The soccer field buzzed with kids playing, their laughter echoing in her ears. Her heart pounded as she approached the field, feeling the weight of her worn soccer shoes on the freshly mowed grass. A tall coach with a big smile stopped her. "New here?" he asked kindly. Kate mumbled, "Yes," his smile making her feel better. The coach's warm smile and encouraging words helped calm Kate's racing heart as he explained the practice drills to the players. Kate found unexpected joy in kicking the ball, the cool autumn air refreshing her with each pass. With each successful dribble, the coach offered a high five and a word of encouragement, "Nice footwork, Kate! Keep it up!" By the end, Kate not only felt excited but also like a star! Walking home, Kate realized that she had talent in soccer. She couldn't wait to get back on the field for her next practice to show off her skills!

*buzz: 시끌벅적하다　**mow: (잔디를) 깎다

① envious   →   ashamed
② frustrated →   grateful
③ nervous   →   confident
④ indifferent →   pleased
⑤ thrilled   →   disappointed

02 다음 글의 요지로 가장 적절한 것은?

A human body starts out as a handful of cells. It grows, matures, ages and dies. Then it decomposes. At the molecular level, it constantly changes. With every breath, we inhale billions of atoms from the environment — each one modifying our physical make-up to some degree. Moreover, 98% of our atoms are renewed every year; if this were not so, we would die within hours, poisoned by our own waste. The body is like a building whose bricks are constantly replaced. We grow a new skin and liver every few months and the skeleton, which appears so solid, regenerates every six months. Not one cell remains from the body you occupied two years ago. Even the brain cells, where your personality and memories are stored, die off and are replaced every year or so.

① 인간의 신체를 이루고 있는 구성 요소는 끊임없이 바뀐다.
② 노화는 자연스러운 과정이므로 인정하고 받아들여야 한다.
③ 신체는 복잡해 보이지만 실은 다양한 분자 활동의 총합체이다.
④ 대부분의 신체 조직과 장기는 이식할 수 있지만 뇌는 그렇지 않다.
⑤ 정신 작용은 신체의 물질 작용과 어느 정도 독립적으로 이루어진다.

03 다음 글의 제목으로 가장 적절한 것은?

Elephants, one of the largest animals on earth, eat well and excrete a lot, too. Some zookeepers recently decided to try to find a way to deal with this huge amount of waste. They noticed that elephant excrement was full of fibers, so they developed elephant waste paper. The paper is thick, with a texture similar to traditional Korean paper. To make it, elephant excrement is dried, boiled and washed many times until only the high-quality fibers remain. The fibers are cut into small pieces and dye is added. Once dried in the sun, it is complete. Any odor or germs disappear in the process. Some zoos sell good luck charms with phrases like "pass the test" printed on paper made of elephant excrement. They say it brings luck as big as an elephant.

*excrete: 배설하다

① Various Types of Paper in Use
② Elephant Wastes Recycled as Paper
③ Elephants Are an Endangered Species
④ Making Paper from Recycled Materials
⑤ Elephants: An Animal Bringing Good Luck

04 Children's Art Festival Poster Contest에 관한 다음 안내문의 내용과 일치하는 것은?

Children's Art Festival Poster Contest

Design a poster for the Children's Art Festival and see your artwork on the festival's poster and T-shirt!

Applicants

Applicants are limited to the residents in this city. Applicants under 18 require parental signature.

Poster requirements

• Entries should represent the theme "Summer Fun."
• Entries will not be returned.
• Entries are for single applicants only. Group artwork will not be accepted.
• Entries are due by March 7.

Prizes

• The winning entry will be featured on a limited number of Children's Art Festival posters and T-shirts.
• The first five runners-up will have their works displayed at the Children's Art Festival on Saturday, May 26.

① 거주지에 상관없이 누구나 신청할 수 있다.
② 포스터의 주제에는 제한이 없다.
③ 탈락된 작품은 참가자에게 돌려준다.
④ 단체로 출품하는 것은 허용되지 않는다.
⑤ 상위 5명의 작품은 3월 7일에 전시될 예정이다.

05 다음 글의 밑줄 친 부분 중, 문맥상 낱말의 쓰임이 적절하지 <u>않은</u> 것은?

What if you were unable to see the color red? Would you be less likely to be ① <u>tempted</u> by an apple or a beverage in a red glass? Ask color-blind individuals this question, and they will emphatically answer no. They can still ② <u>recognize</u> an apple, and know that it would taste good. They can still learn to associate a colored glass with a sweet beverage. Just think of the times you have watched a black-and-white television show. You quickly forget that it's black-and-white, and your mind matches the shades of ③ <u>gray</u> to colors you would expect to see. People who are born missing one of their photopigments are just as tempted by a juicy red apple as those whose color vision is ④ <u>impaired</u>. The color they see may be different from the one the rest of us see, but they will still have learned to associate it with an ⑤ <u>emotional</u> response.

*photopigment: 광색소

06 다음 빈칸에 들어갈 말로 가장 적절한 것은?

There is no one who does not know what it is to feel angry. In fact, according to a recent poll by the Mental Health Organization, more than a quarter of people worry about just how angry they sometimes feel. Yet the red mist of rage _____; anger was a motivating force that drove us to achieve the innately driven goal of survival of our DNA. Our angry ancestors were more likely to fight for food, shelter and mates than their more laid-back contemporaries. If our ancestors had not got angry about others stealing their food and resources or about predators trying to kill them, they wouldn't have taken preventative action and they wouldn't have survived.

① made them feel happy
② helped our ancestors survive
③ had a negative effect on health
④ prevented fights between people
⑤ motivated us to steal food from others

07 다음 빈칸에 들어갈 말로 가장 적절한 것은?

To those who fear monopolies and believe that some producers should be protected from other producers by the government, such antitrust suits can be considered morally necessary. But the issue is not whether antitrust legislation is moral; it is whether it serves the free market and our folk economic intuitions. Antitrust actions are based on a win-lose, zero-sum, producer-driven economy, but the economy is not zero sum. And it is our folk intuitions that lead us to believe that the economy must have been designed from the top down, and thus can only succeed with continual managing and control from the top. But in his evolutionary, bottom-up model of the economy, Adam Smith provided plenty of evidence that disapproves this myth. He insisted that the economy prospers when

_____.

*antitrust suit: 독점 금지법

① a moral government is firmly established
② it distributes the resources evenly to people
③ the efficiency of mass-production is realized
④ the free pursuits of individual interests are allowed
⑤ the antitrust policies are accepted by the producers

08 다음 글에서 전체 흐름과 관계 없는 문장은?

Goods we all benefit from but only some of us pay for, or which damage us all but only some of us produce — what economists call 'public goods' — are not naturally 'market goods'. ① Economic theory defines public goods as those which are non-rival and non-excludable, i.e. our use of them does not reduce the ability of others to use them, and once they are provided we cannot prevent others from using them. ② It may be that some of the environmental public goods, such as clean air or biodiversity, need to be protected by centralized expenditure derived from taxation. ③ People are free to exchange private goods in the marketplace, and public systems provide a minimal level of oversight to ensure that exchanges are fair. ④ Yet those who will pay these taxes may not value the public goods sufficiently, or have a real sense of their value, and thus will resent having to pay for them, and hence a market economy may struggle to allocate them efficiently. ⑤ So a market system may result in too much pollution and too few footpaths.

*expenditure: 지출 **allocate: 배분하다

09 주어진 글 다음에 이어질 글의 순서로 가장 적절한 것은?

A psychological identification between self and site is part of place-making, in an ongoing social process.

(A) They have fond memories of a special childhood place that they bonded with and can still vividly describe. Yet in all too many cases this landscape of childhood has been altered or even destroyed, and "people relate similar stories about how their special places have changed."

(B) Interviews with environmental activists from all parts of the world reveal a striking thematic pattern: whether the person is from an Asian tropical rain forest, an African savanna, a Latin-American city, a European valley, or a North American farm, they tell a similar story.

(C) It demands a personal investment in a particular location whose appearance, sounds, and smells become part of a daily round. Creating a sense of place in an unfamiliar space establishes somewhere to belong. Human geographers and other researchers consider this process of identification to be fundamental to place.

① (A) – (C) – (B) ② (B) – (A) – (C)
③ (B) – (C) – (A) ④ (C) – (A) – (B)
⑤ (C) – (B) – (A)

10 글의 흐름으로 보아, 주어진 문장이 들어가기에 가장 적절한 곳은?

But it is worth questioning rules along the way.

Most people choose to follow the rules. (①) However, rules are often meant to be broken. (②) It is important to keep in mind that there are often creative ways to work around the rules, to jump over the traditional hurdles, and to get to your goal by taking a side route. (③) While most people wait in a never-ending line of traffic on the main route to the highway, others who are more adventurous try to find a side road to get to their destinations more quickly. (④) Of course, some rules are in place to protect our safety, to keep order, and to create a process that works for a large number of people. (⑤) Sometimes side roads around the rules can get you to your goal when the traditional paths appear blocked.

11 글의 흐름으로 보아, 주어진 문장이 들어가기에 가장 적절한 곳은?

If these creatures are then food for larger ones, the accumulated toxins are concentrated even further.

Certain amounts and types of pollution are cleansed by natural processes. (①) When we create waste that nature cannot handle, or that cannot be absorbed as fast as we create it, pollution builds up. (②) The problems become more and more serious as the activity continues. (③) Some pollutants can create serious hazards even when thoroughly diluted. (④) Small amounts of toxic materials, after being absorbed by tiny organisms, can accumulate in the flesh of the creatures that eat them. (⑤) Through this biological accumulation, some poisons, although thinly dispersed, can be found in dangerous concentrations — for example, in fish from polluted water and in the humans who eat those fish.

[12-14] 다음 글을 읽고, 물음에 답하시오.

(A)

Many years ago, when I worked as a volunteer at Stanford Hospital, I got to know a little girl named Liza, who was suffering from a rare and serious disease. Her only chance of recovery appeared to be a blood transfusion from her five-year-old brother, Kevin, who had miraculously survived the same disease and had developed the antibodies needed to combat the illness.

*blood transfusion: 수혈

(B)

As the transfusion progressed, (a)he lay in a bed next to his sister and smiled, seeing the color returning to her cheeks. Then his face grew pale and his smile faded. He looked up at the doctor and asked (b)him with a trembling voice, "Will I start to die right away?" His eyes were full of tears.

(C)

Being young, the boy had misunderstood the doctor. (c)He thought he was going to have to give her all his blood. He had made the decision to die in order to save his sister. Every time when people ask me what courage is, I always tell them this story about the little boy who risked (d)his life to save his sister.

(D)

The doctor explained the situation to her little brother, and asked the boy if (e)he would be willing to give his blood to his sister. I saw him hesitate for only a moment before taking a deep breath and saying, "Yes, I'll do it if it will save Liza."

12 주어진 글 (A)에 이어질 내용을 순서에 맞게 배열한 것으로 가장 적절한 것은?

① (B) – (D) – (C) ② (C) – (B) – (D)
③ (C) – (D) – (B) ④ (D) – (B) – (C)
⑤ (D) – (C) – (B)

13 밑줄 친 (a)~(e) 중에서 가리키는 대상이 나머지 넷과 다른 것은?

① (a) ② (b) ③ (c) ④ (d) ⑤ (e)

14 윗글의 Kevin에 관한 내용으로 적절하지 않은 것은?

① 희귀병을 앓고 있는 누나가 있었다.
② Liza와 같은 병을 앓은 적이 있다.
③ 수혈이 진행되는 동안 Liza 옆 침대에 누워 그녀를 바라보았다.
④ 수혈을 하면 목숨을 잃는 것으로 생각했다.
⑤ 망설임 없이 수혈을 해 주기로 결심했다.

지문의 문장으로 점검하는 수능 빈출 주요문법!

빈칸에 주어진 단어를 올바른 형태로 쓰거나, 네모 안에서 알맞은 것을 고르시오.

1 Kate found unexpected joy in kicking the ball, the cool autumn air refreshed / refreshing her with each pass. 01번

2 Even the brain cells, which / where your personality and memories are stored, die off and are replaced every year or so. 02번

3 The color they see may be different from the one the rest of us see, but they will still have learned to associate it / one with an emotional response. 05번

4 Yet the red mist of rage helped our ancestors survive; anger was a motivating force that / what drove us to achieve the innately driven goal of survival of our DNA. 06번

5 To those who fear monopolies and believe that some producers should be protected from other producers by the government, such antitrust suits can be considered morally necessary / necessarily . 07번

6 It may be that some of the environmental public goods, such as clean air or biodiversity, need / needs to be protected by centralized expenditure derived from taxation. 08번

7 It demands a personal investment in a particular location in which / whose appearance, sounds, and smells become part of a daily round. 09번

8 While most people wait in a never-ending line of traffic on the main route to the highway, others who are more adventurous try to find a side road get / to get to their destinations more quickly. 10번

9 The problems become more and more serious / seriously as the activity continues. 11번

10 Her only chance of recovery appeared _____(be)_____ a blood transfusion from her five-year-old brother, Kevin, who had miraculously survived the same disease and had developed the antibodies _____(need)_____ to combat the illness. 12-14번

01 다음 글의 목적으로 가장 적절한 것은?

Dear Editors,

Teens Life used to be my favorite magazine. Articles that question people's morals, values, and current event are what I like to read about. The May 2022 issue included a column on the subject of teen refugees surviving wars. In the July 2023 issue, you ran a column about teens living with AIDS. Granted, newspapers can also give worldwide news stories, but a teenager wants to read articles in a magazine that will relate those harsh subjects to a teenager's life. However, to my dismay, most of the issues in recent months have been full of ads. This has greatly reduced the number of interesting articles. I used to buy *Teens Life* on the first of every month. Now I rarely ever buy it. Please make *Teens Life* into the magazine it used to be, because changes are not always good.

Sincerely,
Morris Jackson

① 기사의 잘못된 점을 지적하려고
② 잡지 구독료 인상에 항의하려고
③ 잡지사의 신규 기자직에 지원하려고
④ 잡지에 시사 기사를 다시 늘릴 것을 요청하려고
⑤ 잡지에서 다루어 주기를 바라는 장소를 소개하려고

02 다음 글에서 필자가 주장하는 바로 가장 적절한 것은?

One large-scale project measured to see whether using your brain can cause new growth of neurons and dendrites. In the project, computers were programmed so that an individual computer could evaluate a subject's ability in math. Then, the computer started a test for its subject that stayed in line with the person's ability. Once the computer pushed the limit of each person's ability, the researchers were able to see growth of neurons and dendrites. The best part is that people didn't need to get the answers right to reap the benefits. Simply working with math problems beyond their capabilities was enough to cause the regrowth. So for you, if you get barely half of the answers to Sunday's crossword puzzle, the best thing for your brain would be to continue working on it. Just like an athlete becomes faster and stronger by training to attain goals that are just out of reach, you can train your brain to stay smarter and sharper.

＊dendrite: (신경 세포의) 수상 돌기(정보를 받아들이는 뉴런 부분)

① 수학 공부는 어린이의 뇌 발달에 도움이 된다.
② 컴퓨터는 인간의 사고 능력을 능가할 수 없다.
③ 자신의 능력을 뛰어넘는 문제를 풀면 뇌의 발달에 좋다.
④ 문제 풀이에 실패했을 때의 좌절감은 자아 형성에 나쁘다.
⑤ 학습 능률 향상을 위해 개별화된 프로그램을 제공해야 한다.

03 밑줄 친 Coeliacs of France, rejoice.가 다음 글에서 의미하는 바로 가장 적절한 것은?

There's a very important interaction between food and human health. We all know the importance of a balanced and varied diet, but what if one of the components of a typical diet is the very thing that makes you ill? Coeliac disease affects about 1% of the population. In this condition, the body's immune system increases a harmful reaction to the gluten proteins found in wheat. This damages the lining of the gut, resulting in diarrhoea and vomiting, and in its most extreme forms it can lead to malnutrition and gut cancers. A research group in Cordoba, Spain, used gene editing to inactivate 35 of the 45 genes in wheat that produce the specific gluten proteins that trigger the immune over-reaction. Delightfully, they reported that the resulting flour was good enough to create baguettes, but not suitable for baking sliced white loaves. Coeliacs of France, rejoice.

*coeliac disease: 만성 소화 장애증 **diarrhoea: 설사
***inactivate: 비활성화시키다

① The prevalence of coeliac disease in France remains steady.
② French people respond to coeliac disease rather indifferently.
③ Coeliac disease is considered very common among French people.
④ Coeliac disease can be treated by French's gene editing technology.
⑤ French people with coeliac disease are less likely to suffer from it.

04 다음 글의 주제로 가장 적절한 것은?

When we talk about boomerangs, we usually mean the curved devices that return to you when you throw them, but there are actually two different kinds of boomerangs. The kind we're familiar with, returning boomerangs, are lightweight pieces of wood, plastic or other material. They are not suited for hunting, as they are very hard to aim. On the other hand, non-returning boomerangs are also curved pieces of wood, but they are usually heavier and longer, typically 3 feet or more across. They do not have the special wing design that causes returning boomerangs to travel back to the thrower, but their curved shape does cause them to fly easily through the air. They are effective hunting weapons because they are easy to aim and they travel a good distance at a high rate of speed. There is also such a thing as a battle boomerang, which is basically a non-returning boomerang used in hand-to-hand combat.

① the history of studying boomerangs
② characteristics and usage of boomerangs
③ Westerners' misconceptions about boomerangs
④ differences between boomerangs and other weapons
⑤ the development of boomerangs for recreational purposes

05 다음 도표의 내용과 일치하지 <u>않는</u> 것은?

U.S. Adults Who Don't Go Online

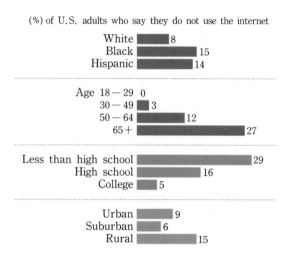

(%) of U.S. adults who say they do not use the internet

The above graph shows the percentage of U.S. adults who say they do not use the internet, categorized by ethnic group, age, education level, and community type. ① Higher percentages of both Black and Hispanic Americans say that they don't go online than White Americans. ② The percentage of adults who chooses not to use the internet is 0% in the 18-29 age group, and is in the single digits in the 30-49 age group. ③ The percentage of non-internet users aged 65 and older is 15 percentage points higher than that of adults aged 50-64. ④ Over three-in-ten adults with less than a high school education say they do not use the internet, but that share falls as the education level increases. ⑤ The percentage of U.S. adults who do not use the internet is less than 10% in both urban and suburban populations, whereas 15% of the U.S. adult rural population says they are non-internet users.

06 (A), (B), (C)의 각 네모 안에서 어법에 맞는 표현으로 가장 적절한 것은?

The fact that construction is a project-based industry is an important issue. When attempting to manage a dynamic, changing environment, such as a construction site, it should be kept in mind (A) [that / which] there needs to be an appropriate organization structure to deal with the changing nature of the project. As it moves from design to construction, and as problems arise (such as late delivery of materials) on a day-to-day basis, (B) [there / where] is a need for rapid decision-making and a flexible form of organization. This engenders a free, independent spirit in construction site workers and (C) [has / having], traditionally, led to a disregard for authority. In many cases, this disregard has been taken too far and caused problems.

	(A)		(B)		(C)
①	that	……	there	……	has
②	that	……	there	……	having
③	that	……	where	……	has
④	which	……	where	……	having
⑤	which	……	where	……	has

07 다음 빈칸에 들어갈 말로 가장 적절한 것은?

Every intelligence has to be _____. A human brain, which is genetically primed to categorize things, still needs to see a dozen examples as a child before it can distinguish between cats and dogs. That's even more true for artificial minds. Even the best-programmed computer has to play at least a thousand games of chess before it gets good. Part of the AI breakthrough lies in the incredible avalanche of collected data about our world, which provides the schooling that AIs need. Massive databases, self-tracking, web cookies, online footprints, terabytes of storage, decades of search results, Wikipedia, and the entire digital universe made AI smart. Andrew Ng explains it this way: "AI is akin to building a rocket ship. You need a huge engine and a lot of fuel. The rocket engine is the learning algorithms but the fuel is the huge amounts of data we can feed to these algorithms."

*primed: 준비가 되어 있는 **avalanche: 쇄도

① taught
② believed
③ assessed
④ predicted
⑤ controlled

08 다음 빈칸에 들어갈 말로 가장 적절한 것은?

In 2008, the management book *Who Moved My Cheese?* became the bestselling business book ever with 22 million copies sold worldwide in 37 languages — thus demonstrating the interest in _____. This simple story tells of two people and two mice who live in a maze with plenty of cheese. But one day their cheese disappears, and they must look for cheese elsewhere. The mice do this. However, one of the humans refuses to accept reality and adapt, demanding to know who moved his cheese. The other human, while initially resistant, realizes that he must leave his comfort zone and embrace change. Think of people you know who may have gone through corporate changes, layoffs, restructuring, or mergers. Do you think they acted like the mice or the resistant humans in the book?

① individual lifestyle
② openness to change
③ curiosity about the world
④ the need for global education
⑤ healthy relationships with peers

09 다음 글에서 전체 흐름과 관계 없는 문장은?

Even when the direct use of force is barred among a group of countries, military power can still be used politically. ① During the Cold War each superpower used the threat of force to deter attacks by other superpowers on itself or its allies; its deterrence ability thus served an indirect, protective role, which it could use in bargaining on other issues with its allies. ② This bargaining tool was particularly important for the United States, whose allies were concerned about potential Soviet threats and which had fewer other means of influence over its allies than did the Soviet Union over its Eastern European partners. ③ The United States had, accordingly, taken advantage of the Europeans' (particularly the Germans') desire for its protection and linked the issue of troop levels in Europe to trade and monetary negotiations. ④ A key component of sustainable economic development is the absence of military conflict and tension, which can only be achieved through close coordination among countries. ⑤ Thus, although the first-order effect of deterrent force was essentially negative — to deny effective offensive power to a superpower opponent — states could use that force positively — to gain political influence.

*bar: 금지하다   **deter: 저지하다   ***ally: 동맹국

10 주어진 글 다음에 이어질 글의 순서로 가장 적절한 것은?

In Africa it is hot, and for months on end it doesn't rain. In many regions very little grows. These are deserts, as are the lands on either side of Egypt. Egypt also gets very little rain.

(A) The mud was rich in nutrients. There, under the hot sun, the grain grew as it did nowhere else. Which is why, from earliest times, the Egyptians worshipped the Nile as if it were God himself.

(B) Then people were forced to take to boats to move among the houses and the palm trees. And when the waters withdrew, the earth was wonderfully drenched and rich with oozing mud.

(C) But here they don't need it, because the Nile flows right through the middle of the country, from one end to the other. Twice a year, when heavy rain filled its sources, the river would swell and burst its banks, flooding the whole land.

① (A) – (C) – (B)
② (B) – (A) – (C)
③ (B) – (C) – (A)
④ (C) – (A) – (B)
⑤ (C) – (B) – (A)

11 글의 흐름으로 보아, 주어진 문장이 들어가기에 가장 적절한 곳은?

So when it happened, I started to do some mental work right away and referred to my finger as having a lot of sensation.

Someone at one of my lectures was going through a lot of turmoil, and the word *pain* kept coming up in the conversation. (①) She asked if there was another word that she could use. (②) I thought about the time I had smashed my finger by slamming a window on it. (③) I knew if I gave into the pain, I was going to go through a very difficult period. (④) By viewing what happened in that particular way, I think it helped to heal the finger much more quickly and to handle what could have been a very unpleasant experience. (⑤) Sometimes if we can alter our thinking a little bit, we can completely change a situation.

12 다음 글의 내용을 한 문장으로 요약하고자 한다. 빈칸 (A), (B)에 들어갈 말로 가장 적절한 것은?

If you were a billiard-table dealer, which would you first show a potential buyer — a $329 model or a $3,000 model? You would probably promote the lower-priced item and hope to interest customers in the higher-priced item when they come to buy. But G. Warren Kelley, a business promotion manager at Brunswick, says you could be wrong. To prove his point, Kelley has actual sales figures from a representative store. During the first week, customers were shown the low end of the line and then encouraged to consider more expensive models — the traditional *trading-up* approach. The average table sale that week was $550. However, during the second week, customers were led instantly to a $3,000 table, regardless of what they wanted to see, and then allowed to shop the rest of the time in declining order of price and quality. The result of selling down was an average sale of more than $1,000.

⬇

G. Warren Kelley's case shows that showing customers ___(A)___ items first could ___(B)___ the amount of sales.

	(A)		(B)
①	pricey	......	increase
②	pricey	......	decrease
③	inexpensive	......	increase
④	new	......	decrease
⑤	new	......	maintain

[13-14] 다음 글을 읽고, 물음에 답하시오.

Most people spend their time at work trying to look intelligent, and for the last fifty years or more, people have tried to look intelligent by trying to look like scientists; if you ask someone to explain why something happened, they will generally give you a plausible-sounding answer that makes them seem intelligent, rational or scientific but that may or may not be the (a)real answer. The problem here is that real life is not a (b)conventional science — the tools which work so well when designing a Boeing 787, say, will not work so well when designing a customer experience or a tax program. People are not nearly as flexible or predictable as carbon fiber or metal alloys, and we should not (c)pretend that they are.

Adam Smith, the father of economics, identified this problem in the late eighteenth century, but it is a lesson which many economists have been ignoring ever since. If you want to look like a scientist, it pays to cultivate an air of certainty, but the problem with attachment to certainty is that it causes people completely to (d)understand the nature of the problem being examined, as if it were a simple physics problem rather than a psychological one. There is hence an ever-present (e)temptation to pretend things are more 'logical' than they really are.

*plausible-sounding: 그럴듯하게 들리는

13 윗글의 제목으로 가장 적절한 것은?

① Don't Forget to Find Evidence for Your Theory
② Why We Ignore Our Inner Voice to Reason So Often
③ Differences Between Fake Science and Real Science
④ Beware of the Desire to Look for Certainty in Reality
⑤ Our Scientific Tools Fail to Explain Natural Phenomena

14 밑줄 친 (a)~(e) 중에서 문맥상 낱말의 쓰임이 적절하지 않은 것은?

① (a)   ② (b)   ③ (c)   ④ (d)   ⑤ (e)

GRAMMAR REVIEW

지문의 문장으로 점검하는 수능 빈출 주요문법!

빈칸에 주어진 단어를 올바른 형태로 쓰거나, 네모 안에서 알맞은 것을 고르시오.

1 Granted, newspapers can also give worldwide news stories, but a teenager wants to read articles in a magazine it / that will relate those harsh subjects to a teenager's life. 01번

2 This damages the lining of the gut, ____(result)____ in diarrhoea and vomiting, and in its most extreme forms it can lead to malnutrition and gut cancers. 03번

3 When we talk about boomerangs, we usually mean the curved devices that return to you when you throw them / themselves , but there are actually two different kinds of boomerangs. 04번

4 In many cases, this disregard has been ____(take)____ too far and caused problems. 06번

5 AI is akin to ____(build)____ a rocket ship. 07번

6 The other human, while initially resistant, realizes that / what he must leave his comfort zone and embrace change. 08번

7 This bargaining tool was particularly important for the United States, whose allies were concerned about potential Soviet threats and which had fewer other means of influence over its allies than did / was the Soviet Union over its Eastern European partners. 09번

8 So when it happened, I started to do some mental work right away and referring / referred to my finger as having a lot of sensation. 11번

9 During the first week, customers were shown the low end of the line and then encouraging / encouraged to consider more expensive models — the traditional *trading-up* approach. 12번

10 The problem here is that real life is not a conventional science — the tools which work so well when ____(design)____ a Boeing 787, say, will not work so well when ____(design)____ a customer experience or a tax program. 13-14번

01 다음 글에 드러난 Joe의 심경 변화로 가장 적절한 것은?

For about a month, Joe noticed a shortness of breath and pressure in his chest while warming up to play tennis. After about 10 minutes, these feelings would go away. The pain was not sharp, and it was certainly not of sufficient concern to stop the match. So he didn't think much of it. After waiting one week to see if these feelings would clear up on their own, he made an appointment with his family doctor. She seemed concerned during his examination and sent him to a cardiologist. One test led to several tests. The diagnosis was far from what Joe had expected. "Joe, you have coronary heart disease," the doctor said. "As it's serious, I recommend immediate surgery within the next few days." Joe fell to the ground after hearing her words and couldn't stand up for quite a while.

*cardiologist: 심장병 전문의 **coronary: 관상 동맥의

① anxious   →   relieved
② regretful   →   confident
③ disappointed →   grateful
④ interested   →   indifferent
⑤ unconcerned →   shocked

02 다음 글의 요지로 가장 적절한 것은?

Although it's a difficult habit to break, it's not only enjoyable but actually peaceful to have the quiet confidence to be able to surrender your need for attention and instead share in the joy of someone else's glory. Rather than jumping right in and saying, "Once I did the same thing" or "Guess what I did today," bite your tongue and notice what happens. Just say, "That's wonderful," or "Please tell me more," and leave it at that. The person you are speaking to will have so much more fun, and because you are so much more "present," because you are listening so carefully, he or she won't feel in competition with you. The result will be that the person will feel more relaxed around you, making him or her more confident as well as more interesting. You too will feel more relaxed because you won't be on the edge of your seat, waiting your turn.

① 대화 중간에 끼어드는 습관은 무례하다는 인상을 줄 수 있다.
② 진심이 담기지 않은 형식적인 응답이라도 하지 않는 것보다는 낫다.
③ 상대방의 말에 대해 긍정적인 반응을 보여야 대화가 발전할 수 있다.
④ 다른 사람의 말을 기억해 두었다가 화제에 올리면 관계가 돈독해진다.
⑤ 말하지 않고 경청하면 마음이 느긋해지며 상대방은 대화를 즐길 수 있다.

03 다음 글의 제목으로 가장 적절한 것은?

Athletes in training are increasing their muscle levels and, therefore, the total amount of protein in their bodies. Many people think that this means they need more protein in their diets, and this is correct to a certain extent. However, even in children recovering from severe malnutrition, who show rapid catch-up growth, the gain in body protein is less than half the total amount of protein that is synthesized and broken down each day. Because average intakes of protein are sufficiently in excess of requirements, there is no need for more protein in the diet, especially from taking protein supplements, to permit an increase in the total amount of protein in the body as muscle is gained through training. On the other hand, there is a need for increased energy intake to meet both the cost of new protein synthesis and the energy cost of training and increased physical activity. If an athlete eats a larger quantity of their usual types of food, he or she will automatically increase not only energy but also protein intake. The protein supplements that are marketed for athletes therefore seem to be unnecessary.

① Myth about Protein Supplements for Athletes
② What Happens When You Eat Too Much Protein
③ The More Protein in Your Diet, the Healthier You Are
④ Fierce Competition Between Protein Synthesis Processes
⑤ Protein Supplements: A Plausible Temptation for Athletes

04 Aaron Copland에 관한 다음 글의 내용과 일치하지 않는 것은?

Aaron Copland was born on November 14, 1900, in Brooklyn, New York, the youngest of five children. One of Copland's sisters showed him how to play the piano when he was eleven years old, and soon afterward he began taking lessons from a teacher in the neighborhood. In 1921, he went to France to study and completed his studies in 1924, when he returned to America and composed the *Symphony for Organ and Orchestra*, his first major work. In the late 1920s, Copland turned to an increasingly experimental style, featuring irregular rhythms and often jarring sounds. Beginning in the mid-1930s through 1950, Copland made a serious effort to widen the audience for American music and took steps to change his style when writing pieces requested for different occasions. He composed music for theater, ballet, and films, as well as for concert situations. Aaron Copland was one of the most important figures in American music during the second quarter of the twentieth century, both as a composer and as a spokesman who was concerned about making Americans aware of the importance of music.

*jarring: 귀에 거슬리는

① 이웃의 한 선생님으로부터 피아노 수업을 받기 시작했다.
② 1921년에 공부하러 프랑스에 갔고 1924년에 공부를 마쳤다.
③ 1930년대 중반부터 점점 더 실험적인 형식을 시도했다.
④ 콘서트뿐만 아니라 연극, 발레, 영화를 위한 음악도 작곡했다.
⑤ 미국인들이 음악의 중요성을 알게 만드는 것에 관심을 가졌다.

05 다음 글의 밑줄 친 부분 중, 문맥상 낱말의 쓰임이 적절하지 않은 것은?

Hydropower's air pollution emissions are negligible because no fuels are burned in the production of electricity. However, if a large amount of vegetation is growing along the riverbed when a dam is built, it can ① decay in the lake that is created, causing the buildup and release of methane. Hydropower often requires the use of dams, which can greatly affect the flow of rivers, thereby ② altering ecosystems and affecting the wildlife and people that depend on those waters. Often, water at the bottom of the lake created by a dam is ③ hospitable to fish because it is much colder and oxygen-poor compared with water at the top. When this colder, oxygen-poor water is released into the river, it can kill fish living downstream that are accustomed to warmer, oxygen-rich water. Eroded material from upstream sources also ④ collects in dams, and over time, they become filled with huge deposits of silt that must be dredged. Nutrients and stream load (sediments) necessary for the health and balance of the waterway, which would have naturally been carried down river, become trapped in the reservoir behind the dam. This can have ⑤ negative effects.

*silt: 미사(微砂)(모래보다 곱고 진흙보다는 거친 침적토(沈積土))
**dredge: (강바닥 등에서) 건져 올리다

06 다음 빈칸에 들어갈 말로 가장 적절한 것은?

_____ is a commonly observed paradox. I recall being surprised at first to hear Charlotte Linde's observation that policemen whose conversations she had studied talked frequently about what "bad boys" they had been, trading stories about their youthful escapades and how cleverly they had broken the law in their wild days. This seeming puzzle was not solved until I came to understand the view of the world as a hierarchical social order. "Born rebels" who defy authority are not oblivious of it, but oversensitive to it. Defying authority is a way of asserting themselves and refusing to accept subordinate positions. When they are old enough, or established enough, to take the dominant position, reinforcing authority becomes the way to assert themselves, since the hierarchy is now operating to their advantage.

*escapade: 무모한 행위

① The law-abiding citizen who suffers a great loss
② Today's loser who becomes a winner in the future
③ The rebellious youth who turns into an authoritarian adult
④ The democratic politician who encourages a hierarchical order
⑤ The self-assertive person who has had traumatic experiences

07 다음 빈칸에 들어갈 말로 가장 적절한 것은?

What does boredom have to do with the creative process? Apparently plenty. To really exercise the creative muscle, _____. This doesn't happen when the mind is preoccupied and heavily engaged with social media posts, binge watching, or video gaming. The mind needs quiet time to engage all aspects of the creative process. However, today people are so consumed with their screen devices that the creative process is stifled. Creativity experts now agree that boredom is essential to the creative process. They suggest unplugging from one's screen devices and setting aside dedicated time to give the mind a chance to do nothing. Learning to quiet the mind is considered an essential precursor in allowing the creative process to unfold. In the words of the Chinese philosopher Confucius, "A seed grows with no sound, but a tree falls with a huge noise. Destruction has noise, but creation is quiet. This is the power of silence."

*binge watching: (TV 프로그램 등의) 몰아서 보기 **stifle: 방해하다
***precursor: 선구자

① we have to keep our mind functioning
② idleness can do nothing for our brains
③ the mind needs downtime to incubate ideas
④ old ideas should be combined with new ideas
⑤ accepting our drifting minds as normal is important

08 다음 글에서 전체 흐름과 관계 <u>없는</u> 문장은?

Like all forms of humor, the use of humor for coping with adversity usually takes place in a social context. ① People typically do not begin laughing and cracking jokes about their problems when they are all alone. ② Instead, coping humor commonly takes the form of joking and laughing with other people, either in the midst of an adverse situation or shortly afterwards. ③ For example, when the events of a particularly stressful day are discussed among a group of close friends later in the evening, difficulties that earlier seemed distressing and overwhelming can be perceived as humorously incongruous and become the basis of a great deal of hilarity and lively laughter. ④ Genuine laughter often comes from joyful situations, and forcing laughter when someone is going through a tough time may come across as insensitive to others. ⑤ The greater the emotional arousal and tension engendered by the stressful events, the greater the pleasure and the louder the laughter when joking about them afterwards.

*incongruous: 얼토당토않은 **hilarity: 유쾌 ***arousal: 흥분

09 주어진 글 다음에 이어질 글의 순서로 가장 적절한 것은?

The biggest difference between your sensory organs and other organs is that their malfunctioning doesn't have life-threatening implications — more like life-altering ones.

(A) Blind since birth, Feliciano had had to adjust the way he lives — especially in areas most people take for granted, like figuring out the difference between a $1 bill and a $20 bill.

(B) If your heart or brain stops working, so do you. But that's not the case with your sensory organs. In fact, some people, like singer Jose Feliciano, even embrace the loss of their senses.

(C) But when asked about whether he wished to have eyesight, he said he wouldn't — because he didn't want to be thought of as ungrateful for all the talents and gifts he has been given.

① (A) – (C) – (B)　　② (B) – (A) – (C)
③ (B) – (C) – (A)　　④ (C) – (A) – (B)
⑤ (C) – (B) – (A)

10 주어진 글 다음에 이어질 글의 순서로 가장 적절한 것은?

All human beings are born with brains divided into three parts. One part, the cortex (the cerebral hemispheres), handles learning, abstract thought, and imagination. The cortex comes into practical use in most children after they are seven years old.

(A) If you roll one of the balls into the shape of a snake and ask the child which piece of clay is larger, however, the child is likely to pick one or the other.

(B) Before that age, children do not have the mental tools to make intellectual assessments. If you take two identical balls of clay and ask a child, "Are they the same?" the child will say, "Yes."

(C) Ask the same question of a child older than seven, though, and he or she is likely to say, "Do you think I'm dumb or something?" The cortex is where logic resides and where we do the higher-level reasoning that separates us from all other animals.

*cortex: 대뇌 피질　**cerebral hemisphere: 대뇌 반구

① (A) – (C) – (B)　　② (B) – (A) – (C)
③ (B) – (C) – (A)　　④ (C) – (A) – (B)
⑤ (C) – (B) – (A)

11 글의 흐름으로 보아, 주어진 문장이 들어가기에 가장 적절한 곳은?

> Occasions when effective verbal messages depend on careful and exact phrasing are the few exceptions to the general rule of avoiding manuscript speaking.

Perhaps you remember the first speech you ever had to give, maybe as long ago as elementary school. Chances are that you wrote out your message and read it to your audience. Unfortunately, manuscript speaking is rarely done well enough to be interesting. (①) Most speakers who rely on a manuscript read it either in a monotone or with a pattern of vocal inflection that makes the speech "sound read." (②) They are so afraid of losing their place that they keep their eyes glued to the manuscript and seldom look at the audience. (③) These challenges are significant enough that most speakers should avoid reading from a manuscript most of the time. (④) For example, because an awkward statement made by the U.S. Secretary of State could cause an international crisis, his or her remarks on critical issues are usually carefully scripted. (⑤) If you ever have to speak on a sensitive, critical, or controversial issue, you too might need to deliver a manuscript speech.

*manuscript: 원고 **inflection: 억양
***Secretary of State: (미국의) 국무 장관

[12-14] 다음 글을 읽고, 물음에 답하시오.

(A)

Refining cane syrup in one boiling cauldron after another was not only dangerous; it was terribly inefficient. The man who figured out a safe, reliable way to accomplish the same thing with far less labor was himself a product of slave society. Nobert Rillieux was born in New Orleans in 1806. His father was a wealthy white man and engineer who recognized that the boy whom (a) he had fathered with a free woman of color was unusually smart.

*cauldron: 가마솥

(B)

Now, one person, instead of a team, could oversee the operation, and far less heat would be needed, since the heat could be transferred from one pan to another. Rillieux first demonstrated (b) his invention in the 1840s, and sugar producers were quick to see its value. But even being a noted inventor who had been given his legal freedom by his father was not guarantee of safety to a black man in Louisiana, so (c) he returned to France.

(C)

So Nobert's father sent (d) him to France to be educated. There, he learned the rational, scientific approach to testing and experimenting that had proven that sugar from beets is the same as the sugar from cane. And when he returned home to Louisiana, he applied his knowledge of engineering to refining sugar. Rillieux figured out that if the sugar syrup was heated in a series of special sealed pans, instead of an open cauldron, the whole process would be simplified.

(D)

Though he was not in danger of being enslaved in France, he suffered through a series of conflicts with others who claimed they had invented his process. Frustrated, (e) he turned his sharp mind to other tasks, such as the study of ancient Egyptian characters. Rillieux, who died in Paris in 1894, is a perfect example of the changing world of sugar in the 1800s. He himself was free but had to struggle against prejudice throughout his life.

12 주어진 글 (A)에 이어질 내용을 순서에 맞게 배열한 것으로 가장 적절한 것은?

① (B) – (D) – (C) ② (C) – (B) – (D)
③ (C) – (D) – (B) ④ (D) – (B) – (C)
⑤ (D) – (C) – (B)

13 밑줄 친 (a)~(e) 중에서 가리키는 대상이 나머지 넷과 다른 것은?

① (a) ② (b) ③ (c) ④ (d) ⑤ (e)

14 윗글의 Nobert Rillieux에 관한 내용으로 적절하지 않은 것은?

① 백인 아버지와 유색인 어머니 사이에서 태어났다.
② 1840년대에 자신의 발명을 처음으로 시연했다.
③ 루이지애나에서는 안전을 보장받을 수 없어서 프랑스로 돌아갔다.
④ 프랑스에서 배운 것을 설탕 정제 방법에 적용했다.
⑤ 사망할 때까지 계속 설탕 정제 방법에 관해 연구했다.

GRAMMAR REVIEW

지문의 문장으로 점검하는 수능 빈출 주요문법!

빈칸에 주어진 단어를 올바른 형태로 쓰거나, 네모 안에서 알맞은 것을 고르시오.

1 The diagnosis was far from which / what Joe had expected. 01번

2 The result will be that the person will feel more relaxed around you, ____ (make) him or her more confident as well as more interesting. 02번

3 In 1921, he went to France to study and completed his studies in 1924, which / when he returned to America and composed the *Symphony for Organ and Orchestra*, his first major work. 04번

4 However, if a large amount of vegetation is growing along the riverbed when a dam is built, it can decay in the lake that is created, ____ (cause) the buildup and release of methane. 05번

5 Learning to quiet the mind is considered an essential precursor in allowing the creative process ____ (unfold) . 07번

6 For example, when the events of a particularly stressful day are discussed among a group of close friends later in the evening, difficulties that earlier seemed distressing and overwhelming can be perceived as humorously incongruous / incongruously and become the basis of a great deal of hilarity and lively laughter. 08번

7 The biggest difference between your sensory organs and other organs is / are that their malfunctioning doesn't have life-threatening implications — more like life-altering ones. 09번

8 If you roll one of the balls into the shape of a snake and ask the child that / which piece of clay is larger, however, the child is likely to pick one or the other. 10번

9 They are so afraid of losing their place that they keep their eyes ____ (glue) to the manuscript and seldom look at the audience. 11번

10 Rillieux figured out that if the sugar syrup was heated in a series of special sealed pans, instead of an open cauldron, the whole process would ____ (simplify) . 12-14번

01 다음 글의 목적으로 가장 적절한 것은?

Dear Mr. Verbanks,

We thank you for the order you placed on January 10 for 500 steel bookshelves to be delivered by February 10. You changed the design on January 15, which we accepted. However, while we were checking our inventory, we found that some parts are out of stock right now. Your previous design didn't require those parts, but your present design does. We placed an order to our provider for the parts, and they are going to arrive on January 20. To complete the shelves, we will need to work on them for three or four more days. Thus, we ask you to understand our situation and accept the delivery on February 14. We shall get in touch with you as soon as we complete your order. We once again thank you for offering us your business.

Yours truly,
Frederick Furniture

① 결함이 있는 제품의 환불을 요구하려고
② 주문받은 제품의 배송일 연기를 알리려고
③ 주문한 제품의 배송 지연에 대해 항의하려고
④ 주문한 제품의 디자인 변경 가능 여부를 확인하려고
⑤ 주문 제작 제품의 가격 책정 방식에 대해 설명하려고

02 다음 글에서 필자가 주장하는 바로 가장 적절한 것은?

The true financial plan for retirement is never finished because your needs are always going to change. Let's say you're retiring at age 60 and you have a plan in place to generate $2,000 a month of income, based on what your needs are today. That might be great for the first two, three or four years of retirement. But things are always changing in your life personally, and things are also changing in the economy and in the world. A big factor regarding those changes is inflation. Just because you need $2,000 a month today in 2024, that $2,000 a month is not going to go as far in 2027, because of inflation. You need to regularly revise your plan for that reason. You need to create a plan that will continue to increase your income to keep up with inflation.

① 퇴직 후의 재정 계획은 퇴직하기 전에 세워야 한다.
② 정부는 퇴직자의 노후 생활을 위한 정책을 마련해야 한다.
③ 인플레이션에 맞춰 퇴직 후 재정 계획을 수정해 나가야 한다.
④ 정년 연장 논의는 사회의 전반적인 차원에서 검토되어야 한다.
⑤ 인플레이션 시기에는 자산을 증식할 수 있는 투자를 해야 한다.

03 밑줄 친 disappear into the population of the rest of the country가 다음 글에서 의미하는 바로 가장 적절한 것은?

The attitudes of 19th-century racism and evolutionism are no longer unquestioningly accepted throughout the world, but a certain neo-evolutionism has taken their place. Indigenous (or tribal) societies are rarely called "savage" these days, at least not in public, but they are normally considered "backward!" It may no longer be considered acceptable to remove them by massacring them (though this still happens), but it is everywhere the case that governments feel that such peoples should be helped or forced to overcome their "backwardness." To overcome its backwardness, an indigenous society is urged to abandon its traditional way of life and often its language as well, usually in the hope that in so doing it will cease to exist as a society altogether. Its individual members, now no longer embedded in their "backward" society, will disappear into the population of the rest of the country.

① go back to their savage state
② create their own new society
③ lose their traditional way of life
④ be in conflict with the government
⑤ fail to overcome their "backwardness"

04 다음 글의 주제로 가장 적절한 것은?

Strange as it may seem, the killer whale affects the diet of the bald eagle in Alaska! Researchers have found that an increase in killer whales results in a decrease in sea otters, one of their favorite prey items. Otters eat sea urchins. Therefore, the fewer otters, the more sea urchins there are. Sea urchins feed on the large algae that serve as hiding places for fish along banks. Thus, the more sea urchins, the fewer algae and the fewer hiding places! As a result, the fish move elsewhere. In Alaska, bald eagles are raptors who feed mainly on the fish in shallow waters on the edges of the ocean. Without these fish, they have to find other food. Accordingly, scientists discovered that the decline of sea otters in Alaska thanks to the predation of killer whales, forces bald eagles to change their diet and choose marine birds as prey. A puzzle indeed!

＊sea urchin: 성게 ＊＊raptor: 맹금

① the impacts of climate change
② the bonds linking animal species
③ how to increase food productivity
④ the ways to conserve endangered species
⑤ the importance of preserving natural habitats

05 Recycled Art Contest에 관한 다음 안내문의 내용과 일치하지 <u>않는</u> 것은?

Recycled Art Contest

We are looking for the best piece of Trash Art! The Earth Day Festival Planning Committee invites you to participate in our Recycled Art Contest.

PARTICIPANTS
All the residents in Berkeley city

ENTRY DATE
Bring the entry form and your work to Berkeley Community Center by Friday, April 22.

SPECIFICATIONS
1. You have to use the materials that would have been trash. The project must convey the three Rs(Reduce, Reuse, Recycle).
2. Any media will be accepted(painting, digital, photos, textile, etc.).

JUDGING & AWARDS
Contestants will be judged on the use of recyclable materials and the message conveyed. Prizes will be awarded for 1st, 2nd, and 3rd place.

① Berkeley 시의 거주자라면 누구나 참가할 수 있다.
② 참가 신청서와 작품을 4월 22일까지 제출해야 한다.
③ 공정성을 기하기 위해 작품 표현 수단에 제한이 있다.
④ 작품 평가에는 재활용 가능한 재료의 사용 여부가 고려된다.
⑤ 대회에 참가한 사람들 중 1위부터 3위까지 상이 주어진다.

06 다음 글의 밑줄 친 부분 중, 어법상 <u>틀린</u> 것은?

The ancient Greeks conceptualized time as either chronos or kyros. Chronos is clock time ①<u>measured</u> in seconds, minutes, and hours, and it is the root of words such as "chronology" and "chronological." Kyros is timelessness, living in the here and now, synchronicity and carpe diem — seizing the moment. Chronos and kyros represent quantity and quality, which reflect ②<u>that</u> our struggle with time is all about. While chronos is fixed at an objective rate, kyros varies ③<u>considerably</u> because it is subjective and can be a positive or negative experience. To most people 45 minutes spent in the dentist's chair will feel longer than the same period of time spent ④<u>reading</u> a fascinating book. How can we experience more positive kyros time and less chronos? Doing one thing at a time, refusing to live an over-scheduled life, and making time for the important people and activities in our lives ⑤<u>are</u> key ways to help us balance the quantity and the quality of our time.

07 다음 빈칸에 들어갈 말로 가장 적절한 것은?

There is an ancient cemetery outside the Glasgow Cathedral in Scotland that may hold a forgotten secret of health. In the early 1990s, researcher George Davey Smith conducted a study that asked a creative and strange question: Could the grave markers at the old cemetery hold any information about the health and longevity of the deceased? To answer this question, he compared the height of each grave marker to the age of the person buried beneath it at the time of death. What he discovered points out the error of assuming that good health is a matter of genetic good luck, a Spartan diet and running like a hamster on a treadmill. Smith found that the taller the grave marker, the longer the life. The deceased men with tall obelisks had lived an average of three years longer than those with shorter markers, and the same test held true for the women. Of course, buying yourself a tall gravestone now won't make you live longer. But it would in the past. Smith was looking for correlations between _____ and health and longevity.

① habit
② height
③ religion
④ affluence
⑤ achievement

08 다음 빈칸에 들어갈 말로 가장 적절한 것은?

Consider a series of studies by Nicholas Epley and colleagues in which subjects were greeted at the laboratory and given a $50 check. During the explanation of why they were receiving the check, one group of subjects heard the check described as a "bonus" and another group heard it described as a "tuition rebate." Epley and colleagues conjectured that the bonus would be mentally coded as a positive change from the status quo, whereas the rebate would be coded as a return to a previous wealth state. They thought that the bonus framing would lead to more immediate spending than the rebate framing, because spending from the status quo is more easily coded as a(n) _____. This is exactly what happened. In one experiment, when the subjects were contacted one week later, the bonus group had spent more of the money. In another experiment, subjects were allowed to buy items from the university bookstore (including snack foods) at a good discount. Again, the subjects from the bonus group spent more in the laboratory discount store.

*rebate: 환불   **conjecture: 추측하다   ***status quo: 현재 상황

① relative loss
② wise purchase
③ unexpected gain
④ future investment
⑤ financial recovery

09 다음 글에서 전체 흐름과 관계 없는 문장은?

Inequality, we have to keep in mind, is not the same thing as poverty. ① When people like Timothy Noah complain that "income distribution in the United States is now more unequal than in Uruguay, Nicaragua, Guyana, and Venezuela," they act as if it's irrelevant that almost all Americans are rich compared to the citizens of those countries. ② Economic inequality is perfectly compatible with widespread affluence, and rising inequality is perfectly compatible with a society in which the vast majority of citizens are getting richer. ③ If the incomes of the poorest Americans doubled while the incomes of the richest Americans tripled, that would dramatically increase inequality even though every single person would be better off. ④ More economic growth does not necessarily mean increased inequality. ⑤ Inequality refers not to deprivation but difference, and there is nothing suspicious or objectionable about differences *per se*.

10 주어진 글 다음에 이어질 글의 순서로 가장 적절한 것은?

Several studies have shown that changing lifestyle causes changes in gene expression, "turning on" genes that prevent chronic diseases and "turning off" genes that can cause heart disease and other illnesses.

(A) Their genes had changed to metabolize food more slowly, which, if you are starving, gives you a survival advantage but in the presence of adequate nutrition makes you more likely to gain weight and develop diabetes and high blood pressure. These genetic changes were passed on to their children and grandchildren as well.

(B) Equally amazing is that these changes in your genes can be passed down to future generations. An article published in June 2009 listed over 100 well-documented cases suggesting that these inheritances happen much more often than scientists previously thought.

(C) For example, in one case, women who were pregnant during the 1944 winter famine in the Netherlands had babies who were much more likely to develop diabetes even though the babies were given adequate nutrition by the time they were born.

① (A) – (C) – (B)　　② (B) – (A) – (C)
③ (B) – (C) – (A)　　④ (C) – (A) – (B)
⑤ (C) – (B) – (A)

11 글의 흐름으로 보아, 주어진 문장이 들어가기에 가장 적절한 곳은?

Historically, there was an informal contract between the employer and employee, between the leader and the led.

The ways in which we look at the role of the leader have changed. Leadership today comes less from the person at the top of the organizational chart than it once did. Leadership can come from anywhere in the library. There may be several leaders, each with special information, responsibilities, and/or skills. (①) The leader is part of the community and leads not just from a position of authority but also as a result of consensus of those being led. (②) If the individual being led was loyal to the leader, that individual's job was secure. (③) That contract no longer exists, largely because employees are unwilling to give loyalty as easily as was once true. (④) If a contract between a staff member and a leader still exists, it has become one in which mutual respect and appreciation have replaced the earlier, more paternalistic model. (⑤) "Leadership has become a reciprocal relationship between those who choose to lead and those who decide to follow."

*paternalistic: 가부장적인 **reciprocal: 호혜적인

12 다음 글의 내용을 한 문장으로 요약하고자 한다. 빈칸 (A), (B)에 들어갈 말로 가장 적절한 것은?

The earliest known theories of art in Western philosophy were proposed by Plato and his student Aristotle. The particular artform that most concerned them was drama. In his *Republic*, Plato presented a design for an ideal state. In the course of outlining his utopia, he argued that poets — particularly dramatists — should be outlawed. In order to justify the argument, Plato had to give reasons. And the reasons Plato found had to do with what he regarded as the nature of drama. According to Plato, the essence of drama was imitation — the simulation of appearances. That is, actors in plays imitate the actions of whomever they represent. In *Medea*, the actors, for example, imitate having arguments. Plato thought that this was problematic primarily because he believed that appearances appeal to the emotions and that stirring up the emotions is socially dangerous. An emotional citizenry is apt to be influenced by political agitation rather than by good sense.

⬇

In a utopia Plato presented as an ideal state, dramatists ought to be ___(A)___ , for he believed the actors who copy the actions of whomever they represent make citizens ___(B)___ to political agitation.

	(A)		(B)
①	imitated	······	subject
②	expelled	······	subject
③	expelled	······	immune
④	welcomed	······	indifferent
⑤	welcomed	······	immune

[13-14] 다음 글을 읽고, 물음에 답하시오.

There are unethical scientists, and there are certainly scientific advances that occurred because the unfortunate implications could not be predicted at the time, but the point is that science does directly and explicitly (a)examine the possible consequences of discovery. The precautionary principle dictates that questions concerning the possible implications of actions be considered before the fact. A direct manifestation of this can be seen in the requirement that any research involving human subjects be examined by an (b)outside group of reviewers to determine if there are any risks to the people involved. Institutional review boards are required whenever any research that involves humans is going to be conducted. Couple this requirement with the precautionary principle and the first question in science becomes "Should this be done?"

Technology, by contrast, asks the question, "Can this be done?" Technology is interested in how things will be done and how they will be applied but is woefully (c)deficient in terms of ethical analysis. In many ways all that (d)limits technological experimentation is what material it is possible to obtain. Certainly, some of this relates to the profit motive and consumerism. However, much of this lack of attention to ethical issues is a product of the (e)ability to consider the implications amid the rapidly changing nature of the technological landscape. Everything has become transient and there is no time to think about that which will be obsolete tomorrow.

13 윗글의 제목으로 가장 적절한 것은?

① Ethical Technology: Making Ethics a Priority
② On the Universality of Science and Technology
③ Technological Progress and Potential Risks in Future
④ New Ethical Problems That Technology Introduced
⑤ Science and Technology from an Ethical Perspective

14 밑줄 친 (a)~(e) 중에서 문맥상 낱말의 쓰임이 적절하지 않은 것은?

① (a)　　② (b)　　③ (c)　　④ (d)　　⑤ (e)

GRAMMAR REVIEW

정답 및 해설 88쪽

지문의 문장으로 점검하는 수능 빈출 주요문법!

빈칸에 주어진 단어를 올바른 형태로 쓰거나, 네모 안에서 알맞은 것을 고르시오.

1 Its individual members, now no longer ___(embed)___ in their "backward" society, will disappear into the population of the rest of the country. 03번

2 Researchers have found that an increase in killer whales | result / results | in a decrease in sea otters, one of their favorite prey items. 04번

3 Doing one thing at a time, refusing to live an over-scheduled life, and | make / making | time for the important people and activities in our lives are key ways to help us balance the quantity and the quality of our time. 06번

4 There is an ancient cemetery outside the Glasgow Cathedral in Scotland | where / that | may hold a forgotten secret of health. 07번

5 In one experiment, when the subjects were contacted one week later, the bonus group | spend / had spent | more of the money. 08번

6 Economic inequality is perfectly compatible with widespread affluence, and rising inequality is perfectly compatible with a society | which / in which | the vast majority of citizens are getting richer. 09번

7 An article published in June 2009 listed over 100 well-documented cases | suggested / suggesting | that these inheritances happen much more often than scientists previously thought. 10번

8 That contract no longer exists, largely because employees are unwilling to give loyalty as | easy / easily | as was once true. 11번

9 The earliest known theories of art in Western philosophy | was / were | proposed by Plato and his student Aristotle. 12번

10 Couple this requirement with the precautionary principle and the first question in science | becomes / to become | "Should this be done?" 13-14번

PART

고난도
모의고사

01 밑줄 친 **takes on a new cast**가 다음 글에서 의미하는 바로 가장 적절한 것은?

Our first embrace of sociable robotics is a window onto what we want from technology and what we are willing to do to accommodate it. From the perspective of our robotic dreams, networked life takes on a new cast. We celebrate its "weak ties," the bonds of acquaintance with people we may never meet. But that does not mean we prosper in them. We often find ourselves standing depleted in the hype. When people talk about the pleasures of these weak-tie relationships as "friction free," they are usually referring to the kind of relationships you can have without leaving your desk. Technology ties us up as it promises to free us up. Connectivity technologies once promised to give us more time. But as the cell phone and smartphone eroded the boundaries between work and leisure, all the time in the world was not enough. Even when we are not "at work," we experience ourselves as "on call."

*hype: (과장된) 광고

① helps resolve unexpected conflicts
② restrains our extended sphere of life
③ sets the boundary between work and leisure
④ makes people afraid of technological development
⑤ allows human relationships to function more efficiently

02 다음 글의 제목으로 가장 적절한 것은?

Increasingly, we recognise that today's poorer countries are developing in a very different context to the historical context in which Western countries developed. For a start there are new pollutants and modern technology is capable of extracting resources much more rapidly than in the nineteenth and early twentieth centuries. Trade allows for importing existing technologies rather than developing them domestically, which could be environmentally beneficial if efficiency is prioritised. But trade also allows 'pollution havens' to emerge. Many of today's developing countries are former colonies. Western countries developed by extracting raw materials from their colonies. Many of these now-independent countries remain locked into an extractionist development model. They can only seek higher incomes through expanded extraction and export of natural resources, not by moving towards another 'stage' of development. Some wonder whether China is becoming a 'colonial power' in its quest for growth, but most developing countries do not have this option. We should therefore be very cautious about using the West's experience to anticipate the development paths of today's poorer countries.

*haven: 피난처

① Why Efficiency Is Prioritised over Fairness in Trade
② When and How Culture Influences International Trade
③ Do Poorer Countries Develop Just as Western Countries Did?
④ Let's Provide Economic Assistance for Underdeveloped Countries!
⑤ Expanded Extraction of Natural Resources: The Key to Development

03 다음 글의 밑줄 친 부분 중, 문맥상 낱말의 쓰임이 적절하지 않은 것은?

Whatever the motivation, welfare is now on the fish farming agenda and several members of the aquaculture community have begun collaborating with fish scientists to identify which current practices ①adversely affect farmed fish. Researchers have already identified various routine handling practices that are stressful for the fish and in some cases this has led to ②changes in practice. Size-grading, for example, was once a very labour-intensive process ③requiring fish to be netted and handled, but now pumps and wide-diameter hoses fitted with counters are used to move fish of different size between tanks or ponds. This ④increases both the amount of direct handling and the time fish spend out of water. The results are clearly beneficial for the fish: grading is now a less stressful process and the fish recover more quickly. The positive experience of improving grading procedures has led to an ⑤interest in finding other ways of improving routine aspects of husbandry.

*husbandry: (낙농·양계 따위를 포함하는) 농업

04 다음 빈칸에 들어갈 말로 가장 적절한 것은?

The microeconomic approach for studying climate change adaptation explores who has an edge in coping with change and how one builds this capacity. For example, those who love a specific city and a specific leisure activity within that city will be less nimble in coping with a city-specific climate shock because they will be less willing to move elsewhere. Someone who loves skiing and is unwilling to substitute a different leisure activity will lose more than other people if local temperatures in winter often rise above freezing. The same issue of _____ arises in evaluating the impact of climate change. Consider your diet. Suppose you enjoy eating strawberries and prunes equally, but climate change raises the price of strawberries (perhaps because of the water needed to grow them). In this case, you will not suffer much because you can substitute prunes for strawberries. This key economic idea of substitution arises again and again. Those who are unwilling or unable to substitute will suffer more as climate change disrupts past routines and consumption habits.

*microeconomic: 미시 경제학의 **nimble: 민첩한

① improving their own surroundings
② engaging in various hobbies actively
③ exhibiting a willingness to substitute
④ attributing climate change to global warming
⑤ being enthusiastic about specific leisure activities

05 다음 빈칸에 들어갈 말로 가장 적절한 것은?

Although in principle the production of an agrarian surplus became possible, for thousands of years this did not lead to a large accumulation of human-made complexity other than for the fulfillment of daily needs or to a rapidly growing social complexity. If current traditional agrarian societies provide a reasonably good model of what may have happened in the past, any produced surplus was mostly, if not entirely, consumed in competitive feasting and other social obligations, which would have had a strong economic leveling effect within such societies. Such exchanges bring about a network of social obligations, which are helpful in surviving leaner times. As a result of this situation, no substantial surplus would have accumulated, which very much limited the emergence of more elaborate forms of social or technical complexity characteristic of 'civilized' societies. It may even be that such people _____.
This tendency may well be a fundamental human characteristic, which would have evolved simply because generating more complexity requires more energy.

*agrarian: 농업의

① converted any produced surplus into alternative energy sources
② put the complexity of social inclusion and exclusion under control
③ strived to solve complicated social problems caused by competition
④ created an environment for prosperity rather than economic equality
⑤ preferred to keep the complexity of their societies as low as possible

06 주어진 글 다음에 이어질 글의 순서로 가장 적절한 것은?

Whenever genes, situations, or therapy changes our personalities, they must do so by changing the brain. In that sense, all personality differences are biological, regardless of whether they are influenced by genetics or not, because they must go through the brain.

(A) Higher levels of testosterone lead us toward aggressive behaviors; lower levels lead us toward politeness. Testosterone levels are affected by the triad of factors — genes, culture, and opportunity. Situations such as a successful hunt, driving a fast car, being in the public eye, or being in charge of a large number of people can increase testosterone levels.

(B) These neurobiological changes are accompanied by chemical changes in the brain. As an example, assertiveness, competitiveness, dominance, and belligerence all are influenced by testosterone across genders.

(C) The normal process of aging tends to lower them. A typical professional career trajectory finds one gaining more power as one gets older — this can compensate for biologically lowered levels of testosterone in some individuals.

*testosterone: 테스토스테론(남성 호르몬) **belligerence: 호전성
***trajectory: 경로

① (A) – (C) – (B)　　② (B) – (A) – (C)
③ (B) – (C) – (A)　　④ (C) – (A) – (B)
⑤ (C) – (B) – (A)

07 글의 흐름으로 보아, 주어진 문장이 들어가기에 가장 적절한 곳은?

> So when we are talking about loneliness, we are not just talking about lonely minds, but also lonely bodies.

We often imagine a lonely person as passive, quiet, muted. Indeed, when many of us remember the loneliest times in our lives we don't immediately recall a hammering heart, racing thoughts or other typical signs of a high-stress situation. (①) Loneliness instead evokes associations of stillness. (②) Yet the chemical presence of loneliness in the body — where it lives and the hormones it sends coursing through our veins — is essentially identical to the 'fight or flight' reaction we have when we feel under attack. (③) It's this stress response that fuels some of the most insidious health effects of loneliness. (④) These can be far-reaching and even, in the worst cases, deadly. (⑤) The two are of course intertwined.

*insidious: 잠행성의(서서히 진행되는)

08 다음 글의 내용을 한 문장으로 요약하고자 한다. 빈칸 (A), (B)에 들어갈 말로 가장 적절한 것은?

Richard LaPiere, a sociologist at Stanford University in the 1930s, traveled around the United States with a young Chinese couple. During the time of LaPiere's study, widespread prejudice against Chinese people was quite common, and many restaurant and hotel managers expressed negative attitudes toward Chinese people. To test how well these attitudes would predict behavior, LaPiere took this couple on a 10,000-mile trip throughout the United States, which included visits to 251 restaurants, campgrounds, and hotels. What happened? In all 184 restaurants, the Chinese couple was accepted — and they were received with considerable hospitality in 72 of the restaurants. In visits to 66 hotels, they were refused only once. Two months after the trip, LaPiere wrote to all of the places they had visited and asked whether they would accept Chinese patrons. Of those who responded, 91% said they would not accept such guests, even though such a couple had clearly been served within the last few months.

*patron: (상점, 여관 따위의) 고객

⬇

> In LaPiere's study, the fact that the Chinese couple was not ___(A)___ at most of the restaurants and accommodations during their trip shows that the link between attitude and behavior is not as ___(B)___ as is assumed.

	(A)		(B)
①	welcomed	······	close
②	welcomed	······	direct
③	served	······	common
④	rejected	······	strong
⑤	rejected	······	indirect

01 밑줄 친 half metal and half idea가 다음 글에서 의미하는 바로 가장 적절한 것은?

Coding has always had a mysterious hint of magic about it. It's a form of engineering, sure. But unlike in every other type of engineering — mechanical, industrial, civil — the machines we make with software are woven from words. Code is speech; speech a human utters to silicon, which makes the machine come to life and do our will. This makes code oddly literary. Indeed, the law reflects this nature of code. While physical machines like car engines or can openers are governed by patent law, software is also governed by copyright, making it a weird sister of the poem or the novel. Yet software is also, obviously, quite *different* from a poem or a novel, because it wreaks such direct physical effects on how we live our lives. (This is part of why some coders think it's been ruinous to regulate code with copyright.) Code straddles worlds, half metal and half idea.

*straddle: (양쪽으로) 다리를 걸치고 앉다

① being the most poetic discipline in the scientific field
② consisting of words but controlling the physical world
③ being the written signs that can be translated into human language
④ being subjective in interpretation but objective in expression
⑤ expressing the workings of machines in machine language

02 다음 글의 주제로 가장 적절한 것은?

The art of literature probably derived from that of the primitive story-teller. He was not merely providing entertainment, but passing down to his listeners a tradition of who they were, where they had come from, and what their lives signified. By making sense and order out of his listeners' existence, he was enhancing their feeling of personal worth in the scheme of things and therefore increasing their capacity to deal effectively with the social tasks and relationships which made up their lives. The myths of a society usually embody its traditional values and moral norms. Repetition of these myths therefore reinforces the coherence and unity of the society, as well as giving each individual a sense of meaning and purpose. Literature can be understood as having developed from activities which, originally, were adaptively useful.

*the scheme of things: 일이 돌아가는 상황

① literary devices commonly used in myths
② daily life as the main source of literary themes
③ functional aspects of literature for social adaptation
④ the basic instinct of humans for entertainment
⑤ myths as a means of creating moral values

03 다음 글의 밑줄 친 부분 중, 어법상 틀린 것은?

Managers and supervisors in today's workforce are faced with motivating a diverse group of employees. ① Make people of all ages and cultural backgrounds feel important, connected, useful, and motivated is a major challenge. In these ② highly competitive times of shrinking budgets, some unconventional and cost-effective means are necessary to increase staff motivation and retention. Retention is a key player in corporate costs, with some estimates to replace a ③ departing employee ranging as high as 250 percent of that person's annual salary. Turnover losses ④ are said to impose a $5 trillion annual drain on the U.S. economy and are often the most ignored business expense. The workers leaving may be the very employees you don't want to lose, making the loss ⑤ even more painful.

04 다음 빈칸에 들어갈 말로 가장 적절한 것은?

Many aspects of our experiences are not what they seem. Take the clear experience that you are having right now as you read these words. As your eyes flit across the page, your visual world seems continuous and rich, but you are actually only sampling a fraction of the text one bit at one time, rarely reading all the letters in between. Your peripheral vision is smeared and colorless, yet you could swear that it is perfectly clear just like the center of your visual field. There are two blindspots, the size of lemons at arm's length, just off-center from your field of view that you do not even notice. Everything in your visual world is unbroken, yet your visual world is blacked out for a fraction of a second between eye movements. You are not made aware of any of these imperfections because your brain provides such a convincing cover story. The same _____ is true for all human experience, from the immediacy of our perception to the contemplation of inner thoughts, and that includes the self.

*flit: 스쳐 지나가다 **peripheral vision: 주변 시야
***smeared: 얼룩진

① empathy　　　　　　② autonomy
③ deception　　　　　④ availability
⑤ competition

05 다음 빈칸에 들어갈 말로 가장 적절한 것은?

Estimating fluxes in and out of a carbon reservoir is even trickier than estimating the reservoir size because it is often difficult to quantify the rates of the processes (such as photosynthesis, respiration and decomposition) that contribute to these fluxes. In practice, many of the processes _____. For example, the rate at which various types of organic material decompose may be estimated in the field by the loss in mass over a given time period of a bag containing litter such as leaves: the bag is made of a mesh through which organisms can move freely, decomposing the litter to CO_2. Similarly, gross primary production may be measured by monitoring the CO_2 decrease or O_2 increase in a sealed box containing a plant or leaf, and net primary productivity may be estimated by the change in the weight of plant biomass over a given area at the beginning of and at the peak of the growing period.

*photosynthesis: 광합성
**gross primary production: 총1차 생산량   ***biomass: 생물량

① have similar structures
② are measured indirectly
③ are being handled manually
④ are related to climate change
⑤ remove CO_2 from the atmosphere

06 주어진 글 다음에 이어질 글의 순서로 가장 적절한 것은?

Much of our lives are spent in familiar situations: the rooms in our homes, our yards, our routes to and from school or work, our offices, neighborhood parks, stores, restaurants, etc.

(A) In addition to having a pattern for your home, your brain has one for homes in general. It biases your perception of all homes, familiar and new. In a kitchen, you expect to see a stove and a sink. In a bathroom, you expect to see a toilet, a sink, and a shower or a bathtub (or both).

(B) For example, you know most rooms in your home well enough that you need not constantly scrutinize every detail. You know how they are laid out and where most objects are located. You can probably navigate much of your home in total darkness. But your experience with homes is broader than your specific home.

(C) Repeated exposure to each type of situation builds a pattern in our minds of what to expect to see there. These perceptual patterns, which some researchers call frames, include the objects or events that are usually encountered in that situation.

① (A) – (C) – (B)   ② (B) – (A) – (C)
③ (B) – (C) – (A)   ④ (C) – (A) – (B)
⑤ (C) – (B) – (A)

07 글의 흐름으로 보아, 주어진 문장이 들어가기에 가장 적절한 곳은?

> But evolution does not know where it is going; it has no ultimate objective, no endgame.

Natural selection is essential to understanding all things human, including our societies. For behavioral traits, just as for physical traits, evolution works by the "survival of the fittest." (①) In each generation, chance mutations mean that an organism's progeny will have small genetic changes that might increase or decrease the likelihood that an individual will survive and reproduce (the changes can also be neutral). (②) This is where natural selection comes in — the environment in which an organism is located will naturally favor some individuals but not others, and those that are favored will have more descendants. (③) The environment acts like an animal breeder, modifying selected traits over the course of a few generations by choosing who gets to reproduce. (④) Genes, individuals, and species have no way of predicting what traits will be useful in the future or which traits might set the stage for subsequent modifications. (⑤) Genes are just a way that biological systems store and transmit information.

*mutation: 돌연변이 **progeny: 자손

08 다음 글의 내용을 한 문장으로 요약하고자 한다. 빈칸 (A), (B)에 들어갈 말로 가장 적절한 것은?

The Stanford professor Baba Shiv carried out a fantastic experiment. He gave half his volunteers a two-digit number to remember (representing a low cognitive load) and gave the other half a seven-digit number (a high cognitive load). The volunteers were then told to walk to another room and in so doing pass a table where they had to choose between chocolate cake or fruit salad. Of the people with the high load, 59 percent opted for cake whereas only 37 percent of the people with the low load did. Shiv speculates that remembering a seven-digit number required cognitive resources that had to come from somewhere, and in this case were taken from our ability to control our urges! Anatomically this is plausible because working memory (where we 'store' numbers) and self-control are both located in our prefrontal cortex. The neurons that would normally be helping us make healthy food choices were otherwise engaged in remembering a seven-digit number. In those instances we have to rely on our more impulsive emotions.

*prefrontal cortex: 전두엽 피질

↓

> The Stanford professor Baba Shiv's experiment on the cognitive load shows that having ___(A)___ to hold in the head might ___(B)___ the level of self-control.

	(A)		(B)
①	plenty	⋯⋯	lower
②	control	⋯⋯	lower
③	impulse	⋯⋯	influence
④	numbers	⋯⋯	increase
⑤	memories	⋯⋯	increase

01 밑줄 친 paralysis by analysis가 다음 글에서 의미하는 바로 가장 적절한 것은?

There is a great challenge of introspection. How can we observe our own experiences without tainting them, since the act of observation itself is an experience? We face this problem quite often. Try to observe what your fingers are doing as you type at a computer keyboard and you will quickly find yourself typing slowly and making many errors, if you can still type at all. Try to observe yourself enjoying a movie or a game, and the enjoyment can quickly fade away. Some call this "paralysis by analysis," and others refer to it as the Heisenberg principle. This principle, in reference to the Heisenberg Uncertainty Principle from quantum mechanics, points out that the motion of a particle cannot be observed without disturbing the motion of that particle. Similarly, the nature of an experience cannot be observed without disturbing the nature of that experience. This makes introspection sound hopeless.

*taint: 손상시키다　**quantum mechanics: 양자역학

① remembering the past mistakes and trying to prevent them
② stopping thinking about what is being done and slowing down
③ feeling intimidated by other's criticism and not trying anything
④ getting less richer feelings from the experience when self-monitored
⑤ showing inferior performance in familiar activities with an audience

02 다음 글의 제목으로 가장 적절한 것은?

Time hasn't changed. An hour is still an hour and a day a day. What has changed is our *perception of time*. Neuroscience research has highlighted that how the brain perceives time passing determines whether our days feel luxuriously long or short and harried. This is also something we have control over. By *paying attention* and actively *noticing new things*, we can slow time down. There is an old saying, "The days are long, but the years are short." And for good reason. In very familiar events, such as the morning commute, and then those days we get stuck in traffic, we complain and moan about the hellish experience. But a few days later we can hardly recall the event. A neuroscientist by the name of David Eagelman concludes that this is because our brain isn't taking in much new information. If nothing new is happening and there are no new events to look back on, you have little to remember at all. So, how do we deal with this issue of time racing by? Just try to *notice* things more, and this means *focused attention on the here and now*.

*harried: 어찌할 바를 모르는　**moan: 투덜대다

① Living in the Present: Easier Said than Done
② Positive Impacts of Aging on Time Perception
③ Don't Ruin Your Present by Dwelling on the Past
④ How Memory Occurs: Still a Mystery to Scientists
⑤ Extending Time with Mindfulness and Newness

03 다음 글의 밑줄 친 부분 중, 문맥상 낱말의 쓰임이 적절하지 <u>않은</u> 것은?

When purpose and pleasure are brought together work becomes play. Every bit of work done in this ① <u>spirit</u> strengthens the man who does it. It is ② <u>recreative</u> as well as creative. Artist and carpenter — they make pictures and chairs, but even more they make men, themselves. Think on what you are doing more than on the result, or what you are going to do afterwards. You will not then ③ <u>miss</u> the pleasure of little things. I pick up my pen; there is a sheer and undiluted pleasure in this, if I ④ <u>allow</u> myself to experience it. It is natural and pure, and mine when I stop fighting it. In such little things thought, love and will can flow and grow. And then arise peace and strength and — in active life — the ⑤ <u>separation</u> of work and play.

04 다음 빈칸에 들어갈 말로 가장 적절한 것은?

In the United States, the Supreme Court functions solely as the highest appeal court of the state. It is not possible, as it is in France or Germany, for a legislative leader to request a ruling in advance on whether a proposed law would be constitutional, and it is certainly not possible for an ordinary citizen to request a ruling on a law. The only way that a case can reach the Supreme Court is after _____. A law's constitutionality cannot be tested in the Supreme Court until the law has been passed by Congress and the president, and then challenged in cases in lower federal courts. If a person has lost a case in a federal appeals court, that person can present the case as an appeal to the Supreme Court, arguing on the question of whether the law is constitutional. The Court does not accept all cases that are submitted to it, but if it does so, the Justices of the Court will consider whether the law is consistent with the Constitution and with all earlier Supreme Court interpretations of what the Constitution means.

① the story behind it has been fully told
② the Court has agreed to check on its progress
③ it has promoted any enormous national interest in it
④ it has been ruled on in a lower federal court of appeals
⑤ a lower federal court has made a change in their ruling

05 다음 빈칸에 들어갈 말로 가장 적절한 것은?

A key principle in the authoritative parenting model that conveys to children a parent's caring is that children are treated firmly, with dignity and respect. Treating children with dignity means honoring their position and their abilities and seeing them as worthy of esteem. Treating children with respect means showing regard for their basic human right of expression and believing in their ability to manage their own lives successfully. Respect requires listening and sincerely considering what children are saying. With authoritative parenting, it is taken for granted that parents have more knowledge and skill, control more resources, and have more physical power than their children, but parents believe that the rights of parents and children are reciprocal. Reciprocity is a key word. Children _____. They have reciprocal rights.

*reciprocal: 상호적인

① become a source of information that adds to the family
② are punished when they don't pay due respect to their parents
③ have the right to spend their spare time enjoying themselves
④ are viewed as capable and significant and are treated respectfully
⑤ participate in making family rules and voluntarily follow them

06 주어진 글 다음에 이어질 글의 순서로 가장 적절한 것은?

Scientists have found that certain materials, such as wood and plants and volcanic rocks, change slowly but regularly over a very long period of time.

(A) They were different from the Neanderthal people who appeared about seventy thousand years earlier and inhabited the earth for about two hundred thousand years.

(B) This means that we can work out when they grew or were formed. And since the discoveries in Germany, people have carried on searching and digging, and have made some startling finds.

(C) In Asia and Africa, in particular, more bones have been found, some at least as old as the Heidelberg jaw. These were our ancestors who may have already been using stones as tools more than a hundred and fifty thousand years ago.

① (A) – (C) – (B)
② (B) – (A) – (C)
③ (B) – (C) – (A)
④ (C) – (A) – (B)
⑤ (C) – (B) – (A)

07 글의 흐름으로 보아, 주어진 문장이 들어가기에 가장 적절한 곳은?

> However, the more interesting form of the phenomenon occurs when the one who basks in the glory of another has done nothing to bring about the other's success.

It is a common and understandable tendency for people who have been successful in some positive way to make others aware of their connection with that accomplishment. (①) However, there also appears to be a seemingly less rational but perhaps more interesting tendency for people to publicize a connection with *another person* who has been successful. (②) This latter inclination might be called the tendency to bask in reflected glory (BIRG). (③) That is, people appear to feel that they can share in the glory of a successful other with whom they are in some way associated; one manifestation of this feeling is the public trumpeting of the association. (④) Such a phenomenon is not hard to understand when the one wishing to share in another's success has been instrumental to that success. (⑤) Here, a simple case of affiliation or membership is sufficient to stimulate a public announcement of the critical connection.

*bask in: (관심 · 칭찬 등을) 누리다 **affiliation: 소속

08 다음 글의 내용을 한 문장으로 요약하고자 한다. 빈칸 (A), (B)에 들어갈 말로 가장 적절한 것은?

According to the anthropologist Joe Henrich, human beings learn skills from each other by copying prestigious individuals, and they innovate by making mistakes that are very occasionally improvements — that is how culture evolves. The bigger the connected population, the more skilled the teacher, and the bigger the probability of a productive mistake. Conversely, the smaller the connected population, the greater the steady deterioration of the skill as it was passed on. Because they depended on wild resources, hunter-gatherers could rarely live in bands larger than a few hundred and could never achieve modern population densities. This had an important consequence. It meant that there was a limit to what they could invent. A band of a hundred people cannot sustain more than a certain number of tools, for the simple reason that both the production and the consumption of tools require a minimum size of market. People will only learn a limited set of skills and if there are not enough experts to learn one rare skill from, that skill will disappear.

⬇

> A skill in a given society needs to be kept alive by ____(A)____ in order not to be ____(B)____ .

	(A)		(B)
①	numbers	......	lost
②	numbers	......	abused
③	incentives	......	banned
④	institutions	......	lost
⑤	institutions	......	abused

01 밑줄 친 more like ships passing in the night가 다음 글에서 의미하는 바로 가장 적절한 것은?

Some parents provide for the basic necessities of their children and are polite and kind to their children, but in a way one would reserve for acquaintances. An acquaintance relationship has no depth to it. It lacks intimacy. Gottman, a renowned relationship expert, refers to the depth of information people have for their loved ones as a "cognitive love map." He also highlights the importance of accepting a bid for attention from loved ones and valuing one another by sharing dreams and admiring each other's venerable attributes. The more detailed the map, the more attention that is given to one another, and the more people admire one another, the more easily people navigate their relationship. Acquaintance parents' love map, ability to give meaningful attention, and ability to express admiration for the children and adult children are stunted. Their relationship with their children is more like ships passing in the night.

*venerable: 훌륭한 **stunt: (정상적인 발달 등을) 방해하다

① mutually beneficial
② not worth the effort
③ unlikely to get better
④ happier than it really is
⑤ not close or deep enough

02 다음 글의 주제로 가장 적절한 것은?

Green invaders are taking over America. They are plants from other countries brought here to make gardens and yards look pretty. But now these plants are killing the native plants that have lived here since before human settlers arrived. That's a serious problem, says Dr. Doug Tallamy, an entomologist. He explains that almost all the plant-eating insects in the United States eat only certain plants. Monarch butterfly caterpillars, for example, dine on milkweed, a native plant. If people cut down milkweed and replace it with an introduced plant, the caterpillars will not have the food source they need to survive. But the trouble doesn't stop there, because it goes right across the food web. When insects can't get the right plants to eat and they die off, then the birds don't have enough bugs for their meals and they die off, too. The bottom line is that introduced plants threaten nature's delicate food web.

*entomologist: 곤충학자

① reasons we should plant many trees
② good examples of introduced plants
③ how to get rid of plant-eating insects
④ types of weeds and their strong survival
⑤ harmful effects of introduced plants on the food web

03 다음 글의 밑줄 친 부분 중, 어법상 틀린 것은?

Peripherally coded objects are objects in which software has been embedded, but where the software is incidental to the primary function of the object. There are relatively few such objects and, in most cases, the code merely augments use, but ① is by no means essential to its functioning. Often, the presence of code is merely an adornment that serves the purpose of product marketing, to differentiate ② it from predecessors or acts as a token of added value. For example, an oven might have a digital timer ③ embedded in it, but if this ceases to function, then the appliance will continue to cook food. Similarly, an exercise bike might have a device that digitally displays the speed ④ at which the cyclist is pedaling, but if this ceases to work, the equipment still enables exercise to take place. In both cases, the code does little more than augment the object's use by enabling the chef to know how long a dish has been cooking and the cyclist ⑤ knows the traveling speed. Both are simply digital replacements for analog technology.

*peripherally: 지엽적으로　**augment: 증대시키다
***adornment: 장식

04 다음 빈칸에 들어갈 말로 가장 적절한 것은?

One reason why it's tough being a teenager is that you have to be an adolescent at the same time. Actually, adolescence is _____.
In the 1800s, a person went directly from childhood to adult responsibilities like work and family. A mere three generations later, a person might spend the years between 13 and 24 going to high school, then college, then graduate school without dipping more than a toe into the real world. There is no social track record for what is supposed to happen during this long and often tough period. Since only three generations have passed since we began to consider adolescence as a natural process of human development, there are few proven ways to alleviate the symptoms and pains people suffer from during these years.

① a recent invention
② a groundless myth
③ a period of changes
④ an emotional period
⑤ a different point of view

05 다음 빈칸에 들어갈 말로 가장 적절한 것은?

The Soviet Union's demise in 1991 may be one of the few historical events that has not seemed inevitable after the fact to large numbers of historians, both lay and professional. The fall of the Roman Empire, the rise of the Third Reich, and the American success in reaching the moon before the Russians, not to mention less momentous events, are routinely seen as inevitable by commentators, who, one strongly suspects, could not have predicted them. We tend to have two problems when we try to "predict" the past. One is believing that, at least in retrospect, events could not have turned out other than they did. The other is even thinking that in fact one easily could have predicted in advance that events would have turned out as they did. A lot of evidence shows that people overestimate the extent to which they could have _____.

① controlled the outcome of a bet
② acted in response to a sudden threat
③ explained the consequence of a crisis
④ predicted the outcome of a given event
⑤ influenced the development of future events

06 주어진 글 다음에 이어질 글의 순서로 가장 적절한 것은?

Machine learning algorithms are useful even for jobs that a human could do better. One repetitive task that people are automating with AI is analyzing medical images.

(A) There are similar problems with self-driving cars — driving is mostly repetitive, and it would be nice to have a driver who never gets tired, but even a tiny glitch can have serious consequences at sixty miles per hour.

(B) Lab technicians spend hours every day looking at blood samples under a microscope, counting platelets or white or red blood cells or examining tissue samples for abnormal cells. Each one of these tasks is simple, consistent, and self-contained, so in that way they're good candidates for automation.

(C) But the stakes are higher when these algorithms leave the research lab and start working in hospitals, where the consequences of a mistake are much more serious.

*glitch: (작은) 결함 **platelet: 혈소판

① (A) – (C) – (B)   ② (B) – (A) – (C)
③ (B) – (C) – (A)   ④ (C) – (A) – (B)
⑤ (C) – (B) – (A)

07 글의 흐름으로 보아, 주어진 문장이 들어가기에 가장 적절한 곳은?

> Synthetic fertilizers were developed on the "reductionist" premise that production could be enhanced simply by increasing the total amounts of the major plant nutrients — nitrogen, phosphorus, and potassium — in the soil.

In the early days of the transition to industrial agriculture, farmers had access to few external inputs. (①) Fertilizers consisted of composts and manures produced on the farm. (②) By the early 20th century, however, fertilizers produced by chemists working in the emerging agribusiness sector began making their way onto farms, replacing what livestock produced in the barn and fields. (③) The chemists, however, lacked the deep appreciation for the soil that is required by those whose job it is to produce large quantities of food for extended periods of time. (④) While crop yields from synthetic fertilizers were quite good initially, they eventually wore out the soil. (⑤) Yields declined and susceptibility to disease and pests increased.

*reductionist: 환원주의의(다양한 현상을 단순한 원리로 설명하려는 경향의)
**phosphorus: 〈화학〉 인

08 다음 글의 내용을 한 문장으로 요약하고자 한다. 빈칸 (A), (B)에 들어갈 말로 가장 적절한 것은?

The good news about stereotype threat is that it can be defused by subtle interventions. The most intriguing fact about these interventions is that the question of the malleability of intelligence is actually hotly debated by psychologists and neuroscientists. Although scores on achievement tests like the SAT can certainly be affected by training of different kinds, the purest kind of intelligence is not very malleable at all. But a psychologist at Stanford named Carol Dweck has discovered a remarkable thing: Regardless of the facts on the malleability of intelligence, students do much better academically if they *believe* intelligence is malleable. Dweck divides people into two types: those who have a fixed mindset, who believe that intelligence and other skills are essentially static and inborn, and those who have a growth mindset, who believe that intelligence can be improved. She has shown that students' mindsets predict their academic trajectories: those who believe that people can improve their intelligence actually do improve their grades.

*malleability: 가변성 **trajectory: 궤적

⬇

> Students believing in the malleability of intelligence showed ___(A)___ performance, while purely ___(B)___ intelligence did not change much, which disproved the power of stereotype threat.

	(A)		(B)
①	persistent	......	social
②	persistent	......	testable
③	superior	......	social
④	superior	......	inherited
⑤	worse	......	inherited

01 밑줄 친 play follow the follower가 다음 글에서 의미하는 바로 가장 적절한 것은?

In order to create a fulfilling career, you must make conscious career decisions. You can't simply play follow the follower (as opposed to follow the leader), traipsing down a path that others are following just as blindly. Don't compromise. If you find yourself on a path without a heart, get off of it as quickly as you can. Other people may protest loudly, but a few years later, you'll notice that something rather funny happens. The same people who hated you for leaving will turn around and ask your advice on how they can do what you did. The reason people get angry in such situations is that you force them to face the unpleasant truths they've been avoiding as well. You'll be an inspiration for others who wished they had your courage. This is true even if the strongest resistance comes from your own family members.

＊traipse: 터벅터벅 걷다

① look for an easy shortcut to success
② rely on your family for advice and help
③ live as an ideal-looking member of society
④ get a job that you don't feel passionate for
⑤ pretend that money is most important to you

02 다음 글의 제목으로 가장 적절한 것은?

The oddest manner in which a new sweetener came to light was when, one day in 1976, a foreign research student at King's College in London misheard the instructions of his professor, L. Hough. Hough was searching for possible synthetic industrial applications of sucrose, the common sugar of cane and beet, and several derivatives had been produced in the laboratory. One of these was a trichlorosucrose (sucrose into which three atoms of chlorine had been introduced). Hough asked Shashikant Phadnis to 'test' the substance, but, his ear being imperfectly attuned to the language, Phadnis instead 'tasted' it. Sucralose, as it became known, is one of the sweetest of all substances and can replace sucrose at less than one-thousandth of the concentration.

＊sucrose: 자당(사탕무와 사탕수수에 함유되어 있는 당)
＊＊chlorine: 염소

① Kinds of Sweeteners on the Market Today
② Too Much Sucralose Causes Mood Swings
③ Differences between Sucralose and Sucrose
④ Communicate Clearly What Your Intention Is
⑤ A Hearing Mistake Leads to the Discovery of Sucralose

03 다음 글의 밑줄 친 부분 중, 문맥상 낱말의 쓰임이 적절하지 않은 것은?

Despite the fact that science matters so much for our culture, we often treat it as if it were somehow ① beyond culture. Science is assumed to progress by its own momentum as discovery piles up on discovery. From this point of view, science often looks like a force of nature rather than of culture. It is something unique about science itself that makes it progress, and there is something ② inevitable about its progress. Science therefore doesn't need culture to move forwards, it simply carries on under its own steam. Culture gets in the way sometimes, but in the end science always ③ wins. If science exists outside culture like this, then it should not really matter where it happened. This means that the history of science should not really matter either. At best, it can tell us who did what when, but that is a matter of chronicle rather than history, which tries to interpret the past as well as simply record it. ④ Deniers of this sort of view of science often talk about the scientific method as the key to understanding its success. Some experts now talk about peer review or double blind testing as the hallmarks of scientific objectivity, for example, despite the fact that these are ⑤ cultural institutions of very recent provenance.

*chronicle: 연대기 **hallmark: 특징 ***provenance: 유래

04 다음 빈칸에 들어갈 말로 가장 적절한 것은?

How does "batching" tasks work? Suppose the issue on your mind right now is the excessive workload your team's currently facing. Everyone's worn down. You're catching your breath while having dinner in a buzzing restaurant with an open kitchen, and you reflect on those analogy-seeking questions while you're waiting for your food. First, you notice that the kitchen staff are deluged with customer orders, like your own team. What's different is that the restaurant staff seems pretty calm, despite the demands they're facing. And while your team allocates work depending on who's got spare capacity, each person in the kitchen has a clear job to do: some make salads, others hot food or desserts. What does that make you think? You consider that maybe you could do more to _____, so that everyone isn't flipping from one thing to another all the time. You think that this might reduce people's stress. An idea takes shape in your mind.

*batch: (일괄 처리를 위해) 함께 묶다 **deluge with: ~이 쇄도하다

① ask team members to cover the tired colleague's work
② invite your team members to the restaurant to relax
③ help your team see the problem from different views
④ tag each team member to particular types of requests
⑤ keep the working environment friendly and peaceful

05 다음 빈칸에 들어갈 말로 가장 적절한 것은?

Reflexes, forming the second level of behavior next to the first level of the processing of sensory input, are truly hardwired and independent of conscious thought, except in later memory. The sneeze is a reflex, as are the knee jerk, involuntary eyeblink, blushing, yawn, and salivation. The most complex reflex is the startle response. Imagine coming up unseen and very close behind someone, almost touching, and making a loud noise (I don't recommend that you actually try this). The person will instantly slump forward, drop the head, close the eyes, and open the mouth. The function of the startle reflex is defense. Think of a Paleolithic hunter who, when stalked from behind and attacked by a predator (say a leopard), instantly rolls forward and away in an overall relaxed posture. Thus correct decision and swift action _____.

* Paleolithic: 구석기 시대의

① is independent of the intervention of reflexes
② comes along with limitation of sensory input
③ is attained with no conscious thought needed
④ requires the mind to assess the given situation
⑤ doesn't come as a product of human evolution

06 주어진 글 다음에 이어질 글의 순서로 가장 적절한 것은?

Attachment to place and attachment to people share an evolutionary pathway, and a quality of uniqueness is central to both.

(A) As a result, the notion of place in contemporary life has increasingly been reduced to a backdrop and the interaction, if there is any, tends to be of a transient nature, rather than a living relationship that might be sustaining.

(B) These days we are surrounded by functional places lacking in character and individuality, like supermarkets and shopping malls. While they provide us with food and other useful things, we don't develop affectionate bonds for them; in fact, they are often deeply unrestorative.

(C) The feeding of an infant is not enough on its own to trigger bonding, because we are biologically encoded to attach through the specificity of smells, textures, and sounds as well as pleasurable feelings. Places too evoke feelings, and natural places are particularly rich in sensory pleasures.

* unrestorative: 회복시키지 않는

① (A) – (C) – (B)   ② (B) – (A) – (C)
③ (B) – (C) – (A)   ④ (C) – (A) – (B)
⑤ (C) – (B) – (A)

07 글의 흐름으로 보아, 주어진 문장이 들어가기에 가장 적절한 곳은?

The same thing would happen if the top were spinning in space and you poked it slightly off center.

When I was a kid, my parents bought me a toy top. I used to love to spin it, watching it move across the floor in funny patterns. (①) I also noticed that as it began to slow its spin, it would start to wobble. (②) I was too young to understand it then, but I now know that the wobble is due to the interplay of complicated forces on the spinning top. (③) If the axis of the top is not exactly vertical, gravity pulls the top off-center, which is called a *torque*. (④) Because the top is spinning, you can think of that force being deflected horizontally, making the top slowly wobble. (⑤) The axis would wobble, making little circles; the bigger the poke, the bigger the circle it would make.

*wobble: 흔들리다; 흔들림 **torque: 회전력
***deflect: 방향을 바꾸다

08 다음 글의 내용을 한 문장으로 요약하고자 한다. 빈칸 (A), (B)에 들어갈 말로 가장 적절한 것은?

In years past, when shipbuilders were planning on making a great ship, they knew that the life of the crew and the safety of the cargo depended upon the ship's mainmast. To make the mainmast, they would find a straight, tall tree on the top of a mountain near the coast. Then they would cut down all the other trees around it so that it would be exposed to the full force of the angry winds and mighty gusts that blew off the sea. After many years of exposure to such harshness, the tree would become stronger and stronger, its very fiber being strengthened by the intense buffeting it was experiencing day after day. Finally, after many testing storms alone on the mountaintop, the tree was ready to be trusted as the mainmast of a great ship.

⬇

Being exposed to ____(A)____ for a long time makes a tree ____(B)____, until it could be used as the mainmast of a great ship.

	(A)		(B)
①	warmth	······	flexible
②	adversity	······	strong
③	strictness	······	smooth
④	abundance	······	powerful
⑤	indifference	······	endurable

부록

· WORDS LIST

· WORDS REVIEW

WORDS LIST

01
ail 앓다
obvious 분명한
confirm 확인하다
spirit 기분, 정신
demonstrate 보여 주다, 입증하다
arrange 정하다, 마련하다
treat 특별한 선물, 대접
be in touch 연락하다

02
tropical 열대의
seaweed 해초
still 고요한
reside (~에) 있다, 살다
endure 견디다

03
privilege 특권
holding public office 공직 재임
distinction 구별
residence 거주
distribute 분배하다
discriminate 차별하다
deliberate 의도적인
infliction (고통·벌·타격을) 가함[줌]

04
perspective 원근법; 관점
Renaissance 르네상스
conception 개념
gaze 응시, 시선
landscape 풍경
beholder 보는 사람
object 대상
spatial 공간의
realm 영역
sociologist 사회학자
describe 묘사하다
disenchantment 각성, 깨어남

05
in-demand 수요가 많은
post 일자리
sought-after 수요가 많은, 인기 있는
demand 수요
job posting 채용 공고
immediately 바로, 즉시

06
foster 육성[촉진]하다
innovation 혁신

attract 끌어들이다
recruit 고용하다
instrument 도구, 기구
identify 식별하다, 확인하다
interplay 상호 작용
ultimately 결국, 궁극적으로
proven 입증된
approach 접근 (방식)
contribute 기여하다

07
stretch assignment 현재 전문 지식을
넘어서는 과제
comfort zone 안전지대
experiment 실험하다; 실험
cheer on ~를 응원하다
cheer up ~를 격려하다
ensure 보장하다

08
incandescent 백열등의
fluorescent 형광등의
promote 홍보하다
sound 건전한
skeptic 회의론자
criterion (pl. criteria) 기준
slant 경향을 띠게 하다
conventional 전통적인
replacement 교체

09
intuition 직관
hinder 방해하다
folk 민속(의), 민간(의)
means 수단
boundary 경계(선), 한계
phenomenon 현상
validity 타당성, 정당성
portray 묘사하다
degree 정도
measure 측정하다
identical 동일한, 똑같은
sustain 유지하다
conceptual 개념적인, 개념의

10
range 범위
molecular 분자의
sufficiently 충분히
interfere with ~을 방해하다
appropriate 적절한
density 농도, 밀도

variability 변동(성)
translate into (결과적으로) ~이 되다,
~으로 바뀌다
carbon dioxide 이산화탄소
carbon monoxide 일산화탄소
poisonous 유독한, 유해한
modest 알맞은
property 속성, 특성
tolerate 견디다, 참다
given that ~을 고려하면
essential 필수적인

11
authoritative 권위 있는
compile 모으다; 편찬하다
clipping 오려낸 기사
unregulated 규제되지 않은
requirement 자격 조건
legally 합법적으로
fatality 사망자
regulation 규제
hold back 방해하다, 저지하다
estimate 추산하다

12
particular 특정한
permanently 영원히
overturn 뒤집다
adjust 조정하다
reorganize 재조직하다
neuronal 신경 단위의
examine 검사하다, 조사하다
carry out 수행하다
degeneration 악화, 퇴보
neural 신경의

13-14
optimal 최적의
reputation 평판
irrationality 불합리성
negotiate 뚫고 나가다; 협상하다
bottom line 결론, 요점
disrupt 방해하다
immune to ~에 영향을 받지 않는
unpredictable 예측 불가능한
prone to ~하는 경향이 있는
impulsive 충동적인
function 작동하다, 기능하다
disastrous 비참한

WORDS LIST

01
courtyard 안뜰
daffodil 수선화
agog at ~에 설레어, ~에 흥분하여
compact (공간이) 작은; 밀집한
contained 조심스러운
encircle 둘러싸다
canal 운하

02
generous 관대한
translate 적용되다
moral 도덕적인
inconsistent 일관적이지 않은
deed 행동, 행위
liberate 자유롭게 하다
engage in ~을 하다
unethical 비윤리적인
for fear of ~할까 봐 (두려워서)
donate 기부하다
charity 자선 (단체)
trait 특성
reflect on ~을 반성하다

03
pass (판단 등을) 내리다
imprint 각인하다
isolated 단 한 번의, 고립된
immediate 직속의, 직계의
circle (관심·직업 등으로 연결된 사람들의) …계[사회]
trace 흔적
pale 희미한, 약한
label 꼬리표[딱지]
turn into ~으로 바뀌다
be subjected to ~을 받다
charge 부담, 짐
resistance 저항(력)
believe it or not 믿거나 말거나
attach 달다, 붙이다
endeavor 노력

04
epic 서사시(의)
consist of ~로 이루어지다
cite 인용하다
Norse 노르웨이의
Danish 덴마크의
anonymous 익명의, 이름이 알려지지 않은
manuscript 원고
masterpiece 걸작
imaginative 상상력이 뛰어난

05
attribute to ~의 덕분으로 돌리다
initiate 시작하다
state 말하다, 진술하다
statement 진술, 말
observation 관찰
constant 끊임없는, 지속적인
flux 흐름, 유동
infer 추론하다
modify 변형하다
extinct 사라진, 멸종된

06
truthful 진실한
emphasize 강조하다
pronoun 대명사
analyze 분석하다
predictor 예측 변수
deception 기만
abnormally 비정상적으로
stimulus (pl. stimuli) 자극
cue 단서, 신호
gut feeling 직감

07
convince 납득시키다
attribute A to B A를 B가 가지고 있다고 생각하다
fabulous 환상적인
foundation 기관
grant 보조금
budget 예산
strategic 전략적인
flattery 아첨
detect 간파하다
indulge 탐닉하다

08
interlink 연결되다
hypothesis (pl. hypotheses) 가설
prayer 기도
involve 포함하다, 수반하다
open question 미해결 문제
secure 확고한, 안전한
refinement 개선
revision 수정
rejection 거부
interconnection 연관성
evidence 증거
assess 가늠하다, 평가하다
prior probability 사전 확률
claim 주장

accordingly 그에 따라

09
please 기쁘게 하다
persist 고집스럽게 계속하다
unwilling 하고 싶어 하지 않는, 마지못해서 하는
powerlessness 무력감
obtain 얻다
on the lookout for ~을 찾는

10
redeem 벌충하다, 만회하다
mechanism 방법, 메커니즘
up-close 근거리에서의
malfunction 오작동하다
prevention 예방
detection 발견

11
point out ~을 언급[지적]하다
vacant 비어 있는
revolution 혁명
be involved in ~에 관여하다
paradigm shift 패러다임 전환
frustration 좌절
go against ~과 맞지 않다, ~에 위배되다
procedure 절차
calculation 계산
opening 틈, 구멍
assumption 가정, 추측
allow for 고려하다, 참작하다
properly 적절히

12-14
stray 길을 잃은, 주인이 없는
ginger 황[적]갈색의
scrap 남은 음식
nevertheless 그럼에도 불구하고
nurture 보살피다
affectionate 다정한
vet clinic 동물병원
trap 덫[올가미]으로 잡다
vote with one's feet 가거나 가지 않는 것으로 의사 표시를 하다

WORDS LIST

01
register 등록하다
thrilled 몹시 흥분한
enthusiastic 열렬한
entry 출품작
inform 알리다, 공지하다
adjustment 수정, 조정
diverse 다양한
unexhibited 전시되지 않은
review 살펴보다, 검토하다

02
innovate 혁신하다
punish 벌을 주다
mixed 엇갈리는
exploration 탐색 과정, 탐구
wild 엉뚱한, 무모한
pay off 좋은 성과를 거두다
thrive 번창하다
readily 선뜻
daring 대담한

03
cognitive psychology 인지 심리학
psychotherapy 심리 치료
deliberately 의도적으로
curiously 기묘하게도, 이상하게도
obsessively 강박적으로, 집요하게
pose 제시하다, 자세를 취하다
cursed 저주받은
pioneer 선도하다, 개척하다
fancy 복잡한, 화려한
necessity 불가피한 일, 필수품
suppression 억누르기, 억압
challenge 도전, 난제

04
alter 바꾸다
living organism 생물체
fertile 비옥한
competitor 경쟁 상대
tame 길들이다
hide 가죽
hoof (pl. hooves) 발굽
breed 사육하다
prosper 번성하다
gene 유전자

05
refuge 보호소, 보호 시설
kindergarten 유치원
edit 편집하다

magnified 확대된
submission 제출(물)
overall 종합적인, 전체의
display 전시하다
announce 발표하다
award ceremony 시상식

06
numeral 숫자
era 시대
decimal 십진법의
astrologer 점성술사
Nestorian 네스토리우스(교파)의
bishop 주교
superior to ~보다 우월한
prophet 선지자
founder 창시자
border 국경
expansion 팽창
acquire 습득하다
astronomical 천문학의

07
astronomy 천문학
gravitation 중력
atom 원자
emit 발산하다
wavelength 파장
spectrum 스펙트럼
reveal 밝히다
relativity 상대성
astronomically 천문학적으로
Mercury 수성
gravitational field 중력장

08
lack ~이 없다, ~이 부족하다
fertilize 수정시키다
profound 심오한
govern 지배하다
hive 벌집
honeycomb 벌집
forager 식량 징발자
successive 연속된
promotion 승진
asset 자산
indignity 모욕
accompany 동반하다
efficiency 효율성
assignment 배치

09
assume 생각하다, 추측하다
remarry 재혼하다
reject 거절하다
poet 시인
compose 쓰다, 구성하다
legendary 전설적인
in disguise 변장한

10
great man theory 위인설
justify 정당화하다
royal 왕족(의 일원), 왕실의
maintain 유지하다; 주장하다
in many respects 많은 점에서
obligatory 필수적인, 의무적인
equipped ~을 갖추고 있는

11
unbelievable 믿기 어려운
sea star 불가사리
regrow 재생하다
limb 팔[다리]
rearrange 재배치하다
symmetrical (좌우) 대칭적인
crucial 대단히 중요한
contract 수축하다
stumble upon ~을 우연히 마주치다
symmetrization 대칭화

12
tanker 대형 선박, 유조선
odd-looking 이상하게 보이는
transform 바꾸어 놓다
commerce 상업
handle 다루다
standardize 규격화하다
merchant 상인
automated 자동화된
complication 혼란, 복잡
strictly 엄격히

13-14
temporal 시간의
precede 선행하다
simultaneous 동시의
tempting 마음이 당기는
classic 전형적인
superstition 미신
forward 전달하다
arise 비롯되다

WORDS LIST

01
bang 쾅 부딪치다
chill 오싹한 느낌, 한기
spine 척추, 등뼈
remainder 나머지
bother 성가시게 하다
honk (경적 등을) 울리다
exhale 숨을 내쉬다
slump 털썩 주저앉다

02
motivate 동기부여하다
meaningful 의미 있는
stand in the way of ~에 방해가 되다
colleague 동료
undervalue 과소평가하다
quest 추구, 탐색
undermine 해치다, 약화시키다
organizational 조직의
suffer 피해를 입다
recruiter 채용자
climb the ladder (성공을 위한) 사다리
[단계]를 오르다

03
inflammation 염증
accumulation 축적
artery 동맥
oral 구강의
established 확인된
factor 요인, 요소
obesity 비만

04
perception 인식
adequate 적절한
staffing 직원 규모
pace 속도
physician 의사
proportion 비율

05
imperfection 불완전한 상태
acceptance 수용
passive 순순히 따르는, 수동적인
shrug (어깨를) 으쓱하다
mature 성숙한
reform 개혁
inevitability 필연성
governance 통치
ill 해악, 문제
draw ~을 끌다

by instinct 본능적으로
sell out 신념[원칙]을 버리다
black-and-white 흑백 논리적인
distortion 왜곡

06
clan 가문, 씨족
gorgeous 화려한
theory 이론, 학설
ornament 장식
fit 몸이 좋은, 건강한
mutation 돌연변이
flaw 결함
prospect 전망, 가망

07
physical 물리적인
dependent on ~에 의존하는
primarily 주로
active agent 활성제
reciprocal 상호의
definitely 분명히
housebuilder 목수
politician 정치가

08
longevity 수명
slaughter 도살하다
tusk (코끼리의) 엄니
median 중간값의
poach 밀렵하다
shattered 산산조각이 난
turn to ~에 의지하다
gang 집단으로 행동하다
primitive 원시 시대의
aggregation 집합
disperse 흩어지다
continual 끊임없는
break up 헤어지다

09
rein 제어하다, 지배하다
bias 편향, 편견
perseverance 인내, 버팀
disconfirm 부당성을 증명하다
death penalty 사형
deter 단념시키다, 방해하다
refute 논박하다, 반박하다
strengthen 강화하다
conviction 신념, 확신
capital punishment 사형

10
sail out 날아가다
surrounding 주변의, 부근의
accommodate 충분한 공간을 제공하다,
수용하다
reframe 재구성하다
drive (공이) 날아가다
rejoice 기뻐하다

11
disbelief 불신
convert 전환하다
recognition 인식
incredible 정말 놀라운
wonder 의심하다, 이상하게 여기다
voluntary 자발적인
sceptical 회의적인
pinch 꼬집다
external 외부의
self-reflective 자기 반성적인
critical 비판적인

12-14
inning (야구·소프트볼의) 회
on base 출루하여
sprint 전속력으로 달리다
give out (기능이) 정지하다
burst out 갑자기 ~하다
shed tears 눈물을 흘리다
step in 끼어들다, 개입하다
all-time 전대미문의
umpire 심판
resume 재개하다
substitute A for B A로 B를 대신하다
single 1루타
erase 지우다, 무효로 하다

WORDS LIST

01
economic recession 경기 침체, 경기 후퇴
static 고정적인, 정적인
manufacturer 제조업체
dealer's price 소매가
effective (법률 등이) 시행되는
invoice (물품 대금·작업비 등의) 청구서[송장]를 보내다
across-the-board 전반적인
association 관계, 관련

02
get caught up in ~에 사로잡히다
end up 결국 ~하게 되다
reason (논리적으로) 생각하다
may as well ~하는 편이 낫다
live life to the fullest 마음껏 즐기며 삶을 살다
debate 논쟁하다; 논쟁

03
prove 증명하다
to one's satisfaction ~가 만족할 만큼
worship 숭배하다
permanent 영구적인
accuracy 정확성
triumph 승리
funeral 장례식
maturity 성숙
unrestricted 구속[제약]이 없는
revolutionary 혁명적인
in progress 진행 중인
proceed 전진하다
ignorance 무지

04
refer to ~을 언급[지칭]하다
heritage 계승, 유산
by force 강압에 의해
voluntarily 자발적으로
extinction 사멸
closely 밀접하게
be identified with ~과 밀접한 관계를 맺다; ~과 동일시되다
academia 학계
invariably 예외[변함] 없이
dominant 지배적인
indigenous 토속의, 토착의
distinct 별개의
dialect 방언

05
nonprofit 비영리의

micro 초소형의, 아주 작은
feature 특별히 포함하다, 특징으로 삼다
educator 교육자
donation 기부
significant 상당한
backing 지원, 후원
hedge fund 헤지 펀드 (국제 증권 및 외환 시장에 투자해 단기 이익을 올리는 민간 투자 자금)
tutorial 개별 지도

06
contemporary 현대의, 당대의
account for ~을 설명하다
wear out (차츰) 닳다
cell 세포
regulate 통제하다, 조절하다
contribute to ~의 요인이 되다
dysfunction 기능 장애
activate 활성화하다
deposit 찌꺼기, 퇴적물
accumulate 축적하다, 모으다

07
esteem 생각하다, 존중하다
in addition to ~ 이외에
detour 우회(로)
wilderness 황야, 황무지
conquer 정복하다
obscure 보기 어렵게 하다
despondent 실의에 빠진, 낙담한
retreat 퇴각, 후퇴
commitment 전념, 헌신

08
chapel 성당, 예배당
execute (실)행하다
discomfort 불편
posture 자세
odd 이상한
inversion 전도, 도치
upside down 거꾸로
perceptual 지각의
flip 뒤집히다

09
anxiety 불안(감)
apply 붙이다, 적용하다
personality 성격, 인격
character 개성, 특성
define 규정하다
overcome 극복하다
incompetent 무능한

stuck (무엇을 할지 몰라서) 막막한
hopeless 가망 없는

10
word of mouth 입소문, 구전
exchange 대화; 교환
spark 촉발시키다
in turn 결국
echo ~에 반향을 일으키다
response 응답, 반응
view 조회(수)
additional 추가적인
exposure 노출

11
crew 조정 경기
meditation 명상
unite 단결하다
stroke (노를) 젓기, 스트로크
instructor 교관, 지도자
enhance 높이다
effectiveness 효과성
in spite of ~에도 불구하고
irony 역설
turn out ~으로 밝혀지다
in harmony (~와) 조화되어

12
statistics 통계
staple food 주식
devote 바치다
indication 징후, 암시
marginal 수지가 안 맞을 정도의
fertilizer 비료
tremendous 엄청난
implication 관련

13-14
equitable 공평한
access 이용하다, 접근하다
launch 시작하다
densely 밀집하여
initially 처음에
install 설치하다
resident 주민
oversight 간과
marginalization 사회적 무시
expand 확대[확장]되다
evenly 고르게
overrepresent 실제보다 많게 표시하다
barrier 장벽

WORDS LIST

01
examiner 시험관
instruct 지시하다
pull away (차량이) 움직이기 시작하다
wipe 닦다
sweaty 땀에 젖은
thigh 허벅지
rearview mirror (자동차의) 백미러
curtly 퉁명스럽게
parallel 평행의; 평행선, 평행면
licensing office 면허 발급 사무실
with flying colors 우수한 성적으로

02
edge 경계
unfamiliar 익숙하지 않은
territory 영역, 영토
stay up all night 밤을 새다
altogether 완전히
stick with ~을 계속 하다
missing 빠진, 없어진
paralyze 마비시키다
prevent A from B A가 B하지 못하게 하다

03
electronic device 전자 장치
circuit board 회로판
connectivity 연결(성)
negligible 무시해도 될 정도의
extract 추출하다
ore 광석
yield (결과 따위를) 내다, 산출하다
urban mining 도시 광산업
diffusion 보급, 확산
sincere 진심 어린, 진실된

04
participant 참가자
reservation 예약
in advance 미리
cancellation 취소

05
incentive 유인, 인센티브
accompany 수반하다, 포함하다
check-out 계산(대)
retail store 소매점
profit 이익
indicate 나타내다
cover (무엇을 하기에 충분한 돈을) 대다
shift 옮기다, 이동하다

conversely 정반대로, 역으로
indicative of ~을 나타내는
relative to ~에 비해
characterize 특징짓다
enlarge 증대하다, 확대하다
flow 흐름

06
when it comes to ~에 관한 한
perspective 균형 있는 시각; 관점
contrary to ~와는 반대로
suggest 시사하다, 암시하다
revolution 혁명
complicated 복잡한
prospect 전망, 예상
scenario 시나리오
disrupt 중단시키다, 혼란시키다
contain 억제하다, 봉쇄하다

07
menacing 위협적인
alien 외계인
set the stage for ~의 발판을 마련하다
apparently 명백하게, 분명히
star ~을 주연으로 하다
introduction 소개, 도입
big idea 의도, 목적
representative 대표

08
unprecedented 전례가 없는
dawn 시작, 새벽
signal 암시하다, 시사하다
archaeologically 고고학적으로
chipped stone 뗀석기
artifact 유물
game 사냥감
confront 대면하다
characteristic 특성, 특징
convey 뜻하다, 전하다
natural selection 자연 선택
survival of the fittest 적자생존
undermine 약화시키다
adaptive 적응의
trait 형질, 특성
fit 적합한
trap (위험한 장소·궁지에) 가두다
inheritance 유전

09
per capita 1인당

have something to do with ~와 관계가 있다
gross 총체의, 전체의
relatively 상대적으로
pursue 추구하다
at all costs 무슨 수를 써서라도
put forth 내놓다, 제안하다
internal 내적인

10
universal 보편적인
observe 관찰하다
address 다루다, 처리하다
depending on ~에 따라
outcome 결과
phenomenon 현상
preexisting 기존의
inquiry 탐구, 연구
make sense of ~을 이해하다
hypothesize 가설을 세우다
be composed of ~으로 구성되다
be made up of ~으로 구성되다
particle 입자
reveal 나타내다, 보이다
stance 입장

11
military campaign 군사 작전
consequently 따라서
sentimentalize 감상적으로 다루다
legitimate 정당한; 합법적인
nostalgia 향수병
longing 갈망, 동경
remarkable 현저한, 주목할 만한

12-14
enduring 영원한, 지속하는
basis 토대, 기초
struggle 노력, 분투
adversity 역경
prior to ~ 이전에
stroke 뇌졸중, 발작
note 주목하다
incorporate 짜 넣다, 통합하다
triumphant 승리를 거둔
distort 왜곡하다
sturdy 튼튼한
sensitive 민감한, 예민한
intrusion 침범, 방해, 침입
deform 흉하게 하다
pasture 목초지
encircle 둘러싸다

WORDS LIST

01
recommend 권장하다
tub 통
elevated 높아진, 높은
impaired 손상된, 약화된
absorption 흡수
bowel 장(腸)(의 일부)

02
statistics 통계 (자료)
vital 필수적인
take pride in ~을 자랑스러워하다
beard 수염
accountant 회계사
pull together (여러 곳에서 모아) 만들다
readable 읽기 쉬운
reasonable 합리적인, 타당한

03
collaborative 협력적인
advance 진보, 발전
along with ~과 더불어
reward 보상하다; 보상
investigator 연구자
recount 이야기하다[말하다]
egg-laying 산란의
hen 암탉
productive 생산적인
breed 번식하다
latter 후자의
exclaim 외치다
department 학과

04
contemporary 동시대의
rationalize 합리화하다
bureaucracy 관료제
hierarchy 위계질서[구조]
application 적용, 응용
undemocratic 비민주의적인
adherence 고수
inhibit 방해하다

05
share 점유율, 비율
wind-generated 풍력 발전의
supplier 공급자
account for (부분·비율을) 차지하다
slightly 약간

06
literate 글을 읽고 쓸 수 있는
assuredly 분명히
maturationally 성숙하게
cognitive 인지적인
other than ~을 제외하고
availability 이용 가능성
extensive 광범위한
confine 국한시키다
fraction 일부, 부분
substantial 상당한, 중요한

07
sidestep 외면하다, 회피하다
high-minded 고결한, 고상한
punishing 극도로 힘든
depletion 고갈, 소모
be in the mood 마음이 내키다
cast 종류, 성질
suffering 고통
empathetically 감정 이입적으로
unfortunate 불행한 사람; 불행한
endure 견디다
argument 논의, 논쟁
counterbalance 효과를 상쇄하다
excessively 지나치게
sentimental (지나치게) 감상적인

08
narrate 이야기하다, 서술하다
overall 전반적인
emphasize 강조하다
de-emphasize 덜 강조하다
filter 거르다
nonjudgmental 개인적인 판단을 피하는
bear on ~와 관계되다

09
transmission 전파, 전송
absence 부재, 없음
simplicity 단순성
aid 돕다; 도와주는 것
sacrifice 희생하다
for the sake of ~을 위해서
rhyme 운을 맞추다; 압운
verse 가사, 시
appropriate 적절한
substitute 대체물

10
experiment 실험하다
inevitable 피할 수 없는
dissect 해부하다
manually 수동으로
charge 책임, 임무
neuroscience 신경 과학
neurophysiology 신경 생리학

11
dimension 차원, 치수
capture 포착하다
eliminate 제거하다
load (카메라에) 필름을 넣다
audible 들리는
fake 가짜의, 위조의
dial tone 발신음

12
episode (라디오·텔레비전 연속 프로의) 1회 방송분
deal with ~을 다루다
neutral 감정을 드러내지 않는; 중립적인
highlight 강조하다
retention 기억(력), 보유
immediate 즉각적인

13-14
literature 문헌
fundamental 기본적인, 근본적인
assumption 가정
rational 합리적인
strategic 전략적인
in action 활동 중인
cast doubt on ~에 의구심을 제기하다
engage in ~을 하다
formal 공식적인
analyze 분석하다
grasp (기회를) 붙잡다
on the wing 진행 중에, 비행 중에
intuitively 직관적으로
emerge 생겨나다, 나타나다

WORDS LIST

01
finale 마지막 (부분)
nationals 전국 대회
crushing 참담한
sour 시큼둥한, (맛이) 신
whisper 속삭이다
spot 자리
wave 손을 흔들다
prove 증명하다

02
landscape ~계, 분야
efficient 효과적인
subscription 구독
generate 발생시키다
equate to ~와 같다
approximately 대략
take into account ~을 고려하다
publication 출판[간행]물
wastage 낭비, 소모
scarce 부족한, 적은
distribute 배포하다
consume 소비하다

03
date back to ~로 거슬러 올라가다
certain (어느) 특정한
definite 일정한; 명확한
fascinate 매혹시키다
figure out ~을 알아내다
flower bed 화단
clock face 시계 문자판

04
extraordinary 비범한, 비상한
memorize 암기하다
experimentation 실험
treatment 치료
flock 몰려들다
miracle 기적
rely on ~에 의존하다
physics 물리학
chemistry 화학
supernatural 초자연적인
status 지위
qualified 자격을 갖춘

05
commerce 상업, 무역
dense 밀집한
autonomous 독립한, 자율적인

prescription 처방
extinction 멸종
pool 공동으로 모으다
revenue stream 수입원
autonomy 자율성
in return for ~에 대한 대가로
entrepreneurial 기업가의
outsourcing 아웃소싱(외부 용역이나
부품으로 대체하는 것)
norm 기준

06
distress 고통
release 해방; 해방하다
tension 긴장
consequence 결과
adapt 적응시키다, 적응하다
investment 투자
discredit 믿지 않다, 의심하다
maintain 유지하다
consciousness 의식
entirely 완전히

07
invasive species 침입종
invasion 침괴
minimize 최소화하다
colonize 대량 서식하다
initial 처음의
hold ~ in check ~을 저지[억제]하다
hamper 방해하다
predict 예측하다
approach 접근(법)
spread 확산

08
alter 바꾸다
conservation 보존
define 정의하다
management 관리
woodland 삼림(지)
logic 논리
industrialization 산업화
agriculture 농업
exploitative 자원을 개발하는
conservative 보수적인, 보존하는
integral 필수적인
commitment 책임; 의지
sustainable 지속 가능한
intervention 개입
override 우선하다

09
ski pole 스키 지팡이
snap 딱 부러지다
hopeless 절망적인, 희망이 없는
uphill 오르막의
attention 관심, 집중
benefactor 은인
marvelous 놀라운
hand 건네다
make up for ~을 만회[벌충]하다

10
infant 유아
expose 노출하다
attend to ~에 주의를 기울이다
anchor (~에) 단단히 기반을 두다
point out ~을 언급[지적]하다
irrespective of ~에 관계없이
sensible 합리적인
pre-program 미리 설정하다
built-in 타고난, 내장된
encode 암호화하다
determine 결정하다

11
destruction 파괴
volcanic eruption 화산 폭발
warning 경고
skeleton 해골
entomb 파묻다
uncover 발견하다, 밝히다
excavator 발굴자
faithfulness 충성스러움
finely 섬세하게, 세밀하게
etch ~에 식각(飾刻)[에칭]하다
inscription 적힌[새겨진] 글
ambush 매복 공격
futile 헛된, 소용없는

12-14
personally 직접
buzz for ~을 버저로 부르다
wrap up ~을 마무리하다
take ~ by surprise ~을 깜짝 놀라게 하다
comprehend 이해하다
incapable 할 수 없는
obstacle 장애물
stunned 깜짝 놀란
genius 천재
immediately 즉시
notice 알아차리다

WORDS LIST

01
retriever 되찾는 사람[것]
bin 용기, 저장소
landscaping 조경
cardboard 마분지
fundraising 자금 조달, 모금

02
startup 신생 기업
entrepreneur 기업가
corporation 기업
handsome 상당한
profile 수준, 개요, 분석표
realign 조정하다, 변경하다
match 일치하다
annual 연간의, 1년의
incentivize (인센티브를 주어) 장려하다
tackle 해결하다

03
grain 한 알, 낟알
recipe 처방
fig 무화과
rue 루타(지중해 연안 원산의 귤과의 상록 다년초)
pound (가루가 되도록) 찧다[빻다], 두드리다
proverbial 속담에 나오는
proof (~에) 견디는, (~의) 작용을 받지 않는
poison 독
figurative 비유적인
biblical 성경의
commentator 주석가, 논평가
warrant 정당화하다
a pinch of 소량의
take in ~을 받아들이다, ~을 흡수[섭취]하다
in that ~이라는 점에서
appeal 호소

04
deck (카드 패의) 한 벌
emotional 감정의
stereotypical 전형적인, 진부한
dexterity 손재주
empathy 감정이입, 공감
ambition 야망
diplomacy 외교술
assertiveness 자기 주장
tweak (기계·시스템을) 수정[변경]하다

05
gymnastics 체조
strength 체력, 힘
theme 주제

(column 2)

pre-registration 사전 등록
non-refundable 환불되지 않는
deposit 보증금
tuition 수업료
balance 잔액

06
dispute 논란, 논쟁
archaeologist 고고학자
settlement 정착지
civilization 문명
predate ~을 앞서다
temple 사원
dwelling 주거지
cultivate 경작하다
abundant 풍부한
reliable 확실한, 믿을 만한
drought 가뭄
make do with ~으로 때우다
edible 먹을 수 있는

07
conductor 지휘자
authority 권위
exercise 행사하다
visible 눈에 보이는
opposite 정반대
confusion 혼란
hands on 손을 움직이는, 손으로 하는
physicality 신체적 특징
instrumentalist (기악) 연주자
fingering 운지법
mechanics 역학
orchestral 오케스트라의

08
waggle 흔들다
consistent 일관된
bounce 튀기다
sequence 순서
routine 정해진 절차
systematically 체계적으로
specific 특정한
evident 분명한, 눈에 띄는
execution 실행
self-paced 자기 진도에 의한
extensively 광범위하게
psychologist 심리학자
competitive 경쟁의

09
make sense 타당하다
narrow down ~을 줄이다[좁히다]

(column 3)

potential 잠재적인
imitate 모방하다
work out ~을 알아내다
rule out ~을 배제하다
hairdo 헤어스타일
range from ~ to ... 범위가 ~에서 …까지 이르다
stir 휘젓다
determinant 결정 요소

10
previous 이전의
quality 질, 품질
systematic 체계적인
presumptuous 주제넘은
conveyor 전달자
ignore 무시하다
icing (과자 등의) 당의(糖衣)

11
compensate 보충하다, 상쇄하다
supervise 감독하다
discipline 훈육하다
socialization 사회화
pronounced 두드러진, 현저한
available 도움이 되는, 이용 가능한
neglect 방치, 소홀, 태만
abuse 학대

12
broadcaster 방송인
devise 계획하다, 고안하다
on-demand 주문식의
tune in 채널을 맞추다

13-14
analogy 비유
geographic 지리적인
equipment 장비
formulate ~을 명확하게 나타내다, 공식화하다
precision 정확성
categorization 분류, 범주화
in all likelihood 아마, 십중팔구
alternative 대안적인
nonobvious 분명치 않은
arena 활동 무대, 경기장, (각축의) 장
adapt to ~에 적응하다
fierce 맹렬한
bracket 부류
convenience 편리함
flexibility 융통성
aspire 갈망하다

WORDS LIST

01
blast 강타하다
freeze 얼리다, 얼다
itinerary 여행 일정표
what little 있을까 말까 한 정도의, 거의 없는
charm 매력
coach 이코노미석, 보통석
bump 올리다; 승진시키다
nestle 기분 좋게 앉다

02
genetics 유전적 특징, 유전학
ancestor 조상
crucial 매우 중요한
kin 친족
forerunner 선조
fungus (pl. fungi) 균류, 버섯
merge 합치다, 어우러지다
limb 큰 가지
fungal 균류의, 버섯의
molecular 분자의
affinity 관련성; 친밀감
illogic 비논리, 불합리
transcendence 초월(성), 탁월(성)

03
honor 존중하다
mind you 말하자면, 그러니까
ignorance 무지
denial 부인, 거부
awareness 인식
lingering 오래 끌고 있는
illusion 착각, 환상

04
gender (사회적) 성
compared to ~과 비교하여
female 여성의
counterpart (동일한 지위나 기능을 갖는) 상대, 대응 관계에 있는 사람[것]

05
habitat 서식지
captivity 감금, 속박
replicate 복제하다
surrounding (보통 pl.) 환경
predator 포식자
tame 길들이다
cruel 잔인한
median 중간의
lifespan 수명
excessive 지나친

06
sophistication 정교함
domain 영역
responsible 책임감 있는
miserable 비참한
grip 지배력; 파악
divine 신의
precede 선행하다
synthesis 종합

07
associate ~ with ... ~를 …과 결부시키다, 연관 짓다
context 맥락, 문맥
conservancy 보호, 보존
casually 평상복으로
chinos 치노 바지
shorts 반바지
prep school 사립 중등학교
overdressed 지나치게 치장한

08
possess 가지다, 소유하다
geographical 지리적인
by virtue of ~의 덕분에
region 지역
cultural exchange 문화 교류
vocation 소명; 천직
millennium 천 년
majority (대)다수
contract 계약
short-term 단기의
allow for ~을 고려[참작]하다
citizenship 시민권
ownership 소유(권)
property 재산
expose A to B A가 B를 받게[접하게] 하다
interference 방해, 간섭
meddling 간섭, 참견
neighboring 이웃의
particularly 특히
defend 방어하다
vulnerable to ~에 취약한

09
attachment 애착
artifact 인공물
essentially 근본적으로
look up 나아지다
depict 묘사하다

memoir 회고록
dashboard 계기판
curse 악담을 퍼붓다

10
disability 장애
entrance 출입구
non-disablist 장애인 차별이 없는
permanently 영구적으로
appreciate 이해하다
set aside ~을 따로 마련하다
layer (시스템 등의 일부를 이루는) 층[단계]
ground 이유, 근거
discrimination 차별
inclusive 포용적인
means 수단

11
association 관련, 연상
clue 단서
causation 인과 관계
cause 유발하다, 일으키다; 원인
sufficient 충분한
necessary 필요한, 필수의
correlation 연관성, 상관관계
stepchild 의붓자식, 냉대받는 사람[것]
play trick on ~을 속이다
owe 빚지다

12-14
stove 난로
flame 화염
unconscious 의식을 잃은
resolve 결심하다
persistence 인내
resolute 굳은
determination 결의
faintly 희미하게
devastate 황폐시키다, 유린하다
physician 의사, 내과 의사
mortal 치명적인
be doomed to ~할 운명이다
cripple 신체 장애인

WORDS LIST

01
sponsor 후원하다
job fair 채용[취업] 박람회
appreciate 높이 평가하다, 감사하다
stimulate 활성화하다
applaud 박수를 보내다
worthy 가치 있는
cause 대의
climate 상황, 분위기
charitable 자선의
commit 책정하다, (돈·시간을) 사용하다
budget 예산
sincerely 진심으로
fundraising 모금

02
appreciation 감사
perceive 인지하다, 지각하다
attend to ~을 돌보다
assume 가정하다
thank-you note 감사장
in order 제대로 된, 적절한
exception 예외

03
literature 문헌
persist 지속하다
considerably 상당히
developing country 개발도상국
import substitution 수입 대체(개발도상국 등이 종래 수입해온 상품 대신에 국내 제품으로 수요를 만족시키려고 하는 것)
in conjunction with ~과 함께
nonuniform 비일률적인
sector 부문, 영역
promarket 시장 친화적인
macroeconomic 거시 경제적인
liberalization 자유화
ingredient 구성 요소, 재료

04
utter 말하다, 입 밖에 내다
occasional 때때로의, 가끔의
aspect 측면, 양상
emission 배출
chitchat 잡담
encounter 만남
oppressive 숨이 막힐 듯한
horrendous 끔찍한, 참혹한
privation 결핍, 궁핍

05
contribute (글을) 기고하다
periodical 정기 간행물
landscape 조경, 풍경
Capitol 미국 국회의사당
arboretum 식물원, 수목원
autobiography 자서전

06
memorable 기억에 남는
poetic 시적인
literally 문자 그대로
reinforce 강화하다
stereotype 고정 관념
commit to ~에 전념[헌신]하다
devotion 헌신, 전념, 몰두
tendency 경향

07
reawaken 되살리다
apply 적용하다
caring 보살피는
asset 자산
vanish 사라지다
consciousness 의식, 자각
cliché 상투적인 문구

08
briefly 짧게, 잠시
pulse 파동, 맥박
instruct 지시하다
roughly 대략
intensity 강도; 격렬
benefit 혜택, 이득
gradually 점진적으로

09
bluffer 허풍꾼
break 틈, 구멍
moist 습한
queer 괴상한
mess 엉망인 상태
harbor 품다
sprout 싹이 나다
relentlessness 매정함, 가차 없음
ingenuity 독창성
claw 고난을 이기고 나아가다; 할퀴다

10
manual labor 육체노동
restrain 속박하다, 구속하다
imprint 각인시키다
in place 자리를 잡은
handler 조련사
break free 탈출하다
come up with 생각해 내다
self-imposed 자신에게 부과한
chew 씹다

11
discriminate 식별[구별]하다
detect 감지하다, 간파하다
dramatic 인상적인, 극적인
champ(=champion) 챔피언
discern 알아차리다, 파악하다

12
criterion (pl. criteria) 기준
monoculture 단일 경작
outcome 결과
cultivate 양성하다
overlapping 중복된
redundant 불필요한, 여분의
diverse 다양한
cognitive 인지적인
policy 정책
metric 측정 기준
substantially 실질적으로
underperform ~만큼 잘 못하다

13-14
potential 가능성, 잠재력
discrete 개별의
preference 선호
perspective 관점
autobiographical 자전적인
narrator 화자
inattentive 주의를 기울이지 않는
content 내용
interpretive 설명의
alter 바꾸다
adjust 조정하다, 적응하다
confront 마주치다, 직면하다
implication 함축적 의미
deliberation 숙고

WORDS LIST

01

clutch (꽉) 움켜잡다
echo (소리가) 울리다, 메아리치다
pound (심장이) 마구 뛰다
approach 다가가다, 접근하다
mumble 중얼거리다
encouraging 격려하는
drill 반복 연습
refresh 상쾌하게 하다, 생기를 되찾게 하다
footwork (운동선수의) 발놀림
talent 소질, 재능
show off ~을 뽐내다[자랑하다]

02

mature 성숙하다
decompose 분해되다
molecular 분자의
inhale 숨을 들이쉬다
modify 바꾸다, 수정하다
constantly 끊임없이
liver 간
skeleton 뼈대, 골격
regenerate 재생되다, 재생성하다

03

excrement 배설물
fiber 섬유(질)
texture (직물의) 질감, 감촉
similar to ~와 비슷한
high-quality 질 좋은
dye 염료
odor 냄새
germ 세균
good luck charm (행운의) 부적

04

artwork 예술품
applicant 신청자
resident 주민, 거주자
signature 서명
represent 표현하다, 나타내다
limited 한정된, 제한된
runner-up 입상자

05

tempt (마음을) 끌다, 유혹하다
color-blind 색맹의
emphatically 단호히
recognize 인식하다
color vision 색각(색을 식별하는 감각)
emotional 감정적인

06

poll 여론 조사
rage 격노
innately 선천적으로
shelter 쉼터, 주거지
laid-back 느긋한
contemporary 동년배, 동시대인
predator 포식자

07

monopoly 독점
morally 윤리적으로
legislation 법률
folk 민간의
intuition 직관
top down 위에서 아래로
evolutionary 진화의
bottom-up 아래에서 위로
disapprove 반박하다, 비난하다
prosper 번영[번성]하다

08

benefit 이익을 얻다
define 정의하다
non-rival 비경합적인
non-excludable 비배제적인
i.e. 즉(라틴어 id est의 약어)
biodiversity 생물 다양성
centralize 중앙 집권화 하다
derived from ~에서 비롯된
taxation 과세, 징세
sufficiently 충분하게
resent 억울하다고 여기다, 분개하다
struggle to do ~하는 데 어려움을 겪다
result in ~을 초래[야기]하다
footpath 보도(사람이 통행하는 길)

09

psychological 심리적인
identification 동일시
ongoing 계속되는
fond 행복한
bond 유대를 형성하다
vividly 생생하게
relate 이야기하다, 말하다
reveal 밝히다
thematic 주제의
tropical rain forest 열대 우림
investment 투자
human geographer 인문 지리학자
fundamental 기본이 되는

10

hurdle 장애물
side route 옆길, 샛길
adventurous 모험적인
destination 목적지, 도착지
in place 가동 중인, 가동할 준비가 된
keep order 질서를 유지하다

11

creature 생물
accumulate 축적하다
toxin 독소
concentrate 농축하다
cleanse 정화하다
absorb 흡수하다
pollutant 오염 물질
hazard 위험
thoroughly 철저하게
dilute 희석하다
disperse 퍼뜨리다, 흩어지게 하다

12-14

miraculously 기적적으로
antibody 항체
combat 싸우다
pale 창백한
fade 사라지다, 희미해지다
trembling 떨리는
risk (목숨 등을) 걸다
hesitate 망설이다

WORDS LIST

01
moral 윤리
refugee 난민
run (이야기·사진 등을) ~에 게재하다
granted 분명히, 확실히
harsh 가혹한, 모진
dismay 실망, 낙담, 당황

02
measure 측정하다
neuron 신경 세포, 뉴런
in line with ~와 비슷한
reap (보답 등을) 받다, 얻다
regrowth 다시 자라남
athlete 운동선수
attain 이루다, 도달하다
out of reach 손이 닿지 않는 곳에

03
component 구성 요소
immune 면역의
lining 내벽
gut 장
vomiting 구토
malnutrition 영양실조
trigger 유발하다
rejoice 기뻐하다

04
curved 휘어진
lightweight 가벼운, 경량의
aim 겨냥하다
hand-to-hand combat 백병전

05
urban 도시의
suburban 교외의
rural 농촌의, 시골의
categorize 분류하다
ethnic group 인종 집단
Hispanic American 히스패닉계 미국인
share 비율

06
construction 건설 공사
dynamic 역동적인
keep in mind ~을 명심하다
appropriate 적절한
engender (감정·상황 등을) 생기게 하다, 낳다, 발생시키다
disregard 경시, 무시

07
distinguish 구별하다
artificial 인공의, 인위적인
breakthrough 혁신적 발전
massive 거대한
self-tracking 자체 추적
footprint 발자국
storage 저장
akin 유사한, 비슷한
fuel 연료

08
demonstrate 입증하다
maze 미로
adapt 적응하다
initially 처음에
resistant 저항하는
comfort zone 안락 지대
corporate 기업[회사]의
layoff 해고
restructuring 구조 조정
merger 합병

09
the Cold War 냉전
superpower 초강대국
bargaining 협상, 흥정
Soviet (구) 소련의
troop 병력, 부대
monetary 통화의, 금전의
first-order 일차적인
deny 허락하지 않다

10
on end 계속하여
nutrient 영양분, 영양소
worship 숭배하다
palm tree 야자나무
withdraw 물러나다
drench 흠뻑 적시다
ooze 질척거리다, 스며 나오다
bank 제방

11
refer to A as B A를 B로 보다[칭하다]
sensation 감각
turmoil 혼란
smash (단단한 것을 세게) 부딪치다
slam 쾅 닫다
give into ~에 굴복하다
handle 처리하다, 다루다

12
billiard-table 당구대
promote 홍보하다
interest ~ in ... ~이 …에 관심을 갖게 하다
business promotion manager 영업부장
sales figures 매출액
representative 대표(의)
low end of the line 저가 종류의 상품
instantly 즉시
regardless of ~과 상관없이

13~14
rational 합리적인
conventional 전통적인
tax 세금
flexible 유연한
predictable 예측 가능한
carbon 탄소
alloy 합금
identify 파악하다
pay (~에게) 이득이 되다
cultivate 구축하다, 함양하다
certainty 확실성
attachment 애착, 지지
physics 물리적 현상; 물리학
hence 따라서
ever-present 영원히 존재하는
temptation 유혹
logical 논리적인

WORDS LIST

01

pressure 압박
chest 가슴
sufficient 충분한
appointment (진료) 예약, 약속
examination 검사
diagnosis 진단
immediate 즉각적인
surgery 수술

02

enjoyable 즐거운
confidence 자신감, 확신
surrender 포기하다, 버리다
attention 주목
jump in (대화에) 불쑥 끼어들다
bite one's tongue 말하지 않고 참다
leave it at that 그대로 두다
on the edge of one's seat 의자에서 몸을 내밀고; 긴장하여

03

protein 단백질
recover from ~에서 회복하다
catch-up growth 회복 성장
synthesize 합성하다
break down ~을 분해하다
intake 섭취
in excess of ~을 초과하여
requirement 필요(조건), 요구
supplement 보충제
automatically 자동적으로
market 광고하다, 내놓다
unnecessary 불필요한

04

neighborhood 이웃
compose 작곡하다
experimental 실험적인
feature ~을 특징으로 하다
widen 확대하다, 넓히다
take a step 조치하다
occasion 행사, 때
figure 인물
spokesman 대변자
be concerned about ~에 관심을 가지다

05

negligible 무시해도 좋은 정도의
vegetation 식물
decay 썩다
release 방출, 배출

hospitable (기후 조건이 사람·동물이) 지내기 좋은
be accustomed to ~에 익숙하다
deposit 침전물
sediment 퇴적물
waterway 수로
reservoir 저수지

06

recall 생각해 내다, 회상하다
hierarchical 계층[계급]에 따른
rebel 반항아
defy 도전하다, 반항하다
oblivious 의식하지 못하는
oversensitive 지나치게 민감한
assert (단호하게) 자기 주장을 하다
subordinate 종속적인
dominant 지배적인
rebellious 반항적인
authoritarian 권위적인

07

boredom 무료함, 지루함, 권태
apparently 분명히
exercise 발휘하다
preoccupied 몰두한
engage 관여하다
consumed with ~에 열중한
set aside 따로 마련하다
dedicated 전용의
unfold 펼쳐지다
philosopher 철학자
destruction 파괴
downtime 비가동 시간

08

cope with ~에 대처하다
adversity 역경, 불운
context 맥락, 상황
typically 대체로, 일반적으로
in the midst of ~이 한창인 중에
adverse 부정적인, 불리한
distressing 고통스러운, 괴로움을 주는
overwhelming 압도적인, 굉장한
perceive ~ as ... ~을 …으로 인식하다
lively 활기찬

09

sensory organ 감각 기관
malfunction (기계 등이) 제대로 작동하지 않다
take ~ for granted ~을 당연하게 여기다

embrace 포용하다, 받아들이다
ungrateful 은혜를 모르는

10

practical 실질적인, 실용적인
roll 굴리다
mental 정신적인
intellectual 지적인
assessment 평가
identical 똑같은, 동일한
dumb 바보 같은, 멍청한
reside 존재하다
reasoning 추론, 추리

11

verbal 구두의, 말에 관한
phrasing 표현(법), 말씨
monotone 단조로운 어조
vocal 발성의, 음성의
lose one's place (읽던) 부분을 놓치다
glue 고정하다, 눈[귀]를 떼지 않다
significant 매우 큰, 중요한
awkward 서투른, 어색한
statement 성명, 진술
crisis 위기
remark 발언, 언급
critical 중대한, 결정적인
script 대본을 작성하다
sensitive 민감한
controversial 논란이 되는

12-14

refine 정제하다
cane 사탕수수
father ~의 아버지가 되다
oversee 감독하다, 가만히 보다
demonstrate 시연하다
guarantee 보장
beet 사탕무
sealed 밀봉된
conflict 분쟁
prejudice 편견

WORDS LIST

01
steel 강철
inventory 재고 [목록]
part (보통 pl.) 부품
out of stock 재고가 없는
provider 공급업체, 공급자

02
retirement 퇴직, 은퇴
generate 창출하다, 생산하다
income 소득
factor 요인
regarding ~에 관한
revise 수정하다
keep up with ~을 따라잡다

03
racism 인종 차별주의
evolutionism (사회) 진화론
unquestioningly 의심의 여지 없이, 무조건
indigenous 토착의
tribal 부족의
savage 야만인; 야만적인
massacre 대학살하다; 대학살
abandon 버리다, 포기하다
embed 끼워 넣다

04
killer whale 범고래
bald eagle 흰머리독수리
sea otter 해달
prey 먹이
alga (pl. algae) 해조류
shallow 얕은
predation 포식

05
committee 위원회
participate in ~에 참가하다
community center 지역 문화 회관
convey 전달하다, 전하다
medium (pl. media) (화가·작가·음악가의)
표현 수단[기법]
textile 직물
award 상; (상을) 수여하다

06
conceptualize 개념화하다
root 어원, 뿌리
chronology 연대기
timelessness 영원함
synchronicity 동시성

seize the moment 현재를 즐기다
reflect 반영하다
struggle 분투, 싸움
fixed 고정된
objective 객관적인
rate 속도
subjective 주관적인
refuse 거부하다, 거절하다

07
cemetery 공동묘지
cathedral 대성당
longevity 장수
the deceased 고인
beneath ~의 아래에
genetic 유전적인
hold true 딱 들어맞다, 유효하다
correlation 상관관계, 연관성

08
subject 피실험자
laboratory 실험실; 실험(실)용의
tuition 수업료[등록금]
code 부호화[암호화]하다
positive 양[플러스]의, 영(0)보다 더 큰
frame (특정한 방식으로) 표현하다
lead to ~을 유발하다, ~으로 이어지다
experiment 실험
contact 연락하다

09
inequality 불평등
poverty 가난
distribution 분배
irrelevant 문제가 되지 않는
compatible 양립할 수 있는
affluence 풍요로움
deprivation 박탈
suspicious 미심쩍은
objectionable 못마땅한
per se 그 자체로

10
gene 유전자
chronic 만성적인
metabolize 대사 작용을 하다
presence 존재함
diabetes 당뇨병
pass on 전달하다, 넘겨주다
list 목록을 작성하다
well-documented 문서에 의해 충분히
입증된

11
contract 계약
organizational chart 조직도
authority 권위
consensus 합의
loyal 충성스러운
unwilling 꺼려하는
mutual 상호의
appreciation 인정, 이해
replace 대체하다

12
concern 관심을 끌다
outline 개요를 서술하다
outlaw 추방하다
justify 정당화하다
argument 주장
imitation 모방
simulation 흉내 내기, 가장하기
problematic 문제가 있는
stir up ~을 선동하다
citizenry 시민
agitation 선동, 동요

13-14
unethical 비윤리적인
implication 결과, 영향
predict 예측하다
explicitly 명시적으로
consequence 결과
precautionary principle 예방 원칙(사전
배려 원칙)
dictate 지시하다
before the fact 사전에
manifestation 표명, 표현
determine 결정하다
institutional 제도적인, 제도상의
conduct 수행하다
woefully 비참하게
deficient 불완전한
analysis 분석
profit motive 이익을 염두에 둔 동기
consumerism 소비자 운동
transient 덧없는
obsolete 쓸모없는

WORDS LIST

01

embrace 수용, 용인
accommodate 수용하다
perspective 관점
take on (일 등을) 맡다
cast 배역
bond 유대
acquaintance 친분
prosper in ~에 성공하다
deplete 고갈시키다
friction 마찰
refer to ~을 가리키다
tie up ~을 묶다
free up ~을 자유롭게 하다
connectivity 연결
erode 침식시키다
boundary 경계
on call 대기 중인, 전화만 하면 언제든지 달려가는

02

pollutant 오염 물질
extract 추출하다
domestically 국내에서
efficiency 효율성
prioritise 우선하다
emerge 출현하다
colony 식민지
colonial 식민지의, 식민지풍의
quest 추구
cautious 신중한
anticipate 예측하다, 예상하다

03

welfare 복지
agenda 의제
aquaculture 양식업
collaborate with ~과 협력하다
practice 관행
adversely 부정적으로, 불리하게
labour-intensive 노동 집약적인
diameter 직경
fitted with ~ 설비가 갖춰진
counter 계측기
beneficial 이로운

recover 회복하다
procedure 절차

04

adaptation 적응
edge 우위, 우세
cope with ~에 대처하다
substitute 대체하다
evaluate 평가하다
prune 자두
substitution 대용품
disrupt 어지럽히다, 혼란케 하다
routine 일상적인 일
consumption 소비

05

surplus 잉여(물)
accumulation 축적
complexity 복잡성
fulfillment 충족
feasting 연회, 잔치
obligation 의무
leveling effect 평준화 효과
lean 수확이 적은
emergence 출현
elaborate 정교한
characteristic 특징
may well 아마 ~일 것이다, ~은 당연하다

06

therapy 치료
personality 성격
genetics 유전적 특질
aggressive 공격적인
politeness 공손함
triad 3인조
in the public eye 대중의 이목을 받고 있는
neurobiological 신경 생물학적인
be accompanied by ~을 동반하다
assertiveness 단호함
competitiveness 경쟁력
dominance 지배
compensate for ~을 보상하다

07

loneliness 외로움, 고독
passive 수동적인
muted 말이 없는
hammering 망치로 두드리는
evoke 불러일으키다
association 연상
stillness 고요함
vein 정맥
identical 동일한
far-reaching 광범위한
deadly 치명적인
intertwine 뒤얽히다, 엮다

08

sociologist 사회학자
prejudice 편견
common 흔히 있는
considerable 상당한
hospitality 환대
refuse 거절하다

WORDS LIST

01

engineering 공학
mechanical 기계의
civil engineering 토목 공학
weave 짜다, 짜서 만들다
utter 말하다
oddly 이상하게
literary 문학적인, 문어적인
reflect 반영하다
govern ~에 적용되다, 지배하다
patent 특허
copyright 저작권
wreak 입히다, 가하다
ruinous 파괴적인
regulate 규제하다

02

derive from ~에서 유래하다
primitive 원시의
pass down ~을 전승하다
tradition 구전, 전통
signify 의미하다
make up ~을 구성하다
embody 구체적으로 표현하다
moral 도덕의, 도덕적인
norms 규범
repetition 반복
reinforce 강화하다
coherence 일관성
adaptively 순응적으로

03

supervisor 감독자
workforce 노동 인구
diverse 다양한
background 배경
motivated 동기가 부여된, 의욕을 가진,
자극받은
highly 매우
competitive 경쟁력 있는
shrink 줄어들다
budget 예산
unconventional 관습에 얽매이지 않는
retention 잔류, 유지
corporate 기업[회사]의
annual salary 연봉

turnover 이직(률)
impose 부과하다
drain 고갈시키는 것
expense 비용, 경비

04

fraction 부분
swear 장담하다, 맹세하다
blindspot 사각지대, 맹점
at arm's length 어느 정도 거리를 두고
black out ~을 깜깜하게 하다
imperfection 결함
convincing 설득력 있는
cover story 꾸며낸 이야기
immediacy 직접성
contemplation 사색

05

estimate 추정하다; 추정(치)
flux 흐름
reservoir 저장고
tricky 까다로운
quantify 정량화하다
respiration 호흡
decomposition 분해
mass 질량
litter 쓰레기
mesh 그물 천
seal 밀봉하다, 봉인하다

06

in general 일반적으로
stove 가스레인지
scrutinize 면밀히 조사하다
lay out ~을 배치하다
navigate 걸어 다니다
exposure 노출
encounter 우연히 마주치다

07

ultimate 궁극적인
objective 목표
endgame 최종 단계
natural selection 자연 선택
trait 특성, 특징
chance 우연한

likelihood 가능성
reproduce 번식하다
neutral 중립적인
favor 선호하다
descendant 후손
breeder 사육사
modify 수정하다
subsequent 이후의

08

digit 자릿수
opt for ~을 선택하다
speculate 추측하다
urge 충동
anatomically 해부학적으로
plausible 그럴듯한
neuron 신경세포
otherwise 다른 상황에서는, 만약 그렇지
않으면

WORDS LIST

01
introspection 자기 성찰
observe 관찰하다
fade away 사라져 버리다, 희미해지다
refer to A as B A를 B라고 부르다
in reference to ~에 관련하여
particle 입자
disturb 방해하다
hopeless 가망 없는

02
perception 인식, 지각
highlight 강조하다
luxuriously 사치스럽게
commute 통근(하다)
hellish 지옥 같은
look back on ~을 되돌아보다
deal with ~을 처리하다

03
purpose 목표
bring together 합치다, 묶다
every bit of 모든, 일체의
strengthen 강화시키다
recreative 기분 전환이 되는
carpenter 목수
sheer 순전한
undiluted 희석되지 않은
pure 순수한
will 의지
arise 생기다
strength 힘

04
Supreme Court 대법원
appeal court 항소 법원
legislative 입법의
ruling 판결
in advance 미리
constitutional 합헌의
Congress 의회
challenge 이의를 제기하다
federal court 연방 법원
submit 제출하다
justice 판사, 재판관

be consistent with ~에 부합하다
[일치하다]
constitution 헌법
interpretation 해석

05
principle 원칙
authoritative 권위 있는, 권위적인
parenting 양육, 가정 교육
convey 전달하다
firmly 확고하게, 단호하게
dignity 위엄
honor 존중하다
esteem 존중
regard 배려, 고려
expression 표현
require 필요로 하다
sincerely 진지하게
take it for granted that ~을 당연하게
여기다
resource 자원
reciprocity 상호성

06
material 물질
volcanic 화산의
regularly 규칙적으로
inhabit 거주하다
carry on 계속 수행하다
dig 파다, 파내다
startling 놀라운
jaw 턱

07
phenomenon 현상
bring about ~을 유발하다
tendency 경향
aware of ~을 알고 있는
seemingly 겉보기에는
rational 합리적인
publicize 알리다, 공개하다
latter 후자의
inclination 성향
associate 연관시키다
manifestation 표현
instrumental 도움이 되는, 유용한

membership 회원의 지위[자격]
sufficient 충분한
stimulate 고무하다
critical 중요한

08
anthropologist 인류학자
prestigious 명망 있는
innovate 혁신하다
occasionally 가끔, 때때로
evolve 진화하다
probability 가능성
productive 생산적인
deterioration 악화
density 밀도
sustain 유지하다, 지속하다
disappear 사라지다

WORDS LIST

01
necessity 필수품
acquaintance 지인, 아는 사람
intimacy 친밀감
renowned 저명한
cognitive 인지적인
bid 시도, 노력
attribute 자질, 속성
navigate 처리하다[다루다], 항해하다

02
invader 침입자
take over 접수하다; 인계받다
native 토종의, 토착의
settler 정착민
Monarch butterfly 왕나비
caterpillar 애벌레
milkweed 아스클레피아스(쌍떡잎식물
용담목 박주가리과의 한 속)
replace 대체하다
introduce 도입하다
survive 살아남다
food web 먹이 그물, 먹이망
die off 차례로 죽다, 죽어 없어지다
bottom line 결론, 최종 결과
threaten 위협하다
delicate 깨지기 쉬운, 연약한

03
object 물건, 물체
embed (기기에) 내장하다[장착하다]
incidental to ~에 부수적인
primary 주요한, 주된
relatively 비교적, 상대적으로
merely 단지
by no means 결코 ~이 아닌
differentiate 차별화하다, 구별하다
predecessor 전에 있던 것[모델], 전임자
token 징표, 표시
added value 부가 가치
appliance (가정용) 기기, 장비
display (화면에) 표시하다, 보여주다
pedal 페달을 밟다; 페달
analog 아날로그의

04
adolescent 청소년
adolescence 청소년기
directly 바로
dip 살짝 담그다
track record 추적하여 기록한 것, 실적
process 과정
alleviate 완화하다

05
demise 소멸, 종말
inevitable 불가피한, 필연적인
lay 전문가가 아닌
professional 전문적인
Third Reich 제3제국(1933~1945년,
히틀러 정권 하의 독일)
momentous 중대한
routinely 일상적으로, 늘
commentator 논평자
suspect 의심하다
in retrospect 되돌아보면
overestimate 과대평가하다

06
algorithm 알고리즘
repetitive 반복적인
automate 자동화하다
analyze 분석하다
consequence 결과, 영향
microscope 현미경
tissue 세포
abnormal 비정상적인
consistent 일관된
self-contained 자체로서 완비된
candidate 후보(자)
stakes 위험성, 리스크

07
fertilizer 비료
premise 전제
enhance 향상하다
nutrient 영양소
nitrogen 질소
potassium 칼륨, 포타슘
transition 이행, 이동
have access to ~을 이용하다, ~에 접근하다

external 외부의
compost 퇴비
manure 거름
emerging 신생의, 최근 생겨난
agribusiness 농업 관련 산업
extended 장기의; 늘어난
initially 처음에
wear out 못쓰게 만들다, 마모시키다
susceptibility 민감성

08
stereotype 고정 관념
defuse 완화하다
intervention 개입, 조정
intriguing 아주 흥미로운
neuroscientist 신경 과학자
mindset 사고방식

WORDS LIST

01
fulfilling 성취감을 주는
conscious 의식적인
path 길, 경로
compromise 타협하다
protest 항의하다
unpleasant 불편한, 불쾌한
inspiration 영감을 주는 사람[것]
courage 용기
resistance 저항, 반대

02
odd 이상한
manner 방식
sweetener 감미료
come to light (사람들에게) 알려지다
[밝혀지다]
mishear 잘못 듣다[알아듣다]
instruction 지시 사항
synthetic 인조의, 합성의
application 응용
beet 사탕무
derivative 파생물
laboratory 실험실
trichlorosucrose 트리클로로수크로오스
(세 개의 염소 원자가 넣어진 자당)
introduce 끼워 넣다
substance 물질
imperfectly 불완전하게
be attuned to ~에 적응되다
Sucralose 수크랄로스(설탕에 비해
600배의 단맛을 가진 무열량 감미료)
concentration 농도

03
matter 중요하다
treat 여기다, 간주하다
assume 가정하다
progress 진보하다
momentum 추진력, 여세
pile up (양이) 누적되다, 쌓이다
unique 고유한, 독특한
under one's own steam 자체의 힘으로,
스스로
get in the way 방해하다
at best 기껏해야

interpret 해석하다
peer review 동료 검토
double blind testing 이중 맹검 실험
objectivity 객관성
institution 제도, 관례

04
excessive 과도한
worn down 기진맥진한
catch breath 한숨 돌리다
buzzing 와글와글거리는
reflect on ~을 곰곰이 생각하다
allocate 할당하다
capacity 생산 능력, 수용력
flip 휙 뒤집다

05
reflex 반사 작용
hardwired 타고난, 내장된
sneeze 재채기
knee jerk 무릎 반사
involuntary 무의식적인
blushing 얼굴 붉힘
yawn 하품
salivation 타액 분비
startle response 놀람 반응
instantly 즉시
slump 털썩 쓰러지다
defense 방어
stalk 몰래 접근하다
posture 자세

06
notion 관념, 개념
contemporary 현대의
backdrop 배경
transient 일시적으로 머무르는
trigger 촉발하다
encode 부호화하다
specificity 특별함
texture 촉감
sensory 감각의

07
top 팽이
spin 회전하다, 돌리다; 회전
poke (쿡) 찌르다; (쿡) 찌름
slightly 약간, 조금
off center 중심에서 벗어나
interplay 상호 작용
complicated 복잡한
axis 축
vertical 수직의
gravity 중력
horizontally 수평으로

08
crew 선원
cargo 화물
depend upon ~에 달려 있다
mainmast 큰 돛대
be exposed to ~에 노출되다
mighty 강력한, 힘센
gust 돌풍
harshness 거친 상태
fiber 섬유질
intense 강렬한
buffeting 난타

WORDS REVIEW

A 다음 영어 단어에 해당하는 우리말 뜻을 빈칸에 쓰시오.

01	confirm	_____	11	density	_____
02	discriminate	_____	12	variability	_____
03	perspective	_____	13	tolerate	_____
04	realm	_____	14	authoritative	_____
05	sought-after	_____	15	compile	_____
06	recruit	_____	16	fatality	_____
07	interplay	_____	17	adjust	_____
08	skeptic	_____	18	degeneration	_____
09	conventional	_____	19	reputation	_____
10	validity	_____	20	disastrous	_____

B 다음 우리말과 의미가 같도록 빈칸에 알맞은 말을 [보기]에서 골라 쓰시오. (필요시 형태를 변형할 것)

> ─ 보기 ─
> ensure   intuition   impulsive   endure   privilege

01 Citizens must have unique _____ of participation in government: voting and holding public office.

시민에게는 선거권과 공직 재임권이라는 고유의 정부 참여 권리(참정권)가 있어야 한다.

02 Sometimes our _____ help us develop scientific understandings of the world, and sometimes they hinder them.

때로 우리의 직관은 우리가 세상에 대한 과학적 이해를 발전시키는 데 도움이 되기도 하고 때로 그것은 그런 이해에 방해가 되기도 한다.

03 You can _____ any stressful or difficult situation, while remaining calm within yourself, because your spirit resides in an untouchable place within you.

여러분은 내적 평온을 유지하면서 스트레스가 많거나 힘든 어떤 상황도 견딜 수 있는데, 여러분의 정신이 내면의 건드릴 수 없는 곳에 있기 때문이다.

04 The single most important thing you can do to _____ your future success is to find someone who has an interest in your development.

여러분이 미래의 성공을 보장하기 위해 할 수 있는 단 하나의 가장 중요한 일은 여러분의 발전에 관심을 가지고 있는 누군가를 찾는 것이다.

05 Instead, they show poor and unpredictable judgment and are prone to engage in highly _____ behavior patterns that mess up their lives badly.

대신, 그들은 형편없고 예측 불가능한 판단력을 보여 주며 자신들의 삶을 엉망으로 만드는 매우 충동적인 행동 패턴에 빠지는 경향이 있다.

WORDS REVIEW

A 다음 영어 단어에 해당하는 우리말 뜻을 빈칸에 쓰시오.

01	contained	_____	11	deception	_____
02	generous	_____	12	convince	_____
03	deed	_____	13	budget	_____
04	trait	_____	14	indulge	_____
05	resistance	_____	15	hypothesis	_____
06	endeavor	_____	16	assess	_____
07	masterpiece	_____	17	unwilling	_____
08	flux	_____	18	malfunction	_____
09	modify	_____	19	vacant	_____
10	extinct	_____	20	nurture	_____

B 다음 우리말과 의미가 같도록 빈칸에 알맞은 말을 [보기]에서 골라 쓰시오. (필요시 형태를 변형할 것)

보기
imprint	stimulus	procedure	encircle	cite

01 You could walk every street within its _____ canal in a day or so.

하루 정도면 그것을 둘러싼 운하 내의 모든 거리를 걸어 다닐 수 있었다.

02 But if it comes repeatedly from someone we are close to, and is confirmed by others as well, it would be deeply _____ in our minds and would become a label.

하지만 그것이 우리에게 가까운 사람에게서 반복적으로 들려오고 다른 사람에 의해서도 또한 확인된다면, 그것은 우리 마음 속에 깊이 각인되어 하나의 꼬리표가 될 것이다.

03 It is possibly the oldest surviving long poem in Old English and is commonly _____ as one of the most important works of Old English literature.

그것은 아마도 고대 영어로 쓰인 남아 있는 가장 오래된 시일 것이며 고대 영어 문학의 가장 중요한 작품들 중 하나로 흔히 인용된다.

04 While humans can be deceived by a number of visual _____, computers detect only the given cues, which can be relied on as truthful.

인간이 많은 시각적인 자극들에 의해 속을 수 있는 반면, 컴퓨터는 주어진 단서들만을 탐지하는데, 그것은 참이라고 신뢰될 수 있다.

05 While the most likely explanation is that one made a mistake in a _____ or calculation, there is always the chance that it represents an opening through which new light will be shown.

가장 그럴듯한 설명은 절차나 계산에서 실수를 저질렀다는 것이지만, 그것이 새로운 빛이 통과해서 보이게 될 틈을 나타내는 가능성이 항상 존재한다.

WORDS REVIEW

A 다음 영어 단어에 해당하는 우리말 뜻을 빈칸에 쓰시오.

01	expansion	11	justify
02	adjustment	12	obligatory
03	innovate	13	equipped
04	thrive	14	exploration
05	pioneer	15	symmetrical
06	suppression	16	crucial
07	fertile	17	commerce
08	prosper	18	precede
09	compose	19	arise
10	in disguise	20	superior to

B 다음 우리말과 의미가 같도록 빈칸에 알맞은 말을 [보기]에서 골라 쓰시오. (필요시 형태를 변형할 것)

---- 보기 ----

reveal	successive	alter	assume	contract

01 Because he is gone for a long time, everyone _____ he is dead, and they demand that Penelope remarry.

그가 오랫동안 돌아오지 않아서, 모든 사람이 그가 죽었다고 생각하고, 그들은 페넬로페에게 재혼하라고 강요한다.

02 Later in the nineteenth century, these solar observations _____ the existence of new elements, such as helium, that were previously unknown on Earth.

그 이후 19세기 중에, 이러한 태양의 관측은 이전에는 지구상에서 알려지지 않았던 헬륨과 같은 새로운 원소의 존재를 밝혀 냈다.

03 For Abrams' test animal to achieve that, muscles _____ in its body, which pushed and pulled the remaining arms until they were once again evenly spaced.

Abrams의 실험 동물이 그것을 성취하기 위해 근육이 그것의 몸에서 수축했는데, 그것은 남아 있는 팔들이 다시 고른 간격으로 떨어지게 될 때까지 그것들을 밀고 당겼다.

04 A bee is like a worker in industry who is rewarded for her experience and length of service with _____ raises and promotions, until the employee is considered a cost rather than an asset.

벌은 마치 고용인이 자산보다는 비용으로 여겨질 때까지, 연속적인 임금 인상과 승진으로 경험과 근속 기간을 보상받는 산업체의 근로자와 같다.

05 The use of technology to _____ living organisms for human use is almost as old as the human race.

인간이 사용하기 위해 생물체를 바꾸는 기술의 사용은 거의 인류만큼이나 오래되었다.

WORDS REVIEW

A 다음 영어 단어에 해당하는 우리말 뜻을 빈칸에 쓰시오.

01 remainder _____ 11 disbelief _____

02 exhale _____ 12 recognition _____

03 undervalue _____ 13 sceptical _____

04 accumulation _____ 14 external _____

05 shattered _____ 15 burst out _____

06 proportion _____ 16 resume _____

07 acceptance _____ 17 mutation _____

08 surrounding _____ 18 distortion _____

09 accommodate _____ 19 substitute A for B _____

10 rejoice _____ 20 dependent on _____

B 다음 우리말과 의미가 같도록 빈칸에 알맞은 말을 [보기]에서 골라 쓰시오. (필요시 형태를 변형할 것)

┌─ 보기 ───┐
│   ill   deter   reciprocal   convert   disperse   │
└──┘

01 This disbelief can be increased and _____ into the recognition that we are, in fact, dreaming.

이러한 불신은 증가하여 우리가 사실상 꿈을 꾸고 있다는 인식으로 전환될 수 있다.

02 They gave both groups two sets of research findings: one set that supported the claim that the death penalty _____ crime and the other set refuting that position.

그들은 양쪽 집단에 모두 두 세트의 연구 결과를 제공했는데, 한 세트는 사형이 범죄를 단념시킨다는 주장을 지지하는 것이었고, 다른 세트는 그 입장을 논박하는 것이었다.

03 Rather, we work in full knowledge of the limits of politics, knowing that good governance will never be perfect governance, and nor will it cure all the _____ of the world.

오히려 우리는 정치의 한계를 충분히 인식하며 일을 해 나가는데, 좋은 통치가 결코 완벽한 통치가 될 수 없으며, 그리고 그것이 세상의 모든 해악을 고칠 수도 없다는 것을 알고 있다.

04 There is a _____ (or dialectic) relation between 'self' and place.

'자아'와 장소 사이에는 상호의 (또는 변증법적) 관계가 있다.

05 In ages past, these aggregations were temporary, and elephants _____ when the danger was gone.

과거의 시대에, 이러한 집합은 일시적이었고, 위험이 지나가면 코끼리들은 흩어졌다.

WORDS REVIEW

A 다음 영어 단어에 해당하는 우리말 뜻을 빈칸에 쓰시오.

01	contemporary	_____	11	devote	_____
02	indication	_____	12	implication	_____
03	debate	_____	13	equitable	_____
04	worship	_____	14	densely	_____
05	proceed	_____	15	oversight	_____
06	inversion	_____	16	feature	_____
07	exchange	_____	17	distinct	_____
08	association	_____	18	activate	_____
09	meditation	_____	19	esteem	_____
10	extinction	_____	20	end up	_____

B 다음 우리말과 의미가 같도록 빈칸에 알맞은 말을 [보기]에서 골라 쓰시오.

┌ 보기 ┐
| dominant | exposure | obscure | static | statistics |

01 Since about the mid-1990s, _____ have shown that the yearly rate of increase for the crops is decreasing.

1990년대 중반 정도부터, 통계는 작물의 연간 증가율이 줄어들고 있음을 보여 주었다.

02 In spite of the global economic recession, we've kept the prices of our products _____ until now, but it seems we can no longer do so.

전 세계적인 경기 불황에도 불구하고, 저희는 지금까지 저희 제품의 가격을 동결해 왔습니다만, 더는 그렇게 할 수 없을 것 같습니다.

03 Similarly, when a YouTube video attracts so many views that it lands on the YouTube home page, that additional _____ is responsible for more views.

마찬가지로, 어떤 YouTube 영상이 매우 많은 조회를 기록해서 YouTube 홈페이지에 올라갈 때, 그 추가적인 노출이 더 많은 조회의 원인이 된다.

04 When storms blow in and _____ the top of the mountain, the climbers grow discouraged and despondent and consider retreat.

폭풍우가 불어와서 산 정상을 보기 어렵게 할 때, 등반가들은 낙담하고 실의에 빠져 퇴각을 고려한다.

05 In a colonization situation, the smaller culture invariably must accommodate the _____ culture, and this is when language shift will most likely take place.

식민지 상황에서는, 더 작은 규모의 문화가 예외 없이 지배적인 문화를 수용해야만 하고, 이때가 언어 전이가 일어날 가능성이 가장 높은 때이다.

WORDS REVIEW

A 다음 영어 단어에 해당하는 우리말 뜻을 빈칸에 쓰시오.

01	territory	_____	11	intrusion	_____
02	stick with	_____	12	disrupt	_____
03	yield	_____	13	unprecedented	_____
04	parallel	_____	14	diffusion	_____
05	gross	_____	15	adaptive	_____
06	pursue	_____	16	menacing	_____
07	hypothesize	_____	17	inheritance	_____
08	legitimate	_____	18	triumphant	_____
09	inquiry	_____	19	prior to	_____
10	distort	_____	20	contrary to	_____

B 다음 우리말과 의미가 같도록 빈칸에 알맞은 말을 [보기]에서 골라 쓰시오. (필요시 형태를 변형할 것)

┌ 보기 ┐
| phenomenon | extract | incorporate | artifact | paralyze |

01 Some trees had _____ the wires into their trunks, and grew strong and upright despite the barbed wire.

몇몇 나무들은 그 철조망을 자신들의 몸통에 파묻었고, 그 가시철조망에도 불구하고 강인하고 똑바르게 자랐다.

02 While only 5 grams of gold can usually be _____ from 1 ton of ore, 1 ton of mobile phones yields 150 grams of gold, 30 times the amount from ore.

단 5그램의 금이 보통 1톤의 광석에서 추출될 수 있는 반면에, 1톤의 휴대전화는 광석에서 나오는 양의 30배에 달하는 150그램의 금을 내놓는다.

03 The dawn of the technological era is signaled archaeologically by the first chipped stone _____ — a tool or weapon plausibly used for killing big game.

기술 시대의 시작은 고고학적으로 최초의 뗀석기 유물, 즉 큰 사냥감을 죽이는 데 그럴듯하게 사용된 도구나 무기에 의해 암시된다.

04 That is, scientists shape the outcome to some extent by their interaction with the _____.

다시 말해서, 과학자들은 현상과의 상호 작용을 통해 어느 정도 결과를 형성한다.

05 In sum, fear of the unknown can _____ us and prevent us from acting rationally.

요컨대, 미지의 것에 대한 두려움은 우리를 마비시키고 우리가 합리적으로 행동하지 못하게 할 수 있다.

WORDS REVIEW

A 다음 영어 단어에 해당하는 우리말 뜻을 빈칸에 쓰시오.

01	accountant	_____	11	cognitive	_____
02	collaborative	_____	12	substitute	_____
03	exclaim	_____	13	extensive	_____
04	bureaucracy	_____	14	confine	_____
05	absorption	_____	15	substantial	_____
06	manually	_____	16	narrate	_____
07	dimension	_____	17	emphasize	_____
08	depletion	_____	18	for the sake of	_____
09	grasp	_____	19	along with	_____
10	emerge	_____	20	other than	_____

B 다음 우리말과 의미가 같도록 빈칸에 알맞은 말을 [보기]에서 골라 쓰시오. (필요시 형태를 변형할 것)

보기
inhibit   transmission   rational   retention   experiment

01 Much of the literature on strategy makes a fundamental assumption that strategy making is a _____ process.

전략에 관한 많은 문헌은 전략 수립이 합리적 과정이라는 기본적인 가정을 내린다.

02 They claim that bureaucratic authority is undemocratic and the blind adherence to rules may _____ the exact actions necessary to achieve organizational goals.

그들은 관료주의적 권위가 비민주적이고 규칙들에 대한 맹목적인 고수는 조직의 목표를 성취하는 데 필요한 정확한 조치를 방해할 수도 있다고 주장한다.

03 It is also nearly impossible to learn anything without doing it yourself, by _____ along the way, and by recovering from the inevitable failures.

또한 어떤 것을 배운다는 것은 그 방식으로 그것을 직접 실험해 보고 또 불가피한 실패들로부터 회복해 보지 않고서는 거의 불가능하다.

04 _____ by voice and hearing is the most basic definition of a folk song.

목소리와 듣기에 의한 전파는 민요의 가장 기본적인 정의이다.

05 The differences between the two groups were still evident one week later, indicating that the discussion enhanced _____ as well as immediate learning.

두 집단 사이의 차이는 일주일 후에도 여전히 분명했는데, 그것은 그 논의가 즉각적인 학습뿐만 아니라 기억력도 향상시켰다는 것을 보여 주었다.

WORDS REVIEW

A 다음 영어 단어에 해당하는 우리말 뜻을 빈칸에 쓰시오.

01 crushing _____   11 hamper _____
02 scarce _____   12 define _____
03 distribute _____   13 sustainable _____
04 fascinate _____   14 benefactor _____
05 status _____   15 expose _____
06 qualified _____   16 destruction _____
07 autonomous _____   17 excavator _____
08 norm _____   18 futile _____
09 adapt _____   19 obstacle _____
10 invasion _____   20 stunned _____

B 다음 우리말과 의미가 같도록 빈칸에 알맞은 말을 [보기]에서 골라 쓰시오. (필요시 형태를 변형할 것)

| 보기 |
| distress   subscription   override   encode   prescription |

01 For example, a single annual _____ to *The New York Times* roughly generates 520 pounds of waste, which equates to approximately 4.25 trees being cut down per reader per year.

예를 들어, '뉴욕 타임즈'의 단 1년 정기 구독이 대략 520파운드의 쓰레기를 발생시키는데, 그것은 1년에 구독자 한 명당 약 4.25그루의 나무가 베이는 것과 같다.

02 Today, going it alone is a _____ for extinction.

오늘날, 혼자 힘으로 하는 것은 멸종을 위한 처방이다.

03 The _____, great or small, causes them to seek release from the tension and anxiety.

그 고통은 크든 작든 그들로 하여금 그 긴장과 불안으로부터의 해방을 추구하게 한다.

04 In sum, financial expediency tended to _____ best farming practice in relation to conservation of the natural environment.

요컨대, 재정적 편의는 자연 환경의 보존과 관련하여 최고의 농업 관행에 우선하는 경향이 있었다.

05 This proves that there is a built-in, uniquely human capacity to learn language, which must be genetically _____, but that the actual language acquired is determined by the environment.

이것은 유전적으로 암호화된, 타고나고 특유한 인간의 언어 학습 능력이 있으며, 습득되는 실제 언어는 환경에 의해 결정된다는 것을 증명한다.

WORDS REVIEW

A 다음 영어 단어에 해당하는 우리말 뜻을 빈칸에 쓰시오.

01 fundraising _____
02 startup _____
03 realign _____
04 figurative _____
05 warrant _____
06 diplomacy _____
07 deposit _____
08 dispute _____
09 dwelling _____
10 authority _____

11 confusion _____
12 execution _____
13 competitive _____
14 potential _____
15 determinant _____
16 presumptuous _____
17 discipline _____
18 devise _____
19 analogy _____
20 aspire _____

B 다음 우리말과 의미가 같도록 빈칸에 알맞은 말을 [보기]에서 골라 쓰시오.

| 보기 |
| edible   balance   alternative   abuse   stereotypical |

01 Studies of gifted teenagers confirm that intelligence and academic excellence are associated more with cross-gender abilities and less with _____ gender roles.

재능이 있는 십 대들에 대한 연구는 지능과 학업 우수성이 성의 교차적인 능력들과 더 많이 관련되어 있고 전형적인 성 역할들과는 덜 관련되어 있다는 것을 입증한다.

02 Camp tuition _____ will be charged to the credit card provided and due August 1 for all camp weeks.

캠프 수업료 잔액은 제공된 신용카드로 청구될 것이며, 모든 캠프 주에 대해 8월 1일까지 지불해야 할 것입니다.

03 A drought or blight may have come along, or the populations outgrew the wild food supply, and the settlers had to find ways to make do with whatever _____ plants remained.

가뭄이나 마름병이 찾아왔을 수도 있고, 아니면 인구가 야생 식량 공급을 초과하여 증가해서, 정착민들은 먹을 수 있는 식물이 남기는 어떤 것이라도 그것으로 때울 방법을 찾아야만 했다.

04 The driver of categorization will in all likelihood be the outcomes that particular customers seek ("jobs to be done") and the _____ ways those outcomes might be met.

분류를 추진하는 것은 아마도 특정한 소비자들이 추구하는 결과물('이루어져야 할 일들')일 것이고 그러한 결과물이 충족될 수 있는 대안적인 방법일 것이다.

05 In the United States, however, child care became a big social problem, leading in some cases to child neglect and _____.

그러나 미국에서는 보육이 큰 사회적 문제가 되었고, 이것은 어떤 경우들에는 자녀에 대한 방치와 학대로 이어졌다.

WORDS REVIEW

A 다음 영어 단어에 해당하는 우리말 뜻을 빈칸에 쓰시오.

01	itinerary	_____	11	property	_____
02	affinity	_____	12	meddling	_____
03	molecular	_____	13	look up	_____
04	illusion	_____	14	depict	_____
05	replicate	_____	15	curse	_____
06	predator	_____	16	discrimination	_____
07	excessive	_____	17	inclusive	_____
08	sophistication	_____	18	causation	_____
09	miserable	_____	19	devastate	_____
10	conservancy	_____	20	cripple	_____

B 다음 우리말과 의미가 같도록 빈칸에 알맞은 말을 [보기]에서 골라 쓰시오. (필요시 형태를 변형할 것)

┌─ 보기 ─
│   nestle   denial   resolve   counterpart   vocation
└

01 Not necessarily liking it, mind you, but coming to seeing how it shaped you, and making adult choices based not in ignorance and _____ but in courage and awareness of your past.

꼭 그것을 좋아하지는 않아도 되지만, 말하자면 그것은 여러분을 형성한 방식을 알게 되는 것과 여러분의 과거에 대한 무지와 부인이 아니라 용기와 인식에 근거한 어른스러운 선택을 하는 것을 포함한다.

02 Only men in the two oldest age groups made more walking trips per person than their female _____.

두 개의 최고 연령대의 남성만 동년배의 여성보다 1인당 도보 이동 횟수가 더 많았다.

03 That, after all, was its _____ a millennium ago, and it is the role that the United Arab Emirates has been successfully recreating as the Middle East's trading and tourist center.

결국 그것은 천 년 전 그곳의 소명이었고, 그것이 바로 아랍 에미리트 연합국이 중동의 무역과 관광의 중심지로서 성공적으로 재창출하고 있는 역할이다.

04 I boarded the plane and _____ down in a wide seat with extra leg room.

나는 비행기에 탑승했고 다리를 뻗을 수 있는 여분의 공간이 있는 넓은 좌석에 기분 좋게 앉았다.

05 Then, he began dragging himself along the fence, _____ that he would walk.

그리고 나서 그는 자신이 걸을 것이라고 결심하며 울타리를 따라 자신의 몸을 끌고 가기 시작했다.

WORDS REVIEW

A 다음 영어 단어에 해당하는 우리말 뜻을 빈칸에 쓰시오.

01 sponsor _____

02 applaud _____

03 perceive _____

04 discrete _____

05 nonuniform _____

06 ingredient _____

07 emission _____

08 privation _____

09 autobiography _____

10 reinforce _____

11 vanish _____

12 benefit _____

13 sprout _____

14 restrain _____

15 detect _____

16 discern _____

17 criterion _____

18 redundant _____

19 persist _____

20 deliberation _____

B 다음 우리말과 의미가 같도록 빈칸에 알맞은 말을 [보기]에서 골라 쓰시오. (필요시 형태를 변형할 것)

보기
confront   utter   contribute   literally   bluffer

01 Every day we _____ thousands of words.

매일 우리는 수천 개의 말을 입 밖으로 쏟아 낸다.

02 Between 1934 and 1938 he _____ articles to the periodical *Landscape and Gardening*.

1934년과 1938년 사이에 그는 정기 간행물 'Landscape and Gardening'에 글을 기고했다.

03 Less poetic but certainly more _____ representative of the whole of the human race!

덜 시적이지만, 분명히 더 글자 그대로 인류 전체를 대표하는 것이다!

04 Sailors have an expression about the weather: they say, the weather is a great _____.

선원들에게는 날씨에 관한 표현이 있다. 그들이 말하기를, 날씨는 굉장한 허풍꾼이다.

05 In my own classes, I have adjusted a lecture when _____ with what appeared to be a tired or uninterested group of students.

내 수업에서, 피곤하거나 흥미가 없는 학생들로 보이는 집단과 마주쳤을 때 나는 강의를 조정했다.

WORDS REVIEW

A 다음 영어 단어에 해당하는 우리말 뜻을 빈칸에 쓰시오.

01	clutch	11	disapprove
02	mature	12	biodiversity
03	decompose	13	resent
04	odor	14	identification
05	applicant	15	bond
06	signature	16	fundamental
07	recognize	17	hurdle
08	rage	18	absorb
09	show off	19	hazard
10	folk	20	antibody

B 다음 우리말과 의미가 같도록 빈칸에 알맞은 말을 [보기]에서 골라 쓰시오. (필요시 형태를 변형할 것)

— 보기 —
mumble	accumulate	excrement	hesitate	monopoly

01 Kate _____, "Yes," his smile making her feel better.

Kate는 "네"라고 중얼거렸고, 코치의 미소에 그녀의 기분이 나아졌다.

02 They noticed that elephant _____ was full of fibers, so they developed elephant waste paper.

그들은 코끼리 배설물에 섬유질이 가득하다는 점에 착안해, 코끼리 배설물 종이를 개발했다.

03 To those who fear _____ and believe that some producers should be protected from other producers by the government, such antitrust suits can be considered morally necessary.

독점을 두려워하고 정부에 의해 몇몇 생산자들이 다른 생산자들로부터 보호받아야 한다고 생각하는 사람들에게는, 그런 독점 금지법이 윤리적으로 필요하다고 여겨질 수 있다.

04 If these creatures are then food for larger ones, the _____ toxins are concentrated even further.

만약 이러한 생물들이 그다음에 더 큰 것들의 먹이가 되면, 그 축적된 독소들은 훨씬 더 농축된다.

05 I saw him _____ for only a moment before taking a deep breath and saying, "Yes, I'll do it if it will save Liza."

나는 그가 잠시 망설이고 나서 깊은 숨을 쉬고는 "네, 그것이 Liza를 살릴 수 있는 일이라면 하겠어요."라고 말하는 것을 보았다.

WORDS REVIEW

A 다음 영어 단어에 해당하는 우리말 뜻을 빈칸에 쓰시오.

01 refugee _____
02 harsh _____
03 measure _____
04 attain _____
05 trigger _____
06 categorize _____
07 rural _____
08 appropriate _____
09 disregard _____
10 cultivate _____

11 attachment _____
12 distinguish _____
13 artificial _____
14 storage _____
15 demonstrate _____
16 merger _____
17 monetary _____
18 withdraw _____
19 refer to A as B _____
20 give into _____

B 다음 우리말과 의미가 같도록 빈칸에 알맞은 말을 [보기]에서 골라 쓰시오. (필요시 형태를 변형할 것)

보기
predictable   suburban   component   turmoil   resistant

01 The other human, while initially _____, realizes that he must leave his comfort zone and embrace change.

처음에는 저항을 했던 다른 인간은 자신의 안락 지대를 떠나 변화를 수용해야 한다는 것을 깨닫는다.

02 People are not nearly as flexible or _____ as carbon fiber or metal alloys, and we should not pretend that they are.

사람들은 탄소 섬유나 금속 합금처럼 유연하거나 혹은 예측 가능하지 않으며, 우리는 그들이 그러하다고 가장해서도 안 된다.

03 We all know the importance of a balanced and varied diet, but what if one of the _____ of a typical diet is the very thing that makes you ill?

우리 모두는 균형 잡히고 다양한 식단의 중요성을 알고 있지만, 만약 일반적인 식단의 구성 요소 중 하나가 여러분을 아프게 하는 바로 그것이라면 어떻게 될까?

04 The percentage of U.S. adults who do not use the internet is less than 10% in both urban and _____ populations, whereas 15% of the U.S. adult rural population says they are non-internet users.

인터넷을 사용하지 않는 미국 성인의 비율은 도시와 교외 인구 모두에서 10% 미만인 반면, 미국 성인 농촌 인구의 15%가 자신이 인터넷 사용자가 아니라고 답했다.

05 Someone at one of my lectures was going through a lot of _____, and the word *pain* kept coming up in the conversation.

내 강의들 중 하나를 듣던 어떤 사람이 많은 혼란을 겪고 있었는데, '고통'이라는 단어가 대화 중에 계속 나왔다.

WORDS REVIEW

A 다음 영어 단어에 해당하는 우리말 뜻을 빈칸에 쓰시오.

01	diagnosis	11	controversial
02	confidence	12	refine
03	surrender	13	occasion
04	vegetation	14	conflict
05	release	15	assert
06	embrace	16	subordinate
07	identical	17	apparently
08	reside	18	cope with
09	significant	19	take ~ for granted
10	remark	20	in excess of

B 다음 우리말과 의미가 같도록 빈칸에 알맞은 말을 [보기]에서 골라 쓰시오. (필요시 형태를 변형할 것)

┌─ 보기 ───┐
    assessment   critical   adversity   oblivious   sufficient
└──┘

01 Like all forms of humor, the use of humor for coping with _____ usually takes place in a social context.

모든 형태의 유머와 마찬가지로, 역경에 대처하기 위한 유머의 사용은 대개 사회적 맥락에서 이루어진다.

02 Before that age, children do not have the mental tools to make intellectual _____.

그 나이 이전에는 아이들은 지적인 평가를 할 수 있는 정신적 도구가 없다.

03 For example, because an awkward statement made by the U.S. Secretary of State could cause an international crisis, his or her remarks on _____ issues are usually carefully scripted.

예를 들어, 미국 국무 장관의 서투른 성명은 국제적 위기를 초래할 수 있기 때문에 중요한 사안에 대한 그의 발언은 보통 대본 작성이 신중하게 이루어진다.

04 The pain was not sharp, and it was certainly not of _____ concern to stop the match.

통증이 심하지는 않았고, 그것이 확실히 경기를 멈출 만큼 충분히 걱정스러운 것은 아니었다.

05 "Born rebels" who defy authority are not _____ of it, but oversensitive to it.

권위에 도전하는 '타고난 반항아들'은 그것(권위)을 의식하지 못하는 것이 아니라, 그것에 대해 매우 과민하다.

WORDS REVIEW

A 다음 영어 단어에 해당하는 우리말 뜻을 빈칸에 쓰시오.

01 retirement _____   11 objective _____
02 factor _____   12 agitation _____
03 genetic _____   13 imitation _____
04 consequence _____   14 determine _____
05 evolutionism _____   15 obsolete _____
06 abandon _____   16 laboratory _____
07 prey _____   17 irrelevant _____
08 chronology _____   18 convey _____
09 consensus _____   19 keep up with _____
10 mutual _____   20 pass on _____

B 다음 우리말과 의미가 같도록 빈칸에 알맞은 말을 [보기]에서 골라 쓰시오. (필요시 형태를 변형할 것)

┌─ 보기 ──┐
│ deficient   root   appreciation   deprivation   indigenous │
└──┘

01 If a contract between a staff member and a leader still exists, it has become one in which mutual respect and _____ have replaced the earlier, more paternalistic model.

직원과 리더 사이의 계약이 여전히 존재한다면, 상호 존중과 인정이 이전의 가부장적 모델을 대체한 계약이 되었다.

02 Technology is interested in how things will be done and how they will be applied but is woefully _____ in terms of ethical analysis.

기술은 일이 어떻게 이루어질 것인지 그리고 그것이 어떻게 적용될지에 관심이 있지만 윤리적 분석의 측면에서는 비참할 정도로 불완전하다.

03 _____ (or tribal) societies are rarely called "savage" these days, at least not in public, but they are normally considered "backward!"

토착(혹은 부족) 사회는 오늘날 적어도 공공장소에서는 거의 '야만인'이라고 불리지 않지만, 그들은 보통 '뒤떨어졌다'고 여겨진다!

04 Inequality refers not to _____ but difference, and there is nothing suspicious or objectionable about differences *per se*.

불평등은 박탈이 아니라 차이를 의미하며, 차이 '그 자체로' 미심쩍거나 못마땅한 것은 없다.

05 Chronos is clock time measured in seconds, minutes, and hours, and it is the _____ of words such as "chronology" and "chronological."

chronos는 초, 분, 시간으로 측정되는 시계 시간이고, '연대기', '연대기적인'과 같은 단어의 어원이다.

WORDS REVIEW

A 다음 영어 단어에 해당하는 우리말 뜻을 빈칸에 쓰시오.

01 erode _____   11 consumption _____

02 deplete _____   12 surplus _____

03 friction _____   13 obligation _____

04 prioritise _____   14 elaborate _____

05 colony _____   15 therapy _____

06 welfare _____   16 aggressive _____

07 agenda _____   17 muted _____

08 diameter _____   18 vein _____

09 evaluate _____   19 intertwine _____

10 assertiveness _____   20 prejudice _____

B 다음 우리말과 의미가 같도록 빈칸에 알맞은 말을 [보기]에서 골라 쓰시오. (필요시 형태를 변형할 것)

보기
anticipate   hospitality   dominance   evoke   acquaintance

01 We celebrate its "weak ties," the bonds of _____ with people we may never meet.

우리는 그것의 '약한 유대', 즉 우리가 결코 만나지 못할 사람들과의 친밀함의 유대를 찬양한다.

02 We should therefore be very cautious about using the West's experience to _____ the development paths of today's poorer countries.

따라서 우리는 오늘날 더 가난한 국가들의 발전 경로를 예측하기 위해 서구의 경험을 이용하는 것에 대해 매우 신중해야 한다.

03 As an example, assertiveness, competitiveness, _____, and belligerence all are influenced by testosterone across genders.

예를 들어, 단호함, 경쟁력, 지배, 그리고 호전성은 모두 남녀를 막론하고 테스토스테론의 영향을 받는다.

04 Loneliness instead _____ associations of stillness.

대신에 외로움은 고요함이라는 연상을 불러일으킨다.

05 In all 184 restaurants, the Chinese couple was accepted — and they were received with considerable _____ in 72 of the restaurants.

모든 184곳의 식당에서 그 중국인 부부를 받아 주었고, 그 식당 중 72곳에서 상당한 환대와 함께 그들을 맞이했다.

WORDS REVIEW

A 다음 영어 단어에 해당하는 우리말 뜻을 빈칸에 쓰시오.

01 weave _____   11 reservoir _____

02 patent _____   12 quantify _____

03 primitive _____   13 decomposition _____

04 coherence _____   14 breeder _____

05 shrink _____   15 encounter _____

06 unconventional _____   16 ultimate _____

07 turnover _____   17 likelihood _____

08 impose _____   18 neutral _____

09 blindspot _____   19 speculate _____

10 convincing _____   20 urge _____

B 다음 우리말과 의미가 같도록 빈칸에 알맞은 말을 [보기]에서 골라 쓰시오.

┌─ 보기 ─
│ plausible   contemplation   regulate   embody   scrutinize
└─

01 This is part of why some coders think it's been ruinous to _____ code with copyright.

부분적으로는 이것이 일부 코딩하는 사람들이 코드를 저작권법으로 규제하는 것이 파괴적이라고 생각하는 이유이다.

02 The myths of a society usually _____ its traditional values and moral norms.

한 사회의 신화는 일반적으로 그 사회의 전통적 가치와 도덕규범을 구체적으로 표현한다.

03 The same deception is true for all human experience, from the immediacy of our perception to the _____ of inner thoughts, and that includes the self.

우리 인식의 직접성에서부터 내면의 생각에 대한 사색에 이르기까지 똑같은 기만이 모든 인간 경험에도 적용되는데, 그것은 자아도 포함한다.

04 For example, you know most rooms in your home well enough that you need not constantly _____ every detail.

예를 들어, 여러분은 모든 세부 사항을 지속적으로 면밀히 조사할 필요가 없을 정도로, 여러분 집에 있는 대부분의 방을 잘 알고 있다.

05 Anatomically this is _____ because working memory (where we 'store' numbers) and self-control are both located in our prefrontal cortex.

해부학적으로 이것은 그럴듯한데, 왜냐하면 (우리가 숫자를 '저장하는') 작동 기억과 자제심은 둘 다 우리의 전두엽 피질에 위치해 있기 때문이다.

WORDS REVIEW

A 다음 영어 단어에 해당하는 우리말 뜻을 빈칸에 쓰시오.

01	introspection	_____	11 firmly	_____
02	particle	_____	12 parenting	_____
03	highlight	_____	13 dignity	_____
04	commute	_____	14 reciprocity	_____
05	recreative	_____	15 inhabit	_____
06	sheer	_____	16 associate	_____
07	ruling	_____	17 inclination	_____
08	constitutional	_____	18 stimulate	_____
09	submit	_____	19 anthropologist	_____
10	interpretation	_____	20 prestigious	_____

B 다음 우리말과 의미가 같도록 빈칸에 알맞은 말을 [보기]에서 골라 쓰시오. (필요시 형태를 변형할 것)

> ┌ 보기 ┐
> startling   manifestation   strengthen   deterioration   perception

01 What has changed is our _____ *of time.*

달라진 것은 우리의 '시간에 대한 인식'이다.

02 Every bit of work done in this spirit _____ the man who does it.

이런 정신으로 이루어지는 모든 일은 그것을 행하는 사람을 강화시킨다.

03 And since the discoveries in Germany, people have carried on searching and digging, and have made some _____ finds.

그리고 독일에서의 발굴들 이후, 사람들은 찾고 파내기를 계속 수행했고, 몇 가지 놀라운 발견을 해냈다.

04 That is, people appear to feel that they can share in the glory of a successful other with whom they are in some way associated; one _____ of this feeling is the public trumpeting of the association.

즉, 사람들은 어떤 방식으로 자신과 연관된 성공한 타인의 영광을 공유할 수 있다고 느끼는 것 같은데, 이런 기분의 한 가지 표현은 그 연관성을 떠벌리는 것이다.

05 Conversely, the smaller the connected population, the greater the steady _____ of the skill as it was passed on.

역으로, 연결된 인구가 적으면 적을수록, 기술의 점진적인 악화는 그것이 전해지면서 더 커진다.

WORDS REVIEW

A 다음 영어 단어에 해당하는 우리말 뜻을 빈칸에 쓰시오.

01 extended	_____	11 alleviate	_____
02 threaten	_____	12 delicate	_____
03 replace	_____	13 abnormal	_____
04 suspect	_____	14 premise	_____
05 intimacy	_____	15 intriguing	_____
06 differentiate	_____	16 take over	_____
07 momentous	_____	17 by no means	_____
08 susceptibility	_____	18 have access to	_____
09 necessity	_____	19 bottom line	_____
10 adolescence	_____	20 incidental to	_____

B 다음 우리말과 의미가 같도록 빈칸에 알맞은 말을 [보기]에서 골라 쓰시오. (필요시 형태를 변형할 것)

┌─ 보기 ───┐
| inevitable   stereotype   attribute   transition   consistent |
└──┘

01 In the early days of the _____ to industrial agriculture, farmers had access to few external inputs.

산업적 농업으로 이행하던 초기에, 농부들은 외부의 자원을 거의 이용하지 못했다.

02 The Soviet Union's demise in 1991 may be one of the few historical events that has not seemed _____ after the fact to large numbers of historians, both lay and professional.

1991년의 소련 붕괴는 그 사건 이후 많은 수의 비전문 역사가들뿐만 아니라 전문 역사가들에게도 불가피해 보이지 않았던 몇 안 되는 역사적 사건들 중 하나일 것이다.

03 The good news about _____ threat is that it can be defused by subtle interventions.

고정 관념의 위협(고정 관념에 의해 행동이 제약받는 것)에 대한 좋은 소식은 그것이 미묘한 개입에 의해 완화될 수 있다는 것이다.

04 Each one of these tasks is simple, _____, and self-contained, so in that way they're good candidates for automation.

이러한 과업들 각각은 단순하고, 일관되며, 그 자체로 완비되어 있어서, 그런 방식으로 그것들은 자동화의 좋은 후보이다.

05 He also highlights the importance of accepting a bid for attention from loved ones and valuing one another by sharing dreams and admiring each other's venerable _____.

그는 또한 사랑하는 사람들로부터 관심을 끌려는 시도를 받아들이는 것과 꿈을 공유하고 서로의 훌륭한 자질을 칭찬함으로써 서로를 존중하는 것의 중요성을 강조한다.

WORDS REVIEW

A 다음 영어 단어에 해당하는 우리말 뜻을 빈칸에 쓰시오.

01	compromise	_____	11	conscious	_____
02	instruction	_____	12	hardwired	_____
03	derivative	_____	13	allocate	_____
04	institution	_____	14	concentration	_____
05	defense	_____	15	transient	_____
06	momentum	_____	16	be attuned to	_____
07	protest	_____	17	get in the way	_____
08	spin	_____	18	come to light	_____
09	poke	_____	19	pile up	_____
10	complicated	_____	20	be exposed to	_____

B 다음 우리말과 의미가 같도록 빈칸에 알맞은 말을 [보기]에서 골라 쓰시오. (필요시 형태를 변형할 것)

---/ 보기 /---

substance   progress   intense   flip   vertical

---

01 After many years of exposure to such harshness, the tree would become stronger and stronger, its very fiber being strengthened by the _____ buffeting it was experiencing day after day.

그런 거친 상태에 수년 동안 노출된 후에, 그 나무는 점점 더 강해지곤 했는데, 그것이 매일같이 경험하고 있던 강렬한 난타에 의해 나무의 바로 그 섬유질이 강화된 것이었다.

02 Sucralose, as it became known, is one of the sweetest of all _____ and can replace sucrose at less than one-thousandth of the concentration.

알려진 바와 같이, 수크랄로스는 모든 물질 중에서 가장 단맛이 나는 물질들 중 하나이고, 농도를 1000분의 1보다 적게 해서 자당을 대체할 수 있다.

03 If the axis of the top is not exactly _____, gravity pulls the top off-center, which is called a *torque*.

만일 팽이의 축이 정확하게 수직이 아니라면, 중력은 중심에서 벗어나 그 팽이를 잡아당기는데, 그것은 '회전력'이라고 불린다.

04 Science is assumed to _____ by its own momentum as discovery piles up on discovery.

과학은 발견에 발견이 누적되어 그 자체의 추진력에 의해 진보한다고 가정된다.

05 You consider that maybe you could do more to tag each team member to particular types of requests, so that everyone isn't _____ from one thing to another all the time.

여러분은 모두가 항상 한 가지 일에서 다른 일로 휙 넘어가지 않도록, 각각의 팀원에게 특정 유형의 요청이라는 꼬리표를 붙이기 위해 여러분이 아마도 더 많은 일을 할 수 있을 것이라고 생각한다.

이 책을 검토해 주신 선생님

강원

김나은 나은영어학원
김보라 전문과외
김세진 세진쌤영어
김안나 이루다영어학원
김영남 엘리쌤 영어교실
안서아 숲영어전문학원
연지원 이투스247원주
오진아 라온영어학원
이승주 이상학원
이지애 수학전문학원
임지은 더써밋학원
전수지 에리카영어학원
최가영 나의, 영어
최수남 강릉 영수 배움교실
최현주 최샘영어
하지현 하이디영어과외방

경기

강동수 찐공스터디
강수현 중동엠마영어
강승희 전문과외
강예진 YJ 영어의 정원
고승환 세움학원
고혜경 전문과외
곽억훈 최강영어학원
권계미 A&T+영어
권소희 부천 권소희영어
권응경 애니랑영어
권정현 수잔잉글리쉬학원
권종혁 고등바른공부학원
권지영 호수영어
김강인 전문과외
김고은 전문과외
김광수 더배움 잉글리쉬
김규리 전문과외
김규은 분당소피아영어학원
김민선 HC 영수전문학원
김민정 이화영어
김상겸 물푸레스쿨
김세종 데이비드영어교습소
김승민 룩스영어 영어 교습소
김승훈 진접최강학원
김인종 S4국영수학원 고덕국제점
김완혁 단칼영어학원
김원동 미래인학원
김유경 더 웨이퍼스 어학원
김유림 리드해법영어교습소
김윤경 상승영어교습소
김종윤 감자 국영수 학원
김진희 하이노크영어학원
김창훈 영품학원
김태무 전문과외
김하늘 훈선생영어학원
김현영 영스타영어교습소
김현정 시흥 파머스어학원 은행캠퍼스
김후중 동탄더플랜영어학원
김희용 동탄에이블영어학원
나병찬 베스트교육 호매실
남준현 프로미스영어학원
노연웅 알찬교육학원
문은영 삼성영어 쎈수학 은계학원

문징균 스카이학원
박경란 더하다학원
박도희 전문과외
박민희 아이린영어
박상유 콕수학오드리영어
박선영 잉글리쉬머핀
박선이 썬영어
박소희 청라 정상어학원
박수정 가온학원
박시은 파머스영어 용인 씨엘캠퍼스
박영심 전문과외
박영철 이즈원 영어수학 전문학원
박정현 JH 스파르타 영어학원
박정훈 안양외국어고등학교
박지연 시작
박천형 한빛에듀
박치옥 Park's Room English
박현석 전문과외
박혜원 넘버원 원더레슨
백은진 리한에듀영어학원
백재원 서윤희 입시영어학원
서다혜 Cloe English
서동기 모티프온 영어국어학원
서정원 엉클제이 영어학원
손영화 옥정 푸르지오 공터영어
송동섭 송동섭영어
송상종 캐피타운학원
송정은 송스 잉글리시
송희승 아이리스플러스
신다영 김포 우리학원
신상훈 엘피다학원
신연우 목동영어 카트리나
신혜원 해밀영어
안웅희 서윤희 입시영어학원
안지미 이엔영어학원
안지선 드림빅잉글리시
안효상 더오름영어수학학원
양상현 개런티영어학원
양창현 조셉입시학원
염지민 전문과외
오동산 이랩스영어학원
오수혜 훈에듀라하잉글리시
오주향 대치힐영어학원
오희교 마이티영어학원
우승완 조셉입시학원
우아림 최선어학원
유경민 Judy English
유미주 송린중학교
유혜선 앨리스영어학원
윤겸서 운양에듀플렉스
윤석호 야탑고등학교
윤연정 오스카빌 영어
윤정원 윤앤강학원
윤지후 오산 락수맘 앤 윤영어
윤현정 위너영수
이경민 에린영어
이계집 PROMIS영어학원
이광열 열강영어교습소
이권우 수원 레볼리쉬 어학원
이규섭 학생애학원
이다온 스타디온 학원
이동준 리프영어학원
이민영 윤앤영수학원
이보라 김쌤보습 이쌤영어 학원

이보라 디오영어
이서윤 계윰학원
이선구 인코(EnCORE)어학원
이선미 정현영어학원
이수정 exam4you
이수진 백암고등학교
이승봉 평촌이지어학원
이예녹 목동엘리엔학원
이연경 명품M수학영어
이영민 상승공감학원
이오석 오성학원
이유진 에셀영어
이유진 팍스어학원
이재협 사차원학원
이주현 웅진정자학원
이지연 러닝센터
이지은 캡틴제이 영어학원
이진성 필탑교육
이충기 영어나무
이혜랑 PerfectPoint+
이희성 맨투맨학원
임수정 이화영어
임은희 Eunice English
장미래 안성종로엠
장서희 더프라임학원
장소정 메가스터디 러셀
장은주 휘 영어교습소
장현정 도프(DOPE)영어학원
장혜민 아발론 어학원 김포한강캠퍼스
전성훈 훈선생영어학원
전영인 전영인영어학원
전주원 필업단과전문학원
정다움 카인드학원
정무건 중앙학원
정미영 미셸영어과외
정보경 블룸영어학원
정성봉 한강미래인재
정성 JK영어수학전문학원
정성태 에이든영어학원
정연우 최강학원
정연욱 인크쌤영어학원
정영선 시퀀트영수전문학원
정영훈 채움국어학원
정윤하 전문과외
정인하 뮤엠영어 별가람영어교습소
조민수 평촌 프로미스영어학원
조용원 이티엘영어교습소
조은쌤 조은쌤&장쌤영어전문학원
조정휘 유하이에듀 학원
조준모 베스트교육호매실캠퍼스
조춘화 뮤엠영어발곡학원
주지은 지은잉글리시클래스영어교습소
채연우 와이더블유클래스
채희수 보라동 영어과외
최상이 엄마영어아빠수학학원
최세열 JS수학영어학원
최아란 알짱영어학원
최유나 수원@una_englishtutor
최정준 전문과외
최주현 일품 영어
최진 전문과외
최희정 SJ클쌤영어학원
하사랑 덕계한샘학원
하이디 하이디드림팀

한송이 쏭쌤영어
한지선 G1230파주문산점
현윤아 중동그린타운스마트해법영어
홍형근 제임스M어학원
황인아 별내고래영어학원
황인옥 하이탑학원

경남

강나경 ASK 배움학원
고성관 T.O.P 에듀학원
곽정현 꿀잼영어
김민범 전문과외
김선우 호이겐스학원
김성은 이엠스터디학원
김소민 다올영어수학학원
김재훈 하이퍼영어학원
김준 거제 정상어학원
김지혜 ASK 배움학원
김태리 전문과외
김현주 삼성영어셀레나 프리미엄신명점
박영하 전문과외
박재형 인투잉글리쉬어학원
배승빈 에스영어전문학원
배현령 배선생영어
손선영 이화멘토영어학원
신형섭 크림슨어학원
양경화 봄공부방
양기영 다니엘어학원
윤지연 에이프릴 유진학원
이근호 레이첼 잉글리쉬
이수길 명성영수전문학원
이연홍 대치퍼스트학원
임나영 삼성영어셀레나 남양영어교습소
임진 윌플러스학원
임진희 진해씨쌤영어학원
장서영 어썸영어학원
장은정 케이트어학원
장재훈 ASK 배움학원
정나래 아이피영어전문학원
정상락 비상잉글리시아이 대운점 영어교습소
정수정 지탑영어
조서은 창원 EFG어학원
채유진 다름학원 율하캠퍼스
최숭관 창선고등학교
최지영 시퀀스영수학원
최지윤 호이겐스
최환준 Jun English
최효정 인에이블잉글리시
하동권 네오시스템영어학원
하상범 진동삼성수학영어학원
하수미 삼성수학학원
한지용 성민국영수학원
황은영 에이블어학원

경북

강민표 현일고등학교
강은석 미래인재학원
강혜성 EiE 고려대 어학원
김광현 전문과외
김주훈 아너스영어
김지훈 알앤비
김형표 표쌤영어학원
문상헌 에이원영어
박계민 영광중학교

한규정 베네치아 영어
박주연 아이린영어학원
박지연 케일리 영어
배세왕 BK영수전문학원(고등관)
변민준 The 채움영어
성유진 국영수과오름학원
손누리 이든영어수학학원
신보연 위잉글리시영어
장가은 앨리스영어학원
장미 잉글리시아이 원리학원
정상원 정상어학원 영천분원
정선린 포항항도중학교
정진욱 현일고등학교
정현주 필즈수학영어학원
천예슬 그린트리영어교습소
최동희 전문과외
허미정 레벨업영어 교습소

광주

고태연 원더영어
김도엽 스카이영어전문학원
김병남 위즈덤 영어
김영연 AnB영어학원
김원경 전문과외
김유경 프라임 아카데미
김유희 김유희영어학원
김인화 김인화영어학원
김종익 전문과외
김혜원 엘위스 영어학원
나혜영 윤선생우리집앞영어교실 동천빛고을
문장엽 엠제이영어수학전문학원
박주형 광주 봉선동 한수위 영어
봉병주 철수와영수
송수빈 전문과외
신지수 온에어영어학원
심연우 문미승 영어클리닉
양신애 윤학당오름국어영어학원
오승리 이지스터디
오평안 상무지산한길어학원
우진일 블루페스 영어학원
유현주 유즈영어교습소
윤상혁 하이엔드 영어 사회 학원
이민정 롱맨 어학원
이현미 IGSE풍암아카데미
이현창 진월유앤아이어학원
임지상 상무 외대어학원
전솔 서강고등학교
채성문 마하나임영수학원
한기석 이유국어영어한문학원
한방엽 531학원인산학원

대구

강영미 강선생영어
강정임 공부방
곽민경 조성애세움영어수학학원
권보현 씨즈더데이어학원
권오길 공부를 디자인하다
권익재 제이슨영어교습소
권하련 아너스이엠에스학원
김근아 블루힐영어학원
김기목 목샘영어교습소
김미나 메이쌤 영어
김민재 열공열강 영어수학 학원
김유환 범어지성학원

김종석 보습학원	심효령 삼부가람학원	이혜린 스카이영어학원	박진경 제이즈잉글리쉬	최유송 목동 씨앤씨학원
김지영 김지영영어	안수정 궁극의 사고	임정연 안은경영어학원	박찬경 펜타곤영어	최정문 한성학원
김하나 하나로운영어	오봉주 새미래영수학원	장혜인 민락능률이엠학원	박현진 e. Class	최형미 전문과외
김희정 탑에이스학원	유수민 대치이강	정성덕 학장중학교	반향진 세레나영어수학	최희재 표현어학원
노태경 윈스잉글리쉬	윤영숙 전문과외	정영훈 제이앤씨영어전문학원	배지은 빛나는영어교습소	표호진 전문과외
문창숙 지앤비(GnB)스페셜입시학원	이보배 비비영어교습소	채지영 리드앤톡영어도서관학원	배현경 전문과외	하다님 연세 마스터스 학원
민승규 민승규영어학원	이성구 청명대입학원	최승빈 다온학원	백미선 최종호어학원	한성호 티포인트에듀
박고은 스테듀입시학원	임혜지 파라곤어학원	최우성 초이English&Pass	백희영 서초토피아어학원	한인혜 레나잉글리쉬
박라율 열공열강영어수학학원	장유리 삼성영어셀레나 도안학습관	최이내 전문과외	신경훈 탑앤탑수학영어학원	한혜주 함영원입시전문학원
박소현 워싱턴어학원	장윤정 이지탑학원	탁아진 에이블영어국어학원	심나현 성북메가스터디	허미영 삼성영어 창일교실 학원
박예빈 영재키움영어수학전문학원	정예슬 소로영어	하현진 브릿츠영어학원	안미영 스카이플러스학원	홍대균 홍대균 영어
박지환 전문과외	정윤지 Alex's English		양하나(바이올렛) 목동 씨앤씨	홍영민 성북상상학원
방성모 방성모영어학원	정현지 전문과외	**서울**	엄태열 대치차오름학원	황선애 앤스영어학원
백재민 에소테리카 영어학원	정혜수 쌜리영어	가혜림 위즈스터디	오유림 헬리오 오쌤 영어	황혜진 이루다 영어
서정인 서울입시학원	최성호 에이스영어교습소	강경표 최선어학원 중계캠퍼스	오은경 전문과외	
신혜경 전문과외	한형식 서대전여자고등학교	강은 더이룸학원	용혜영 SWEET ENGLISH 영어전문 공부방	**세종**
심경아 전문과외	허욱 Ben class(전문과외)	강이권 네오어학원	유경미 서울	강홍구 세종시 더올림 입시학원
엄재경 하이엔드영어학원	황지현 공부자존감영어입시학원	강준수 전문과외	유연이 오세용어학원	김세인 이룸영어교습소
우유진 이듀 잉글리쉬		강현숙 토피아어학원 중계지점	유은주 리프영어	방종영 세움학원
원현지 원샘영어교습소	**부산**	강호영 인투엠학원	윤성 대치동 새움학원	성민진 EiE 반곡 캠퍼스
유경아 티나잉글리시	강민주 에듀플렉스 명륜점	공진 리더스	윤은미 CnT영어학원	손대령 강한영어학원
유지연 에스피영어	고경외 JS영수학원	김경수 탑킴입시컨설팅진학지도	이계윤 이지영어학원	안성주 더타임학원
윤이강 윤이강 영어학원	김경희 거제동 니키영어	김명열 대치명인학원 은평캠퍼스	이남규 전문과외	
이가나 이나영어교실	김대영 엘리트에듀 학원	김미은 오늘도맑음 영어교습소	이명순 Top Class 영어	**울산**
이근성 헬렌영어학원	김도담 도담한영어교실	김미정 전문과외	이상윤 주연학원	강상배 전문과외
이동현 쌤마스터입시학원	김도윤 코어영어교습소	김배성 정명영어교습소	이석현 지구촌고등학교	김경수 핀포인트영어학원
이미경 전문과외	김동혁 코어영어수학전문학원	김상희 스카이플러스학원	이선미 범블비 영어 교습소	김경현 에린영어
이샛별 전문과외	김동휘 장정호 영어전문학원	김선경 마크영어학원	이선정 제이나영어학원	김문정 천곡고려학원
이수희 이온영어학원	김미혜 더멘토영어교습소	김성근 더원잉글리시	이성택 엠아이씨영어학원	김은주 공부발전소학원
이승현 학문당입시학원	김소림 엘라영어학원	김성연 대치청출어람학원	이수정 영샘영어	김주희 하이디영어교습소
이지현 지니영어	김소연 전문과외	김승환 Arnold English	이승혜 스텔라 영어	김한중 스마트영어전문학원
이하욱 이하욱 영어학원	김은정 클라라 잉글리쉬	김영재 제니퍼영어 교습소	이승희Edward 임팩트7영어학원 목동	서예원 해법멘토영어수학학원
이현지 리즈영어	김재경 탑클래스영어학원	김용봉 SKY PLUS 학원	2단지 고등관	송희철 꿈꾸는고래학원
인솔내 제인영어학당	김진규 의문을열다	김은영 LCA 영어학원	이연주 Real Iris Class	엄여은 준쌤영어교습소
임형주 사범대단과학원	김효은 김효은 영수 전문학원	김은정 전문과외	이은선 드림영어하이수학학원	윤주이 고도영어학원
전윤애 올리영어교습소	남재호 제니스학원	김은진 ACE영어교습소	이은영 한국연예예술학교	이서경 이서경영어학원
전윤영 뮤엠영어 경동초점	류미향 류미향입시영어	김정민 W영어	이자임 자몽영어교습소	이수현 제이엘영어학원
전지영 제이제이영어	문희진 베아투스학원	김종현 김종현영어	이정혜 수시이룸교육	이승준 전문과외
정대웅 유신학원	박미진 MJ영어학원	김지윤 비타윤영어	이지윤 전문과외	이은선 스마트영어전문학원
정용희 에스피영어학원	박수진 제이엔씨 영어학원	김태성 전문과외	이철웅 비상하는 또또학원	이재은 잉크영어학원
진보라 메이킹어학원	박인혜 정철어학원	김현지 전문과외	이혜정 이루리학원	임재희 임재희영어전문학원
최효진 너를 위한 영어	박정아 전문과외	김혜영 스터디원	이희영 이쌤아카데미 영어교습소	정은선 한국esl어학원
한정아 능인고등학교	박지우 영어를 ON하다	나영은 전문과외	임광영 러셀 메가스터디	정혜미 전문과외
황윤슬 사적인영어	박지은 박지은영어전문과외방	노현회 전문과외	임서y 형설학원	조승현 스마트영어전문학원
	박창헌 오늘도,영어그리고수학	도선혜 중계동 영어	임소례 윤선생영어교실우리집앞신내키움	조충일 YBM 잉글루 울산연양 제1학원
대전	배슬기 전문과외	류하영 유니슨영어	영어교습소	최아현 jp영어학원
Tony Park Tony Park English	배찬원 에이플러스 영어	맹혜선 휘경여자고등학교	임은옥 전문과외	한건수 한스영어
고우리 영어의꿈	백은비 비앙카 영어 교습소	명가은 명가은 영어하다 학원	임해림 그레이스학원	허부배 비즈단과학원
김근범 딱쌤학원	변혜련 전문과외	문명기 문명기 영어학원	장서인 함께 자라는 스마트올클래스	
김기형 상승학원	성장우 전문과외	문슬기 문쌤 전문영어과외	전지영 탑클래스영수학원	**인천**
김민정 전문과외	손소희 에스 잉글리쉬 사이언스	박기철 한진연 입시전략연구소	정경록 미즈원어학원	강재민 스터디위드제이쌤
김아영 전문과외	송석준 스카이영수전문학원	박남규 알짜영어교습소	정연우 전문과외	김미경 김선생영어/수학교실
김영철 빅뱅잉글리시리더스	송초롱 최상위영어교습소	박미애 명문지혜학원	정유하 크라센어학원	김민영 YBM Homeschool 영종자이센터
김주리 위드제이영어	안정아 GnB어학원양성캠퍼스	박미정 위드멘토학원	정재욱 씨알학원	김민정 김민영어
김현지 영어과외	예다슬 전문과외	박병석 주영학원	조길영 이앤조영어	김서애 제이플러스영어
나규성 대전 비전21학원	오세창 범천반석단과학원	박선경 씨투엠학원	조미연 튼튼영어마스터클럽구로학원	김선나 지니어스영어학원
남영종 엠베스트SE학원 대전 전민점	오지은 이루다영어	박소영 JOY	조미지 책읽는영어교습소 제니쌤영어	김영태 에듀터학원
노지혜 제일학원	옥지윤 더센텀영어학원	박소하 전문과외	조민석 더원영수학원	김영호 조주석수학&영어클리닉학원
노현서 앨리잉글리쉬아카데미	윤지영 잉글리쉬무무영어교습소	박솔이 Sole English	조봉현 대치명인학원 중계캠퍼	김옥경 잉글리쉬 베이
박난정 제일학원	윤진희 위너드영어전문교습소	박숭규 이지수능교육	채보경 개인과외	김주영 아너스영어학원
박성희 청담프라임학원	이미정 탑에듀영어교습소	박정미 드림영어 하이수학학원	채상우 클레영어	김지연 송도탑영어학원
박정민 율영수학원	이상석 엠베스트se 공부습관365 학원	박정효 성북메가스터디학원	채에스더 문래중학교 방과후	김현미 송도탑영어학원
박지현 더브라이트학원	이순실 하단종로엠학원	박준육 G1230학원	최미림 밀리에듀영어학원	김현섭 전문과외
박효진 박효진 영어	이영준 개금국제어학원	박지훈 청담어학원	최민주 전문과외	김현준 JKD영어전문학원

나일지 두드림하이학원
문지현 전문과외
박가람 전문과외
박나혜 TOP과외
박민아 하이영어 공부방
박승민 대치세정학원
박주현 Ashley's English Corner
신나리 이루다교육학원
신은주 명문학원
신현경 GMI 어학원
오희정 더제니스엣지영어학원
윤효주 잉글리시브릿지
윤희영 세실영어
이가희 S&U영어
이미선 고품격EMEDU
이수진 전문과외
이영태 인천부흥고등학교
이은정 인천논현고등학교
이진희 이진희영어
장승혁 지엘학원
전혜원 제일고등학교
정도영 스테디 잉글리시
정춘기 정상어학원
조윤정 인천이음중학교
최민솔 영웅아카데미
최민지 빅뱅영어
최수련 업앤업영어교습소
최창영 학산에듀넷
최하은 정철어학원
홍영주 홍이아쎈영어

조예진 에이펙스 영어학원
조형진 대니아빠앤디영어교습소
최미화 MH노블영어학원
최석원 전주에듀캠프학원
한주훈 알파스터디영어수학전문학원
황보희 에임드영수학원

제주
Brian T.K Top Class Academy
고보경 제주여자고등학교
고승용 진정성학원제주노형센터
김진재 함성소리학원
김평호 서이현아카데미학원
김현정 유비고영어학원
문재웅 문&YES 중고등 내신수능 영어
배동환 뿌리와샘
이승우 늘다올 학원
이윤아 에이투지어학원
이재철 함성소리학원
임정열 엑셀영어
정승현 J's English
지광미 지샘입시영어학원

충남
강유안 전문과외
고유미 고유미영어
김인영 더오름영어
김일환 김일환어학원
김창현 타임영어학원
박서현 EIE고려대어학원
박재영 로제타스톤 영어교실
박희진 박쌤영어과외
우경희 우쌤'클라쓰
윤현미 비비안의 잉글리쉬 클래스
이규현 글로벌학원
이상진 마틴영어학원
이영롱 대승학원
이종화 오름에듀
임진주 원더크라운영어학원
장성은 상승기류
장완기 장완기학원
정래 (주)탑씨크리트교육
조남진 천안 불당PYO영어국어학원
채은주 위너스 학원

전남
강용문 강용문영수입시전문
김숙진 지니쌤 공부방
김아름 전문과외
김은정 BestnBest 공부방
김임열 태강수학영어학원
김재원 나주혁신위즈수학영어학원
박민지 벨라영어
박주형 해룡고등학교
배송이 JH공터영어전문학원
손성호 아름다운 11월학원
양명승 엠에스어학원
오은주 순천금당고등학교
이상호 스카이입시학원
이용 해룡고등학교
이정원 앤더슨 영어학원
조소을 수잉글리쉬
차형진 상아탑학원

충북
김보경 더시에나영어학원
박광수 폴인어학원
박수열 전문과외
박현자 박샘영어
신유정 비타민 영어클리닉
안지영 전문과외
양미정 전문과외
양미진 JEC지니영어교실
윤선아 타임즈영어학원
윤홍석 대학가는길
이경수 더애스에이티영수단과학원
이재욱 대학 가는 길 학원
이재은 파머스영어와이즈톡학원
조현국 업클래스학원
하선빈 어썸영어수학학원

전북
길지만 비상잉글리시아이영어학원
김나은 애플영어학원
김보경 최영훈영수학원
김설아 전주 에듀캠프학원
김수정 베이스탑영어
김예исл 옥스포드 어학원
김예진 카일리영어학원
이경훈 리더스영수전문학원
이수정 씨에이엔영어학원
이진주 전문과외
이한결 DNA영어학원
이효상 에임하이영수학원
장길호 장길호영어학원

수능·내신 영어의 모든 것을 마스터하세요!

MASTER
Series

독해를 마스터

듣기를 마스터

명단어를 마스터

최신 수능 경향 반영!
수준별 독해서

"유형 - 실전 - 고난도"로
영어 독해 체계적 완성

1등급 목표!
수능 영어 듣기 훈련서

유형 학습부터 고난도까지
완벽한 3단계 난이도 구성

반드시 알아야 할
빈출 어휘 영단어장

학습앱&워크북, 미니북
온&오프 복습 시스템

워드마스터
학습앱

바로가기

• 이투스북 도서는 전국 서점 및 온라인 서점에서 구매하실 수 있습니다. • 이투스북 온라인 서점 | www.etoosbook.com

이투스북

수학의 바이블

2022개정 교육과정이 ON:온 다!

전국 선생님 1,700명
검토단 검수 완료

"검토하는 내내 감탄했어요!"

모든 유형+유사+기출변형
내신 끝내기 유형서

"같이 병행하면 진짜 좋아요!"

개념 학습

기본 개념은 물론,
궁금할만한
개념까지
놓치지 않았다

유형 학습

기본부터 유사,
기출 변형까지
내신에 필요한 유형을
빠짐없이 담았다

개념과 문제 풀이
방법 익히기

개념:유형
매칭 학습법

익힌 개념 별
모든 유형 풀어보기

• 이투스북 도서는 전국 서점 및 온라인 서점에서 구매하실 수 있습니다.   • 이투스북 온라인 서점 | www.etoosbook.com

이투스북

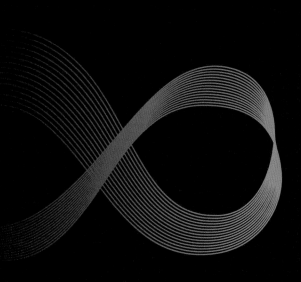

READING MASTER

정답 및 해설

수능
실전

READING MASTER

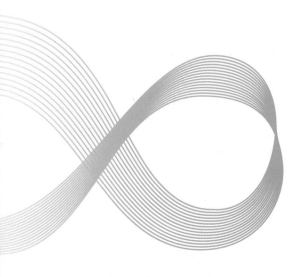

수능
실전

정답 및 해설

본문 10쪽

하프 모의고사 01회

01 ②	02 ⑤	03 ④	04 ⑤	05 ③
06 ③	07 ①	08 ①	09 ④	10 ⑤
11 ③	12 ③	13 ③	14 ②	

01
정답 ②

Joan, Jane, Beth에게:
내가 이 편지를 쓰는 것이 정말이지 다소 어렵지만, 그것은 중요한 일이라고 생각해. 나는 어제 식료품점에서 Harriet과 그녀의 남편 Hank를 봤어. 우리는 모두 그녀가 한동안 앓았다는 것을 알고 있지만 이제는 그녀가 심하게 아픈 것이 분명해. Hank가 그것을 확인해 주지만 그녀의 기분은 좋으며 대부분의 모든 면에서 그녀는 우리가 오랫동안 알고 사랑해 온 바로 그 Harriet이라고 말해. 나는 지금이야말로 우리의 우정이 얼마나 강한지 보여줄 때라고 생각해. 나는 소수의 친구들을 모아 집으로 그녀를 방문하고 싶어. 우리는 Hank와 적절한 시간을 정하고 특별한 선물들도 몇 개 가져갈 수 있어. 나는 우리가 다음 주에 뭔가 준비하려고 할 수 있으면 좋겠어. 내가 곧 연락할게.
진심을 담아,
Monica 드림

해설
다음 주에 아픈 친구 Harriet을 문병하자고 친구들에게 제안하는 내용의 글이다. 따라서 글의 목적으로 가장 적절한 것은 ②이다.

TEXT FLOW

도입	아픈 친구 Harriet의 최근 상황을 전함
요지	Harriet을 문병하자는 제안을 함
부연	문병을 위한 준비 사항을 이야기함

구문

• **It is** with some difficulty **that** I write this letter, but I think it is important.
: 「It is ~ that ....」 강조구문이 사용되어 with some difficulty가 강조되었다.

• Hank confirms it, but says [her spirits are good and in most every way she is the Harriet {we have known and loved for so long}].
: [ ]는 says의 목적어 역할을 하는 명사절이고, 그 안의 { }는 the Harriet을 수식하는 관계절이다.

02
정답 ⑤

여러분이 폭풍우가 몰아치는 가운데 열대 바다에서 헤엄치고 있다고 상상해 보라. 여러분은 파도와 바람에 아무렇게나 이리저리 휩쓸리고 있다. 그래서 여러분은 몇 마일 바닷속으로 잠수하기로 결심한다. 거친 바다 표면을 뚫고 물고기와 해초를 지나 점점 더 깊이 헤엄쳐 들어가자, 여러분은 고요하고 평화로운 바다에 도달한다. 물은 따뜻하고 여러분은 더 이상 물살에 이리저리 휩쓸리지 않는다. 여러분이 깊이 잠수할수록 여러분 주변의 바다는 더 조용하고 더 잔잔해진다. 수면 위에서는 폭풍우가 사납게 몰아쳐도 여러분이 머무는 깊은 바닷속은 고요하고 잔잔하다. 바다 밑바닥의 평온함처럼, 여러분의 육체에 있는 정신은 여러분 주변의 사건의 폭풍우가 건드릴 수 없다. 여러분은 내적 평온을 유지하면서 스트레스가 많거나 힘든 어떤 상황도 견딜 수 있는데, 여러분의 정신이 내면의 건드릴 수 없는 곳에 있기 때문이다. 그것이 여러분이 해야 하는 바이다.

해설
어떤 고난도 내면의 자기 정신은 건드릴 수 없으므로 내적 평온을 유지하며 삶의 고난을 견뎌내라는 내용의 글이다. 따라서 필자의 주장으로 가장 적절한 것은 ⑤이다.

⊗ 매력적인 오답 주의!
③ 글을 제대로 읽지 않고 고난에도 긍정적인 면이 있다는 통념에 의존하면 고를 수 있는 오답이다.
④ 고난에도 자기 정신이 무너지지 않는다는 내용에만 집중하면 고를 수 있는 오답이다.

TEXT FLOW

도입	폭풍우가 몰아치는 바다에서 잠수하는 것을 상상하게 함
전개	깊은 바닷속은 고요하고 잔잔하여 폭풍우로부터 안전함
결론	삶의 고난에도 내적 평온을 유지하라고 조언함

구문

• **The deeper** you dive, **the quieter** and **calmer** the waters around you become.
: '~할수록 더 ...하다'라는 의미의 「the+비교급, the+비교급」이 사용되었다.

• Just like the tranquility at the bottom of the ocean, the spirit [residing in your physical body] is untouchable by the storm of events around you.
: [ ]는 문장의 주어인 the spirit을 수식하는 분사구이다.

03
정답 ④

시민에게는 선거권과 공직 재임권이라는 고유의 정부 참여 권리(참정권)가 있어야 한다. 그렇지 않으면 시민과 외국인의 구별에 의미가 없을 것이다. 시민에게는 또한 거주의 혜택에 대한 특별한 권리, 예를 들어 비자를 거부당할 수 있는 외국인에게는 없는, 해외에 있을 때 그 나라에 입국할 수 있는 권리가 있을 수 있다. 정부는 시민들과 다른 거주민들을 위한 보살핌과 배려의 특별한 책임이 있다. 한 국가의 경제 정책은 주로 자국민들에게 유리하도록 설계될 수 있으며, 그것은 다른 나라들에 살고 있는 사람들에게는 할당하지 않는 복지 및 기타 혜택을 그들에게 분배할 수도 있다. 이 모든 면에서, 국가는 자국민에게 이익이 되도록, 그 때문에 자국민이 아닌 사람들에게는 불리하도록 차별할 수도 있고, 어느 정도는 차별해야 한다. 그러나 의도적으로 상해를 가하는 것은 다르며, 정부는 자국민에게 상해를 가하도록 허용되지 않을 이유 때문에 또는 그런 상황에서 의도적으로 외국인에게 상해를 입힐 권리나 권한이 없다. 이것은 상해가 심각할 때 단연코 그러하다. 인권의 영역에는 <u>여권이 설 자리가 없다</u>.

해설
시민에게는 선거권과 공직 재임권이라는 고유의 참정권이 있고, 국가는 그런 시민들을 외국인과 구별하여 돌보고 배려해야 하는 책임이 있으며 자국민에게 이익이 되도록 외국인을 차별할 수 있지만, 인권의 영역에서는 자국민과 외국인을 구별해서는 안 된다는 내용의 글이다. 여권은 자국민과 외국인을 구별하는 문서로, 인권의 영역에서는 그런 구별이 설 자리가 없다는 것은 외국인이라는 이유로 그들을 차별해서는 안 된다는 것을 의미한다. 따라서 밑줄 친 부분이 글에서 의미하는 바로 가장 적절한 것은 ④ '모든 사람을 차별 없이 대하는 것에 근거를 둔다'이다.
① 복잡한 절차를 단순화하는 데 초점을 맞춘다
② 국가의 경제적 번영과 밀접한 관련이 있다
③ 모든 시민이 가고 싶은 곳을 방문하는 것을 허용한다
⑤ 고유의 참정권을 보장한다

TEXT FLOW

도입	외국인과 구별되는 시민의 참정권(선거권, 공직 재임권, 거주권)이 있음
부연	정부는 시민과 다른 거주민을 보살피고 배려할 책임이 있으며, 외국인들에게는 주지 않는 복지 및 기타 혜택을 할당함
주장	자국민에게 상해를 가할 수 없듯이 외국인 역시 동일하게 상해를 입힐 권리나 권한이 국가에게 없음
재진술	인권의 영역에는 자국민과 외국인의 차별이 있을 수 없음

구문

• A nation's economic policy may be designed primarily [to favor its own residents], and it may distribute welfare and other benefits to them [that it does not distribute to people {living in other countries}].
: 첫 번째 [ ]는 목적의 의미를 나타내는 부사적 용법의 to부정사구이고, 두 번째 [ ]는 welfare and other benefits를 수식하는 관계절이다. 두 번째 [ ] 안의 { }는 people을 수식하는 현재분사구이다.

• But the deliberate infliction of injury is different, and government has no right or authority deliberately [to injure foreigners for reasons or in circumstances {in which it would not be permitted to injure its own citizens}].
: [ ]는 right or authority를 수식하는 형용사적 용법의 to부정사구이고, 그 안의 { }는 reasons와 circumstances를 수식하는 관계절이다.

04
정답 ⑤

초기 르네상스 시대에 원근법이 미술에 처음 사용되었을 때, 그것은 공간에 대한 인간의 개념에 있어서 혁명이었다. 처음으로, '인간의' 응시가 위의 하늘로부터 저 너머의 '풍경'으로 바뀌었다. 원근법은 개인을 처음으로 자기 세계의 중심으로 둔다. 우리는 바라보는 사람의 눈을 통해 상황을 본다. 우리가 저 너머의 세상을 보는 것은, 바로 인간의 눈을 통해서이지 신의 은총이 아니다. 그리고 시야에 있는 모든 것은 인간이 주목할 대상이 된다. 원근법은 주체-객체 관계의 새로운 공간 영역으로 인간을 인도한다. 그것은 사회학자 Max Weber가 나중에 '세상의 각성'이라고 부른 것의 시작점이다.

해설
초기 르네상스 시대에 도입된 원근법은 인간의 시선을 하늘에서 지상의 풍경으로 바꾸게 했고, 개인을 세계의 중심으로 두게 만든다는 내용이므로, 글의 주제로는 ⑤ '미술에서의 원근법 도입의 의의'가 가장 적절하다.
① 원근법은 처음에 어떻게 발명되었는가
② 전형적인 착시로서의 미술의 원근법
③ 초기 르네상스 시대의 예술가들과 그들의 작품들
④ 미술에 표현된 신을 향한 강한 욕망

TEXT FLOW

도입	초기 르네상스 시대에 미술에 도입된 원근법은 공간에 대한 인간의 개념에 있어 혁명이었음
전개	원근법을 통해 인간은 하늘이 아니라 지상의 풍경을 보기 시작했음
결론	원근법은 주체-객체 관계의 새로운 공간 영역으로 인간을 인도함

구문

• **It is** through man's eyes, and not God's grace, **that** we view the world beyond.
: 「It is ~ that ...」 강조구문이 사용되어 전치사구 through man's eyes, and not God's grace가 강조되었다.

05
정답 ③

위 그래프는 2021년부터 2022년까지 미국과 유럽에서의 채용 공고 수를 기준으로 가장 수요가 많은 프로그래밍 언어들을 보여 준다. 미국에서는 이 기간 동안 Python 프로그래머들에 대한 수요가 가장 많았으며, 약 13만 개의 채용 공고가 있었다. 하지만, 유럽에서는 Java가 11만 개가 넘는 채용 공고로 가장 수요가 많은 언어였는데, JavaScript와 Python이 바로 그 뒤를 이었다. 미국에서는 C# 프로그래머들에 대한 수요가 가장 적었는데, 채용 공고 수는 5만 건 미만이었다. 유럽에서는 C와 C++ 프로그래머 둘 다에 대한 채용 공고 수가 모두 5만 건 미만이었다. 반면에, 유럽의 C# 프로그래머들에 대한 채용 공고 수는 5만 건을 넘었다.

해설
미국에서 C# 프로그래머들의 채용 공고 수는 5만 건을 조금 넘었으므로, 도표의 내용과 일치하지 않는 것은 ③이다.

구문

• In Europe, however, Java was the most sought-after language, with more than 110,000 job postings, [immediately followed by JavaScript and Python].
: [ ]는 주절의 상황에 부수하는 상황을 나타내는 분사구문이다.

06
정답 ③

여러분의 조직에서 혁신을 촉진하려면 혁신적인 사람을 끌어들여 고용해야 한다. 여러분이 혁신적 인재를 식별하는 기술과 도구를 개발하고 나서 그들을 고용해야 한다고 보일 수 있다. 하지만 그것은 그렇게 간단하지 않다. 물론, 어떤 사람들이 다른 사람들보다 더 선천적으로 혁신적이지만, 그 사람과 그 사람의 환경 간의 상호 작용이 결국 혁신성의 수준을 결정한다. 혁신적일 수 있는 능력이 입증된 사람이라도 창의성을 육성하지 않는 문화와 상황에

놓이게 되면 계속 혁신하는 것이 불가능하지는 않더라도 어렵다는 것을 알게 될 것이다. 그 문화는 그 사람의 혁신을 억누를 수도 있는데, 그 문화가 그 사람에게 너무 편안해서 새로운 접근 방식이 생각나지 않기 때문이거나, 그 문화가 너무 낯설고 불편해서 그것이 일하고 기여하는 그 사람의 능력을 방해하기 때문이다.

해설

③ 주어의 핵이 interplay이므로 술어 동사를 단수형 동사 determines로 고쳐야 한다.
① '~인 것 같다'는 의미의 「It seems that ~」 구문의 that절을 이끄는 접속사 that은 적절하다.
② 앞 문장의 to develop techniques ~ and then hire them을 가리키는 대명사 it은 적절하다.
④ find의 목적격 보어 역할을 하는 형용사 difficult는 적절하다.
⑤ 'A이거나 B'라는 의미의 「either A or B」에 의해 연결되어 이유의 부사절을 이끄는 접속사 because는 적절하다.

⊗ 매력적인 오답 주의!

④ find가 목적격 보어를 취하지 않는다고 생각하면 고를 수 있는 오답이다.
⑤ because가 이끄는 두 개의 절이 「either A or B」로 연결되어 있다는 것을 놓치면 고를 수 있는 오답이다.

TEXT FLOW

도입	혁신적인 사람들을 식별하는 것의 어려움
주제	선천적 특성과 환경 간의 상호 작용이 혁신성의 수준을 결정함
전개	혁신적인 사람을 혁신적이지 못하게 만드는 문화와 상황이 존재함

구문

• To foster innovation in your organization, you need to attract and recruit people [who will be innovative].
: [ ]는 people을 수식하는 관계절이다.

• Even a person [who has a proven ability to be innovative] would find innovating on an ongoing basis difficult, if not impossible, [if put in a culture and situation {that do not foster creativity}].
: 첫 번째 [ ]는 a person을 수식하는 관계절이다. 두 번째 [ ]는 조건의 부사절로 if the person is put in a culture and situation ~으로 이해할 수 있고, 그 안의 { }는 a culture and situation을 수식하는 관계절이다.

07
정답 ①

이끌어 가는 일에 있어서나 어떤 일에서든 최고가 되기 위해, 여러분은 스스로에게 도전하고, 현재 자신의 지식 수준을 넘어서는 과제를 떠맡고, 자신의 안전지대 밖으로 나가며, 일하는 새로운 방식을 실험하고, 실수를 하고, 그리고 실패로부터 배워야 한다. 여러분이 최고의 지도자가 될 수 있는 법을 배우고 있을 때, 이것들은 모두 그 과정의 자연스러운 일부일 뿐이다. 그것은 모두 좋고 괜찮다. 하지만 여러분을 가르치고, 향상하는 방법에 관해 여러분을 코치해 주고, 여러분을 응원하고, 여러분을 격려하고, 여러분이 넘어질 때 붙잡아 주고, 여러분이 벽에 부딪힐 때 여러분을 위로해 줄 사람이 그곳에 아무도 없다면, 여러분은 이런 일들을 하지 못할 것이다. 이끌어 가는 것을 배우는 것은 다른 사람으로부터 도움을 받는 것을 필요로 한다. 사회적 지지는 특히 그 학습이 도전적일 때, 성장과 발전을 위한 필요조건이다. 전 세계 2,700만 명 이상의 고용인들을 대상으로 한 갤럽 기구의 조사에 따르면, "여러분이 미래의 성공을 보장하기 위해 할 수 있는 단 하나의 가장 중요한 일은 여러분의 발전에 관심을 가지고 있는 누군가를 찾는 것이다."

해설

이끌어 가는 일에 있어서나 어떤 일에서든 최고가 되기 위해서는 스스로에게 도전하고, 자신의 안전지대 밖으로 나가고, 새로운 방식을 실험하며, 실수와 실패로부터 배우는 것뿐만 아니라, 옆에서 자신을 가르치고, 향상하는 방법을 코치해 주고, 응원하고, 격려하고, 위로해 줄 누군가의 도움이 필요하다는 내용의 글이다. 따라서 빈칸에 들어갈 말로는 ① '사회적 지지'가 가장 적절하다.

② 내적 갈등   ③ 반복되는 실패
④ 행동 변화   ⑤ 합리적 결정

TEXT FLOW

도입	어떤 일에서든 최고가 되려면 자신의 한계를 넘어서는 일과 실수와 실패를 통한 학습이 필요함
부연	최고의 지도자가 되기 위해서는 옆에서 자신을 가르치고, 향상하는 방법을 코치해 주고, 응원하고, 격려하고, 위로해 줄 수 있는 다른 사람의 도움, 즉 사회적 지지가 필요함
결론	미래의 성공을 보장하기 위해서 할 수 있는 가장 중요한 일은 자신의 발전에 관심을 가지고 있는 누군가를 찾는 것임

구문

• [To become the best at leading, or at anything], you have to **challenge** yourself, **take** on stretch assignments, **step** outside your comfort zone, **experiment** with new ways of doing things, **make** mistakes, and **learn** from failure.
: [ ]는 목적의 의미를 나타내는 부사적 용법의 to부정사구이다. challenge, take, step, experiment, make, learn은 콤마(,)와 and에 의해 연결되어 모두 have to에 이어진다.

• "The single most important thing [you can do to ensure your future success]," according to the Gallup organization's study of more than 27 million employees worldwide, "is [to find someone {who has an interest in your development}]."
: 첫 번째 [ ]는 The single most important thing을 수식하는 관계절이다. 두 번째 [ ]는 is의 주격 보어 역할을 하는 to부정사구이고, 그 안의 { }는 someone을 수식하는 관계절이다.

08
정답 ①

여러분은 백열전구를 소형 형광전구와 비교하는 그런 광고들을 본 적이 있을 텐데, 둘 중 후자가 환경적으로 건전하다고 홍보되고 있다. 여러분이 지구 온난화 회의론자이거나, 개인적인 이해관계와 같은 더 흔한 기준에 근거하여 구매를 한다면, 그 광고들은 여러분에게 장기적인 비용 절감 측면에서 판매하는 경향을 띠게 된다. 많은 광고들 중 하나의 사례만 보면, 60와트짜리 전통적인 전구는 75센트가 들고 1천 시간 동안 지속되는데, 14와트짜리 소형 형광전구는 2달러가 들고 1만 시간 동안 지속된다. 여러분은 두 전구에서 같은 양의 빛을 얻는다. 각각의 전구를 1만 시간 동안 사용하는 전체 비용은 전구 교체 비용까지 합해서 백열전구는 59달러이고 소형 형광전구는 12달러이다. 여러분은 어떤 것을 사야 할 것인가?

빈칸 뒤에 이어지는 사례가 장기적으로 봤을 때 백열전구보다 형광전구를 사용하는 것이 더 경제적이라는 것을 나타내므로, 빈칸에 들어갈 말로는 ① '장기적인 비용 절감'이 가장 적절하다.
② 손실 혐오 경향
③ 새로운 것의 자연스러운 매력
④ 각각의 기구의 이용 가능성
⑤ 기구 가격의 상승

TEXT FLOW

도입	백열전구와 형광전구를 환경적 측면에서 비교하는 광고들이 있음
전환	장기적인 비용 절감 측면에서 백열전구와 형광전구를 비교하는 광고들도 있음
예시	개당 가격은 백열전구가 더 싸지만, 1만 시간의 사용 시간을 기준으로 하면 형광전구가 더 쌈

구문

• You have probably seen those ads comparing incandescent light bulbs with compact fluorescent light bulbs, [the latter of which are being promoted as environmentally sound].
: [ ]는 앞 문장의 내용을 부연 설명하는 계속적 용법의 관계절로, the latter는 '후자'를 의미하므로 the latter of which의 선행사는 compact fluorescent light bulbs이다.

09 정답 ④

때로 우리의 직관은 우리가 세상에 대한 과학적 이해를 발전시키는 데 도움이 되기도 하고 때로 그것은 그런 이해에 방해가 되기도 한다. 가장 중요한 것은, 민속 이론은 현상의 경계를 구성하는 신뢰할 수 있는 수단이 아니고 설명적 타당성이 있다고 여겨져서는 안 된다는 것이다. 예를 들어, 진화 생물학은 동물 종들 간 차이가 분류학적 종류의 차이가 아니라 유전적 근접성으로 측정된 정도의 차이로 정확하게 묘사된다고 우리에게 말한다. 게다가, 종들은 보이는 것보다 더 유사할 수 있다. 예를 들어, 수컷 카푸치노(조류)는 유전적으로 거의 동일함에도 불구하고 종에 따라 생김새와 소리가 매우 다를 수 있다. (민속 지식은 수 세기 동안 전 세계 여러 지역에서 사회와 그 사회의 환경을 유지하는 광범위한 활동의 기반이 되어 왔다.) 따라서 민속 이론이 종교를 포함한 물질세계의 작동 방식에 대한 과학적 이론을 발달시키는 데 유용하고 정확한 개념적 토대를 항상 제공하는 것은 아니다.

해설
민속 이론이 물질세계의 작동 방식에 대한 과학적 이론을 발달시키는 데 항상 도움이 되지는 않는다는 내용의 글이다. 따라서 수 세기 동안 사회와 그 사회의 환경을 유지하는 광범위한 활동의 기반이 되어 온 민속 지식의 역할에 관한 내용인 ④는 글의 전체 흐름과 관계가 없다.

TEXT FLOW

도입	직관은 세상에 대한 과학적 이해를 발전시키는 데 도움이 되기도 하고 방해가 되기도 함
주제	민속 이론은 현상의 경계를 구성하는 신뢰할 수 있는 수단이 아니며 설명적 타당성이 있다고 여겨져서는 안 됨
예시	진화 생물학에 의해 밝혀진 민속 이론의 한계

구문

• For instance, evolutionary biological science tells us [that the differences among animal species are **not** accurately portrayed {as taxonomic differences in kind} but {as differences in degree as measured by genetic proximity}].
: [ ]는 tells의 직접목적어 역할을 하는 명사절이고, 그 안에서 두 개의 { }가 'A가 아니라 B'라는 의미의 「not A but B」에 의해 연결되어 있다.

• Therefore, folk theories do not always provide a useful and accurate conceptual foundation [from which to develop scientific theories about {how the material world, including religion, works}].
: [ ]는 a useful and accurate conceptual foundation을 수식하는데, from which we can develop scientific theories about ~ 정도로 이해할 수 있다. 그 안의 { }는 전치사 about의 목적어 역할을 하는 명사절이다.

10 정답 ⑤

탄소 없이는 물리적 생명체가 있을 수 없다. 생명체가 필요로 하는 광범위한 복합적 분자 구조를 형성하는 데 필요한 풍부한 화학적 행동을 보이는 (탄소 외의) 다른 원소는 없다. (C) 물리적 생명체가 탄소 기반이어야 한다는 것을 고려한다면, 신은 왜 그렇게 적은 탄소로 우주를 만들었는가? 탄소가 생명체에 필수적이지만 또한 생명체에 파괴적일 수도 있기 때문에 탄소량은 꼭 알맞은 양과 너무 많지 않은 양 사이에 면밀한 균형을 맞춰야 한다는 것을 연구자들이 알아냈다. (B) 탄소가 너무 많으면 이산화탄소, 일산화탄소, 메탄이 너무 많이 생성된다. 양이 많으면 이들 기체는 유독하다. 양이 알맞으면 그것들의 온실 속성이 생명체에게 충분히 따뜻하도록 지구를 유지한다. 양이 더 많으면 그것들은 물리적 생명체가 견딜 수 있는 수준 이상으로 지구 표면을 가열할 수 있다. (A) 지구의 한 가지 경이로움은 그것에 탄소가 충분히 풍부하면서 부족하다는 것이다. 지구는 생명체가 살기에 충분한 탄소를 지니고 있지만, 폐의 효율적인 작동을 위한 적절한 기압과 농도, 그리고 매우 다양한 활성 발달 종들이 생존할 수 있게 하는 기온 범위(와 변동) 같은 생명체의 대기의 필요를 방해할 정도로 많은 양은 아니다.

해설
물리적 생명체에게 탄소가 필수적이라는 내용의 주어진 글 뒤에는 우주에 탄소가 적게 존재하는 이유에 대해 궁금해하면서 알맞은 양의 탄소가 생명체에 중요한 이유에 관한 연구자들의 연구 결과를 소개하는 (C)가 이어져야 한다. 그 연구 결과의 내용을 구체적으로 설명하는 내용의 (B)가 이어지고 난 다음에, 지구의 사례를 들어 알맞은 양의 탄소의 중요성을 보여 주는 (A)가 오는 것이 글의 흐름상 가장 자연스럽다.

⊗ 매력적인 오답 주의!
② 탄소의 장점이 언급된 주어진 글에서 탄소의 단점이 언급된 (B)로 바로 연결되는 흐름의 어색함을 파악하지 못하면 고를 수 있는 오답이다.

TEXT FLOW

도입	탄소는 물리적 생명체에 필수적임
주제	탄소량은 꼭 알맞은 양과 너무 많지 않은 양 사이에 면밀한 균형을 맞춰야 함
예시	탄소량이 면밀한 균형을 맞추고 있는 지구

- No other element displays the rich chemical behavior [needed to form the range of complex molecular structures {life requires}].
  : [ ]는 the rich chemical behavior를 수식하는 분사구이고, 그 안의 { }는 the range of complex molecular structures를 수식하는 관계절이다.

- In larger quantities, they can heat a planet's surface beyond [what physical life can tolerate].
  : [ ]는 전치사 beyond의 목적어 역할을 하는 명사절이다.

11 정답 ③

20세기 초반에, 미국 내 비행은 거의 완전히 규제를 받지 않았다. 그 국가는 면허 체제가 없었고 훈련에 대한 자격 조건도 없었다. 아무나 어떤 조건에서든 비행기를 살 수 있었고, 유료 승객을 합법적으로 태울 수 있었다. 미국은 비행에 대해 너무나 느슨해서 심지어 비행기 추락 사고와 사망자의 수를 계속 파악하고 있지도 않았다. 가장 권위 있는 정보원인 '비행 연감'은 그 수치들을 신문 기사로부터 모았다. 그 연간 보고서의 저자들은 규제의 부재가 진보를 방해하고 불필요한 사망을 유발한다고 확신했다. 그들은 비행기가 처음으로 사용 가능해진 후 300명 이상의 사람들이 사망하고 500명 이상이 부상을 입었다고 추산했다. 그들은 또한 상업적인 항공기 운행을 규제하는 법이 있었더라면 많은 사고들이 예방되었을 것이라는 점을 분명히 했다.

해설

주어진 문장은 '비행 연감'이라는 책이 어떤 수치에 대한 정보를 포함하고 있다는 내용으로, the figures는 ③ 앞 문장의 the number of airplane crashes and fatalities를 가리키며, ③ 뒷문장의 that annual report는 주어진 문장의 '비행 연감'을 지칭하는 것이므로 주어진 문장은 ③에 들어가는 것이 가장 적절하다.

TEXT FLOW

도입	20세기 초반, 미국은 비행에 대한 규제를 거의 하지 않았음
전개	미국은 심지어 비행기 추락 사고와 사망자 수도 파악하고 있지 않았음
결론	'비행 연감'의 저자들은 규제 부재로 인해 불필요한 사망과 사고가 발생했다고 주장함

구문

- They also made **it** clear [that many accidents **would have been** prevented {**had** there **been** a law regulating the operation of commercial aircraft}].
  : it은 made의 가목적어이고 [ ]가 진목적어이다. [ ]에는 말하는 시점보다 과거에 일어났던 사실의 반대를 가정하는 가정법이 쓰였는데, { }는 if가 생략된 조건절의 「had+과거분사」의 had가 there 앞으로 도치된 형태이다.

12 정답 ③

많은 사람들이 한때 성인 뇌의 특정 부위가 손상을 입게 되면, 신경 세포들이 새로운 연결을 생성하거나 재생하는 것이 불가능하여, 뇌의 그 부위에 의해

조절되는 기능들이 영원히 상실될 것으로 생각했다. 그러나, 동물과 인간에 관한 새로운 연구가 이러한 잘못된 오래된 관점을 뒤집었다. 오늘날, 과학자들은 뇌가 지속적으로 조정하고 재조직한다고 확신한다. 사실, 원숭이를 연구하면서, 그들은 뇌의 많은 부위에서 신경 단위의 연결이 검사될 때마다 매번 다르게 구성되어 나타나는 것을 발견했다. 활성화되지 않거나 다른 목적들로 사용되는 기존의 신경 연결 통로들은 약화되어 상실된 기능들을 대신하여 수행하는 능력을 보여 주고, 성인 뇌의 재조직이 심지어 새로운 신경 단위의 연결 형성을 수반할 수 있다는 증거가 있다.

➡ 전통적인 믿음과는 반대로, 성인의 뇌는 새로운 신경 단위의 연결을 형성함으로써 역동적으로 스스로를 재조직할 수 있는 능력을 가지고 있다.

해설

한때 많은 사람들이 생각했던 것과는 달리, 성인 뇌는 특정 부위가 손상되더라도 재조직과 신경 세포의 재생을 통해 그 기능을 복구할 수 있다는 내용의 글이므로, 요약문의 빈칸 (A)에는 conventional(전통적인)이, (B)에는 reorganize(재조직할)가 들어가는 것이 가장 적절하다.

① 현대적인 – 재조직할
② 현대적인 – 통제할
④ 전통적인 – 통제할
⑤ 전통적인 – 감지할

TEXT FLOW

도입	한때 성인 뇌의 특정 부위가 손상을 입으면 그 부위와 관련된 기능들을 할 수 없다고 생각했음
전환	최근의 연구에 따르면 뇌 속의 신경 세포들은 끊임없이 재조직됨
결론	성인 뇌는 스스로를 재조직하고 재생할 수 있는 능력을 가지고 있음

구문

- [Existing neural pathways {that are inactive or used for other purposes}] show the ability **to take over** and **carry out** functions lost to degeneration, ~.
  : [ ]가 문장의 주어로, 그 안의 { }는 Existing neural pathways를 수식하는 관계절이다. to take over와 (to) carry out은 앞의 the ability를 수식하는 형용사적 용법의 to부정사구로 and에 의해 병렬 구조를 이루고 있다.

13~14 정답 13 ③ 14 ②

감정은 인지 처리와 의사 결정에 영향을 미치지만, 항상 최적의 결과를 만들어 내는 것은 아니다. 감정은 불합리하다는 평판의 일부를 받을 만도 하지만, 반면에 감정이 부족한 사람들은 인간의 사회 생활을 통해 자신들의 길을 뚫고 나가는 데 상당한 어려움을 겪는 것처럼 보인다. 결론은 비록 결과가 완벽과는 거리가 멀더라도, 감정이 틀림없이 해보다 더 이득이 된다는 것이다. 감정이 주로 사고를 방해한다면, 그러면 상대적으로 감정에 영향을 받지 않는 사람들이 더 현명하고 더 합리적일 것이다. 이 관점은 옛날 '스타 트렉' 텔레비전 프로그램의 Mr. Spock이라는 등장인물에 의해 부정되었다(→ 대중화되었다). Spock은 다른 행성과 인종 출신이었고, 비록 대부분의 면에서 인간과 비슷했지만, 그에게는 감정이 없었다. 그는 자신의 지구인 동료들에게 감정보다 오히려 이성과 논리에 근거하여 결정을 내려야 한다는 것을 설명하는 데 결코 지치지 않았고, 그 프로그램에서 그는 가장 합리적이고 신뢰할 수 있는 인물들 중 하나였다.
그러나 인간의 현실은 꽤 다르다. Antonio Damasio 같은 연구원들은 뇌

손상이나 그들이 감정을 갖지 못하게 하는 다른 문제들을 겪은 사람들을 연구해 왔다. 그들은 Mr. Spock처럼 대단히 현명하고 침착하며 합리적인 존재는 아니다. 대신, 그들은 형편없고 예측 불가능한 판단력을 보여 주며 자신들의 삶을 엉망으로 만드는 매우 충동적인 행동 패턴에 빠지는 경향이 있다. 감정은 합리적인 사고에 중요한 보조 도구로 남아 있다. 오늘날 인간 사회에서 살기 위해서는, 전체 시스템이 제대로 작동하게 하는 것이 중요하다. 여러분의 행동을 이끄는 데 도움이 되는 감정이 없는 것은 단지 감정만을 바탕으로 행동하는 것만큼이나 비참할 것이다.

해설

13 감정이 인지 처리와 의사 결정에서 항상 최적의 결과를 만들어 내는 것은 아니지만, 감정 없이 이성과 논리로 의사 결정을 한다고 해서 최적의 결과가 도출되는 것 또한 아니라는 내용이 제시된 후, 감정이 인간의 합리적 사고에 없어서는 안 될 중요한 도구라는 점을 말하고 있다. 따라서 글의 제목으로 가장 적절한 것은 ③ '감정은 합리적 사고에 필수불가결하다'이다.
① 감정을 넘어선 이성의 우월성
② 실수를 하는 인간의 불가피한 성향
④ 지나치게 충동적인 행동의 부정적인 결과
⑤ 이성과 감정 사이의 서로 다른 기능

14 감정이 사고를 방해한다면 감정에 영향을 받지 않는 사람이 더 현명하고 더 합리적일 것이라는 내용이 언급되고 난 후, '스타 트렉' 텔레비전 프로그램의 Mr. Spock이라는 등장인물을 통해 예를 들고 있으므로, (b) denied(부정된)를 popularized(대중화된)와 같은 단어로 바꿔야 한다.

TEXT FLOW

도입	감정이 인지 처리와 의사 결정에 영향을 미치지만, 그것이 항상 최적의 결과를 만들어 내지는 않음
주제	비록 완벽하지 않다고 해도 감정은 해보다는 이득이 됨
예시/반론	'스타 트렉' 텔레비전 프로그램의 Mr. Spock이라는 등장인물을 통해 감정이 없는 사람이 더 현명하고 합리적일 것이라는 반론 제시
부연	인간의 현실은 텔레비전 프로그램과 다르며, 연구에 따르면 감정이 없는 사람들은 미숙한 판단력과 충동적인 행동 패턴에 빠지는 경향이 있음
재진술	감정은 합리적인 사고에 중요한 보조 도구이며 행동을 이끄는 데 유익함

구문

• **If** emotions mainly **disrupted** thinking, then people [who were relatively immune to emotions] **would be** wiser and more rational.
: 「If+주어+과거 동사 ~, 주어+would+동사원형 ...」 형태의 가정법 과거 구문으로, 현재 사실에 반대되는 가정을 하고 있다. [ ]는 people을 수식하는 관계절이다.

• He never tired of explaining to his earthling colleagues [that decisions should be made on the basis of reason and logic **rather than** on emotions], and in the show he was [one of the most rational and reliable characters].
: 첫 번째 [ ]는 explaining의 목적어 역할을 하는 명사절이다. 「A rather than B(B보다는 오히려 A)」 구문에서 전치사구 on the basis of reason and logic과 on (the basis of) emotions가 병렬 구조를 이루고 있다. 두 번째 [ ]에서 「one of the+최상급+복수 명사」는 '가장 ~한 것들 중 하나'를 의미한다.

• [Having no emotions {to help guide your behavior}] would be just **as** disastrous **as** [acting solely on the basis of emotions].
: 「as+형용사[부사]의 원급+as」 동등 비교 구문으로, 첫 번째 [ ]와 두 번째 [ ]는 모두 동명사구로 병렬 구조를 이루고 있다. 첫 번째 [ ] 안의 { }는 emotions를 수식하는 형용사적 용법의 to부정사구이다.

GRAMMAR REVIEW

본문 17쪽

1 that	2 being	3 what
4 was	5 that	6 sustain
7 though	8 available	9 controlled
10 them		

1 「It is ~ that ....」 강조구문을 이루어야 하므로 that이 적절하다.

2 의미상 수동태의 진행형 「be+being+과거분사」를 이루어야 하므로 being을 써야 한다.

3 describe의 목적어 역할을 하면서 접속사 역할을 해야 하므로 선행사를 포함하는 관계대명사 what이 적절하다.

4 주어의 핵이 demand이므로 술어 동사는 단수형 동사인 was가 적절하다.

5 '매우 ~해서 ...하다'의 의미인 「so ~ that ....」을 이루는 접속사 that이 적절하다.

6 선행사 the wide range of activities가 관계절의 주어이므로 sustain이 적절하다.

7 essential 앞에 it is가 생략된 것으로 볼 수 있으므로 절을 이끄는 접속사 though가 적절하다.

8 「make+목적어+목적격 보어(형용사)」를 수동태로 바꾼 형태이므로 형용사 available이 적절하다.

9 the functions를 수식하며 수동의 의미이므로 과거분사 controlled를 써야 한다.

10 관계절 안의 prevent의 목적어는 people이고 prevent의 주어는 other problems이므로 them이 적절하다.

하프 모의고사 02회

01 ③	02 ③	03 ③	04 ⑤	05 ④
06 ④	07 ③	08 ③	09 ③	10 ②
11 ④	12 ③	13 ④	14 ④	

01
정답 ③

나는 하루 동안 Bruges에 갔었다. 나는 하루 동안 입을 다물지 못하고 걸어 다녔다. 나는 Groeninge 미술관을 들여다보고 그 유명한 Béguinage 수녀원과 수선화가 만발한 그곳의 안뜰 잔디밭을 방문했지만, 대부분은 그런 완벽함이 모여 있는 것에 설레며 그저 거리들을 걸어 다녔다. 심지어 그곳의 규모조차 완벽했다. 즉, 도시가 되기에 충분할 정도로, 서점들과 흥미로운 음식점들이 있을 정도로 크지만, 조심스럽고 친근하게 느낄 수 있을 정도로 작았다. 하루 정도면 그것을 둘러싼 운하 내의 모든 거리를 걸어 다닐 수 있었다. 내가 바로 그렇게 했는데 그렇게 살고 싶은 거리를 본 적이 없었고 내가 사는 곳의 풍경이라 부르고 싶은 풍경을 본 적이 없었다. 그곳이 현실에 존재한다는 것, 즉 사람들이 이런 집들에 매일 밤 돌아오고 이런 가게들에서 쇼핑을 하고 이런 거리들에서 개들을 산책시키고 이것이 세상사(世上事)이 치라고 생각하면서 삶을 살아 나간다는 것을 받아들이기 어려웠다.

해설
필자는 Bruges라는 도시를 구경하면서 그 도시의 완벽한 규모와 아름다움에 깊은 인상을 받았고 그 아름다움에 행복해하고 있으므로, 글에 드러난 'I'의 심경으로는 ③ '감명받고 감탄하는'이 가장 적절하다.
① 질투심이 나고 죄책감을 느끼는
② 겁을 먹고 불안한
④ 감사하고 동정심을 느끼는
⑤ 실망하고 짜증난

TEXT FLOW
도입	Bruges에서 하루를 보내게 됨
묘사	도시가 완벽할 정도로 멋지고 도시의 규모도 완벽함
심경	비현실적으로 멋진 도시에 감명을 받고 감탄함

구문
• It was hard to accept [that it was real] — that people **came** home to these houses every night and **shopped** in these shops and **walked** their dogs on these streets and **went** through life thinking [that this is the way of the world].
: 첫 번째 [ ]는 accept의 목적어 역할을 하는 명사절이다. came, shopped, walked, went는 모두 people을 주어로 하는 동사들이다. 두 번째 [ ]는 thinking의 목적어 역할을 하는 명사절이다.

02
정답 ③

사람들이 어느 한 상황에서 친절하고 관대하더라도 그것이 반드시 모든 상황에 적용되는 것은 아니다. 이것은 '도덕적 자기 면허'라고 알려져 있는데, 어느 한 상황에서 도덕적 방식으로 행동하는 사람들이 나중에 다른 상황에서는 일관적이지 않은 행동을 보이는 경우이다. 과거의 선행은 비도덕적이거나 비윤리적이거나 그렇지 않으면 문제가 되는 행동, 즉 그러지 않는다면(자유로워지지 않는다면) 비도덕적인 느낌이 들거나 그런 모습으로 보일까 봐 두려워서 피할 행동을 하도록 사람들을 자유롭게 할 수 있다. 가난한 사람들을 돕기 위한 자신들의 교회 모금 행사에서 일손을 돕는 자원봉사를 하는 누군가는 나중에 다른 자선 단체에 기부하지 않기로 결정할 수 있다. 자신의 긍정적인 도덕적 특성이나 부정적인 도덕적 특성에 대해 써 보라는 요청을 받았을 때, 자신을 더 관대하다고 기술하는 사람들은 자선 단체에 더 적게 기부하지만, 자신이 얼마나 나쁜 사람인지에 대해 반성하는 사람은 더 많이 기부한다.

해설
사람들은 도덕적 행동을 하고 나면 평소에는 피할 비도덕적 행동을 자유롭게 한다는 '도덕적 자기 면허'에 관한 글이다. 따라서 글의 요지로 가장 적절한 것은 ③이다.

⊗ **매력적인 오답 주의!**
① '도덕적 자기 면허'의 내용을 정반대로 이해하면 고를 수 있는 오답이다.
④ 마지막 문장을 제대로 이해하지 못하고 도덕적 행동에 대한 상식에만 근거하면 고를 수 있는 오답이다.

TEXT FLOW
도입	도덕적 행동의 비일관성 및 '도덕적 자기 면허' 개념 소개
요지	과거의 선행은 평소에는 피할 비도덕적 행동을 자유롭게 하게 함
예시	모금 행사 자원봉사 후 또는 긍정적/부정적 도덕적 특성 기술 후 자선 단체 기부 사례

구문
• This is known as 'moral self-licensing', [where individuals {who behave in a moral way in one situation} can later display behaviours that are inconsistent in another].
: [ ]는 moral self-licensing을 부가적으로 설명하는 관계절이고, 그 안의 { }는 individuals를 수식하는 관계절이다.

• [When asked to write either about their positive or negative moral traits], those [that describe themselves as more generous] donate less to a charity, whereas those [who reflect on {how bad they are}], donate more.
: 첫 번째 [ ]는 접속사 When을 명시한 때를 나타내는 분사구문이고 asked 앞에 being이 생략된 것으로 이해할 수 있다. 두 번째와 세 번째 [ ]는 각각 those를 수식하는 관계절이다. 세 번째 [ ] 안의 { }는 전치사 on의 목적어 역할을 하는 명사절이다.

03
정답 ③

판단이 우리를 둘러싼 사람들에 의해 내려지면, 그것은 우리 마음속에 각인되는데, 우리 뇌의 뉴런이 작동하여 아주 작은 데이터가 우리의 감각을 통해 입력될 때조차도 서로 연결을 이룬다. 그것이 단 한 번의 판단이거나 직속 사회 밖에 있는 사람에 의해 내려진다면, 그것이 남기는 흔적은 희미하고 약하며 현재 또는 미래의 우리의 전반적인 행동에 영향을 미치지 않을 것이다. 하지만 그것이 우리에게 가까운 사람에게서 반복적으로 들려오고 다른 사람에 의해서도 또한 확인된다면, 그것은 우리 마음속에 깊이 각인되어 하나의 꼬리표가 될 것이다. 꼬리표가 신념으로 바뀔지의 여부는 주로 시간, 즉 우리가 얼마나 오랫동안 그것의 영향을 받았는지, 우리에게 영향을 미치는 그것의 감정적인 부담, 그것에 대한 우리의 저항력에 달려 있다. 믿거나 말거나, 우리가 누구인지에 대한 우리 생각의 일부가 된 우리에게 달린 꼬리표의 영향을 받아 우리는 우리 성격의 자질을 형성하고, 그것(자질)은 결국 모든 우리 노력의 성패를 결정한다.

해설

타인의 판단이 가까운 사람에게서 오면 우리의 마음속에 각인되어 우리의 정체성에 영향을 미친다는 내용의 글이다. 따라서 글의 제목으로 가장 적절한 것은 ③ '타인의 판단: 우리의 정체성에 반영된다'이다.
① 가깝지 않은 사람들에게는 판단을 아껴라
② 긍정적인 자기 이미지: 인생에서 성공의 열쇠
④ 우리의 감각: 흔히 진짜인 것을 포착하지 못한다
⑤ 타인의 판단은 그것이 반복될 때만 귀 기울여라

TEXT FLOW

도입	주변 사람에 의한 판단은 우리 마음속에 각인됨
전개	가까운 사람에게서 반복적으로 오는 판단이 큰 영향력을 가짐
결론	타인의 판단이 우리 정체성의 일부를 이루어 성격의 자질을 형성함

구문

• If it is an isolated judgment, or is passed by a person outside our immediate circle, the trace [it leaves] [is pale and weak] and [would not affect our overall behavior now, or in the future].
: 첫 번째 [ ]는 the trace를 수식하는 관계절이다. 두 번째와 세 번째 [ ]는 and로 연결되어 주절의 술어를 이룬다.

• But if it comes repeatedly from someone [we are close to], and is confirmed by others as well, it would be deeply imprinted in our minds and would become a label.
: [ ]는 someone을 수식하는 관계절이다.

04   정답 ⑤

'베어울프'는 3,182행의 긴 행들로 이루어진 고대 영어 서사시이다. 그것은 아마도 고대 영어로 쓰인 남아 있는 가장 오래된 시일 것이며 고대 영어 문학의 가장 중요한 작품들 중 하나로 흔히 인용된다. 그 서사시는 절반은 노르웨이 신화에, 절반은 6세기 덴마크 역사에 뿌리를 두고 있다. 그것은 8세기와 11세기 초반 사이의 어느 시점에 영국에서 쓰였다. 작가는 작자 미상의 앵글로 색슨 시인이었다. 그 시 전체가 대영 도서관에 있는 Nowell Codex라고 알려진 원고에 남아 있다. 수년간, 학자들은 그 서사시를 문학적인 걸작으로보다는 역사적이고 언어적인 자료로 취급했다. 독자들이 '베어울프'의 유혈과 폭력이 난무하는 환상적인 요소들을 높이 평가해야 한다고 주장한 최초의 사람들 중 한 명이 바로 '반지의 제왕'의 저자인 옥스퍼드 대학 교수 J.R.R. Tolkien이었다. 그는 1936년의 '괴물들과 비평가들'이라는 강연에서 '베어울프'의 알려지지 않은 저자를 위대한 시인이지, 지나치게 상상력이 뛰어난 역사가는 아니라고 칭했다.

해설

J.R.R. Tolkien은 '베어울프'의 유혈과 폭력이 난무하는 환상적인 요소들을 높이 평가했으며 그것을 쓴 저자를 위대한 시인이지, 상상력이 뛰어난 역사가는 아니라고 칭했다고 했으므로 ⑤는 글의 내용과 일치하지 않는다.

구문

• One of the first [to argue {that readers should value the gory and fantastic elements of *Beowulf*}] **was** the Oxford professor J.R.R. Tolkien, author of *The Lord of Rings*.
: 문장의 주어는 One ~ *Beowulf*이고, 동사는 was이다. [ ]는 One of the first를 수식하는 형용사적 용법의 to부정사구이고, 그 안의 { }는 argue의 목적어 역할을 하는 명사절이다.

05   정답 ④

진화론은 Charles Darwin의 덕분이라고 여겨지지만, 진화 연구를 시작한 사람이 바로 Darwin인 것은 아니었다. 솔로몬 왕은 "태양 아래 새로운 것은 없다."라고 말했는데, 이것은 세상이 끊임없는 흐름의 상태라는 관찰을 언급하는 철학적인 진술이다. 주어진 어떤 시간에든, 우리는 우리 주변의 현재 상황을 보지만, 우리는 또한 일생 동안 발생하는 변화를 따라가며 우리가 직접적으로 관찰할 수 없는 시간 동안에 걸쳐 발생하는 변화를 인식한다. 과거에 일어난 변화와 관련된 증거는 종종 무엇이 그러한 변화를 유발했는지를 우리가 추론하는 것을 막는다(→ 가능하게 한다). 그것은 바위, 동식물 같은 물리적인 세계와 행동 방식, 패션, 문학, 의학적인 관행, 기술을 포함하는 사회에 둘 다 적용된다. 그 변화는 그 자체의 메커니즘에 따라 발생한다. 가끔 무엇이 살아남는지, 무엇이 변형되는지, 그리고 무엇이 사라지는지가 우리에게 분명하지만, 그 메커니즘을 파악하는 것이 언제나 쉬운 것은 아니다.

해설

우리는 현재 상황만 보는 것이 아니라 과거의 변화를 참고하여 현재 일어나는 변화를 인식한다는 내용의 글로, 과거의 변화에 관련된 증거들은 우리의 추론을 가능하게 한다는 흐름이 적절하므로 ④ forbids(막는다)를 enables(가능하게 한다)와 같은 단어로 바꿔야 한다.

TEXT FLOW

도입	세상은 끊임없는 흐름의 상태임
전개 1	우리는 현재 상황을 보지만, 관찰할 수 없는 시간 동안 발생하는 변화도 인식함
전개 2	과거의 변화를 참고하여 현재 일어난 변화를 추론할 수 있음
전환	변화는 분명히 발생하지만, 변화의 메커니즘을 파악하는 것은 쉽지 않음

구문

• Sometimes **it** is clear to us [what survives], [what is modified], and [what becomes extinct], but **it** is not always easy [to identify the mechanism].
: 두 개의 절이 but으로 연결된 문장이다. 첫 번째 절에서 it은 가주어이고, and로 연결된 세 개의 절 [ ]가 진주어이다. but 뒤에 이어지는 절의 it은 가주어이고, to부정사구 [ ]가 진주어이다.

06   정답 ④

거짓말을 하는 사람은 자신의 말을 소유하고 싶어 하지 않는다. 어떤 사람이 진실한 말을 할 때, 그는 '나는', '우리는', 그리고 '우리를' 같은 대명사들을 문장의 나머지만큼 혹은 그 이상 강조한다. "네, 저는 그래요."라는 말 대신, 거짓말을 하고 있는 사람은 간단하게 '네'라고 대답할지도 모른다. 이런 견지로 보면, 컴퓨터가 우리보다 거짓말을 더 잘 탐지하는 것은 놀랍지 않다. 그것은 객관적으로 관찰되는 기만을 예측하게 하는 변수들의 패턴을 찾아 글을 분석한다. 컴퓨터는 비정상적으로 낮은 수의 1인칭 대명사를 찾기 위해 빠르게 글을 검토할 수 있다. 인간이 많은 시각적인 자극들에 의해 속을 수 있는 반면, 컴퓨터는 주어진 단서들만을 탐지하는데, 그것은 참이라고 신뢰될 수 있다. 많은 연구들이 허구와 진실을 구별하는 우리의 능력이 우연이나 다름없다는 것을 보여 주는데, 그 이유는 우리가 소위 '직감'이라고 불리는 무의식적인 정신에 의존하기 때문이다.

해설

1인칭 대명사를 자주 사용하는 것이 진실을 말하고 있는지 아닌지를 탐지하는 데 있어 중요한 지표인데, 컴퓨터는 이것을 정확하게 분석해 주기 때문에 인간보다 정확하게 거짓말 여부를 가릴 수 있다는 내용의 글이다. 따라서 빈칸에 들어갈 말로는 ④ '우리보다 거짓말을 더 잘 탐지하는'이 가장 적절하다.
① 거짓말의 언어적인 단서들을 무시하는
② 종종 성급한 결론에 도달하는
③ 우리에게 불완전한 증거를 제공하는
⑤ 갑작스러운 일탈을 다룰 수 있는

TEXT FLOW

도입	진실을 말할 때 우리는 1인칭 대명사를 강조하여 사용하는 경향이 있음
전개	이런 단서를 활용해 거짓말 여부를 판단하는 것은 컴퓨터가 인간보다 뛰어남
부연	(컴퓨터와 달리) 인간은 직감에 의존하기 때문에 거짓말을 구별하는 것이 우연이나 다름없음

구문

• When a person is making a truthful statement, he emphasizes the pronouns, *I*, *we*, and *us* **as much as** or **more than** the rest of the sentence.
: as much as와 more than은 모두 the rest of the sentence와 연결되어 '문장의 나머지만큼'과 '문장의 나머지 이상'의 뜻을 나타낸다.

07
정답 ③

우리는 너무나 사랑받고 싶어 해서 가끔 친구들이 우리가 했다고 생각하는 것을 정말로 했고 그들이 우리가 가졌다고 여기는 옳은 동기를 정말로 가졌다고 스스로를 납득시킬 수 있다. 한 상사는 자신이 상사가 되었을 때 자신의 농담이 더 재미있어졌다고 생각하도록 스스로를 속일 수 있다. 나는 시험이 채점되고 학생들이 조용해진 후에도 내 수업이 정말로 환상적이라고 쉽게 믿게 될 수 있으며, 보조금으로 수백만 달러를 나눠주는 기관에 있는 내 친구는 예산에 대한 그의 통제는 ("정말 멋져 보이시네요!"라고) 사람들이 그에게 살이 빠졌는지를 계속 묻는 이유와 전혀 무관하다고 정말로 믿을 수 있다. 전략적인 아첨은 <u>우리가 받는 찬사가 사실이라고 우리가 믿고 싶어 하기</u> 때문에 성공적일 수 있다. 일단 사람들이 사랑받고 멋져 보이는 것에 대해 두는 중요성을 여러분이 파악하면, 여러분은 전략적인 아첨을 조금 더 잘 간파하게 된다. 그리고 아마도 여러분 스스로는 그것에 덜 탐닉할 수 있을 것이다.

해설

우리는 사랑받고 멋져 보이고 싶은 욕구가 너무나 강해서 누군가 아첨을 하면 그것을 우리가 정말 그렇다고 믿고 싶어 한다는 내용의 글이므로, 빈칸에 들어갈 말로 가장 적절한 것은 ③ '우리가 받는 찬사가 사실이라고 우리가 믿고 싶어 하기'이다.

① 그것이 부분적으로 우리가 가지고 있는 긍정적인 특성에 근거해 있기
② 아첨하는 사람의 의도가 다른 사람들에 의해 쉽게 간파되지 않기
④ 그것이 제공하는 보상이 그것의 적은 비용보다 너무나 크기
⑤ 더 높은 지위가 더 많은 특권을 가져오는 것을 우리가 당연하게 여기기

TEXT FLOW

도입	우리는 사랑받고 싶은 욕구에 의해 스스로를 속일 수 있음
예시	상사, 학생들을 가르치는 필자, 보조금을 지급하는 기관에 있는 친구
부연	전략적 아첨은 사랑받고 싶어 하는 우리의 욕구로 인해 성공함
결론	사람들의 이런 욕구를 파악하면 전략적 아첨을 간파할 수 있음

구문

• I can easily come to believe [my class really is fabulous] [even after the exam is graded and the students are quiet], and [my friend at the foundation {handing out millions of dollars in grants}] can really believe [that his control of the budget has nothing to do with {why people keep asking if he has lost weight}].
: 첫 번째 [ ]는 believe의 목적어 역할을 하는 명사절로 앞에 접속사 that이 생략되어 있고, 두 번째 [ ]는 시간을 나타내는 부사절이다. 세 번째 [ ]는 and 뒤에 오는 절의 주어이며, 그 안의 { }는 the foundation을 수식하는 현재분사구이다. 네 번째 [ ]는 believe의 목적어 역할을 하는 명사절로, 그 안의 { }는 with의 목적어 역할을 하는 명사절이다.

08
정답 ③

과학은 관찰, 설명, 모형, 가설을 포함하는 이론들끼리 연결된 망이며, 일부는 확실히 확인되었고 일부는 더 잠정적이다. 기존의 과학 지식 체계와 다양한 종류의 의존 관계를 갖지 않는 과학에서의 새로운 생각을 도입하는 것은 불가능하다. 과학에서 훈련을 받는다는 것의 의미 중 하나는 이 망의 자기 전문 분야에 대한 이해를 습득하는 것이다. (때로 과학은 선을 넘기도 하지만, 대부분의 경우 그것은 가난한 사람들을 위한 더 많은 식량과 질병에 대한 치료법을 구하는 우리 기도에 대한 귀중한 응답이다.) 이것에는 미해결 문제가 어디에 있는지, 어떤 부분이 가장 확고한지, 어떤 부분이 개선, 수정 또는 거부에 열려 있는지에 대한 훌륭한 이해를 키우는 것이 포함된다. 이러한 상호 연관성과 각각에 대한 증거의 중대성에 대한 올바른 판단력을 키우면 평범한 것이든 혁명적인 것이든 어떤 주장의 사전 확률을 가늠하고 그에 따라 회의의 정도를 조정할 수 있다.

해설

과학에서의 훈련은 이론의 연결된 망 속의 자기 전문 분야의 미해결 문제, 이미 입증된 부분, 개선, 수정, 혹은 거부할 수 있는 부분을 이해하는 것이라는 내용의 글이다. 따라서 과학이 더 많은 식량과 질병 치료법을 구하는 귀중한 방편이라는 내용의 ③은 글의 전체 흐름과 관계가 없다.

TEXT FLOW

도입	관찰, 설명, 모형, 가설을 포함하는 이론들끼리 연결된 망으로서의 과학
주제	과학 훈련은 자기 전문 분야(미해결, 기입증, 개선/수정/거부 부분)를 이해하는 것
결론	과학에 대한 올바른 판단력은 주장의 사전 확률 가능과 회의의 정도를 조정 가능하게 함

구문

• Science is a web of interlinking theories [containing observations, explanations, models, and hypotheses], [some highly confirmed, some more tentative].
: 첫 번째 [ ]는 a web of interlinking theories를 수식하는 분사구이다. 두 번째 [ ]는 주절의 상황에 부수하는 상황을 나타내는 분사구문인데, some 뒤에는 각각 being이 생략되었다.

• **It** is not possible [to introduce a new idea in science {that would not have dependency relationships of various sorts with the existing body of scientific knowledge}].
: It은 가주어이고 [ ]는 진주어이다. [ ] 안의 { }는 a new idea in science를 수식하는 관계절이다.

09 정답 ③

아이들은 모두 아주 기꺼이 부모를 기쁘게 해 주려 하고, 그래서 그들은 정말이지 열심히 노력한다. (B) 그 결과, 아이들은 흔히 조숙하게 유능하고 책임감이 강하다. 그러나 그 힘은 성장하기 위해 그들 자신이 필요로 하는 사랑과 보살핌을 얻을 수 없는 내적 무력감의 토대 위에 세워진다. (C) 그런 다음 그들은 그 '무기력한 힘'을 성인 생활까지 가져온다. 그들은 어린 시절에 결코 성취할 수 없었던 것을 성인 생활에서 성취하기 위해 그 힘을 사용할 또 한 번의 기회를 무의식적으로 찾는다. (A) 그런 이유로 사람들은 수년 동안, 때로는 평생 기뻐할 능력이 없는 사람을 계속 고집스럽게 기쁘게 하려고 한다. 혹은 사랑을 주고 싶어 하지 않거나 그럴 능력이 없는 사람에게서 사랑을 얻으려고 한다. 혹은 구원받지 않기로 결심한 사람을 '구원'하려고 한다.

해설

부모를 기쁘게 하려는 아이들의 노력을 언급한 주어진 글 뒤에는, 그런 결과로 생기는 아이들의 조숙한 유능함과 책임감을 언급하면서 성장에 필요한 사랑과 보살핌을 얻을 수 없는 내적 무력감을 토대로 그런 힘이 생기는 것이라고 말하는 (B)가 와야 한다. 이어서 성인 생활까지 그 힘을 가져와서 무의식적으로 사랑과 보살핌을 얻으려 한다고 말하는 (C)가 오고, 그다음에는 그러한 성인이 보이는 행동 사례를 제시하는 (A)가 오는 것이 글의 흐름상 가장 자연스럽다.

⊗ 매력적인 오답 주의!

② (A)에서 사례로 언급된 행동들이 성인들이 보이는 행동이라는 것을 파악하지 못하면 고를 수 있는 오답이다.

TEXT FLOW

도입	부모를 기쁘게 하려는 아이들
전개	조숙한 유능함 및 강한 책임감 ↔ 사랑과 보살핌을 얻지 못하는 무력감
결론	성인 생활에서도 사랑과 보살핌을 얻으려는 노력을 지속함

구문

• That is why people persist for many years, sometimes for a whole lifetime, in trying to please someone [who is not capable of being pleased].
: [ ]는 someone을 수식하는 관계절이다.

• But that power is built on a foundation of inner powerlessness to obtain the love and care [they themselves

need to grow up].
: [ ]는 the love and care를 수식하는 관계절이다.

10 정답 ②

전통적으로, 우리는 암을 신체의 용으로 보았다. 즉, 어떻든 간에 그것은 전혀 별충할 만한 효용성이 없다는 것이다. (B) 그러나 보다 최근에, 우리는 그것이 스승이 될 수도 있다는 것을 알게 되었다. 암을 공부하고, 연구하고, 치료하는 어떤 의사이든 신체가 어떻게 작동하게 되어 있는지와 그것이 그러지 않을 때 어떻게 반응하는지에 대한 자세한 모습을 얻는다. (A) 그것이 의사들의 가장 큰 희망들 중 하나이다. 즉, 암세포들을 죽이는 방법을 발견하거나, 아니면 애초에 그것들이 자라지 못하게 하는 것이다. 우리에게는, 그것이 우리가 암에 대해 배워야 하는 가장 중요한 이유들 중 하나이다. (C) 인간 신체의 경이와 여러분의 신체가 오작동하면 무슨 일이 일어나는지에 대해 약간 배움으로써, 여러분은 그것이 더 잘 작동하게 하는 더 나은 방법들을 배울 수 있다. 사실, 암이 항상 생명을 앗아가는 것은 아니다. 그러나 여러분은 똑똑한 예방 전략과 조기 발견으로 스스로를 도울 수 있다.

해설

주어진 글은 암에 대해 사람들이 가진 기존의 믿음에 관한 내용이다. 이어서 최근 암에 대해 바뀐 인식과 의사들의 연구를 언급하는 (B)가 온 후, 의사들이 암 연구를 하며 갖게 된 희망에 관한 내용인 (A)가 오고, (A)에서 언급한 우리가 암에 대해서 배워야 하는 이유를 부연 설명한 (C)가 이어지는 것이 글의 흐름상 가장 자연스럽다.

TEXT FLOW

도입	기존에는 암을 벌충할 만한 효용성이 없는 것으로 여겼음
전환	암 연구를 통해 신체의 작동과 오작동에 관해 더욱 잘 알 수 있게 됨
부연	암세포를 죽이거나 자라지 못하게 하는 방법을 알아내는 것이 암에 대해 배우는 이유 중 하나임
주제	예방 전략 및 조기 발견을 통해 암으로부터 스스로를 도울 수 있음

구문

• By learning a little about [the wonders of the human body] and [what happens when your body malfunctions], you can learn better ways to make it work better.
: 첫 번째 [ ]인 명사구와 두 번째 [ ]인 의문사절이 전치사 about의 목적어로 and로 이어져 병렬 구조를 이루고 있다.

11 정답 ④

과학 혁명의 구조에 대한 Thomas Kuhn의 영향력 있는 역사적, 철학적 연구의 한 가지 효과는 과학자들이 패러다임의 전환에 관여한다는 생각을 좋아한다는 것이다. 따라서 과학자들은 어떤 실험, 혹은 어떤 새로운 관찰 결과가 예상과 맞지 않는 경우에 좌절과 흥분이 뒤섞인 감정을 느낀다. 가장 그럴듯한 설명은 절차나 계산에서 실수를 저질렀다는 것이지만, 그것이 새로운 빛이 통과해서 보이게 될 틈을 나타내는 가능성이 항상 존재한다. 일반적인 회의적 태도는 이런 가능성에 열려 있게 해 준다. 이것이 영구히 열린 마음을 가져야 한다는 말은 아닌데, 왜냐하면 철학자 Bertrand Russell이 지적한 것처럼 그것은 비어 있는 마음일 것이기 때문이다. 그러나 과학자들은 증거가 그 분야에서 오랫동안 유지되어 온 가정에 위배되기 시작하면 심지어 그것에 대해서도 의문을 제기해야 한다. 적절히 균형 잡히고 조정된 판단을 고려하는 마음의 습관을 길러야 한다.

해설
④ 앞뒤의 문장이 모두 과학자가 기존 가정에 대해 가지는 회의적 태도에 대해 긍정적인 입장을 보이고 있는데, ④ 뒤의 문장은 역접의 접속사 However로 시작하고 있으므로 글의 흐름이 어색하다. 주어진 문장은 과학자의 회의적 태도에 대해 철학자 Bertrand Russell이 비어 있는 마음이라고 지적한 내용이므로, 주어진 문장이 들어가기에 가장 적절한 곳은 ④이다.

⊗ 매력적인 오답 주의!
⑤ ④ 뒤의 문장 맨 앞에 있는 역접의 접속사 However를 놓치고 해석하면 고를 수 있는 오답이다.

TEXT FLOW
도입	예상과 맞지 않는 증거에 대해 느끼는 좌절과 흥분
전개	일반적인 회의적 태도의 중요성
결론	적절히 균형 잡히고 조정된 판단을 고려하는 회의적 태도의 필요성

구문
• This is not to say [that one must be perpetually open-minded] for, as the philosopher Bertrand Russell pointed out, that would be a mind [that is vacant].
: 첫 번째 [ ]는 say의 목적어 역할을 하는 명사절이고 for는 이유를 나타내는 접속사이다. 두 번째 [ ]는 a mind를 수식하는 관계절이다.

• While the most likely explanation is that one made a mistake in a procedure or calculation, there is always the chance [that it represents an opening {through which new light will be shown}].
: [ ]는 the chance와 동격인 명사절이고, 그 안의 { }는 an opening을 수식하는 관계절이다.

12~14
정답 12 ③ 13 ④ 14 ④

(A) 2008년 8월에, 나는 황갈색의 떠돌이 고양이 한 마리가 내 정원에 들어오는 것을 알게 되었다. 그는 내가 가끔 새들을 위해 먹다 남은 음식들을 던져 놓는다는 것을 발견했었던 것이다. 나는 그를 위해 음식들을 내놓기 시작했지만, 그는 무척 야생적이어서 나는 그에게 가까이 다가갈 수 없었다. 그럼에도 불구하고, 그는 대부분의 저녁 시간에 계속해서 음식을 찾아왔다.
(C) 그 후, 11월 말에 나는 지난 2월에 그가 2킬로미터 떨어진 동물병원에서 탈출했었다는 것을 알게 되었다. 그를 잡아서 동물병원으로 돌려보내 그의 주인과 다시 만나게 해 준 다음, 나는 내가 그를 마지막으로 본 것이라고 생각했다. 하지만 12일 후, 그는 다시 내 정원에 와 있었으며, 나는 내 눈을 의심했다.
(D) 나중에, 나는 그 고양이가 너무 야생적으로 변해 버렸기에 그 주인이 그를 감당할 수 없게 되었음을 알게 되었다. 그래서 그는 그를 놓아줘야만 했다. 그 고양이는 직접 발로 뛰어 자신의 의사를 밝히고, 2킬로미터 거리의 여행을 떠나 그가 있고 싶어 하는 곳으로 돌아왔던 것이다. 그렇게 노력했는데, 내가 어찌 그를 받아들이지 않을 수 있었겠는가?
(B) 그를 보살피고 그에게 용기를 북돋아 준 지 수개월 만에, 그는 마침내 자

신의 두려움을 극복하고 내가 그를 만지도록 허락해 주었다. 그 순간 이후로 우리는 결코 뒤를 돌아보지 않았는데, 그는 이제 사랑을 듬뿍 받는, 우리 가족의 매우 다정한 구성원이다.

해설
12 주어진 글 (A)에서 정원에 들어오는 고양이가 떠돌이 고양이인 줄 알았다는 내용이 있으므로, 사실은 주인이 있는 고양이가 동물병원에서 탈출한 것이었음을 알게 되었다는 내용의 (C)가 (A) 다음에 오고, 그 고양이를 동물병원에 보내 주인을 만나게 해 주었지만 원래 주인을 떠나 필자의 정원으로 되돌아왔다는 내용의 (D)가 그다음에 이어지며, 마지막으로 수개월 후 그 고양이를 마침내 가족으로 받아들이게 되었다는 내용의 (B)가 이어지는 것이 글의 흐름상 가장 자연스럽다.

13 (d)는 고양이의 원래 주인을 가리키고, 나머지는 모두 고양이를 가리킨다.

14 고양이를 주인에게 돌려보냈을 때 너무 야생적으로 변해 있어서 주인이 그를 감당할 수 없게 되었다고는 했지만 주인이 학대를 했다는 언급은 없으므로, 글의 내용으로 적절하지 않은 것은 ④이다.

TEXT FLOW
시간 순서/사건 전개에 따른 흐름:
(A) 필자의 정원에 들어오는 떠돌이 고양이에게 음식을 챙겨 줌 → (C) 동물병원에서 탈출한 고양이인 것을 알고 주인을 찾아 주었지만 다시 돌아옴 → (D) 원래 주인이 야생적으로 변한 고양이를 놓아준 것이고 필자를 찾아온 것임을 알게 됨 → (B) 극진한 보살핌에 고양이가 마음을 열고 가족의 구성원이 됨

구문
• Then, in late November, I discovered that back in February, he **had escaped** from a vet clinic 2 kilometers away.
: had escaped는 과거완료 시제로 대과거의 의미를 나타낸다. 필자가 이야기하고 있는 시점(in late November)보다 더 앞선 과거(back in February)에 일어난 사건이었기 때문에 과거완료 시제가 사용되었다.

GRAMMAR REVIEW
본문 25쪽

1 asked	2 establishing	3 cited
4 it	5 that	6 what
7 be saved	8 doesn't	9 them
10 had become		

1 접속사 When이 명시된 분사구문의 의미상의 주어 those가 동사 ask의 대상이므로 과거분사 asked를 써야 한다.

2 술어 동사 do가 있으므로 주절의 부수적인 상황을 나타내는 분사구문을 이끄는 establishing을 써야 한다.

3 cite는 '인용하다'라는 뜻의 타동사로, 주어인 It이 cite의 행위를 당하는 대상이므로 수동 의미의 과거분사 cited를 써야 한다.

4 「it was ~ who」 강조구문을 이루고 있으므로 대명사 it이 적절하다.

5 「so ~ that ...」 구문으로 '너무나 ~해서 …하다'의 의미를 나타내므로 접속사 that이 적절하다.

6 관계절 안에서 means의 목적어 역할을 하면서 전치사 of의 목적어 역할도 해야 하므로 선행사를 포함하는 관계대명사 what이 적절하다.

7 save는 타동사인데 목적어가 없으므로 be saved가 적절하다.

8 work이 뒤에 생략되어 있으므로 doesn't가 적절하다.

9 의미상 long-held assumptions in the field를 대신해야 하므로 복수형 대명사인 them이 적절하다.

10 그 주인이 고양이를 감당할 수 없게 되었음을 알게 된 것보다 고양이가 너무 야생적으로 변해 버린 것이 먼저 일어난 일이기 때문에 과거완료 had become을 써야 한다.

하프 모의고사   03회

01 ③	02 ⑤	03 ③	04 ⑤	05 ⑤
06 ⑤	07 ①	08 ⑤	09 ③	10 ⑤
11 ②	12 ④	13 ①	14 ⑤	

01
정답 ③

참가자 여러분께,

Langley Community 미술 대회에 등록해 주신 모든 분께 감사드립니다! 저희는 열렬한 반응에 몹시 흥분해 있으며 여러분의 창의적인 출품작을 보게 되는 것을 기대하고 있습니다. 이 이메일은 대회 기준에 대한 중요한 변경 사항을 여러분에게 알려 드리기 위한 것입니다. 신중한 검토와 지역 예술 공동체의 피드백을 거친 후, 저희는 참가자들의 다양한 재능과 예술적 표현을 더 잘 반영하기 위해 기존의 대회 기준을 약간 수정했습니다. 원래는 전시되지 않은 작품만 출품할 수 있었습니다. 이제 주요 상을 받지 않았기만 하면 이전에 전시된 작품도 환영합니다. 변경된 기준은 현재 저희 웹사이트인 www.LCAC.net에서 확인하실 수 있습니다. 이를 주의 깊게 살펴보시고 출품작에 필요한 조정을 거치시기를 바랍니다. Langley Community 미술 대회에 대한 여러분의 이해와 지속적인 참여에 감사드립니다.

진심을 담아,

Timothy Jones 드림

해설

Langley Community 미술 대회에 참가자로 등록한 사람들에게 기존의 대회 기준을 약간 수정했다고 안내하고 있으므로, 글의 목적으로 가장 적절한 것은 ③이다.

TEXT FLOW

도입	미술 대회 참가 등록자에 대한 감사와 기대감 표시
안내	기존의 대회 기준을 수정
부연	이전에 전시된 작품도 출품이 가능해짐
결론	변경된 기준을 검토하여 출품작에 필요한 조정 요청

구문

• [After careful consideration and feedback from the local art community], we have made minor adjustments to the original contest criteria [to better reflect {the diverse talents and artistic expressions of our participants}].

: 첫 번째 [ ]는 시간을 나타내는 전치사구이다. 두 번째 [ ]는 목적의 의미를 나타내는 부사적 용법의 to부정사구이며, 그 안의 { }는 reflect의 목적어 역할을 하는 명사구이다.

02
정답 ⑤

회사가 직원들에게 혁신하도록 장려하면서 그들의 새로운 접근 방식이 실패했을 때 그들에게 벌을 준다면 이는 엇갈리는 신호를 보내는 것이다. 실패를 처벌하는 것은 사람들이 위험을 감수하고 새로운 아이디어를 시도하는 것을 방해한다. 심지어 더 나쁜 것은 사람들이 실패를 숨기려고 애쓰기 때문에 실패로부터 배울 수 있는 능력을 떨어뜨릴 수 있다는 것이다. 실수를 받아들이고 그것에 대한 논의와 학습을 장려하는 문화에서는 더 많은 위험의 감수와 더 많은 실패가 발생하지만, 궁극적으로는 더 많은 성공이라는 결과를 낳을 수 있다. 탐색 과정을 고려하고 심지어 매우 엉뚱한 아이디어도 장려하는 회사 문화를 조성하라, 그러면 아마 좋은 성과를 거둘 수도 있다. 인정하건대, 그것은 말처럼 쉬운 일은 아니다. 성취 수준이 높고 성취 지향적이며 경쟁심이 강한 개인이 번창하는 동시에 자신의 실수를 공유하고 공개적으로 분석하는 것을 편안하게 느낄 수 있는 환경을 조성하는 것은 어려울 수 있다. 하지만 모두가 실패를 선뜻 인정할 마음이 생기는 문화가 애초에 실패하는 것에 대한 줄어든 두려움으로 자연스럽게 이어질 수 있다는 점을 기억하라. 이러한 환경에서는 대담한 혁신이 번창할 것이다.

해설

혁신하는 과정에서 발생하는 실수를 받아들이고 그것에 대한 공개적인 논의와 학습을 장려하는 회사 문화를 조성하면, 실패하는 것에 대한 줄어든 두려움으로 이어지며 이런 환경에서는 대담한 혁신이 번창할 것이라는 내용이므로, 필자가 주장하는 바로 가장 적절한 것은 ⑤이다.

TEXT FLOW

도입	혁신을 장려하는 과정에서 실패할 때 벌을 주는 것은 엇갈리는 신호를 보내는 것임
부연	실패를 처벌하면 위험을 감수하고 새로운 아이디어를 시도하는 것을 방해함
주제	실수를 받아들이고 그것에 대한 논의와 학습을 장려하는 문화는 성공을 낳을 수 있음
부연	실패를 인정할 마음이 생기는 문화가 실패하는 것에 대한 줄어든 두려움으로 이어짐

구문

• **It** can be challenging [to create an environment {in which high-performing, achievement-driven, competitive individuals can thrive but also feel comfortable sharing and publicly analyzing their mistakes}].
: It은 가주어이고 [ ]는 진주어이다. 그 안의 { }는 an environment를 수식하는 관계절이다.

• But remember, [a culture {in which everyone feels like they can readily admit failures naturally}] **extends** to a reduced fear of [making them in the first place].
: 첫 번째 [ ]는 문장의 주어이고, 주어의 핵심어구가 a culture이므로 술어 동사로 단수형 동사 extends가 사용되었다. 그 안의 { }는 a culture를 수식하는 관계절이다. 두 번째 [ ]는 전치사 of의 목적어 역할을 하는 동명사구이다.

03 정답 ③

심리 치료 및 명상 수행 경험과 더불어 인지 심리학에 대한 연구는 우리가 단지 원하는 것만으로는 생각을 없앨 수 없다는 것을 매우 명확하게 가르쳐 준다. 사실, 구체적인 무언가를 생각하는 것을 의도적으로 멈추려고 하면 기묘하게도 정반대의 효과를 얻게 되는데, 바로 이와 같은 주제에 대해 강박적으로 생각하게 된다. Fyodor Dostoyevsky는 'Winter Notes on Summer Impressions'에서 "북극곰을 떠올리지 않으려고 노력하는 과업을 자신에게 제시해 보세요. 그러면 여러분은 매 순간 그 저주받은 것(북극곰)이 떠오르는 것을 보게 될 것입니다."라고 말했다. 이 직관적 지식은 이후

에 '역설적 과정'이라고 이름 붙여진 현상에 관하여 고인이 된 Dan Wegner가 선도한 훌륭한 연구로 이후에 뒷받침되었다. 생각을 멈추려고 애쓰는 것은 실험실 환경에서 하려고 따로 준비해 둔 어떤 복잡한 실험적 과제가 아니라 오히려 우리 모두에게 일상적으로 불가피한 일이다. Freud와 다른 이들이 설명한 것처럼, 생각과 감정을 억누르는 것에서부터 다양한 트라우마에 관해 생각하는 것을 피하려고 애쓰는 것, 그리고 지나치게 걱정하지 않음으로써 통제력을 유지하려고 애쓰는 것에 이르기까지, 생각하지 않는 것은 끊임없는 도전이다.

해설

구체적인 무언가를 생각하는 것을 의도적으로 멈추려고 하면 오히려 그 주제에 대해 강박적으로 생각하게 된다는 내용의 글이다. 따라서 밑줄 친 부분이 글에서 의미하는 바로 가장 적절한 것은 ③ '생각을 억누르려는 시도는 그것의 증가된 발생으로 이어진다.'이다.

① 필요는 가장 충격적인 상황에서 생겨날 수 있다.
② 무언가를 추구하는 것이 그것을 획득하는 것보다 더 큰 성취감을 줄 수 있다.
④ 가장 준비된 사람이 흔히 가장 예상치 못한 상황에 직면한다.
⑤ 공감 능력이 높은 사람은 자신의 감정적 욕구를 소홀히 하는 경향이 있다.

⊗ 매력적인 오답 주의!

① 글 전체의 중심 내용을 이해하지 않고 an everyday necessity for all of us / avoid thinking about various traumas 등과 같은 단편적인 어휘와 표현을 근거로 고를 수 있는 오답이다.

TEXT FLOW

도입	단지 원하는 것만으로는 생각을 없앨 수 없음
요지	무언가를 생각하는 것을 의도적으로 멈추려고 하면 강박적으로 생각하게 됨
부연	사고 억제의 역설적 과정에 관한 연구로 뒷받침됨
결론	생각하지 않는 것은 일상에서 늘 마주하는 도전임

구문

• [Research in cognitive psychology, {combined with experience with psychotherapy and the practice of meditation}], teaches us very clearly [that we cannot get rid of thoughts just by wishing].
: 첫 번째 [ ]는 문장의 주어부이고, 그 안의 { }는 분사구로 주어의 핵심어구인 Research in cognitive psychology를 수식한다. 두 번째 [ ]는 teaches의 직접목적어 역할을 하는 명사절이다.

• From [suppression of thoughts and feelings], as has been described by Freud and others, to [{trying to avoid thinking about various traumas}, and {trying to stay in control by not worrying too much}], not thinking is a constant challenge.
: 두 개의 [ ]가 'A에서부터 B까지'의 의미를 나타내는 「from A to B」 구문으로 연결되어 있다. 두 번째 [ ] 안에서 동명사구인 두 개의 { }가 and로 연결되어 전치사 to에 이어진다.

04 정답 ⑤

인간이 사용하기 위해 생물체를 바꾸는 기술의 사용은 거의 인류만큼이나 오래되었다. 최초의 인간들이 농사를 시작했을 때, 그들은 곧 몇몇 씨앗과 농작물이 더 많은 식량을 생산하는 데 있어 다른 것들보다 더 낫다는 것을 알게

되었다. 인간들은 그 씨앗들을 보관했고, 그것들을 비옥한 토양에 심었으며, 그 경쟁 상대들을 소멸시켰다. 이것이 식물들에게는 자신들의 유전자를 퍼뜨릴 좋은 기회였다. 인간들은 또한 몇몇 동물들이 길들여졌을 때 이 동물들의 고기뿐만 아니라 가죽, 발굽, 뿔과 다른 신체 부위들에 대한 많은 쓰임새가 발견되었다는 것을 알아차리기 시작했다. 예를 들어, 초기의 인간들은 털을 위해 어떤 종류의 양이 사육될 수 있다는 것을 발견했고 다른 종류의 양보다 그 선택한 양을 키우려 노력했다. 그런 종들은 인간들과 함께 번성했고 그들의 도움에 힘입어 자신들의 유전자를 쉽게 퍼뜨렸다.

해설
인간이 자신들에게 이로운 식물과 동물을 선별하여 키움에 따라 이 식물과 동물은 자기 유전자를 쉽게 퍼뜨리게 되었다는 내용이므로, 글의 주제로는 ⑤ '종의 경쟁에 있어서 인간의 개입'이 가장 적절하다.
① 우월한 것에 대한 자연 선택
② 다른 것들에 비해 초기의 농작물이 가졌던 장점
③ 농사를 위한 식물 선택의 기준
④ 농경이 유럽과 아시아에서 시작된 이유

TEXT FLOW

도입	오랫동안 인간은 사용하기 위해 생물체(식물/동물)를 바꿔 옴
예시 1	인간은 농사를 시작하며 특정 식물을 선별하여 재배하고, 경쟁 상대를 소멸시킴
	↓
	인간에게 선택된 식물들이 유전자를 더 잘 퍼뜨림
예시 2	인간은 가죽, 털 등을 사용하기 위해 몇몇 동물을 길들임
	↓
	인간에게 선택된 동물들이 유전자를 쉽게 퍼뜨림
주제	선택된 종들이 인간과 함께 번성함

구문
• Humans also began to notice [that {when some animals were tamed}, many uses were found not only for the meat of these animals, but also for their hides, hooves, horns, and other body parts].
: [ ]는 notice의 목적어 역할을 하는 명사절이고, 그 안의 { }는 시간의 의미를 나타내는 부사절이다.

05　　　　　　　　　　　　　　　　　　　　　정답 ⑤

Sherburne 국립 야생 동물 보호소 청소년 사진 공모전

규정
• 유치원부터 12학년까지
• 낮 시간대에 일반인에게 공개되는 지역에서 촬영된 것
• 참가자들에 의해 촬영 및 편집된 것

부문
• 큰 사진: 풍경, 야생 동물, 오락
• 자세히 보기: 식물, 곤충, 야생 동물의 확대 사진

제출
• 8″ x 10″, 사진 전용 인화지에 인쇄한 것
• 10월 8일 금요일 오후 5시까지 우편 발송분
• sherburne@fws.gov로 디지털 복사본을 송부할 것

수상
• 종합 1위: 30달러 / 사진은 Oak Savanna Learning Center에서 전시됩니다.
• 범주별: 1위: 20달러 / 2위: 15달러 / 3위: 10달러
수상자는 11월 17일 시상식에서 발표됩니다.

더 많은 정보를 원하시면, 저희 웹사이트를 방문하십시오.

해설
수상자는 11월 17일 시상식에서 발표될 것이라고 했으므로, 안내문의 내용과 일치하지 않는 것은 ⑤이다.

구문
• The winners **will be announced** at our award ceremony on November 17.
: The winners는 announce의 행위를 당하는 대상이므로 수동태가 사용되었으며, 조동사가 포함된 수동태 문장은 「조동사+be+과거분사」 형태로 쓴다.

06　　　　　　　　　　　　　　　　　　　　　정답 ⑤

우리 자신의 '아라비아' 숫자인 0, 1, 2, 3, 4, 5, 6, 7, 8, 그리고 9를 생각해 보라. 그것들은 사실상 인도에서 왔는데, 그곳에서 기독교 시대의 첫 몇 세기 동안 그것들의 사용이 전개되었다. 정수의 십진법은 인도의 점성술사 Aryabhatta(서기 476년)에게 알려졌던 것으로 보인다. 이 체계는 670년경 메소포타미아 지방에 도달했고, 그곳에서 네스토리우스 교파의 주교인 Severus Sebokht는 그것이 그리스인들에 의해 사용되던 체계보다 우월하다고 칭찬했다. 이슬람교의 창시자인 선지자 마호메트의 사망(서기 632년) 후 100년 이내에, 이슬람교의 영향력은 북아프리카, 스페인의 많은 지역, 그리고 동쪽으로는 중국 국경까지 확장되었다. 이러한 팽창의 결과로, 이슬람교도들은 외국의 학문을 습득하기 시작했고, 칼리프 알 만수르의 시대에 인도와 페르시아의 천문학 문서들은 아랍어로 번역되었으며 다음에는 이러한 새로운 지식의 많은 부분이 이슬람교를 믿는 스페인으로 도입되었다.

해설
⑤ much of this new knowledge가 bring의 동작 대상이므로 수동태로 써야 한다. 따라서 현재분사 bringing을 과거분사 brought로 고쳐야 한다.
① India를 수식하는 관계절을 이끌며, 관계절이 완전한 형태의 절이므로 관계부사 where는 적절하다.
② 주어가 A decimal system for whole numbers이고 주어의 핵은 system이므로 단수 동사 seems는 적절하다.
③ the system을 대신하여 사용되었으므로 단수 대명사 that은 적절하다.
④ 주어가 Muslim influence이므로 이와 연결되는 술어 동사로 과거 동사 extended는 적절하다.

TEXT FLOW

도입	'아라비아' 숫자의 유래
전개	인도에서 아라비아 숫자 발명 → 메소포타미아 지방에 도달 → 이슬람 문화권으로 전파 → 스페인으로 전파

구문
• This system reached Mesopotamia around 670 [where the Nestorian bishop Severus Sebokht praised **it** as being

superior to that used by the Greeks].
: [ ]는 Mesopotamia를 부연 설명하는 관계절이고, it은 This system을 가리키는 대명사이다.

07

한 가지 용도가 천문학에는 남아 있는데, 그것은 계속해서 우리의 자연 법칙의 발견에서 매우 중요한 역할을 맡고 있다. 뉴턴을 자신의 운동과 중력의 법칙의 발견으로 이끌었던 것은 바로 행성의 운동 문제였다. 원자가 특정한 파장만으로 빛을 발산하고 흡수한다는 사실은, 20세기에 양자 역학의 발전으로 이어졌는데, 그것은 19세기 초반에 태양의 스펙트럼 관측에서 발견된 것이다. 그 이후 19세기 중에, 이러한 태양의 관측은 이전에는 지구상에서 알려지지 않았던 헬륨과 같은 새로운 원소의 존재를 밝혀냈다. 20세기 초반에, 아인슈타인의 '일반 상대성 이론'은 처음에는 자신의 예측을 관측된 수성의 움직임과 비교하고, 그런 다음 태양의 중력장에 의한 별빛의 굴절에 대한 성공적인 예측을 통해 천문학적으로 검증되었다.

해설
천문학적인 탐구를 통해 운동과 중력의 법칙이 발견되었고 이후 양자 역학의 발전으로 이어졌으며, 새로운 원소의 존재 및 '일반 상대성 이론'이 밝혀졌다는 내용의 글이므로, 빈칸에 들어갈 말로는 ① '자연 법칙'이 가장 적절하다.
② 지구의 외로움
③ 보편적인 이야기
④ 지성의 한계
⑤ 과학의 실용적 사용

TEXT FLOW

주제	천문학은 자연 법칙의 발견에서 중요한 역할을 함
예시	뉴턴의 발견 → 양자 역학의 발전으로 이어짐 → 새로운 원소의 존재를 밝힘
부연	아인슈타인의 '일반 상대성 이론' → 자신의 예측을 수성의 움직임과 비교 → 추후 천문학적으로 검증됨

구문
• Early in the twentieth century, Einstein's General Theory of Relativity was tested astronomically, at first [by **comparison of** his theory's predictions **with** the observed motion of the planet Mercury], and then [through the successful prediction of the deflection of starlight {by the gravitational field of the Sun}].
: 첫 번째와 두 번째 [ ]는 각각 전치사 by와 through로 유도되는 전치사구이다. 「comparison of A with B」의 구조가 사용되어 'A와 B에 대한 비교'의 의미를 나타낸다. 두 번째 [ ] 안의 { }는 '~에 의한'의 의미를 나타내는 전치사구이다.

08
정답 ⑤

일벌들은 수정란을 생산하는 능력이 없는 암컷들이다. 일벌의 삶은 생물학적인 시간표에 의해 조절되는데, 그것은 벌집을 지배하는 심오한 수수께끼 중 하나이다. 그녀의 짧은 생애 동안, 그녀는 간호사, 밀랍 생산자, 벌집 건설자, 집 관리자, 식량을 구해 오는 자, 물을 가져오는 자, 문지기, 그리고 병사와 같은 많은 다양한 역할들을 한다. 그녀는 나이와 경험에 따라 이런 역할들 중 하나에서 다른 역할로 옮겨간다. 벌은 마치 고용인이 자산보다는 비용으로 여겨질 때까지, 연속적인 임금 인상과 승진으로 경험과 근속 기간을 보상받는 산업체의 근로자와 같다. 벌은 나이가 든다 해서 모욕을 받는 경우가 거의 없다. 개별적인 지위나 직업상의 배치가 아니라 효율성과 벌집의 요구가 일생에 걸쳐 죽을 때까지 그녀의 역할들을 결정한다.

해설
일벌들은 나이를 먹으면서 점차 다른 역할을 하게 되며, 효율성과 벌집의 요구에 의해 일련의 역할을 한 다음 생애를 마친다는 내용의 글이므로, 빈칸에 들어갈 말로는 ⑤ '생물학적인 시간표에 의해 조절되는'이 가장 적절하다.
① 그것의 영양 공급에 달려 있는
② 사회 연결망에 의해 지탱되는
③ 세 가지 주요 단계로 구성되는
④ 여왕벌의 명령을 따르는

TEXT FLOW

도입	일벌의 삶은 나이에 따라 조절됨
부연	일벌은 나이와 경험에 따라 다양한 역할을 함
재진술	일벌은 효율성과 벌집의 요구에 따라 일련의 역할을 하게 됨

구문
• A bee is like a worker in industry [who is rewarded for her experience and length of service with successive raises and promotions, {until the employee is considered a cost **rather than** an asset}].
: [ ]는 관계절로 선행사 a worker (in industry)를 수식한다. 부사절 { }에서 「A rather than B(B보다는 오히려 A)」 구문이 쓰였으며 A와 B는 명사로 병렬 구조를 이루고 있다.

09
정답 ③

'오디세이'라고 불리는 고대 서사시에서, 호머는 오디세우스라는 남자와 그의 아내인 페넬로페의 이야기를 해 준다. 오디세우스와 페넬로페는 서로 깊이 사랑한다. 어느 날, 오디세우스는 트로이 전쟁에 불려간다. 그가 오랫동안 돌아오지 않아서, 모든 사람이 그가 죽었다고 생각하고, 그들은 페넬로페에게 재혼하라고 강요한다. 남자들은 각각 자신들이 오디세우스에 못지않게 훌륭하다고 주장하면서 이곳저곳에서 오지만 페넬로페는 그들 모두를 거절한다. ('오디세이'는 그리스 시인인 호머의 작품으로 믿어지는데, 그는 전설적이거나 역사적인 영웅들에 대한 장편 서사시인 '일리아드'도 썼다.) 곧 모든 면에서 오디세우스에 못지않게 정말 훌륭한 한 베일에 싸인 이방인이 나타난다. 페넬로페에게는 다행스럽게도, 그 남자는 오랫동안 행방불명이었던 바로 그 오디세우스가 변장한 것으로 밝혀진다.

해설
'오디세이'의 전체 줄거리에 대한 내용이므로, '오디세이'가 호머의 작품으로 믿어지고 그가 '일리아드'도 썼다는 내용의 ③은 글의 전체 흐름과 관계가 없다.

발단	서로 깊이 사랑한 오디세우스와 페넬로페는 오디세우스가 전쟁에 불려가면서 헤어지게 됨
전개	오디세우스가 오래도록 돌아오지 않자 사람들은 그가 죽었다고 여김
발전	남자들이 페넬로페에게 재혼을 요구하며 찾아오지만 그녀는 모두 거절함
결말	페넬로페를 찾아온 베일에 싸인 이방인이 오디세우스 본인인 것으로 밝혀짐

구문

• Men come from far and wide, [each one claiming to be just as good as Odysseus] but Penelope rejects every one of them.

: [ ]는 분사구문으로, 주절의 주어(Men)와 분사구문의 주어(each one)가 달라서 분사(claiming) 앞에 주어를 밝혀 주었다.

10 정답 ⑤

위인설(偉人設)에 따르면, 리더로 태어난 사람은 항상 지도자가 될 것이지만, 특정 유전적 특성 없이 태어난 사람은 절대 리더가 될 수 없다. 이 이론은 19세기까지 널리 받아들여졌으며 왕족과 일반인의 신분 차이를 정당화하는 데 사용되었다. (C) 과거에는 왕실이나 귀족 가문에서 태어났다는 것은 여러분이 '명문가 출신', 즉 리더십 역할을 위해 유전적으로 필요한 것을 갖추고 있다는 것으로 정의되었다. 이 이론에 따르면 모든 뛰어난 리더는 동일한 목록의 특성을 가지고 있다고 가정해야 한다. 하지만 그런 목록은 실제로 존재하지 않는다. (B) 마하트마 간디, 윈스턴 처칠, 그리고 마틴 루서 킹을 생각해 보라. 그들이 같은 특성을 가지고 있을까? 물론 그렇지 않고 이들은 많은 점에서 서로 다르다. 물론 몇 가지 공통적인 특성은 존재하겠지만, 리더십을 위해 필수적이라고 할 수 있는 특성은 거의 없다. 이로 인해 새로운 리더십 이론이 개발되었는데, 그중 하나가 상황적 리더십 이론이다. (A) 이 견해에 따르면 리더는 유전적 특성의 결과로 부상하는 존재가 아니라 적시 적소에 있는 사람이다. 이러한 사람은 추종자들과 상황에 의존하여 자신들의 리더십 자리를 유지한다.

해설

리더의 특성은 유전적으로 타고난 것이라는 위인설을 설명하는 주어진 글 다음에, 과거에는 왕실이나 귀족 가문과 같은 명문가 출신에서 태어나면 이런 유전적 특징을 갖추고 있다고 정의되었다는 내용의 (C)가 오고, 위인설에 따르면 모든 뛰어난 리더는 동일한 특성을 가지고 있다고 가정해야 한다고 언급한 (C) 뒤에는, 간디, 처칠, 마틴 루서 킹과 같은 위인들이 실제로 같은 특성을 가졌는지에 대해 반문하며 상황적 리더십 이론을 소개하는 (B)가 이어져야 한다. 그리고 상황적 리더십 이론이 규정하는 리더의 모습을 설명하는 (A)가 마지막으로 오는 것이 글의 흐름상 가장 자연스럽다.

⊗ 매력적인 오답 주의!

② 주어진 글에서 위인설을 설명하며 genetic traits에 대해서 언급하는데, 이것을 (B)에서 간디, 처칠, 마틴 루서 킹과 같은 위인들이 identical traits를 가졌는지에 대해 질문하는 내용과 섣불리 연결 지어 주어진 글에서 (B)로 이어지는 것으로 오인하면 고를 수 있는 오답이다.

도입	위인설에 따르면 리더십은 타고난 유전적 특성에서 비롯되고 동일한 특성이 있다고 가정해야 함
전환	가정과 달리 모든 리더가 동일한 유전적 특성이 있지는 않으며, 위인설의 대안으로 상황적 리더십이 등장함
부연	상황적 리더십에 따르면 리더는 적시 적소에 있는 사람이며 추종자들과 상황에 의존하여 리더십을 유지함

구문

• This has led to the development of new leadership theories, [one of which is situational leadership theory].

: [ ]는 new leadership theories를 부가적으로 설명하는 관계절이다.

• In the past, [being born into a royal or aristocratic family] defined you as [{having "blue blood,"} that is, {being genetically equipped for a leadership role}].

: 첫 번째 [ ]는 문장의 주어로 사용된 동명사구이다. 두 번째 [ ]는 전치사 as의 목적어로 사용된 동명사구이며, 그 안의 두 번째 { }는 첫 번째 { }를 구체적으로 설명하는 동명사구이다.

11 정답 ②

도롱뇽과 불가사리와 같은 몇몇 동물들은 신체의 일부를 잃으면 그 부위를 재생시킬 수 있다. 그것이 바로 생물학자인 Michael Abrams가 어린 무럼해파리의 8개의 팔 중 2개를 제거했을 때 일어날 것으로 예상했던 것이다. 그러나 Abrams가 그 실험을 확인했을 때, 그는 믿기 어려운 것을 발견했다. 팔을 재생시키는 대신, 그 해파리는 남아 있는 그것의 팔들을 다시 배치해서 몸을 빙 둘러 같은 거리의 간격으로 떨어져 있게 했다. 어린 무럼해파리에게, 혹은 성체에게, 좌우 대칭적인 것은 움직임과 먹이를 먹는 데 대단히 중요하다. Abrams의 실험 동물이 그것을 성취하기 위해 근육이 그것의 몸에서 수축했는데, 그것은 남아 있는 팔들이 다시 고른 간격으로 떨어지게 될 때까지 그것들을 밀고 당겼다. 과학자들은 과학에 완전히 새로운 현상과 우연히 마주쳤으며, 그들은 그것을 '대칭화'라고 부른다.

해설

주어진 문장은 생물학자인 Michael Abrams가 이전에는 알려지지 않았던 실험 결과를 얻었다는 내용이므로, 어린 무럼해파리가 잃은 팔을 재생시키는 것이 아니라 남은 것으로 대칭화하는 내용이 나오기 전인 ②에 들어가는 것이 가장 적절하다.

도입	잃어버린 신체 부위를 재생시키는 도롱뇽과 불가사리
전개	무럼해파리의 팔을 잘라 내는 실험 소개
발전	무럼해파리는 신체 재생 대신 남아 있는 팔들을 재배치해서 같은 간격으로 떨어지게 함
결론	'대칭화' 현상의 우연한 발견

구문

• **For Abrams' test animal** to achieve that, muscles contracted in its body, [**which** pushed and pulled the remaining arms until they were once again evenly spaced].

: For 다음에 나온 Abrams' test animal은 to achieve의 의미상 주어

이고, [ ]에서 계속적 용법의 관계대명사 which는 의미상 and it[that]으로 생각할 수 있다.

12

1956년에, 한 오래된 대형 선박이 이상한 모양의 금속 상자 한 짐을 날랐는데, 그것들은 컨테이너였다. 이 기술은 세계 상업을 극적인 방식으로 바꾸는 데 도움을 주었다. 컨테이너의 발명 전에는, 상품들이 근로자들에 의해 다루어졌다. 각각의 상품은 특정한 포장재들, 상자들, 그리고 근로자들을 필요로 했다. 대조적으로, 컨테이너는 기계들에 의해 운반되고 다뤄질 수 있는 규격화된 금속 상자였다. 컨테이너 덕분에, 상인들은 고도로 자동화된 상품 운반 체계를 최소한의 비용과 혼란만 들이고도 사용할 수 있었다. 항구들과 경제가 모두 극적으로 변모했다. 1956년 이전에, 지역 시장들은 대개 소규모의 지역 산업체에 의해 물건을 공급받았다. 오늘날에는 엄격히 현지의 물건만 사고파는 시장을 찾는 것이 어렵다. 컨테이너가 있어서, 사람들은 중국, 싱가포르, 또는 베트남처럼 먼 곳에서 극도로 낮은 가격에 생산된 다양한 종류의 소비재를 사용할 수 있게 되었다.
➡ 컨테이너의 발명과 사용은 운송의 <u>효율성</u>을 높였고 동시에 경제를 <u>세계화했다</u>.

해설
기계로 운반될 수 있는 규격화된 컨테이너를 사용함으로써 화물 운반 비용을 절감하고 자동화가 가능해졌으며 이에 힘입어 세계 무역이 발달했다는 내용의 글이므로, 요약문의 빈칸 (A)에는 efficiency(효율성)가, (B)에는 globalized(세계화했다)가 들어가는 것이 가장 적절하다.
① 비용 – 세계화했다
② 비용 – 불경기로 만들었다
③ 안전 – 불경기로 만들었다
⑤ 효율성 – 고정시켰다

TEXT FLOW

도입	1956년에 최초로 화물 운송에 컨테이너가 사용됨
전개	기계로 운반하고 다룰 수 있는 컨테이너가 세계 경제를 변모시켰음
결론	컨테이너 덕분에 세계 무역이 발달됨

구문
• With containers, people gained access to [a wide range of consumer goods {produced at extremely low prices as far away as China, Singapore or Vietnam}].
: 전치사 to의 목적어는 명사구인 [ ]이다. 그 안의 { }는 과거분사구로 a wide range of consumer goods를 수식한다.

13-14

시간적 순서는 사건이 시간 순서대로 발생하는 순서이다. 2시에 발생한 사건이 3시에 발생한 사건에 선행한다. 어떤 원인이 시간상 그것의 결과 이후에 발생할 수 없다는 것은 사실이다. 오늘 비가 온다고 해서 지난달 농작물에 도움이 되지 않으며, 다음 주 토요일에 치는 홈런이 지난주 경기에서 이길 수 있게 만들지 못한다. 모든 원인이 결과보다 선행하는 것은 아니며, 일부는 결과와 동시에 발생하는 것도 사실이다. 예를 들어, 야구공이 창문에 부딪히면 창문이 깨지지만 부딪히는 것과 깨지는 것은 동시에 일어난다. 그러나 한 사

건이 다른 사건에 선행하기 때문에 첫 번째 사건이 두 번째 사건을 유발한다고 생각할 마음이 나기 쉬운데, 특히 이러한 사건이 매우 빈번하게 쌍을 이룰 때 더욱 그렇다.
사다리 밑을 걷거나 검은 고양이가 여러분이 가던 길을 가로지르도록 두면 불운이 온다거나, 행운의 양말을 신으면 여러분의 팀이 승리하도록 돕는다던가, 사랑이나 우정에 관한 이메일을 전달하지 않으면 불운이 온다는 등의 전형적인 미신을 생각해 보라. 이러한 미신은 종종 현실을 통제하려는 인간의 욕망에서 비롯된다. 만약 여러분이 게임에서 이기면 다음 게임에서 이기는 데 도움을 받기 위해 사용할 수 있는 원인을 찾기 시작할 수 있다. "오늘 참으로 공교롭게도 내가 빨간 양말을 신었는데, 이것이 우리가 승리한 이유인지도 몰라!" 여러분이 다음 경기에서도 같은 양말을 신고 이긴다면 미신이 확인된 것이고 빨간 양말을 신으면 경기에서 더 잘할 수 있다고 생각하는 것을 망설일(→ 내키게 할) 수도 있다.

해설
13 한 사건이 시간적 순서에 의해 다른 사건에 선행하게 되는 것이 당연한데, 그것을 한 사건이 다른 사건을 유발한다고 잘못 이해하기 쉬우며, 이런 생각의 오류가 생활 속에서 다양한 미신을 만들어 낸다는 내용의 글이다. 따라서 글의 제목으로 가장 적절한 것은 ① '시간적 순서를 인과 관계로 오인하는 것이 미신을 만드는 방식'이다.
② 미래는 쓰이지 않았다: 미신에서 벗어나기
③ 상관관계 대 인과 관계: 그 차이를 이해하기
④ 시간에 대한 정신의 인식을 왜곡하는 요인들
⑤ 미신이 정서적 안정을 제공하는 이유

14 빨간 양말을 신은 것이 승리한 이유라고 생각하게 된 상황에서, 다음 경기에도 같은 양말을 신고 이긴다면 미신이 확인된 것이라는 내용으로 보아, 빨간 양말을 신으면 경기에서 더 잘할 수 있다고 자연스럽게 생각하게 된다는 것이 문맥상 자연스럽다. 따라서 (e) hesitant(망설일)를 tempted(내키게 할)와 같은 단어로 바꿔야 한다.

⊗ 매력적인 오답 주의!

13 ② 본문에서 시간적 순서를 인과 관계로 오인하는 것으로 생기는 미신이 언급되는데, 미신에서 벗어나는 것을 글의 중심 내용으로 오인하면 고를 수 있는 오답이다.

14 ④ 시간적 순서를 인과 관계로 오인하여 생기는 미신이 결국 현실을 통제하려는 인간의 욕망에서 비롯된 것이라는 내용을 잘 이해하지 못하면, 오히려 현실을 통제할 수 없어서 미신에 빠진다고 잘못 생각하여 고를 수 있는 오답이다.

TEXT FLOW

도입	모든 사건은 시간적 순서에 따라 발생하므로 결과가 원인보다 시간적으로 선행할 수 없음
주제	한 사건이 다른 사건보다 앞서 일어나서 인과 관계가 성립된다고 오인하기 쉬움
부연 1	이러한 오인이 여러 전형적인 미신을 만들어 냄
부연 2	이러한 미신은 현실을 통제하려는 인간의 욕망에서 비롯됨

구문
• If you win a game, you might begin looking for some cause [that you can use {to help you win the next game}].
: [ ]는 some cause를 수식하는 관계절이다. { }는 목적의 의미를 나타내는 부사적 용법의 to부정사구이다.

• [If you win the next game {wearing the same socks}],

you might be tempted to think [{that the superstition is confirmed} and {that ⟨wearing your red socks⟩ causes you to play better}].
: 첫 번째 [ ]는 조건의 부사절이고, 그 안의 { }는 부사절의 주어인 you의 부수적인 동작을 설명하는 분사구문이다. 두 번째 [ ]는 think의 목적어인데, 그 안에 명사절인 두 개의 { }가 and로 연결되어 있다. ⟨ ⟩는 명사절인 세 번째 { }의 주어 역할을 하는 동명사구이다.

GRAMMAR REVIEW
본문 33쪽

1 look	2 trying	3 producing
4 began	5 determine	6 remarry
7 which	8 to happen	9 automated
10 tempting		

1 문장의 주어는 We이고 and에 의해 두 개의 동사구가 병렬 구조로 연결되어 이어지고 있으므로 복수형 동사 look이 적절하다.

2 「from A to B」 구문이 사용되고 있는데, 전치사인 to 이하에서 두 개의 동명사구가 and를 중심으로 대등하게 연결되어야 하므로 동명사 trying을 써야 한다.

3 전치사 in의 목적어이며 능동의 의미이므로 동명사 producing을 써야 한다.

4 주어 Muslims와 연결되는 술어 동사가 필요하므로 과거 동사 began이 적절하다.

5 Efficiency and hive demands and not personal status or job assignment를 주어로 하는 술어 동사 자리이므로 determine이 적절하다.

6 demand(요구하다)의 목적어로 that절이 와서 주어인 Penelope 다음에 조동사 should가 생략된 것으로 볼 수 있으므로 동사원형인 remarry가 적절하다.

7 두 개의 절이 접속사가 없이 콤마(,)로 연결되어 있으므로, 접속사와 대명사의 역할을 동시에 할 수 있는 관계대명사 which가 적절하다.

8 expected의 목적어가 필요하므로 to부정사구를 이루는 to happen을 써야 한다.

9 뒤에 이어지는 명사 system을 수식하며 수동의 의미이므로 과거분사 automated를 써야 한다.

10 문맥상 어떤 사람이 무언가를 하고자 하는 마음을 느끼는 것이 아니라, 내용상의 주어인 to부정사구를 하고자 하는 마음이 생기는 것이므로 현재분사 tempting이 적절하다.

하프 모의고사   04회

01 ④	02 ⑤	03 ①	04 ⑤	05 ④
06 ④	07 ③	08 ④	09 ④	10 ③
11 ②	12 ⑤	13 ③	14 ③	

01
정답 ④

밤늦게 Dave는 자신의 배에 있는 모든 것이 괜찮은지 확인하러 물가로 내려갔다. 그가 자신의 오두막으로 이어지는 작은 오솔길로 돌아올 때, 그는 갑자기 쾅하는 소리를 들었다. 등골이 오싹해졌다. 천천히, 그는 그것을 향해 걸어가 그 방향으로 손전등을 향하게 했다. 빛은 오두막 앞의 곰 한 마리를 비추었고, 그것은 남은 음식을 찾아 쓰레기통을 주의 깊게 뒤지고 있었다. 그는 자신의 자동차로 가서 시동을 걸고 천천히 그 동물을 향해 몰았다. 전조등이 그 곰에게 집중되었지만, 그것은 전혀 개의치 않는 것 같았다. 그런 다음 Dave는 그 곰이 마침내 도망갈 때까지 경적을 울렸다. 그 동물이 어둠 속으로 사라진 뒤, Dave는 깊게 숨을 내쉬었다. 간신히 오두막에 들어가 문을 잠근 후, 그는 바닥에 털썩 주저앉았다.

해설
밤늦게 오두막 앞 쓰레기통을 뒤지러 온 곰과 마주쳐 겁에 질렸지만, 차의 경적을 울려 곰을 쫓아내고 문을 잠근 후 깊게 숨을 내쉬며 바닥에 주저앉았다고 했으므로, Dave의 심경 변화로는 ④ '겁에 질린 → 안도한'이 가장 적절하다.
① 충격을 받은 → 자랑스러운
② 궁금한 → 자신감 있는
③ 만족한 → 짜증이 난
⑤ 혼란스러운 → 동정하는

TEXT FLOW

시간 순서/사건 전개에 따른 흐름:
Dave는 밤늦게 배를 확인하고 오두막으로 돌아오는 길에 쾅하는 소리를 들음 → 오싹함을 느끼고 손전등을 비춘 후 그것이 곰인 것을 알게 됨 → 자동차에 타서 전조등을 비추고 경적을 울려 곰을 쫓아냄 → 간신히 오두막에 들어와 문을 잠근 후 바닥에 주저앉음

구문
• The headlights were focused on the bear, [which **seemed not to be bothered** in the least].
: [ ]는 the bear를 부연 설명하는 관계절이다. seem은 뒤에 to부정사가 오는데, 수동의 의미이므로 「to be+p.p.」 형태인 to be bothered로 쓰였다.

02
정답 ⑤

다른 사람들이 내재적으로 동기부여되고 싶어 한다는 것, 즉 그들이 자신이 좋아하는 사람들과 함께 흥미롭고 의미 있는 일을 하고 싶어 한다는 사실을 깨닫지 못하면 가족, 친구, 그리고 동료와의 관계에 방해가 될 수 있다. 부모가 자녀의 학교에서의 내재적 동기 추구를 의미 있고 삶을 변화시키는 경험

을 가지는 것보다 높은 성적에 신경 쓴다고 생각하여 과소평가하면 그들의 관계를 해칠 수 있다. 그리고 직장에서 고용주가 직원의 내재적 동기를 과소평가하고 동시에 직원이 고용주의 내재적 동기를 과소평가하면 조직의 위계 전반에 걸쳐 상호 작용이 피해를 입는다. 한 연구는 구직자들이 구직 면접에서 내재적 동기를 충분히 강조하지 않는다는 점을 밝혀냈다. 그 이유는 구직자들은 내재적으로 동기부여가 되기를 원하지만, 그들은 채용자가 내재적 동기에 대한 표현에 얼마나 관심이 있는지, 따라서 얼마나 감명을 받는지 과소평가하기 때문이다. 구직자들은 고용주가 (성공을 위한) 사다리를 오르고 싶어 하는 사람을 찾고 있다고 생각하여, 그 직업이 얼마나 의미 있게 느껴질 수도 있을지에 대해 언급하지 않는다.

해설
다른 사람이 내재적으로 동기부여가 되고 싶어 한다는 점을 과소평가했을 때는 가족, 친구, 동료와의 관계에 방해가 되며, 고용주와 직원이 서로의 내재적 동기를 과소평가하면 관계에 있어서 중요한 상호 작용이 피해를 입는다는 내용의 글이다. 따라서 글의 요지로 가장 적절한 것은 ⑤이다.

⊗ **매력적인 오답 주의!**
② 글의 중반부에 고용주와 직원이 서로의 내재적 동기를 과소평가한다는 내용이 언급되는데, 이를 외적인 보상과 잘못 연결 지으면 고를 수 있는 오답이다.

TEXT FLOW

주제	다른 사람이 내재적으로 동기부여가 되고 싶어 한다는 점을 깨닫지 못하면 관계에 방해가 될 수 있음
예시 1	부모가 자녀의 내재적 동기 추구를 과소평가하면 관계를 해칠 수 있음
예시 2	직원과 고용주가 서로의 내재적 동기를 과소평가하면 조직 내 상호 작용이 피해를 입음
부연	채용자들의 내재적 동기에 관한 관심의 정도를 과소평가하여 구직자들이 내재적 동기를 충분히 강조하지 않음

구문
• [When a parent undervalues a child's quest for intrinsic motivation in school, {assuming ⟨she cares for high grades **rather than** having a meaningful, life-changing experience⟩}], it can undermine their relationship.
: [ ]는 시간의 부사절이고, 그 안의 { }는 부사절의 주어인 a parent의 부수적인 동작을 설명하는 분사구문이다. ⟨ ⟩는 assuming의 목적어 역할을 하는 명사절이며 전치사 for의 목적어로 high grades와 having ~ experience가 rather than에 의해 병렬 연결되어 있다.

• The reason: [although candidates want to be intrinsically motivated], they underestimate [how much recruiters care **about**, and therefore are impressed **by**, {expressions of intrinsic motivation}].
: 첫 번째 [ ]는 양보의 부사절이다. 두 번째 [ ]는 underestimate의 목적어 역할을 하는 명사절이고, 그 안의 { }는 전치사 about과 by의 목적어이다.

03
정답 ①

지난 20년간 신체의 염증이 막힌 동맥의 축적에 주요한 역할을 한다는 점이 동의되어 왔다. 이것을 입증하기 위해, Richard Watt와 그의 팀은 스코틀

랜드 건강 조사에 참가한 11,000명 이상의 성인들로부터 얻은 자료를 분석했다. 그 결과는 그들의 구강 건강 행동이 대체로 좋았다는 것을 보여 주었는데, 62%의 참가자들이 6개월마다 치과를 방문한다고 말했으며, 71%가 매일 두 번 양치질을 한다고 보고했다. 일단 그 자료가 사회 계층, 비만, 흡연, 그리고 심장병 가족력과 같은 확인된 심장병의 위험 요인들에 의해 조정되고 나자, 저자들은 비록 전체적인 위험도가 꽤 낮긴 했지만, 양치질을 덜 자주 한다고 보고한 사람들이 하루에 두 번 양치질을 한 사람과 비교했을 때 70% 더 높은 심장병의 위험을 갖고 있다는 점을 발견했다.

해설
양치질을 덜 자주 하는 사람들이 심장병과 관련해 더 높은 위험도를 갖게 된다는 내용의 글이므로, 글의 제목으로는 ① '깨끗한 구강: 건강한 심장으로 가는 길'이 가장 적절하다.
② 잦은 양치질을 둘러싼 근거 없는 믿음
③ 양치질이 어떻게 긴장을 완화시키는가
④ 구강 건강: 경제적 지위의 척도
⑤ 세균: 심장을 강화하는 여러분의 지지자

TEXT FLOW

주제	신체의 염증과 막힌 동맥의 축적이 관련 있다는 의견이 있음
근거	11,000명 이상의 성인들의 건강 조사 결과 분석
결론	양치질을 덜 자주 하는 사람들이 심장병 위험이 더 높음

구문
• [Once the data were adjusted for established heart disease risk factors such as social class, obesity, smoking and family history of heart disease], the authors found [that individuals {who reported less frequent toothbrushing} had a 70% higher risk of heart disease compared to individuals {who brushed their teeth twice a day}, although the overall risk remained quite low].
: 첫 번째 [ ]는 조건의 부사절이다. 두 번째 [ ]는 found의 목적어이며, 두 개의 관계절 { }는 각각 앞의 선행사 individuals를 수식한다.

04
정답 ⑤

위 도표는 2021년 환자 안전을 위한 적절한 직원 규모 수준과 업무 속도에 대한 7개국 병원 의료 분야 종사자들의 인식을 세 가지 직군(관리직, 의사, 간호사)으로 분류하여 보여 준다. 7개국 중 6개국에서 직원 규모 수준과 업무 속도가 적절하다고 응답한 관리 직원의 비율은 의사의 비율보다 높았다. 도표에 제시된 국가 중 콜롬비아가 직원 규모 수준과 업무 속도가 적절하다고 응답한 간호사 비율이 가장 높았고, 비율이 가장 낮은 국가는 벨기에였다. 튀르키예, 미국, 그리고 콜롬비아에서는 40%가 넘는 의사가 직원 규모 수준과 업무 속도가 환자 안전을 위해 적절하다고 응답했다. 포르투갈, 폴란드, 그리고 한국에서는 의사보다 간호사가 더 큰 비율로 직원 규모 수준과 업무 속도가 적절하다고 응답했다. 7개국 중에서 벨기에가 직원 규모 수준과 업무 속도가 적절하다고 응답한 의사의 비율이 가장 낮았으며, 35%를 조금 넘었다.

해설
7개국 중에서 직원 규모 수준과 업무 속도가 적절하다고 응답한 의사의 비율이 가장 낮았던 국가는 34%를 기록한 포르투갈과 폴란드이므로, 도표의 내용과 일치하지 않는 것은 ⑤이다.

구문

- In six of the seven countries, [the percentage of management staff {who responded that staffing levels and work pace were adequate}] **was** higher than that of physicians.

: [ ]는 문장의 주어이고, 그 안의 { }는 management staff를 수식하는 관계절이다. 주어의 핵심어가 percentage이므로 술어 동사로 단수형 동사 was가 쓰였다.

05
정답 ④

현실적으로 그것이 불가능할 때 상황이 달라져야 한다고 불평하는 것은 감정적 에너지의 낭비이며, 세상의 불완전한 상태에 대처하지 않으려는 유아적인 마음이다. 그러한 수용은 순순히 이루어지지 않아도 된다. 예를 들어, 사랑의 과정은 순조롭게 진행되는 경우가 드물다. 그렇다고 해서 우리가 사랑에 대해서 전혀 고민하지 말아야 한다거나, 혹은 일이 잘못되면 '그럴 줄 알았어!'라고 하며 어깨를 으쓱하면서 그냥 외면하고 떠나야 한다는 뜻인가? 물론 아니다. 불완전한 상태에서 일을 해 나가는 것이 성숙한 행동이다. 정치 개혁도 마찬가지이다. 우리는 그것을 포기하지도 않고, 모든 것이 눈물로 끝날 수밖에 없다는 필연성을 받아들이지도 않는다. 오히려 우리는 정치의 한계를 충분히 인식하며 일을 해 나가는데, 좋은 통치가 결코 완벽한 통치가 될 수 없으며, 그리고 그것이 세상의 모든 해악을 고칠 수도 없다는 것을 알고 있다. 이것은 하기 쉬운(→ 어려운) 일인데, 정치에 끌리는 많은 사람이 본능적으로 이상주의자이고, 이들은 그 외에 다른 것이 된다는 것은 포기하는 것이며 신념을 버리는 것이라고 두려워하기 때문이다. 이는 세상에 대한 단순한 흑백 논리적 관점에 기반한 두려움이며, 그 관점 자체가 잘못된 불평으로 이어지는 일종의 도덕적 왜곡의 원천이다.

해설

세상만사와 마찬가지로 정치 개혁도 불완전한 상태에서 일을 해 나가는 것이 성숙한 행동인데, 정치에 끌리는 많은 사람이 본능적으로 이상주의자이기 때문에 본인의 이상이 아닌 다른 것이 되는 것에 대해 신념을 버리는 것이라고 두려워하는 경향이 있어, 정치의 한계를 충분히 인식하며 일을 해 나가기가 쉽지 않을 것임을 추론할 수 있다. 따라서 ④ easy(쉬운)를 hard(어려운)와 같은 단어로 바꿔야 한다.

TEXT FLOW

주제	현실적으로 상황이 달라지는 것이 불가능할 때 불평하는 것은 세상의 불완전한 상태에 대처하지 않으려는 유아적인 마음임
예시	사랑의 과정은 순조롭지 않으나 그렇다고 사랑에 대해서 고민하지 않거나 그냥 외면하는 것은 잘못된 행동임
전환	정치 개혁도 세상만사와 마찬가지로 불완전한 상태에서 일을 해 나가야 하는 과정임
부연	현실과 타협하는 것을 신념을 버리는 것으로 보는 것은 잘못된 불평으로 이어짐

구문

- [To complain {that things ought to be different ⟨when they can never realistically be so⟩}] is a waste of emotional energy, an infantile unwillingness [to deal with the imperfection of the world].

: 첫 번째 [ ]는 문장의 주어 역할을 하는 to부정사구이다. 그 안의 { }는 complain의 목적어 역할을 하는 명사절이며, ⟨ ⟩는 시간의 부사절이다.

두 번째 [ ]는 an infantile unwillingness를 수식하는 형용사적 용법의 to부정사구이다.

- This is a fear [based on a simplistic black-and-white view of the world], [which is itself a source of the kind of moral distortion {which leads to wrong complaint}].

: 첫 번째 [ ]는 a fear를 수식하는 분사구이다. 두 번째 [ ]는 앞 절의 a simplistic black-and-white view of the world를 부가적으로 설명하는 관계절이고, 그 안의 { }는 moral distortion을 수식하는 관계절이다.

06
정답 ④

큰 집안에서 그렇듯, 닭기러기류의 가문에는 몇몇 화려한 구성원들과 몇몇 수수하게 생긴 구성원들이 있다. 흥미롭게도, 최근의 연구에 의하면 가장 화려한 닭기러기류의 수컷들이 가장 좋은 유전자들을 후손에게 전달하고 있지 않을 수 있다고 한다. 진화생물학자인 Judith Mank는 "장식들, 아름다운 색들과 큰 꼬리들이 가장 몸이 좋은 수컷들에 의해 소유된다는 많은 이론들이 있습니다. 우리는 그 이론을 시험해 보고 있었습니다."라고 말한다. Mank와 그녀의 동료들은 화려하고 수수한 여섯 종의 새들로부터 유전 물질들을 분석했다. 그들은 화려하게 생긴 새들에게서 급격하지 않은 유전자 돌연변이들에 의해 표시되는 빠르게 진화하는 게놈을 발견했는데, 그것은 열등한 특징을 유발할 수 있다. 반면, 수수하게 생긴 새들에게서는 그것을 발견하지 못했다. 암컷들이 화려하게 생긴 수컷들과 짝짓기를 하게 되면, 그런 유전적인 결함이 전달된다. 그것은 장래에 그 종의 전망에 영향을 미칠 수 있다.

해설

화려하게 생긴 수컷들이 열등한 특징을 유발하는 유전자 변이를 겪고 있으며, 이러한 유전적 결함이 후손에게 전해질 수도 있다는 내용의 글이므로, 빈칸에 들어갈 말로는 ④ '가장 좋은 유전자들을 후손에게 전달하고'가 가장 적절하다.
① 배경에 섞여 들어가고
② 암컷들에 대한 자신들의 관심을 보여 주고
③ 열등한 경쟁자들을 배제하고
⑤ 자신들의 색을 다른 것들과 구별하고

TEXT FLOW

주제	화려하게 생긴 닭기러기류 수컷들이 가장 좋은 유전자들을 후손에게 전달하는 것은 아님
전개	화려하게 생긴 새들은 유전자 돌연변이를 겪는데 이것은 열등한 특징을 유발할 수 있음
부연	화려하게 생긴 수컷들의 자손은 유전적 결함을 갖게 될 수 있음

구문

- In the gorgeous-looking birds they found [a rapidly evolving genome {marked by mild gene mutations}, {which can cause inferior characteristics}]; in the plain-looking **ones** they didn't find **that**.

: [ ]는 동사 found의 목적어로 쓰인 명사구이다. 그 안의 첫 번째 { }는 과거분사구로 a rapidly evolving genome을 수식하고, 두 번째 { }는 관계절로 역시 a rapidly evolving genome을 부연 설명한다. ones는 birds를, that은 a rapidly evolving genome을 가리킨다.

07
정답 ③

우리는 육체를 가지고 있고, 다른 사람들과의 사회적 관계에 의존하며, 우리의 삶에서 의미를 찾아야 한다. 물리적 본질, 사회적 관계, 그리고 의미의 이러한 혼합은 주로 <u>그것이 장소와 공간에서의 활동을 포함하기</u> 때문에 이해가 가능하다. 장소는 우리 '자아'를 형성하는 데 있어 활성제가 된다. '자아'와 장소 사이에는 상호의 (또는 변증법적) 관계가 있다. 우리는 우선 우리의 '자아' 형성에 영향을 미치는 부모님의 집과 고향에서 어린아이로서 삶을 시작한다. 하지만 그러고 나서 우리는 공부를 하기 위해 또는 세계 여행을 시작하기 위해 다른 장소로 이동할지도 모른다. 우리에게는 자신의 '뿌리'가 있지만, '자아'의 발달은 새로운 장소에서의 새로운 경험을 통해 영향을 받는다. 어느 정도 우리는 또한 우리가 오게 된 장소들, 특히 우리 주변의 사회생활, 친구, 연인, 틀림없이 다른 사람들에 대한 '의미', 그리고 때로는 물리적인 구조에도 영향을 미친다. 만약 우리가 농부, 목수, 또는 정치가로 종사한다면 분명히 그러하다.

해설
부모님의 집과 고향이라는 장소에서 어린아이로서 삶을 시작하고, 다른 장소로 이동하여 공부 또는 여행이라는 활동을 하며, 새로운 장소에서 새로운 경험(활동)을 함으로써 자아의 발달이 영향을 받는다는 내용이므로, 빈칸에 들어갈 말로 가장 적절한 것은 ③ '그것이 장소와 공간에서의 활동을 포함하기'이다.
① 우리 모두는 살 수 있는 안전한 장소를 필요로 하기
② 공적인 공간이 더 안전해지고 있기
④ 사회적 관계가 중립적 공간을 안식처로 바꾸기
⑤ 장소와 공간의 구별이 중요하기

TEXT FLOW

도입	우리는 육체를 가지고 있고, 사회적 관계에 의존하며, 삶에서 의미를 찾음
	↓
	이러한 물리적 본질(육체), 사회적 관계, 의미의 혼합은 장소와 공간에서의 활동을 포함하므로 이해 가능함
주제	'자아'와 장소 사이에는 상호 관계가 있음
예시	고향이나 공부 또는 여행을 위해 이동한 장소 등에서 상호 영향을 받게 됨

구문
• [We have a physical body], [we are dependent on social relations with others], and [we need to find a meaning with our lives].
: 세 개의 절 [ ]가 and로 병렬 연결되어 문장을 구성하고 있다.

• But then we may move to another place [to study or start traveling in the world].
: [ ]는 목적의 의미를 나타내는 부사적 용법의 to부정사구이다.

08
정답 ④

코끼리 세계에서 뭔가 잘못되었다는 첫 번째 신호는 나이가 많은 집단 구성원이 없다는 것이다. 자연 상태의 수명이 거뜬히 50년이나 60년까지 가는 종에서, 엄니를 얻으려는 밀렵꾼들의 그 동물들에 대한 도살은 아프리카코끼리의 나이 중간값을 35.9세까지 끌어내렸다. 밀렵에서 간신히 살아남은 동물들은 고아가 될 가능성이 있으며, 더 이상은 모계 지도자가 없는 산산조각 난 가족 단위에 속하게 된다. 지도자가 없는 이러한 집단들은 무리를 짓는 경향이 있는데, 아마도 원시 시대의 인간들에 대항해 자신들을 지키기 위해 집단으로 행동하던 그들의 본능에 의지하는 것 같다. 과거의 시대에, 이러한 집합은 일시적이었고, 위험이 지나면 코끼리들은 흩어졌다. (주로 아프리카 남부에서 아프리카코끼리의 일부 개체군이 안정적이며 확대되고 있기는 하지만, 다른 지역에서 숫자가 계속 줄어들고 있는데, 특히 아프리카 중부와 아프리카 동부의 일부 지역에서 그러하다.) 그러나, 코끼리들이 끊임없는 압박을 받고 있는 현대의 아프리카에서 그 집단들은 더 이상 헤어지지 않는다.

해설
아프리카코끼리가 집단을 이루고 그 집단이 서로 흩어지지 않은 채 유지되는 상황과 그 이유를 설명하고 있는 글이다. 따라서 아프리카코끼리의 지역별 개체수에 관해 언급하고 있는 ④는 글의 전체 흐름과 관계가 없다.

TEXT FLOW

도입	코끼리의 세계에서 나이가 많은 집단 구성원이 없다는 문제점이 있음
원인	엄니를 얻으려는 코끼리 도살로 코끼리들의 중간 나이가 낮아짐
전개	지도자 없이 살아남은 코끼리들이 본능에 의해 무리를 지음
결과	현대의 아프리카코끼리는 집단을 이루고 있음

구문
• In a species [whose wild longevity is easily 50 or 60 years], [poachers slaughtering the animals for their tusks] has driven the median age of the African elephant down to 35.9 years.
: 첫 번째 [ ]는 a species를 수식하는 관계절이고, 두 번째 [ ]는 문장의 주어인 동명사구로, poachers는 slaughtering의 의미상 주어이다.

09
정답 ④

우리가 자신의 믿음에 대한 편향과 자신의 직관에 대한 맹목적인 신뢰의 힘을 제어하기를 원한다면, 우리는 믿음에 대한 고수라는 심리적 현상을 인식해야 한다. 일단 우리가 뭔가를 믿는다고 결심했다면, 우리는 그것의 부당성을 증명하는 증거 앞에서도 그것을 계속 믿는 경향이 있을 것이다. (C) 1979년에, 심리학자인 Charles Lord와 그의 동료들은 믿음을 변화시키는 것이 얼마나 어려운지를 보여 주는 고전적인 연구를 제시했다. 그들은 사형에 대해 반대되는 견해를 가진 사람들을 연구했다. (A) 그들은 양쪽 집단에 모두 두 세트의 연구 결과를 제공했는데, 한 세트는 사형이 범죄를 단념시킨다는 주장을 지지하는 것이었고, 다른 세트는 그 입장을 논박하는 것이었다. 실험 대상자들은 결국 자신들의 원래의 믿음을 지지하는 연구에 더 깊은 인상을 받았다. (B) 따라서, 그 쟁점에 대한 더 주의 깊은 고려로 이어지는 대신에 양쪽 입장에 대한 연구의 혼합은 사형에 찬성하는 파와 반대파 집단들이 자신들의 원래 신념을 강화시켰다는 것을 보여 주었다.

해설
주어진 글은 우리가 무언가를 믿기로 하면 그 믿음을 고수하는 경향이 있다는 내용이다. 이어서 이를 뒷받침하는 연구 사례를 제시하는 내용인 (C)가 오고, 그 연구에서 실험 대상들에게 각각 사형 제도에 대해 찬성하는 연구 결과와 반대하는 연구 결과를 제시했을 때 그들의 반응에 관한 내용이 언급된 (A)가 와야 한다. 마지막으로 결국 실험 대상자들이 자신들의 믿음을 굳건히 하는 경향을 보였다는 실험 결과가 드러나는 (B)가 이어지는 것이 글의 흐름상 가장 자연스럽다.

주제	우리는 자신의 믿음을 고수하려는 경향이 있음
근거	사형에 대해 상반되는 견해를 가진 양쪽 집단을 대상으로 실험을 실시함
결론	자신들의 원래 믿음을 지지하는 연구에 공감하는 것이 관찰됨

구문

• Thus, **instead of** leading to a more mindful consideration of the issue, the mix of studies on both sides showed [that {the pro- and anti-death-penalty groups} strengthened their original convictions].
: instead of는 '~ 대신에'를 뜻하는 전치사구로 뒤에 동명사구가 이어진다. [ ]는 showed의 목적어인 명사절로, 그 안의 { }가 명사절의 주어이다.

10
정답 ③

1980년대 프로 골퍼 Jack Nicklaus가 Grand Cayman 섬의 골프 코스 설계를 맡도록 고용되었을 때 그는 난제에 직면했다. 폭이 6마일이고 길이가 22마일에 불과한 이 섬은 너무 작아서 표준 크기의 골프 코스를 위한 충분한 공간을 제공할 수 없었다. Nicklaus와 그의 팀은 이 문제를 해결하기 위한 첫 번째 시도로 서로 다른 티에서 두 번 플레이할 수 있는 아홉 홀 코스를 영리하게 설계했다. 그럼에도 불구하고 골퍼들은 스윙을 짧게 할 수 없었고, 공은 너무 쉽게 주변 수면으로 날아갔다. 이 시점에서 Nicklaus는 코스의 크기에 계속 집중하는 대신 '골프공이 멀리 날아가지 않는다면 어떨까?'라고 문제를 재구성했다. Nicklaus와 MacGregor Golf Company는 많은 시험과 연구 끝에 제한적으로 날아가는 'Cayman ball'을 개발했는데, 이 공은 같은 정도의 스윙으로 일반 골프공의 절반의 거리를 날아갔다. 작은 섬의 호텔과 곳곳에 있는 뒷마당에서 (골프에) 서투른 사람들이 기뻐했다.

해설

③의 앞 부분은 Nicklaus와 그의 팀이 작은 섬의 문제를 해결하기 위해 아홉 홀로 된 골프 코스를 설계하였다는 내용이고, ③의 뒷문장은 코스의 크기에 계속 집중하는 대신 골프공의 비거리를 짧게 만드는 것으로 문제를 재구성했다는 내용이므로, 골퍼들이 스윙을 짧게 할 수 없었고 공이 너무 쉽게 수면으로 날아갔다는 내용의 주어진 문장은 ③에 들어가는 것이 가장 적절하다.

⊗ **매력적인 오답 주의!**

⑤ 같은 정도의 스윙으로 일반 골프공의 절반의 거리를 날아가는 'Cayman ball'을 개발했다는 내용이 ⑤ 앞에 나오는데, 이를 주어진 문장에서 언급하는 스윙과 관련지어 오인하면 고를 수 있는 오답이다.

도입	Jack Nicklaus가 Grand Cayman 섬의 골프 코스 설계를 맡도록 고용됨
문제	섬의 크기가 너무 작아서 표준 크기의 골프 코스를 위한 공간을 제공할 수 없었음
해결 1	아홉 홀 코스를 설계하여 문제 해결을 시도했으나, 골퍼들이 스윙을 짧게 할 수 없어서 공이 너무 쉽게 수면으로 날아가는 문제가 발생함
해결 2	같은 스윙으로 일반 골프공의 절반의 거리만 날아가는 공을 개발하여 문제를 해결함

구문

• In his first attempt [to deal with the problem], Nicklaus and his team cleverly designed a nine-hole course [that could be played twice from different tees].
: 첫 번째 [ ]는 his first attempt를 수식하는 형용사적 용법의 to부정사구이다. 두 번째 [ ]는 a nine-hole course를 수식하는 관계절이다.

• After heavy testing and research, Nicklaus and the MacGregor Golf Company developed the limited-flight "Cayman ball," [which drives half the distance of a regular golf ball with the same amount of swing].
: [ ]는 the limited-flight "Cayman ball"을 부가적으로 설명하는 관계절이다.

11
정답 ②

대부분의 꿈에서 우리는 자신이 깨어 있다고 확신한다. 그러나 때때로 꿈에서 일어나는 사건은 우리를 의심하게 만들 정도로 정말 놀랍다. 이러한 불신은 증가하여 우리가 사실상 꿈을 꾸고 있다는 인식으로 전환될 수 있다. 따라서 자각몽이라고 할 때, 우리는 흔히 잃게 되는 깨어 있는 의식의 중요한 측면, 즉 주로 우리가 처한 상태에 대한 정확한 인식을 꿈을 꾸는 동안 다시 획득하는 것을 의미한다. 우리가 깨어 있을 때 우리는 그것을 알고 있으며 우리의 지식에 이상이 없는지를 매우 쉽게 확인할 수 있다. 우리는 자발적으로 움직일 수 있고, 생각을 통제할 수 있으며, 만약 우리가 회의적일 경우 심지어 스스로를 꼬집어 우리가 외부 자극과 관련하여 사물을 느끼고 행동하고 있는 것을 볼 수 있다. 꿈을 꾸는 동안 우리는 일반적으로 이러한 자기 반성적 자각을 잃고, 우리가 처한 상태를 인식하지 못하며, 우리의 생각을 통제할 수 없고, 그리고 비판적 판단을 내릴 수 없다.

해설

주어진 문장에서의 This disbelief는 ② 앞에 언급된, 꿈에서 일어나는 사건이 우리를 의심하게 만들 정도로 정말 놀랍다는 내용을 가리킨다. 또한 주어진 문장의 내용에 따르면 이러한 불신이 증가하면 우리가 실제로는 꿈을 꾸고 있다는 인식으로 전환되는데, 이것이 ② 뒤에서 언급되는 자각몽의 의미, 즉 우리가 처한 상태에 대한 정확한 인식을 다시 획득하는 것을 의미한다는 내용과 자연스럽게 연결된다. 따라서 주어진 문장이 들어가기에 가장 적절한 곳은 ②이다.

⊗ **매력적인 오답 주의!**

③ 우리가 처한 상태에 대한 정확한 인식을 다시 획득한다는 내용을 This disbelief로 오인하면 고를 수 있는 오답이다.

도입	우리는 꿈을 꾸는 동안 자신이 깨어 있다고 확신함
전환	하지만 꿈에서 일어나는 사건은 우리를 의심하게 만들 정도로 놀라움
주제	자각몽이란 우리가 처한 상태에 대한 정확한 인식을 다시 획득하는 것을 의미함
부연	꿈을 꾸는 동안 우리는 자기 반성적 자각을 잃고 자신이 처한 상태를 인식하지 못함

구문

• This disbelief can **be increased** and **converted** into the recognition [that we are, in fact, dreaming].

: This disbelief가 increase와 convert의 주체가 아닌 대상이므로 수동태가 사용되었다. [ ]는 the recognition의 구체적인 내용을 설명하는 동격절이다.

- By lucid dreaming, we thus mean the reacquisition during dreaming [of an important aspect of waking consciousness {that is usually lost}], mainly the accurate recognition of the state [that we are in].
: 첫 번째 [ ]는 the reacquisition을 수식하는 전치사구이고, 그 안의 { }는 an important aspect of waking consciousness를 수식하는 관계절이다. 두 번째 [ ]는 the state를 수식하는 관계절이다.

12-14

정답 12 ⑤ 13 ③ 14 ③

(A) 어느 아름다운 봄날 오후, 라이벌인 Central Washington 대학과 Western Oregon 대학 사이에 소프트볼 경기가 있었다. Western의 Sara Tucholsky는 한 번도 홈런을 쳐 본 적이 없었는데, 심지어 타격 연습에서조차 없었다. 그때, 2회에 그녀는 공을 세게 쳐서 중앙의 담장 너머로 보냈다. 두 명의 주자가 출루해 있는 상황에서, 그것은 3점포가 될 것이었다. Tucholsky는 무척 흥분해서 1루를 향해 질주했다. 하지만 공이 담장을 통과하는 것을 보면서, 그녀는 1루를 놓쳤다. 그녀가 돌아가서 그것에 닿기 위해 재빨리 멈추어 섰을 때, 그녀의 무릎 속 무엇인가가 멈춰 버렸다. 그녀는 땅바닥에 쓰러지고 말았다.
(D) 극심한 고통 속에서, Tucholsky는 먼지를 뚫고 1루로 다시 기어갔다. Western 팀의 코치가 필드로 달려왔다. 심판들은 코치에게 Tucholsky의 Western 팀 동료들이 그녀를 도와 베이스를 도는 것은 규정에 어긋난다고 말했다. 코치는 그녀 대신 대주자를 기용할 '수도 있었다'. 하지만 그렇게 하면 그 타격은 1루타로 판정될 것이었다. Tucholsky의 4년간의 선수 경력 중 유일한 홈런이 지워질 것이었다. 코치는 어떻게 해야 할지를 몰랐다.
(C) 바로 그때 Mallory Holtman이 끼어들었다. Holtman은 상대팀의 1루수였다. 그녀는 또한 Central Washington 팀에서 전대미문으로 홈런을 리드하고 있었다. 만약 그녀의 팀이 그 경기에서 진다면, 그들의 결승전 희망이 아마도 사라질 것이라는 점을 그녀는 알고 있었다. 하지만 코치와 심판이 하는 말을 잠시 듣고 난 후, 그녀는 질문을 했다. '우리가 그것을 할 수 있나요? 상대팀은 그녀를 데리고 베이스를 돌아도 되나요?' 심판들은 그것을 금하는 그 어떤 것도 규정집에 없다고 말했다. 그래서 Holtman과 Central 팀의 유격수인 Liz Wallace가 Tucholsky에게 걸어가서 그녀를 부축하여 일으켰다. 그녀를 데리고 다니면서, 그들은 홈런 걸음을 재개했다.
(B) 각 베이스에서, 그들은 Tucholsky가 그녀의 부상당하지 않은 다리로 베이스에 닿게 하기 위해 잠시 멈추었다. 2루에서, Holtman은 "나는 이것이 다른 사람들에게는 어떻게 보이는지 궁금해."라고 말했다. 그 세 명의 선수들은 웃음을 터뜨렸다. 하지만 경기장에 있던 다른 사람들은 웃고 있지 않았다. 그들은 울고 있었다. Western Oregon 팀, 코치들, 그리고 군중들은 그토록 감동적인 스포츠맨십의 행위를 보고서 눈물을 흘리고 있었다.

해설

12 Tucholsky가 선수 경력 중 처음으로 홈런을 쳤는데 실수로 1루를 밟지 않고 지나가는 바람에 다시 1루로 돌아가려는 순간 무릎에 이상이 생겨 땅바닥에 쓰러졌다는 내용의 주어진 글에 이어, Tucholsky가 1루로 다시 기어갔지만 대주자를 기용하게 되면 Tucholsky의 3점 홈런이 1루타로만 인정받게 되므로 코치가 어떻게 해야 할지 몰랐다는 내용의 (D)가 오고, 이 말을 듣고 있던 상대팀의 Holtman이 자신의 팀 동료와 함께 Tucholsky를 도와 홈런 걸음을 재개했다는 내용의 (C)가 이어진 다음, 마지막으로 그 모습을 보고 감동하여 Western Oregon 팀, 코치들, 그리고 군중들이 모두 눈물을 흘렸다는 내용의 (B)가 이어지는 것이 글의 흐름상 가장 자연스럽다.

13 (c)는 Holtman을 가리키고, 나머지는 모두 Tucholsky를 가리킨다.

14 2루에 도착했을 때 자신을 부축해 주던 Holtman의 말을 듣고 Tucholsky가 상대팀 선수들과 함께 웃음을 터뜨렸다고 했으므로, 아파서 눈물을 터뜨렸다는 ③은 글의 내용과 일치하지 않는다.

TEXT FLOW

시간 순서/사건 전개에 따른 흐름:
(A) 두 대학의 소프트볼 경기에서 Sara Tucholsky는 생애 첫 홈런을 쳤지만 1루를 밟지 못하고 부상을 당함 → (D) 그녀는 간신히 1루로 갔지만 팀 동료들의 도움을 받을 수도 없고, 대주자를 기용하면 홈런이 아닌 1루타로 인정받아야 하는 상황임 → (C) 상대팀 선수들이 Sara가 홈으로 들어올 수 있도록 도와줌 → (B) 선수들과 코치, 군중들이 그들의 스포츠맨십에 감동받음

구문
- The umpires told the coach [it was against the rules for Tucholsky's Western teammates **to help** her around the bases].
: [ ]는 told의 직접목적어 역할을 하는 명사절로, 앞에 접속사 that이 생략되어 있다. 명사절의 it은 가주어, to help 이하는 진주어이며, for Tucholsky's Western teammates는 to부정사의 의미상 주어이다.

GRAMMAR REVIEW

본문 41쪽

1 Thinking	2 saying, reporting	3 categorized
4 do	5 that	6 which
7 themselves	8 refuting	9 which
10 that		

1 주절의 주어인 candidates를 의미상 주어로 하는 분사구문을 유도하고, candidates가 think의 주체이므로 현재분사 Thinking을 써야 한다.

2 「with+목적어+분사」 구문으로 '~가 …하는 상황에서'라는 뜻이며, 능동의 의미이므로 각각 현재분사 saying과 reporting을 써야 한다.

3 완전한 절인 The graph ~ in 2021 뒤에 접속사가 없이 콤마(,)로만 이어지고 있으므로 준동사를 사용해야 한다. 문맥상 종사자들의 인식이 세 가지 직종으로 분류되어 제시된 것이므로 과거분사 categorized를 써야 한다.

4 부정의 의미를 나타내는 nor 뒤에는 주어와 조동사가 도치되는데, 도치된 주어가 we이므로 do가 적절하다.

5 lots of theories와 의미상 동격을 이루는 절을 이끌고 있으므로 접속사 that이 적절하다.

6 influences의 주어 역할을 하면서 두 개의 절을 이어주는 주격 관계대명사가 필요한데, 선행사가 사물이므로 which가 적절하다.

7 defend의 동작 주체는 These leaderless groups이고 대상도 역시 같으므로 재귀대명사 themselves가 적절하다.

8 the other set을 수식하는 분사구를 이끌고 있으며 능동의 의미이므로 현재분사 refuting을 써야 한다.

9 주어와 술어 동사를 모두 갖춘 완전한 절이 접속사 없이 뒷내용과 콤마 (,)로 연결되어 있으므로, 접속사와 대명사의 역할을 동시에 할 수 있는 관계대명사 which가 적절하다.

10 주어와 동사, 그리고 목적어를 모두 갖춘 완전한 절이 뒤에 이어지고 있으므로 접속사 that이 적절하다.

하프 모의고사　05회

01 ③	02 ④	03 ⑤	04 ①	05 ⑤
06 ⑤	07 ①	08 ②	09 ③	10 ②
11 ③	12 ④	13 ②	14 ⑤	

01　　　　　　　　　　　　　　　　　　정답 ③

Sniper 씨께,
전 세계적인 경기 침체에도 불구하고, 저희는 지금까지 저희 제품의 가격을 동결해 왔습니다만, 더는 그렇게 할 수 없을 것 같습니다. 이탈리아에 있는 우리의 제조업체가 급작스럽게 가격을 인상하는 바람에, 수입되는 모든 돼지 가죽으로 만드는 여성 신발(모든 사이즈와 모든 색상)의 소매 가격을 9월 1일부로 4.7% 올릴 수밖에 없게 되었습니다. 그날 '이전에' 들어온 주문들은 예전 가격 수준으로 청구서를 보내 드릴 것입니다. 인상된 가격의 필요성에 대해 진심으로 유감의 뜻을 표합니다. 하지만 더 높아진 생산비와 인건비뿐만 아니라 인플레이션에 의한 이런 전반적인 인상이 어쩔 수 없는 일임을 이해해 주실 것으로 알고 있습니다. 귀사에게 정말로 고마움을 표하며 귀사와 계속된 관계를 맺기를 고대합니다.
Sylvia Trager 드림

해설
제조업체의 급작스러운 가격 인상과 인플레이션 등의 이유 때문에 제품의 가격을 인상할 수밖에 없음을 거래처에게 알리고 그에 대한 양해를 구하고 있으므로, 글의 목적으로는 ③이 가장 적절하다.

TEXT FLOW

도입	제조업체의 급작스러운 가격 인상 때문에 불가피하게 제품의 가격을 올리게 되었음
부연	돼지가죽으로 만드는 모든 여성 신발의 소매 가격을 4.7% 올리게 되었음
결론	생산비, 인건비, 인플레이션에 의한 가격 인상의 필요성을 이해해 주기를 바람

구문
• However, we know you will understand [that this across-the-board increase, {which is caused by inflation as well as higher production and labor costs}, is beyond our control].
: [ ]는 동사 understand의 목적어 역할을 하는 명사절이고, 그 안의 { }는 계속적 용법의 관계절로 명사절의 주어 역할을 하는 선행사 this across-the-board increase를 부연 설명한다.

02　　　　　　　　　　　　　　　　　　정답 ④

'언젠가 우리는 죽는다.'라는 생각을 숙고해 보라. 우리 대부분은 이것이 사실이라는 데 동의하지만, 그 생각에 사로잡히는 것은 여러분에게 도움이 되지 않을 수 있다. 아마도 여러분은 결국 삶이 얼마나 위험한지에 관해 생각하게 될 것이고, 위험한 일을 피하기 위해 여러분은 집을 떠나고 싶어 하지 않을 것이다. 그렇지 않으면 어쩌면 여러분은 어차피 죽을 것이므로 마음껏 즐기며 삶을 살고 원하는 것은 무엇이든지 하고, 먹는 편이 나을 수도 있다고 생각할 것이다. 둘 중 어떤 반응도 여러분을 여러분의 가치로 다가가게 할 것 같지는 않다. 그러니 지금 하고 있는 생각이 진실인지 아닌지에 대해 자기 자신과 논쟁하기보다는 그 생각이 여러분을 여러분의 가치로 다가가게 할지 아니면 여러분의 가치에서 멀어지게 할지를 물어보라. 만약 그 생각이 여러분을 가치로 다가가게 한다면, 좋다. 그 생각을 따르라! 만약 그 생각이 여러분을 여러분의 가치에서 멀어지게 한다면, 그 생각을 여러분에게 준 사람들에게 공유해 준 데 대한 심심한 감사를 표하고 어쨌든 여러분의 가치로 다가가라.

해설
생각이 진실인지 아닌지는 신경 쓰지 말고 자신의 가치에 부합하여 그것에 가까워지게 해 주는 생각이라면 따르고, 멀어지게 하는 생각이라면 잊고 자신의 가치를 향해 나아가라는 내용의 글이다. 따라서 필자의 주장으로 가장 적절한 것은 ④이다.

😵 **매력적인 오답 주의!**
③ 글의 요지와 관계없이 글의 마지막 문장에 언급된 내용에만 집중하면 고를 수 있는 오답이다.

TEXT FLOW

도입	어떤 생각이 사실이라도 해로울 수 있음
주제	생각과 자기 가치와의 관계에 대한 질문의 중요성
결론	생각이 자신의 가치에 맞으면 따르고, 맞지 않으면 잊고 자신의 가치를 향해 나아가는 것이 중요함

구문
• Or perhaps you'll reason [that {since you're going to die anyway}, you might as well live life to the fullest and do and eat {whatever you want}].
: [ ]는 reason의 목적어 역할을 하는 명사절이다. 그 안의 첫 번째 { }는 이유를 나타내는 부사절이고, 두 번째 { }는 eat의 목적어 역할을 하는 명사절이다.

• So rather than debating with yourself about [whether the thought {you're having} is true or not], ask [if the thought will move you toward or away from your values].
: 첫 번째 [ ]는 about의 목적어 역할을 하는 명사절이고, 그 안의 { }는 the thought를 수식하는 관계절이다. 두 번째 [ ]는 ask의 목적어 역할을 하는 명사절이다.

03　　　　　　　　　　　　　　　　　정답 ⑤

실제로 과학을 하는 즐거움 중 하나는 누군가가 틀렸다는 것을 증명하는 것인데, 심지어는 더 이전 시기의 여러분 자신도 해당한다. 과학자들은 어떻게 자신이 어떤 것을 알고 있는 때를 확실히 알 수 있는가? 언제 어떤 것이 그들이 만족할 만큼 알려지게 되는가? 사실은 언제가 최종적인가? 실제로는, 오로지 거짓 과학만이 '사실'을 숭배하며, 그것을 영구적인 것으로 생각하고 모든 것을 알고 정밀한 정확성으로 예측할 수 있다고 주장한다. 사실, 새로운 증거로 인해 어쩔 수 없이 과학자들이 자신의 이론을 수정해야 하는 경우에, 그것은 패배가 아니라 승리로 간주된다. 현재 양자 역학이라고 알려진 물리학의 혁명을 이끈 훌륭한 물리학자인 Max Planck는 과학적 지식이 얼마나 자주 바뀌는지 질문을 받았다. 그는 "장례식이 있을 때마다요."라고 답했다. 새로운 젊은 과학자들이 성숙해지고 이전 세대의 생각과 '사실'에 의한 구속

이 없어지면서 개념과 이해는 혁명적이면서도 점진적인 방식으로 자유롭게 바뀐다. 진정한 과학은 언제나 진행 중인 수정이다. 그것은 무지가 있었다 없었다 하면서 전진한다.

해설
과학은 수정을 통해서 변화하고 발전한다는 내용의 글이다. 밑줄 친 부분은 과학적 지식의 변화 시기에 관한 질문에 대한 답이고, 바로 뒤에 새로운 젊은 과학자들이 성숙해지고 이전 세대의 생각과 사실에 의한 구속이 없어지면서 개념과 이해가 바뀐다는 설명이 이어지고 있다. 따라서 밑줄 친 부분이 의미하는 바로 가장 적절한 것은 ⑤ '과학은 낡은 통찰이 새로운 통찰로 대체될 때 발전한다'이다.
① 과학은 결국 무지를 이긴다
② 과학적 변화는 급진적일 뿐만 아니라 점진적이다
③ 과학은 때때로 그것의 이전 접근법으로 돌아간다
④ 과학 이론은 항상 수정의 과정에 있다

😵 **매력적인 오답 주의!**
③ 장례식이라는 말을 과학의 진보와 반대 의미로 잘못 파악하면 고를 수 있는 오답이다.
④ 밑줄 친 부분과 관계없이 요지만을 근거로 판단하면 고를 수 있는 오답이다.

TEXT FLOW

도입	과학에서 사실이 틀림을 증명하는 것의 의미
전개	과학 진보에 대한 Max Planck의 의견
결론	진정한 과학은 늘 수정되는 것

구문
• In reality, only false science [worships "facts,"] [thinks of them as permanent] and [claims to be able to {know everything} and {predict with exact accuracy}].
: 세 개의 [ ]는 and로 연결되어 문장의 술어 역할을 한다. 세 번째 [ ] 안의 두 개의 { }는 and로 연결되어 be able to에 이어진다.

• Max Planck, [the brilliant physicist {who led the revolution in physics ⟨now known as quantum mechanics⟩}], was asked how often science changed.
: [ ]는 Max Planck와 동격 관계이다. 그 안의 { }는 the brilliant physicist를 수식하는 관계절이고, ⟨ ⟩는 the revolution in physics를 수식하는 분사구이다.

04　　　　　　　　　　　　　　　　　정답 ①

사람들은 사회적, 경제적, 그리고 정치적 요인들 때문에 다른 언어보다 한 언어를 말하기를 선택하고, 이것이 언어 전이를 유발한다. 언어 전이는 자신들이 계승한 언어를 외면하고, 화자들이 강압에 의해서든 자발적이든 다른 언어를 택하는 것을 말한다. 계승한 언어를 포기하는 것은 결국 그것의 사멸로 이어진다. 계급, 지위, 민족성, 그리고 매체와 교육 같은 외부의 영향력이 언어에 영향을 미치고 언어 전이에 영향을 미친다. 예를 들어, 멕시코에서 스페인어는 글을 읽고 쓸 줄 아는 능력 및 학계와 가장 밀접하게 관계되어 있고, 궁극적으로는 더 높은 사회 경제적 계급과 관계되어 있다. 식민지 상황에서는, 더 작은 규모의 문화가 예외 없이 지배적인 문화를 수용해야만 하고, 이때가 언어 전이가 일어날 가능성이 가장 높은 때이다. 멕시코에는 공식적으로 인정받은 68개의 토속 언어들과, 364개의 별개의 방언들이 있기는 하지

만, 인구의 6%만이 그것들 중 한 가지 언어를 말하고, 다른 모든 사람은 스페인어를 말한다.

해설

언어 전이가 무엇인지 정의하고 나서, 멕시코에서 일어난 언어 전이를 그 예로 들어 부연 설명을 하고 있으므로, 글의 주제로는 ① '언어 전이의 정의와 그것의 사례'가 가장 적절하다.
② 그렇게 많은 방언들이 세상에 존재하는 이유들
③ 언어와 사고의 밀접한 관계
④ 한 언어에서 다른 언어로 이동하는 것의 어려움
⑤ 소수 언어들이 사라지는 것을 막는 것의 중요성

TEXT FLOW

도입	언어 전이는 자신들이 계승한 언어를 외면하고 화자들이 다른 언어를 택하는 것을 말함
부연	계급, 지위, 민족성, 매체, 교육 같은 것들이 언어와 언어 전이에 영향을 미침
예시	멕시코에는 많은 토속 언어와 방언이 있지만, 인구의 대부분이 사회 경제적 계급과 관계가 있는 스페인어를 말함

구문

• Language shift refers **to** speakers **turning** away from their heritage language and **adopting** another language, either by force or voluntarily.
: turning과 adopting은 and에 의해 병렬 구조를 이루어 전치사 to에 연결되고, speakers는 동명사 turning과 adopting의 의미상 주어 역할을 한다.

05
정답 ⑤

Khan Academy는 '모든 곳의 모든 이들에게 무료로 세계적인 수준의 교육'을 제공하기 위해 교육자인 Salman Khan에 의해 2006년에 만들어진 비영리 교육 기관이다. 그 기관은 유튜브 영상의 형태로 초소형 강의들을 제작한다. 초소형 강의들에 더하여, 그 기관의 웹사이트는 교육자들을 위한 연습 문제들과 (교수) 도구들을 특별히 제공한다. 그것은 기부에 의해 자금이 조달된다. 그것은 Bill & Melinda Gates 재단, Ann and John Doerr, 브라질에 본부를 두고 있는 Lemann 재단, 그리고 Google로부터 상당한 지원을 받는다. Salman Khan은 MIT로부터 세 개의 학위를 받고 헤지 펀드 매니저로 일을 시작했다. 자신의 여동생, 친척들, 그리고 친구들의 수학을 돕기 위해, 그는 교습 동영상을 만들어 그것들을 유튜브에서 배포했다. 그 프로젝트는 거의 즉각적으로 커졌고, Khan은 그 교습 동영상들에 집중하기 위해 일을 그만두었다.

해설

Khan은 프로젝트가 커지자 교습 동영상에 집중하기 위해 일을 그만두었다고 했으므로, 글의 내용과 일치하지 않는 것은 ⑤이다.

구문

• Khan Academy is a nonprofit educational organization [created in 2006 by educator Salman Khan {to provide "a free, world-class education for anyone, anywhere}]."
: [ ]는 과거분사구로 a nonprofit educational organization을 수식한다. { }는 '~하기 위해'라는 뜻의 목적을 나타내는 to부정사의 부사적 용법으로 사용되었다.

06
정답 ⑤

노화에 대한 현대의 이론들은 인간이 왜 늙는지를 설명할 수 없다. 마모 이론이라는 한 이론에서는, 신체는 단지 시간이 지나면서 차츰 닳는 것이라고 주장한다. 어떤 이론들은 세포 그 자체 내에 있는 변화들을 다루는 반면, 다른 이론들에서는 노화란 계획되어 있고 노화의 과정은 시상하부에 있는 노화 시계에 의해 통제된다고 말한다. 유전자 이론에서는 신체의 기능 장애의 요인이 되는 어떤 특정한 유전자들이 있으며 이러한 유전자들은 인간이 더 늙어갈수록 활성화되는 것 같다고 주장한다. 더 나아가, 세포 속에는 축적되는 어떤 특정한 찌꺼기들이 있으며 이것이 노화, 그리고 궁극적으로는 죽음에 이르는 기능 장애를 일으킨다고 주장하는 세포 찌꺼기 이론도 있다.

해설

⑤ 앞에서 there are certain deposits로 완전한 문장을 갖추었기 때문에 accumulate는 주어인 certain deposits를 수식하는 과거분사 accumulated로 고쳐야 한다.
① '나이가 들다'라는 의미의 동사로 사용되었고 주어가 people이므로 age는 적절하다.
② 주어가 One theory이므로 단수 동사인 maintains는 적절하다. the wear and tear theory는 One theory와 동격어구이다.
③ '~에 위치한'의 의미로 located는 적절하다. an aging clock 다음에 주격 관계대명사 that[which]과 be동사 is가 생략된 형태로 볼 수 있다.
④ which ~ dysfunctions가 앞에 나오는 certain genes를 수식하고 있으므로, 관계절을 이끄는 주격 관계대명사 which는 적절하다.

TEXT FLOW

도입	노화에 대한 현대의 이론들은 인간이 늙는 이유를 설명하지 못함
전개	노화를 설명하고자 하는 이론에 마모 이론과 유전자 이론이 있음
부연	노화를 설명하고자 하는 이론으로 세포 찌꺼기 이론도 있음

구문

• Some theories deal with the changes within the cells themselves, **while** still others state [that aging is programmed], and [that the aging process is regulated by an aging clock located in the hypothalamus].
: while은 대조를 나타내는 접속사로 '~하는 반면에'라는 뜻으로 해석된다. 두 개의 [ ]는 명사절로서 and로 연결되어 있으며 state의 목적어이다.

07
정답 ①

소유할 말한 가치가 있는 것은 무엇이든 시간이 걸린다. "우리가 너무 쉽게 얻는 것을, 우리는 너무 가볍게 생각한다."라고 Thomas Paine은 썼다. 그러나 열심히 일하는 것과 가끔씩 오래 기다리거나 황야를 지나 우회로로 가는 것 이외에, 핵심적인 요소는 비전이다. 예를 들어, 수천 명의 사람들이 에베레스트 산을 정복하려고 노력해 왔다. 시도를 하는 사람들 중에서, 일곱 명 중 단 한 명만이 정상에 도달한다. 성공 대(對) 실패의 가장 큰 요소들 중 하나는 자신들이 어디로 향하는지를 볼 수 있는 등반가들의 능력이다. 폭풍우가 불어와서 산 정상을 보기 어렵게 할 때, 등반가들은 낙담하고 실의에 빠져 퇴각을 고려한다. 그러나 폭풍우가 있는 대기가 맑아지고 등반가들이 다시 정상을 볼 때, 여정은 더 쉬워지고, 전념이 다시 시작되며, 믿음은 강화된다. 갑자기 거기에 도달하는 것이 가능한 것처럼 생각된다.

해설

에베레스트 산 정상 등반에 성공하기 위해서 중요한 것은 자신들이 어디로 향하는지를 볼 수 있는 등반가들의 능력이라고 한 것에서 '비전'이 성공의 핵심적인 요소라는 것을 알 수 있으므로, 빈칸에 들어갈 말로는 ① '비전'이 가장 적절하다.

② 인내 ③ 창의성 ④ 관용 ⑤ 협동

TEXT FLOW

도입	성공의 핵심적인 요소는 비전임
전개	에베레스트 산 정상 등반 시 성공과 실패를 가르는 가장 큰 요소 중 하나는 자신들이 어디로 향하는지를 볼 수 있는 등반가들의 능력임
결론	산 정상을 볼 수 있으면 거기에 도달하는 것이 가능한 것처럼 보여 성공 가능성이 높아짐

구문

• "[What we obtain too easily], we esteem too lightly," Thomas Paine wrote.
: [ ]는 동사 esteem의 목적어로, 강조를 위해 도치되었다. 목적어가 문두에 나가 도치될 때는 「목적어＋주어＋동사」의 어순을 취한다.

• [One of the greatest factors in success versus failure] is the climbers' ability [to see {where they are headed}].
: 첫 번째 [ ]는 문장의 주어이고 동사는 is이다. 두 번째 [ ]는 to부정사의 형용사적 용법으로 the climbers' ability를 수식하며, 그 안의 { }는 간접의문문으로 see의 목적어 역할을 한다.

08

정답 ②

미술사가 Giorgio Vasari는 미켈란젤로가 Sistine 성당에 그림을 그릴 때, 거의 천장까지 비계를 세우고 20개월 동안 그림을 그렸다고 말한다. Vasari가 기록하듯이, "그 일은 매우 불편한 상태에서 이루어졌는데, 왜냐하면 미켈란젤로가 머리를 뒤로 젖힌 채 서 있어야만 했기 때문이었고, 그의 시력이 크게 손상되어 몇 달 동안 그는 그 자세로 설계도를 읽고 볼 수 있었을 뿐이었다." 이것은 그의 뇌가 적응했던 그 이상한 자세에서만 볼 수 있도록 <u>그것의 회로를 바꾼</u> 경우였을지도 모른다. Vasari의 주장은 믿을 수 없는 것처럼 보일지도 모르지만, 연구에 따르면 세상을 거꾸로 뒤집혀 보이게 하는 프리즘 전도 안경을 쓸 때, 사람들은 잠시 후에 그들의 지각 중심이 '뒤집히고', 그 결과 세상을 똑바로 지각하고 심지어는 뒤집혀 있는 책들을 읽기도 한다는 것을 발견한다. 그 안경을 벗으면, 그들은 미켈란젤로가 그랬던 것과 마찬가지로, 재적응할 때까지 마치 거꾸로 뒤집혀 있는 것처럼 세상을 본다.

해설

미켈란젤로가 머리를 뒤로 젖힌 채 거꾸로 그림을 그린 결과 그 자세로만 글을 읽고 설계도를 볼 수 있었다는 것은 뇌가 세상을 지각하는 회로를 바꾸었다는 의미이므로, 빈칸에 들어갈 말로는 ② '그것의 회로를 바꾼'이 가장 적절하다.

① 창의성이 부족한   ③ 미래를 예언한
④ 현실로부터 도피한   ⑤ 불편함을 느낀

TEXT FLOW

도입	미켈란젤로는 머리를 뒤로 젖힌 자세로 Sistine 성당 벽화를 20개월 동안 그렸음
전개	그 자세로 그림을 그리다 보니 미켈란젤로의 뇌가 그 상황에 익숙해짐
부연	프리즘 전도 안경을 쓰면 세상이 똑바로 보이는 것도 지각 중심이 뒤집혀서 뇌가 상황에 익숙해진 결과임

구문

• The work was executed in great discomfort, [as Michelangelo had to stand {with his head thrown back}], and he so injured his eyesight that for several months he could only read and look at designs in that posture.
: [ ]는 이유를 설명하는 부사절이고, 그 안의 { }는 부대상황의 분사구문으로 목적어와 분사의 관계가 수동이라서 「with＋목적어＋과거분사」 형태로 쓰였다.

• [Taking the glasses off], they see the world **as though** it were upside down, until they readapt, as Michelangelo **did**.
: [ ]는 분사구문으로 After they take the glasses off로 바꿔 쓸 수 있다. as though는 '마치 ~처럼'이라는 뜻으로 가정법 과거 구문을 이끈다. did는 대동사로 내용상 saw the world as though it were upside down 전체를 대신한다.

09

정답 ③

꼬리표 붙이기라는 사고 오류는 여러분 자신, 상황, 혹은 다른 사람에 대한 여러분의 감정을 부정적인 꼬리표로 요약하는 것을 포함한다. 사회적 불안을 가진 사람들은 매우 흔히 다른 사람이 아닌 그들 자신에게 부정적인 꼬리표를 붙인다. 이러한 꼬리표는 여러분이 불만족스러울 수도 있는 특정한 것(여러분이 한 말이나 행동)에서 여러분의 성격이나 개성에 대한 전체적인 부정적 판단으로 여러분의 주의를 옮기기 때문에 문제를 일으킨다. (여러분의 성격이나 개성을 규정하는 것은 실패가 아니라 여러분이 어떻게 회복해서 그 실패를 극복하느냐이다.) 이것은 프로젝트에서 몇몇 실수를 했다고 여러분 자신에게 말하는 것과 여러분 자신을 '무능한 멍청이'라고 부르는 것의 차이이다. 그 꼬리표는 여러분의 기분을 나쁘게 할 뿐만 아니라 여러분에게 무엇이든 바꾸는 것에 대해 막막하고 가망이 없게 느끼도록 만들 수 있다.

해설

꼬리표 붙이기는 자신의 성격이나 개성에 대해 전체적인 부정적 판단이 들게 하는 사고 오류라는 내용의 글이다. 실패가 아니라 어떻게 회복해서 그 실패를 극복하느냐가 성격이나 개성을 규정하는 것이라는 내용의 ③은 글의 전체 흐름과 관계가 없다.

TEXT FLOW

도입	꼬리표 붙이기라는 사고 오류 소개
주제	성격이나 개성에 대한 전체적인 부정적 판단을 야기하는 꼬리표 붙이기
부연	꼬리표 붙이기의 문제점 → 변화하려는 의지를 없앰

구문

• [What defines your personality or character] is **not** [your failure], **but** [how you get back and overcome that failure].

: 첫 번째 [ ]는 주어 역할을 하는 명사절이다. 두 번째 [ ]와 세 번째 [ ]는 'A가 아니라 B'라는 의미의 「not A but B」로 연결되었다.

- **Not only does the label make** you feel bad, it can make you feel stuck and hopeless about changing anything.
  : 부정어 Not only가 문장 맨 앞으로 가면서 「조동사＋주어＋동사」의 어순이 되었다.

10   정답 ②

Twitter, YouTube, 그리고 Facebook과 같은 소셜 미디어는 진정 '사회적'이어서, 공적인 메시지들과 오로지 친구들에게만 보이는 메시지들을 통해서 입소문을 퍼뜨린다. (B) 결국, 다른 소비자들이 그 원래의 메시지를 다시 포스팅하거나 다시 트윗을 하고, 자신들의 말로 그것에 반향을 보이거나, 영상 응답을 녹화함으로써, 또는 다른 방식들로 그 대화를 계속 이어 나가게 할 수 있다. (A) 여러 가지 방식을 통한 이런 사회적 대화들은 그것들 자체로 입소문을 촉발시키고 더 많은 소비자들이 그 대화와 상표 또는 상품에 참여하도록 할 수 있다. 예를 들어, Twitter에서 어떤 상품이나 상표가 인기가 있으면, 다른 사람들이 무엇을 트윗하고 있는가를 보려고 많은 사용자들이 클릭을 할 것이다. (C) 마찬가지로, 어떤 YouTube 영상이 매우 많은 조회를 기록해서 YouTube 홈페이지에 올라갈 때, 그 추가적인 노출이 더 많은 조회의 원인이 된다.

해설
주어진 글은 소셜 미디어가 공적 또는 사적인 메시지를 통해 입소문을 퍼뜨린다는 내용이다. 이어서 원래의 메시지에 다른 사람들이 여러 가지 방식들로 반응함으로써 대화를 이어간다는 입소문 전파 양상에 대한 내용인 (B)가 오고, 그런 여러 가지 방식을 통한 사회적 대화의 예를 Twitter를 통해 들고 있는 (A)가 (B) 다음에 이어지며, YouTube 영상으로 다시 비슷한 예를 드는 (C)가 마지막에 오는 것이 글의 흐름상 가장 자연스럽다.

TEXT FLOW

도입	사회적인 성격을 지닌 소셜 미디어가 입소문을 퍼뜨림
전개	사용자들이 여러 가지 방식으로 대화를 계속 이어 나감
결론	그러한 대화는 Twitter나 YouTube의 예에서 알 수 있듯이, 입소문을 촉발시키고 더 많은 사람들의 참여와 관심을 유도함

구문

- In turn, other consumers may keep the conversation going **by reposting** or **retweeting** the original message, **echoing** it in their own words, **recording** a video response, or in other ways.
  : 「by+동명사」는 '~함으로써'의 의미를 나타내며, reposting, retweeting, echoing, recording이 by에 연결되어 병렬 구조를 이루고 있다.

11   정답 ③

세계 조정 선수권 대회를 준비하면서 어느 일류 조정 팀의 코치가 명상 교관을 초빙했다. 그는 그 교관이 자신의 조정 팀에게 집중, 휴식, 그리고 스트레스 관리 기술을 가르쳐 주기를 원했다. 그는 그러한 훈련이 노를 젓는 효과를 높이고 단결심을 향상시켜 줄 것이라고 믿었다. 조정 팀이 명상에 관해 더 많은 것을 배울수록, 그들은 더욱 단결하게 되었고 그들의 노 젓기는 더욱 부드

러워졌으며 저항도 적어졌다. 이러한 이점들에도 불구하고, 역설적인 것은 그들의 성적이 꾸준히 저하했고 그들이 더 천천히 갔다는 점이다. 놀랍게도, 그 팀의 선수들이 이기는 것보다 조화를 이루는 데 더 관심이 많아졌다는 것이 밝혀졌다. 그들은 이기는 것이 유일한 목표는 아니라는 것을 깨닫고 경기를 함께 즐길 수 있는 방법을 찾아냈다.

해설
주어진 문장은 명상 훈련을 통해 조정 팀이 얻게 된 이점에 관한 내용이므로, 그러한 이점들에도 불구하고 성적은 꾸준히 저하했고 더 천천히 갔다는 내용 앞인 ③에 들어가는 것이 가장 적절하다.

TEXT FLOW

도입	일류 조정 팀의 코치가 명상 교관을 초빙해서 집중, 휴식, 스트레스 관리 기술을 팀원들에게 가르치고자 함
전개	그 결과 팀원들이 단결하게 되고, 노 젓기가 부드러워졌으며, 저항도 적어졌지만, 그들의 성적이 저하했고 속도가 느려짐
결론	팀원들은 이기는 것보다 조화를 이루는 데 더 관심이 많아져서 경기에 이기는 것만을 추구하지 않고 경기를 함께 즐기는 방법을 찾아냄

구문

- In spite of these benefits, the irony was [that their performance decreased steadily and they went slower].
  : [ ]는 동사 was의 보어 역할을 하는 명사절이다.

- They **realized** that winning is not the only goal and **found** the way to enjoy games together.
  : realized와 found는 문장의 동사로 주어 They에 공통으로 연결된다.

12   정답 ④

1990년대 중반 정도부터, 통계는 작물의 연간 증가율이 줄어들고 있음을 보여 주었다. 또한 다른 지역들의 생산성 증가가 느려졌다는 증거도 있다. 예를 들어, 많은 개발도상국가들의 주식 작물 중 하나는 카사바로 알려진 열대 뿌리 작물이다. 1970년 이후, 카사바 생산에 투입된 땅의 면적은 43% 정도 증가한 반면, 생산량은 그 시간 동안 고작 20% 증가했다. 이것은 질이 더 좋지 않은 땅이 생산에 투입되고 있다는 징후이다. 많은 지역에서 인구가 폭발적으로 증가했기 때문에, 새로운 농부들은 수지가 안 맞을 정도의 땅에서 농사를 짓는 수밖에 없었다. 결과적으로, 더 많은 물과 비료가 농사에 투입되지만 에이커당 더 적은 식량을 생산할 뿐이다. 이것은 사람들에게 먹을 것을 주는 것뿐만 아니라 환경에 미치는 영향에도 엄청난 관련이 있다.
➡ 인구 증가로 인해, 더 많은 <u>불모의 땅</u>이 농업에 사용되어, 농사의 <u>생산성</u>을 떨어뜨리고 있다.

해설
인구가 증가하면서 생산성이 떨어지는 땅이 농사에 사용되고, 그에 따라 에이커당 생산되는 식량이 줄어든다는 내용이므로, 요약문의 빈칸 (A)에는 barren land(불모의 땅)가, (B)에는 productivity(생산성)가 들어가는 것이 가장 적절하다.
① 보조금 – 성과 상여금
② 보조금 – 생산성
③ 불모의 땅 – 복잡성
⑤ 지하수 – 성과 상여금

도입	작물의 연간 증가율이 줄어드는 현상
전개	인구의 증가로 인해 질이 더 좋지 않은 땅이 농사에 사용되고, 그에 따라 더 많은 물과 비료가 투입됨
결론	식량 공급과 환경에 좋지 않은 영향을 가져옴

구문

• [Since the population exploded in many areas], new farmers **had no choice but to farm** on marginal land.

: [ ]는 원인을 나타내는 부사절이고, 「have no choice but to+동사원형」은 '~할 수밖에 없다'의 의미를 나타낸다.

13~14
정답 13 ② 14 ⑤

공평한 투자를 필요로 하는 것은 단지 자전거 도로뿐만 아니라 그것을 이용하게 해 주는 수단도 그렇다. Minneapolis의 자전거 공유 시스템인 Nice Ride는 미국 최초의 그런 프로그램 중 하나이다. 2010년에 그것이 시작되었을 때, 짧은 거리를 이동하는 많은 사람들에게 서비스를 제공할 수 있게 하기 위해 65개의 스테이션과 700대의 자전거로 구성된 비교적 소규모의 시스템이 서로 근접하여 위치하도록 그 도시의 인구가 가장 밀집한 지역에 스테이션을 배분했다. 시범적인 프로그램의 성공을 입증하는 데는 효과적이긴 했지만, 그 첫 공개는 North Minneapolis에 충분한 자전거 공유 스테이션이 없다는 결과를 남겼다.

처음에는, North Minneapolis에 자전거 공유 스테이션이 전혀 설치되지 않았다. 이듬해에 Nice Ride는 Minneapolis 보건부 보조금을 통해 추가 자금을 지원받아 11개의 스테이션을 설치했지만, 주민들은 이러한 간과를 사회적 무시의 신호로 읽었다. 그것은 라틴계, 흑인계, 아시아계 미국인 주민 사이에서 자전거 이용이 가장 빠르게 증가하고 있는데도 자전거 공유가 유색 인종 사회를 위한 것이 아니라는 생각을 연상시켰다. 이 이야기는 Minneapolis에만 특유하지 않다. 공공 자전거 공유가 미국 전역으로 확대되었지만, 그것이 항상 고르게 분포되는 것은 아니다. 연구에 따르면 유색 인종 사회는 자전거 공유 이용자가 <u>실제보다 많게 표시되는(→ 실제보다 적게 표시되는)</u> 경우가 많다고 한다. 자전거 공유 스테이션의 부족은 이들 집단을 제한하는 한 가지 요인일 뿐이다. 비용, 결제 선택권의 부족, 생소함은 다른 장벽이다.

해설

13 유색 인종 사회가 자전거 공유 스테이션 부족 등의 이유로 공공 자전거 공유 서비스를 이용하는 데 불리하다는 내용의 글이다. 따라서 글의 제목으로 가장 적절한 것은 ② '인종 차별이 공공 자전거 공유에도 영향을 미친다!'이다.

① 더 나은 미래 세상을 위해 여러분의 자전거를 공유하라!
③ 자전거 공유가 정말로 친환경적인 도시 통근의 수단인가?
④ 일부 인종은 특정한 교통수단을 선호한다
⑤ 자전거 공유 스테이션이 도시에서 어디에 설치되어야 하는가?

14 North Minneapolis에 공유 자전거 스테이션을 많이 설치하지 않아서 자전거 공유가 유색 인종 사회를 위한 것이 아니라는 생각을 연상시킨 것이 그대로 재현된 상황이므로, 유색 인종 사회는 자전거 공유 이용자가 실제보다 적게 표시되어야 한다. 따라서 (e) overrepresented(실제보다 많게 표시되는)를 underrepresented(실제보다 적게 표시되는)와 같은 단어로 바꿔야 한다.

13 ③ 자전거 공유에 문제점이 있다는 것은 이해했지만 문제점의 내용을 잘못 파악하면 고를 수 있는 오답이다.

14 ④ North Minneapolis의 상황과 미국 전역에서 벌어지는 상황의 관계를 파악하지 못하면 고를 수 있는 오답이다.

도입	Minneapolis의 자전거 공유 시스템인 Nice Ride의 도입 소개
전개 1	유색 인종 사회에서 자전거 공유 스테이션의 부족
전개 2	유색 인종 사회를 제한하는 자전거 공유 이용에의 여러 장애물

구문

• When it launched in 2010, stations were distributed in the most densely populated parts of the city [**so that** a relatively small system of sixty-five stations and seven hundred bikes could be located close together {to serve many people taking short trips}].

: [ ]에는 '~하도록'이라는 의미의 「so that ~」이 사용되었고, 그 안의 { }는 목적의 의미를 나타내는 부사적 용법의 to부정사구이다.

• It formed the association [that bike sharing was not for communities of color even when the fastest growth in bicycling was among the Latinx, Black, and Asian American populations of the city].

: [ ]는 the association과 동격 관계인 명사절이다.

GRAMMAR REVIEW
본문 49쪽

1 life is	2 predict	3 to create
4 discouraged	5 changing	6 apply
7 that	8 that	9 to produce
10 is		

1 about의 목적어 역할을 하는 간접의문문 형태가 되어야 하므로 「의문사+형용사+주어+동사」의 어순이 적절하다.

2 의미상 be able to 뒤에 know everything과 and로 연결되어 병렬 구조를 이루고 있으므로 동사원형 predict가 적절하다.

3 that절의 동사는 are이므로 술어 동사가 또 나올 수 없다. 따라서 목적을 나타내는 부사적 용법의 to create가 적절하다.

4 grow는 주격 보어를 취하는 동사이며 the climbers가 discourage의 행위를 당하는 대상이므로 수동의 의미를 나타내는 과거분사 discouraged를 써야 한다.

5 전치사 of의 목적어 역할을 하는 동명사구가 되도록 changing을 써야 한다. his brain은 changing의 의미상 주어이다.

6 주어의 핵이 people이므로 복수형 동사 apply가 적절하다.

7 '매우 ~해서 …하다'의 의미를 나타내는 「so ~ that …」 구문이므로 that이 적절하다.

8 동사 believed의 목적어 역할을 하는 명사절을 이끌어야 하며 뒤에 완전한 형태의 절이 이어지므로 접속사 that이 적절하다.

9 only와 연결되어 결과를 나타내는 부사구를 이루고 있으므로 to부정사구를 만드는 to produce를 써야 한다.

10 주어의 핵이 Lack이므로 단수형 동사 is가 적절하다.

하프 모의고사 06회

01 ②	02 ②	03 ②	04 ③	05 ④
06 ①	07 ④	08 ④	09 ②	10 ③
11 ⑤	12 ⑤	13 ⑤	14 ③	

01
정답 ②

시험관은 조수석에 올라타 Ginny에게 연석에서 차를 빼서 출발하라고 지시했다. 그녀는 땀에 젖은 양쪽 손바닥을 자신의 허벅지에 닦은 다음 조심스럽게 백미러를 확인했다. 그녀는 백미러를 통해 어머니가 자신을 향해 손을 흔드는 모습을 보았다. 시험관은 자신의 클립보드에 메모를 하면서 "좌회전하세요… 우회전하세요… 여기서 멈추세요."라는 말만 되풀이하며 퉁명스럽게 말했다. Ginny는 평행 주차가 가장 걱정스러웠다. 그들이 평행 주차를 할 때쯤, Ginny는 뜨거운 난로 위의 얼음덩이처럼 땀을 흘리고 있었다. 시험관은 Ginny의 주차 기술을 테스트하기 위해 두 개의 빈 공간이 있는 곳을 골랐고, 그녀는 그곳에 차를 겨우 주차했다. "아주 좋아요, Ms. Ginny." 시험관이 차가 면허 발급 사무실에 다시 돌아오자 말했다. "우수한 성적으로 합격하셨어요." Ginny는 그를 껴안을 뻔했다. 그 대신에 그녀는 차에서 뛰어내려 그녀의 어머니에게 달려갔다. "나 합격했어요! 엄마, 나 합격했어요!"

해설

Ginny는 긴장해서 땀을 흘리며 운전면허 시험을 보다가 가장 걱정스러웠던 평행 주차 성공 후 시험관에게서 합격했다는 말을 듣고 크게 기뻐하고 있으므로, Ginny의 심경 변화로 가장 적절한 것은 ② '긴장한 → 아주 기뻐하는'이다.
① 질투하는 → 후회하는
③ 좌절한 → 감사하는
④ 호기심이 나는 → 부끄러운
⑤ 실망한 → 만족한

TEXT FLOW

도입	Ginny가 운전면허 시험을 시작함
전개	Ginny가 긴장하면서 여러 과제를 무사히 완수함
결론	Ginny가 검사관에게서 합격했다는 말을 듣고 기뻐함

구문

• She saw her mother [waving at her] in the rearview mirror.
: [ ]는 saw의 목적격 보어 역할을 하는 분사구이다.

• The examiner spoke curtly, [saying little more than, "Turn left … turn right … stop here,"] as he made notes on his clipboard.
: [ ]는 동시 동작을 나타내는 분사구문이다.

02
정답 ②

성장하는 여정에서, 우리는 앞에 무엇이 놓여 있는지 확신하지 못한 채, 미지의 것의 경계에 서 있는 자신을 발견할 때가 있다. 이 익숙하지 않은 영역에 직면할 때, 우리의 마음은 때때로 이해가 많이 되는 것처럼 보이지 않는 방식으로 반응할 수 있다. 중요한 이벤트 전날 밤을 상상하라. 최선을 다해 준비가 되어 있음에도 불구하고, 일어날지도 모르는 일에 대한 좀체 사라지지 않는 불안감이 여전히 존재한다. 이러한 불안감은 밤을 새우거나 상황을 완전히 피하는 것과 같은, 논리적으로 보이지 않을 수도 있는 결정으로 이어질 수 있다. 마찬가지로, 우리의 미래에 대한 결정을 내리거나 새로운 일을 시도하는 것에 관한 한, 실수를 하는 것에 대한 두려움은 우리를 제지하여, 우리로 하여금 모험을 하기 보다는 우리가 알고 있는 것을 계속하게 만들 수 있다. 그것은 마치 빠진 조각을 가지고 퍼즐을 풀려고 하는 것과 같은데, 우리의 뇌는 상황이 명확하고 예측 가능하기를 좋아하지만, 그렇지 않은 경우, 우리는 비합리적으로 보이는 방식으로 행동할 수 있다. 요컨대, 미지의 것에 대한 두려움은 우리를 마비시키고 우리가 합리적으로 행동하지 못하게 할 수 있다.

해설
성장하는 과정에서 우리는 우리 앞에 무엇이 놓여 있는지 모르는 상태에서 미지의 것에 대한 두려움과 실수에 대한 두려움에 사로잡혀 비논리적인 행동을 하게 된다는 내용의 글이다. 따라서 글의 요지로 가장 적절한 것은 ② 이다.

⊗ 매력적인 오답 주의!
⑤ 글 전체의 내용을 파악하지 않고, the fear of making a mistake라는 어구에 집중하여 실수에 대한 두려움으로 인해 비판에 민감해질 수 있다고 오인하면 고를 수 있는 오답이다. 인간이 비판에 민감해질 수 있다는 내용은 언급되지 않았기 때문에 글의 요지로 적절하지 않다.

TEXT FLOW
도입	앞에 무엇이 놓여 있는지 모른 채 미지의 것의 경계에 서 있을 때가 있음
부연	일어날지도 모르는 일에 대한 불안감과 실수를 하는 것에 대한 두려움 때문에 비논리적인 결정을 하게 됨
결론	미지의 것에 대한 두려움 때문에 우리는 마비가 되고 비합리적으로 행동함

구문
• [When faced with this unfamiliar territory], our minds can sometimes react in ways [that don't seem to make much sense].
: 첫 번째 [ ]는 시간의 부사절에서 When과 faced 사이에 we are가 생략된 것으로 이해할 수 있다. 두 번째 [ ]는 ways를 수식하는 관계절이다.

03
정답 ②

휴대전화 한 대에는 평균 6.8밀리그램의 금이 들어 있다. 그것은 휴대전화 1,000대에는 약 6.8그램의 금이 들어 있다는 것을 의미한다. 더 가볍고 더 작은 것이 첨단 기술 전자 장치의 절대적인 기준이다. 대부분의 휴대전화는 그것의 회로판에 금을 사용하는데, 그것이 연결성이 높기 때문이다. 사용된 양이 무시해도 될 정도는 아니다. 단 5그램의 금이 보통 1톤의 광석에서 추출될 수 있는 반면에, 1톤의 휴대전화는 광석에서 나오는 양의 30배에 달하는 150그램의 금을 내놓는다. 현재, 세계는 광물 가격이 매일 오르는 가운데 자원 전쟁을 하고 있다. 우리는 이제 우리의 눈을 도시 광산업으로 돌려야 한다. 한국의 휴대전화 보급률은 매우 높고, 많은 사람들이 유행을 좇으려고 매년 자신의 휴대전화를 바꾸는 나라이다. 사람들의 서랍 안에 놓여 있는 휴대전화를 수거하려는 진심 어린 캠페인이 있다면, 우리는 많은 양의 자원, 즉 금을 모을 수 있을 것이다.

해설
평균 6.8밀리그램의 금이 들어 있는 휴대전화가 각 가정에 방치되는 경우가 많이 있는데, 그것을 수거할 수 있다면 많은 양의 금을 모을 수 있다는 요지의 글이므로, 글의 제목으로는 ② '휴대전화를 향한 새 금광지로의 쇄도'가 가장 적절하다.
① 대한민국: 자원이 부족한 나라
③ 휴대전화가 여러분에게서 개성을 빼앗는다
④ 모든 기능의 통합으로서의 휴대전화
⑤ 더 많은 휴대전화는 더 많은 자원 낭비를 의미한다

TEXT FLOW
도입	휴대전화의 회로판에 금이 사용되는데, 한 대당 평균 6.8밀리그램의 금이 들어 있음
전개	광물 가격이 매일 오르는 상황에서 도시 광산업으로 눈을 돌려야 함
결론	가정에 방치된 사용하지 않는 휴대전화를 수거하면 많은 양의 금을 모을 수 있음

구문
• If there **were** a sincere campaign to collect cell phones sitting in people's drawers, we **would be** able to collect a great amount of resources, gold.
: 「If+주어+were ~, 주어+would+동사원형 ....」 형태의 가정법 과거 구문으로 현재 사실에 반대되는 가정을 하고 있다. 가정법 과거에서 if절의 be동사는 인칭과 수에 상관없이 were를 쓴다.

04
정답 ③

Sunrise 여름 테니스 강습

이번 여름에 테니스 강습을 받을 계획이신가요? Welcome Center에 377-8803으로 전화해서 일정만 잡으시면 됩니다.

강습
– 개인 테니스 강습
– 소규모 테니스 강습 (2~3명의 선수)

개인별 시간당 요금
– 개인 강습: 비회원 60달러, 회원 40달러
– 소규모 강습:
• 참가자 2명: 비회원 40달러, 회원 25달러
• 참가자 3명: 비회원 30달러, 회원 20달러

테니스 코트
• 회원은 48시간 전까지 예약할 수 있습니다.
• 취소 통보는 24시간 전에 이루어져야 합니다.
• 예약한 모든 코트에 대해 15분 유예 시간이 허용됩니다.
• 비회원은 코트가 이용 가능 시 경기할 수 있습니다(예약 필요 없음).

더 많은 정보를 원하시면, 저희 웹사이트 www.sunrisesummertennis.com을 방문해 주세요.

해설
회원은 48시간 전까지 코트를 예약할 수 있다고 했으므로, 안내문의 내용과 일치하는 것은 ③이다.

구문

• A twenty-four-hour notice **should be given** for cancellations.

: 조동사가 포함된 문장의 수동태는 「조동사+be+과거분사」 형태로 쓴다.

05

정답 ④

시장에 의해 발생하는 유인 구조는 분주한 소매점의 계산이나 고속도로 운전을 수반하는 유인 구조와 매우 비슷하다. 차선에 있는 사람 수처럼, 이익과 손실은 시장 참여자에게 여러 다른 경제 활동의 장점과 단점에 대한 정보를 제공한다. 손실은 어떤 경제 활동이 혼잡하여 결과적으로 생산자가 자신의 비용을 댈 수 없다는 것을 나타낸다. 그런 경우에, 성공적인 시장 참여자는 자신의 자원을 그런 활동에서 빼서 가치가 더 큰 다른 용도로 옮긴다. 정반대로, 수익은 혼잡한(→ 비어 있는) 차선, 즉 단위당 비용에 비해 가격이 높은 활동으로 옮기면 이익을 경험할 수 있는 기회를 나타낸다. 생산자와 자원 공급자가 혼잡함으로 특징지어지는 활동에서 수익의 기회로 특징지어지는 활동으로 옮기면 경제 활동의 흐름이 증대한다.

해설

시장의 유인 구조는 소매점의 계산이나 고속도로 운전을 수반하는 유인 구조와 같아서 생산자와 자원 공급자는 경제 활동을 혼잡한 차선이 아니라 비어 있는 차선에서 하려고 한다는 내용의 글이다. 수익은 비어 있는 차선에서 발생할 것이므로 ④ crowded(혼잡한)를 open(비어 있는)과 같은 단어로 바꿔야 한다.

⊗ 매력적인 오답 주의!

② 경제적 활동이 혼잡하다는 것을 사업 경쟁자가 많다는 것으로 이해하지 못하면 고를 수 있는 오답이다.

TEXT FLOW

도입	시장의 유인 구조와 소매점의 계산 또는 고속도로 운전과의 유사성
주제	차선에 있는 사람의 수처럼 이익과 손실은 여러 경제 활동의 장단점에 대한 정보를 제공함
부연	자원을 혼잡한 차선에서 비어 있는 차선으로 옮기는 경제 활동

구문

• The incentive structure [generated by markets] is a lot like **that** [accompanying the check-out at a busy retail store or driving on the freeway].

: 첫 번째 [ ]는 문장의 주어인 The incentive structure를 수식하는 분사구이고, 동사는 is이다. that은 the incentive structure를 대신하는 대명사이고, 두 번째 [ ]는 that을 수식하는 분사구이다.

• Conversely, profits are indicative of an open lane, [the opportunity to experience gain if one shifts into an activity {in which the price is high relative to the per-unit cost}].

: [ ]는 an open lane과 동격 관계의 명사구이다. 그 안의 { }는 an activity를 수식하는 관계절이다.

06

정답 ①

뉴스와 관련하여, 균형 있는 시각을 가지는 것은 과거의 사건들과 현재의 사건들을 비교하는 능력을 포함한다. 균형 있는 시각을 염두에 두면, 우리는 뉴스가 시사하는 것과는 반대로 거의 아무것도 완전히 새로운 것이 없으며 소수의 일들만 정말 놀랍고 거의 아무것도 절대적으로 끔찍하지 않다는 것을 곧 알게 된다. 혁명은 역사의 종말을 의미하지 않을 것이고, 그것은 여러 다양하고 사소하고 복잡한 방식들로 많은 것을 바꿀 뿐일 것이다. 경제적인 전망은 어둡지만, 우리는 지난 세기 동안 여러 번 경기 하강을 경험했다. 심지어 최악의 시나리오들마저 우리가 몇십 년 전의 생활 수준으로 돌아갈 것이라고 예측할 뿐인데, 그때도 생활은 여전히 가능했다. 독감은 잠시 해외 여행을 중단시키고 알려진 약으로는 듣지 않을 것이지만, 연구실이 결국 그것을 파악하고 억제할 것이다. 홍수는 극적인 것처럼 보이지만, 결국 그것은 그저 인구의 일부에게만 영향을 줄 것이다.

해설

빈칸 뒤에 오는 사례들은 현재의 비극은 새롭거나 놀랍거나 끔찍한 것이 아니며, 과거에도 유사한 일이 있었고 결국 인류는 이것을 극복하리라는 것을 말하고 있다. 따라서 빈칸에 들어갈 말로는 ① '과거의 사건들과 현재의 사건들을 비교하는'이 가장 적절하다.
② 비극을 겪고 있는 다른 사람들에게 공감하는
③ 위기의 해결책을 아는 전문가들을 찾는
④ 인류를 구해 온 기술의 힘을 신뢰하는
⑤ 특정한 집단들의 의견들을 입증된 사실들과 구별하는

TEXT FLOW

주제	뉴스를 볼 때 균형 있는 시각은 과거와 현재의 사건들을 비교하는 능력을 말함
부연	균형 있는 시각을 갖게 되면 절대적으로 새롭거나 놀랍거나 끔찍한 것은 거의 없다는 것을 알게 됨
예시	혁명, 어두운 경제 전망, 독감, 홍수

구문

• Even the worst scenarios only predict [that we will return to a standard of living we had a few decades ago, {when life was still possible}].

: [ ]는 predict의 목적어 역할을 하는 명사절이고, 그 안의 { }는 관계부사절로 a few decades ago를 부연 설명한다.

07

정답 ④

1970년대 어느 영화 제작팀이 위협적인 외계인과 관련된 아이디어를 구상하고 있었다. Dan O'Bannon과 Ron Shusett은 그 이야기에 관해 함께 작업했고, 대부분의 영화 제작자들과 마찬가지로, 그것을 스튜디오에 홍보할 방법을 필요로 했다. 그들은 '우주 속의 Jaws'라는 단순한 세 단어를 사용하여 영화를 홍보했다. Steven Spielberg가 감독한 영화 'Jaws'는 1975년에 극장가에 히트를 쳤는데, 그것은 대히트였다. 수백만 명이 그 영화를 보았고, 보지 않았던 사람들도 그 이야기를 알고 있었다. O'Bannon과 Shusett은 'Jaws'라는 이름을 들먹임으로써 그들의 아이디어에 대한 발판을 마련했다. 그것은 명백하게 효과가 있었다. 그들의 아이디어는 오스카 수상작 'Alien'이 되었는데, Sir Ridley Scott이 감독했고 Sigourney Weaver가 주연을 맡았다. 1979년에 개봉한 이후 그것은 전 세계적으로 1억 달러 이상을 벌어들였다. 'Alien'을 본 적이 있는 사람이면 누구나 '우주

속의 Jaws'가 그 영화의 의도에 유용한 소개였다는 것을 알 수 있다. 그것이 왜 효과가 있었을까? 왜냐하면 O'Bannon과 Shusett은 그들의 아이디어를 관객이 이미 이해하고 있던 어떤 것에 연결시킬 수 있었기 때문이었다. 스튜디오 대표들은 아마 'Jaws'를 봤고 이 지식을 사용하여 'Alien' 뒤에 숨겨진 의도를 상상할 수 있었다.

해설

영화 'Alien'의 제작 배경에 관한 글로, 영화 홍보를 위해 '우주 속의 Jaws'라는 세 단어를 사용하였는데 이것이 매우 효과적인 홍보였으며 영화가 크게 흥행하였다는 내용이다. 모든 사람이 'Jaws'를 알고 있었기 때문에 그들의 홍보 전략이 효과가 있었으므로, 빈칸에 들어갈 말로 가장 적절한 것은 ④ '그들의 아이디어를 관객이 이미 이해하고 있던 어떤 것에 연결시킬'이다.
① 우주에서 진짜 외계인들을 만나는 것에 큰 흥미를 느낄
② 그들의 새 영화에 훌륭하고, 인기 있고, 유명한 배우들을 투입할
③ 그들의 과학 지식을 참신하고 낯선 상황에 응용할
⑤ 많은 사람에게 일어나지 않은 창의적인 아이디어를 생각해 낼

TEXT FLOW

도입	한 영화 제작팀이 새 영화 홍보를 위해 'Jaws in Space'라는 세 단어를 이용함
전개 1	당시 'Jaws'는 대히트작으로 'Jaws in Space'는 효과적인 소개였음
전개 2	덕분에 오스카 수상작인 'Alien'이 탄생했고 대성공을 거두게 되었음
주제	성공의 이유는 아이디어를 청중이 이미 이해하고 있던 어떤 것에 연결시킬 수 있었기 때문이었음

구문

• Dan O'Bannon and Ron Shusett [**worked** together on the story] and, {like most moviemakers}, [**needed** a way ⟨to pitch it to studios⟩].
: 두 개의 동사구 [ ]가 and로 연결되어 병렬 구조를 이루고 있다. { }는 삽입어구이고, ⟨ ⟩는 앞의 a way를 수식하는 형용사적 용법의 to부정사구이다.

• Anyone [who has seen *Alien*] can see [that "*Jaws* in Space" was a useful introduction to the big idea of the movie].
: 첫 번째 [ ]는 Anyone을 수식하는 관계절이고, 두 번째 [ ]는 see의 목적어 역할을 하는 명사절이다.

08

정답 ④

오늘날 기술의 힘은 전례가 없긴 하지만, 그 티핑 포인트는 250만 년이 넘는 기간 전에 일어났다. 기술 시대의 시작은 고고학적으로 최초의 뗀석기 유물, 즉 큰 사냥감을 죽이는 데 그럴듯하게 사용된 도구나 무기에 의해 암시된다. 그 시점 이후에, 인간을 대면하는 동물들에게는, 보통은 (생물학적) 적합성을 뜻하게 될 특성이 점점 더 불리한 것이 될 수 있었다. 자연 선택과 적자생존의 과정이 약화되었다. (자연 선택은 다양한 환경에서 생존을 위한 적응 형질을 만들어 내도록 (생물) 종을 유도했다.) 무기를 가진 지적인 인간은 적합하든 부적합하든, 어리든 늙었든, 크든 작든, 원하는 동물은 어떤 것이나 죽일 수 있었고, 유전의 생물학에 갇힌 동물들은 효과적인 대응을 전혀 하지 못했다.

해설

인간이 기술의 힘을 이용하게 되면서 유전의 생물학에만 의존했던 동물들을 능가하게 되었다는 내용의 글이다. 따라서 자연 선택으로 인해 생물 종이 적응 형질을 가지게 되어 다양한 환경에서 생존할 수 있었다는 내용의 ④는 글의 전체 흐름과 관계가 없다.

TEXT FLOW

도입	뗀석기 유물부터 시작된 기술 시대
주제	동물의 생물학적 적합성이 점점 더 불리한 것이 됨
부연	자연 선택과 적자생존 과정이 약화됨

구문

• After that point, for animals confronted by humans, the characteristics [that would ordinarily convey fitness] could increasingly become a liability.
: [ ]는 the characteristics를 수식하는 관계절이다.

• Intelligent humans with weapons could kill [whichever animals they liked], [fit or unfit, young or old, large or small], and the animals, trapped by the biology of inheritance, had no effective response.
: 첫 번째 [ ]는 kill의 목적어 역할을 하는 명사절이고, any animals they liked의 의미로 이해할 수 있다. 두 번째 [ ]는 첫 번째 [ ]에 대해 부가적으로 설명하는 형용사구이다.

09

정답 ②

히말라야의 동쪽 맨 끝에 위치하고 있는 부탄은 인구가 약 70만 명이고, 1인당 GDP가 약 2,000달러인 작은 왕국이다. 텔레비전은 1999년에 처음 소개되었고, 인터넷은 2000년에 처음 등장했다. (B) 상대적으로 경제와 인구 규모가 작고 과학 기술 발전이 부족함에도 불구하고, 부탄은 세계에서 여덟 번째로 행복한 나라로 선정되었다. (A) 부탄 사람들이 그와 같은 높은 수준의 행복감을 느끼는 이유는 1972년 선왕 Jigme Singye Wangchuck에 의해 도입된 생각인, 그 나라의 GNH(국민 총 행복) 정책과 관계가 있다. (C) 그는 무슨 수를 써서라도 경제 발전을 추구하는 대신에, 환경과 동등하게 분배된 부(富)를 보호하는 정책을 내놓았다. 돈보다도 내적인 만족감에 더 많은 중요성을 두었다.

해설

부탄이라는 나라에 대한 개략적인 소개에 해당하는 주어진 글 다음에는, 경제와 인구 규모가 작고 부족한 과학 기술 발전에도 불구하고, 세계에서 여덟 번째로 행복한 나라로 선정되었다는 내용의 (B)가 오고, 그렇게 높은 수준의 행복감을 느끼는 이유에 대해 언급하는 (A)가 (B) 다음에 온 후에, Jigme Singye Wangchuck 왕이 펼친 정책에 대해 설명하는 (C)가 마지막에 오는 것이 글의 흐름상 가장 자연스럽다.

TEXT FLOW

도입	부탄은 경제와 인구 규모가 작고 과학 기술도 많이 발전하지 않은 왕국임
전개	부탄은 세계에서 여덟 번째로 행복한 나라로 선정되었는데, 부탄 사람들의 높은 행복지수는 Jigme Singye Wangchuck 왕에 의해 도입된 정책과 관계가 있음
부연	그 정책은 돈보다도 내적인 만족감에 중점을 두었음

• The reason [why Bhutanese feel such a great level of happiness] has something to do with the county's policy of GNH (Gross National Happiness), ~.
: [ ]는 관계부사절로 문장의 주어인 The reason을 수식하고, 동사는 has이다.

10 정답 ③

20세기에, Werner Heisenberg와 Albert Einstein을 비롯한 물리학자들은 보편적이고 객관적인 '진리'의 가능성에 의문을 제기하기 시작했다. 그들은 동일한 질문을 다루기 위해 고안된 다양한 실험이 질문의 방식에 따라 서로 다른 결과를 낸다는 사실을 관찰했다. (B) 예를 들어, 빛이 파동으로 이루어진다는 가설이 세워지면, 실험은 그것(빛)이 파동임을 시사하는 패턴을 내놓았다. 그러나 빛이 입자로 구성되어 있다는 가설이 세워지면, 실험은 입자의 패턴을 나타냈다. (C) 빛이 동시에 파동이면서 입자이고, 에너지이면서 물질인 것이 가능했던 것일까? Heisenberg는 실험 과정 자체가 현실과 상호 작용하며, 진리를 바라보는 완전히 객관적인 입장이라는 것은 없다고 결론지었다. (A) 다시 말해서, 과학자들은 현상과의 상호 작용을 통해 어느 정도 결과를 형성한다. 심지어 과학적 해석조차도 기존의 관점에 기반을 두고 있고, 무엇을 관찰하고 그것을 어떻게 이해해야 하는지에 대한 규칙을 가진, 특정 탐구 문화에 기반을 두고 있다.

해설

실험이 질문 방식에 따라 다른 결과를 낸다는 물리학자들의 관찰 결과를 언급한 주어진 글 뒤에는, 빛을 사례로 들어 가설에 따라 파동 혹은 입자, 에너지 혹은 물질이 되는 실험 결과를 예시한 (B)가 와야 한다. (B) 뒤에는 빛이 다양한 모습이 되는 이유를 실험 과정과 현실의 상호 작용으로 설명하는 (C)가 와야 한다. (C) 뒤에는 (B)에서 언급한 실험 과정과 현실의 상호 작용을 과학자의 현상과의 상호 작용이라고 풀어서 다시 진술하는 (A)가 오는 것이 글의 흐름상 가장 자연스럽다.

TEXT FLOW

주제	실험이 질문 방식에 따라 다른 결과를 냄
예시	파동이면서 입자이고 에너지이면서 물질인 빛
재진술	과학자들은 현상과의 상호 작용을 통해 어느 정도 결과를 형성함

구문

• For example, when light was hypothesized to be composed of waves, the experiments produced a pattern [that suggested it was waves].
: [ ]는 a pattern을 수식하는 관계절이다.

11 정답 ⑤

향수병은 오랫동안 감상적으로 다뤄져 와서 처음으로 부모와 떨어진 아이들이나 그것을 앓아야만 정당화될 정도가 되었다. 그렇지만 1688년에 Johannes Hofer는 향수병이나 고향을 그리워하는 것은 의학적인 질병이라고 썼다. 집으로 돌아가는 것을 나타내는 'nostos'와 고통이나 갈망을 나타내는 'algos'는 아픈 사람이 고향으로 돌아가기를 바라고 고향을 다시 보지 못할 것이라고 두려워하기 때문에 느끼는 고통으로 이해되었다. Hofer의

입장에서 보면, 그것은 강대국들이 항상 전쟁을 하던 시대에 속한 질병이었다. 그 시대에, 병사들은 고국에 다시 발을 들여놓지 못할 것이라고 의심하면서 한 번에 몇 년씩 외국 땅에서 보낼 수도 있었다. 군사 작전들로 인해 거의 죽기 직전이어서 가족이 있는 곳에서 죽기 위해 고향으로 보내지는 사람들이 생겨났다. 그러나 그들은 자신들의 도시나 나라를 보자마자 현저히 회복되었다.

해설

주어진 문장은 군사 작전 중에 사망할 지경에 이르러 고향으로 보내지는 사람들이 있었다는 내용이므로, 전쟁 때문에 병사들이 외국 땅에서 몇 년씩 보냈다는 내용과 이 사람들이 고향을 보자마자 현저히 회복되었다는 내용 사이인 ⑤에 들어가는 것이 가장 적절하다.

TEXT FLOW

도입	향수병에 대한 과거의 인식
전환	Johannes Hofer는 향수병을 의학적인 질병으로 이해함
부연	역사적으로 강대국들이 전쟁을 하던 시기에 이 질병이 발생했는데, 군사 작전으로 죽어 가던 사람들이 고향을 보자마자 현저히 회복됨

구문

• At that time, soldiers **might** spend years at a time in foreign lands, [suspecting that they might never again set foot in their native countries].
: 불확실한 가정을 나타내기 위해 조동사 might를 사용했다. [ ]는 분사구문으로 '~하면서'라는 의미의 동시동작을 나타낸다.

12-14 정답 12 ⑤ 13 ⑤ 14 ③

(A) Edgar Jackson은 '단풍나무의 메시지'라는 자신의 고전적인 이야기로 유명한데, 그 이야기는 모든 사람들을 위한 영원한 메시지를 담고 있다. 그 이야기의 토대는 자신의 인생에 닥친 거대한 역경의 벽을 극복하기 위한 Jackson의 노력에서 나왔다. 그 이야기를 쓰기 전에, Jackson은 뇌졸중을 겪고 말을 할 수 없게 되었다. 그가 회복했을 때, 그는 Vermont의 Corinth에 있는 농장으로 이사했고, 그곳에서 Edward Zieglar라는 작가를 만났다.

(D) Zieglar는 '리더스 다이제스트' 지의 저자였고, Jackson의 책을 여러 권 읽었다. 그 자신도 작가로서, 그는 Jackson을 굉장히 존경했었다. 그는 여러 심각한 개인적인 문제들을 경험하고 있었기에, Jackson에게 도움을 청하러 갔다. Jackson은 Zieglar와 잠시 이야기를 나누고는, 자신의 목초지로 가자고 그를 초대했다. 그들은 이전 주인에 의해 심어진 단풍나무들로 둘러싸인 3에이커의 목초지로 걸어서 갔다. Jackson은 나무들을 가리키며, 이전 주인이 그가 울타리를 위한 말뚝들을 세울 필요가 없도록 그것들을 심었다고 설명했다.

(C) 그 주인은 그 나무들이 튼튼해질 때까지 기다린 다음, 한 나무에서 옆의 나무로 가시철조망을 연결했다. Jackson이 Zieglar와 이 나무에서 저 나무로 걸어가고 있을 때, 그는 여러 다른 단풍나무들이 그것들의 민감한 껍질을 둘러싼 가시철조망에 어떻게 반응했었는지 가리켰다. 몇몇 나무들은 그 철조망을 자신들의 몸통에 파묻었고, 그 가시철조망에도 불구하고 강인하고 똑바르게 자랐다. 그렇지만 몇몇 나무들은 가시철조망의 침범에 전혀 적응하지 못했고, 그것들은 뒤틀리고 흉하게 자랐다.

(B) Jackson은 사람들이 그 단풍나무들과 비슷하다는 점에 주목했다. 어떤 사람들은 문제에 직면하고, 그 문제들을 자신들의 삶에 짜 넣음으로써 그것

들에 적응하고, 그런 다음 계속 살아가고, 그 과정에서 키가 자라고 승리하게 된다. 다른 사람들은 그 어려움들이 자신들의 삶을 휘게 하고, 왜곡하며, 망치도록 허용한다. 나무들과 사람들의 차이점은 사람들은 자신들이 어떻게 자랄 것인지 선택할 수 있다는 점이다. Jackson은 그가 겪어 내었던 그의 뇌졸중이나 고통스러운 과정에 관해 한마디도 하지 않았지만, Zieglar는 그의 메시지를 완전히 이해할 수 있었다. 결국, 그도 역경을 딛고 자란 단풍나무였다.

해설

12 뇌졸중에서 회복한 Jackson이 이사를 갔고 그곳에서 Zieglar를 만나게 되었다는 내용의 (A)에 이어, Zieglar에 대한 소개 내용과 그가 Jackson과 이야기를 나눈 후에 단풍나무들에 둘러싸인 목초지를 걷는 내용인 (D)가 온 다음, 철조망이 얽히게 된 단풍나무들의 두 가지 반응에 대한 내용인 (C)가 온다. 이어서 Jackson이 하는 말을 듣고 난 Zieglar가 사람도 단풍나무와 같아서, 시련을 자신의 일부로 받아들이고 적응하여 극복해야 한다는 점을 깨달았다는 내용의 (B)가 오는 것이 글의 흐름상 가장 자연스럽다.

13 (e)는 목초지의 이전 주인을 가리키고, 나머지는 모두 Jackson을 가리킨다.

14 (B)에 Jackson은 자신이 겪은 뇌졸중이나 그 고통스러운 과정에 관해 Zieglar에게 한마디도 하지 않았다는 언급이 있으므로, ③은 Jackson에 관한 내용으로 적절하지 않다.

TEXT FLOW

시간 순서/사건 전개에 따른 흐름:
(A) 뇌졸중에서 회복한 Jackson이 Vermont로 이사를 가서 Zieglar를 만나게 됨 → (D) 함께 목초지를 걸으며 Jackson이 그곳에 있는 단풍나무에 관해 이야기함 → (C) 가시철조망이 나무를 둘러쌀 때, 철조망을 몸속에 파묻고 자란 나무들과 철조망을 피해 뒤틀리며 자란 나무들이 있음 → (B) Jackson은 사람들도 이와 같이 어려움을 대하는 태도가 다름에 주목함

구문

• Some people **encounter** problems, **adjust** to those problems by incorporating them into their lives, and then **continue** on, [growing tall and triumphant in the process].
: encounter, adjust, continue는 and로 병렬 연결되어 주어 Some people에 이어지는 동사이다. [ ]는 연속 동작을 나타내는 분사구문으로, 의미상 주어는 Some people이다.

• Jackson pointed to the trees and explained [that the former owner **had planted** them so that he wouldn't have to set posts for a fence].
: [ ]는 explained의 목적어 역할을 하는 명사절로, 과거의 어느 시점보다 더 이전에 일어난 사실을 분명하게 하기 위해 대과거 had planted를 사용했다.

GRAMMAR REVIEW

본문 57쪽

1 to pull	2 are	3 rising
4 those	5 what	6 knew
7 used	8 it	9 at which
10 where		

1 instruct는 목적격 보어로 to부정사를 취하는 동사이므로 to pull이 적절하다.

2 they는 things를 가리키고 are not clear and predictable에서 clear and predictable이 생략된 것이므로 are가 적절하다.

3 「with+목적어+분사」 구문으로 mineral prices가 rise의 주체이므로 현재분사 rising을 써야 한다.

4 activities를 대신하는 대명사이어야 하므로 those가 적절하다.

5 contrary to의 목적어인 관계절을 이끌고 선행사가 없으므로 관계대명사 what이 적절하다.

6 관계절 who did not (see the movie)의 수식을 받는 those가 절의 주어이며 동사가 필요하다. 문맥상 과거 시제이므로 knew가 적절하다.

7 a tool or weapon을 수식하는 분사가 와야 하는데, a tool or weapon이 동사 use의 대상이므로 과거분사 used를 써야 한다.

8 의미상 what to observe를 대신해야 하므로 단수형인 it이 적절하다.

9 the point를 수식하는 관계절을 이끌고 완전한 형태의 절이므로 「전치사+관계대명사」인 at which가 적절하다. 관계대명사 뒤에는 불완전한 형태의 절이 온다.

10 선행사 a farm in Corinth, Vermont가 장소를 나타내며, 뒤에 완전한 형태의 절이 이어지므로 이를 부연 설명하는 관계부사 where가 적절하다.

하프 모의고사 07회

01 ⑤	02 ①	03 ③	04 ②	05 ③
06 ⑤	07 ②	08 ⑤	09 ③	10 ④
11 ③	12 ⑤	13 ⑤	14 ③	

01
정답 ⑤

칼슘은 뼈를 만들고 유지하는 데 필수적이지만, 설문 조사에 따르면 50%에 달하는 아시아 여성이 일일 권장량보다 칼슘을 덜 섭취할지 모른다고 한다. 유제품은 그것을 쉽게 얻을 수 있는 하나의 방법인데, 매일 저지방 요구르트 한 통과 고칼슘 우유 300밀리리터면 권장량의 대부분을 얻을 수 있다. 하지만 칼슘을 너무 많이 섭취하기란 매우 어렵다. 대부분의 성인들은 하루에 2,000밀리그램까지는 안전하게 섭취할 수 있지만, 더 많은 양은 혈액 속 높아진 칼슘 농도, 손상된 신장 기능, 다른 무기질들의 흡수 저하를 포함하는 문제들을 일으킬 수 있다. 그러나 최근 연구에 따르면, 높은 칼슘 농도는 대장암에 걸릴 위험성을 줄여 준다. 따라서 매일 충분한 칼슘을 섭취하는 것이 적극적으로 권장된다.

해설
칼슘이 뼈를 만들고 유지하는 데 필수적이며 대장암에 걸릴 위험성을 줄여 주는 기능이 있어 매일 충분한 칼슘 섭취를 할 필요가 있다고 권장하는 내용의 글이므로, 글의 목적으로는 ⑤가 가장 적절하다.

TEXT FLOW

도입	칼슘은 뼈를 만들고 유지시키는 데 필수적임
전개	유제품으로 쉽게 칼슘 섭취를 할 수 있음에도 불구하고 많은 사람들이 충분한 칼슘 섭취를 못하고 있음
결론	높은 칼슘 농도가 대장암에 걸릴 위험성을 줄여 주므로 매일 충분한 칼슘을 섭취할 것을 권장함

구문
• However, **it** is very hard [to get too much calcium].
: it은 가주어이고 [ ]가 진주어이다.

02
정답 ①

오늘날의 기자에게 있어 대차 대조표의 형태이든, 혹은 통계 자료 한 묶음의 형태이든 통계 자료와 수치는 필수적인 업무의 일부이다. 많은 기자가 "아, 저는 수학을 못 해요."라고 말하는 것을 마치 채식주의자이거나 수염을 기르는 것과 같은 생활 양식의 선택인 마냥 자랑스러워하는 것처럼 보인다. 분명히 그들이 재능 있는 수학자였다면 회계사 혹은 수학자, 아니면 통계학자로 일하고 있을 것이다. 그들은 자신의 역량이 다른 곳에 있어서 기자로 일하고 있다. 그러나 우리가 통계학자나 회계사가 그들의 통계 자료나 대차 대조표에 대한 읽기 쉬운 보고서를 만들 수 있기를 기대하고, 그렇지 못했을 때 비웃을 수도 있는 것과 꼭 마찬가지로, 똑똑한 기자라면 기본적인 대차 대조표를 이해하고 읽을 수 있으며 통계의 기본을 이해할 수 있기를 기대하는 것이 합리적이다.

해설
통계 자료와 수치는 오늘날의 기자에게 있어서 필수적인 업무의 일부이며 똑똑한 기자라면 대차 대조표와 통계의 기본을 이해할 수 있어야 한다는 내용의 글이므로, 필자가 주장하는 바로 가장 적절한 것은 ①이다.

✕ 매력적인 오답 주의!
④ 글의 중심 생각을 제대로 이해하지 못하고 글에서 언급되는 reporter, statistics와 같은 단편적인 어휘를 근거로 고를 수 있는 오답이다.

TEXT FLOW

주제	기자에게 있어서 통계와 수치는 필수적인 업무의 일부임
부연 1	많은 기자가 자신이 수학을 못 하는 것을 하나의 선택처럼 인식함
부연 2	똑똑한 기자라면 기본적인 대차 대조표와 통계의 기본을 이해하고 읽을 수 있어야 함

구문
• Statistics and figures are a vital part of the reporter's job these days, **whether** in the form of [a balance sheet] **or** [a sheaf of statistics].
: 명사구인 두 개의 [ ]가 '~이든지 …이든지 간에'의 의미를 나타내는 「whether ~ or ....」로 연결되어 있다.

• But **just as** we [would expect a statistician or accountant to be able to pull together a readable report about their statistics or balance sheets], and [might sneer if they couldn't], **so** it is reasonable to expect an intelligent reporter [to be able to {understand and read a basic balance sheet} and {understand the basics of statistics}].
: 「just as ~, so ....」는 '~인 것과 꼭 마찬가지로 …하다'라는 의미이다. 첫 번째 [ ]와 두 번째 [ ]는 부사절의 술어로 and로 연결되어 부사절의 주어인 we에 이어진다. 세 번째 [ ]는 expect의 목적격 보어 역할을 하는 to부정사구인데, 그 안에 있는 두 개의 { }가 and로 연결되어 be able to에 이어진다.

03
정답 ③

과학적 진보의 파생적이고 협력적인 특성을 더 강조하는 문화와 더불어, 과잉 경쟁적 행동에 대한 보상과 '명망 있는' 연구자 추종에 관한 줄어든 강조는 과학을 발전시킬 수 있을 것이다. 진화생물학자 David Sloan Wilson은 Purdue 대학교 연구원인 William Muir의 산란계 생산성 향상 시도에 관해 이야기한 바 있다. 다음 세대를 번식시키기 위해 각 집단에서 가장 생산성이 높은 암탉을 선발하는 접근 방식과 가장 생산성이 높은 암탉 집단을 선발하는 방법이 비교되었다. 예상외로 후자의 접근 방식이 가장 성공적이었는데, 그 이유는 성공적인 집단에 속한 개체가 협력하여 활동하는 법을 배웠고, 더 행복한 암탉일수록 더 많은 알을 낳았기 때문이다. 우수한 암탉을 한 집단으로 편성했을 때는 생산성이 급감했고, 실험이 끝날 무렵 이 집단의 암탉 세 마리를 제외한 모든 암탉이 죽었다. 이러한 결과를 설명하는 강의가 끝나자 청중에 있던 한 교수가 이렇게 외쳤다. "저건 우리 학과가 어떤지를 말하고 있어요! 저 닭 세 마리의 이름을 알아요!"라고 외쳤다. 안타깝게도 우리 중 많은 이들이 각자의 학과에서 비슷한 닭들을 알고 있다.

해설
과학에서 과잉 경쟁적 행동과 명망 있는 연구자 추종에 대한 줄어든 강조가 과학을 발전시킬 수 있을 것이고 이것과 관련하여 예시가 소개되는데, 닭의 생산성을 향상하려는 실험에서 가장 생산성이 높은 암탉을 선발하여 한 집단으로 편성했을 때 오히려 생산성이 급감했으며 세 마리의 암탉만 살아남았고, 이 실험 결과를 들은 한 교수가 이 결과가 본인이 속한 학과의 상황을 나타내는 것이라고 말했다는 내용이다. 따라서 밑줄 친 부분이 글에서 의미하는 바로 가장 적절한 것은 ③ '팀워크보다 개인의 성취를 더 우선시하는 연구자들'이다.

① 학문적 명성을 얻는 데 관심이 없는 학자들
② 원하는 결과를 얻기 위해 데이터를 조작하는 과학자들
④ 실용적인 응용보다 이론에 더 집중하는 교수들
⑤ 참신한 아이디어가 부족하여 기존 연구에만 기반하는 연구자들

TEXT FLOW

주제	과학적 진보의 파생적이고 협력적인 특성을 강조하고 과잉 경쟁적 행동을 덜 강조하는 것이 과학을 발전시킴
실험	David Sloan Wilson의 산란계 생산성 향상 실험에서 닭의 생산성을 비교함
결과	우수한 암탉을 한 집단으로 편성했을 때 오히려 생산성이 급감하고 다른 닭들이 죽게 됨

구문

• A culture [that places a greater emphasis on {the derivative and collaborative nature of scientific advances}, along with a reduced emphasis on {rewarding hypercompetitive behavior and the cult of the "rock star" investigator}], would improve science.
: [ ]는 A culture를 수식하는 관계절이고, 두 개의 { }는 각각 전치사 on의 목적어 역할을 한다.

• [The approach of selecting the most productive individual hens from each group {to breed the next generation}] was compared with [selecting the most productive groups of hens].
: 첫 번째 [ ]는 문장의 주어이고, 그 안의 { }는 목적의 의미를 나타내는 부사적 용법의 to부정사구이다. 두 번째 [ ]는 전치사 with의 목적어 역할을 하는 동명사구이다.

04
정답 ②

현대 사회에서, 한 개인의 운명은 동시대의 삶의 크기와 복잡성에 매우 깊이 영향을 받는다. 예를 들어, 관료제라고 하는 조직의 합리화된 형태가 마침내 카리스마적인 리더십과 전통을 대체했다. 규칙, 규율, 그리고 권위의 위계질서에 근거한 관료제는 사람들을 객관적으로 다루도록 만들어진 보편적인 규칙들에 따라 기능한다. 원칙적으로, 관료제는 많은 수의 사람들에게 관련된 일을 통제하는 가장 효과적인 수단이다. 그러나 관료제는 흔히 그 자체의 문제점들을 만들어 내는데, 특히 객관적인 규칙들을 결국 분별 없이 적용하게 되는 그것의 경향과 관련하여 그렇다. 그래서, 일부 사람들은 관료제가 사실 통제 불능이라고 주장한다. 그들은 관료주의적 권위가 비민주적이고 규칙들에 대한 맹목적인 고수는 조직의 목표를 성취하는 데 필요한 정확한 조치를 방해할 수도 있다고 주장한다.

해설

현대 사회의 관료제는 사람들을 객관적인 기준으로 대한다는 점에서 많은 사람이 관련된 일을 통제하는 가장 효과적인 수단이지만 그 특성으로 인해 여러 가지 문제점들도 양산한다는 내용의 글이므로, 글의 주제로는 ② '관료제의 이상과 한계'가 가장 적절하다.

① 관료제의 기본 원칙
③ 관료주의적 조직의 혁신적인 측면
④ 공정한 법 적용의 필요성
⑤ 사람들이 권위적인 인물들에게 복종하고자 하는 경향

TEXT FLOW

도입	관료제가 카리스마적인 리더십과 전통을 대체함
전개	원칙적으로 관료제는 많은 사람들과 관련된 일을 통제하는 가장 효과적인 수단임
반론	그러나 관료제가 비민주적이고 규칙을 맹목적으로 고수하면 조직의 목표를 성취하는 데 방해가 될 수 있음

구문

• They claim that [bureaucratic authority is undemocratic] and [the blind adherence to rules may inhibit the exact actions {necessary to achieve organizational goals}].
: 두 개의 [ ]가 접속사 that에 이어져 claim의 목적어 역할을 한다. 두 번째 [ ] 안의 { }는 the exact actions를 수식하는 형용사구이다.

05
정답 ③

위의 두 개의 파이 그래프는 2010년과 2019년에 영국의 4개 구성국의 풍력 발전 전력의 점유율을 보여 준다. 2010년에는 스코틀랜드가 영국 4개 구성국 중 가장 큰 풍력 발전 전력 점유율을 가졌다. 하지만 2019년에는 잉글랜드가 영국에서 가장 많은 풍력 발전 전력을 공급하는 구성국이었다. 2010년과 2019년 둘 다에서 스코틀랜드는 영국의 전체 풍력 발전 전력의 40퍼센트 이상을 차지했다. 2010년부터 2019년까지 북아일랜드와 웨일스 풍력 발전 전력 점유율은 둘 다 약간 감소했다. 북아일랜드는 2010년과 2019년 모두 4개 구성국 중 풍력 발전 전력 비중이 각 해 7퍼센트 미만으로 가장 낮았다.

해설

2019년에 스코틀랜드는 영국 전체 풍력 발전 전력의 34.8퍼센트를 차지했으므로, 도표의 내용과 일치하지 않는 것은 ③이다.

구문

• From 2010 to 2019, [the shares of wind-generated electricity in both Northern Ireland and wales] slightly fell.
: [ ]는 문장의 주어이고, 동사는 fell이다.

06
정답 ⑤

과학자들처럼, 글을 읽고 쓸 수 있는 인간은 태어나는 것이 아니라 만들어진다. 과학처럼, 읽을 수 있는 능력은 가장 분명하게, 성숙하게 타고난 인지 기술이 '아니다'. 과학 말고 더 많은 연습을 필요로 하는 어떤 지적 기술이 있는가? 읽고 쓰는 방법을 배우는 것은 단지 수년간의 노력과 교육뿐만 아니라 쓰고 읽을 수 있는 자료의 이용 가능성을 필요로 한다. 한 아동의 삶에서 다년간 지속되는 인쇄 자료와 학교 교육 시스템의 광범위한 이용 가능성은 독특하게 현대적인 현상으로, 그것은 오늘날까지 주로 세계에서 가장 부유한 절반의 국가에만 국한되어 있다. 과학이 인류 역사에서 그렇게 드물었던 주

된 이유는 그것이 의존하는 부자연스러운 인지적 성취, 즉 읽고 쓰는 능력 그 자체가 인류 역사에서 매우 드물었기 때문이다. 대부분의 문화는 쓰기 체계를 발달시키지 않았고, 심지어 쓰기 체계를 채택한 문화 중 극히 일부만이 상당한 언어 자료를 만들어 냈을 뿐이다.

해설

⑤ and 다음에 절이 나와야 하는데, only a fraction of those that even adopted one이 주어이고 술어 동사가 필요하므로 having을 have로 고쳐야 한다.

① 동사 requires의 주어 역할을 하면서 선행사 any intellectual skill을 수식하는 관계대명사가 필요하므로 that은 적절하다. other than science는 선행사 any intellectual skill과 관계대명사 that 사이에 쓰인 삽입어구임에 유의한다.

② to write on이 앞의 명사 materials를 수식하는 형용사적 용법의 to부정사구로 명사가 전치사 on의 목적어이므로 전치사 on을 쓴 것은 적절하다.

③ a uniquely modern phenomenon이 '국한되어 있는' 수동의 의미이므로 과거분사 confined는 적절하다.

④ the unnatural cognitive accomplishment를 수식하면서 뒤에 완전한 형태의 절이 이어지므로 「전치사+관계대명사」는 적절하다. depend on의 전치사 on이 관계대명사 앞에 쓰인 것으로 볼 수 있다.

TEXT FLOW

주제	과학자들처럼, 글을 읽고 쓸 수 있는 인간은 태어나는 것이 아니라 만들어짐
부연	읽고 쓰는 방법을 배우는 것은 단지 수년간의 노력과 교육뿐만 아니라 쓰고 읽을 수 있는 자료의 이용 가능성을 요구하며 이는 독특하게 현대적인 현상임
근거	인류 역사에서 과학이 드물었던 이유는 읽고 쓰는 능력 그 자체가 인류 역사에서 매우 드물었기 때문임

구문

• [Learning to read and write] calls **not merely** [for years of hard work and tutelage] **but** [for the availability of materials to write on and to read].
: 첫 번째 [ ]는 문장의 주어 역할을 하는 동명사구이고, 두 번째와 세 번째 [ ]는 '단지 A뿐만 아니라 B(도)'라는 의미의 「not merely A but (also) B」 구문으로 연결되어 있다.

• The principal reason [that science has been so rare in human history] is [that the unnatural cognitive accomplishment {on which it depends}, literacy, has itself been so rare in human history].
: 첫 번째 [ ]는 The principal reason을 수식하는 관계절이고, 두 번째 [ ]는 is의 주격 보어 역할을 하는 명사절이다. 두 번째 [ ] 안의 { }는 the unnatural cognitive accomplishment를 수식하는 관계절이다.

07 정답 ②

현대의 청중들이 고결한 소비를 위한 기회를 외면할 가능성이 있는 한 이유가 있는데, 그들이 <u>지쳐 버렸기</u> 때문이다. 현대의 업무는 참여자에게 극도로 힘든 양의 일을 요구한다. 우리는 보통 고갈된 상태로 직장으로부터 돌아온다. 그런 상태에서는 우리가 마음이 내키게 되는 제품과 서비스가 매우 독특한 종류의 것이어야 한다. 우리는 너무 무정하게 되어서 다른 사람의 고통에 그다지 관심을 가지지 않거나, 멀리 떨어진 차 농장이나 목화밭의 불행한

사람들에 대해 감정 이입하여 생각하지 못할 수도 있다. 우리는 지루함을 너무 많이 견뎌서 지적으로 조심스럽고 학문적으로 미묘한 논의에 관하여 인내심을 유지하지 못했을 수도 있다. 우리는 너무 불안해서 우리 마음의 더 진심어린 부분을 탐구할 힘을 갖지 못할 수도 있다. 우리는 자신을 약간 지나치게 미워해서 자신에게 좋은 것만 먹고 마시고 싶지 않을 수도 있다. 우리의 삶은 의미 있는 것에만 집중하기에는 너무 의미가 부족할 수 있다. 직장에서 일어난 것의 효과를 상쇄하기 위해 우리는 지나치게 달고, 짜고, 산만하고, 쉽고, 화려하고, 일촉즉발이고, 그리고 감상적인 것을 향해 본능적으로 접근할 수 있다.

해설

현대 사회에서는 직장에서 극도로 힘든 양의 일을 요구하기 때문에 우리는 보통 고갈된 상태에서 직장에서 돌아오는데, 그런 상태에서는 고결한 소비를 하기보다는 자극적이고 감상적인 것에 본능적으로 접근한다는 내용의 글이다. 따라서 빈칸에 들어갈 말로는 ② '지쳐 버렸기'가 가장 적절하다.

① 이상적이기　　　　　　③ 위선적이기
④ 물질만능주의적이기　　⑤ 야망이 지나치기

⊗ 매력적인 오답 주의!

④ 글의 내용을 정확하게 파악하지 않고 고결한 소비를 하지 못하는 이유를 배경지식에만 의존해서 찾으면 고를 수 있는 오답이다.

TEXT FLOW

주제	현대의 청중들이 고결한 소비를 위한 기회를 외면하는 이유는 지쳐 버렸기 때문임
부연 1	우리는 고갈된 상태로 직장에서 돌아와 너무 무정하고 불안하게 됨
부연 2	직장에서 일어난 일의 효과를 상쇄하기 위해 자극적이고 감상적인 것에 본능적으로 접근함

구문

• We may be **too** brutalised [**to** care much about the suffering of others], or [**to** think empathetically of unfortunates in faraway tea plantations or cotton fields].
: 두 개의 [ ]는 or로 병렬 연결되어 too brutalised에 이어져서 '너무 ~해서 …할 수 없는'의 의미를 나타내는 「too ~ to부정사」 구문을 이룬다.

• [To counterbalance {what has happened at work}], we may instinctively move towards [what is excessively sweet, salty, distracting, easy, colourful, explosive, and sentimental].
: 첫 번째 [ ]는 목적의 의미를 나타내는 부사적 용법의 to부정사구이다. 그 안의 { }는 counterbalance의 목적어 역할을 하는 명사절이다. 두 번째 [ ]는 전치사 towards의 목적어 역할을 하는 명사절이다.

08 정답 ⑤

여러분이 자신의 소설을 이야기하게끔 선택한 인물이 여러분의 작품의 전반적인 목소리, 어조, 그리고 문체에 영향을 끼칠 것이다. 그것은 또한 그 이야기가 어떻게 말해지는가, 어떤 사건들이 강조되거나 덜 강조되는가, 그리고 그 사건들이 그 인물을 통해서 여러분의 독자에게 어떻게 걸러지는가에 영향을 끼칠 것이다. 예를 들어, 소설의 주요 사건들이 발생한 때에 아이였던 Scout에 의해 이야기되지 않았더라면 'To Kill a Mockingbird(앵무새 죽이기)'는 어떻게 변했을까? Scout는 악의가 없으면서 개인적 판단도 피하는데, 그것이 분명히 사건들의 서술 그 자체와 관계가 있게 된다. 최근의 소설

'The Lovely Bones(러블리 본즈)'는 어떤가? 이 소설은 Susie Salmon에 의해 이야기되는데, 그녀는 소설의 첫 문장에서 자신이 이미 죽었으며 사후 세계에서 이야기를 하고 있다고 선언한다. 만약 다른 인물이 그것을 이야기했다면, 완전히 다른 본질을 가진 소설이 되었을 것이다. 내가 상상하건대, 독자들이 그토록 빠르게 어떤 소설에 끌리는 이유들 중 한 가지는 이야기의 시점 때문이다.

해설

소설 작품에서 누가 소설을 이야기하느냐가 소설의 구성에 많은 영향을 끼치고 독자를 끌어들이는 데에도 큰 영향을 끼친다는 내용이므로, 빈칸에 들어갈 말로는 ⑤ '이야기의 시점'이 가장 적절하다.
① 저자의 인기
② 이야기의 진실성
③ 다른 독자들의 반응들
④ 유명한 비평가들의 논평들

TEXT FLOW

주제	소설을 이야기하는 인물이 작품에 큰 영향을 끼침
예시	'To Kill a Mockingbird(앵무새 죽이기)'나 'The Lovely Bones(러블리 본즈)'의 경우처럼, 소설을 이야기하는 인물은 소설의 서술 그 자체와 관계가 있음
결론	독자들이 어떤 소설에 빠르게 끌리는 한 가지 이유는 그 소설이 어떤 시점에서 서술되느냐에 달려 있음

구문

• It will also affect [how the story gets told], [what events are emphasized or de-emphasized], and [how the events are filtered, through the character, to your reader].
: and로 연결된 세 개의 의문사절 [ ]가 동사 affect의 목적어 역할을 한다.

• The novel **would have been** an entirely different entity altogether [**had** a different character **narrated** it].
: 과거 사실에 반대되는 가정을 하는 가정법 과거완료 구문 「if+주어+had+과거분사 ~, 주어+would have+과거분사 ....」가 쓰였다. [ ]는 조건절에서 if가 생략되어 주어와 동사가 도치된 형태이다.

09
정답 ③

목소리와 듣기에 의한 전파는 민요의 가장 기본적인 정의이다. 문자로 되어 있는 글의 부재와 듣고 기억해야 하는 필요성은 여러 가지 방식으로 민요에 영향을 끼친다. 단순성이 주요한 특성인데, 그것이 가사, 음조, 그리고 노래의 기본적인 의미를 기억하는 데 도움을 주기 때문이다. (어느 민요와 마찬가지로, 의미는 압운을 맞추기 위해 희생된다.) 후자가 중요한데, 가사의 일부를 잊어버리면, 기본적인 취지를 알고 있는 것이 빠진 부분의 복구나 적절한 대체물의 창작을 허용할 수도 있기 때문이다. 압운, 반복되는 코러스, 또는 음악적으로 상기시키는 것들의 형태로 기억을 도와주는 것이 민요에 공통된다.

해설

목소리와 듣기에 의해 전파되는 특징을 지닌 민요는 단순성이 주요한 특성이라는 내용이므로, 압운을 맞추기 위해 의미가 희생된다는 내용의 ③은 글의 전체 흐름과 관계가 없다.

TEXT FLOW

도입	구전은 민요의 기본적인 특징임
전개	문자로 되어 있는 글 없이, 듣고 기억해야 하는 민요는 단순성을 주요한 특성으로 지님
결론	단순성은 여러 가지 장치를 통해 민요의 기본적인 의미를 기억하는 데 도움이 됨

구문

• **The latter** is important, [for if one forgets part of a verse, {knowing the basic message} may allow recovery of the missing part or the creation of an appropriate substitute].
: The latter(후자)는 ② 문장의 '노래의 기본적인 의미를 기억하는 것'을 의미한다. [ ]는 이유를 나타내는 부사절로, 그 안의 { }는 부사절의 주어 역할을 하는 동명사구이다.

10
정답 ④

가장 강력한 배움은 성공들뿐만 아니라 실패들을 경험하는 것으로부터 나온다. 또한 어떤 것을 배운다는 것은 그 방식으로 그것을 직접 실험해 보고 또 불가피한 실패들로부터 회복해 보지 않고서는 거의 불가능하다. (C) 경험을 통한 배움이 무엇인지에 대해 생각할 때마다, 나는 신경 과학 분야의 대학원생이었을 때의 나의 시간이 생각난다. 나는 우리가 신경 생리학의 원리들을 '배웠던' 몇몇 강의들을 들었다. (A) 나는 그 자료에 대한 지필 시험은 통과할 수 있었지만, 실험실에서 현미경을 보며 신경들을 해부하고 역전류 검출관의 다이얼들을 수동으로 돌려 보고 나서야 비로소 완전히 그 개념들을 이해할 수 있었다. (B) 마찬가지로, 여러분은 리더십에 관한 많은 책들을 원하는 대로 읽을 수는 있지만, 진짜 지도자들이 직면하는 도전 과제들을 경험하고 나서야 비로소 책임을 떠맡을 준비가 되어 있을 것이다.

해설

주어진 글은 실제적인 경험을 통해서만 진정한 배움을 얻을 수 있다는 내용이므로, 이를 자신의 대학원생 시절의 경험을 예로 들며 설명하는 (C)와 (A)가 연이어 이어지고 나서, 리더십의 경우도 그와 마찬가지라고 부연해서 설명하는 (B)가 마지막에 오는 것이 글의 흐름상 가장 자연스럽다.

TEXT FLOW

도입	실제적 경험을 통해서만 진정으로 무언가를 배울 수 있음
전개	신경 과학을 배울 당시 경험했던 것을 통한 배움
부연	직접 경험을 통해서만 진짜 리더십을 배울 수 있음

구문

• Although I could pass a written test on the material, **it wasn't until** I was in the lab, [dissecting nerves under a microscope] and [manually turning the dials on the oscilloscope], **that** I fully understood the concepts.
: 「It was not until A that B」 구문은 직역하면 'A하기 전까지는 B하지 못했다'라는 뜻이지만, 보통 'A하고 나서야 비로소 B했다'라고 해석한다. 두 개의 [ ]는 연속 동작을 나타내는 분사구문이다.

11

정답 ③

일반적으로 디지털 카메라는 사용자에게 필름 카메라보다 더 나은 피드백을 제공한다. 매번 촬영을 하고 나서, 사진사는 방금 포착된 이미지의 작은 형태를 볼 수 있다. 이것은 필름 시대에 흔히 있는 온갖 실수들, 필름을 제대로 넣지 못하는 것에서부터, 렌즈 뚜껑을 여는 것을 깜박하거나, 사진의 중앙에 있는 인물의 머리를 자른다거나 하는 것들까지를 없애 준다. 그러나 초기 디지털 카메라는 한 가지 중대한 차원의 피드백에서 실패했다. 사진이 찍힐 때, 그 이미지가 포착됐다는 것을 나타내는 청각 신호가 없었다. 현대의 모델들은 이제 사진이 찍힐 때 매우 만족스럽지만 완전히 가짜인 '셔터가 찰칵하는' 소리를 포함한다. 오늘날 대부분의 휴대전화들은 비슷한 이유에서 가짜 발신음을 포함하기도 한다.

해설
However(그러나)로 시작하는 주어진 문장은 초기 디지털 카메라가 한 가지 피드백에서 실패했다는 내용이므로 그에 대한 구체적인 내용, 즉 이미지가 포착되었다는 것을 나타내는 청각적인 신호가 없었다는 내용이 나오기 전인 ③에 들어가는 것이 가장 적절하다.

TEXT FLOW

도입	디지털 카메라는 필름 카메라보다 더 나은 피드백을 제공함
전환	하지만 초기 디지털 카메라에 이미지 포착을 나타내는 청각 신호가 없었던 것은 중대한 피드백 결함이었음
결론	현대의 휴대전화들에는 그러한 청각 신호가 있음

구문
• This eliminates all kinds of errors that were common in the film era, [**from** failing to load the film properly, {**to** forgetting to remove the lens cap}, and {**to** cutting off the head of the central figure of the picture}].
: [ ]에는 'A에서부터 B까지'라는 의미의 「from A to B」 구문이 쓰였으며, 그 안에 있는 두 개의 { }가 and에 의해 병렬 연결되어 있다.

12

정답 ⑤

한 연구에서, 네 살짜리와 다섯 살짜리 아이들이 가족 시간대 프로그램인 'Adam-12'의 1회 방송분을 시청했다. 그 1회 방송분은 학생들이 학교를 무단결석하고 문제를 일으키는 것을 다룬 것이었다. 한 집단의 학생들은 "여기 앉아서 TV 프로그램을 보자."와 같은 감정을 드러내지 않는 말을 한 교사와 함께 그 프로그램을 시청했다. 두 번째 집단은 똑같은 교사와 시청했지만, 그 교사는 중요한 정보를 강조했고 "오, 안 돼! 저 소년은 어려움에 처해 있구나. 그는 가야만 하는데 학교에 가지 않았단다. 그건 나쁜 일이지."와 같은 말로 프로그램에서 일어나고 있는 일을 설명했다. 두 번째 집단의 아이들은 그 프로그램에 관한 더 구체적인 세부 사항을 배웠고, 무단결석에 대한 지식을 늘렸으며, 교사의 논평이 향하는 방향으로 자신들의 긍정적인 태도를 증진시켰다. 두 집단 사이의 차이는 일주일 후에도 여전히 분명했는데, 그것은 그 논의가 즉각적인 학습뿐만 아니라 기억력도 향상시켰다는 것을 보여 주었다.
➡ TV 프로그램에서 일어나고 있는 일을 설명함으로써, 교사는 학생들의 학습과 긍정적인 태도뿐만 아니라 그들의 기억력도 증진시켰다.

해설
프로그램에서 일어나고 있는 일에 대해 중요한 정보를 강조하고 설명해 줌으로써 아이들이 무단결석에 대해 더 많은 지식을 알게 되었고 교사의 논평대로 긍정적인 태도 증진과 기억력 향상을 보였다는 내용의 글이므로, 요약문의 빈칸 (A)에는 interpreting(설명함)이, (B)에는 promoted(증진시켰다)가 들어가는 것이 가장 적절하다.
① 모방함 – 증진시켰다
② 예측함 – 손상시켰다
③ 예측함 – 증진시켰다
④ 설명함 – 손상시켰다

TEXT FLOW

도입	한 연구에서 4~5살 아이들을 대상으로 문제를 일으키는 학생들을 다룬 방송을 시청하게 함
부연	두 집단으로 나눠 한 집단에서는 교사가 감정을 드러내지 않는 말을 하게 하고, 나머지 집단에서는 중요한 정보를 강조하고 사건을 설명하게 함
결과	정보를 강조하고 사건을 설명한 집단의 아이들은 프로그램에 관해 구체적인 세부 사항과 지식을 배웠고 교사의 논평이 가리키는 방향으로 긍정적인 태도 증진과 기억력 향상을 보여 줌

구문
• The episode dealt with students [being truant from school and getting into trouble].
: [ ]는 with의 목적어 역할을 하는 동명사구이고, students는 동명사구의 의미상 주어이다.

• The differences between the two groups were still evident one week later, [indicating {that the discussion enhanced retention **as well as** immediate learning}].
: [ ]는 앞의 내용 전체를 부연 설명하는 분사구문이고, 그 안의 { }는 indicating의 목적어 역할을 하는 명사절이다. 「B as well as A」는 'A뿐만 아니라 B도 역시'의 의미이다.

13~14

정답 13 ⑤ 14 ③

전략에 관한 많은 문헌은 전략 수립이 합리적 과정이라는 기본적인 가정을 내린다. 경영자는 자신의 조직과 환경에 대한 충분한 지식을 바탕으로 전략적 결정을 내린다. 그러한 결정은 증거를 고려하고 가능한 최선의 해결책을 생각해 냄으로써 합리적으로 이루어진다.
그러나 활동 중인 경영자를 대상으로 한 연구는 전략이 실제로 이런 방식으로 이루어지는지에 대한 의구심을 제기해 왔다. 캐나다의 교수 Henry Mintzberg는 1970년대 'Harvard Business Review'에 실린 일련의 기사와 이후 일련의 저서에서 대부분의 경영자가 실제로는 공식적인 계획 세우기와 전략 수립에 매우 많은(→ 적은) 시간을 소비한다고 주장했다. 매일매일의 업무 압박은 경영자가 끊임없이 주변의 사건과 사람에 반응해야 한다는 것을 의미한다. 모든 사실을 수집하고 상세히 분석할 시간이 있기도 전에 빠르게 결정이 요구되는 경우가 많다. 기회는 사라지기 전에 붙잡아야 한다. 이러한 상황에서는 결정이 거의 즉시 입수할 수 있는 정보를 바탕으로 직관적으로 내려지며, 전략은 '진행 중에' 결정되는 경향이 있다. Mintzberg는 극소수의 경영자만 실제로 공식적이고 합리적인 방식으로 전략을 수립한다고 생각한다. 대신 전략은 조직의 다양한 부분에서 이루어지는 일련의 결정의 결과로 비공식적이고 '임시방편적인' 방식으로 '생겨난다'.

해설
13 흔히 기업 경영에서 전략이라는 것은 합리적인 과정으로 이루어진다고 생각하지만 실제로는 극소수의 경영자만 합리적인 방식으로 전략을 수립하

며 보통의 경우 비공식적이고 임시방편적인 방식으로 생겨난다는 내용의 글
이므로, 글의 제목으로는 ⑤ '합리적인 전략 짜기의 그릇된 통념: 경영자들이
실제로 전략을 수립하는 방법'이 가장 적절하다.
① 성격 특성이 경영 스타일에 미치는 방법
② 사업에서의 의사결정: 더 빠를수록 더 좋다
③ 사업 기회 포착을 위한 다양한 경영 전략
④ 불확실성의 시대에서 장기적인 사업 계획에 대한 재고

14 경영자는 매일매일의 업무 압박으로 인해 끊임없이 주변의 사건과 사람
에 반응해야 하고, 모든 사실을 수집하고 상세히 분석할 시간이 있기도 전에
빠르게 결정을 내려야 한다는 맥락이므로, (c) much(많은)를 little(적은)과
같은 단어로 바꿔야 한다.

❌ 매력적인 오답 주의!

13 ② 본문에서 기회는 사라지기 전에 붙잡아야 한다는 내용을 토대로 의사
결정이 빠를수록 더 좋다는 것을 글의 중심 내용으로 오인하면 고를 수 있는
오답이다.

14 ④ (d) 뒤에 there is time ~ in detail의 내용을 결정을 내리기 전에
자료를 수집하고 자세히 분석할 시간이 있는 것으로 오인하면 고를 수 있는
오답이다.

TEXT FLOW

도입	전략에 관한 많은 문헌은 경영자들의 전략 수립이 합리적이라고 가정함
전환	연구 결과는 이러한 가정에 의구심을 제기함
주제	대부분의 경영자가 실제로는 공식적인 계획 세우기와 전략 수립에 매우 적은 시간을 소비함
부연	전략은 즉시 입수할 수 있는 정보를 바탕으로 직관적으로 수립되는 경우가 많음

구문

• [Much of the literature on strategy] makes a fundamental
assumption [that strategy making is a rational process].
: 첫 번째 [ ]는 문장의 주어이고, 두 번째 [ ]는 a fundamental
assumption의 구체적 내용을 설명하는 동격절이다.

• In these situations, strategy tends to be made 'on the wing',
[with decisions taken more or less intuitively based on the
information {that is immediately available}].
: [ ]에서 부수적인 상황을 나타내는 「with+명사(구)+분사(구)」 구문이 사
용되었고, 그 안의 { }는 the information을 수식하는 관계절이다.

GRAMMAR REVIEW 본문 65쪽

1 was	2 designed	3 both
4 to think	5 that	6 remembering
7 in which	8 satisfying	9 explained
10 taken		

1 The approach ~ generation이 문장의 주어이므로 뒤에 술부를
이끌 수 있는 술어 동사가 필요하다. 따라서 술어 동사의 역할을 할 수
있는 was가 적절하다.

2 bureaucracy functions가 문장의 주어와 동사이므로 according
to 다음에는 명사구가 나와야 한다. universal rules를 수식하며 수동
의 의미이므로 과거분사 designed를 써야 한다.

3 'A와 B 둘 다'의 의미를 나타내는 「both A and B」 구문이 쓰였으므
로 both가 적절하다.

4 '너무 ~해서 …할 수 없는'의 의미인 「too ~ to+동사원형」이 사용되었
고, or를 중심으로 두 개의 to부정사구가 병렬 구조를 이루어야 하므로
to think가 적절하다.

5 Susie Salmon을 부연 설명하는 주격 관계대명사가 이끄는 절 안에
서 announces의 목적어 역할을 하는 명사절이 필요하므로 접속사
that이 적절하다.

6 전치사 in의 목적어 역할을 하는 명사구를 이끌면서 the words,
tune, and basic meaning of the song을 목적어로 취하는 동사
의 역할을 해야 하므로 동명사 remembering을 써야 한다.

7 뒤에 주어, 동사, 목적어를 모두 갖춘 완전한 형태의 절이 이어지므로
in which가 적절하다.

8 satisfy는 '만족스럽게 하다'라는 뜻의 타동사로, 'shutter click'
sound가 satisfy의 행위를 하는 주체이므로 능동의 의미를 나타내는
현재분사 satisfying을 써야 한다.

9 but 이하에서 and에 의해 동사 highlighted와 병렬 구조를 이루도록
explained를 써야 한다.

10 부수적인 상황을 나타내는 「with+명사(구)+분사(구)」 구문이 사용되
었는데, decisions가 take라는 동작의 주체가 아니라 대상이므로 과
거분사 taken이 적절하다.

01   정답 ①

그리고 이제 대망의 마지막, 솔로 댄스, 전국 대회에 진출할 수 있는 기회…. 모든 것이 이 순간으로 모아지고 있었다. "우리 마지막 부문은 솔로 댄스입니다! 3위는, Ruby Taylor입니다!" '3위라고? 그녀는 2등은 참담한 패배라고 생각하는 댄서이다.' 아니나 다를까, 그녀는 시큰둥한 얼굴로 무대로 향했다. "내가 정말 그녀를 이긴 것인가? 내가 2등을 한 것인가?" 나뭇잎처럼 떨면서, 나는 속으로 속삭였다. "2등은, Malia Scott!" '뭐라고? 2위는 내가 늘 차지하던 자리잖아. 나는 전혀 순위에 들지 못했나? 아니면… 아니면…' 나는 숨을 죽였다. 'Kate Baker라고 말해라, Kate Baker라고 말해라…' "그리고 우리의 솔로 댄스 1위는… Kate Baker입니다!" '오, 세상에. 내가 해냈어! 내가 해냈어! 내가 이겼다!!' 나는 미친 듯이 무대로 달려갔다. 거기에서 나는 군중 속의 엄마와 아빠가 격하게 나를 향해 손을 흔드는 것을 보았다. 나는 내가 한 일에 대해 기분이 좋았다. 나는 전국 무대에서 경쟁할 준비가 되었다는 것을 증명했다. '전국 대회. 뉴욕시야, 내가 간다!'

해설
필자는 솔로 댄스 부분 수상자를 발표할 때 3등, 2등까지 자신의 이름이 불리지 않아서 긴장하고 있다가 1등 수상자로 자신의 이름이 불리자 스스로에 대해 자랑스러워하고 있으므로, 필자의 심경 변화로 가장 적절한 것은 ① '긴장한 → 자랑스러워하는'이다.
② 질투하는 → 부끄러워하는
③ 화가 난 → 고마워하는
④ 안도하는 → 무서워하는
⑤ 기대하는 → 실망한

TEXT FLOW
도입	솔로 댄스 수상자 발표 시작
전개	3위와 2위 수상자로 호명되지 않음
결론	1위 수상자로 호명되어 자신을 자랑스러워함

구문
- She's a dancer [who considers second place a crushing defeat].
  : [ ]는 a dancer를 수식하는 관계절이다.
- I'd proven [I was ready to compete on a national stage].
  : [ ]는 had proven의 목적어 역할을 하는 명사절이다.

02   정답 ④

신문은 친환경적이지 않으므로 현대 언론계에서 설 자리가 없다. 뉴스가 유포될 수 있는 많은 다른 효과적인 방법들이 있을 때 그것들은 종이의 낭비이다. 예를 들어, '뉴욕 타임즈'의 단 1년 정기 구독이 대략 520파운드의 쓰레기를 발생시키는데, 그것은 1년에 구독자 한 명당 약 4.25그루의 나무가 베이는 것과 같다. 전 세계에서 인쇄되는 모든 다른 간행물들을 고려할 때, 이것은 피할 수 있었던 점점 더 부족해지는 천연자원의 많은 낭비와 같다. 꼭 구매되거나 소비되지 않아도 될 때조차도 제품이 인쇄되는 인쇄 매체 수단보다는 내용이 실제로 필요할 때 공급원을 이용하기만 하면 되기 때문에 뉴스를 배포하기 위해 디지털 도구를 사용하는 것이 더 효과적이다.

해설
신문이 친환경적이지 않다는 점을 종이 낭비를 근거로 주장하고 있으며, 뉴스를 배포하는 데 있어서도 필요할 때만 이용하면 되는 디지털 도구를 사용하는 것이 더 효과적이라는 점을 피력하고 있으므로, 글의 요지로 가장 적절한 것은 ④이다.

TEXT FLOW
도입	신문은 친환경적이지 않아 현대 언론계에서 설 자리가 없음
전개	신문은 종이 낭비이며 천연자원의 큰 손실임
결론	뉴스를 배포하는 데 있어서 디지털 도구를 사용하는 것이 더 효과적임

구문
- Using digital tools to distribute news is more efficient as you only use [resources when the content is actually required] **rather than** [the print media method {in which the product is printed even when it may not be necessarily purchased and consumed}].
  : 「A rather than B」 구문은 'B보다는 오히려 A'라는 의미로 두 개의 [ ]가 병렬 구조를 이루고 있다. { }는 선행사 the print media method를 수식하는 관계절이다.

03   정답 ②

어떤 정원사들은 일하는 곳에서 시계를 필요로 하지 않는다. 그들은 그냥 꽃들을 보면 된다. 꽃들을 보고 시간을 아는 것은 1700년대로 거슬러 올라간다. 그 시기의 과학자들은 어떤 특정한 종류의 꽃들이 하루 중 일정한 시간에 피고 진다는 것을 이미 알고 있었다. 이것이 스웨덴의 과학자 Carolus Linnaeus를 매혹시켰다. 그는 자기 주위의 꽃들의 일과를 연구했다. 그리고 나서 그는 정원사가 하루 종일 시간을 알려 주는 화단을 어떻게 가꿀 수 있는지를 알아냈다. Linnaeus는 하루 중 특정한 시간에 피거나 지는 꽃들의 목록을 만들었다. 그는 흐리거나 추운 날에도 시간에 맞춰 '작동할' 토종 꽃들을 선택했다. 몇 년 후에, 한 예술가가 Linnaeus의 생각의 형태를 시계 문자판에 옮겨다 놓았다. 12시간의 낮시간 각각은 그 시간에 피거나 지는 꽃의 종류를 보여 준다.

해설
스웨덴의 과학자 Carolus Linnaeus는 어떤 특정한 종류의 꽃들이 일정한 시간에 피고 진다는 것을 알고 하루 종일 시간을 알려 주는 화단을 가꿀 수 있는 방법을 알아냈고, 한 예술가가 Linnaeus의 생각을 이용해서 각 시간에 피거나 지는 꽃들을 문자판에 옮겨 시계로 만들었다는 내용이므로, 글의 제목으로는 ② '시간을 알려 주는 시계로서의 꽃들'이 가장 적절하다.
① Linnaeus가 분류한 꽃들
③ Linnaeus의 과학적 업적들
④ 꽃들과 소통하는 정원사들
⑤ 꽃들을 성공적으로 기르기 위한 조건들

도입	어떤 특정한 종류의 꽃들은 하루 중 정해진 시간에 피고 짐
전개	스웨덴의 과학자 Carolus Linnaeus는 꽃을 보고 시간을 알 수 있도록 하루 중 특정한 시간에 피거나 지는 꽃들의 목록을 만듦
결론	Linnaeus의 생각을 차용하여 한 예술가가 꽃으로 시간을 알려 주는 시계를 만듦

구문

• Then he figured out [how a gardener could plant a flower bed that would keep time all day long].
: [ ]는 figured out의 목적어 역할을 하는 의문사절이다.

• Each of the 12 daylight hours shows a kind of flower [that opens or closes at that time of day].
: [ ]는 a kind of flower를 수식하는 관계절이다.

04
정답 ④

Ibn-Sina로도 알려진 Avicenna는 페르시아의 사만 왕조에서 태어났다. 어릴 때부터, Avicenna는 비범한 지능과 기억력을 보여 주었다. 10살 무렵, 그는 전체 코란을 암기했다. 하지만, 이것은 Avicenna에게 충분하지 않았다. 그는 자신이 세상을 이해할 수 있도록 세상에 대해 더 많이 배우고 싶어 했다. Avicenna는 이미 과학과 철학에 큰 관심을 보이고 있었다. 그는 배움에 너무 능숙해서 14살이 되었을 무렵에 자신의 선생님들보다 더 많은 것을 알고 있었다. 16살 무렵, 그는 의학을 공부하기 시작했다. 그는 의학 이론을 배우고 나서 자신만의 실험을 시작했으며, 새로운 치료 방법을 발견했다. 곧, 아픈 사람들이 치료를 받기 위해 그의 집으로 몰려들기 시작했다. 그의 명성은 그가 그들을 자주 무료로 치료하면서 퍼졌고, 그는 다른 의사들이 할 수 없는 '기적' 치료법을 전할 수 있었다. 사람들을 치료하기 위해, 당연히 Avicenna는 초자연적인 것보다는 오로지 과학, 물리학, 그리고 화학에만 의존하고 있었다. 18살 무렵, 그는 자격을 갖춘 의사로서 완전한 지위를 얻었다.

해설

Avicenna의 명성은 그가 자주 무료 치료를 하면서 퍼졌고, 그는 다른 의사들이 할 수 없는 '기적' 치료법을 전할 수 있었다고 했으므로, 글의 내용과 일치하는 것은 ④이다.

구문

• He was **so** good at learning **that** by the time he was fourteen years old, he knew more than his teachers.
: 「so ~ that ....」은 '매우 ~해서 …하다'의 의미이다.

• [To cure people], Avicenna was, of course, relying solely [on science, physics and chemistry] **rather than** [on anything supernatural].
: 첫 번째 [ ]는 목적의 의미를 나타내는 부사적 용법의 to부정사구이다. 두 번째와 세 번째 [ ]는 rather than에 의해 연결된 전치사구로 relying에 이어진다.

05
정답 ④

국제적인 상업은 더욱 밀집되고 속도가 빨라져 가고 있다. 어떤 단일 회사도

오로지 시장 교환 메커니즘만을 통해 일하는 독립 에이전트로서는 효과적인 경쟁을 할 수 없다. 오늘날, 혼자 힘으로 하는 것은 멸종을 위한 처방이다. 네트워크에 기반한 관계에서 오직 자원을 공동으로 모으고 위험과 수입원을 공유함으로써만 회사는 생존할 수 있다. 이것은 네트워크화된 처리 방식과 함께 오는 기업가의 이익과 안정에 대한 대가로 얼마간의 자율성을 획득하는 것(→ 포기하는 것)을 뜻한다. 경쟁이 여전히 회사들 사이에 존재하지만, 시장이 가까운 시일 내에 사라지지는 않을 테고, 아웃소싱, 공동 공급, 그리고 수익 공유라는 형태의 협력과 공유된 절약 합의가 점점 더 기준이 되어 가고 있다.

해설

네트워크에 기반한 국제적인 상업에서는 어떤 회사도 단독으로는 효과적인 경쟁이 어려우며, 공동 공급이나 수익 공유 등의 형태로 함께해야 살아남을 수 있다는 내용의 글이다. 이익과 안정에 대한 대가로 얼마간의 자율성을 포기해야 한다는 문맥이 되어야 자연스러우므로 ④ gaining(획득하는 것)을 abandoning(포기하는 것)과 같은 단어로 바꿔야 한다.

주제	단일 회사가 시장 교환 메커니즘만을 통해서는 효과적인 경쟁을 할 수 없음
전개	네트워크에 기반한 관계를 맺고 자원, 위험, 수입원을 공유해야만 회사가 생존할 수 있음
부연	아웃소싱, 공동 공급, 수익 공유라는 형태의 협력과 공유된 절약 합의가 점점 더 기준이 되어 가고 있음

구문

• [Only by pooling resources and sharing risks and revenue streams in network-based relationships] **can firms** survive.
: 부사구 [ ]가 문두로 나가면서 주어(firms)와 조동사(can)가 도치되었다.

06
정답 ②

사람들은 자신들이 이미 믿고 있는 것과 반대되는 새로운 정보를 받을 때 불편해진다. 그 고통은 크든 작든 그들로 하여금 그 긴장과 불안으로부터의 해방을 추구하게 한다. 만약 그 사건에 덧붙여지는 결과가 거의 없다면, 그 새로운 관점을 포함하도록 현실을 보는 우리의 눈을 적응시키는 것은 충분히 간단하며 긴장은 해소된다. 반면에, 한 사람이 논쟁 중인 그 문제에 개인적인 투자를 한다면, 그 사람은 원래의 견해를 지지하거나 새로운 정보를 불신하는 다른 정보를 구할 것이다. 원래의 관점에 감정적으로나 경제적으로 더 많이 투자가 되어 있는 사람일수록, 그것을 유지하는 데 더 많은 노력이 들어간다. 만약 수백만 달러나 일생의 노동이 투자되어 있다면, 그 관련자들은 표현되고 있는 것과 반대인 말을 듣기 위해 새로운 정보를 뒤집어 버리거나, 아니면 그냥 그것을 의식 밖으로 완전히 차단해 버릴 가능성이 있다.

해설

사람들은 이미 믿고 있는 것과 반대되는 새로운 정보를 받을 때 불편해진다고 했고, 이것은 논쟁 중인 문제에 대해 개인적인 투자를 많이 하면 할수록 더 그렇다는 내용의 글이므로, 빈칸에는 그런 경우에 변화를 싫어하는 사람들이 취할 수 있는 조치인 ② '새로운 정보를 뒤집어 버리거나'가 들어가야 적절하다.
① 원래의 관점을 바꾸거나
③ 변화를 이해하고 받아들이거나
④ 망설임 없이 스스로를 희생하거나
⑤ 새로운 것에 대한 그들의 투자를 늘리거나

😵 매력적인 오답 주의!

⑤ 글 전체를 포괄하는 요지를 파악하지 못하고 new, more, invest와 같은 단편적인 어휘를 근거로 고를 수 있는 오답이다.

TEXT FLOW

주제	사람들은 이미 믿고 있는 것과 반대되는 새로운 정보를 받을 때 불편해짐
전개	논쟁 중인 문제에 대해 개인적 투자를 한 사람은 원래의 관점을 유지하거나 새로운 정보를 거부하는 조치를 취하게 됨
부연	논쟁 중인 문제에 감정적 또는 경제적으로 큰 투자를 한 사람은 새로운 정보를 뒤집거나 차단해 버릴 수 있음

구문

• If little of consequence is attached to the issue, **it** is simple enough [to adapt our vision of reality {to include the new perspective}] and the tension is released.
: it은 가주어이고 진주어는 [ ]이다. 그 안의 { }는 '~하기 위해서'라는 의미로 목적을 나타내는 부사적 용법의 to부정사구이다.

07   정답 ①

침입종의 영향을 제한할 두 가지 주요한 방법이 있다. 첫 번째는 새로운 침입을 막는 것이고, 두 번째는 그것들이 일단 어떤 지역에 대량 서식하게 되면 그 영향력을 최소화하는 것이다. 처음의 침입은 격리 조치를 이용해서 저지될 수 있지만, 이런 조치는 어느 종이 침입하게 될 수 있을지를 예측할 수 없는 것 때문에 방해를 받는다. 게다가, 미국과 호주 같은 나라들은 대개 무역에 대한 제한을 피하기 위해서, 들어오는 종에게 '죄가 입증될 때까지 무죄' 접근법을 적용한다. 다시 말해서, 모든 종은 그것들이 해롭다는 것을 우리가 알 때까지 들어온다. 이런 접근법이 가진 주요 문제는 어떤 종이 해롭다는 것을 일단 우리가 알면, 그것의 확산을 제어하기에 흔히 너무 늦다는 것이다.

해설

처음의 침입은 격리 조치를 통해 저지될 수 있지만, 미국과 호주 같은 나라에서는 해로움이 입증되기 전까지는 격리 조치가 이루어지지 않는다고 했으므로, 빈칸에 들어갈 말로는 ① '그것들이 해롭다는 것을 우리가 알 때까지 들어온다'가 가장 적절하다.
② 비슷한 진화론적인 과정과 특성을 가지고 있다
③ 그것들이 무리 지어 있을 때 무고한 것으로 믿어진다
④ 침입종으로부터 보호받을 권리가 있다
⑤ 그것들이 불완전한 상태로 태어났다는 점에서 취약하다

TEXT FLOW

도입	침입종의 영향을 제한하는 두 가지 방법이 있음
전개	처음의 침입은 격리 조치를 통해 저지될 수 있지만, 미국과 호주 같은 나라들에서는 '죄가 입증될 때까지 무죄' 접근법을 적용함
결론	해롭다는 것이 입증되기 전까지는 계속해서 들어오고, 나중에는 흔히 확산을 제어하기에 어려운 상황에 이르게 됨

구문

• In addition, countries [such as the United States and Australia] apply an "innocent until proven guilty" approach to incoming species, [mostly to avoid limits on trade].

: 첫 번째 [ ]는 주어인 countries를 수식하고, 두 번째 [ ]는 목적을 나타내는 부사적 용법의 to부정사구이다.

08   정답 ③

생산주의 시대에 일어난 가장 중요한 변화들 중 하나는 자연 환경(자연)에 대한 행동을 바꾸어야 한다는 농부들에 대한 압력이 증가했다는 것이다. 비록 이것(환경의 보존)이 토양, 농경지, 그리고 황무지의 관리와 같은 특징들의 관점에서 좁게 정의되는 경향이 있었지만, 농부들은 환경의 보존에 항상 민감했다. 그러나 농업의 산업화 논리는 농부들에게 그들의 천연자원 기반을 향한 보수적인 행동보다는 오히려 자원을 개발하는 행동을 취하도록 압력을 가했다. (모든 천연자원의 보존은 지속 가능한 발전에 대한 책임의 필수적인 부분이다.) 예를 들어, 정부의 개입은 농업 전문화와 관련된 위험을 줄였고, 농산물에 대한 가격을 보호했으며, 그 외에, 새로운 농업 기술은 비용 절감뿐만 아니라 생산량을 증가시키는 것이었다. 요컨대, 재정적 편의는 자연 환경의 보존과 관련하여 최고의 농업 관행에 우선하는 경향이 있었다.

해설

③은 모든 천연자원의 보존은 지속 가능한 발전에 대한 책임의 필수적인 부분이라는 내용으로, 농업의 산업화가 농부들에게 자연을 개발하는 행동을 취하도록 압력을 가했다는 내용과 그러한 압력의 예를 들고 있는 내용 사이에 오는 것은 글의 흐름상 적절하지 않다.

TEXT FLOW

주제	생산주의 시대에 농부들은 자연 환경에 대한 행동을 바꾸도록 압력을 받음
부연	이전에는 농부들이 환경 보존에 민감했으나 산업화 논리는 자원을 개발하는 행동을 취하게 함
예시	농업 전문화 위험 축소, 농산물 가격 보호, 비용 절감, 생산량 증가 등의 여러 재정적 편의가 자연 환경 보전이라는 농업 관행보다 우선시됨

구문

• [One of the most important changes to occur during the productivist era] **was** the increased pressure on farmers to alter their behaviour towards the natural environment (nature).
: [ ]는 문장의 주어이고 주어의 핵은 One이므로 단수 동사 was가 쓰여 수일치를 이루고 있다.

• For example, intervention by the state [reduced the risks {associated with agricultural specialization}], and [protected prices for farm products]: besides which, new farming technology was output-increasing as well as cost-reducing.
: 두 개의 [ ]가 and로 연결되어 동사구를 이루고 있다. 첫 번째 [ ] 안의 { }는 the risks를 수식하는 과거분사구이다.

09   정답 ⑤

캐나다인 Sarah Harmer가 크로스 컨트리 단체 스키 경기에서 팀의 선두를 달리던 중 그녀의 오른쪽 스키 지팡이가 딱 부러지고 말았다. 그녀는 절망적이었다. 오르막 경사지에서, 여러 스키 선수들이 그녀를 지나쳐 갔

다. (C) 그때 놀라운 일이 벌어졌다. 한 남자가 코스 옆에서 앞으로 걸어 나오더니 Harmer에게 다른 지팡이를 건네주었다. 그녀는 경기에 다시 임했고, 허비한 시간을 만회하여 결국에는 캐나다가 은메달을 획득했다. (B) Harmer는 자신을 도와준 은인이 4위를 차지한 노르웨이 팀의 코치인 Asle Fagestroem이었다는 사실을 경기가 끝나고 나서야 알았다. 그는 그 즉시 캐나다에서 영웅이 되었다. (A) 그러나 그는 그 모든 관심을 이해하지 못했다. 그는 한 신문에서 말했다. "올림픽 정신은 우리가 따르고자 하는 방침입니다. 이기긴 했지만 누군가를 도와주었어야만 했던 상황에서 도와주지 않는다면, 이기는 게 무슨 소용이 있습니까?"

해설

주어진 글은 크로스 컨트리 단체 스키 경기를 치르고 있던 캐나다의 Sarah Harmer가 스키 지팡이가 부러지는 절망적인 상황에 처했다는 내용이다. 이어서 한 남자로부터 다른 스키 지팡이를 건네받은 덕에 그녀가 경기를 계속하여 결국 그녀의 팀이 은메달을 획득했다는 내용의 (C)가 오고, 경기가 끝난 후에 그녀에게 도움을 준 사람이 4위를 차지한 노르웨이 팀의 코치였다는 것을 알게 되었다는 내용의 (B)가 이어지며, 이 일로 인해 캐나다에서 영웅이 된 그 노르웨이 코치가 올림픽 정신에 맞는 당연한 일을 했다고 말하는 인터뷰에 대한 내용인 (A)가 마지막에 오는 것이 글의 흐름상 가장 자연스럽다.

TEXT FLOW

시간 순서/사건 전개에 따른 흐름:
캐나다의 Sarah Harmer가 크로스 컨트리 단체 스키 경기 도중 그녀의 스키 지팡이가 부러졌음 → 한 남자로부터 다른 스키 지팡이를 건네받고 경기를 마쳐 그녀의 팀이 결국 은메달을 땄고, 그녀에게 도움을 준 사람이 4위를 차지한 노르웨이 팀의 코치였다는 것을 알게 됨 → 노르웨이 팀의 코치는 올림픽 정신에 비추어 당연한 일을 했다고 말함

구문

• **It was not until** after the race **that** Harmer learned that her benefactor was Asle Fagestroem, ~.
  : 「It was not until A that B」 구문으로 'A하고 나서야 비로소 B했다'의 의미를 나타낸다.

10

정답 ⑤

우리에게는 기회의 창이 있고 환경으로부터의 특정 정보에 주의를 기울이도록 미리 설정되어 있다는 증거가 정말로 있는 듯하다. 예를 들어, 인간의 언어 발달은 대개 특유하게 인간적이면서 생물학적으로 단단한 기반이 있는 뇌 기반 능력의 가장 좋은 예 중 하나로 자랑스럽게 알려져 있다. 'The Language Instinct'에서 Steven Pinker는 거의 모든 아이는 어디에서 자랐는지에 관계없이 거의 동시에 거의 노력하지 않고 언어를 배우지만, 같은 가정에서 키우는 그들의 반려 햄스터는 그렇지 않다고 언급한다. 여러분이 반려동물에게 아무리 말을 걸어도 반려동물이 여러분에게 대답하게 할 수 없을 것이다. 이에 대한 유일한 합리적인 설명은 인간의 뇌는 언어를 배우도록 미리 설정되어 있지만, 반려 햄스터의 뇌는 그렇지 않다는 것이다. 어떤 환경에서 자랐든 모든 유아는 자신이 노출된 언어를 배울 수 있다. 이것은 유전적으로 암호화된, 타고나고 특유한 인간의 언어 학습 능력이 있으며, 습득되는 실제 언어는 환경에 의해 결정된다는 것을 증명한다.

해설

언어 학습 능력은 인간에게 특유하고 타고난 능력이며, 실제 습득되는 언어는 노출되는 언어라는 내용의 글이다. ⑤ 앞까지는 햄스터와 달리 인간은 언

어를 학습할 수 있다는 내용이 이어지다가 ⑤ 뒤에서는 이를 통해 인간에게 특유한 언어 학습 능력과 환경에 의한 실제 습득 언어의 결정이 입증된다고 서술하고 있다. 따라서 노출된 환경에 의해 실제 습득 언어가 결정된다는 내용이 ⑤ 앞에서는 언급된 적이 없으므로, 주어진 문장이 들어가기에 가장 적절한 곳은 ⑤이다.

⊗ 매력적인 오답 주의!

② 주어진 문장을 습득하는 언어를 한정하는 내용으로 파악하지 않고 인간의 언어 습득 능력을 강조하는 내용으로 파악하면 고를 수 있는 오답이다.

TEXT FLOW

도입	인간에게는 뇌 기반 능력으로서의 언어 학습 능력이 있음
예시	아이와 햄스터의 언어 습득 가능성 비교
결론	인간은 내재된 언어 학습 능력이 있고 노출된 환경에 의해 습득 언어가 결정됨

구문

• There **does** appear to be evidence [that we have windows of opportunity and are preconfigured to attend to certain information from the environment].
  : does는 동사 appear를 강조하기 위해 쓰인 조동사이고, [ ]는 evidence와 동격 관계인 명사절이다.

• This proves [that there is a built-in, uniquely human capacity to learn language, {which must be genetically encoded}], but [that the actual language acquired is determined by the environment].
  : 두 개의 [ ]는 but으로 연결되어 proves의 목적어 역할을 하는 명사절이다. 첫 번째 [ ] 안의 { }는 a built-in, uniquely human capacity to learn language에 대해 부가적으로 설명하는 관계절이다.

11

정답 ④

기원후 79년 8월 24일 화산 폭발에 의한 폼페이의 파괴는 너무나 급작스러워서 사람들은 단 한순간의 경고만을 받았고 도망칠 수가 없었다. 그러나 거의 19세기가 지난 후에 발견된 2천 점의 해골들 중에서, 한 아이의 형체 위로 보호하듯 몸을 뻗은 어느 개의 형체에 대한 이야기만큼 마음을 저리게 하는 이야기는 없었다. 뜨거운 재가 도시에 비 내리듯 내려 모든 것을 파묻어 버렸다. 고대의 개와 아이의 몸들을 발견하면서, 발굴자들은 최후까지 이어진 조용한 충성의 장면에 감동을 받았다. 그러나 그들은 그 개의 목걸이에 있는 글을 해독했을 때 훨씬 더 놀랐다. 그것 위에 섬세하게 새겨진 글은 그 개가 어떻게 그 아이의 아버지인 Severinus를 세 번, 즉 익사로부터 한 번, 매복 공격을 당하는 동안 도둑들로부터 한 번, 그리고 늑대로부터 한 번 구해 냈었는지를 알려 주었다. 죽어 가는 그 개의 행동은 자신이 사랑하는 아이를 보호하기 위해 용감하게, 그러나 헛되이 자신의 몸을 던진 것이었다.

해설

주어진 문장은 그들(the excavators)이 개의 목걸이에 새겨진 글을 해독했을 때 훨씬 더 놀랐다는 내용으로, 목걸이에 새겨진 글을 통해 그 개가 아이의 아버지를 세 번 구해 냈다는 것을 알게 되었다는 문장이 나오기 전인 ④에 들어가는 것이 가장 적절하다.

TEXT FLOW

도입	기원후 79년 8월 24일, 화산 폭발에 의해 폼페이가 파괴됨
전개	거의 19세기가 지난 후에 발견된 폼페이의 해골들 중 아이를 보호하듯 몸을 뻗은 감동적인 개의 형체가 있었음
결론	그 개가 아이의 아버지를 세 번이나 구해 낸 적이 있었고, 마지막까지 아이를 구하기 위해 자신의 몸을 던졌다는 것이 밝혀짐

구문

• But of the 2,000 skeletons [found almost nineteen centuries later], **none** told a story **so** heartbreaking **as that** of the form of a dog stretched protectively over **that** of a child.
: [ ]는 과거분사구로 the 2,000 skeletons를 수식한다. none 이하는 원급 비교 문장이지만, 「부정 표현(none) ~ so ... as」의 형태로 최상급의 의미를 나타낸다. as 다음에 있는 that과 over 다음의 that은 모두 지시대명사로 각각 a story와 the form을 가리킨다.

12-14

정답 12 ③ 13 ⑤ 14 ⑤

(A) 아동 심리학자인 Mr. Watson은 아동 발달에 관한 연구를 하고 있었다. 100명이 넘는 아이들을 직접 인터뷰하고 나서, 이제 그는 마지막 세 아이만 남겨 두고 있었다. 그는 비서를 버저로 불러 그녀에게 그 세 아이 중 첫 번째 아이를 데려와 달라고 했다. 몇 분 후에 비서는 Tom이라는 어린 소년을 데리고 돌아왔다. Mr. Watson은 그 소년에게 일련의 질문을 하고 그의 대답을 자신의 클립보드에 기록했다. 자신의 일련의 질문을 마무리하면서 그는 그 소년에게 "Tom, 너는 무엇이 되고 싶니?"라고 물었다. 그 어린아이는 곧바로 "저는 의사가 되고 싶어요."라고 대답했다.
(C) Mr. Watson이 그 소년에게 이유를 묻자, 그는 "의사는 돈을 많이 벌잖아요. 저는 부자가 되고 싶어요."라고 대답했다. 심리학자는 그 소년의 이름 옆에 '보통'이라는 단어를 썼다. 그러고 나서 그는 비서에게 그다음 아이를 데려와 달라고 했다. 이번에 비서는 Sarah라는 이름의 어린 소녀를 데려왔다. Mr. Watson은 그녀에게 똑같은 질문을 했고, 그가 그녀에게 무엇이 되고 싶은지 묻자, 그녀는 "저는 발레리나가 되고 싶어요."라고 대답했다. 그가 그녀에게 이유를 묻자, 그녀는 "발레리나는 아름다워요. 저는 아름다워지고 싶어요."라고 대답했다. 그 소녀의 이름 옆에 그는 또한 '보통'이라는 단어를 썼다.
(D) Rick이라는 이름의 마지막 아이가 들어왔을 때, Mr. Watson은 이 소년이 눈이 멀었다는 것을 즉시 알아차렸다. 그는 그 눈이 먼 소년에게 똑같은 질문을 했다. 그가 그 소년에게 무엇이 되고 싶은지 묻자, 그 어린 소년은 그것에 대해 잠시 생각하고 나서 "아직 잘 모르겠지만 저는 제가 성공할 거라는 걸 알아요."라고 말했다. Mr. Watson은 그 소년에게 성공하리라는 것을 그가 어떻게 그렇게 확신할 수 있느냐고 물었다. 그 말에 대한 대답으로, 그 어린 소년은 "제가 눈이 멀었기 때문이죠."라고 말했다.
(B) 그 소년의 대답은 Mr. Watson을 정말로 깜짝 놀랐게 했는데, 그는 왜 그 소년이 눈이 먼 것이 어쨌든 그가 인생에서 더 성공하는 데 도움이 될 수 있다고 생각하는지 이해하지 못했고, 그런 이유로 그는 "너는 왜 그렇게 생각하니?"라고 물었다. 그 어린 소년은 심리학자의 목소리가 나는 방향으로 몸을 돌려 "다른 모든 이들과 달리 저는 제 장애물을 볼 수 없기 때문이죠."라고 대답했다. 의사는 깜짝 놀라며 그 소년의 이름 옆에 '천재'라는 단어를 썼다.

해설

12 아동 심리학자인 Mr. Watson이 연구를 위해 마지막 세 아이 중 첫 번째 아이 Tom과의 인터뷰를 시작하는 내용의 글 (A) 뒤에는, Tom에 대한 평가를 하고 나서 두 번째 아이 Sarah와 인터뷰를 하고 평가를 하는 내용의 글

(C)가 와야 한다. 이어서 세 번째 아이 Rick과의 인터뷰를 시작하는 내용의 (D)가 오고, 마지막으로 Rick이 스스로의 장애에 대해 생각하는 바에 대해 경탄하며 평가하는 (B)가 오는 것이 글의 흐름상 가장 자연스럽다.

13 (a), (b), (c), (d)는 Mr. Watson을 가리키고, (e)는 마지막 인터뷰 대상자인 Rick을 가리킨다.

14 Rick이라는 이름의 마지막 아이가 들어왔을 때, Mr. Watson은 이 소년의 눈이 멀었다는 것을 즉시 알아차렸다고 했으므로, Mr. Watson에 관한 내용으로 적절하지 않은 것은 ⑤이다.

TEXT FLOW

도입	아동 심리학자인 Mr. Watson이 아동 발달 연구를 위한 인터뷰를 실시함
전개	Tom, Sarah, Rick과의 인터뷰를 진행함
결론	Rick의 자기 장애에 대한 견해를 듣고 Mr. Watson이 경탄함

구문

• The boy's answer really took Mr. Watson by surprise, and he failed to comprehend [why the boy thought {that being blind could somehow help him to be more successful in life}]; ~.
: [ ]는 comprehend의 목적어 역할을 하는 명사절이고, 그 안의 { }는 thought의 목적어 역할을 하는 명사절이다.

GRAMMAR REVIEW

본문 73쪽

1 waving	2 in which	3 shows
4 discovering	5 effectively	6 that
7 defined	8 handed	9 are
10 being		

1 술어 동사가 saw이고, 목적어인 my mom and dad in the crowd가 동사 wave의 주체이므로 목적격 보어 자리에 현재분사 waving이 적절하다.

2 뒤에 주어와 동사가 모두 있는 완전한 형태의 절이 이어지므로 in which가 적절하다.

3 「each of+복수 명사」는 단수 취급하므로 단수 동사 shows가 적절하다.

4 연속 동작을 나타내는 분사구문이 되도록 현재분사 discovering을 써야 한다.

5 동사 compete를 수식하는 부사가 필요하므로 effectively를 써야 한다.

6 뒤에 완전한 문장이 이어지므로 is의 주격 보어 역할을 하면서 명사절을 이끄는 접속사 that이 적절하다.

7 접속사 although가 이끄는 절의 주어 this가 가리키는 것이 the conservation of the environment이고 define의 행위를 당하는 대상이므로 수동 의미의 과거분사 defined를 써야 한다.

8 A man을 주어로 하여 동사 stepped와 and에 의해 연결되어 병렬

구조를 이루도록 handed를 써야 한다.

9 are not pre-programmed를 대신해야 하므로 be동사 are가 적절하다.

10 that절 안의 주어 역할을 해야 하므로 동명사 being을 써야 한다.

하프 모의고사 **09회**

01 ③	02 ③	03 ④	04 ③	05 ②
06 ⑤	07 ①	08 ②	09 ④	10 ②
11 ⑤	12 ③	13 ②	14 ③	

01   정답 ③

학부모님들께,

우리 학교에 Paper Retriever라고 불리는 종이 재활용 프로그램이 있다는 것을 알고 계셨습니까? 여러분의 모든 신문, 잡지, 쇼핑 카탈로그, 사무실과 학교의 서류와 우편물을 매일 바로 이곳에 있는 초록색과 노란색 함에 재활용하실 수 있습니다. 이것은 여러분이 우리가 운동장, 조경, 도서, 그리고 기타 학교에 필요한 것들과 같은 프로젝트들을 위한 돈을 모을 수 있도록 도와주시는 손쉬운 방법입니다. 종이를 재활용함으로써, 여러분이 에너지를 절약하시는 것뿐만 아니라, 우리 학교는 여러분이 도와주셔서 저희가 모으게 되는 종이에 대해 파운드당 돈을 벌게 됩니다. 여러분의 모든 잡지, 우편물, 신문, 그리고 사무실 서류를 우리 학교 주차장에 있는 초록색과 노란색 함에 넣어 주시되, 마분지나 전화번호부는 포함시키지 말아 주십시오. 이런 중요한 기금 마련 운동에 대한 여러분의 지속적인 후원에 대해 감사드립니다.

Green 고등학교 교감

Tom Duffy 올림

해설

Paper Retriever라는 교내 종이 재활용 프로그램을 소개하면서 재활용 종이를 모아 돈을 벌어서 필요한 사업을 할 수 있도록 기금 마련 운동에 동참해 줄 것을 요청하고 있으므로, 글의 목적으로 가장 적절한 것은 ③이다.

TEXT FLOW

도입	Paper Retriever라는 교내 종이 재활용 프로그램을 소개함
전개	종이를 재활용함으로써 학교가 여러 프로젝트를 위한 자금을 마련할 수 있음을 피력함
결론	기금 마련 운동에 대한 지속적인 후원에 대해 감사를 표함

구문

• By recycling paper, **not only** do you save energy, **but** our school earns money for every pound of paper [you help us collect].

: 「not only A but (also) B(A뿐만 아니라 B도)」 구문이 사용되었고, 부정어구인 not only가 문장 앞에 와서 do you save로 주어와 조동사가 도치되었다. [ ]는 선행사 paper를 수식하는 관계절로 목적격 관계대명사 that(which)이 생략되어 있다.

02   정답 ③

혁신 생태계에서는 보상이 재고될 필요가 있다. 신생 기업에서 10억 달러라는 점증적인 가치를 창출하는 것은 그 배후의 세력인 기업가들에게 커다란 부를 창출할 수 있다. 대기업에서 10억 달러라는 점증적인 가치를 창출하면 상당한 보상을 받을 수 있는데, 그것은 신생 기업의 처지와 같은 수준과는 거리가 멀다. 분명히, 두 개의 환경에는 많은 차이점과 위험 수준이 있지만, 기업이 최대 가치 창출자를 잃지 않으려면 내부 혁신가와 기업가가 자신들이 창출하도록 도운 이익을 훨씬 더 많이 공유할 수 있도록 보상 체계가 조정되어야 한다. 성공에 대한 보상은 창출한 가치와 일치해야 하며, 승진이나 넉넉한 연봉 보너스는 극단적인 가치 창출에 대한 인센티브를 통한 장려가 되지 못한다. 10억 달러의 점증적인 가치를 만들어 낸 사람에게 왜 2천만 달러나 그 이상을 지급하지 않는가? 이는 새로운 세대의 가치를 창출하려는 열망이 있다면 조직의 지도부가 반드시 해결해야 할 문제이다.

해설
신생 기업도 큰 가치 창출을 지속하려면 대기업처럼 창출한 가치와 일치하는 보상을 지급하도록 보상 체계를 조정해야 한다는 내용의 글이다. 따라서 필자의 주장으로 가장 적절한 것은 ③이다.

⊗ 매력적인 오답 주의!
① 신생 기업이 가진 문제를 자체의 보상 체계가 아니라 대기업과의 관계에서 비롯된 것이라고 잘못 판단하면 고를 수 있는 오답이다.
⑤ 보상책으로의 승진을 적절한 보상 체계로 잘못 판단하면 고를 수 있는 오답이다.

TEXT FLOW
도입	신생 기업에서의 10억 달러라는 점증적인 가치 창출의 의미
주제	신생 기업의 보상 체계 조정의 필요성
전개	성공에 대한 보상은 창출한 가치와 일치해야 함

구문
• [Creating a billion dollars of incremental value at a startup] generates great wealth for the entrepreneurs [who are the forces behind it].
: 첫 번째 [ ]는 문장의 주어 역할을 하는 동명사구이고, 두 번째 [ ]는 the entrepreneurs를 수식하는 관계절이다.

• Clearly, the two settings have many differences and risk profiles, but if corporations don't want to lose their greatest value creators, the rewards system needs to be realigned [so that internal innovators and entrepreneurs share far more in the benefits {they helped create}].
: [ ]는 '~하도록'이라는 목적의 의미를 나타내는 「so that ~」 구문이 쓰인 부사절이고, 그 안의 { }는 the benefits를 수식하는 관계절이다.

03
정답 ④

어떤 것에 대해 회의적이거나 비판적인 태도를 권할 때 흔히 그것은 '소금 한 알과 함께' 받아들여야 한다고 말한다. 이 표현은 고대 그리스어, 특히 Pliny 장로의 'Naturalis Historia'까지 거슬러 올라가는데, 거기서 그는 독을 해독하는 전통적인 처방을 설명한다. 말린 두어 개의 호두, 두어 개의 무화과, 스무 개의 루타 잎을 가져다가 함께 찧고 속담에 나오는 소금 한 알을 더하라. 이 혼합물 1회분을 복용하라. 그러면 '하루 동안의 모든 독을 견딜 수' 있을 것이다. 그 비유적 의미는 오류를 피하기 위해 회의가 정당화될 때 성경 주석가들이 특정 성경의 주장에 적용되는 것처럼 나중에 생겨났다. 소량의 회의적인 소금은 위험한 거짓 주장을 받아들이지 않도록 도와준다. 회의적인 테스트는 그런 독에 대한 방어이다. 무언가를 테스트하는 것과 무언가를 맛보는 것은 기본적인 호소가 경험의 증거에 대한 것이라는 점에서 비슷하다. 이런 의미에서, 회의는 <u>과학의 소금</u>이다.

해설
과학에서 회의는 위험한 거짓 주장을 받아들이지 않도록 도와준다는 내용의 글이다. 회의를 과학의 소금이라고 정의하고 있으므로, 밑줄 친 부분이 의미하는 바로 가장 적절한 것은 ④ '정보에 대한 맹목적인 수용에 대한 방어'이다.
① 객관적 진실의 가능성에 대한 오해
② 과학적 지식의 적용 결과
③ 과학 연구에서 흔히 발생하는 오류의 원인
⑤ 과학적 진실과 종교적 진실 추구 사이의 균형

⊗ 매력적인 오답 주의!
① 본문에 언급된 회의의 긍정적 역할이 아니라 상식에 근거한 회의의 부정적 기능에만 집중하면 고를 수 있는 오답이다.
⑤ 본문에 언급된 biblical의 의미를 확대 해석하여 과학에서의 거짓 주장에 대한 대안으로 생각한다면 고를 수 있는 오답이다.

TEXT FLOW
도입	소금에 대한 비유적 표현의 소개
전개	소금에 대한 비유적 표현의 기원(Pliny 장로의 'Naturalis Historia')
결론	회의는 과학에서 소금의 역할을 함

구문
• The expression goes back to the ancient Greeks, specifically to Pliny the Elder's *Naturalis Historia*, [in which he describes a traditional recipe for an antidote].
: [ ]는 Pliny the Elder's *Naturalis Historia*를 부가적으로 설명하는 관계절이다.

• Take a couple of dried walnuts, a couple of figs, twenty rue leaves and pound **them** together, [adding the proverbial grain of salt].
: them은 a couple of dried walnuts, a couple of figs, twenty rue leaves를 대신한다. [ ]는 주절의 상황에 부수적인 상황을 나타내는 분사구문이다.

04
정답 ③

남아들과 여아들은 정말로 서로 다른 흥미, 능력, 그리고 개성을 갖고 있다. 하지만 어떤 남아나 여아가, 혹은 남성이나 여성이, 더 완전한 한 벌의 인지 기술과 감정 기술을 가지고도 더 성공하지 못하는가? 재능이 있는 십 대들에 대한 연구는 지능과 학업 우수성이 성의 교차적인 능력들과 더 많이 관련되어 있고 전형적인 성 역할들과는 덜 관련되어 있다는 것을 입증한다. 우리 세상에서 성공은 점점 남성과 여성의 능력을 혼합한 것, 즉 같은 정도의 감정이입과 야망, 외교술과 자기 주장에 덧붙여, 말하기, 읽기, 쓰기, 수학, 공간적 능력, 기계적인 손재주, 그리고 신체적 기능을 요구하는 데는 의심할 여지가 없을 것이다. 우리가 더 일찍 개입하여 아이들의 성장하는 뉴런과 시냅스를 변경해 줄 수 있을수록, 균형 잡힌 일련의 기술을 갖춘 남아들과 여아들을 기를 가능성은 더 커진다.

해설
지능과 학업 우수성은 전형적인 성 역할보다는 성의 교차적인 능력과 더 크게 관련되어 있으며, 미래에 더 성공할 수 있는 남아와 여아를 기를 가능성을 높이기 위해서는 성 교차적인 기술을 갖게 해야 한다는 취지의 글이므로, 글의 주제로 가장 적절한 것은 ③ '성 교차적인 능력을 갖추는 것이 성공에 미치는 영향'이다.
① 전형적인 성 역할의 위험성
② 자녀를 정서적으로 성숙하게 만드는 방법
④ 학습 패턴에 있어 남아와 여아의 차이점들
⑤ 지능과 학업 우수성 간의 관계

TEXT FLOW

도입	남아와 여아는 서로 다른 특성을 갖고 있음
전개	지능과 학업 우수성은 성의 교차적인 능력과 더 많은 관련성이 있음
부연	성공은 점점 더 남성과 여성의 능력을 혼합한 여러 능력을 필요로 함

구문

• **The earlier** we can step in and tweak kids' growing neurons and synapses, **the better** our chances of raising both boys and girls with well-balanced sets of skills.
: '~하면 할수록 더 …하다'의 의미를 나타내는 「the+비교급 ~, the+비교급 …」 구문이 쓰였다.

05
정답 ②

Decal의 여름 체조 캠프

이 캠프는 체조 기술, 팀 빌딩 경기, 그리고 체력 및 컨디션 조절 활동을 포함할 것입니다. 모든 활동은 각 주간마다 다른 주제에 초점을 맞출 것입니다.

저희 체조 캠프는 사전 등록이 필요하며, 등록 시 캠프가 있는 주마다 환불되지 않는 20달러의 보증금이 요구됩니다. 캠프 수업료 잔액은 제공된 신용카드로 청구될 것이며, 모든 캠프 주에 대해 8월 1일까지 지불해야 할 것입니다.

* **주간 캠프 참가비**: 170달러 (20달러 보증금 포함)
* **연령**: 3~12세 (캠프 참가자들은 적절한 연령대별로 나누어질 것입니다.)
* **일정**: 모든 여름 캠프는 월요일부터 금요일까지이고, 오전 9시부터 오후 1시까지입니다.
* 부모님들은 자녀들을 위해 점심, 음료, 그리고 건강에 좋은 간식을 준비하셔야만 합니다.

해설
등록할 때 캠프가 있는 주마다 환불되지 않는 20달러의 보증금이 요구된다고 했으므로 ②는 안내문의 내용과 일치하지 않는다.

구문

• Camp tuition balance **will be charged** to the credit card **provided** and **due** August 1 for all camp weeks.
: charged와 due는 and에 의해 병렬 구조로 연결되어 will be에 이어진다. provided는 과거분사로 the credit card를 수식한다.

06
정답 ⑤

고고학자들 사이에서 농경이 정착지들, 궁극적으로는 문명들이 시간이 지남에 따라 번성하는 것을 가능하게 했다는 점에 대해서는 거의 논란의 여지가 없다. 그러나 많은 정착지들이 농경을 앞섰다는 증거도 있다. 최초로 경작된 작물이 나타나기 훨씬 전에 형성된, 사원과 종신 주거지가 딸린 종교 유적지가 있었다. 페루 서부의 Pikimachay와 터키 동부의 Gobekli Tepe와 같은 곳들은 기원전 10,000년경, 고기잡이에 알맞은 강 근처나 식량 공급이 쉬운 채집이었던 지역에 위치해 있었다. 곡식, 과일, 단백질의 야생 공급원은 풍부하고 확실했는데, 그것들이 그렇지 않을 때까지(곡식, 과일, 단백질의 야생 공급원이 풍부하고 확실하지 않을 때까지) 그랬다. 가뭄이나 마름병이 찾아왔을 수도 있고, 아니면 인구가 야생 식량 공급을 초과하여 증가해서, 정착민들은 먹을 수 있는 식물이 남기는 어떤 것이라도 그것으로 때울 방법을 찾아야만 했다.

해설
⑤ until they were not abundant and reliable의 의미이므로 didn't를 weren't로 고쳐야 한다.
① that절의 가목적어 it에 대한 진목적어이므로 to thrive를 쓴 것은 적절하다.
② evidence와 동격인 명사절을 이끄는 접속사이므로 that을 쓴 것은 적절하다.
③ 수식을 받는 temples and permanent dwellings는 establish의 주체가 아니라 대상이므로 과거분사 established는 적절하다.
④ 주어가 Places이므로 복수형 동사 were는 적절하다. such as ~ Turkey는 Places를 수식하는 전치사구이다.

TEXT FLOW

도입	농경으로 인해 정착지, 문명이 번성함
반론	농경 이전에 정착이 이루어졌다는 증거가 있음
근거	최초로 경작된 작물이 나타나기 훨씬 전에 형성된 종교 유적지의 흔적

구문

• There's little dispute among archaeologists [that farming made **it** possible for settlements, and ultimately for civilizations, **to thrive over time**].
: [ ]는 dispute를 부연 설명해 주는 동격절이다. it은 가목적어이고, to thrive over time이 진목적어이다.

• Places [such as Pikimachay in western Peru and Gobekli Tepe in eastern Turkey] were located, circa l0,000 BC, near fishable rivers or in regions [where the food supply was easy pickings].
: 첫 번째 [ ]는 Places를 수식하는 전치사구이고, 두 번째 [ ]는 관계부사 where가 이끄는 절로 regions를 수식한다.

07
정답 ①

지휘자는 대중 앞에서 권위를 행사하는 몇 안 되는 사람들 중 하나이다. 그 역할의 매우 잘 보이는 특성 때문에 무대 뒤에 있는 사람의 일보다 이해하기 쉽다고 생각하겠지만, 정반대의 경우도 있는 것 같다. 혼란을 일으키는 것은 분명히 지휘자의 모습이다. 지휘자들은 대부분의 지도자들보다 더 많이 손을 움직인다. 혼란의 원인은 지휘자들이 사용하는 언어가 비유적이고, 그들의 의사소통 방식은 아마도 그것이 작동하는 것을 전혀 보지 못하게 되어 있는 청중들에게는 의문스럽게 보일 수 있다는 것이다. 공연장에 있는 대중들이 지휘자의 신체적 특징을 관찰하는 것을 피하기가 어렵지만, 연주자의 운지법이 목적을 위한 수단이 아니듯 그들의 몸짓도 목적을 위한 수단이 아니다. 지휘자가 어떻게 생겼는지가 듣는 사람에게 중요해야 하는지 모르겠지만, 실황

오케스트라 콘서트의 시각적 역학에 관한 모든 것은 그것이 중요하다고 시사하는 것 같다.

해설
지휘자의 손동작이 오히려 지휘자의 의사소통 방식을 알지 못하는 청중들에게 의문스럽게 보일 수 있다고 했으므로, 빈칸에 들어갈 말로 가장 적절한 것은 ① '모습'이다.
② 경력 ③ 능력 ④ 리더십 ⑤ 성격

TEXT FLOW
도입	지휘자의 모습으로 인해 혼란이 일어남
부연	지휘자는 손을 많이 움직이고, 청중은 그 의사소통 방식을 이해하기 어려움
주제	청중은 무대 위 지휘자의 신체적 특징을 볼 수밖에 없지만, 지휘자의 몸짓이나 생김새는 중요하지 않음

구문
• The complication is [that the language {conductors use} is figurative, and their mode of communication can appear questionable to an audience {that is probably not meant to see it at work at all}].
: [ ]는 is의 주격 보어 역할을 하는 명사절이다. 그 안의 첫 번째 { }는 the language를 수식하는 관계절이고, 두 번째 { }는 an audience를 수식하는 관계절이다.

08
정답 ②

운동은 매우 의례적인 활동이다. 예를 들어, 골프 선수들은 공을 치기 전에 수차례 일관되게 자신들의 골프채를 '흔드는' 경향이 있고, 테니스 선수들은 서브를 하기 전에 정해진 기준대로 여러 번 공을 튀기는 것을 좋아한다. 이렇게 선호되는 행동의 순서들은 '(의식 등의) 수행 전 정해진 절차(PPRs)'라고 불리고 운동선수들이 자신들의 특정한 운동 기술을 수행하기 전에 체계적으로 참여하는 과업과 관련된 생각과 행동을 포함한다. 보통, PPRs는 테니스에서 서브를 하거나, 농구에서 자유투를 하거나, 골프에서 퍼팅을 하는 것과 같은 자기 진도에 따른 활동들을 실행하기 전에 분명히 나타난다. 그러한 정해진 절차들은 집중력을 향상시키고 경쟁의 성과를 향상시키기 위한 정신적 준비의 한 형태로서 운동선수들에 의해 광범위하게 사용되고 코치와 심리학자들에 의해 추천된다.

해설
골프 선수들과 테니스 선수들이 공을 치기 전이나 서브를 하기 전에 습관적으로 하는 행동들이 있다는 내용과, 이렇게 선호되는 행동의 순서들을 '수행 전 정해진 절차'라고 부른다는 설명으로 미루어 볼 때, 빈칸에 들어갈 말로 가장 적절한 것은 ② '매우 의례적인 활동'이다.
① 목표 지향적인 활동
③ 상당히 보편적인 언어
④ 일종의 위안, 도피처
⑤ 여러 세대를 통해 전해진 유산

TEXT FLOW
도입	운동은 매우 의례적인 활동이며, 공을 치거나 서브를 하기 전 골프 선수와 테니스 선수의 행동을 통해 이를 확인할 수 있음
전개	'수행 전 정해진 절차'라고 불리는 것은 운동선수들이 특정한 운동 기술을 수행하기 전에 하는 일련의 행동임
결론	정해진 절차들을 수행하는 것은 집중력 및 경쟁의 성과 향상의 긍정적 효과를 낳기 때문에 광범위하게 사용되고 추천됨

구문
• [These preferred action sequences] **are called** "pre-performance routines" (PPRs) and **involve** task-relevant thoughts and actions [which athletes engage in systematically prior to their performance of specific sport skills].
: 첫 번째 [ ]가 주어이고 동사 are called와 involve가 접속사 and로 연결되어 있는 구조이다. 두 번째 [ ]는 task-relevant thoughts and actions를 수식하는 관계절이다.

09
정답 ④

누구에게 배울 것인가에 대한 문제를 해결하려면, 먼저 누가 잘하는지를 살펴봄으로써 시작할 수 있다. Alex는 요리 실력이 뛰어나고, Renee는 좋은 사회적 관계를 유지하는 데 능숙하므로 그들에게서 배우는 것이 타당하다. 하지만 이런 식으로 그 문제를 줄였다고 해도 모방할 수 있는 많은 잠재적 행동이 남는다. 우리는 Alex가 어떻게 그리고 왜 그렇게 훌륭한 요리를 만들 수 있었는지 어떻게 정확히 알아내는가? 우리의 직관이 몇 가지 요인 — 아마도 그의 헤어스타일은 아니겠지만 — 을 배제하는 데 도움이 되겠지만, 범위가 재료나 조리 시간처럼 가장 명백한 것부터, 사소하게는 사용한 양파의 구체적인 종류나 쌀을 휘저은 방법과 같은 것에 이르기까지 많은 가능성이 남아 있다. (좋은 요리사는 음식의 원산지, 전통적으로 음식이 어떻게 사용되는지, 그것이 어떻게 자신에게 도달했는지, 그것을 어떻게 가장 잘 조리할지 등 그 말의 모든 면에서 음식을 존중한다.) 요리사의 조리법을 그대로 따라 해보면 알 수 있듯이, 성공의 결정 요소는 때로 매우 불분명할 수 있다.

해설
성공하기 위해 배울 대상자를 결정한다고 해도 배움의 대상 행동이 여러 가지여서 성공의 결정 요소가 불분명하다는 내용으로, 요리사의 조리법 모방을 예로 들며 설명하고 있다. 따라서 훌륭한 요리사의 자질로서 음식을 존중하는 태도를 언급하고 있는 ④는 글의 전체 흐름과 관계가 없다.

TEXT FLOW
도입	누구에게 배울 것인가에 대한 문제 해결은 잘하는 사람을 살펴봄으로써 시작할 수 있음
전개	배움 대상 행동의 모방 가능한 잠재적 행동이 여전히 남아 있음
결론	성공의 결정 요소에는 불분명성이 있음

구문
• How do we work out exactly [how and why Alex was able to cook such a great dish]?
: [ ]는 work out의 목적어 역할을 하는 명사절이다.

• ~ but there remain many possibilities, [ranging from the most obvious, such as the ingredients or the cooking time,

to the least, such as the specific type of onions used or how the rice was stirred].
: [ ]는 many possibilities를 부가적으로 설명하는 분사구이다.

10
정답 ②

너무나 많은 교사들이 마치 어린이가 배울 것이거나 배울 필요가 있는 것은 그들이 학교에서 가졌던 이전의 학습 경험에 달려 있는 것처럼 계획한다. (B) 하지만 이것은 학교 환경에서 벗어나서 어린이들이 학습하는 것의 지대한 영향을 무시하는 것이다. 어린이들은 학교 학습의 모든 측면에 영향을 주는 경험들이 풍부한 가정, 가족, 지역 사회로부터 온다. 학교에서의 학습은 케이크 위에 뿌려진 당의이다. (A) 그것의 질이 좋을 때 그것은 학습을 더 체계적이게 만들지만, 학교는 절대 자신들이 지식의 유일한 전달자인 것처럼 행동할 정도로 주제넘어서는 안 된다. (C) 교사들은 어떤 새로운 것을 소개하려고 계획할 때, 늘 '이 수업의 어린이들이 이미 알고 있는 것은 무엇인가?', 즉 '그 아이들의 일부는 그들의 경험 중 이러한 측면에 대해 서로에게, 그리고 나에게, 무엇을 가르쳐 줄 수 있을까?'라는 질문을 해야 한다.

해설
많은 교사들이 어린이가 배워야 할 것이 그들의 학교에서의 이전 학습 경험에 달려 있는 것처럼 계획한다는 주어진 글에 이어, 그것이 학교 환경 밖의 학습 영향을 무시하는 것이며 어린이들은 학교 밖의 여러 환경으로부터 경험을 얻는다는 내용의 (B)가 오고, (B)의 the icing을 받는 it으로 시작하여 학교가 지식의 유일한 전달자인 것처럼 행동해서는 안 된다는 내용의 (A)가 이어지고, 마지막으로 앞의 내용을 바탕으로 새로운 것을 소개하려고 할 때 적절한 교사의 자세를 언급한 (C)가 오는 것이 글의 흐름상 가장 자연스럽다.

TEXT FLOW

도입	많은 교사들이 어린이의 학습이 학교에서의 이전 학습 경험에 달려 있는 것처럼 계획을 하는데, 이것은 학교 환경 밖의 학습 영향을 무시하는 것임
전개	학교에서의 학습은 학교 밖의 다양한 경험들로부터 영향을 받으며, 학교 학습은 그것을 마무리하는 장식에 불과함
결론	새로운 것을 소개하려고 계획할 때 교사는 학생들이 이미 알고 있는 것과 경험을 고려해야 함

구문
• When it is of good quality it can **make learning more systematic**, but schools should never be so presumptuous as to act **as though** they are the only conveyors of knowledge.
: 「make+목적어+목적격 보어」의 구문으로 목적격 보어 자리에 형용사 (more systematic)가 쓰인 구조이다. as though는 '마치 ~인 것처럼'이라는 뜻의 접속사이다.

11
정답 ⑤

가족의 사회화 기능은 1세기 전에 더 많이 두드러졌는데, 이는 부분적으로 성인 가족 구성원들이 오늘날에 그러한 것보다 더 기꺼이 보육에 도움이 될 수 있었기 때문이다. 미국 전역에서 산업이 성장함에 따라, 가족은 도시의 공장과 사무실에서 일하기 위해 농장을 떠났다. 특히 1950년대 이후, 많은 여성들이 임금을 위해 집 밖에서 일을 해야만 했다. 아버지들은 자신들의 자녀

들과 더 많은 시간을 보냄으로써 (여성들이 아이들과 보내지 못하는 시간을) 보충하지 않았다. 사실, 이혼율이 증가했고 많은 아버지들이 이혼 이후 자녀들과 덜 접촉하기 때문에, 자녀들은 아마도 평균적으로 자신들의 아버지들을 1세기 전에 그랬던 것보다 지금 덜 볼 것이다. 스웨덴과 프랑스 같은 일부 국가들에서는 국가가 자금을 지원하는 보육 시설을 만들어 어린이들을 교육하고, 감독하고, 훈육하는 것을 도움으로써 이러한 발달을 보충했다. 그러나 미국에서는 보육이 큰 사회적 문제가 되었고, 이것은 어떤 경우들에는 자녀에 대한 방치와 학대로 이어졌다.

해설
주어진 문장은 스웨덴과 프랑스에서는 국가가 지원하여 보육 시설을 만들어 보육을 지원했다는 내용이므로, 역접의 연결사 however를 포함하여 그와 반대되는 미국의 상황에 대한 서술이 이어지는 문장 앞인 ⑤에 들어가는 것이 가장 적절하다.

TEXT FLOW

도입	성인 가족 구성원들의 도움으로 가족의 사회화 기능은 1세기 전에 더 두드러졌음
전개	미국 전역에서 산업이 성장할수록 부모가 자녀와 보내는 시간이 감소함
결론	일부 국가에서는 국가가 지원하는 보육 시설을 만들어 자녀 양육의 부족한 시간을 보충했으나 미국에서는 보육이 큰 사회적 문제가 되었음

구문
• [In some countries, such as Sweden and France], the creation of state-funded child care facilities compensated for these developments **by helping** teach, supervise, and discipline children.
: [ ]는 전치사구로서 부사의 역할을 하고, 「by+동명사」는 '~함으로써'의 의미로 수단이나 도구의 의미를 나타낸다.

12
정답 ③

과거에, 방송인들은 연구를 하고, 고객의 관심을 평가하고, 시장을 위해 콘텐츠를 개발하고, 일정(방송 순서)을 계획했다. 그 당시에, 시청자들은 방송인들이 제공한 것을 시청할 수밖에 없었다. 그러나 오늘날에는 형세가 변했다. 주문식의 상호작용 환경에서는, 고객에게 선택권이 있다. 그렇다, 시청자는 미식축구 경기, 뉴스 방송, 또는 주간 시트콤의 첫 방송과 같은 여전히 예정된 프로를 위해 채널을 맞출 수도 있지만, 그 '채널 맞춤'은 '방송'이 재생되고 있을 때 일어나지 않을 수도 있다. 대부분의 경우, 어떤 방송국에 채널을 맞추고 있기보다는, 시청자는 방송 프로 편성의 다중매체 데이터베이스에 접속할 것이다. 그 결과, 방송인들의 역할은 시청자들을 위해 일정을 짜는 것에서 그들이 시청하고 즐길 좋은 데이터베이스를 제공하는 것으로 이동한다.

➡ 과거에, 방송인들은 시청자들과의 관계에서 지배적인 위치를 가지고 있었던 반면에, 오늘날 그들은 주로 콘텐츠 제공자들로서 역할을 한다.

해설
과거에는 방송인들이 연구 평가, 개발, 계획 등의 일을 하는 지배적인 위치에 있었지만, 오늘날에는 주로 시청자들에게 좋은 데이터베이스를 제공하는 역할을 한다는 내용이므로, 요약문의 빈칸 (A)에는 dominant(지배적인)가, (B)에는 content providers(콘텐츠 제공자들)가 들어가는 것이 가장 적절하다.

① 중립적인 – 콘텐츠 제공자들
② 지배적인 – 이윤 창출자들
④ 종속적인 – 정보 감독관들
⑤ 종속적인 – 이윤 창출자들

TEXT FLOW

도입	과거에 방송인들은 방송과 관련된 연구, 평가, 개발, 계획 등의 일을 함
전환	현대의 주문식 상호작용 환경에서는 선택권이 고객에게 있음
부연	이제 방송인들의 역할은 시청자들이 시청하고 즐길 좋은 데이터베이스를 제공하는 것으로 이동함

구문

• As a result, the role of broadcasters shifts **from scheduling** for the viewers **to offering** a good database **for them** [to watch and enjoy].
: 'A에서 B로'를 의미하는 「from A to B」 구문이 쓰였는데, 이때 from과 to는 전치사이므로 목적어로 동명사를 취했다. [ ]는 to부정사의 형용사적 용법으로 a good database를 수식하며, for them은 to부정사구의 의미상 주어이다.

13-14

정답 13 ② 14 ③

군대의 비유를 사용하자면, 전투는 특정한 지리적 위치에서, 특정한 장비를 가지고, 특정한 맞수를 무찌르기 위해 이루어진다. 점점 더 사업 전략은 그 정도의 정확성으로 체계적으로 나타낼 필요가 있게 되었다. 분류를 추진하는 것은 아마도 특정한 소비자들이 추구하는 결과물('이루어져야 할 일들')일 것이고 그러한 결과물이 충족될 수 있는 대안적인 방법일 것이다. 이것은 매우 중요한데, 주어진 이점에 대한 가장 중요한 위협은 주변부 또는 분명치 않은 장소에서 발생할 가능성이 있기 때문이다.
이것은 더 나아가 어떤 회사가 그것이 참여하는 모든 활동 무대에 대해 한 가지 접근법을 가지지 않을 것이라는 문제를 야기한다. 대신, 그 접근법은 일반적인(→ 특정한) 활동 무대와 그것이 직면하는 경쟁자들에 맞추어 적응될 수 있다. 예를 들어, 언어를 가르치는 회사인 Berlitz의 전략을 고려해 보라. 그들의 전 회장이었던 브라질인 Marcos Justus가 나에게 말했듯, 브라질에서 대중적인 시장을 위한 경쟁은 맹렬했지만, 상위 소득 부류의 소비자에 대한 경쟁은 그보다는 덜했다. 그곳에서는, 더 높은 계층에 주안점을 두고 우수한 상품으로서 그 브랜드의 위치를 선정한 전략이 이치에 맞았다. 소비자들의 다수가 중간 어딘가에 있는 미국에서는, 편리함과 융통성을 특징으로 하는 다른 위치 선정이 이치에 맞았다. 이것은 두 개의 서로 다른 전략이고 두 개의 서로 다른 활동 무대의 요구에 대응하는 것이다. 그러나 이러한 두 가지 전략 모두 Berlitz가 되기를 갈망하는 문화적인 자문 회사를 향한 Berlitz의 발전을 추진한다.

해설

13 자신이 참여하는 활동 무대의 특성을 잘 파악하고, 각각의 경쟁의 장에서 필요한 개별적이고 구체적인 접근법을 만들어 그에 맞는 전략을 구사해야 한다는 내용의 글이므로, 글의 제목으로 가장 적절한 것은 ② '모든 서로 다른 활동 무대를 위해 전략을 다양화하라'이다.
① 인생은 전투가 아니고 일련의 협상이다
③ 자신감과 용기를 가지고 모든 도전에 대처하라
④ 세상을 성공을 위한 하나의 거대한 활동 무대로 생각하라
⑤ 자신에 대한 지식: 전투를 위한 강력한 무기

14 각각의 구체적인 경쟁의 장을 위해 개별화된 전략을 수립해야 한다는 내용의 글이므로, (c) general(일반적인)을 particular(특정한)와 같은 단어로 바꿔야 한다.

TEXT FLOW

도입	전투의 비유(특정한 전장에 대한 구체적인 전략 필요)
주제	회사 또한 특정한 소비자군에 대한 구체적인 접근이 필요함
예시	브라질과 미국에서 각기 다른 전략을 활용한 Berlitz

구문

• The driver of categorization will in all likelihood be the outcomes [that particular customers seek] ("jobs to be done") and the alternative ways [those outcomes might be met].
: 첫 번째 [ ]는 the outcomes를 수식하는 관계절이다. 두 번째 [ ]는 the alternative ways를 수식하는 관계절로, 앞에 관계부사 how가 생략되어 있다.

• As Marcos Justus, their former Brazilian president, told me, [in Brazil, {competition for the mass market} was fierce, but {competition for customers in the upper income brackets} was less **so**].
: [ ]는 told의 직접목적어 역할을 하는 명사절이다. 첫 번째 { }는 but 앞에 있는 절의 주어로 쓰인 명사구이고, 두 번째 { }는 but 뒤에 오는 절의 주어로 쓰인 명사구이다. so는 fierce 대신 사용되었다.

GRAMMAR REVIEW

본문 81쪽

1 called	2 Creating	3 Take
4 gifted	5 that	6 whose
7 putting	8 remain	9 that
10 are		

1 동사 call의 목적어가 the Paper Retriever로 존재하고, 의미상 수식을 받는 a paper recycling program이 call의 주체가 아니라 대상이므로 수동의 의미를 갖는 과거분사 called를 써야 한다.

2 문장의 주어 역할을 해야 하는 구를 이끌어야 하므로 동명사 Creating이 적절하다.

3 '~하라, 그러면 …할 것이다'라는 의미의 「명령문, and ...」 구문을 이루어야 하므로 Take가 적절하다.

4 수식을 받는 teenagers가 gift라는 행위를 하는 주체가 아니라 그 대상이 되므로 수동의 의미를 갖는 과거분사 gifted를 써야 한다.

5 dispute를 부연 설명하는 동격절을 이끄는 접속사 that이 적절하다.

6 the few people이 관계절 내에서 authority의 소유격(the few people's authority) 역할을 하고 있으므로 소유격 관계대명사 whose가 적절하다.

7 serving ~, free-throwing ~과 함께 such as에 대등하게 이어져 병렬 구조를 이루고 있으므로 동명사 putting을 써야 한다.

8 주어가 many possibilities이므로 복수 동사 remain이 적절하다.

9 관계절의 수식을 받는 experiences가 관계절의 동사 touch에 대한 주어 역할을 하므로 주격 관계대명사 that이 적절하다.

10 they are readily available for child care에서 readily available for child care가 생략된 것이므로 are가 적절하다.

하프 모의고사   10회

01 ②	02 ④	03 ④	04 ③	05 ②
06 ③	07 ④	08 ③	09 ⑤	10 ③
11 ⑤	12 ④	13 ④	14 ⑤	

01   정답 ②

26번 탑승구에서 그 승객을 보았는가? 그 친구는 발권 담당 직원을 강아지 눈으로 쳐다보고 있었다. 그 사람은 바로 나였다. 북쪽에서 온 전선(前線)이 중서부를 강타하여 시카고의 O'Hare 공항을 얼렸고 내 것을 비롯한 수천 개의 여행 일정표를 날려 버렸다. 나는 San Antonio로 향하는 그날의 마지막 비행기를 탈 수 있는지 묻고 있었다. 나는 내가 가진 얼마 안 되는 매력을 친절하지만 지쳐 있는 발권 담당 직원에게 퍼붓고 있었다. 나는 다음날 취업 면접이 있었고 그녀가 내 미래를 손에 쥐고 있었다. "남는 좌석이 있습니까?" 나는 윙크를 하고 있었지만, 그녀는 알아차리지 못했다. 그녀는 그저 화면을 들여다보고 한숨을 쉬었다. "유감스럽지만 …" 무엇이 유감스럽다는 말일까? 나는 그녀가 자신의 문장을 끝마치기를 기다렸다. "유감스럽지만 이코노미석에는 더 이상 자리가 없습니다. 귀하를 일등석으로 승급해 드려야 할 겁니다. 그렇게 해도 괜찮으시겠습니까?" 나는 거의 소리를 쳤다. "제가 당신에게 포옹해도 괜찮으시겠어요?" 나는 비행기에 탑승했고 다리를 뻗을 수 있는 여분의 공간이 있는 넓은 좌석에 기분 좋게 앉았다.

해설
악천후 때문에 공항에 발이 묶인 상태에서 발권 담당 직원에게 San Antonio로 가는 마지막 비행기에 좌석이 있는지 초조하게 물었고, 발권 담당 직원이 이코노미석은 더 이상 좌석이 없다고 하며 일등석으로 좌석을 승급해 준 덕분에 편안하게 비행기를 탈 수 있었다는 내용의 글이므로, 필자의 심경 변화로는 ② '불안한 → 기쁜'이 가장 적절하다.
① 감사하는 → 궁금한
③ 안도하는 → 겁먹은
④ 짜증난 → 동정하는
⑤ 고대하는 → 실망하는

TEXT FLOW

시간 순서/사건 전개에 따른 흐름:
악천후이지만 San Antonio행 마지막 비행기를 타야 하는 상황 → 발권 담당 직원에게 남는 좌석이 있는지 물어봄 → 발권 담당 직원이 이코노미석 대신 일등석 좌석 승급을 제안함 → 일등석으로 편히 여행함

구문

• I was pouring [what little charm I had] on the kind but tired ticket agent.
  : [ ]는 동사 was pouring의 목적어 역할을 하고, I had 앞에는 목적격 관계대명사인 that[which]이 생략되었다.

02   정답 ④

우리가 가장 단순한 종류의 동물과 그들 조상들의 유전적 특징을 주의 깊게

검토하면, 우리는 우리 자신에 대해 매우 중요한 것을 배울 수 있다. 동물 생명체 나무의 토대 저 아래쪽, 선조들의 뿌리 깊은 곳에서, 우리의 친족과 버섯의 선조들을 구분하는 것은 불가능해진다. 동물과 균류는 합쳐지고, 둘을 혼합하는 10억 살 된 강인한 가지를 만든다. 이 연합의 증거는 동물과 균류의 DNA를 비교하는 데서 나온다. 이 분자 계통 발생론적인 작업은 30년 동안 진화상의 관련성을 알아내기 위해 널리 퍼져 왔다. 방법이 치밀해지고 데이터 세트가 확장되면서, 동물과 균류의 관련성에 대한 주장은 강화되었다. 그러므로, 우리가 잔디밭에서 보는 버섯에 대한 (우리의) 초월성에 대한 비논리를 넘어서, 우리는 그것들과 연관되어 있다. 우리는 식물이나 혹은 다른 어떤 주요한 생물 집단보다도 균류와 더 유사하다.

해설
유전적 특징의 검토를 통해 DNA를 비교해 보면 인간은 균류와 매우 유사하다는 내용의 글이므로, 글의 요지로 가장 적절한 것은 ④이다.

TEXT FLOW
도입	동물 기원을 살펴보면 인간의 친족과 버섯의 선조 구분이 어려움
부연	DNA의 비교 연구를 통해 이에 대한 증거가 제시됨
주제	우리는 다른 어떤 주요한 생물 집단보다 균류와 더 유사함

구문
• [Down at the base of the tree of animal life, deep in the ancestral roots], it becomes impossible [to tell the difference between our kin and the forerunners of mushrooms].
: 첫 번째 [ ]는 위치를 나타내는 부사구이다. it은 가주어이고 두 번째 [ ]는 진주어인 to부정사구이다.

03
정답 ④

있는 그대로의 삶에 편안해지는 것은 여러분이 어디에서 왔는지를 존중하는 것을 포함한다. 꼭 그것을 좋아하지는 않아도 되지만, 말하자면 그것은 여러분을 형성한 방식을 알게 되는 것과 여러분의 과거에 대한 무지와 부인이 아니라 용기와 인식에 근거한 어른스러운 선택을 하는 것을 포함한다. 알다시피, 우리가 자신의 초기 상황이 우리 인생에 미치는 지속적인 영향을 무시하려고 애쓸 때, 우리는 결국 착각의 세계를 돌아다니게 된다. 우리는 자신이 그다지 영리하지 못하다거나 중요하지 않다거나 어울리지 않는다고 생각할지도 모르지만, 그것은 사실이 아니다. 일단 우리가 그러한 착각들을 놓아주고 현재의 우리 자신이 된 방식에 직면할 수 있으면, 우리는 우리 자신의 내부에서 괜찮을 수 있는 능력을 개발하여, 우리가 어디에서 왔든 무슨 일이 일어나든 우리는 괜찮으리라는 것을 인식할 수 있다.

해설
있는 그대로의 삶에 편안해지려면 자신의 과거를 존중해야 하며, 초기 상황이 인생에 미치는 지속적인 영향을 무시하려고 애쓰면 착각 속에 빠지게 된다고 했으므로, 글의 제목으로 가장 적절한 것은 ④ '자신의 과거를 이해하는 것: 진정한 자아를 발견하는 방법'이다.
① 자신을 존중하라, 자신을 보호하라
② 긍정적으로 생각하라, 일이 잘 풀릴 것이다
③ 용서하고 나아가는 법: 스스로를 가르쳐라
⑤ 더 나은 원가를 희망하는 것: 평범한 삶에 안주하기를 거부하는 것

TEXT FLOW
요지	자신의 과거를 존중하게 되면 삶이 편안해짐
전개	초기 상황이 인생에 미치는 영향을 무시하려고 하면 결국 자신의 능력에 대한 부정적인 착각에 빠지게 됨
부연	착각에서 벗어나 현재의 자신이 된 방식에 직면할 수 있으면 과거가 어떻든 무슨 일이 일어나든 괜찮을 것이라는 인식을 갖게 됨

구문
• **Once** we can let go of those illusions and face how we became who we are, we can develop the capacity to be all right within ourselves, **to recognize** [that no matter where we came from or what happens, we'll be all right].
: Once는 부사절을 이끄는 접속사로 '일단 ~하면'의 뜻이다. to recognize는 결과를 나타내는 부사적 용법의 to부정사이고, [ ]는 recognize의 목적어로 쓰인 명사절이다.

04
정답 ③

위 그래프는 2020년 잉글랜드의 연령별 및 성별 1인당 도보 이동 횟수를 보여 준다. 평균적으로, 여성이 남성보다 1인당 도보 이동 횟수가 더 많았는데, 남성의 207회와 비교하여 여성은 265회였다. 두 개의 최고 연령대의 남성만 동년배의 여성보다 1인당 도보 이동 횟수가 더 많았다. 남성의 도보 이동 횟수는 대부분의 연령대에서 대략 200회에 머물렀고, 70세 이상에서 가장 많았다. 반면에, 여성은 40~49세의 사람들이 모든 연령대에서 1인당 도보 이동 횟수가 가장 많았다. 17~20세 남성과 여성은 둘 다 1인당 도보 이동 횟수가 가장 적었다.

해설
남성의 도보 이동 횟수는 17~20세와 21~29세는 200회에 미치지 못하고, 16세 이하의 연령대에서 가장 많았으므로, 도표의 내용과 일치하지 않는 것은 ③이다.

구문
• [The number of walking trips for men] stayed around 200 for most of the age groups, and it was the highest for those [aged 70 and over].
: 첫 번째 [ ]는 문장의 주어이고, 두 번째 [ ]는 those를 수식하는 분사구이다.

05
정답 ②

동물들은 야생에서 그들의 자연 그대로의 서식지들에 속해 있다. 우리 자신의 목적을 위해서 강제로 그들을 가두어 두는 것은 그들의 자연권을 침해하는 것이다. 그들은 자신들만의 먹이를 모으지 못하게 되고, 자신들만의 사회 질서를 발전시키지 못하게 되며, 대개 자신들에게 자연스러운 방식으로 행동하지 못하게 된다. 우리가 동물원에 그들의 환경을 복제해 주려고 아무리 애쓸지라도, 우리는 결코 충분한 결과를 얻지 못할 것이다. 포식자들은 사냥할 필요가 있는데 그들을 길들임으로써 그들에게서 그렇게 하는 능력을 앗아 가는 것은 잔인함을 넘어서는 일이다. '사이언스' 지의 2008년 한 연구에서는 아시아의 벌목장에 있는 야생 코끼리들의 41.7년에 비교하여 유럽의 동물원들에 있는 아시아 코끼리들의 중간 수명은 고작 18.9년이었다는 것을 발견했다. 먹이 순환에 대한 인간의 지나친 개입은 그것을 상당히 교란시켰다.

자연이 제 갈 길을 가게 놓아 두라.

해설

(A) 야생에 속해 있는 동물들의 자연권을 침해하는 경우와 관련 있어야 하므로 captivity(감금)가 적절하다.
(B) 길들인다는 내용과 관련지어 동물원에 동물들이 살던 환경을 옮겨 놓는 경우이므로 replicate(복제하다)가 적절하다.
(C) 포식자들을 사냥하지 못하게 하고 그러한 능력을 앗아가는 것은 그들을 길들이는 것에 대한 내용이므로 taming(길들임)이 적절하다.

TEXT FLOW

도입	동물을 가두어 두는 것은 동물의 자연권을 침해하는 것임
전개	동물들의 환경을 복제해 주려고 해도 충분한 결과를 얻지 못함
결론	인간의 개입은 부정적인 결과를 가져오므로 자연을 있는 그대로 두어야 함

구문

• They are prevented from [gathering their own food], [developing their own social orders] and [generally behaving in ways that are natural to them].
: 전치사 from의 목적어로 세 개의 동명사구 [ ]가 and에 의해 병렬 구조로 연결되어 있다.

06

정답 ③

우리가 지식의 본체들이 서로 어떻게 연결되어 있는지에 대해 생각하기 시작할 수 있는 것은 바로 그것들이 특정 수준의 정교함에 이르렀을 때인 것 같다. 우리는 부분들의 의미를 이해했을 때만 전체 그림의 의미를 이해할 수 있다. 분석은 종합에 선행한다. 서구 사회에서, 20세기 초반은 딱 알맞은 때였다. 사회 과학이라는 영역은 인구 대다수의 비참한 생활 조건에 대해 몇 명의 책임감 있는 사람들이 느낀 점점 커져 가는 분노감의 결과로 등장하게 되었다. 종교적인 믿음들의 지배력, 특히 사람들에게 죽음 이후 그들의 고난에 대한 보상의 기대를 약속한 것들은 그들의 지배력을 잃어 가기 시작하고 있었다. 신의 개입을 기다릴 필요 없이 우리 자신의 노력을 통해 우리가 이 생애에서 인간의 조건을 개선시킬 수 있다는 생각이 점점 증가하고 있었다.

해설

빈칸 앞에서는 부분의 의미를 이해했을 때만 전체 그림의 의미를 이해할 수 있다는 내용이 제시되고, 빈칸 다음의 예시에서는 20세기 초반 서구 사회에서 비참한 생활 조건에 대한 분노감(분석)의 결과로 사회 과학(종합)이 등장하게 되었다는 내용이 제시되었으므로, 빈칸에 들어갈 말로 가장 적절한 것은 ③ '분석은 종합에 선행한다'이다.
① 불완전은 아름다움이다
② 운은 대담한 사람들을 좋아한다
④ 악을 악으로 갚아 봐야 좋을 게 없다
⑤ 나무는 보고 숲은 보지 못한다

TEXT FLOW

도입	부분들을 이해하고 나서야 전체를 이해할 수 있음
요지	분석이 종합에 선행함
부연	20세기 초반은 서구 사회에 사회 과학이 등장하기에 딱 맞는 시기였음

구문

• It seems that **it is** [only when bodies of knowledge have reached a certain level of sophistication] **that** we can begin to think about how they connect with each other.
: 「It seems that ....」 구문의 that절에 「it is ~ that ....」 강조구문이 사용되어 시간의 부사절인 [ ]를 강조하고 있다.

07

정답 ④

우리는 단 한 가지의 뉘앙스와 농담을 결부시키지는 않는다. 그것은 결국 맥락이 전부이다. 여러분의 프레젠테이션의 요소에 대해서도 마찬가지다. 한번은 국제 자연 보호 협회의 한 현장 생물학자가 청중들이 모두 평상복 차림을 하고 있을 때 정장을 입고 넥타이를 맨 채 발표회에 나타난 적이 있었다. 만약 여러분이 현장 생물학자에 대해 조금이라도 알고 있다면, 그들이 숲에서 웅크리고 앉아 있거나 진흙이 무릎까지 올라온 채로 많은 시간을 보낸다는 것을 안다. 일을 하는 중에 그들은 청바지나 치노 바지, 반바지를 많이 입는다. 그래서 한 사립 중등학교의 세미나실에서 이 발표를 하고 있던 그 현장 생물학자는 자신이 지나치게 차려 입은 특이한 입장에 처해 있다는 것을 알게 되었다. 그는 넥타이를 내려다보고 청중을 올려다보고 다시 넥타이를 응시하다가 다시 청중 쪽으로 눈을 들어 "여러분 중에 저를 아시는 분들은 제 어머니가 항상 자랑스러워하시는 어떤 것을 알고 조금 놀라실 것입니다. 저는 말끔하게 차려입었습니다."라고 말했다. 청중 모두가 웃었다. 그의 발표 맥락에서는, 평범한 정장과 넥타이가 농담이었다.

해설

농담은 단 한 가지의 뉘앙스와 결부되는 것이 아니라 맥락과 관련이 있으며 프레젠테이션의 요소에서도 마찬가지라고 했는데, 프레젠테이션에서 일상적인 복장과 달리 정장 차림을 하고 온 현장 생물학자가 발표의 맥락상 자신의 차림새를 유머의 요소로 활용했으므로, 빈칸에 들어갈 말로 가장 적절한 것은 ④ '평범한 정장과 넥타이가 농담이었다'이다.
① 그의 외모는 중요하지 않았다
② 유머 감각은 타고난 것이었다
③ 그의 차림새는 전혀 그와 어울리지 않았다
⑤ 성공의 열쇠는 진실성이었다

TEXT FLOW

주제	프레젠테이션의 요소에 있어 농담은 맥락과 관련이 있음
전개	일을 하는 평상시와 달리 정장 차림으로 프레젠테이션을 하는 현장 생물학자
결론	발표 맥락에서 현장 생물학자의 복장이 유머 요소였음

구문

• So the field biologist [making this presentation in the seminar room of a prep school] found **himself** in the unusual position of being overdressed.
: [ ]는 the field biologist를 수식하는 분사구이다. 주어와 목적어가 같은 사람이므로 목적어에 재귀대명사 himself를 썼다.

• He looked down at his tie and looked up at the audience and returned his gaze to his tie and lifted his eyes again to his audience and said, "Those of you [who know me] may be a little surprised to learn something [my mother has always been proud of]: I clean up well."
: 첫 번째 [ ]는 Those of you를 수식하는 관계절이고, 두 번째 [ ]는

something을 수식하는 관계절로 목적격 관계대명사 that이 생략되었다.

08 정답 ③

중동은 세계의 다른 어느 지역에서도 보지 못한 지리적인 환경을 가지고 있다. 긍정적인 면에서, 유럽과 아시아 사이에 있는 그곳의 위치 덕분에, 그 지역은 확실히 세계 무역과 문화 교류의 중심이 될 수 있다. 결국 그것은 천 년 전 그곳의 소명이었고, 그것이 바로 아랍 에미리트 연합국이 중동의 무역과 관광의 중심지로서 성공적으로 재창출하고 있는 역할이다. (아랍 에미리트 연합국에서 대부분의 일자리 계약은 단기적이며, 에미리트 연합국들은 시민권이나 토지 혹은 재산의 소유권을 고려하지 않는다.) '중간'에 있다는 것은 또한 그 지역이 인접국들과 멀리 있는 강국들에 의한 수세기에 걸친 방해와 간섭을 받게 했다. 그곳은 아주 많은 방향에서의 공격에 취약하기 때문에 군사적으로 방어하기가 특히 어려운 지역이다.

해설
중동이 세계에서 가지고 있는 독특한 지리적 환경으로 인해, 긍정적인 면에서는 세계 무역, 문화 교류, 관광의 중심지 역할을 할 수 있지만, 부정적인 면에서는 수세기에 걸쳐 여러 나라의 방해와 간섭을 받아야만 했다는 내용의 글이다. 따라서 아랍 에미리트 연합국의 일자리 계약이나 시민권, 소유권에 관해 서술하는 ③은 글의 전체 흐름과 관계가 없다.

TEXT FLOW
도입	중동은 세계적으로 독특한 지리적인 환경을 가지고 있음
전개	긍정적으로는 세계 무역, 문화 교류, 중동 무역, 관광의 중심지가 될 수 있음
부연	부정적으로는 여러 나라의 방해와 간섭을 받아야 했고 군사적 방어가 어려움

구문
• The majority of job contracts in the United Arab Emirates are short-term, [with the emirate nations not allowing for citizenship or the ownership of land or property].
: [ ]는 「with+목적어+분사구」 구문으로 목적어인 the emirate nations와 분사가 능동의 관계이므로 현재분사인 allowing이 쓰였다.

09 정답 ⑤

사람들은 인공물과 애착 및 관계를 형성하고 그것들에게 근본적으로 사회적인 방식으로 반응을 하는 경향이 있다. (C) 예를 들어, 많은 사람들이 자신들의 자동차에 말을 걸고, 그것들에게 이름을 부여하며, 그것들의 계기판을 격려하듯이 토닥거리며, 그것들이 작동하지 않을 때 악담을 퍼붓기도 한다. 그들은 자신의 일과 창조의 과정에서 필수적인 부분인 도구들에게 인간과 같은 애착을 형성할 수도 있다. (B) 첼로 솔로 연주자인 Jacqueline du Pré는 회고록에서, 그녀가 자신의 음악 활동에 대한 요구가 그녀의 삶을 제한하고 있다고 느낄 때 자신의 첼로를 불친절하게 다룬 것으로 묘사되었다. (A) 그녀는 귀중한 골동품 첼로를 호텔 발코니의 눈 속에 내버려두었고, 그것을 택시의 뒷좌석에 두고 여러 번 '잊어버렸다'. 그리고 나서 자신의 삶이 나아지기 시작하면, 그녀는 첼로를 붙잡고서는 그것에 사과했다.

해설
주어진 글은 사람들이 인공물과 애착 및 관계를 형성하고 그것들에게 사회적

인 방식으로 반응한다는 내용으로, 그 예를 제시한 (C)가 바로 다음에 이어지고, (C)의 마지막 부분에서 제시된 창조의 과정에서 필수적인 도구들에 대한 애착 형성의 예로 첼로 솔로 연주자인 Jacqueline du Pré의 이야기를 소개한 (B)가 온 후에, 그녀가 자신의 첼로를 어떻게 다루었는지 구체적으로 묘사한 (A)가 마지막에 오는 것이 글의 흐름상 가장 자연스럽다.

TEXT FLOW
도입	사람들은 인공물과 애착 및 관계를 형성하고 사회적인 방식으로 반응함
예시	사람들이 자신들의 자동차에게 보이는 애착과 사회적 반응
전개	일과 창조의 과정에서 필수적인 도구들에게 인간과 같은 애착을 형성하기도 함
예시	첼로 솔로 연주자인 Jacqueline du Pré가 자신의 첼로에게 보인 애착과 사회적 반응

구문
• People tend to [form attachments and relationships with artifacts], and [respond to them in ways {that are essentially social}].
: 두 개의 [ ]가 and에 의해 병렬 연결되어 tend to에 이어진다. 두 번째 [ ] 안의 { }는 관계절로 ways를 수식한다.

10 정답 ③

대다수의 사람들은 장애인을 반대하지 않는다고 말할 것이고, 그것은 사실일 수 있다. (B) 그러나 대다수는 여전히 장애인을 동등하다고 생각하지 않고, 장애인이 '정상적인' 삶을 살지 못하게 막는, 사회에 존재하는 장애물을 이해하지 못한다. 예를 들어, 일부 사람들은 장애인을 위해 따로 마련된 주차 공간을 이용하여 장애인 운전자가 집으로 돌아가야 할 수도 있는 결과를 초래한다. (C) 장애인 차별은 사회의 모든 층에 스며들어 있다. 경제적 이유에 의한 의식적인 장애인 차별주의(가령, 고용 차별)가 널리 퍼져 있지만, 이것은 무지나 전반적인 이해 부족으로 인한 무의식적인 장애인 차별주의이다. 이는 '차별 정책의 태도', 즉 이동 장애를 가진 사람들은 그들 자신의 건물과 기관, 그리고 교통수단을 가지기 때문에 포용적 계획이 그다지 중요하지 않다는 사회적 시각에서 보일 수 있다. (A) 장애 차별주의는 장애인을 위한 별도의 불평등한 공공건물 출입구가 널리 사용되는 것에서도 드러난다. 장애인 차별이 없는 환경은 노인, 어린 자녀를 동반한 산모, 일시적이거나 영구적인 장애가 있는 사람들이 쇼핑센터와 기타 공공 기관이나 공간을 동등하게 이용할 수 있게 해 준다.

해설
대다수의 사람들이 장애인을 반대하지 않는다고 생각한다는 주어진 글 뒤에는, 그에 반하는 사례를 들어 그런 생각에 반박하는 내용의 (B)가 와야 한다. (B) 뒤에는, 사회에 만연한 장애 차별주의를 지적하면서 의식적, 무의식적인 장애인 차별주의를 사례로 제시하는 (C)가 이어진 후, 장애인을 위한 별도의 불공평한 출입구를 추가적인 사례로 덧붙이는 (A)가 마지막에 오는 것이 글의 흐름상 가장 자연스럽다.

⊗ 매력적인 오답 주의!
② (A)의 첫 문장에 있는 also가 장애인 차별주의가 나타나는 영역을 추가로 제시하게 하는 역할을 한다는 것을 이해하지 못하면 고를 수 있는 오답이다.

TEXT FLOW

도입	장애인에 대한 사람들의 생각과 현실 사이의 괴리
주제	사회에 만연한 장애인 차별주의
예시	의식적/무의식적 장애인 차별주의, 별도의 불공평한 장애인용 출입구

구문

• A non-disablist environment would allow [elderly people], [mothers with small children] and [others {temporarily or permanently impaired}] [equal access to shopping centres and other public institutions or spaces].
: 첫 번째, 두 번째, 세 번째 [ ]는 and로 연결되어 allow의 간접목적어 역할을 하고, 세 번째 [ ] 안의 { }는 others를 수식하는 형용사구이다. 네 번째 [ ]는 allow의 직접목적어이다.

• For example, some people use parking spaces [set aside for people with disabilities] with the result [that disabled drivers may have to turn back home].
: 첫 번째 [ ]는 parking spaces를 수식하는 분사구이고, 두 번째 [ ]는 the result의 구체적인 내용을 나타내는 동격의 명사절이다.

11
정답 ⑤

과학에서 우리는 흔히 어떤 일이나 사건이 또 다른 일이나 사건을 유발하는지 알아내려고 하는데, 대개 이는 두 번째 일이 흔히 첫 번째 일의 뒤를 따른다는 것을 우리가 알아챘기 때문이다. 물어봐야 하는 중요한 질문은 첫 번째 일이 두 번째 일을 유발하기에 '충분'하면서도 '필요'하기도 한지의 여부이다. '충분'하면서도' 필요하다는 것이다. 흔히, 매우 흔히, 여러분은 한 가지 혹은 다른 한 가지만 보여줄 수 있다. 연관성과 비교한 원인에 관한 한, 자연은 설명할 수 없을 정도로 인색하다. 연관성은 원인의 허약한 의붓자식이며, 그것은 항상 여러분을 속인다. 두 일이 시간상으로 서로 가깝게 발생한다고 해서 반드시 하나의 일이 다른 한 가지 일의 원인이라는 의미는 아니거나, 그 점에 있어서는 그것들이 서로에게 어떤 것이라도 빚고 있다는 의미는 아니다. 반면에, 때로는 이런 관련이 인과 관계에 대한 진정한 단서가 될 수도 있다. 여기가 필요와 충분이 등장하는 곳이다.

해설
⑤ 앞의 두 문장은 인과 관계가 아닌 연관성에 관한 내용으로, 충분 혹은 필요 중 하나만을 보여 주기 때문에 인과 관계의 특징인 필요와 충분이 모두 등장하는 관계를 언급하는 내용의 ⑤ 뒷문장과 논리적으로 어울리지 않는다. 주어진 문장은 인과 관계를 보여 주는 단서로서의 두 가지 사건의 관련을 언급하고 있으므로, 주어진 문장이 들어가기에 가장 적절한 곳은 ⑤이다.

⊗ **매력적인 오답 주의!**
① 글의 논리적 흐름을 파악하지 못하고 sufficient와 necessary가 함께 언급된 점에만 집중했을 경우에 고를 수 있는 오답이다.

TEXT FLOW

도입	원인 규명에 대한 단서로서의 사건 발생의 시간적 근접성
주제	사건 원인의 조건으로서의 '충분'과 '필요'
전개	사건 간 연관성과 원인의 차이

구문

• In science we often try to figure out [if some thing or event causes another thing or event], usually because we have noticed [that the first thing is often followed by the second thing].
: 첫 번째 [ ]는 figure out의 목적어 역할을 하는 명사절이고, 두 번째 [ ]는 have noticed의 목적어 역할을 하는 명사절이다.

• [Because two things happen close to each other in time] does **not necessarily** mean [that one is a cause of the other], or for that matter [that they owe anything at all to each other].
: 첫 번째 [ ]는 문장의 주어 역할을 하는 명사절이다. not necessarily는 '반드시 ~은 아니다'라는 의미의 부분 부정을 나타낸다. 두 번째와 세 번째 [ ]는 or로 연결되어 mean의 목적어 역할을 하는 명사절이다.

12-14
정답 12 ④ 13 ④ 14 ⑤

(A) 시골의 한 작은 학교는 석탄 난로로 난방이 되었다. 한 작은 소년이 선생님과 급우들이 도착하기 전에 불을 피워 교실을 따뜻하게 하기 위해 매일 학교에 일찍 오는 일을 맡았다. 어느 날 아침, 그들은 도착하여 학교가 화염에 휩싸인 것을 발견했다. 그들은 불타고 있는 건물 밖으로 의식을 잃은 그 소년을 끌어냈다. 그는 하반신에 큰 화상을 입었고 근처의 병원으로 후송되었다.

(D) 자신의 침대에서 그 소년은 의사가 자신의 어머니에게 말하고 있는 것을 희미하게 들었다. 그는 그의 어머니에게 그 끔찍한 화재가 그의 하반신을 망가뜨려 버렸기 때문에 그녀의 아들은 틀림없이 죽을 것이라고 말했다. 하지만 그 용감한 소년은 죽고 싶지 않았다. 그는 살아남겠다고 결심했다. 그 의사로서는 놀랍게도 그는 정말로 살아남았다. 그 치명적인 위험이 지나갔을 때, 그는 또다시 의사와 자신의 어머니가 조용히 이야기하는 것을 들었다. 그의 어머니는 자신의 아들이 하체를 전혀 쓸 수 없이 평생 장애인으로 살아야 할 운명이라는 말을 들었다. 한 번 더 그 용감한 소년은 결심을 했다. 그는 걸을 것이었다.

(B) 어느 날 그의 어머니가 그를 휠체어에 태워 마당으로 나갔다. 이날, 자신의 휠체어에 앉아 있는 대신에 그는 땅으로 자신의 몸을 던졌다. 그는 풀밭을 가로질러 다리를 질질 끌면서 자신의 몸을 끌었다. 그는 울타리까지 나아갔다. 많은 노력을 기울여, 그는 울타리 위로 자신의 몸을 일으켰다. 그러고 나서 그는 자신이 걸을 것이라고 결심하며 울타리를 따라 자신의 몸을 끌고 가기 시작했다. 그는 울타리 옆 마당 주위로 매끈한 길이 생겨날 때까지 매일 이것을 하기 시작했다.

(C) 마침내 그의 불굴의 인내와 굳은 결의를 통해, 그는 일어서는 능력, 그 다음으로 혼자 걷는 능력, 그 다음으로 뛰는 능력을 정말로 발달시켰다. 그는 학교까지 걸어가기 시작했고, 그 다음엔 학교까지 뛰어가기 시작했으며, 오로지 순수하게 달린다는 기쁨을 위해 달리기 시작했다. 나중에 대학에서 그는 육상부가 되었다. 더 훗날 살아날 것이라고 예상하지 않았고, 틀림없이 결코 걷지 못할 것이었고, 절대 뛰는 것을 희망할 수 없었던 이 결의에 찬 젊은이, Glenn Cunningham은 세상에서 가장 빨리 1마일을 달렸다!

해설
12 소년이 큰 화상을 입고 근처의 병원으로 후송되었다는 내용의 주어진 글에 이어, 병원 침대에 누워 의사와 어머니의 대화를 듣고 자신은 죽지 않을 것이며 반드시 걷고 말겠다는 결심을 한 내용의 (D)가 온 다음, 집에서 걷기 위해 집 울타리 주변에 길이 생겨날 때까지 울타리를 따라 자신을 끌고 가면서 노력했다는 내용의 (B)가 이어지고, 마지막으로 다시 걷고 달릴 수 있게 되어 대학에서 육상부가 되었고 마침내 세상에서 가장 빨리 1마일을 달린 사람이 되었다는 내용의 (C)가 마지막으로 오는 것이 글의 흐름상 가장 자연스럽다.

13 (d)는 의사를 가리키고, 나머지는 모두 Glenn Cunningham을 가리킨다.

14 의사는 소년이 죽게 될 것이라고 했고 살아남은 후에도 평생 장애인으로 살게 될 것이라고 했으므로 ⑤는 글의 내용으로 적절하지 않다.

TEXT FLOW

시간 순서/사건 전개에 따른 흐름:
(A) 한 소년이 교실에서 하반신에 큰 화상을 입음 → (D) 사망할 것이라는 의사의 예측에도 불구하고 소년은 강한 의지로 살아남았고, 하반신 마비를 진단받았으나 반드시 자력으로 걷겠다고 결심함 → (B) 소년은 다리를 끌며 매일 걷기 위해 노력함 → (C) 마침내 소년은 걷고 뛸 수 있게 되었고 훗날 세계에서 가장 빨리 1마일을 달린 사람이 됨

구문

• Still later **this determined young man** [who was not expected to survive], [who would surely never walk], [who could never hope to run], **Glenn Cunningham** ran the world's fastest mile!
: this determined young man이 주어이고, 이를 수식하는 세 개의 관계절 [ ]가 연속으로 제시된 후, 이와 동격인 Glenn Cunningham이 나오는 구조이다.

GRAMMAR REVIEW
본문 89쪽

1 has been	2 involves	3 those
4 is	5 that	6 wearing
7 that	8 that	9 be asked
10 had devastated		

1 30년간 계속되어 온 것이므로 현재완료 시제가 적절하다.

2 주어의 핵인 Becoming이 동명사이고, 동명사는 단수 취급하므로 단수형 동사 involves를 써야 한다.

3 women을 대신하여 사용되었으므로, 복수형 지시대명사 those가 적절하다.

4 be동사의 주어의 핵이 taking(동명사)이고, 동명사는 단수 취급하므로 단수형 동사 is가 적절하다.

5 이어지는 절에서 주어나 목적어 등이 완전하게 갖추어져 있으므로 a growing feeling과 동격인 절을 이끄는 접속사 that이 적절하다.

6 주어인 A field biologist for The Nature Conservancy에 대한 동사가 showed up이므로 부연 설명하는 분사구문이 이어지는 것이 적절하고, 생략된 의미상의 주어 A field biologist for The Nature Conservancy가 '입는/매는(wear)' 행위자이므로 현재분사 wearing을 써야 한다.

7 관계절에서 주어 역할을 해야 하고 선행사 tools가 있으므로 주격 관계대명사 that이 적절하다.

8 뒤에 완전한 문장이 이어지며 the societal view와 동격 관계를 이루어야 하므로 명사절을 이끄는 접속사 that이 적절하다.

9 The important question은 동사 ask의 대상이므로 be asked가 적절하다.

10 그가 말한 것보다 화재로 인해 하반신이 손상된 것이 먼저 일어난 일이므로 과거완료 had devastated를 써야 한다.

01 ①	02 ③	03 ⑤	04 ④	05 ⑤
06 ④	07 ①	08 ②	09 ②	10 ④
11 ②	12 ④	13 ⑤	14 ⑤	

01

정답 ①

Carter 씨께,
Maperville Community 채용 박람회를 후원하도록 저희를 초대해 주셔서 감사합니다. 저희는 지역 경제를 활성화하고자 하는 박람회의 사명을 높이 평가하며, 이러한 가치 있는 대의를 지원하려는 귀하의 노력에 박수를 보냅니다. 안타깝게도 현재의 경제 상황으로 인해 저희를 포함한 많은 기업이 자선 기부 프로그램을 다시 고려하고 있습니다. 이에 따라 저희는 올해 자선 기부금을 위한 저희 예산을 이미 책정했으며, 채용 박람회를 후원할 수 없게 되었습니다. 저희는 Maperville Community 채용 박람회의 중요성을 잘 알고 있으며, 내년 2월 말에 다시 한번 귀하의 요청을 기꺼이 검토해 보겠습니다. 모금 활동에 행운이 함께하시길 진심으로 기원합니다.
진심을 담아,
Claire Adams 드림

해설
채용 박람회 후원 초대를 받았으나 올해 자선 기부금을 위한 예산을 이미 책정하여 채용 박람회를 후원할 수 없게 되었다고 하며 후원 요청을 거절하는 글이다. 따라서 글의 목적으로 가장 적절한 것은 ①이다.

TEXT FLOW
도입	채용 박람회 후원에 초대해 준 것에 대한 감사 표현
요지	올해 기부금을 위한 예산이 이미 책정되어 박람회를 후원할 수 없음
결론	내년 2월 말에 다시 한번 후원 요청을 검토할 예정임

구문
• We appreciate the fair's mission [to stimulate the local economy] and applaud your efforts [to support such a worthy cause].
: 두 개의 [ ]는 각각 the fair's mission과 your efforts를 수식하는 형용사적 용법의 to부정사구이다.

02

정답 ③

다른 사람들이 당신을 위해 하는 일들에 대해 감사를 표시하는 것은 당신이 어떤 사람으로 여겨지는지에 있어 지대한 영향을 끼친다. 누군가가 당신을 위해 하는 모든 일에는 기회비용이 발생함을 명심하라. 그것은 만약 누군가가 당신을 돌보기 위해 자신의 하루 중 시간을 낸다면, 그들이 그들 자신 혹은 다른 누군가를 위해 하지 못한 어떤 일이 있음을 의미한다. 당신 자신을 속여서 당신의 요청이 사소한 것이라고 생각하게 하기는 쉽다. 하지만 누군가가 바쁠 때 사소한 부탁이라는 것은 없다. 그들은 자신들이 하고 있는 일을 멈추고, 당신의 부탁에 집중하며, 응답하기 위해 시간을 들여야 한다. 그것을 염두에 둔다면, 당신을 위해 무언가를 해 준 사람에게 감사하지 말아야 할 시간이란 절대 없다. 사실, 감사의 편지를 제대로 된 것으로 가정하고, 그것을 보내지 못하는 상황들을 예외로 간주하라.

해설
다른 사람이 부탁을 들어주었을 때는 그들이 기꺼이 자신들의 시간을 희생해 준 것인 만큼 항상 감사를 표해야 한다는 요지의 글이므로, 필자의 주장으로는 ③이 가장 적절하다.

TEXT FLOW
요지	타인이 당신을 위해 어떤 일을 해 주는 것에 대해 감사의 표시를 하는 것이 중요함
부연	타인이 당신의 부탁을 들어준다는 것은 그들이 다른 일을 할 수 있는 시간을 대신 썼다는 것을 의미함
결론	부탁을 들어준 사람에게 항상 감사해야 함

구문
• [Showing appreciation for the things {others do for you}] has a profound effect on [how you're perceived].
: 첫 번째 [ ]는 주어 역할을 하는 동명사구이고, 그 안의 { }는 목적격 관계대명사 which(that)가 생략된 관계절로 선행사 the things를 수식한다. 두 번째 [ ]는 전치사 on의 목적어 역할을 한다.

03

정답 ⑤

(경제) 성장 관련 문헌에서 경제 활동에 대한 정부의 개입과 관련된 논쟁만큼 길고 그토록 격렬하게 지속된 논쟁은 없다. 지난 반세기에만 해도 이에 대한 견해와 실제 정책은 상당히 많이 바뀌었다. 1950년대와 1960년대에는 시장이 광범위하게 실패했으며, 경제 변혁 과정과 경제 성장 속도를 높이기 위해서는 정부의 개입이 필요하다고 믿어졌다. 중동과 북아프리카를 포함한 대부분의 개발도상국은 높은 수준의 보호, 중앙 계획, 공공 소유, 그리고 부문 및 (경제) 활동 전반에 걸친 비일률적인 정책과 함께 수입 대체 전략을 채택했다. 1970년대와 1980년대에는 정부도 실패하고, 많은 경우 시장보다 더 많이 실패한다는 사실이 점점 더 분명해졌다. 따라서 추는 반대 방향으로 진동했다. 특히 1980년대에는 세계은행과 IMF의 지원을 받아 시장 친화적 개혁이 자주 채택되었다. 워싱턴 합의는 빠른 경제 성장을 위한 핵심 구성 요소로 거시 경제 안정, 무역 및 가격 자유화, 민영화, 그리고 경쟁을 강조했다.

해설
1950년대와 1960년대에는 시장의 광범위한 실패로 인해 경제 성장을 위해 정부의 개입이 필요하다는 견해가 있었지만, 1970년대와 1980년대에는 정부도 실패할 수 있다는 점이 드러나면서 정부의 민영화와 경쟁을 강조하는 등 시장 친화적이고 정부의 개입이 덜한 방향으로 경제 정책이 변했다는 내용의 글이다. 따라서 밑줄 친 부분이 글에서 의미하는 바로 가장 적절한 것은 ⑤ '정부의 개입이 덜한 시장 중심 정책을 수용하는 것'이다.
① 엄격한 중앙의 계획을 통해 경제를 관리하는 것
② 국제 무역 기구의 영향력을 제한하는 것
③ 빠른 경제 성장보다 경제적 공정성을 우선시하는 것
④ 개발도상국이 시장 실패에 대처하도록 장려하는 것

❌ 매력적인 오답 주의!
④ 시장 실패를 해결하기 위한 정부의 개입이 줄어들게 되었다는 점을 제대로 파악하지 못하면 고를 수 있는 오답이다.

TEXT FLOW

도입	경제 활동에 대한 정부의 개입과 관련된 논쟁은 오랫동안 지속되어 옴
전개	시장의 실패를 해결하고 경제 성장의 속도를 높이기 위해서 정부의 개입이 필요하다고 믿었음
전환	1970년대 이후 정부의 실패가 분명해짐
부연	시장 친화적인 경제 정책이 강조됨

구문

• **No** debate in the development literature has persisted **as long** and with such intensity **as that** [related to government intervention in economic activity].
: 부정의 의미를 가진 No와 원급 비교 구문이 결합되어 최상급의 의미를 나타내고 있다. that은 debate를 가리키며, [ ]는 that을 수식하는 분사구이다.

• In the 1950s and 1960s, **it** was believed [that markets failed widely and government intervention was necessary {to speed up the process of economic transformation and the rate of economic growth}].
: it은 가주어이고 [ ]는 진주어이다. { }는 목적의 의미를 나타내는 부사적 용법의 to부정사구이다.

04   정답 ④

말이 없는 삶을 상상해 보라! 우리들 대부분은 그 어떤 것을 대신하여서도 말을 포기하지 않을 것이다. 매일 우리는 수천 개의 말을 입 밖으로 쏟아 낸다. 우리의 기쁨, 두려움, 의견, 환상, 소망, 요청, 요구, 감정, 그리고 때때로 위협 혹은 모욕까지, 소통하는 것은 인간적인 데 있어서 매우 중요한 측면이다. 대기는 항상 우리의 언어적 배출로 가득 차 있다. 우리가 세상에 알려 주고 싶은 것들이 너무나 많이 있다. 그것들 중 어떤 것들은 중요하고, 그것들 중 어떤 것들은 중요하지 않다. 하지만 우리는 심지어 우리가 말하고 있는 것이 전적으로 중요하지 않다는 것을 알면서도 어쨌든 말을 한다. 우리는 잡담을 사랑하고 말이 없는 만남을 어색하게 여기거나, 심지어 숨이 막힐 것 같다고 느낀다. 말이 없는 삶은 끔찍한 결핍일 것이다.

해설
인간으로서 말을 한다는 것이 얼마나 중요한 측면인지를 강조하고 있는 글이므로, 글의 주제로는 ④ '표현을 위한 말의 중요성'이 가장 적절하다.
① 침묵하는 것의 가치
② 성공적인 말하기 기술들
③ 우리의 의견을 표현하는 방법들
⑤ 단어 선택에 있어 개인적 차이점들

TEXT FLOW

요지	말은 인간적인 데 있어서 매우 중요한 측면임
부연	우리는 말을 통해 소통하고자 하는 강한 욕구를 가지고 있음
결론	말이 없는 삶은 끔찍한 결핍일 것임

구문

• But we talk anyway — even when we know [that {what we are saying} is totally unimportant].
: 대시(—) 이하는 앞의 anyway를 부연 설명해 주는 역할을 한다. [ ]는

05   정답 ⑤

Montague Russell Page는 Lincolnshire에서 Harold Ethelbert Page의 세 아이 중 둘째 아들로 태어났다. 1927년부터 1932년까지 그는 파리에서 미술을 공부했고, 프랑스에서 몇몇 소소한 정원사 일을 했다. 1934년과 1938년 사이에 그는 정기 간행물 'Landscape and Gardening'에 글을 기고했다. 1935년부터 1939년까지 그는 Geoffrey Jellicoe와 동업했다. Page와 Jellicoe는 Somerset의 Longleat 땅에 있는 Cheddar Gorge의 'Caveman Restaurant'의 조경과 건물을 설계했다. Page는 이어서 유럽과 미국에서 정원을 설계하기 시작했다. 그의 작품에는 Washington의 미국 국립 식물원에 있는 국회의사당 기둥이 포함된다. 1962년에 Page의 자서전 'The Education of a Gardener'가 출간되었고, 그는 1985년 1월 4일에 런던에서 사망했다.

해설
Montague Russell Page의 자서전이 출간된 것은 1962년이고 그가 사망한 것은 1985년이므로, ⑤는 글의 내용과 일치하지 않는다.

구문
• In 1962, Page's autobiography, *The Education of a Gardener*, was published and he died on January 4, 1985 in London.
: Page's autobiography와 *The Education of a Gardener*는 콤마(,)에 의해 동격을 이루고 있다.

06   정답 ④

닐 암스트롱이 달에 발을 내디뎠을 때, 그는 기억에 남는 문장을 말했다. "한 사람(man)에게는 작은 발걸음이지만, 인류(mankind)에게는 거대한 도약이다." 만약 그가 1990년대 중반에 달에 도착했더라면, 그는 아마도 훨씬 더 정치적으로 올바른 문장을 말했을 것이다. "한 사람(person)에게는 작은 발걸음이지만, 인류(humankind)에게는 거대한 도약이다." 덜 시적이지만, 분명히 더 글자 그대로 인류 전체를 대표하는 것이다! 특정한 언어는 사회 안에서의 성 역할들에 관한 고정 관념을 강화하는 데 도움을 줄 수 있다. 예를 들면, "책임자는 그의 회사의 안녕에 전념해야 한다."라고 하지만, "간호사는 긴 시간을 일함으로써 그녀의 헌신을 보여 줄 것으로 기대된다."라고 한다. 그러한 단어들의 사용은 특정 직업들을 남성 혹은 여성과 연관 지으려는 경향을 보여 준다.

해설
(A) If절의 시제가 가정법 과거완료이므로 주절의 동사는 「조동사의 과거형 (would)+have+과거분사」 형태가 오는 것이 적절하다.
(B) 문맥상 more literally representative를 수식하는 부사가 오는 것이 적절하다.
(C) 주어의 핵이 The use이므로 단수 동사 shows가 오는 것이 적절하다.

TEXT FLOW

도입	닐 암스트롱이 달에 착륙 후 남긴 유명한 말
전개	그가 1990년대 중반에 달에 착륙했더라면 좀 더 정치적으로 올바른 단어를 선택해서 말했을 것임
결론	특정 직업에 대해 고정된 성 역할을 심어줄 수 있는 단어들이 있음

구문

• **Less poetic** but certainly **more** literally **representative** of the whole of the human race!

: 문장 앞에 It is가 생략되었다고 볼 수 있고, Less poetic과 more representative가 but에 의해 병렬 구조를 이루고 있다.

07

정답 ①

만약 당신이 갓 구운 빵 냄새가 나는 방에 걸어 들어간다면, 당신은 금방 꽤 기분 좋은 향기를 알아차린다. 하지만, 그 방에 몇 분간 머무르면, 그 냄새는 사라지는 것처럼 보일 것이다. 사실, 그것을 되살리는 유일한 방법은 방 밖으로 걸어 나갔다가 다시 들어오는 것이다. 정확히 같은 개념이 행복을 포함하여 우리 삶의 많은 영역에도 똑같이 적용된다. 모든 사람은 행복해할 만한 무언가를 가지고 있다. 아마도 그들은 사랑하는 동반자, 건강함, 흥미로운 취미들, 보살펴 주시는 부모님, 머리 위의 지붕, 마실 수 있는 깨끗한 물, 혹은 먹을 수 있는 충분한 음식을 가지고 있을 것이다. 하지만 시간이 지남에 따라, 그들은 자신들이 가진 것에 익숙해져서, 갓 구운 빵 냄새처럼, 이러한 훌륭한 자산들이 그들의 의식 속에서 사라진다. 오래된 상투적인 문구가 말해 주듯, 당신은 그것이 <u>사라지기</u> 전까지는 당신이 무엇을 가졌는지 알지 못한다.

해설

사람들은 인생에 있어 행복해할 만한 많은 것을 갖고 있음에도 그것들에 너무 익숙해진 나머지 그것들을 의식하지 못한다는 내용의 글이므로, 빈칸에는 가진 것이 사라지기 전까지는 그것의 소중함을 알지 못한다는 문맥에 맞는 ① '사라지기'가 가장 적절하다.

② 사용되기 ③ 알려지기
④ 가시적이기 ⑤ 충분하기

TEXT FLOW

도입	좋은 향기를 맡고 기분이 좋아졌다가도 시간이 지나면 곧 익숙해져서 그 향이 사라진 것처럼 느끼게 됨
전개	우리 삶의 행복도 마찬가지로 익숙하게 느껴지는 것의 소중함을 모르게 됨
결론	우리는 가진 것이 사라지고 나서야 그것의 소중함을 깨닫게 됨

구문

• In fact, [the only way to reawaken it] is [to walk out of the room and come back in again].

: 첫 번째 [ ]가 주어이고, 두 번째 [ ]는 주격 보어 역할을 하는 명사적 용법의 to부정사구이다.

08

정답 ②

여기 약 없이도 경미한 통증을 완화시킬 수 있는 방법이 있다. 그저 숨을 천

천히 쉬도록 하라. 최근의 연구에 의하면, 연구자들은 52명의 여성들의 손바닥에 약간 고통스러운 열기를 주기적으로 짧게 주었다. 자원자들에게 그들의 평소 속도보다 대략 절반 정도의 속도로 숨을 쉴 것을 지시하자, 그들의 고통 강도와 불편함의 정도가 30%까지 떨어졌다. 천천히 숨쉬기는 더 빠른 심박동수나 고혈압과 같은 신체의 스트레스 반응을 느리게 하는 것으로 보인다고 연구 책임자인 애리조나 주립대학의 Alex Zautra는 말한다. 이것은 왜 다른 연구 결과에서 몇몇 명상 기술이 고통을 줄여줄 수 있는 것으로 밝혀졌는지를 설명하는 데 도움을 줄 수 있다. 그 혜택을 보기 위해서는, 당신이 1분에 숨을 몇 번 쉬는지 센 다음, 조용히 앉아서 서서히 그 속도를 줄이라.

해설

숨 쉬는 속도를 늦춤으로써 스트레스 반응을 줄여 고통을 완화시킬 수 있다는 내용의 글이므로, 빈칸에 들어갈 말로는 ② '숨을 천천히 쉬도록 하라'가 가장 적절하다.

① 손바닥을 치라
③ 심박동수를 관찰하라
④ 당신의 증상들을 다른 사람들에게 말하라
⑤ 스트레스를 줄이는 방법을 연구하라

TEXT FLOW

도입	숨을 천천히 쉬는 것은 약 없이 통증을 줄여줄 수 있는 방법임
전개	연구에 의하면 숨을 천천히 쉼으로써 신체의 스트레스 반응 속도를 느리게 만들 수 있음
결론	그 효과를 느끼려면 1분에 몇 번 숨을 쉬는지 센 다음 그 속도를 서서히 줄여야 함

구문

• This may help explain [why other studies have found {some meditation techniques can reduce pain}].

: [ ]는 explain의 목적어 역할을 하는 의문사절이며, 그 안의 { }는 have found의 목적어 역할을 한다.

09

정답 ②

선원들에게는 날씨에 관한 표현이 있다. 그들이 말하기를, 날씨는 굉장한 허풍꾼이다. 우리 인간 사회도 마찬가지인 것 같다. 상황이 어두워 보일 수 있다가도, 구름 사이에 틈이 보이고, 또 때로는 매우 갑자기 모든 것이 변화한다. (구름은 습하고 따뜻한 상승 기류가 대기 안에서 식고 팽창하면서 형성된다.) 인류가 이 행성에서의 삶을 괴상하고 엉망진창으로 만들어 놓은 것은 꽤 분명하다. 하지만 사람으로서 우리는 조건이 맞을 때 싹트기를 기다리며 오랫동안 놓여 있는 선량함의 씨앗을 아마도 품고 있을 것이다. 인간의 호기심, 매정함, 발명성, 독창성은 그를 큰 곤경으로 이끌었다. 우리는 이 똑같은 특성들이 그가 고난을 극복하고 빠져나올 수 있도록 해 주기를 다만 희망할 수 있을 뿐이다.

해설

인간이 스스로를 힘든 상황에 빠뜨렸지만, 시시때때로 변화하고 변덕스러운 날씨처럼, 인간도 언젠가는 문제들을 해결하고 긍정적인 방향으로 발전할 수 있을 것이라는 믿음을 서술하는 내용의 글이므로, 구름의 형성에 관한 과학적 사실을 설명하는 ②는 글의 전체 흐름과 관계가 없다.

TEXT FLOW

도입	선원들은 날씨가 허풍꾼이라고들 말함
전개	예측 불가능한 날씨와 마찬가지로 인간 사회도 암울해 보이다가도 갑자기 변화하여 밝은 미래가 나타날 수 있음
결론	인간을 곤경으로 이끈 인간의 특성들이 인간이 고난을 극복하고 빠져나오는 데도 도움이 되기를 희망함

구문

- **It** is quite obvious [that the human race has made a queer mess of life on this planet].
  : It은 가주어이고 [ ]가 진주어이다.

10
정답 ④

인도에서는 코끼리를 육체노동에 이용한다. 하지만 코끼리가 일하지 않을 때는 코끼리들을 어떻게 해야 할까? 어떻게 코끼리를 속박할까? (C) 코끼리의 조련사들은 코끼리가 아직 어릴 때 자신에게 부과한 생각의 한계를 설정하여 코끼리를 '길들이는' 아이디어를 생각해 냈다. 그것이 어떻게 효과가 있었을까? 코끼리들이 아직 몸무게가 150파운드 정도로 작았을 때, 코끼리들은 매우 무거운 밧줄로 묶여 있었다. 코끼리들은 온종일 밧줄을 제거하려고 애쓰고, 끙끙거렸고, 세게 잡아당겼고, 그리고 일부 코끼리는 심지어 씹으려고 애쓰기도 했다. 하지만 코끼리들은 탈출할 수 없었다. (A) 결국 코끼리들은 포기했고 투쟁은 끝났다. 그리고 이제 흥미로운 부분이 나온다. 그 순간부터 코끼리들은 밧줄을 제거할 수 있는 희망이 전혀 없다고 굳게 믿었다. (B) 그들은 밧줄이 자신을 제한한다는 '사실'을 받아들였다. 그리고 이러한 각인된 믿음이 자리를 잡은 상태에서 그들의 조련사는 아주 작은 밧줄로 코끼리들을 묶을 수 있었다. 그리고 몸무게가 8,000파운드 이상의 다 자란 동물이 되어서도 코끼리들은 탈출할 가능성이 없다는 것을 '알고 있었기' 때문에 절대 탈출을 시도하지 않았다. 코끼리의 한계는 실재하는 것이 아니라 오직 그들의 마음속에만 존재하는 것이었다.

해설

인도에서 육체노동에 이용되는 코끼리를 어떻게 속박할 것인지에 대해 기술한 주어진 글 다음에는, 코끼리의 조련사들이 코끼리들이 어렸을 때 자신에게 부과한 생각의 한계를 설정하여 길들이며, 매우 무거운 밧줄로 어린 코끼리를 묶어서 탈출하지 못하게 만든다는 내용의 (C)가 이어져야 한다. 그다음에는 어린 코끼리가 여러 방법으로 탈출을 시도하지만 끝내 포기하고 그와 동시에 밧줄을 제거할 수 없다고 굳게 믿었다는 내용의 (A)가 이어지고, (B)의 this imprinted belief는 어렸을 때부터 코끼리가 자신에게 부과한 한계를 가리키며 이것 때문에 성장한 후에 아주 작은 밧줄로 묶어도 이에 길들여져 탈출을 시도하지 않게 되었다는 내용의 (B)가 마지막에 오는 것이 글의 흐름상 가장 자연스럽다.

ⓧ 매력적인 오답 주의!

⑤ 코끼리가 조련사에 의해 어렸을 때부터 길들여지는 과정을 충분히 이해하지 못하고 (C)의 후반부에 나오는 they와 (B)의 서두에 언급되는 They를 연결 지을 경우에 고를 수 있는 오답이다.

TEXT FLOW

도입	육체노동에 이용되는 코끼리를 속박하는 방법
전개 1	어린 코끼리를 무거운 밧줄로 묶어 탈출할 수 없게 만듦
전개 2	탈출을 포기한 코끼리는 밧줄이 자신을 제한한다는 사실을 받아들임
결론	다 자란 후 아주 작은 밧줄로 묶어도 코끼리는 절대 탈출을 시도하지 않음

구문

- From that moment on, they strongly believed [that there was absolutely no hope of {getting rid of the rope}].
  : [ ]는 believed의 목적어 역할을 하는 명사절이고, 그 안의 { }는 전치사 of의 목적어 역할을 하는 동명사구이다.

- And even as adults, [weighing 8,000 pounds and more], they never attempted to break free [because they "knew" {they had no chance of **doing so**}].
  : 첫 번째 [ ]는 주절의 주어인 they를 부수적으로 설명하는 분사구문이다. 두 번째 [ ]는 이유의 의미를 나타내는 부사절이고, 그 안의 { }는 knew의 목적어 역할을 하는 명사절이며, doing so는 breaking free를 대신한다.

11
정답 ②

만약 당신이 누군가 당신에게 소리를 질러 운 적이 있다면, 당신은 알 것이다. 말은 감정을 전달한다는 것을 말이다. 당신은 누군가가 무언가를 어떻게 말하고 있는지를 감지함으로써 그들이 무엇을 느끼고 있는지를 알아낼 수 있다. 몇몇 연구가들은 훈련받은 음악가들이 인간의 목소리에서 이러한 감정적 정보를 식별하는 데 있어서 비음악가들에 비해 더 뛰어날 수 있는지를 알아내고 싶었다. 한 연구에서, 영어권 음악가들과 비음악가들에게 그들에게는 외국어인 필리핀 언어 타갈로그어로 표현된 다양한 감정들을 들려주었다. 그들은 자신들이 들은 어떤 감정이라도 구별해 보도록 요청을 받았다. 비록 그들이 그 말을 이해하지도 못하지만, 그들이 그 말 속에서 감정적 정보를 간파하는 데 얼마나 실력이 좋았을까? 결과는 인상적이었다. 훈련받은 음악가들은 매우 잘했지만, 반면에 비음악가들은 놀랍도록 그것을 잘하지 못했다. 음악가들은 특히 슬픔과 공포를 알아차리는 것에 능숙했다.

해설

주어진 문장은 목소리에서 감정적 정보를 식별하는 능력을 알고 싶어 했다는 내용이므로, 말을 통해 감정이 전달된다는 도입부와 이러한 감정 전달을 식별하는 데 있어 음악가들이 비음악가들에 비해 더 뛰어나다는 연구에 관한 내용 사이인 ②에 들어가는 것이 가장 적절하다.

TEXT FLOW

도입	말은 감정을 전달함
전개	음악가와 비음악가를 대상으로 어느 쪽이 감정적 정보를 식별하는 데 더 뛰어난지 알아보기 위한 실험이 실시됨
결론	음악가들이 감정적 정보를 발견하는 데 더 뛰어나다는 결과가 나옴

구문

- They **were asked** to identify [any emotion {they heard}].
  : were asked는 수동태로서 '요청받았다'로 해석하는 것이 자연스럽다. [ ]는 identify의 목적어이며, 그 안의 { }는 목적격 관계대명사 which

〔that〕가 생략된 관계절로 선행사 any emotion을 수식한다.

12   정답 ④

경제에서 숙련된 노동력이 필요한 곳을 찾아서, 그 필요를 충족하기 위해 사람들을 훈련시키고, 정해진 기준에 의거하여 과업 수행에 따른 고용을 위해 그들의 순위를 매기는 모형은 급속하게 발전하는 경제의 움직이는 표적을 놓칠 뿐만 아니라, 지식의 단일 경작 때문에 더 나쁜 결과를 낳게 될 것이다. 인간은 홀로 생각하거나 창조해 내지 않기 때문에, 모두가 최고의 기준에 부합하도록 훈련된 많은 사람들을 양성하는 것은 혁신에 필요한 다양한 인지 도구 세트 대신 그저 서로 중복되고 불필요한 기술 세트를 갖춘 사람들로 구성된 팀을 만들어 낼 뿐이다. 이는 시험과 훈련 정책에 영향을 미친다. 어떤 하나의 측정 기준 또는 심지어 다양한 측정 기준들을 바탕으로 한 기술 측정(말하자면, 사람들을 테스트하여 성적이 최고인 사람들을 고용함으로써)은 모두가 시험을 잘 보는, 즉 모두가 겹치는 사람들로 구성된 팀을 형성할 것이다. 아주 정확히는 동일한 기준에서 모두 탁월했기 때문에 (구성된) 이 '최고의' 팀들은, 비록 그러한 도구 세트가 당장 주어진 과업에 대해서는 가치가 적다고 여겨지더라도 다양한 인지적 도구 세트를 갖춘 구성원들을 포함하는 팀만큼 실질적으로 기량을 발휘하지 못할 것이다.

➡ 모두가 가장 높은 기준을 충족하도록 훈련받은 사람들은 비슷한 능력을 갖게 될 것이며, 따라서 다양한 인지적 도구 세트를 갖춘 사람들로 구성된 팀을 형성하는 것이 혁신에 기여할 것이다.

해설
모두가 최고의 기준에 부합하도록 훈련된 사람들을 양성하는 것은 서로 중복되고 불필요한 기술 세트를 갖춘 사람들로 구성된 팀을 만들어 낼 뿐이라고 했으므로, (A)에 들어갈 말로 가장 적절한 것은 similar(비슷한)이다. 혁신에 다양한 인지 도구 세트가 필요하다고 했고 그런 구성원들을 포함하는 팀이 그렇지 않은 팀보다 더 기량을 발휘할 것이라고 했으므로, (B)에 들어갈 말로 가장 적절한 것은 contribute to(~에 기여할)이다.
① 다양한 - ~을 방해할
② 진보한 - ~에 기여할
③ 독특한 - (결과를) 초래할
⑤ 제한된 - ~을 방해할

TEXT FLOW
주장	숙련된 노동력이 필요한 곳을 찾아 사람들을 훈련시키고 순위를 매기는 모형은 나쁜 결과를 낳을 수 있음
근거	모두가 최고의 기준에 부합하도록 훈련된 사람들을 양성하면 서로 중복된 기술을 가진 사람들로 구성된 팀을 만들어 냄
결론	그러한 최고의 팀은 결국 다양한 인지적 도구 세트를 갖춘 구성원들을 포함하는 팀만큼 실질적으로 기량을 발휘하지 못할 가능성이 있음

구문
• The model of [finding a place in the economy {that needs skilled labor}], [training people to meet that need], and [ranking them for employment according to their performance on set criteria] will **not only** miss the moving target of a rapidly developing economy **but also**, because of knowledge monoculture, produce worse outcomes.
: 세 개의 동명사구 [ ]가 and로 연결되어 전치사 of의 목적어를 이루고 있다. 술어에는 'A뿐만 아니라 B도'라는 의미의 「not only A but also B」의 구문이 사용되었다.

• Measurement of skill on any single metric or even a range of metrics (say, by testing people and hiring those who test the best) will create teams of people [who all tested well — who all overlap].
: 주어의 핵이 Measurement, 동사가 will create이며 [ ]는 people을 수식하는 관계절이다.

13-14   정답 13 ⑤ 14 ⑤

중요한 것은, 처음에 제공되거나 제공되지 않는 것에 듣기가 영향을 미칠 가능성이 있다는 것이다. 다시 말해, 우리는 들리거나 들리지 않음으로 인해서 포함될 (그리고 궁극적으로 고려될) 개별 메시지의 존재를 반드시 가정할 수는 없다. 다른 사람의 말을 듣는 결과로서 우리 자신의 선호와 관점이 바뀔지도 모르는 것처럼, 우리가 제공하는 바로 그 관점이 듣기 관행 자체에 의해 영향을 받을 수도 있다.

예를 들어, 의사소통에 관한 연구는 청중의 듣기 능력이 화자의 메시지를 형성할 수 있다는 것을 발견했다. 구체적으로는, 자서전식 스토리텔링 실험에서 '이야기하는 내용을 바꾸고, 다른 설명의 내용을 제공하고, 이야기의 구조를 바꿈'으로써 '화자는 주의를 기울이지 않는 청자들을 위해 이야기를 바꾼다'는 것을 보여 준다. 내 수업에서, 피곤하거나 흥미가 없는 학생들로 보이는 집단과 마주쳤을 때 나는 강의를 조정했다. 그리고 우리 자신의 일상적인 대화와 개인적인 상호 작용에서, 만약 누군가가 정말로 듣고 있다고 믿는다면, 우리는 흔히 이야기나 의견을 더 나누고 싶어 한다는 것을 발견한다. 말하기와 듣기 사이의 이러한 수동적인(→ 역동적인) 관계는 포함에 대해 중요한 의미를 가지는데, 이는 듣기가 사람들이 숙고할 때 공유하는 바로 그 내용에 영향을 줄 수 있기 때문이다.

해설
13 청자의 반응에 의해 화자가 제공하는 내용이 달라질 수 있다는 내용의 글이므로, 글의 제목으로 가장 적절한 것은 ⑤ '주의 깊게 들으라, 여러분은 다른 사람들이 말하는 것을 바꿀 수 있다'이다.
① 귀를 기울이라! 여러분의 마음이 말하고 있다
② 듣는 법 배우기, 배우는 법 듣기
③ 잘 듣기: 공감적 이해의 기술
④ 말하기 기술: 사람들이 정말로 듣도록 말하는 방법

14 화자는 주의를 기울이지 않는 청자들을 위해 이야기를 바꾼다고 했고, 누군가가 정말로 듣고 있다고 믿는다면, 우리는 흔히 이야기나 의견을 더 나누고 싶어 한다는 것을 발견한다고 했으므로, (e) passive(수동적인)를 dynamic(역동적인)과 같은 단어로 바꿔야 한다.

TEXT FLOW
주제	처음 제공되거나 제공되지 않는 것에 듣기가 영향을 미칠 가능성이 있음
예시	의사소통에 관한 연구에서 청중의 듣기 능력이 화자의 메시지 형성에 영향을 줄 수 있다는 것을 발견함
결론	말하기와 듣기 사이에는 역동적 관계가 있음

구문
• In other words, we can**not necessarily** assume the existence of a discrete message [that either will or will not be heard and therefore included (and ultimately considered)].
: [ ]는 a discrete message를 수식하는 관계절이다. not necessarily

는 부분 부정으로 '반드시 ~인 것은 아니다'의 의미를 나타낸다.

• Specifically, experiments in autobiographical storytelling show [that "narrators change stories for inattentive listeners" by "{changing the content they narrate}, {offering different interpretive content}, and {altering story structure}."]
: [ ]는 show의 목적어 역할을 하는 명사절이다. 그 안에 { }로 표시된 세 개의 동명사구가 and로 이어져 전치사 by의 목적어를 이루고 있다.

GRAMMAR REVIEW

본문 97쪽

1 applaud	2 take	3 adopted
4 is	5 that	6 slowing
7 that	8 expressed	9 that
10 confronted		

1 문장의 주어인 We가 and로 연결된 두 개의 술어와 호응하는 구조이므로, 두 번째 술부를 이끄는 술어 동사는 복수 동사 applaud가 적절하다.

2 stop ~, focus ~와 함께 have to에 and로 연결되어 병렬 구조를 이루고 있으므로 동사원형 take가 적절하다.

3 주어인 Most developing countries에 호응할 수 있는 술어 동사가 필요하므로 과거 동사 adopted가 적절하다.

4 주어의 핵은 Communicating(동명사)이고 동명사 주어는 단수 취급하므로 is가 적절하다.

5 선행사 a room이 관계절에서 동사 smells의 주어 역할을 하므로 주격 관계대명사 that이 적절하다.

6 while ~ 이하는 분사구문으로, 생략된 주어 you가 동사 slow의 행위자이므로 능동의 의미를 갖는 현재분사 slowing이 적절하다.

7 believed 뒤에 유도 부사 there로 시작하는 완전한 절이 이어지고 있으므로 접속사 that이 적절하다.

8 수식을 받는 various emotions가 동사 express의 행위자가 아니라 그 대상이므로 수동의 의미를 갖는 과거분사 expressed를 써야 한다.

9 관계절의 주어 역할을 해야 하고 선행사 teams가 사물이므로 주격 관계대명사 that이 적절하다.

10 when이 이끄는 절의 생략된 주어가 I이고 confront의 목적어가 없는 상황에서 I는 confront의 주체가 아니라 그 대상이므로 과거분사 confronted가 적절하다.

본문 98쪽

하프 모의고사 12회

01 ③	02 ①	03 ②	04 ④	05 ④
06 ②	07 ④	08 ③	09 ⑤	10 ⑤
11 ⑤	12 ④	13 ②	14 ⑤	

01 정답 ③

Kate는 상당히 긴장한 채로 낡은 축구공을 꽉 움켜잡았다. 축구장은 아이들이 노는 소리로 시끌벅적했고 그들의 웃음소리는 그녀의 귓가에 울려 퍼졌다. 그녀가 갓 깎은 잔디 위에서 낡은 축구화의 무게를 느끼며 축구장에 점차 다가가자 그녀의 심장은 마구 뛰었다. 환한 미소를 띤 키가 큰 한 코치가 그녀를 멈춰 세웠다. "여기 처음 왔니?" 그가 친절하게 물었다. Kate는 "네"라고 중얼거렸고, 코치의 미소에 그녀의 기분이 나아졌다. 코치의 따뜻한 미소와 격려의 말은 선수들에게 반복 연습 훈련을 설명하는 동안 Kate의 뛰는 마음을 진정시키는 데 도움이 되었다. Kate는 공을 차는 것에서 뜻밖의 기쁨을 발견했고, 패스 하나하나를 할 때마다 시원한 가을 공기가 한 번씩 그녀를 상쾌하게 해 주었다. 드리블에 성공할 때마다 코치는 하이파이브와 함께 "Kate, 발놀림 좋았어! 계속 그렇게 해!"라고 격려의 말을 건넸다. 연습이 끝날 무렵 Kate는 신이 났을 뿐만 아니라 스타가 된 기분이었다! 집으로 걸어가면서 Kate는 자신이 축구에 소질이 있다는 것을 깨달았다. 그녀는 다음 연습을 위해 빨리 축구장으로 돌아가 자신의 실력을 뽐내고 싶었다!

해설
축구 연습에 처음 합류하게 된 Kate가 처음에는 긴장한 채로 축구장에 들어섰으나, 친절한 코치의 격려 하에 즐겁게 연습에 참여하면서 자신이 축구에 소질이 있다는 것을 깨닫고 다음 연습에서 자신의 실력을 뽐내고 싶다고 했으므로, Kate의 심경 변화로 가장 적절한 것은 ③ '긴장한 → 자신감 있는'이다.
① 부러워하는 → 부끄러운
② 좌절한 → 감사한
④ 무관심한 → 기뻐하는
⑤ 황홀해하는 → 실망한

TEXT FLOW

도입	축구 연습에 처음 참여하여 긴장한 Kate
전개	친절한 코치의 격려 하에 축구 연습에 참여함
결말	연습이 끝난 후 자신이 축구에 소질이 있다는 것을 깨닫고 자신감을 갖는 Kate

구문

• Her heart pounded [as she approached the field, {feeling the weight of her worn soccer shoes on the freshly mowed grass}].
: [ ]는 시간의 부사절이고, 그 안의 { }는 부사절의 주어인 she를 의미상 주어로 하는 분사구문이다.

• Kate found unexpected joy in kicking the ball, [the cool autumn air refreshing her with each pass].
: [ ]는 the cool autumn air를 의미상 주어로 하는 분사구문이다. the cool autumn air가 refresh라는 행위의 주체이므로 현재분사가 사용되었다.

02

인간의 신체는 한 줌의 세포들로 시작된다. 그것은 자라고, 성숙하고, 노화하고, 그리고 죽는다. 그런 다음 그것은 분해된다. 분자 수준에서, 그것은 끊임없이 변화한다. 숨을 쉴 때마다 우리는 환경으로부터 무수한 수의 원자들을 들이쉬고, 각각은 어느 정도 우리의 물리적인 구성을 바꾼다. 게다가, 우리 (몸의) 원자들의 98%가 매년 새로워진다. 그렇지 않으면, 우리는 우리 자신의 독소 때문에 중독되어 몇 시간 안에 죽을 것이다. 신체는 벽돌이 계속 교체되는 건물과 같다. 우리는 몇 달마다 새로운 피부와 간을 키우고, 매우 튼튼해 보이는 뼈대도 6개월마다 재생된다. 여러분이 2년 전에 가졌던 신체에 속한 세포는 하나도 남아 있지 않다. 심지어 여러분의 인격과 기억이 저장되는 뇌세포들도 대략 1년마다 죽어 없어지고 교체된다.

해설
인간의 신체는 분자 수준에서 끊임없이 변화하며, 장기와 뼈대 등을 이루는 세포들도 계속 생성되고 소멸된다는 내용의 글이므로, 글의 요지로 가장 적절한 것은 ①이다.

TEXT FLOW

도입	인간의 신체를 이루는 분자의 끊임없는 변화
전개	지속적인 생성과 소멸을 겪는 신체의 구성 요소들
요지	인간의 신체를 이루고 있는 구성 요소는 계속 변화함

구문
• We grow a new skin and liver every few months and **the skeleton**, [which appears so solid], **regenerates** every six months.
  : [ ]는 the skeleton을 부연 설명하는 관계절이고, and 뒤에 이어지는 절의 주어인 the skeleton과 연결되는 동사는 regenerates이다.

03

지구상에서 가장 큰 동물들 중의 하나인 코끼리는 잘 먹고 배설도 많이 한다. 몇몇 동물원 사육사들은 최근에 이 많은 양의 쓰레기를 처리할 방법을 찾기로 결심했다. 그들은 코끼리 배설물에 섬유질이 가득하다는 점에 착안해, 코끼리 배설물 종이를 개발했다. 그 종이는 두툼하며, 한국의 전통 종이와 비슷한 질감이다. 그것을 만들기 위해서는, 질 좋은 섬유질만 남을 때까지 코끼리 배설물을 말리고, 끓이고, 여러 번 헹군다. 그 섬유질을 잘게 자르고 염료를 첨가한다. 일단 햇볕에 말리기만 하면, 그것은 완성된다. 만드는 과정에서 냄새나 세균은 모두 사라진다. 몇몇 동물원에서는 코끼리 배설물로 만든 종이에 '시험 합격'과 같은 문구를 인쇄해 넣은 부적들을 판다. 그들이 말하기를, 그것이 코끼리처럼 큰 행운을 가져온다고 한다.

해설
코끼리 배설물에 섬유질이 가득하다는 점에 착안하여 코끼리 배설물 종이를 개발했다는 내용의 글이므로, 이 글의 제목으로는 ② '종이로 재활용되는 코끼리 배설물'이 가장 적절하다.
① 사용되고 있는 다양한 종류의 종이
③ 코끼리는 멸종 위기에 처한 종이다
④ 재활용된 물질로 종이 만들기
⑤ 코끼리: 행운을 가져다주는 동물

⊗ 매력적인 오답 주의!
④ 글의 중심 소재를 파악하지 못하고 코끼리 배설물을 이미 재활용된 물질로 잘못 연결지으면 고를 수 있는 오답이다.

TEXT FLOW

도입	몇몇 동물원 사육사들이 많은 양의 코끼리 배설물을 처리할 방법을 찾기로 결심함
전개	코끼리 배설물에 섬유질이 가득한 것에 착안하여 코끼리 배설물 종이를 개발함
결론	몇몇 동물원은 코끼리 배설물로 만든 종이에 문구를 인쇄해 부적으로 판매함

구문
• [**Once dried** in the sun], it is complete.
  : [ ]는 '일단 ~하면'이라는 뜻의 부사절로, Once와 dried 사이에는 it is가 생략되어 있다.

• Some zoos sell good luck charms with phrases like "pass the test" [printed on paper {made of elephant excrement}].
  : [ ]와 { }는 모두 과거분사구로 각각 phrases와 paper를 수식한다.

04

Children's Art Festival 포스터 대회
Children's Art Festival을 위해 포스터를 디자인하고 축제의 포스터와 티셔츠에 있는 여러분의 작품을 보세요!

신청자
신청자들은 이 도시 주민들로 제한됩니다. 18세 미만의 신청자들은 부모의 서명이 필요합니다.

포스터 자격 요건
• 출품작들은 '여름의 즐거움'이라는 주제를 표현해야 합니다.
• 출품작들은 반환되지 않을 것입니다.
• 단독 신청자만 출품할 수 있습니다. 단체 작품은 허용되지 않을 것입니다.
• 출품은 3월 7일까지입니다.

포상
• 우승작은 한정 수량의 Children's Art Festival 포스터와 티셔츠에 특별히 포함될 것입니다.
• 5명의 상위 입상자들은 5월 26일 토요일 Children's Art Festival에서 본인들의 작품들을 전시하게 될 것입니다.

해설
단독 신청자만 출품할 수 있고 단체 작품은 허용되지 않는다고 했으므로 안내문의 내용과 일치하는 것은 ④이다.
① 신청자들은 이 도시 주민들로 제한되어 있다.
② 출품작들은 '여름의 즐거움'이라는 주제를 표현해야 한다.
③ 출품작들은 반환되지 않는다.
⑤ 5명의 상위 입상자들의 작품은 5월 26일에 전시될 것이다.

구문
• The first five runners-up will **have their works displayed** at the Children's Art Festival on Saturday, May 26.
  : 「사역동사(have)+목적어+목적격 보어」의 구문으로, 목적어와 목적격

보어가 수동의 관계이기 때문에 목적격 보어로 과거분사인 displayed가 쓰였다.

05

여러분이 빨간색을 볼 수 없다면 어떻게 될까? 여러분이 사과나 빨간색 잔에 담긴 음료에 끌릴 가능성이 더 낮을 것인가? 색맹인 사람들에게 이 질문을 하면, 그들은 단호히 아니라고 할 것이다. 그들도 여전히 사과를 인식할 수 있으며 그것이 맛이 좋을 것임을 안다. 그들도 여전히 색유리와 달콤한 음료를 연관 짓는 것을 배울 수 있다. 여러분이 흑백의 TV 쇼를 봤던 때를 한번 생각해 보라. 여러분은 그것이 흑백이라는 것을 금세 잊어버리고, 마음속에서 회색의 색조를 여러분이 볼 것으로 예상하는 색에 맞춘다. 광색소 하나가 없는 채 태어난 사람들도 색각이 손상된(→ 온전한) 사람과 똑같이 즙이 많은 빨간색 사과에 끌린다. 그들이 보는 색이 나머지 우리들이 보는 것과 다를 수는 있지만, 그들도 여전히 그것과 감정적인 반응을 연결 짓는 것을 배울 것이다.

해설
광색소가 없는 채 태어나서 색맹인 사람들도 나름대로의 방식으로 빨간색을 인식하고 온전한 색각을 가진 사람처럼 빨간색 사과에 끌린다는 흐름이 적절하므로, ④ impaired(손상된)를 intact(온전한)와 같은 단어로 바꿔야 한다.

TEXT FLOW
도입	색맹인 사람도 사과나 빨간색 잔에 담긴 음료에 끌릴 수 있음
부연 1	색맹이라도 색유리와 달콤한 음료를 연관 지을 수 있음
부연 2	우리가 흑백의 TV 쇼를 볼 때 회색의 색조를 마음속에서 예상되는 색에 맞추는 것과 마찬가지임
결론	색맹인 사람도 색과 감정적인 반응을 연결 짓는 법을 배움

구문
• [People {who are born missing one of their photopigments}] are just **as** tempted by a juicy red apple **as** those [whose color vision is intact].
: 첫 번째 [ ]는 주어이고, 그 안의 { }는 People을 수식하는 관계절이다. '~만큼 …한'이라는 의미의 「as+형용사/부사의 원급+as」 구문이 사용되었으며, 두 번째 [ ]는 those를 수식하는 관계절이다.

06

화나는 기분이 어떤 것인지 모르는 사람은 없다. 사실, 정신 건강 협회에 의해 실시된 최근의 여론 조사에 따르면, 4분의 1이 넘는 사람들이 단지 그들이 때때로 얼마나 화가 나는지에 대해 염려한다. 하지만 극한의 분노는 우리의 조상들이 살아남는 데 도움을 주었다. 즉 분노는 우리가 DNA의 선천적으로 만들어진 생존 목표를 성취하게 만드는 동기를 부여해 주는 힘이었다. 우리의 화난 조상들은 그들의 더 느긋한 동료들보다 음식, 쉼터, 그리고 배우자들을 위해 싸울 가능성이 좀 더 많았다. 우리의 조상들이 그들의 음식과 자원을 훔치는 다른 이들에 대해 혹은 그들을 죽이려고 하는 포식자들에 대해 화가 나지 않았더라면, 그들은 예방 조치를 취하지도 않았을 테고, 그리고 살아남지도 못했을 것이다.

해설
분노라는 감정이 진화론적으로 우리 조상들이 생존하는 데 있어 유용한 감정이었음을 설명하는 내용의 글이다. 분노함으로써 생존에 필요한 것들을 지킬

수 있었으므로, 빈칸에 들어갈 말로는 ② '우리의 조상들이 살아남는 데 도움을 주었다'가 가장 적절하다.
① 그들을 행복하게 만들었다
③ 건강에 부정적인 영향을 끼쳤다
④ 사람들 간의 싸움을 예방했다
⑤ 다른 이들의 음식을 훔치도록 우리를 자극했다

TEXT FLOW
도입	화가 나는 것에 대해 걱정하는 사람들이 많음
전개	하지만 분노라는 감정은 우리 조상들이 살아남는 데 도움을 주었음
결론	분노라는 감정이 없었더라면 우리 조상들은 살아남지 못했을 것임

구문
• In fact, [according to a recent poll by the Mental Health Organization], **more than a quarter of people worry** about just how angry they sometimes feel.
: [ ]는 전치사구로서 문장의 부사 역할을 하고, 문장의 주어는 more than a quarter of people로 복수 명사이므로 복수 동사 worry가 쓰였다.

07

독점을 두려워하고 정부에 의해 몇몇 생산자들이 다른 생산자들로부터 보호받아야 한다고 생각하는 사람들에게는, 그런 독점 금지법이 윤리적으로 필요하다고 여겨질 수 있다. 그렇지만 쟁점은 독점 금지법이 윤리적인가의 여부가 아니며, 자유 시장과 우리의 민간 경제 직관에 그것이 도움이 되는가의 여부이다. 독점 금지 조치는 누군가 이기면 누군가 지는, 제로섬의(쌍방 득실의 차가 무(無)인), 생산자가 주도하는 경제에 근거해 있지만, 경제란 제로섬이 아니다. 그리고 우리가 경제가 위에서 아래로 고안되었음이 틀림없으며, 따라서 위로부터의 끊임없는 경영과 통제를 통해서 성공할 수 있을 뿐이라고 생각하게 만드는 것이 바로 우리의 민간 직관(근거 없는 대중적 직관)이다. 그렇지만 애덤 스미스는 진화론적이고 아래에서 위로 올라가는 그의 경제 모형에서 이 근거 없는 믿음을 반박하는 수많은 증거를 제시했다. 그는 개인의 이익에 대한 자유로운 추구가 허용될 때 경제가 번영한다고 주장했다.

해설
애덤 스미스는 위로부터의 끊임없는 경영과 통제를 통해 성공할 수 있다고 믿는 민간 경제 직관에 반박하는 수많은 증거를 제시했다고 했으므로, 그의 주장에 해당하는 빈칸에 들어갈 말로는 ④ '개인의 이익에 대한 자유로운 추구가 허용될'이 가장 적절하다.
① 윤리적인 정부가 굳건하게 확립될
② 그것(경제)이 자원을 사람들에게 골고루 배분할
③ 대량 생산의 효율성이 실현될
⑤ 독점 금지 정책이 생산자들에 의해 받아들여질

TEXT FLOW
도입	독점 금지법이 윤리적이라고 생각하는 통념이 있지만 쟁점은 그것이 자유 시장과 민간 경제 직관에 도움이 되는가의 여부임
전개 1	경제는 제로섬이 아니며 위에서 아래로 내려오는 것이 아님
전개 2	애덤 스미스는 제로섬 경제관과 민간 경제 직관에 대한 믿음에 반박했음

구문

- But the issue is not [**whether** antitrust legislation is moral]; it is [**whether** it serves the free market and our folk economic intuitions].

  : 두 개의 [ ]는 각각의 문장에서 주격 보어 역할을 하는 명사절로, whether는 '~인지 아닌지'의 의미를 나타낸다.

- And **it is** our folk intuitions **that** lead us to believe [that the economy must have been designed from the top down, and thus can only succeed with continual managing and control from the top].

  :「it is ~ that ...」 강조구문이 사용되어, 주어 our folk intuitions가 강조되었다. [ ]는 believe의 목적어 역할을 하는 명사절이다.

08

정답 ③

경제학자들이 '공공재'라고 부르는, 우리 모두가 이익을 얻지만 우리 중 일부만 비용을 지불하거나, 혹은 우리 모두에게 피해를 주지만 우리 중 일부만 생산하는 재화는 당연히 '시장재'가 아니다. 경제학 이론에서는 공공재를 비경합적이고 비배제적인 것, 즉 그것에 대한 우리의 사용이 다른 사람들이 그것을 사용할 수 있는 능력을 줄이지 않으며, 그리고 일단 제공되면 우리가 다른 사람들이 사용하는 것을 막을 수 없는 것들로 정의한다. 깨끗한 공기나 생물 다양성과 같은 환경 공공재 중 일부는 과세에서 비롯된 중앙 집권화된 지출로 보호해야 할 필요가 있을 수도 있다. (사람들은 시장에서 사적인 재화를 자유롭게 교환할 수 있으며, 공공 시스템은 교환이 공정하게 이루어질 수 있도록 최소한의 감독을 제공한다.) 그러나 이러한 세금을 납부할 사람들은 공공재를 충분히 가치 있게 여기지 않거나 그 가치에 대해 실감하지 못할 수도 있으며, 따라서 공공재의 비용을 지불해야만 하는 것에 대해 억울하다고 여길 것이고, 이런 이유로 시장 경제에서는 효율적으로 공공재를 배분하는 데 어려움을 겪을 수 있다. 따라서 시장 시스템은 너무 많은 오염과 너무 적은 보도(步道)를 초래할 수 있다.

해설

공공재의 특징은 비경합적이고 비배제적이지만 공공재의 가치를 실감하지 못하면 공공재의 비용을 과세로 충당하는 것과 공공재의 효율적 배분이 어려워질 수 있다는 내용의 글이다. 따라서 사람들이 시장에서 사적인 재화를 자유롭게 교환하고 공공 시스템이 공정한 교환을 위한 감독을 제공한다는 내용의 ③은 글의 전체 흐름과 관계가 없다.

⊗ 매력적인 오답 주의!

⑤ 너무 많은 오염과 너무 적은 보도가 공공재와 관련된 내용임을 인지하지 못하여 글의 전체 흐름과 관계가 없다고 오인하면 고를 수 있는 오답이다.

TEXT FLOW

도입	공공재는 비경합적이고 비배제적임
부연	환경 공공재 중 일부는 과세로부터 지출로 보호해야 함
전환	공공재의 가치를 충분히 가치 있게 여기지 않으면 비용 지불에 대해 억울하다고 여길 수 있음
부연	그 결과 시장 경제에서는 효율적인 공공재 배분에 어려움이 발생할 수 있음

구문

- Goods [we all benefit from but only some of us pay for], or [which damage us all but only some of us produce] — [what

economists call 'public goods'] — are not naturally 'market goods'.

  : 첫 번째와 두 번째 [ ]는 or로 연결되어 공통의 선행사인 Goods를 수식하는 관계절이다. 세 번째 [ ]는 Goods ~ produce까지의 주어 부분과 동격 관계를 이루는 명사절로 선행사를 포함하는 관계대명사 what이 사용되었다.

- Yet [those who will pay these taxes] may not [value the public goods sufficiently], or [have a real sense of their value], and thus [will resent having to pay for them], and hence a market economy may struggle to allocate them efficiently.

  : 첫 번째 [ ]는 문장의 주어이다. 두 번째와 세 번째 [ ]는 or로 연결되어 may not에 이어진다. 네 번째 [ ]는 and로 연결되어 주어인 those who will pay these taxes에 이어진다.

09

정답 ⑤

자아와 장소 사이의 심리적 동일시는 계속되는 사회적 과정 속에 있는 공간 창작의 일부이다. (C) 그것은 그것의 외양, 소리, 냄새가 일과의 일부가 되는 특정한 장소에 대한 개인의 투자를 요구한다. 낯선 공간에서 장소에 대한 감각을 조성하는 것은 소속되어야 할 어떤 곳을 설정한다. 인문 지리학자들과 다른 연구자들은 이 동일시의 과정이 장소에 기본이 된다고 생각한다. (B) 세계 각지에서 온 환경 운동가들과의 인터뷰는 놀라운 주제의 패턴을 밝혀 주는데, 그 사람이 아시아 열대 우림 출신이든, 아프리카 사바나 출신이든, 라틴 아메리카의 도시 출신이든, 유럽의 계곡 출신이든, 혹은 북미 농장 출신이든 간에, 그들이 비슷한 이야기를 한다는 것이다. (A) 그들은 자신들이 친밀한 관계를 맺었고 여전히 생생하게 묘사할 수 있는 특별한 유년 시절의 장소에 대한 행복한 기억을 가지고 있다. 그러나 너무나 많은 경우에서 이 어린 시절의 풍경은 바뀌거나 심지어 파괴되었고, '사람들은 자신들의 특별한 장소가 어떻게 변했는지에 대해 비슷한 이야기를 한다.'

해설

주어진 글은 자아와 장소 사이의 심리적 동일시는 계속되는 사회적 과정 속에 있는 공간 창작의 일부라는 내용이므로, 이 내용을 It으로 받아 설명을 이어 가는 (C)가 온 다음, 인문 지리학자들과 다른 연구자들은 이 동일시의 과정이 장소에 기본이 된다고 생각한다는 (C)의 마지막 문장에 이어 동일시의 과정에 대한 환경 운동가들의 인터뷰에 나타난 패턴을 소개한 (B)가 오고, (B)에서 제시된 세계 각지의 환경 운동가들이 어떠한 비슷한 이야기를 했는지 구체화한 (A)가 마지막에 오는 것이 글의 흐름상 가장 자연스럽다.

TEXT FLOW

주제	자아와 장소 사이의 심리적 동일시는 계속되는 사회적 과정 속에 있는 공간 창작의 일부임
부연	동일시의 과정이 장소에 기본이 됨
예시	세계 각지에서 온 환경 운동가들과의 인터뷰에서 나타나는 패턴

구문

- They have fond memories of a special childhood place [that they bonded with and can still vividly describe].

  : [ ]는 a special childhood place를 수식하는 관계절이다.

- [Interviews with environmental activists from all parts of the world] **reveal** a striking thematic pattern: [whether

the person is from an Asian tropical rain forest, an African savanna, a Latin-American city, a European valley, or a North American farm], they tell a similar story.
: 첫 번째 [ ]가 문장의 주어이며 동사는 reveal이다. 두 번째 [ ]는 '~이든 (아니든)'이라는 의미의 양보의 부사절이다.

10   정답 ⑤

대부분의 사람들은 규칙을 따르는 것을 선택한다. 하지만 규칙은 종종 어겨야 하는 것으로 여겨진다. 규칙을 피하면서 일하고, 전통적인 장애물을 뛰어넘으며, 옆으로 난 길을 통해 목표에 다다를 수 있는 창의적인 방법들이 종종 있다는 것을 염두에 두는 것이 중요하다. 대부분의 사람들이 꽉 막힌 고속도로로 통하는 주요 노선의 절대 끝날 것 같지 않은 차량들 속에서 기다리는 반면에, 모험심이 더 강한 다른 사람들은 자신들의 목적지에 더 빨리 도착하기 위해 우회 도로를 찾으려고 노력한다. 물론, 몇몇 규칙들은 우리들의 안전을 보호하고, 질서를 지키며, 상당수의 사람들에게 효과가 있는 과정을 만들기 위해 준비된다. 하지만 그 과정에서 규칙들에 의문을 품어볼 만한 가치가 있다. 전통적인 길들이 막힌 것처럼 보일 때때로 규칙을 피해 가는 옆길들이 당신을 당신의 목적지에 다다르게 할 수 있다.

해설
주어진 문장은 규칙에 의문을 품어 보는 것이 가치 있는 일이라는 내용이고 역접의 의미를 지닌 But으로 시작하고 있으므로, 이와 상반된 내용 다음에 와야 한다. 따라서 규칙을 지켜 나가는 것의 긍정적 측면을 설명한 문장 다음인 ⑤에 들어가는 것이 가장 적절하다.

TEXT FLOW
도입	규칙은 종종 어겨야 하는 것으로 여겨짐
전개	규칙을 피해 목표에 다다를 수 있는 창의적인 방법들이 종종 있음
결론	그 과정에서 규칙에 의문을 품어볼 만한 가치가 있음

구문
• It is important **to keep** in mind [that there are often creative ways {to work around the rules}, {to jump over the traditional hurdles}, and {to get to your goal by taking a side route}].
: It은 가주어, to keep이 진주어이고, [ ]는 keep의 목적절이다. 세 개의 { }는 creative ways를 수식하는 형용사적 용법의 to부정사구이며, and에 의해 병렬 구조를 이룬다.

11   정답 ⑤

특정한 양과 유형의 오염은 자연적인 과정에 의해 정화된다. 자연이 처리할 수 없는, 혹은 우리가 만들어 내는 것만큼 빨리 흡수되지 못하는 폐기물을 우리가 만들어 낼 때 오염이 쌓인다. 그 문제들은 활동이 계속될수록 점점 더 심각해져 간다. 어떤 오염 물질들은 철저하게 희석될 때조차도 심각한 위험을 야기할 수 있다. 적은 양의 독성 물질들은 작은 생물들에 의해 흡수가 된 다음, 그것들을 먹는 생명체들의 몸에 축적될 수 있다. 만약 이러한 생물들이 그다음에 더 큰 것들의 먹이가 되면, 그 축적된 독소들은 훨씬 더 농축된다. 이러한 생물학적 축적을 통해, 어떤 독들은 비록 낮은 농도로 퍼져 있더라도, 예를 들어 오염된 물에서 나온 물고기들과 그 물고기들을 먹는 인간들에게서

위험한 농도로 발견될 수 있다.

해설
주어진 문장에서 이러한 생물들이 더 큰 것들의 먹이가 된다고 했으므로 these creatures가 의미하는 것이 '더 작은 생물들'임을 알 수 있다. 따라서 주어진 문장은 tiny organisms가 언급된 다음인 ⑤에 들어가는 것이 가장 적절하다.

TEXT FLOW
도입	자연이 정화할 수 있는 유형이 아니거나 용량을 초과하면 오염이 쌓임
전개	적은 양의 독성 물질이라도 생물이 흡수하면 몸에 축적됨
결론	낮은 농도로 퍼져 있는 독도 생물학적 축적을 통해 위험한 농도로 축적될 수 있음

구문
• Small amounts of toxic materials, [after being absorbed by tiny organisms], can accumulate in the flesh of the creatures [that eat them].
: 첫 번째 [ ]는 주어와 동사 사이에 삽입된 삽입어구이다. 두 번째 [ ]는 the creatures를 수식하는 관계절이다.

12~14   정답 12 ④   13 ②   14 ⑤

(A) 수년 전에, 내가 Stanford 병원에서 자원봉사자로 일하고 있을 때, 나는 희귀하고 심각한 질병으로 고통받고 있었던 Liza라는 이름의 어린 소녀를 알게 되었다. 그녀가 회복할 수 있는 유일한 기회는 기적적으로 같은 병으로부터 살아남아 그 병과 싸우는 데 필요한 항체가 생성되어 있었던 그녀의 5살짜리 동생 Kevin의 피를 수혈받는 것밖에 없어 보였다.
(D) 의사는 그녀의 어린 동생에게 상황을 설명하고, 그 소년에게 그가 자신의 누나를 위해 자신의 피를 줄 용의가 있는지 물어보았다. 나는 그가 잠시 망설이고 나서 깊은 숨을 쉬고는 "네, 그것이 Liza를 살릴 수 있는 일이라면 하겠어요."라고 말하는 것을 보았다.
(B) 수혈이 진행됨에 따라, 그는 자신의 누나 옆 침상에 누워 미소를 지으며, 그녀의 뺨에 혈색이 돌아오는 것을 지켜보았다. 그러고 나서 그의 얼굴이 창백해지고 미소가 사라져 갔다. 그는 의사를 올려다보며 떨리는 목소리로 그에게 물었다. "저는 곧바로 죽게 되나요?" 그의 두 눈은 눈물로 가득 차 있었다.
(C) 어렸기 때문에, 그 소년은 의사의 말을 오해했던 것이다. 그는 자신의 피를 전부 다 누나에게 주어야 할 것이라고 생각했다. 그는 자신의 누나를 살리기 위해서 죽기로 결심했던 것이다. 사람들이 나에게 용기란 무엇이냐고 물을 때마다, 나는 항상 그들에게 자신의 누나를 살리기 위해 그의 생명을 걸었던 이 어린 소년의 이야기를 들려준다.

해설
12 동생으로부터 수혈을 받는 방법밖에 남지 않은 희귀병을 앓고 있는 Liza에 대한 내용의 주어진 글 다음에, Liza의 남동생인 Kevin이 수혈을 결심하는 내용의 (D)가 이어지고, 수혈하는 동안 자신이 곧 죽을 것이라고 생각했다는 내용의 (B)가 온 후에, 그 소년이 오해했던 것이 밝혀지고 용기가 무엇이냐는 질문을 받을 때마다 필자가 그 이야기를 사람들에게 들려준다는 내용의 (C)가 마지막에 오는 것이 글의 흐름상 가장 자연스럽다.

13 (b)는 의사를 가리키고, 나머지는 모두 Kevin을 가리킨다.

14 수혈을 해 주겠냐는 의사의 물음에 잠시 망설이고 심호흡을 한 뒤에 답변을 했다고 했으므로 ⑤는 글의 내용으로 적절하지 않다.

시간 순서/사건 전개에 따른 흐름:
(A) 희귀병으로 고통받는 소녀 Liza는 남동생에게 수혈을 받아야만 회복할 수 있음 → (D) 의사가 Liza의 남동생에게 수혈해 줄 수 있는지 묻자 소년은 그렇게 하겠다고 답함 → (B) 수혈이 진행되며 누나의 혈색이 돌아오자, 소년은 자신이 곧 죽는지 물어봄 → (C) 소년은 자신의 피를 다 줘야 하는 것으로 오해했음에도, 누나를 위해 수혈을 하기로 결심한 것임

구문
• [As the transfusion progressed], he lay in a bed next to his sister and smiled, [seeing the color returning to her cheeks].
: 첫 번째 [ ]는 때를 나타내는 부사절이고, 두 번째 [ ]는 분사구문으로 동시상황을 나타낸다.

GRAMMAR REVIEW

본문 105쪽

1 refreshing	2 where	3 it
4 that	5 necessary	6 need
7 whose	8 to get	9 serious
10 to be, needed		

1 주절인 Kate ~ the ball과 the cool autumn air ~ each pass가 접속사 없이 콤마(,)로만 연결되어 있으므로, the cool autumn air ~ each pass는 분사구문으로 봐야 한다. 분사구문의 의미상 주어인 the cool autumn air가 refresh라는 행위의 주체이므로 현재분사 refreshing이 적절하다.

2 선행사 the brain cells가 장소를 나타내며, 뒤에 완전한 형태의 절이 이어지므로 이를 부연 설명하는 관계부사 where가 적절하다.

3 The color they see를 가리키므로 부정대명사 one이 아니라 대명사 it이 적절하다.

4 선행사가 a motivating force이고, 관계절의 동사 drove의 주어 역할을 해야 하므로 주격 관계대명사 that이 적절하다.

5 considered의 의미를 보충하고 있으므로, 능동태일 때 consider의 목적격 보어가 될 수 있는 형용사 necessary가 적절하다.

6 that이 이끄는 명사절에서 주어가 「some of+복수 명사」이므로 복수형 동사 need가 적절하다.

7 관계절이 명사구인 주어로 시작되고 선행사인 a particular location이 의미상 관계절 내에서 명사구를 수식하는 소유격의 역할을 하므로 whose가 적절하다.

8 주어 others who are more adventurous에 대한 동사 try가 있으므로 목적을 나타내는 부사적 용법의 to get이 적절하다.

9 동사 become의 의미를 보충하는 주격 보어로 형용사 serious가 적절하다. 부사는 보어 자리에 쓸 수 없다.

10 첫 번째 빈칸은 '~한 것처럼 보이다'는 의미의 「appear+to부정사」를 나타내므로 to be를 써야 한다. 두 번째 빈칸은 수식을 받는 antibodies와 수동의 관계이므로 과거분사 needed를 써야 한다.

하프 모의고사 13회

01 ④	02 ③	03 ⑤	04 ②	05 ④
06 ①	07 ①	08 ②	09 ④	10 ⑤
11 ④	12 ①	13 ④	14 ④	

01

정답 ④

편집자 여러분께,
'Teens Life'는 제가 가장 좋아하는 잡지였습니다. 인간의 윤리와 가치, 그리고 시사에 관해 질문하는 기사들은 제가 읽기를 좋아하는 것입니다. 2022년 5월호에는, 전쟁에서 살아남은 십 대 난민들에 대한 주제를 다룬 칼럼이 포함되어 있었습니다. 2023년 7월호에서 여러분은, AIDS에 걸린 채 살아가는 십 대에 관한 칼럼을 게재했습니다. 분명, 신문은 세계적인 뉴스 기사들도 제공할 수 있습니다만, 십 대는 그런 가혹한 주제들을 십 대의 생활과 연관시키는 기사를 잡지에서 읽고 싶어 합니다. 그렇지만 실망스럽게도, 최근 몇 달의 잡지들 대부분은 광고로 가득 차 있었습니다. 이것은 흥미로운 기사들의 숫자를 크게 줄여 놓았습니다. 저는 'Teens Life'를 매달 초에 사곤 했습니다. 이제 저는 그것을 거의 사지 않습니다. 변화가 항상 좋은 것은 아니므로 'Teens Life'를 예전의 잡지로 만들어 주십시오.
Morris Jackson 드림

해설
필자는 'Teens Life'라는 잡지의 기사를 읽는 것을 좋아하는 애독자인데 최근 시사 기사 분량이 줄어들었고 광고면이 늘어난 데 대해 실망스럽다고 말하고 있다. 글의 마지막 부분에서도 예전의 잡지로 돌아갔으면 좋겠다는 의견을 밝히고 있으므로, 글의 목적으로는 ④가 가장 적절하다.

도입	필자가 'Teens Life'를 좋아했던 이유는 십 대와 관련된 시사 칼럼 때문이었음
전개	최근 'Teens Life'는 시사 기사의 비중이 줄고 광고가 늘어 필자는 거의 구매하지 않음
결론	예전처럼 시사 기사를 다시 강화해 줄 것을 요청함

구문
• Articles [that question people's morals, values, and current events] are [what I like to read about].
: 첫 번째 [ ]는 관계절로 선행사 Articles를 수식하고, 두 번째 [ ]는 선행사를 포함하는 관계대명사 what이 이끄는 명사절로서 주격 보어로 쓰였다.

02

정답 ③

하나의 대규모 프로젝트가 여러분의 뇌를 사용하는 것이 신경 세포들과 수상돌기들의 새로운 성장을 유발할 수 있는지 여부를 알아보기 위해 측정을 했다. 그 프로젝트에서, 개별 컴퓨터가 실험 대상의 수학 능력을 평가할 수 있도록 컴퓨터들이 프로그램되었다. 그런 다음, 그 컴퓨터는 그것의 실험 대상에게 그 사람의 능력과 비슷하게 유지하는 검사를 시작했다. 일단 그 컴퓨터

가 각 사람의 능력의 한계를 밀어붙이자, 연구자들은 신경 세포들과 수상 돌기들의 성장을 볼 수 있었다. 압권은 사람들이 그 혜택을 받기 위해 정답들을 맞힐 필요가 없었다는 점이다. 단지 자신들의 역량을 넘는 수학 문제들을 푸는 것으로 재성장을 유발하기에 충분했다. 그러므로 여러분의 경우, 만약 여러분이 일요일의 크로스워드 퍼즐의 정답을 절반만 간신히 맞힌다면, 여러분의 뇌에 가장 좋은 것은 그것을 계속해서 푸는 일이 될 것이다. 닿지 않는 곳에 있는 목표들에 도달하려고 훈련함으로써 더 빠르고 더 강해지는 운동선수와 똑같이, 여러분은 자신의 뇌가 더 똑똑하고 더 영리해지게 훈련할 수 있다.

해설
실험 대상에게 그 사람의 수준보다 약간 더 높은 수준의 수학 문제를 풀게 했을 때 신경 세포들과 수상 돌기들의 성장을 볼 수 있었다고 하며 우리의 뇌를 위해 어려운 크로스워드 퍼즐을 계속해서 풀라고 격려하고 있으므로, 필자의 주장으로는 ③이 가장 적절하다.

TEXT FLOW

소재	뇌의 사용과 신경 세포들 및 수상 돌기들의 재성장 여부를 측정한 실험
설명	개인의 수학 능력을 뛰어넘는 문제를 풀 때 신경 세포들과 수상 돌기들의 성장이 목격됨
요지	훈련을 통해 뇌를 발달시킬 수 있음

구문
• Then, the computer started a test for its subject [that stayed in line with the person's ability].
: [ ]는 관계절로 선행사 a test for its subject를 수식한다.

03
정답 ⑤

음식과 인간의 건강 사이에는 매우 중요한 상호 작용이 있다. 우리 모두는 균형 잡히고 다양한 식단의 중요성을 알고 있지만, 만약 일반적인 식단의 구성 요소 중 하나가 여러분을 아프게 하는 바로 그것이라면 어떻게 될까? 만성 소화 장애증은 인구의 약 1퍼센트에게서 발생한다. 이 질병에서, 인체의 면역 체계는 밀에서 발견되는 글루텐 단백질에 해로운 반응을 증가시킨다. 이것은 장의 내벽을 손상시켜, 설사와 구토를 유발하며, 가장 극단적인 형태에서 그것은 영양실조와 대장암으로 이어질 수 있다. 스페인 코르도바에 있는 한 연구팀은 면역 과잉 반응을 유발하는 특정 글루텐 단백질을 생산하는 밀의 45개 유전자 중 35개를 비활성화시키기 위해 유전자 편집을 이용했다. 반갑게도, 그들은 그 결과로 만들어진 밀가루가 바게트를 만들기에 적합하지만, 얇게 썬 흰 빵을 굽기에는 적합하지 않다고 보고했다. <u>프랑스의 만성 소화 장애증 환자들이여, 기뻐하라.</u>

해설
만성 소화 장애증 환자들에게 밀에서 발견되는 글루텐 단백질은 해로운데, 특정 글루텐 단백질을 생산하는 밀의 유전자 일부를 비활성화시켜 만든 밀가루가 흰 빵에는 적합하지 않지만 바게트를 만들기에 적합하다는 맥락이므로, 바게트를 주로 먹는 프랑스인의 입장에서는 좋은 소식일 것이다. 따라서 밑줄 친 부분이 글에서 의미하는 바로 가장 적절한 것은 ⑤ '만성 소화 장애증을 앓고 있는 프랑스인들은 그것으로 고생할 가능성이 더 적다.'이다.
① 프랑스에서 만성 소화 장애증은 꾸준히 발병한다.
② 프랑스인들은 만성 소화 장애증에 다소 무관심하게 반응한다.
③ 만성 소화 장애증은 프랑스인들 사이에서 매우 흔한 질병으로 여겨진다.
④ 만성 소화 장애증은 프랑스의 유전자 편집 기술에 의해 치료될 수 있다.

TEXT FLOW

도입	일반적인 식단의 구성 요소 중 하나가 통증을 유발할 수 있음
예시	인구의 1%에서 발생하는 만성 소화 장애증
전개 1	인체의 면역 체계가 밀의 글루텐 단백질에 해로운 반응을 증가시켜 질병을 유발함
전개 2	스페인의 연구팀이 유전자 편집을 이용해 특정 글루텐 단백질을 생산하는 밀 유전자 일부를 비활성화시킴
전개 3	이러한 밀은 바게트를 만들기에 적합함
결론	바게트를 주로 먹는 프랑스의 만성 소화 장애증 환자에게 좋은 소식임

구문
• A research group in Cordoba, Spain, used gene editing [to inactivate 35 of the 45 genes in wheat {that produce the specific gluten proteins ⟨that trigger the immune over-reaction⟩}].
: [ ]는 목적의 의미를 나타내는 부사적 용법의 to부정사구이다. 그 안의 { }와 ⟨ ⟩는 각각 the 45 genes in wheat와 the specific gluten proteins를 수식하는 관계절이다.

• Delightfully, they reported [that the resulting flour was {good enough to create baguettes}, but {not suitable for baking sliced white loaves}].
: [ ]는 reported의 목적어 역할을 하는 명사절이고, 그 안의 두 개의 { }는 but에 의해 병렬 연결되어 was에 이어진다.

04
정답 ②

우리가 부메랑에 관해 이야기할 때, 우리는 대개 던지면 돌아오는 휘어진 기구를 의미하지만, 사실 두 가지 다른 종류의 부메랑이 있다. 우리에게 친숙한 종류인 돌아오는 부메랑은 나무, 플라스틱 또는 다른 재료로 만들어진 가벼운 조각들이다. 그것들은 겨냥하기에 굉장히 힘들기 때문에 사냥에는 적절하지 않다. 반면에, 돌아오지 않는 부메랑도 휘어진 나무 조각이지만, 대개 그것들은 더 무겁고 더 길며, 일반적으로 길이가 3피트이거나 또는 그 이상이다. 그것들은 돌아오는 부메랑이 던진 사람에게 돌아오게 하는 특별한 날개 디자인을 가지고 있지 않지만, 그것들의 휘어진 모양은 그것들이 쉽게 공기 중에서 날아가도록 한다. 그것들은 겨냥하기 쉽고 빠른 속도로 먼 거리를 가기 때문에 효과적인 사냥 무기이다. 전투용 부메랑과 같은 것도 있는데, 그것은 백병전(칼이나 창, 총검 등의 무기를 가지고 적과 직접 몸으로 맞붙어서 싸우는 전투)에서 사용되는, 기본적으로 돌아오지 않는 부메랑이다.

해설
돌아오는 부메랑과 돌아오지 않는 부메랑의 각 특징과 용도에 관해 설명하고 있는 글이므로, 글의 주제로는 ② '부메랑의 특징과 용도'가 가장 적절하다.
① 부메랑 연구의 역사
③ 부메랑에 대한 서양인들의 잘못된 인식
④ 부메랑과 다른 무기들 간의 차이점
⑤ 오락의 목적을 위한 부메랑의 개발

TEXT FLOW

도입	두 가지 다른 종류의 부메랑이 있음
부연 1	던질 때 돌아오는 부메랑의 특징과 용도
부연 2	던질 때 돌아오지 않는 부메랑의 특징과 용도

- There is also such a thing as a battle boomerang, [which is basically a non-returning boomerang {used in hand-to-hand combat}].
  : [ ]는 a battle boomerang을 부연 설명하는 관계절이고, 그 안의 { }는 과거분사구로 a non-returning boomerang을 수식한다.

05 정답 ④

위 그래프는 인터넷을 사용하지 않는다고 답한 미국 성인의 비율을 인종 집단, 연령, 교육 수준, 그리고 지역 사회 유형별로 분류한 것을 보여 준다. 미국 흑인과 히스패닉계 미국인 둘 다 미국 백인보다 더 높은 비율로 인터넷을 사용하지 않는다고 답했다. 인터넷을 사용하지 않는 것을 선택한 성인의 비율은 18~29세 연령 집단에서는 0%였고, 30~49세 연령 집단에서는 한 자릿수였다. 65세 이상의 인터넷 미사용자 비율은 50~64세 성인 인터넷 미사용자 비율보다 15퍼센트포인트 더 높다. 고등학교 미만의 교육을 받은 성인 10명 중 3명 이상이 인터넷을 사용하지 않는다고 답했지만, 교육 수준이 높아질수록 그 비율은 낮아진다. 인터넷을 사용하지 않는 미국 성인의 비율은 도시와 교외 인구 모두에서 10% 미만인 반면, 미국 성인 농촌 인구의 15%가 자신이 인터넷 사용자가 아니라고 답했다.

해설

고등학교 미만의 교육을 받은 성인 중 29%가 인터넷을 사용하지 않는다고 했으므로, 도표의 내용과 일치하지 않는 것은 ④이다.

구문

- [The percentage of non-internet users aged 65 and older] is 15 percentage points higher than that of adults aged 50-64.
  : [ ]는 문장의 주어이고, 주어의 핵심어가 percentage이므로 단수형 동사 is가 사용되었다.

06 정답 ①

건설 공사가 프로젝트에 근거한 산업이라는 사실은 중요한 쟁점이다. 공사장과 같은 역동적이고 변화하는 환경을 운영하려 시도할 때, 프로젝트의 변화하는 속성에 대처할 적절한 조직 구조가 있어야 한다는 점을 명심해야 한다. 설계에서 공사로 이행할 때, 그리고 (자재의 늦은 배송과 같은) 문제들이 매일매일 발생할 때, 빠른 의사결정과 유연한 조직 형태가 필요하다. 이것은 공사장 근로자들에게서 자유롭고 독립적인 정신을 발생시키고, 전통적으로 권위에 대한 경시를 초래해 왔다. 많은 경우에 있어서, 이런 경시가 도를 넘어 문제를 일으켜 왔다.

해설

(A) it이 가주어이고 진주어가 뒤에 이어지는 구조이므로, 주어 역할을 하는 명사절을 이끌 수 있는 접속사 that을 쓰는 것이 적절하다.
(B) as가 이끄는 두 개의 부사절 뒤에 주절이 이어져야 하므로, 주절을 이끌 수 있는 there를 쓰는 것이 적절하다.
(C) This를 주어로 하는 동사인 engenders와 병렬 구조를 이루는 동사가 와야 하므로 has를 쓰는 것이 적절하다. 부사 traditionally가 현재완료 시제인 has led 사이에 쓰인 형태이다.

도입	건설 공사는 프로젝트에 근거한 산업임
전개	프로젝트의 변화하는 속성에 대처할 조직 구조가 필요함
결론	이로 인해 공사장 근로자들은 자유롭고 독립적인 정신을 갖게 되고 권위를 경시하게 되어 문제를 초래해 옴

구문

- The fact [that construction is a project-based industry] is an important issue.
  : [ ]는 The fact와 동격을 이루는 명사절이다.

07 정답 ①

모든 지능은 가르침을 받아야 한다. 유전적으로 사물을 분류할 준비가 되어 있는 인간의 뇌는, 그럼에도 불구하고 고양이와 개를 구별할 수 있기 전에 어릴 때 십여 개의 예를 볼 필요가 있다. 그것은 인공두뇌에 더욱더 그러하다. 가장 잘 프로그래밍이 된 컴퓨터라도 좋아지기 전에 적어도 천 번의 체스 게임을 해야 한다. 인공 지능의 혁신적 발전의 일부는 우리 세계에 관한 믿을 수 없을 정도로 쇄도하는 수집된 자료에 있는데, 그것은 인공 지능에게 필요한 학교 교육을 제공한다. 거대한 데이터베이스, 자체 추적, 웹 쿠키, 온라인 발자국, 테라바이트의 저장, 수십 년에 걸친 연구 결과, 위키피디아, 그리고 전체 디지털 세계는 인공 지능을 똑똑하게 만들었다. Andrew Ng는 그것을 이렇게 설명한다. "인공 지능은 로켓 우주선을 만드는 것과 유사하다. 여러분은 거대한 엔진과 많은 연료가 필요하다. 로켓 엔진은 학습 알고리즘이지만 연료는 이러한 알고리즘에 우리가 공급할 수 있는 거대한 양의 자료이다."

해설

잘 프로그래밍이 된 컴퓨터도 좋아지기 전에는 천 번의 체스 게임을 해야 하는 것처럼, 믿을 수 없을 정도로 많이 수집된 자료를 인공 지능이 배워야 똑똑한 지능이 될 수 있다는 내용의 글이므로, 빈칸에 들어갈 말로는 ① '가르침을 받아야'가 가장 적절하다.
② 믿어져야   ③ 평가되어야
④ 예측되어야   ⑤ 통제되어야

주제	모든 지능은 아무리 준비가 되어 있다 해도 가르침을 받아야 함
전개	인공 지능은 쇄도하는 수집된 자료를 학습해야 하는데, 그것에는 거대한 데이터베이스, 자체 추적, 웹 쿠키, 온라인 발자국, 테라바이트의 저장, 수십 년에 걸친 연구 결과, 위키피디아, 전체 디지털 세계 등이 있음
부연	인공 지능은 로켓 우주선을 만드는 것과 유사해서, 학습 알고리즘인 로켓 엔진에 거대한 양의 데이터를 공급해야 함

구문

- A human brain, [which is genetically primed to categorize things], still needs to see a dozen examples as a child before it can distinguish between cats and dogs.
  : [ ]는 문장의 주어인 A human brain을 부연 설명하는 관계절이며, 동사는 needs이다.

- Part of the AI breakthrough lies in the incredible avalanche of collected data about our world, [which provides the schooling {that AIs need}].

: [ ]는 the incredible avalanche of collected data about our world를 부연 설명하는 관계절이고, 그 안의 { }는 the schooling을 수식하는 관계절이다.

08

2008년에, 'Who Moved My Cheese?(누가 내 치즈를 옮겼을까?)'라는 경영 서적이 전 세계적으로 37개 언어로 2천 2백만 부가 팔리는 베스트셀러 경영학 서적이 되었는데, 그것은 그렇게 해서 변화에의 개방에 대한 관심을 입증한다. 이 단순한 이야기는 많은 치즈가 있는 미로에 사는 두 명의 인간과 두 마리 쥐에 관해 이야기한다. 그러나 어느 날 그들의 치즈가 사라지고, 그들은 다른 곳에서 치즈를 찾아야만 한다. 쥐들은 이것을 한다. 하지만, 인간들 중 한 명은 현실을 받아들이고 적응하기를 거부하면서, 누가 그의 치즈를 옮겼는지를 알고자 한다. 처음에는 저항을 했던 다른 인간은 자신의 안락 지대를 떠나 변화를 수용해야 한다는 것을 깨닫는다. 여러분이 아는 사람들 중에 기업의 변화, 해고, 구조 조정, 또는 합병을 겪었을 수도 있는 사람들을 생각해 보라. 그들이 책에 나온 쥐처럼 행동했다고 생각하는가, 아니면 저항하는 인간들처럼 행동했다고 생각하는가?

해설
'Who Moved My Cheese?(누가 내 치즈를 옮겼을까?)'는 기존에 그들에게 이익을 주는 것(치즈)이 없어졌을 때 그 변화에 적응하는 쪽과 받아들이지 않고 거부하는 쪽에 대한 이야기이므로, 빈칸에 들어갈 말로는 ② '변화에의 개방'이 가장 적절하다.
① 개인적인 생활 양식
③ 세상에 대한 호기심
④ 전 세계적인 교육에 대한 필요성
⑤ 동료들과의 건전한 관계

TEXT FLOW

도입	'Who Moved My Cheese?(누가 내 치즈를 옮겼을까?)'가 전 세계적으로 베스트셀러가 됨
전개	책 내용에 따르면 치즈가 많이 있는 미로에 살던 사람과 쥐는 치즈가 사라졌을 때 각기 다른 방식으로 반응을 함
결론	현실에서 이와 유사한 상황에 처한 사람들이 어떻게 행동했을지 생각해 볼 필요가 있음

구문

• However, one of the humans refuses to accept reality and adapt, [demanding to know who moved his cheese].
: [ ]는 동시 동작을 나타내는 분사구문이다.

• Think of people [you know] [who may have gone through corporate changes, layoffs, restructuring, or mergers].
: 두 개의 [ ]는 모두 people을 수식하는 관계절로, 첫 번째 [ ]는 앞에 목적격 관계대명사 whom이 생략되었다.

09

국가 집단 간 직접적인 무력 사용이 금지된 경우에도 군사력은 여전히 정치적으로 사용될 수 있다. 냉전 기간에 각 초강대국은 자국이나 동맹국에 대한 다른 초강대국의 공격을 저지하기 위해 무력 위협을 사용했으며, 따라서 억지력은 동맹국과의 다른 문제에 대한 협상에서 사용할 수 있는 간접적이며

보호적인 역할을 수행했다. 이 협상 도구는 동맹국들이 소련의 잠재적 위협에 대해 우려하고 있었고, 소련이 동유럽 파트너들에 대해 가졌던 것보다 동맹국들에 영향력을 미치는 다른 수단이 더 적었던 미국에게 특히 중요했다. 따라서 미국은 유럽인들의(특히 독일인들의) 보호에 대한 갈망을 이용했고 유럽 내 병력 수준 문제를 무역 및 통화 협상과 연계했다. (지속 가능한 경제 발전의 핵심 요소는 군사적 충돌과 긴장이 없는 것이며, 이는 국가 간의 긴밀한 협력을 통해서만 달성할 수 있다.) 따라서 억지력의 일차적 효과는 초강대국 상대에게 효과적인 공격력을 허락하지 않는 본질적으로 거부적인 측면이 있었지만, 국가는 정치적 영향력을 얻기 위해 그 힘을 긍정적으로 사용할 수 있었다.

해설
직접적인 무력 사용이 아니더라도 군사력은 여전히 정치적으로 사용될 수 있으며, 냉전 시대의 미국이 군사적 억지력을 동맹국과의 협상에서 유리하게 사용했다는 내용의 글이다. 따라서 지속 가능한 경제 발전의 핵심 요소가 군사적 충돌과 긴장이 없는 것이라는 내용의 ④는 글의 전체 흐름과 관계가 없다.

⊗ 매력적인 오답 주의!
③ 미국이 유럽 내 병력 수준 문제를 무역 및 통화 협상과 연계했다는 내용을 군사력이 정치적으로 사용되었다는 글의 중심 내용과 연결 짓지 못하면 고를 수 있는 오답이다.

TEXT FLOW

주제	직접적인 무력 사용이 금지된 경우에도 군사력은 정치적으로 이용될 수 있음
예시 1	냉전 기간에 군사적 억지력은 동맹국과의 다른 문제에 대한 협상에서 활용이 가능했음
예시 2	미국은 유럽인들의 군사적 보호에 대한 갈망을 무역 및 통화 협상과 연계하여 이용함
재진술	군사적 억지력을 정치적 영향력을 얻기 위해 사용할 수도 있음

구문

• During the Cold War each superpower used the threat of force [to deter attacks by other superpowers on itself or its allies]; its deterrence ability thus served an indirect, protective role, [which it could use in bargaining on other issues with its allies].
: 첫 번째 [ ]는 목적의 의미를 나타내는 부사적 용법의 to부정사구이다. 두 번째 [ ]는 an indirect, protective role을 부가적으로 설명하는 관계절이다.

• This bargaining tool was particularly important for the United States, [whose allies were concerned about potential Soviet threats] and [which had **fewer** other means of influence over its allies **than did the Soviet Union** over its Eastern European partners].
: 두 개의 [ ]는 the United States를 부가적으로 설명하는 관계절이다. 두 번째 [ ]에서 비교급을 나타내는 than 다음에 주어인 the Soviet Union과 had other means of influence를 대신하는 조동사 did가 도치되었다.

10

아프리카에서는 날씨가 더우며 여러 달 동안 계속해서 비가 오지 않는다. 많은 지역에서 거의 아무것도 자라지 않는다. 이곳들은 사막이며, 이집트의 양쪽에 있는 땅도 그렇다. 이집트도 역시 거의 비가 오지 않는다. (C) 그러나 이곳 사람들은 그것(비)을 필요로 하지 않는데, 그 이유는 그 나라의 한쪽 끝에서 다른 쪽 끝까지 정중앙을 관통하여 흐르는 나일강 때문이다. 일 년에 두 번 폭우가 그 수원을 채우면, 강물이 불어나고 제방을 터뜨려서, 땅 전체를 침수시키곤 했다. (B) 그러면 사람들은 어쩔 수 없이 배를 타고 집들과 야자나무들 사이를 움직여야 했다. 그리고 물이 물러가면 그 땅은 놀랍도록 흠뻑 적셔져 있고 질척거리는 진흙으로 비옥해 있었다. (A) 그 진흙은 영양분이 풍부했다. 뜨거운 태양 아래에서, 그곳은 다른 곳과 달리 곡물이 잘 자랐다. 그래서 아주 예전부터 이집트인들이 나일강을 마치 신 그 자체인 것처럼 숭배했던 것이다.

해설
아프리카에서 여러 달 동안 비가 오지 않아 거의 아무것도 자라지 않는 것처럼 이집트에도 거의 비가 오지 않는다는 내용의 주어진 글 다음에는, 이집트는 나라를 관통하여 흐르는 나일강이 있어 비가 필요 없다는 내용의 (C)가 오고, (C)에서 언급된 나일강의 홍수로 인해 이집트 땅은 질척거리는 진흙으로 비옥해진다는 내용의 (B)가 이어진 다음, 영양분이 풍부해진 토양 덕분에 이집트에서는 곡물이 잘 자랐다는 (A)가 마지막에 오는 것이 글의 흐름상 가장 자연스럽다.

TEXT FLOW
도입	아프리카와 이집트의 적은 강우량
발전	이집트에서는 일 년에 두 번 나일강이 범람함
전개	나일강의 범람 후에는 땅이 진흙으로 변해 비옥해짐
결론	영양분이 풍부한 진흙으로 인해 곡물이 잘 자라 예전부터 이집트인들은 나일강을 숭배했음

구문
• Twice a year, when heavy rain filled its sources, the river **would** swell and burst its banks, [flooding the whole land].
: would는 과거에 반복된 행동을 나타내어 '~하곤 했다'의 의미로 해석된다. [ ]는 연속 동작을 나타내는 분사구문이다.

11

내 강의들 중 하나를 듣던 어떤 사람이 많은 혼란을 겪고 있었는데, '고통'이라는 단어가 대화 중에 계속 나왔다. 그녀는 자신이 사용할 수 있는 또 다른 단어가 있는지를 물었다. 나는 창문을 쾅 닫아서 내 손가락을 세게 쳤던 때에 관해 생각했다. 나는 내가 그 고통에 굴복하면 매우 어려운 시기를 겪게 되리라는 것을 알고 있었다. 그래서 그 일이 일어났을 때, 나는 바로 약간의 정신노동을 하기 시작했고 내 손가락을 많은 감각을 가지고 있는 것으로 보았다. 그런 특별한 방식으로 일어난 일을 봄으로써, 나는 그것이 그 손가락을 훨씬 더 빠르게 치유하고 매우 불쾌한 경험이었을 수도 있는 것을 처리하는 데 도움이 되었다고 생각한다. 때때로 우리의 생각을 조금 바꿀 수 있으면, 우리는 상황을 완전히 바꿀 수 있다.

해설
주어진 문장은 창문을 쾅 닫아 손가락을 세게 쳤을 때 약간의 정신노동을 하기 시작해서 손가락이 많은 감각을 가진 것으로 보고 고통을 넘겼다는 내용

이므로, 주어진 문장의 내용을 받는 in that particular way가 있는 문장 앞인 ④에 들어가는 것이 가장 적절하다.

TEXT FLOW
도입	필자의 강의를 듣던 어떤 사람이 '고통'이라는 단어 이외에 또 다른 단어를 사용할 수 있는지 물어봄
전개	손가락을 창문에 세게 부딪쳤을 때 약간의 정신노동을 통해 고통을 극복한 필자의 상황을 언급함
결론	생각을 조금 바꾸면 상황을 완전히 바꿀 수 있음

구문
• I thought about the time [I had smashed my finger by slamming a window on it].
: [ ]는 관계부사 when이 생략된 관계절로 선행사 the time을 수식한다.

• By viewing what happened in that particular way, I think it helped [to heal the finger much more quickly] and [to handle what could have been a very unpleasant experience].
: 두 개의 [ ]는 helped의 목적어로 쓰인 to부정사구로 and에 의해 병렬 구조를 이루고 있다.

12

만약 여러분이 당구대 판매업자라면, 잠재 구매자에게 329달러짜리 모델과 3,000달러짜리 모델 중 어떤 상품을 먼저 보여 주겠는가? 여러분은 아마도 고객이 구매하러 왔을 때 가격이 더 낮은 상품을 먼저 홍보하고 고객이 더 고가의 상품에 관심을 갖게 하고 싶을 것이다. 하지만 Brunswick의 영업부장인 G. Warren Kelley는 여러분의 생각이 틀릴 수 있다고 말한다. Kelley는 자신의 주장을 증명하기 위해 한 대표 매장의 실제 매출액을 제시한다. 첫 주에는 고객들에게 저가 종류의 상품을 보여 준 다음 더 비싼 모델을 고려하도록 권유하는 전통적인 '트레이딩 업' 방식을 사용했다. 그 주 평균 당구대 판매액은 550달러였다. 그러나 두 번째 주에는 고객이 보기를 원하는 것과 상관없이 3,000달러짜리 당구대로 즉시 안내한 다음 나머지 시간에는 가격과 품질이 떨어지는 순서대로 쇼핑할 수 있도록 했다. 비싼 상품을 먼저 보여 준 후 더 저렴한 상품을 제시한 결과는 평균 1,000달러 이상의 매출액으로 이어졌다.

➡ G. Warren Kelley의 사례는 고객에게 <u>값비싼</u> 상품을 먼저 보여 주면 매출액을 <u>늘릴</u> 수 있음을 보여 준다.

해설
G. Warren Kelley에 따르면 고객들에게 저가 종류의 당구대를 먼저 보여주고 더 고가의 모델을 고려하도록 하는 방식보다, 먼저 비싼 당구대를 보여준 후 가격과 품질이 떨어지는 순서대로 고객이 쇼핑하도록 유도하는 방식의 매출액이 더 높았다는 내용의 글이다. 따라서 요약문의 빈칸 (A)에는 pricey(값비싼)가, (B)에는 increase(늘릴)가 들어가는 것이 가장 적절하다.
② 값비싼 – 줄일
③ 저렴한 – 늘릴
④ 새로운 – 줄일
⑤ 새로운 – 유지할

✖ 매력적인 오답 주의!
③ 글의 초반부에 언급된 일반적인 '트레이딩 업' 방식을 사용하여 매출액을 늘렸다고 오인하면 고를 수 있는 오답이다.

TEXT FLOW

도입	가격이 저렴한 상품을 고객에게 먼저 보여 주는 것이 일반적인 생각임
주제	G. Warren Kelley는 이러한 생각이 틀릴 수 있다고 함
전개	전통적인 '트레이딩 업' 방식과 값비싼 상품을 먼저 보여 주는 방식의 주별 평균 매출액을 비교함
결론	비싼 상품을 먼저 보여 주고 이후 더 저렴한 상품을 안내하는 방식이 더 높은 매출액을 기록함

구문

• If you **were** a billiard-table dealer, which **would** you first **show** [a potential buyer] — a $329 model or a $3,000 model?

: 가정법 과거의 표현이 사용되어 if절에는 be동사 were가, 주절에는 과거형 조동사와 동사원형인 would show가 쓰였다. [ ]는 show의 간접목적어이다.

• However, during the second week, customers were [led instantly to a $3,000 table, regardless of {what they wanted to see}], and then [allowed to shop the rest of the time in declining order of price and quality].

: 두 개의 [ ]는 and로 병렬 연결되어 were에 이어져 각각 수동태를 이루고, 첫 번째 [ ] 안의 { }는 regardless of의 목적어 역할을 하는 명사절이다.

13~14

정답 13 ④ 14 ④

대부분의 사람들은 직장에서 지적으로 보이려고 노력하면서 자신의 시간을 보내며, 지난 50년 남짓 사람들은 과학자처럼 보이려고 노력함으로써 지적으로 보이려고 애써 왔다. 만약 여러분이 누군가에게 어떤 일이 왜 발생했는지 설명해 보라고 질문하면 그들은 대체로 여러분에게 그럴듯하게 들리는 대답을 할 것인데, 그것이 그들을 지적이거나, 합리적이거나, 또는 과학적인 것처럼 보이게 하지만, 그것은 진짜 대답일 수도 아닐 수도 있다. 여기서의 문제는 현실 생활은 전통적인 과학이 아니라는 것인데, 이를테면 보잉 787을 설계할 때는 그토록 효과가 좋았던 도구가 소비자의 경험이나 세금 프로그램을 고안할 때는 효과가 없을 수도 있다는 것이다. 사람들은 탄소 섬유나 금속 합금처럼 유연하거나 혹은 예측 가능하지 않으며, 우리는 그들이 그러하다고 가정해서도 안 된다. 경제학의 아버지인 Adam Smith는 18세기 후반에 이 문제를 파악했지만, 그것은 그 이후로 많은 경제학자들에 의해 무시되어 온 가르침이다. 여러분이 과학자처럼 보이고 싶다면, 확실한 분위기를 구축하는 것은 이득이 되지만 확실성에 애착을 갖는 것의 문제는 사람들이 그것 때문에 검토되고 있는 문제의 본질을 마치 그것이 심리학적인 문제가 아니라 간단한 물리학적 문제인 것처럼 완전히 이해하게(→ 잘못 이해하게) 한다는 것이다. 따라서 사물이 사실상 그러한 것보다 더 '논리적인' 것처럼 가장하는 영원히 존재하는 유혹이 있다.

해설

13 우리는 마치 우리가 과학자인 것처럼 현실을 설명하려고 하지만 현실은 과학의 법칙처럼 명료하게 설명될 수 있는 것이 아니며 그렇게 하려 해서도 안 된다는 내용의 글이므로, 글의 제목으로 가장 적절한 것은 ④ '현실에서 확실성을 찾고자 하는 욕구를 경계하라'이다.

① 여러분의 이론에 대한 근거를 찾는 것을 잊지 말라
② 논리적으로 생각하라는 내면의 목소리를 우리가 그토록 자주 묵살하는

이유
③ 가짜 과학과 진짜 과학의 차이
⑤ 우리의 과학적 도구들은 자연 현상을 설명하지 못한다

14 현실 문제는 과학이 아니므로 확실성에 애착을 가지고 표현하는 것은 그것이 심리학적 문제인데 물리학적 문제로 잘못 이해하게 하여 문제의 본질을 흐린다는 맥락이므로, (d) understand(이해하다)를 mistake(잘못 이해하다)와 같은 단어로 바꿔야 한다.

TEXT FLOW

도입	사람들은 과학자처럼 보이려고 함으로써 지적으로 보이고 싶어 함
전환	현실 생활은 전통적인 과학과는 다름
예시	보잉 787을 설계하는 것과 소비자 경험이나 세금 프로그램을 고안하는 것은 다름
결론	확실성에 대한 집착은 현실 생활을 물리학적 문제처럼 잘못 이해하게 함

구문

• ~ if you ask someone to explain [why something happened], they will generally give you a plausible-sounding answer [that makes them seem intelligent, rational or scientific] but [that may or may not be the real answer].

: 첫 번째 [ ]는 explain의 목적어 역할을 하는 명사절이고, 두 번째와 세 번째 [ ]는 a plausible-sounding answer를 수식하는 관계절이다.

• [If you want to look like a scientist], [it pays {to cultivate an air of certainty}], but [{the problem with attachment to certainty} is that it **causes** people completely **to mistake** the nature of the problem being examined], [**as if** it **were** a simple physics problem rather than a psychological one].

: 네 개의 절 [ ]가 연결된 문장으로, 첫 번째 [ ]는 조건의 부사절, 두 번째와 세 번째 [ ]는 접속사 but으로 연결된 주절이다. 두 번째 [ ]에서 it은 가주어이고 { }가 진주어이다. 세 번째 [ ]에서 causes의 목적격 보어로 to mistake로 시작하는 to부정사구가 쓰였다. 네 번째 [ ]에는 「as if+가정법 과거(마치 ~인 것처럼)」 구문이 사용되었다.

GRAMMAR REVIEW

본문 113쪽

1 that	2 resulting	3 them
4 taken	5 building	6 that
7 did	8 referred	9 encouraged
10 designing, designing		

1 a magazine을 수식하는 관계절을 이끌고, 관계절에서 주어의 역할을 하므로 관계대명사 that이 적절하다.

2 주절 This damages the lining of the gut가 원인이 되어 생기는 결과를 나타내는 분사구문으로, 능동의 의미이므로 현재분사 resulting을 써야 한다.

3 throw의 동작 주체는 you이고 대상은 boomerangs이므로 재귀대명사 themselves가 아니라 대명사 them이 적절하다.

4 this disregard가 동작의 대상이므로 현재완료 수동태가 되도록 과거

분사 taken을 써야 한다.

5 to가 전치사이므로 동명사 building을 써야 한다.

6 동사 realizes의 목적어 역할을 하는 명사절을 이끌어야 하며 뒤에 완전한 형태의 절이 이어지므로 접속사 that이 적절하다.

7 문맥상 had other means of influence라는 일반 동사구를 대신해야 하므로, 대동사의 역할을 할 수 있는 조동사 did가 적절하다.

8 I를 주어로 하여 동사 started와 and로 연결되어 병렬 구조를 이루고 있으므로 과거 동사 referred가 적절하다.

9 문장의 주어인 customers가 설득의 주체가 아닌 대상이므로 were에 이어져 수동태를 이룰 수 있는 과거분사 encouraged가 적절하다.

10 각각 시간의 부사절에서 「대명사 주어+be동사」가 생략된 형태이며 능동의 의미이므로 현재분사 designing을 써야 한다.

하프 모의고사   14회

01 ⑤	02 ⑤	03 ①	04 ③	05 ③
06 ③	07 ③	08 ④	09 ②	10 ②
11 ④	12 ②	13 ①	14 ⑤	

01   정답 ⑤

약 한 달 동안, Joe는 테니스를 치기 위해 몸을 푸는 동안 숨참과 가슴의 압박감을 알아차렸다. 약 10분이 지나면, 이러한 느낌들은 사라지곤 했다. 통증이 심하지는 않았고, 그것이 확실히 경기를 멈출 만큼 충분히 걱정스러운 것은 아니었다. 그래서 그는 그것을 대수롭지 않게 생각했다. 일주일을 기다려 이런 느낌들이 저절로 사라질 것인지를 지켜본 후, 그는 가족 주치의와의 진료 예약을 잡았다. 그녀는 그의 검사를 하면서 걱정하는 것 같았고 그를 심장병 전문의에게 보냈다. 한 번의 검사가 여러 번의 검사로 이어졌다. 진단은 결코 Joe가 기대했던 것이 아니었다. "Joe, 당신에게 관상 동맥 심장 질환이 있어요."라고 의사가 말했다. "그것이 심각하기 때문에, 며칠 안으로 수술할 것을 권해요." Joe는 그녀의 말을 들은 후 바닥에 쓰러졌고 한동안 일어설 수가 없었다.

해설

Joe는 테니스를 치기 위해 몸을 푸는 동안 숨참과 가슴의 압박감을 알아차렸으나 금방 사라졌기 때문에 크게 신경 쓰지 않았지만, 일주일 후에 심장병 전문의에게 검사를 받고 나서 관상 동맥 심장 질환으로 며칠 내로 수술을 받아야 한다는 말에 충격을 받고 바닥에 쓰러졌으므로, Joe의 심경 변화로 가장 적절한 것은 ⑤ '개의치 않는 → 충격받은'이다.

① 걱정하는 → 안도하는   ② 후회하는 → 자신감 있는
③ 실망한 → 고마워하는   ④ 관심 있는 → 무관심한

TEXT FLOW

시간 순서/사건 전개에 따른 흐름:
Joe는 테니스를 치기 위해 몸을 푸는 동안 숨참과 가슴의 압박감을 알아차림 → 통증이 곧 사라지고 심하지 않아 대수롭지 않게 생각함 → 일주일 후 심장병 전문의에게 검사를 받음 → 관상 동맥 심장 질환으로 곧 수술을 받아야 한다는 의사의 말을 듣고 충격을 받음

구문

• After waiting one week [to see {if these feelings would clear up on their own}], he made an appointment with his family doctor.
: [ ]는 목적의 의미를 나타내는 부사적 용법의 to부정사구이고, 그 안의 { }는 see의 목적어 역할을 하는 명사절이다.

• Joe [fell to the ground after hearing her words] and [couldn't stand up for quite a while].
: 두 개의 동사구 [ ]는 and로 연결되어 문장의 술어 동사 역할을 한다.

02   정답 ⑤

고치기 어려운 버릇이기는 하지만, 주목을 받고자 하는 욕구를 포기하고 그

대신 다른 사람의 영광의 즐거움을 함께 나눌 수 있는 편안한 자신감을 가지는 것은 즐거울 뿐 아니라 사실상 평화롭기도 하다. 불쑥 곧바로 끼어들어 "나도 전에 같은 일을 했어요." 또는 "내가 오늘 뭘 했는지 맞혀 보세요."라고 말하는 대신, 말하지 말고 참으면서 무슨 일이 일어나는지 알아차려라. 그저 "그거 근사하군요." 또는 "더 말해 주세요."라고 말하고 그대로 두라. 여러분이 말을 주고받고 있는 그 사람은 훨씬 더 즐거워할 것이고, 여러분이 그 자리에 더욱 많이 '존재하기' 때문에, 여러분이 매우 경청하고 있기 때문에, 그 사람은 여러분과 경쟁하고 있다는 느낌을 받지 않을 것이다. 결과는 그 사람이 여러분과 함께 있을 때 더 편안한 기분을 느끼고, 그 사람이 더 재미있다고 느낄 뿐 아니라 더 자신감 있게 느낄 것이라는 것이다. 여러분도 자신의 차례를 기다리며 의자에서 몸을 내밀고 있지 않을 것이므로 더 느긋한 기분을 느낄 것이다.

해설
대화에서 자신이 말을 하여 주목을 끌고자 하는 욕구를 버리고 다른 사람의 말을 경청하면, 상대방은 대화를 통해 즐거움을 느끼게 되며 듣는 사람은 마음이 느긋한 상태로 대화를 즐길 수 있다는 내용이므로, 글의 요지로 가장 적절한 것은 ⑤이다.

TEXT FLOW

도입	주목받고자 하는 욕구를 포기하고 다른 사람의 즐거움을 함께 나눌 것을 권함
전개	말하는 중간에 끼어들지 말고 경청하며 듣고 있다는 정도로만 반응을 보일 것을 제안함
부연	자신의 경청은 상대방에게 즐거움을 느끼게 해 줌
결론	자신 역시 즐겁고 편안하게 대화에 참여할 수 있음

구문
• [The person {you are speaking to}] will have so much more fun, and [because you are so much more "present,"] [because you are listening so carefully], he or she won't feel in competition with you.
: 첫 번째 [ ]는 and 앞에 있는 절의 주어이고, 그 안의 { }는 The person을 수식하는 관계절인데, 목적격 관계대명사가 you 앞에 생략되어 있다. 두 번째와 세 번째 [ ]는 and 뒤에 오는 절에서 이유를 나타내는 부사절이다.

03
정답 ①

훈련을 받고 있는 선수는 자신의 근육 양 증가, 즉 몸 안의 단백질 총량을 증가시키고 있는 중이다. 많은 사람들은 이것이 그들이 식단에 더 많은 단백질을 필요로 한다는 것을 의미하고, 이것이 어느 정도는 맞는 말이라고 생각한다. 그러나, 급격한 회복 성장을 보이는, 심각한 영양실조에서 회복 중인 아이들에게서조차 체내 단백질 증가량은 매일 합성되고 분해되는 단백질 총량의 절반에도 미치지 못한다. 단백질의 평균 섭취가 충분히 필요한 양을 초과하기 때문에, 훈련을 통해 근육을 얻고 있을 때, 체내 단백질의 총량을 증가시키기 위해 식단에 더 많은 단백질, 특히 단백질 보충제 섭취를 통한 더 많은 단백질을 필요로 하지 않는다. 반면에, 새로운 단백질 합성에 드는 노력과 훈련 및 증가한 신체 활동에 드는 에너지 모두를 충족시키기 위해 에너지 섭취를 늘릴 필요가 있다. 만약 어떤 운동선수가 평상시 먹는 음식보다 더 많은 양을 먹는다면, 그 사람은 자동적으로 에너지뿐만 아니라 단백질 섭취를 증가시킬 것이다. 그러므로 운동선수들을 위해 광고되는 단백질 보충제는 불필요해 보인다.

해설
훈련을 받으면서 근육을 키워 가는 운동선수가 식단에 더 많은 단백질 공급을 위해 단백질 보충제를 먹는 것은 불필요해 보인다는 내용의 글이다. 따라서 글의 제목으로 가장 적절한 것은 ① '운동선수를 위한 단백질 보충제에 대한 잘못된 믿음'이다.
② 단백질을 지나치게 많이 섭취할 때 생기는 일
③ 식단에 단백질이 많으면 많을수록 더 건강해진다
④ 단백질 합성 과정 사이의 맹렬한 경쟁
⑤ 단백질 보충제: 운동선수를 위한 그럴듯한 유혹

TEXT FLOW

도입	운동선수가 단백질 총량 증가를 위해 식단에 더 많은 단백질이 필요하다는 것은 어느 정도 맞는 말임
전환	그러나 단백질 총량 증가를 위해 식단에 더 많은 단백질이 필요하지는 않으며, 특별히 단백질 보충제를 섭취할 필요도 없음
부연	평상시 먹는 음식을 더 많이 먹으면 자동적으로 에너지뿐만 아니라 단백질 섭취량이 늘어남
결론	운동선수에게 단백질 보충제는 불필요해 보임

구문
• However, even in children [recovering from severe malnutrition], [who show rapid catch-up growth], the gain in body protein is less than half the total amount of protein [that is synthesized and broken down each day].
: 첫 번째 [ ]는 children을 수식하는 현재분사구이고, 두 번째 [ ]는 children recovering from severe malnutrition을 부연 설명하는 관계절이다. 세 번째 [ ]는 protein을 수식하는 관계절이다.

• On the other hand, there is a need for increased energy intake [to meet **both** the cost of new protein synthesis **and** the energy cost of training and increased physical activity].
: [ ]는 목적을 나타내는 부사적 용법의 to부정사구로 「both A and B」 구문이 쓰였다.

04
정답 ③

Aaron Copland는 New York 주의 Brooklyn에서 1900년 11월 14일에 다섯 자녀 중 막내로 태어났다. Copland의 누나 중 한 명이 그가 11살이었을 때 그에게 피아노 치는 법을 보여 주었고, 곧 그 후 그는 이웃의 어느 선생님으로부터 (피아노) 강습을 받기 시작했다. 1921년에, 그는 공부하러 프랑스에 갔고 1924년에 공부를 마쳤는데, 그때 그는 미국으로 되돌아와서 자신의 첫 주요 작품인 'Symphony for Organ and Orchestra'를 작곡했다. 1920년대 후반에, Copland는 점점 더 실험적인 형식을 시도했는데, 불규칙한 리듬과 흔히 귀에 거슬리는 소리가 그 특징이었다. 1930년대 중반에 시작되어 1950년까지, Copland는 미국 음악에 대한 청중의 저변을 확대하기 위해 진지한 노력을 했고 서로 다른 행사를 위해 요청받은 곡을 쓸 때는 자신의 형식을 바꾸는 조치를 취했다. 그는 콘서트 상황을 위한 음악뿐만 아니라 연극, 발레, 영화를 위한 음악도 작곡했다. Aaron Copland는 20세기 두 번째 분기 동안 미국 음악에서 가장 중요한 인물 중 한 명이었는데, 작곡가이면서 미국인들로 하여금 음악의 중요성을 알게 만드는 것에 관심을 가진 대변자로서 모두 그러했다.

해설
Copland가 점점 더 실험적인 형식을 시도해서 불규칙한 리듬과 귀에 거슬리는 소리를 사용하기 시작한 것은 1920년대 후반이므로, 글의 내용과 일치하지 않는 것은 ③이다.

- In 1921, he [went to France to study] and [completed his studies in 1924, {when he returned to America and composed the *Symphony for Organ and Orchestra*, his first major work}].
: 두 개의 [ ]는 and로 연결되어 문장의 술어 동사 역할을 한다. 두 번째 [ ] 안의 { }는 1924를 부연 설명하는 관계절이다.

- Aaron Copland was [**one of the most** important **figures** in American music during the second quarter of the twentieth century], both as a composer and as a spokesman [who was concerned about making {Americans} {aware of the importance of music}].
: 첫 번째 [ ]는 was의 주격 보어 역할을 하는 명사구로서 「one of the+최상급+복수 명사」 구문이 쓰였다. 두 번째 [ ]는 a spokesman을 수식하는 관계절이고, 그 안의 첫 번째 { }는 making의 목적어, 두 번째 { }는 목적격 보어이다.

- Hydropower often requires the use of dams, [which can greatly affect the flow of rivers, {thereby altering ecosystems and affecting the wildlife and people ⟨that depend on those waters⟩}].
: [ ]는 dams를 부연 설명하는 관계절이고, 그 안의 { }는 관계절 내의 상황에 대한 결과를 나타내는 분사구문이며, 그 안의 ⟨ ⟩는 the wildlife and people을 수식하는 관계절이다.

- Nutrients and stream load (sediments) [necessary for the health and balance of the waterway], [which would have naturally been carried down river], become trapped in the reservoir behind the dam.
: 첫 번째 [ ]는 문장의 주어인 Nutrients and stream load (sediments)를 수식하는 형용사구이고, 두 번째 [ ]는 Nutrients ~ the waterway를 부연 설명하는 관계절이다. 술어 동사는 become trapped이다.

05
정답 ③

수력 전기의 공기 오염 배출은 전력 생산에서 어떤 연료도 연소되지 않기 때문에 무시해도 좋을 정도이다. 그러나, 댐이 건설될 때 강바닥을 따라 많은 양의 식물이 자라고 있다면, 그것이 생성되는 호수에서 썩어 메탄의 증식과 방출을 유발할 수 있다. 수력 전기는 흔히 댐의 사용을 필요로 하는데, 그것이 강물의 흐름에 크게 영향을 미치고, 그로 인해 생태계를 변화시키며 그 물에 의존하는 야생 동물과 사람들에게 영향을 미칠 수 있다. 흔히, 댐에 의해 만들어진 호수 바닥의 물은 꼭대기에 있는 물에 비해 훨씬 더 차갑고 산소가 부족하기 때문에 물고기가 지내기 좋다(→ 지내기 힘들다). 이렇게 더 차갑고 산소가 부족한 물이 강으로 방출되면, 그것은 더 따뜻하고 산소가 풍부한 물에 익숙한 하류에 사는 물고기들을 죽일 수 있다. 상류 수원지에서 침식된 물질들 또한 댐으로 모이고, 시간이 흐르면서 그것들은 건져 올려져야 하는 거대한 미사(微砂) 침전물로 채워지게 된다. 자연스레 강 아래로 내려갔을, 수로의 건전과 균형에 필요한 영양소와 하천 부하(퇴적물)가 댐 뒤쪽의 저수지에 갇히게 된다. 이것은 부정적인 영향을 미칠 수 있다.

해설
수력 전기를 위해 댐이 지어질 때 그것이 생태계를 변화시키고 그 물에 의존하는 야생 동물과 사람들에게 부정적인 영향을 미친다는 내용의 글이다. 댐에 갇힌 호수 바닥의 물은 더 차갑고 산소가 부족해서 물고기가 지내기 힘들다는 흐름이 적절하므로, ③ hospitable(지내기 좋은)을 inhospitable(지내기 힘든)과 같은 단어로 바꿔야 한다.

TEXT FLOW

도입	수력 전기를 위한 댐 건설의 영향에 대한 언급
주제	수력 전기에 쓰일 댐 건설은 강물의 흐름에 영향을 미치고, 그로 인해 생태계가 변화되어 그 물에 의존하는 야생 동물과 사람들에게 영향을 미치게 됨
근거 1	댐에 의해 만들어진 호수 바닥의 물은 더 차갑고 산소가 부족하기 때문에 물고기가 지내기 힘들고, 또한 강에 방출될 경우 따뜻하고 산소가 풍부한 물에 익숙한 하류에 사는 물고기를 죽일 수 있음
근거 2	댐에 거대한 미사(微砂) 침전물이 채워지면서 부정적인 영향을 미칠 수 있음

06
정답 ③

권위주의적인 어른으로 바뀌는 반항적인 젊은이는 흔히 관찰되는 역설이다. 나는 Charlotte Linde가 연구했던 대화를 나눈 경찰관들이, 젊은이 특유의 무모한 행위들과 자신들이 철부지 시절에 얼마나 교묘하게 법을 어겼는지에 대한 이야기를 주고받으면서, 그들이 얼마나 '나쁜 소년들'이었는지에 대해 자주 이야기를 했다는 그녀의 관찰 결과를 듣고, 처음에 놀랐던 것이 생각난다. 퍼즐처럼 보이는 이런 현상은 내가 세상의 모습을 계급적 사회 질서로 이해하게 되기까지는 해결되지 않았다. 권위에 도전하는 '타고난 반항아들'은 그것(권위)을 의식하지 못하는 것이 아니라, 그것에 대해 매우 과민하다. 권위에 도전하는 것은 그들 자신의 주장을 펼치고 종속적인 위치를 받아들이기를 거부하는 한 방법이다. 그들이 지배적인 위치를 차지할 만큼 충분히 나이가 들거나 정착하게 되었을 때는, 이제는 계급 제도가 그들에게 유리하게 작용하고 있기 때문에, 권위를 강화하는 것이 그들이 자기 주장을 펼치는 방법이 된다.

해설
권위에 도전하던 젊은 반항아들이 어른이 되어서는 오히려 그런 권위가 그들에게 이득이 되기 때문에 권위주의자가 된다는 내용이므로, 빈칸에 들어갈 말로는 ③ '권위주의적인 어른으로 바뀌는 반항적인 젊은이'가 가장 적절하다.
① 큰 손해를 보게 되는 준법 시민
② 미래에 승자가 되는 오늘의 패자
④ 위계 질서를 권장하는 민주적인 정치인
⑤ 매우 충격적인 경험이 있는 자기 주장이 강한 사람

TEXT FLOW

도입	어릴 때 반항적이었던 젊은이가 커서 권위주의적인 어른이 되는 역설
전개	반항아들이 권위에 도전하는 것은 그들 자신의 주장을 펼치고 종속적인 위치를 거부하는 한 방법임
주제	그들이 지배적인 위치를 차지하면 그때는 계급 제도가 그들의 이익에 부합하기 때문에 권위주의적이 됨

구문

- I recall being surprised at first to hear Charlotte Linde's

observation [that policemen {whose conversations she had studied} talked frequently about what "bad boys" they had been, {trading stories about their youthful escapades and how cleverly they had broken the law in their wild days}].
: [ ]는 Charlotte Linde's observation의 구체적인 내용을 설명하는 동격절이다. 그 안의 첫 번째 { }는 policemen을 선행사로 하는 관계절이고, 두 번째 { }는 동시 동작을 나타내는 분사구문이다.

• This seeming puzzle was **not** solved **until** I came to understand the view of the world as a hierarchical social order.
: 'B할 때까지는 A하지 않다'를 의미하는 「not A until B」 구문이 쓰였다.

07
정답 ③

무료함은 창의적 과정과 어떤 상관이 있을까? 분명 많은 상관이 있다. 창의력을 진짜 발휘하기 위해서, <u>정신은 아이디어를 배양하기 위한 비가동 시간을 필요로 한다.</u> 이것은 마음이 소셜 미디어 게시물, 몰아서 보기 또는 비디오 게임에 몰두하여 심하게 바쁠 때는 발생하지 않는다. 창의적 과정의 모든 측면에 관여하기 위해서 정신은 조용한 시간을 필요로 한다. 하지만, 오늘날 사람들은 스크린 장치에 너무 열중해서 창의적인 과정이 방해를 받는다. 창의력 전문가들은 이제 무료함이 창의적 과정에 필수적이라는 것에 동의한다. 그들은 정신에 아무것도 하지 않을 기회를 주기 위해 스크린 장치에서 플러그를 뽑고 전용 시간을 마련할 것을 제안한다. 마음을 고요히 하는 법을 배우는 것은 창의적 과정이 펼쳐지도록 하는 데 있어 중요한 전조로 여겨진다. 중국의 철학자인 공자의 말에 따르면 "씨앗은 소리 없이 자라지만, 나무는 큰 소리를 내며 쓰러진다. 파괴에는 소음이 있지만, 창조는 조용하다. 이것이 침묵의 힘이다."

해설
무료함은 창의적 과정과 많은 상관이 있다는 내용의 글이다. 창의적 과정의 모든 측면에 관여하기 위해서 정신은 조용한 시간을 필요로 한다고 했으므로, 빈칸에 들어갈 말로 가장 적절한 것은 ③ '정신은 아이디어를 배양하기 위한 비가동 시간을 필요로 한다'이다.
① 우리는 우리의 마음이 계속 기능하도록 해야 한다
② 게으름은 우리의 뇌를 위해 아무것도 할 수 없다
④ 오래된 생각은 새로운 생각과 결합되어야 한다
⑤ 우리의 표류하는 마음을 정상인 것으로 받아들이는 것이 중요하다

TEXT FLOW
도입	무료함이 창의적 과정과 어떤 상관이 있을지 의문 제기
전개	창의적 과정에 관여하기 위해 정신은 조용한 시간을 필요로 함
결론	마음을 고요히 하는 법을 배우는 것이 창의적 과정에 중요함

구문
• The mind needs quiet time [to engage all aspects of the creative process].
: [ ]는 목적의 의미를 나타내는 부사적 용법의 to부정사구이다.

• However, today people are **so** consumed with their screen devices **that** the creative process is stifled.
: '너무 ~해서 …하다'라는 의미의 「so ~ that ....」 구문이 사용되었다.

08
정답 ④

모든 형태의 유머와 마찬가지로, 역경에 대처하기 위한 유머의 사용은 대개 사회적 맥락에서 이루어진다. 사람들은 대체로 완전히 혼자 있을 때는 자신의 문제에 대해 웃고 농담을 하지 않는다. 대신, (역경) 대처를 위한 유머는 일반적으로 부정적인 상황이 한창인 중에 또는 이후에 얼마 안 있어 다른 사람들과 함께 농담하고 웃는 형태로 나타난다. 예를 들어, 특히 스트레스가 많았던 하루의 사건을 저녁 늦게 친한 친구 몇 명과 이야기할 때, 이전에는 고통스럽고 압도적으로 보였던 어려움이 변덕스럽게도 얼토당토않게 느껴져서 큰 유쾌함과 활기찬 웃음의 바탕이 될 수 있다. (진정한 웃음은 보통 즐거운 상황에서 나오며, 어떤 사람이 어려운 시기를 겪고 있을 때 웃음을 강요하는 것은 타인에게 무신경하게 보일 수도 있다.) 스트레스를 주는 사건으로 인해 생겨난 감정적 흥분과 긴장이 클수록, 나중에 그 사건에 대해 농담을 할 때 더 큰 즐거움과 더 큰 웃음이 나온다.

해설
역경에 대처하기 위한 유머의 사용은 흔히 타인과 함께 있는 사회적 맥락에서 이루어진다는 내용의 글이다. 따라서 진정한 웃음은 즐거운 상황에서 나오고 어떤 사람이 어려운 시기를 겪고 있을 때 웃음을 강요하는 것은 무신경하게 보일 수도 있다는 내용의 ④는 글의 전체 흐름과 관계가 없다.

⊗ 매력적인 오답 주의!
⑤ 타인에 대한 직접적인 언급이 나와 있지 않아 글의 전체 흐름과 관계가 없다고 오인하면 고를 수 있는 오답이다.

TEXT FLOW
주제	역경에 대처하기 위한 유머의 사용은 대개 사회적 맥락에서 이루어짐
부연	사람들은 부정적인 상황에서 다른 사람과 함께 농담하고 웃음
예시	스트레스가 많았던 사건을 친한 친구와 이야기하면 유쾌함과 웃음을 유발할 수 있음
부연	스트레스가 주는 감정적 흥분과 긴장이 클수록 더 큰 즐거움이 유발됨

구문
• For example, [when the events of a particularly stressful day are discussed among a group of close friends later in the evening], difficulties [that earlier seemed distressing and overwhelming] can **be perceived** as **humorously incongruous** ~.
: 첫 번째 [ ]는 시간의 부사절이고, 두 번째 [ ]는 difficulties를 수식하는 관계절이다. 주절의 주어인 difficulties that earlier seemed distressing and overwhelming이 인식의 주체가 아닌 대상이므로 수동태인 be perceived가 사용되었으며, 전치사 as 뒤에는 보어의 역할을 하는 형용사구가 이어지고 있다.

• **The greater** the emotional arousal and tension engendered by the stressful events, **the greater** the pleasure and **the louder** the laughter [when joking about them afterwards].
: '~할수록 더 …한'이라는 뜻의 「the+비교급 ~, the+비교급 ....」 구문이 사용되었다. [ ]는 접속사 when이 명시된 분사구문이다.

09

정답 ②

여러분의 감각 기관들과 다른 기관들 사이의 가장 큰 차이점은 그것들의 기능 불량이 생명을 위협하는 함축적 의미를 가지지 않고, 오히려 삶을 바꾸는 함축적 의미를 가진다는 점이다. (B) 만약 심장이나 뇌가 작동을 멈추면, 여러분도 그렇게 된다. 그렇지만 감각 기관들은 그렇지 않다. 사실, 가수 Jose Feliciano와 같은 몇몇 사람들은 심지어 자신들의 감각 상실을 포용한다. (A) 태어날 때부터 앞을 보지 못했던 Feliciano는, 특히 1달러 지폐와 20달러 지폐 사이의 차이를 알아내는 것과 같이, 대부분의 사람들이 당연하게 생각하는 영역들에서 자신이 살아가는 방식을 조정해야 했다. (C) 그러나 자신이 시각을 가지기를 염원하는지에 대해 질문을 받자, 그는 자신이 받은 모든 재능과 재주에 대해 은혜를 모르는 것으로 생각되고 싶지 않기 때문에 그렇게 바라지 않는다고 말했다.

해설
주어진 글은 감각 기관들의 기능 불량이 다른 기관들의 기능 불량과는 달리 생명을 위협하지 않고 삶을 바꾸는 영향을 준다는 내용으로, 그것에 대한 구체적인 설명을 위해 Jose Feliciano라는 가수의 경우를 예로 든 (B)가 그 다음에 오고, Feliciano의 시각 장애가 그의 삶에 미친 영향을 설명하는 (A)가 이어지고 나서, 그가 자신의 시각 장애를 포용하는 발언이 담겨 있는 내용의 (C)가 마지막에 오는 것이 글의 흐름상 가장 자연스럽다.

TEXT FLOW

주제	감각 기관의 기능 불량은 삶을 바꿀 수 있음
예시	태어날 때부터 앞을 보지 못했던 가수 Jose Feliciano
부연	Jose Feliciano는 시각 장애로 다른 사람들보다 힘든 삶을 살아야 했지만, 시각 장애에 대해 포용하는 마음을 가짐

구문

- But **when asked** about whether he wished to have eyesight, he said he wouldn't — because he didn't want to be thought of as ungrateful for all the talents and gifts [he has been given].
  : 시간의 부사절에서는 주어가 주절의 주어와 같은 경우 「대명사 주어+be동사」가 생략될 수 있다. 여기에서도 when과 asked 사이에 he was가 생략되었다. [ ]는 관계절로 선행사 all the talents and gifts를 수식하며 앞에 목적격 관계대명사가 생략되어 있다.

10

정답 ②

모든 인간은 세 부분으로 나뉜 뇌를 가지고 태어난다. 한 부분인 대뇌 피질(대뇌 반구)은 학습, 추상적 사고, 그리고 상상력을 다룬다. 어린이 대부분은 7세 이후에 대뇌 피질이 실질적으로 사용되기 시작한다. (B) 그 나이 이전에는 아이들은 지적인 평가를 할 수 있는 정신적 도구가 없다. 여러분이 똑같은 점토 공 두 개를 가지고 한 아이에게 "이 두 공이 똑같을까?"라고 물어보면 아이는 "네"라고 대답할 것이다. (A) 그러나 만약 여러분이 점토 공 중 하나를 뱀 모양으로 굴려서 아이에게 어떤 점토 조각이 더 큰지 물어보면, 아이는 둘 중 하나를 선택할 가능성이 크다. (C) 하지만 7세보다 나이가 많은 아이에게 같은 질문을 하면 아이는 "제가 좀 바보 같다고 생각하세요?"라고 말할 가능성이 크다. 대뇌 피질은 논리가 존재하는 곳이며 우리를 다른 모든 동물과 구별하는 고차원적인 추론을 하는 곳이다.

해설
어린이 대부분은 7세 이후부터 학습, 추상적 사고, 상상력을 다루는 대뇌 피질이 사용되기 시작한다는 주어진 글 다음에는, 7세 이전에는 지적인 평가를 할 수 있는 정신적 도구가 없다는 (B)가 이어져야 한다. 그다음에는 지적인 평가를 할 수 없는 상황에 대한 예시로, 같은 크기의 점토 공을 뱀 모양으로 굴려서 두 점토 조각의 크기가 같은지를 물어보면 아이가 두 개가 같다는 것을 인식하지 못한다는 내용의 (A)가 이어지고, 반대로 대뇌 피질을 사용할 수 있게 된 7세보다 나이가 많은 아이에게 같은 질문을 하면, 두 조각의 크기가 같다는 것을 쉽게 안다는 내용의 (C)가 마지막에 오는 것이 글의 흐름상 가장 자연스럽다.

⊗ 매력적인 오답 주의!
③ (B)에서 아이에게 공 크기에 관해 던진 질문을 (C)에서 7세보다 나이가 많은 아이에게 던진 질문과 같다고 오인하면 고를 수 있는 오답이다.

TEXT FLOW

도입/주제	어린이 대부분은 7세 이후에 대뇌 피질이 사용되기 시작함
예시 1	7세 이전에는 똑같은 두 개의 점토 공 중, 하나를 뱀 모양으로 바꾸면 두 개의 점토 조각의 크기가 같다는 것을 인지하지 못함
예시 2	7세보다 나이가 많아지면 대뇌 피질이 사용되어 두 조각의 크기가 같다는 것을 알게 됨
결론	대뇌 피질은 인간을 다른 동물과 구별하는 고차원적인 추론을 하는 곳임

구문

- [If you {roll one of the balls into the shape of a snake} and {ask the child ⟨which piece of clay is larger⟩}], however, the child is likely to pick one or the other.
  : [ ]는 조건의 부사절이고, 그 안에 동사구인 두 개의 { }가 and로 연결되어 부사절의 주어인 you에 이어진다. ⟨ ⟩는 ask의 직접목적어 역할을 하는 명사절이다.

- The cortex is [{where logic resides} and {where we do the higher-level reasoning ⟨that separates us from all other animals⟩}].
  : [ ]는 문장의 주격 보어이고, 그 안에 where(~하는 곳)로 유도되는 명사절인 두 개의 { }가 and로 병렬 연결되어 있다. ⟨ ⟩는 the higher-level reasoning을 수식하는 관계절이다.

11

정답 ④

아마도 여러분은 초등학교 때까지 오래 거슬러 올라가 처음으로 연설을 해야만 했던 기억이 있을 것이다. 여러분은 자신이 전하려는 메시지를 자세히 써서 청중에게 읽었을 가능성이 크다. 안타깝게도 원고에 의존하는 연설은 흥미를 끌 만큼 충분히 잘되는 경우가 드물다. 원고에 의존하는 대부분의 연설자는 단조로운 어조로 읽거나 혹은 '읽는 것 같이 들리게' 만드는 발성 억양 패턴으로 원고를 읽는다. 그들은 (연설을) 읽던 부분을 놓치는 것이 매우 두려워서 원고에 시선이 계속 고정된 상태로 청중을 거의 쳐다보지 않는다. 이러한 문제는 발표자 대부분이 거의 대개 원고로부터 읽는 것을 피해야 할 정도로 매우 크다. 효과적인 구두 메시지가 신중하고 정확한 표현에 달려 있는 경우가 원고에 의존하는 연설을 피해야 한다는 일반적인 규칙의 몇 안 되는 예외이다. 예를 들어, 미국 국무 장관의 서투른 성명은 국제적 위기를 초래할 수 있기 때문에 중요한 사안에 대한 그의 발언은 보통 대본 작성이 신중하게 이루어진다. 만약 여러분이 혹시라도 민감하거나, 중대하거나, 혹은 논란이 되는 사안에 대해 연설해야 한다면, 여러분 또한 원고에 의존한 연설을 해야 할 수도 있다.

해설
원고에 의존하는 연설은 흥미를 끌 만큼 충분히 잘되는 경우가 드물기 때문에 원고로부터 읽어야 하는 연설은 피해야 하지만, 효과적인 구두 메시지가 신중하고 정확한 표현에 달려 있는 경우에는 원고에 의존한 연설이 필요할 수도 있다는 내용의 글이다. 주어진 문장은 효과적인 구두 메시지가 신중하고 정확한 표현에 달려 있는 예외적인 경우에는 원고에 의존하는 연설을 할 수 있다는 내용인데, ④ 앞 문장까지는 원고에 의존하는 연설의 단점을 제시하며 이것을 가급적 피해야 한다는 내용이 기술되다가 ④ 뒷문장에 미국 국무 장관의 예를 들어 중요한 사안에 대한 발언의 경우 사전에 대본 작성이 신중하게 이루어져야 한다는 내용이 이어지고 있으므로, 주어진 문장이 ④에 들어가지 않으면 논리적 단절이 발생한다. 따라서 주어진 문장이 들어가기에 가장 적절한 곳은 ④이다.

⊗ 매력적인 오답 주의!
⑤ ④ 뒤에 예시를 나타내는 접속 부사인 For example을 인지하지 못하고 원고에 의존한 연설이 필요한 상황을 언급하고 있는 ⑤ 뒤의 문장과 내용상 연결된다고 오인하면 고를 수 있는 오답이다.

TEXT FLOW
도입	어렸을 때부터 우리는 원고에 의존한 연설에 익숙함
전개	원고에 의존하는 연설은 흥미를 끌 만큼 충분히 잘되는 경우가 드묾
부연	단조로운 어조로 원고를 읽거나 원고에 시선이 고정되어 청중을 살피지 않음
전환	효과적인 구두 메시지가 신중하고 정확한 표현에 달려 있으면 원고에 의존하는 연설을 예외적으로 할 수 있음
부연	민감하거나 중대한 사안에 대해서는 원고에 의존한 연설을 해야 할 수 있음

구문
• [Occasions {when effective verbal messages depend on careful and exact phrasing}] **are** the few exceptions to the general rule of [avoiding manuscript speaking].
: 첫 번째 [ ]는 문장의 주어로, 주어의 핵심어가 Occasions이므로 술어 동사로 복수형 동사 are가 쓰였다. { }는 Occasions를 수식하는 관계절이다. 두 번째 [ ]는 전치사 of의 목적어 역할을 하는 동명사구이다.

• They are **so** afraid of losing their place **that** they **keep** their eyes **glued** to the manuscript and seldom look at the audience.
: 「so ~ that ....」은 '매우 ~해서 …하다'의 의미를 나타낸다. 「keep+목적어+목적격 보어」 구문이 사용되었고, 목적어(their eyes)와 목적격 보어의 관계가 수동이므로 과거분사 glued가 쓰였다.

12-14
정답 12 ② 13 ① 14 ⑤

(A) 한 개의 끓는 가마솥에서 사탕수수 시럽을 차례로 정제하는 것은 위험하기만 한 것이 아니었으며, 그것은 심하게 비효율적이었다. 같은 것을 훨씬 더 적은 노동으로 성취하는 안전하고 믿을 만한 방법을 알아낸 남자는 그 자신이 노예 사회의 산물이었다. Nobert Rillieux는 1806년에 뉴올리언스에

서 태어났다. 그의 아버지는 그가 자유로운 유색인 여자와의 사이에서 낳은 아들이 비상하게 똑똑하다는 것을 알아차린 부유한 백인이자 공학 기사였다. (C) 그래서 Nobert의 아버지는 교육을 받도록 그를 프랑스로 보냈다. 그곳에서, 그는 사탕무에서 얻은 설탕이 사탕수수에서 얻은 설탕과 같다는 것을 입증한 검사와 실험에 대한 이성적이고 과학적인 접근법을 배웠다. 그리고 그가 루이지애나의 고향으로 돌아왔을 때, 그는 자신의 공학 지식을 설탕 정제에 적용했다. Rillieux는 설탕 시럽이 위가 열린 가마솥 대신에 일련의 특별하게 밀봉된 냄비에서 가열된다면 그 과정 전체가 간소화될 것이라는 점을 알아냈다.
(B) 이제, 한 팀 대신에 한 사람이 그 과정을 감독할 수 있었고, 열이 한 냄비에서 다른 냄비로 옮겨질 수 있어서 훨씬 더 적은 열이 필요할 것이었다. Rillieux는 1840년대에 그의 발명을 처음으로 시연했고, 설탕 생산자들은 빠르게 그 가치를 알아보았다. 그렇지만 아버지에 의해 합법적인 자유를 얻은 유명한 발명가가 된다고 해도 루이지애나에서는 흑인에 대한 안전이 보장되지 못해서 그는 프랑스로 돌아갔다.
(D) 비록 그가 프랑스에서 노예가 될 위기에 처하지는 않았지만, 그는 자신들이 그의 공정을 발명했다고 주장하는 다른 사람들과 일련의 분쟁을 겪었다. 그는 좌절해서 자신의 뛰어난 정신을 고대 이집트 문자 연구와 같은 다른 과업들로 돌렸다. 1894년에 파리에서 사망한 Rillieux는 1800년대의 변모하는 설탕 세계의 완전한 사례이다. 그 자신은 자유로웠지만 평생 편견과 싸워야 했다.

해설
12 Nobert Rillieux가 유색 인종과 혼혈이면서 비상하게 똑똑했다는 내용의 (A)에 이어, 그의 아버지가 그를 교육시키고자 프랑스로 보냈고, 그곳에서 설탕 정제 방법을 발견하고 고향인 루이지애나로 돌아왔다는 내용인 (C)가 온 다음, 그 설탕 정제 방법의 가치를 인정받았지만 루이지애나에서는 흑인에 대한 안전이 보장되지 않아 다시 프랑스로 돌아갔다는 내용의 (B)가 이어지고, 프랑스에서 일련의 분쟁을 겪으면서 유색 인종에 대한 편견에 의해 고통받다가 사망했다는 내용인 (D)가 마지막에 오는 것이 글의 흐름상 가장 자연스럽다.

13 (a)는 Nobert Rillieux의 아버지를 가리키고, 나머지는 모두 Nobert Rillieux를 가리킨다.

14 (D)에서 프랑스로 다시 돌아간 다음에는 일련의 분쟁에 지쳐 고대 이집트 문자 연구와 같은 다른 과업들에 힘썼다는 내용이 제시되므로, ⑤가 Nobert Rillieux에 관한 내용으로 적절하지 않다.

TEXT FLOW
시간 순서/사건 전개에 따른 흐름:
(A) Nobert Rillieux가 태어나고, 아버지는 그가 똑똑하다는 것을 알아차림 → (C) 아버지가 Nobert를 프랑스로 유학 보냈고, 그는 유학 후 루이지애나로 돌아와서 설탕 정제 방법을 알아냄 → (B) 설탕 정제 방법의 가치를 인정받았지만 안전상의 이유로 다시 프랑스로 돌아감 → (D) 프랑스에서도 편견과 싸워야 했고, 일련의 분쟁 이후 다른 과업에 몰두하다가 1894년에 사망함

구문
• His father was a wealthy white man and engineer [who recognized {that the boy ⟨whom he had fathered with a free woman of color⟩ was unusually smart}].
: [ ]는 a wealthy white man and engineer를 수식하는 관계절이다. { }는 명사절로 recognized의 목적어 역할을 하고, 그 안의 ⟨ ⟩는 관계절로 the boy를 수식한다.

- Though he was not in danger of being enslaved in France, he suffered through a series of conflicts with others [who claimed they **had invented** his process].
  : [ ]는 관계절로 others를 수식한다. claimed보다 이전에 일어난 일임을 나타내기 위해 대과거 had invented를 사용했다.

GRAMMAR REVIEW
본문 121쪽

1 what	**2** making	**3** when
4 causing	**5** to unfold	**6** incongruous
7 is	**8** which	**9** glued
10 be simplified		

1 동사 had expected의 목적어 역할을 하면서 선행사를 포함하는 관계대명사 what이 적절하다.

2 의미상 주절에 이어지는 내용을 기술하는 분사구문이고 능동의 의미이므로 현재분사 making을 써야 한다.

3 선행사 1924가 시간을 나타내며, 뒤에 완전한 형태의 절이 이어지므로 이를 부연 설명하는 관계부사 when이 적절하다.

4 주절 it can decay in the lake that is created가 원인이 되어 생기는 결과를 나타내는 분사구문으로 능동의 의미이므로 현재분사 causing을 써야 한다.

5 allow는 목적격 보어로 to부정사를 취하는 동사이므로 to unfold를 써야 한다.

6 '~을 …으로 인식하다'의 의미를 나타내는 「perceive+목적어+as+목적격 보어」가 수동태로 쓰였으므로 as 뒤에는 목적격 보어 역할을 할 수 있는 형용사(구)가 이어져야 한다. 따라서 부사인 humorously의 수식을 받으면서 형용사구를 구성하는 incongruous가 적절하다.

7 주어의 핵이 difference이므로 단수형 동사 is가 적절하다.

8 문맥상 아이에게 두 점토 조각 중에서 어떤 것이 더 큰지를 고르라는 것이므로, 명사절을 유도하면서 의문사의 의미를 나타내는 which가 적절하다.

9 문맥상 they(연설자)의 시선이 원고에 고정되어 있으므로, 동사 keep의 목적어인 their eyes는 고정의 주체가 아닌 대상으로 이해할 수 있다. 따라서 목적격 보어로 과거분사 glued를 써야 한다.

10 the whole process가 simplify(단순화하다)의 대상이므로 수동태인 be simplified를 써야 한다.

본문 122쪽

하프 모의고사 15회

01 ②	02 ③	03 ③	04 ②	05 ③
06 ②	07 ④	08 ①	09 ④	10 ③
11 ②	12 ②	13 ⑤	14 ⑤	

01
정답 ②

Verbanks 씨께,
2월 10일까지 500개의 철제 책장들을 배송해 달라고 1월 10일에 해 주신 주문에 감사드립니다. 귀하께서 1월 15일에 디자인을 변경하셨고, 저희는 그것을 받아들였습니다. 그러나 재고 목록을 확인하는 동안, 저희는 현재 일부 부품의 재고가 없다는 것을 알게 되었습니다. 귀하의 이전 디자인은 그 부품들을 필요로 하지 않지만, 현재의 디자인은 필요로 합니다. 저희는 그 부품을 공급업체에게 주문했고, 그것들은 1월 20일에 도착할 것입니다. 그 책장들을 완성하려면, 3~4일 더 그것들에 공을 들여야 할 것입니다. 그러므로 저희는 귀하가 저희 상황을 이해하셔서 2월 14일에 배송되는 것을 양해해 주실 것을 요청합니다. 주문하신 것이 완성되는 대로 바로 연락드리겠습니다. 저희에게 일을 맡겨 주셔서 다시 한번 감사드립니다.
Frederick 가구 드림

해설
주문자가 변경한 디자인에 필요한 부품이 없어서 공급업체에 주문을 한 상태이고, 이 때문에 부득이하게 제작 기일이 더 걸린다는 점을 설명하면서 배송일 연기에 대해 양해를 요청하고 있으므로, 글의 목적으로 가장 적절한 것은 ②이다.

TEXT FLOW

도입	철제 책장 주문에 대한 감사 인사
전개	변경된 디자인에 필요한 일부 부품의 재고가 없어 공급업체에 주문함
요지	3~4일의 제작 기간이 더 필요하므로 배송일을 연기해야 함

구문
- Thus, we **ask** you **to understand** our situation and **accept** the delivery on February 14.
  : ask가 5형식 동사로 쓰일 때 목적격 보어로 to부정사가 쓰이며, understand와 accept는 and에 의해 to에 이어져 병렬 구조를 이룬다.

02
정답 ③

여러분의 필요성이 항상 달라질 것이기 때문에 퇴직에 대한 진정한 재정 계획은 결코 끝나지 않는다. 여러분이 60세에 퇴직을 하는데, 지금 필요한 것에 근거하여 2,000달러의 월 소득을 창출할 준비가 되어 있는 계획을 가지고 있다고 해 보자. 그것은 퇴직 후 첫 2년, 3년, 또는 4년에는 훌륭한 것일지도 모른다. 하지만 여러분의 삶에서 상황이 개인적으로 항상 변하고 있고, 상황은 또한 경제와 이 세상에서 변하고 있다. 이런 변화에 관한 하나의 큰 요인은 인플레이션이다. 2024년 현재 한 달에 2,000달러가 필요하다고 해서, 월 2,000달러가 2027년까지 계속되지는 않을 텐데, 그것은 인플레이션 때문이다. 그런 이유로 인해 여러분은 자신의 계획을 정기적으로 수정해야 한다. 여러분은 인플레이션을 따라잡기 위해 여러분의 소득을 계속 증가시킬 계획을 만들어야 한다.

해설
퇴직 전에 세운 재정 계획은 인플레이션을 고려하지 않은 것이므로, 인플레이션을 따라잡기 위해 자신의 재정 계획을 정기적으로 수정해 소득을 계속 증가시켜야 한다는 내용의 글이다. 따라서 필자가 주장하는 바로 가장 적절한 것은 ③이다.

TEXT FLOW

도입	필요는 항상 달라지기 때문에 퇴직에 대한 재정 계획은 결코 끝나지 않음
예시	지금 필요한 월 2,000달러의 소득을 퇴직 후 재정 계획으로 세운다면 2~4년은 괜찮을지 몰라도 상황이 바뀜에 따라 모든 것이 달라질 수 있음
주제	인플레이션 때문에 재정 계획을 정기적으로 수정해야 함

구문
• Let's say [you're retiring at age 60] and [you have a plan in place to generate $2,000 a month of income, based on {what your needs are today}].
: 두 개의 [ ]는 and로 연결되어 say의 목적어 역할을 하는 명사절이다. { }는 관계사 what이 이끄는 명사절로 전치사 on의 목적어 역할을 한다.

• You need to create a plan [that will continue to increase your income {to keep up with inflation}].
: [ ]는 a plan을 수식하는 관계절이며, 그 안의 { }는 목적을 나타내는 부사적 용법의 to부정사구이다.

03
정답 ③

19세기 인종 차별주의와 사회 진화론의 태도는 의심의 여지 없이 더 이상 전 세계적으로 받아들여지지 않고 있지만, 특정 신 사회 진화론이 그 자리를 대신해 왔다. 토착(혹은 부족) 사회는 오늘날 적어도 공공장소에서는 거의 '야만인'이라고 불리지 않지만, 그들은 보통 '뒤떨어졌다'고 여겨진다! (비록 이것이 여전히 일어나는데도 불구하고) 그들을 학살함으로써 제거하는 것은 더 이상 용납될 수 없는 일이라고 여겨질 수도 있지만, 정부가 그러한 민족들이 도움을 받거나 그들의 '뒤떨어짐'을 극복하도록 강요받아야 한다고 느끼는 경우가 도처에 있다. 그것의 뒤떨어짐을 극복하기 위해, 원주민 사회는 전통적인 삶의 방식과 또한 흔히 언어도 버리도록 강요받는데, 보통은 그렇게 함으로써 하나의 사회로서의 존재가 완전히 사라질 것이라는 바람에서 그러하다. 이제는 더 이상 그들의 '뒤떨어지는' 사회에 속하지 않게 된 그것의 개별 구성원들은 남은 국가의 인구 속으로 사라질 것이다.

해설
결국 하나의 사회로서의 존재가 완전히 사라질 것이라는 바람에서, '뒤떨어짐'을 극복하기 위해 원주민 사회는 전통적인 생활 방식과 또한 흔히 언어도 버리도록 강요받아 더 이상 '뒤떨어지는' 사회에 속하지 않게 된다고 했으므로, 밑줄 친 부분이 의미하는 바로 가장 적절한 것은 ③ '그들의 전통적인 삶의 방식을 잃을'이다.
① 야만의 상태로 되돌아갈
② 그들 자신의 새로운 사회를 창조할
④ 정부와 갈등을 겪을

⑤ 그들의 '뒤떨어짐'을 극복하는 데 실패할

TEXT FLOW

도입	특정 신 사회 진화론의 관점에서는 토착 사회를 뒤떨어진다고 여김
전개	'뒤떨어짐'을 극복하기 위해 토착 사회는 전통적 생활 방식과 언어를 버리도록 강요당함
결론	결국 하나의 사회로서의 존재가 사라지고 개별 구성원은 남은 국가의 인구 속으로 사라짐

구문
• **It** may no longer be considered acceptable [to remove them by massacring them (though this still happens)], but it is everywhere the case [that governments feel {that such peoples should be helped or forced to overcome their "backwardness."}]
: It은 가주어이고 첫 번째 [ ]가 진주어이다. 두 번째 [ ]는 the case와 동격의 명사절이고, 그 안의 { }는 feel의 목적어 역할을 하는 명사절이다.

• [To overcome its backwardness], an indigenous society is urged to abandon its traditional way of life and often its language as well, usually in the hope [that in so doing it will cease to exist as a society altogether].
: 첫 번째 [ ]는 목적의 의미를 나타내는 부사적 용법의 to부정사구이다. 두 번째 [ ]는 the hope와 동격의 의미를 갖는 명사절이다.

04
정답 ②

이상하게 보일지도 모르지만, 범고래가 알래스카의 흰머리독수리의 먹이에 영향을 준다! 연구자들은 범고래의 증가가 그들이 가장 좋아하는 먹이 중 하나인 해달의 감소를 야기한다는 것을 발견했다. 해달은 성게를 먹는다. 그러므로 해달이 더 적어질수록 성게는 더 많아진다. 성게는 물고기들에게는 모래톱을 따라 숨을 장소의 역할을 하는 큰 해조류를 먹고 산다. 그러므로, 성게가 더 많아질수록 해조류는 더 적어지고 숨을 곳도 더 적어진다! 결과적으로, 물고기는 어딘가 다른 곳으로 이동한다. 알래스카에서, 흰머리독수리는 대양의 가장자리에 있는 얕은 근해에 사는 물고기를 주로 먹고 살아가는 맹금류이다. 이러한 물고기들이 없으면, 그것들은 다른 먹이를 찾아야 한다. 따라서, 과학자들은 범고래의 포식으로 인한 알래스카에서의 해달의 감소는 흰머리독수리가 억지로 그들의 식습관을 바꿔 바닷새를 먹이로 삼게 한다는 것을 발견했다. 정말로 퍼즐과 같다!

해설
범고래의 증가가 해달의 감소와 그 해달의 먹이가 되었던 성게의 증가로 이어지고, 이는 성게의 먹이인 해조류의 감소와 그 해조류를 숨을 곳으로 삼던 물고기들의 이동을 초래하게 되어, 그것들을 먹고 살던 흰머리독수리가 바닷새를 먹이로 삼게 된다는 내용의 글이다. 이는 범고래의 증가가 결과적으로 알래스카의 흰머리독수리의 먹이에 영향을 주게 된 셈이므로, 이 글의 주제로 가장 적절한 것은 ② '동물의 종들을 연결하는 유대'이다.
① 기후 변화의 영향
③ 식품의 생산성을 증가시키는 방법
④ 멸종 위기에 처한 종을 보존하는 방법
⑤ 자연 서식지를 보존하는 것의 중요성

TEXT FLOW

도입	범고래가 알래스카의 흰머리독수리의 먹이에 영향을 미침
전개	범고래의 증가 → 해달의 감소 → 해달의 먹이인 성게의 증가 → 성게의 먹이인 해조류의 감소 → 해조류를 숨을 곳으로 삼던 물고기의 이동
결론	물고기를 먹는 흰머리독수리의 먹이가 바닷새로 바뀜

구문

• Accordingly, scientists discovered [that **the decline** of sea otters in Alaska thanks to the predation of killer whales, **forces** bald eagles **to change** their diet and **choose** marine birds as prey].

: [ ]는 명사절로 동사 discovered의 목적어 역할을 하고, that절의 주어는 the decline이며 동사는 forces이다. 「force+목적어+to부정사」는 '~가 …하도록 강요하다'라는 뜻을 나타내며, to change와 (to) choose가 and에 의해 병렬 구조로 연결되어 있다.

05
정답 ③

재활용 예술 대회
저희는 최고의 쓰레기 예술 작품을 찾고 있습니다! 지구의 날 축제 기획 위원회에서는 여러분을 재활용 예술 대회에 초대합니다.

참가자
Berkeley 시의 모든 거주자

등록일
참가 신청서와 여러분의 작품을 4월 22일 금요일까지 Berkeley 지역 문화 회관으로 가져오세요.

세부 사항
1. 쓰레기가 되었을 재료들을 사용해야 합니다. 프로젝트는 3개의 R(줄이다, 재사용하다, 재활용하다)을 전달해야 합니다.
2. 어떠한 표현 수단들도 허용됩니다(회화, 디지털, 사진, 직물 등).

심사 및 수상
대회 참가자들은 재활용 가능한 재료들의 사용과 전달된 메시지에 근거하여 평가될 것입니다. 1, 2, 3위에 대해서 상이 수여될 것입니다.

해설
세부 사항에 관한 설명에서 회화, 디지털, 사진, 직물 등 어떠한 표현 수단이라도 허용된다고 했으므로 ③은 안내문의 내용과 일치하지 않는다.

구문

• You have to use the materials [that **would have been** trash].

: [ ]는 주격 관계대명사가 이끄는 관계절로 선행사 the materials를 수식한다. 관계절 내의 「would+have+과거분사」는 가정법 과거완료 시제로 과거의 가정을 나타낸다.

06
정답 ②

고대 그리스인들은 시간을 chronos 또는 kyros로 개념화했다. chronos는 초, 분, 시간으로 측정되는 시계 시간이고, '연대기', '연대기적인'과 같

은 단어의 어원이다. kyros는 영원함, 지금 여기에 사는 것, 동시성, 카르페 디엠, 즉 현재를 즐기는 것을 의미한다. chronos와 kyros는 양과 질을 나타내는데, 그것은 우리의 시간과의 분투가 핵심 관건인 것을 반영한다. chronos는 객관적인 속도로 고정되어 있는 반면에, kyros는 주관적이며 긍정적이거나 부정적인 경험이 될 수 있기 때문에 상당히 다양하다. 대부분의 사람들에게 치과용 의자에서 보내는 45분은 매혹적인 책을 읽는 데 보낸 같은 기간보다 더 길게 느껴질 것이다. 우리는 어떻게 긍정적인 kyros 시간은 더 많이, chronos는 더 적게 경험할 수 있을까? 한 번에 한 가지 일을 하는 것, 지나치게 계획된 생활을 하는 것을 거부하는 것, 우리 삶에서 중요한 사람과 활동을 위한 시간을 만드는 것이 우리가 우리 시간의 양과 질의 균형을 맞추는 데 도움이 되는 핵심 방법이다.

해설
② 뒤에 이어지는 절에서 전치사 about의 목적어 역할을 하면서 reflect의 목적어를 이끄는 역할도 해야 하므로 that을 선행사를 포함하는 관계대명사 what으로 고쳐야 한다.
① clock time을 수식하는 분사구이고 clock time이 동사 measure의 대상이므로 과거분사 measured는 적절하다.
③ 동사 varies를 수식하는 부사 considerably는 적절하다.
④ spent 뒤에 전치사 on이 생략된 것이므로 동명사 reading은 적절하다.
⑤ 동명사구 세 개가 and로 연결되어 주어 역할을 하므로 복수 동사 are는 적절하다.

⊗ **매력적인 오답 주의!**

④ spent가 앞의 the same period of time을 수식하는 과거분사라는 것을 모르면 문장의 구조를 파악하지 못하여 고를 수 있는 오답이다.

TEXT FLOW

도입	고대 그리스인들의 chronos와 kyros 개념 소개
전개	chronos와 kyros 개념 비교
결론	삶에서 의미 있는 시간을 만드는 것이 우리 시간의 양과 질의 균형을 맞추는 데 있어 중요함

구문

• Chronos and kyros represent quantity and quality, [which reflect {what our struggle with time is all about}].

: [ ]는 quantity and quality를 부가적으로 설명하는 관계절이다. 그 안의 { }는 reflect의 목적어 역할을 하는 명사절이다.

• To most people 45 minutes [spent in the dentist's chair] will feel longer than the same period of time [spent reading a fascinating book].

: 첫 번째 [ ]는 45 minutes를 수식하는 분사구이고, 두 번째 [ ]는 the same period of time을 수식하는 분사구이다.

07
정답 ④

스코틀랜드의 Glasgow 대성당 밖에는 잊혀진 건강의 비밀을 품고 있을 것 같은 고대의 공동묘지가 있다. 1990년대 초반, 연구자인 George Davey Smith는 창의적이고도 낯선 질문을 하는 연구를 수행했는데, 그것은 '오래된 공동묘지의 비석들이 사망한 사람들의 건강과 장수에 대한 정보를 갖고 있을 수 있는가?'라는 것이었다. 이 질문에 답하기 위해, 그는 각 비석의 높이와 그 아래 묻힌 사람의 사망 당시 나이를 비교했다. 그가 발견한 것은 건강이 유전적인 행운, 스파르타식의 엄격한 식단과 러닝머신 위를 햄스터처럼

달리는 것의 문제라고 추정하는 것의 오류를 지적한다. Smith는 묘지의 비석이 더 높을수록 더 오래 살았다는 점을 발견했다. 높은 오벨리스크들이 있는 사망한 남자들은 더 짧은 비석들이 있는 남자들보다 평균 3년을 더 오래 살았고, 여자들에게도 같은 검사가 딱 들어맞았다. 물론, 오늘날 높은 비석을 사는 것이 더 오래 살게 해 주지는 않을 것이다. 그러나 과거에는 그러했을 것이다. Smith는 부유함과 건강 및 장수 사이의 상관관계를 찾고 있었다.

해설
연구자인 George Davey Smith가 고대의 공동묘지를 연구한 결과, 묘지의 비석이 더 높을수록 더 오래 살았다는 사실을 발견했다는 내용의 글이므로, Smith는 높은 비석을 살 수 있었던 '부유함'과 건강 및 장수 사이의 상호관계를 찾고 있었다고 볼 수 있다. 따라서 빈칸에 들어갈 말로 ④ '부유함'이 가장 적절하다.
① 습관 ② 키 ③ 종교 ⑤ 성취

TEXT FLOW
소재	고대 공동묘지의 비석과 사망자의 건강 및 장수 사이의 관계에 관한 연구
결과	비석이 더 높을수록 더 오래 살았다는 것을 알게 됨
결론	높은 비석을 살 수 있었던 '부유함'은 고대인의 건강 및 장수와 관계가 있었음을 추정할 수 있음

구문
• [What he discovered] points out [the error of assuming that good health is a matter of {genetic good luck}, {a Spartan diet} and {running like a hamster on a treadmill}].
: 첫 번째 [ ]는 문장의 주어로 쓰인 관계절이고, 두 번째 [ ]는 points out의 목적어이다. 세 개의 { }는 and로 연결되어 병렬 구조를 이루며 a matter of에 이어진다.

08
정답 ①

피실험자들을 실험실에서 맞이하고 그들에게 50달러 수표를 준, Nicholas Epley와 동료들이 했던 일련의 연구를 생각해 보라. 그들이 수표를 받는 이유를 설명하면서 한 피실험자 집단은 그 수표를 '보너스'라고 설명하는 것을 들었고, 다른 집단은 '등록금 환불'이라고 설명하는 것을 들었다. Epley와 동료들은 보너스는 현재 상황에서 양의 변화로 마음에 부호화될 것이지만, 환불은 이전의 재산 상태로의 회복으로 부호화될 것이라고 추측했다. 그들은 보너스라고 표현하는 것이 환불이라고 표현하는 것보다 더 즉각적인 지출을 유발할 것이라고 생각했는데, 현재 상황에서의 지출이 상대적 손실로 더 쉽게 부호화되기 때문이다. 바로 이런 일이 일어났다. 한 실험에서, 일주일 뒤에 피실험자들에게 연락해 보니, 보너스 집단은 더 많은 돈을 써 버린 상태였다. 또 다른 실험에서, 피실험자들에게 대학 서점에서 (간식을 포함해서) 다양한 품목을 많이 할인된 가격에 구입할 수 있도록 했다. 이 실험에서도 보너스 집단의 피실험자들은 그 실험용 할인 매장에서 더 많은 돈을 썼다.

해설
'보너스'라고 표현하는 50달러 수표를 받으면 현재 상태에서 플러스되는 변화로 인식해서 더 즉각적이고 더 많은 지출로 이어지지만 '등록금 환불'이라고 표현하는 50달러 수표를 받으면 이전의 재산 상태로의 회복으로 인식해서 지출이 억제된다는 내용의 글이다. 따라서 빈칸에 들어갈 말로 가장 적절한 것은 ① '상대적 손실'이다.
② 현명한 구매 ③ 뜻밖의 이익 ④ 미래 투자 ⑤ 재정적 회복

❌ 매력적인 오답 주의!
③ spending from the status quo의 의미를 제대로 이해하지 못하고 빈칸 뒤에 이어지는 더 많은 돈을 쓰는 실험 사례에만 집중할 경우에 고를 수 있는 오답이다.

TEXT FLOW
도입	Nicholas Epley와 동료들의 실험 소개
결론	보너스라고 표현하는 것이 환불이라고 표현하는 것보다 더 즉각적인 지출을 유발함
부연	추가적인 실험 결과 제시(보너스라고 표현하는 것이 환불이라고 표현하는 것보다 더 많은 지출을 유발함)

구문
• Consider a series of studies by Nicholas Epley and colleagues [in which subjects were {greeted at the laboratory} and {given a $50 check}].
: [ ]는 a series of studies by Nicholas Epley and colleagues를 수식하는 관계절이고, 그 안의 두 개의 { }는 and로 연결되어 were에 이어진다.

• During the explanation of why they were receiving the check, one group of subjects heard the check [described as a "bonus"] and another group heard it [described as a "tuition rebate."]
: 두 개의 [ ]는 각각 heard의 목적격 보어 역할을 하는 분사구이다. it은 the check을 대신한다.

09
정답 ④

우리는 불평등이 가난과 동일한 것이 아니라는 것을 명심해야 한다. Timothy Noah와 같은 사람들이 '미국의 소득 분배가 현재 우루과이, 니카라과, 가이아나, 그리고 베네수엘라보다 더 불공평하다'라고 불평할 때, 그들은 마치 그 나라 국민들에 비해 거의 모든 미국인이 부유한 것은 문제가 되지 않는 것처럼 행동한다. 경제적 불평등은 광범위한 풍요로움과 완벽하게 양립할 수 있고, 늘어나는 불평등은 대다수의 시민들이 부유해지고 있는 사회와 완벽하게 양립할 수 있다. 가장 부유한 미국인들의 소득이 세 배가 되는 동안 가장 가난한 미국인들의 소득이 두 배가 된다면, 비록 모든 사람이 더 잘 살 수 있을지라도, 그것은 불평등을 극적으로 증가시킬 것이다. (더 큰 경제 성장이 반드시 증가한 불평등을 의미하지는 않는다.) 불평등은 박탈이 아니라 차이를 의미하며, 차이 '그 자체로' 미심쩍거나 못마땅한 것은 없다.

해설
대다수의 시민이 부유해지는 사회에서도 불평등은 증가할 수 있으며 불평등은 박탈이 아니라 차이를 의미한다는 내용의 글이므로, 더 큰 경제 성장이 반드시 불평등의 증가를 의미하지는 않는다는 내용의 ④는 글의 전체 흐름과 관계가 없다.

TEXT FLOW
주제	불평등은 가난과 동일한 것이 아님
전개	경제적 불평등은 광범위한 풍요로움과 양립 가능함
예시	미국인들의 소득 증가의 예
결론	불평등은 박탈이 아니라 차이를 의미함

- When people like Timothy Noah complain [that "income distribution in the United States is now more unequal than in Uruguay, Nicaragua, Guyana, and Venezuela,"] they act as if it's irrelevant [that almost all Americans are rich {compared to the citizens of those countries}].

: 첫 번째 [ ]는 complain의 목적어 역할을 하는 명사절이고, 두 번째 [ ]는 as if절의 가주어 it에 대한 진주어 역할을 하는 명사절이다. 두 번째 [ ] 안의 { }는 의미상 주어가 almost all Americans인 분사구문이다.

- Economic inequality is perfectly compatible with widespread affluence, and rising inequality is perfectly compatible with a society [in which the vast majority of citizens are getting richer].

: [ ]는 a society를 수식하는 관계절로, in which는 where로 바꿔 쓸 수 있다.

10 정답 ③

몇몇 연구에 의하면 변화하는 생활 방식은 유전적 발현의 변화를 야기시켜, 만성적인 질병들을 예방하는 유전자들을 '켜고', 심장병과 다른 질병들을 유발할 수 있는 유전자들을 '끈다.' (B) 이와 똑같이 놀라운 것은, 이러한 유전자의 변화가 미래 세대로 전달될 수 있다는 점이다. 2009년 6월에 발표된 한 논문에는 이러한 유전성들이 과학자들이 이전에 생각했던 것보다도 훨씬 더 자주 일어난다는 것을 보여 주는 100개가 넘는 잘 정리된 사례의 목록이 제시되었다. (C) 예를 들어, 한 사례에서는, 1944년 겨울 네덜란드의 기근 당시에 임신한 여성들은, 태어날 때까지 적절한 영양분이 주어졌음에도 훨씬 더 당뇨에 걸릴 가능성이 높은 아기들을 가지게 되었다. (A) 그들의 유전자가 음식을 더 천천히 소화하도록 변화하였는데, 그것은 만약 굶고 있을 때는 생존에 유리함을 주는 것이지만, 적합한 영양분이 존재할 때는 체중이 증가하고 당뇨와 고혈압에 걸릴 가능성을 높여 주는 것이다. 이러한 유전적 변화는 그들의 자녀와 손자, 손녀들에게도 전달되었다.

해설

주어진 글은 생활 방식의 변화가 유전적 발현의 변화를 가져올 수 있다는 내용이므로, 이와 관련하여 그러한 유전자의 변화가 후손으로 전달될 수 있다는 내용의 (B)가 바로 뒤에 오는 것이 적절하다. (B)의 these changes는 주어진 글의 changes in gene expression을 지칭한다. (B)에서 언급한 well-documented cases를 (C)의 in one case에서 언급하고 있으므로 네덜란드 기근 당시 임신한 여성들에 대한 사례인 (C)가 (B) 다음에 이어지고, 기근이라는 상황에 따른 유전자 변화에 대한 내용인 (A)가 마지막에 오는 것이 글의 흐름상 가장 자연스럽다.

TEXT FLOW

도입	생활 방식의 변화는 유전적 발현의 변화를 불러올 수 있음
전개	놀라운 사실은 이러한 유전적 변화는 후손에게 전달될 수 있다는 것임
예시	1944년 겨울 네덜란드의 기근 당시 임신한 여성들에게서 태어난 아기들의 사례

구문

- Their genes had changed to metabolize food more slowly, which, [{if you are starving}, gives you a survival advantage] but [{in the presence of adequate nutrition} makes you

more likely to gain weight and develop diabetes and high blood pressure].

: 계속적 용법의 관계대명사 which 다음에 두 개의 [ ]가 병렬 구조로 연결되어 있다. 각각의 [ ] 안에 있는 { }는 부사의 역할을 하고, which에 이어지는 동사는 gives와 makes이다. gain과 develop은 more likely to에 이어지는 동사원형으로 and에 의해 병렬 구조를 이룬다.

11 정답 ②

리더의 역할을 바라보는 태도가 달라졌다. 오늘날의 리더십은 한때 그랬던 것보다 조직도의 맨 위에 있는 사람에게서 기인하는 경우가 더 적다. 리더십은 도서관 내 어디에서나 기인할 수 있다. 여러 명의 리더가 있을 수 있는데, 각각은 특별한 정보, 책임 및/또는 기술을 가진다. 리더는 공동체의 일원이며 권위가 있는 지위에서 뿐만 아니라 따르는 사람들의 합의의 결과로서도 이끈다. 역사적으로, 고용주와 직원, 리더와 따르는 자 사이에는 비공식적인 계약이 있었다. 따르고 있는 사람이 리더에게 충성하면, 그 사람의 직업은 안정적이었다. 그런 계약은 더는 존재하지 않는데, 대체로 직원들이 예전에 그랬던 것만큼 쉽게 충성심을 보이기를 꺼려 하기 때문이다. 직원과 리더 사이의 계약이 여전히 존재한다면, 상호 존중과 인정이 이전의 가부장적 모델을 대체한 계약이 되었다. "리더십은 이끌기로 선택한 사람과 따르기로 결정한 사람 사이의 호혜적인 관계가 되었다."

해설

③ 뒤의 문장에서 언급된 That contract가 주어진 문장의 an informal contract를 가리키고, ② 뒤의 문장이 an informal contract의 내용에 관한 것이므로, 주어진 문장이 들어가기에 가장 적절한 곳은 ②이다.

⊗ 매력적인 오답 주의!

③ ② 뒤의 문장이 주어진 문장에서 언급된 비공식적인 계약의 내용에 관한 것이라는 것을 파악하지 못하면 고를 수 있는 오답이다.

TEXT FLOW

도입	리더십의 변화
전개	다양한 리더십의 원천(권위의 지위, 따르는 사람들의 합의의 결과)
결론	리더와 따르는 사람 사이의 호혜적인 관계로서의 리더십

구문

- The ways [in which we look at the role of the leader] have changed.

: [ ]는 문장의 주어인 The ways를 수식하는 관계절로 복수형 동사 have가 쓰였다.

- If a contract between a staff member and a leader still exists, it has become one [in which mutual respect and appreciation have replaced the earlier, more paternalistic model].

: [ ]는 one을 수식하는 관계절이고, one은 a contract를 대신한다.

12 정답 ②

서양 철학에서 가장 초기에 알려진 예술 이론은 플라톤과 그의 제자 아리스토텔레스에 의해 제안되었다. 그들의 관심을 가장 많이 끌었던 특정 예술 양식은 드라마[극]였다. 플라톤의 '국가론'에서 그는 이상적인 국가를 위한 설계도를 제시했다. 자신의 유토피아에 대한 개요를 서술하는 과정에서, 그는 시인, 특히 극작가들은 추방되어야 한다고 주장했다. 그 주장을 정당화하기 위해, 플라톤은 이유를 제시해야만 했다. 그리고 플라톤이 찾은 이유들은 그가 드라마의 본질이라고 여겼던 것과 관계가 있었다. 플라톤에 따르면, 드라마의 본질은 모방, 즉 겉모습의 흉내 내기였다. 다시 말해서, 극에 나오는 배우들은 자신들이 표현하는 어떤 사람이든 그들의 행동을 모방한다. 예를 들어, '메데아'에서 배우들은 논쟁하는 것을 모방한다. 플라톤은 주로 겉모습이 감정에 호소하고 감정을 선동하는 것이 사회적으로 위험한 것이라고 믿었기 때문에 이것이 문제가 있다고 생각했다. 감정적인 시민은 분별력보다는 정치적인 선동에 의해 영향을 받기 쉽다.

➡ 플라톤이 이상적인 국가로 제시했던 유토피아에서, 극작가들은 <u>추방되어야</u> 했는데, 왜냐하면 그는 그들이 표현하는 어떤 사람이든 그들의 행동을 모방하는 배우들이 시민들을 정치적인 선동에 <u>영향받게</u> 만든다고 믿었기 때문이었다.

해설

플라톤이 이상적인 국가로 제시한 유토피아에서 시인, 특히 극작가들은 추방되어야 했는데 그들이 쓴 극에 나오는 배우들의 모방 속성으로 인해 시민들이 정치적 선동에 영향을 받기 때문이라는 내용의 글이다. 따라서 요약문의 빈칸 (A)에는 expelled(추방되어야)가, (B)에는 subject(영향받게)가 들어가는 것이 가장 적절하다.
① 모방되어야 – 영향받게
③ 추방되어야 – 영향을 받지 않게
④ 환영받아야 – 무관심하게
⑤ 환영받아야 – 영향을 받지 않게

TEXT FLOW

도입	플라톤과 그의 제자 아리스토텔레스가 제안한 예술 이론 언급
주제	플라톤이 이상적인 국가에서 시인, 특히 극작가들이 추방되어야 한다고 주장한 이유는 행동의 겉모습을 모방하는 극의 속성 때문임
부연	플라톤은 겉모습이 감정에 호소하고 감정을 선동하는 것이 사회적으로 위험한 것이라고 믿었기 때문에 이것이 문제가 있다고 생각했는데, 감정적인 시민은 정치적인 선동에 의해 영향을 받기 쉬움

구문

• And the reasons [Plato found] had to do with [what he regarded as the nature of drama].
: 첫 번째 [ ]는 the reasons를 수식하는 관계절이고, 두 번째 [ ]는 전치사 with의 목적어 역할을 하는 명사절이다.

• Plato thought [that this was problematic primarily because he believed {that appearances appeal to the emotions} and {that ⟨stirring up the emotions⟩ is socially dangerous}].
: [ ]는 thought의 목적어 역할을 하는 명사절이고, 그 안의 두 개의 { }는 and로 연결되어 believed의 목적어 역할을 하는 명사절이다. ⟨ ⟩는 that 절의 주어 역할을 하는 동명사구로, 동명사구 주어는 단수 취급하므로 단수 동사 is가 쓰였다.

13-14
정답 13 ⑤ 14 ⑤

비윤리적인 과학자들이 있고, 그 당시에는 불행한 결과를 예측할 수 없었기

때문에 발생했던 과학적인 발전이 분명히 있지만, 중요한 것은 과학에서는 발견에 따른 가능한 결과를 직접적으로 그리고 명시적으로 조사한다는 것이다. 예방 원칙(사전 배려 원칙)에서는 행위로 인해 발생할 수 있는 영향에 관한 질문이 사전에 고려되어야 한다는 점을 지시한다. 이에 대한 직접적인 표명은 관련된 사람들에 대한 위험성이 있는지를 결정하기 위해서는 인간 피실험자를 포함하는 어떠한 연구도 외부 집단의 검토자에 의해 조사되어야 한다는 요건에서 보여질 수 있다. 인간을 포함하는 어떤 연구든 수행 예정일 때마다 제도적인 검토 위원회가 요구된다. 이 요건을 예방 원칙과 연결시켜 보라, 그러면 과학에서 첫 번째 질문은 "이것이 수행되어야 하는 것인가?"가 된다. 반면, 기술은 "이것이 이루어질 수 있을까?"라는 질문을 던진다. 기술은 일이 어떻게 이루어질 것인지 그리고 그것이 어떻게 적용될지에 관심이 있지만 윤리적 분석의 측면에서는 비참할 정도로 불완전하다. 여러 가지 면에서 기술 실험을 제한하는 모든 것은 어떤 재료를 얻는 것이 가능한가이다. 확실히, 이 중 어떤 것은 이익을 염두에 둔 동기 및 소비자 운동과 관련이 있다. 그러나 윤리적 문제에 대한 이러한 관심 부족의 상당 부분은 빠르게 변화하는 기술 환경의 특징 가운데 내포된 의미를 고려해 볼 수 있음(→ 없음)의 결과이다. 모든 것이 덧없어졌고 내일이면 쓸모없게 될 것에 대해 생각해 볼 시간은 없다.

해설

13 과학에서는 발견에 따른 가능한 결과를 직접적으로 그리고 명시적으로 조사하며, 인간을 포함하는 어떤 연구가 수행될 때는 언제나 제도적인 검토 위원회가 요구되는 등 윤리적 문제가 중요하게 여겨지지만, 기술은 윤리적 분석의 측면에서는 비참할 정도로 불완전하고 윤리적 문제에 대해 관심이 부족하다며 과학과 기술을 비교하는 내용의 글이다. 따라서 제목으로 가장 적절한 것은 ⑤ '윤리적 관점에서 본 과학과 기술'이다.
① 윤리적 기술: 윤리성을 우선순위로 만들기
② 과학과 기술의 보편성에 대하여
③ 기술 발전과 미래의 잠재적 위험성
④ 기술이 도입한 새로운 윤리적 문제

14 마지막 문장에서 모든 것이 덧없어졌고 내일이면 쓸모없게 될 것에 대해 생각해 볼 시간은 없다고 했으므로, 빠르게 변화하는 기술 환경의 특징 가운데 내포된 의미를 고려해 볼 수 없다는 것을 추론할 수 있다. 따라서 (e) ability(~할 수 있음)를 disability(~할 수 없음)와 같은 단어로 바꿔야 한다.

TEXT FLOW

1단락과 2단락의 명확한 대비에 의한 흐름:	
[1단락] 과학에서는 윤리 문제에 주의를 기울임	
도입	과학에서는 예방 원칙에 따라 발견에 따른 가능한 결과를 사전에 조사함
전개	인간을 포함하는 어떤 연구에서든 제도적인 검토 위원회가 요구됨
[2단락] 기술에서는 윤리 문제에 대한 관심이 부족함	
전환	기술에서는 방법과 적용에만 관심이 있고 윤리적 분석이 매우 부족함
부연	윤리적 관심이 부족한 원인은 이익을 염두에 둔 동기 및 빠른 기술 환경 변화 때문임

구문

• There are unethical scientists, and there are certainly scientific advances [that occurred because the unfortunate implications could not be predicted at the time], but the point is [that science **does** directly and explicitly examine the possible consequences of discovery].

: 첫 번째 [ ]는 scientific advances를 수식하는 관계절이고, 두 번째 [ ]는 is의 보어 역할을 하는 명사절이다. 두 번째 [ ] 안의 does는 동사 examine을 강조하기 위해 쓰인 조동사이다.

• A direct manifestation of this can be seen in the requirement [that any research {involving human subjects} **be examined** by an outside group of reviewers {to determine 〈**if** there are any risks to the people involved〉}].
: [ ]는 the requirement와 동격의 의미를 갖는 명사절인데, requirement가 요구의 뜻을 나타내므로 that절에는 「(should+)동사원형」인 be examined가 쓰였다. [ ] 안의 첫 번째 { }는 any research를 수식하는 현재분사구이고, 두 번째 { }는 목적의 의미를 나타내는 부사적 용법의 to부정사구이며, 〈 〉는 determine의 목적어 역할을 하는 명사절로 if는 '~인지 아닌지'의 의미를 나타낸다.

GRAMMAR REVIEW
본문 129쪽

1 embedded	2 results	3 making
4 that	5 had spent	6 in which
7 suggesting	8 easily	9 were
10 becomes		

1 Its individual members가 분사의 의미상 주어인데, embed의 목적어가 없는 상태에서 의미상 행위를 하는 주체가 아니라 대상이므로 수동의 의미를 갖는 과거분사 embedded를 써야 한다.

2 접속사 that이 이끄는 명사절의 주어가 an increase이므로 단수 동사 results가 적절하다.

3 Doing one thing at a time과 refusing to live an over-scheduled life와 함께 and로 연결되어 주어 역할을 해야 하므로 동명사 making이 적절하다.

4 선행사 an ancient cemetery가 관계절에서 동사 may hold의 주어 역할을 하므로 주격 관계대명사 that이 적절하다.

5 보너스 집단에게 연락했을 때 그들이 이미 더 많은 돈을 써버린 상태였으므로 과거완료 had spent가 적절하다.

6 a society를 수식하는 관계절로 뒤에 주어와 동사가 모두 있는 완전한 형태의 절이 이어지므로 in which가 적절하다.

7 문장의 주어 An article published in June 2009에 대한 동사 listed가 있어서 앞의 명사구(over 100 well-documented cases)를 수식하는 분사가 필요한데, that 이하의 목적어가 존재하므로 현재분사 suggesting이 적절하다.

8 의미상 give를 수식하는 부사가 와야 하므로 easily가 적절하다.

9 주어의 핵은 theories이므로 복수 동사 were가 적절하다.

10 the first question을 주어로 하는 술어 동사 자리이므로 becomes가 적절하다.

본문 132쪽

고난도 모의고사 **01**회

| 01 ② | 02 ③ | 03 ④ | 04 ③ |
| 05 ⑤ | 06 ② | 07 ⑤ | 08 ④ |

01 정답 ②

사교 로봇공학을 우리가 처음 수용한 것은 우리가 기술로부터 무엇을 원하고 그것을 수용하기 위해 무엇을 할 것인지를 보여 주는 창이다. 우리의 로봇 꿈의 관점에서 볼 때, 네트워크화된 삶은 새로운 배역을 맡는다. 우리는 그것의 '약한 유대', 즉 우리가 결코 만나지 못할 사람들과의 친밀함의 유대를 찬양한다. 그러나 그것이 우리가 그것에 성공한다는 것을 의미하지는 않는다. 우리는 흔히 우리 자신이 과장 광고에 고갈된 채로 서 있는 것을 발견한다. 사람들이 이런 약한 유대 관계의 즐거움에 관해 '마찰이 없다'고 이야기할 때, 그들은 보통 여러분이 자신의 자리를 떠나지 않고 가질 수 있는 종류의 관계를 가리키고 있는 것이다. 기술은 우리를 자유롭게 해 주겠다고 약속하면서 (동시에) 우리를 구속한다. 연결 기술은 한때 우리에게 더 많은 시간을 주겠다고 약속했다. 하지만 휴대전화와 스마트폰이 일과 여가의 경계를 잠식함에 따라, 세계의 모든 시간은 충분하지 않았다. 우리가 '직장에 있지' 않을 때조차도, 우리는 우리 자신이 '대기 중'이라는 것을 경험한다.

해설

사교 로봇공학에 의해 네트워크화된 삶은 우리에게 약한 유대 관계의 즐거움, 즉 삶을 확장시키는 즐거움을 제공해 주지만, 그로 인해 일과 여가의 경계가 잠식됨에 따라 우리를 제한하는 역할도 한다는 내용의 글이다. 따라서 밑줄 친 부분이 글에서 의미하는 바로 가장 적절한 것은 ② '우리의 확장된 삶의 영역을 제한한다'이다.
① 예기치 않은 갈등을 해결하는 데 도움이 된다
③ 일과 여가의 경계를 설정한다
④ 사람들이 기술 발전을 두려워하게 만든다
⑤ 인간 관계가 더 효율적으로 기능하는 것을 가능하게 한다

TEXT FLOW

도입	네트워크화된 삶은 새로운 배역을 맡음
전개	결코 만나지 못할 수도 있는 사람들과의 친밀함의 유대가 확장되지만 우리가 그것에 성공하는 것은 아님
주제	기술은 우리를 자유롭게 해 줌과 동시에 우리를 구속하기도 함
부연	휴대전화와 스마트폰이 일과 여가의 경계를 잠식함에 따라 세계의 모든 시간은 충분하지 않았으며, 직장에 있지 않아도 우리는 늘 대기 중인 상태에 놓인 것을 경험함

구문

• Our first embrace of sociable robotics is a window onto [what we want from technology] and [what we are willing to do to accommodate it].
: 두 개의 [ ]는 and로 연결되어 onto의 목적어 역할을 하는 명사절이다.

• [When people talk about the pleasures of these weak-tie relationships as "friction free,"] they are usually referring to the kind of relationships [you can have without leaving your desk].
: 첫 번째 [ ]는 시간을 나타내는 부사절이고, 두 번째 [ ]는 the kind of relationships를 수식하는 관계절이다.

02 정답 ③

우리는 오늘날의 더 가난한 국가들이 서구 국가들이 발전했던 역사적 맥락과는 매우 다른 맥락에서 발전하고 있다는 것을 점점 더 많이 인식하고 있다. 우선 새로운 오염 물질이 있고 현대 기술은 19세기나 20세기 초에 비해 훨씬 더 빠르게 자원을 추출할 수 있다. 무역을 통해 기존 기술을 국내에서 개발하는 대신 그것들을 수입할 수 있는데, 그것은 효율성이 우선된다면 환경적으로 유익할 수도 있다. 그러나 무역은 또한 '오염 피난처'가 출현하는 대로 놔두기도 한다. 오늘날의 개발도상국 중 상당수는 과거 식민지 국가이다. 서구 국가들은 자신의 식민지에서 원료를 빼내냄으로써 발전했다. 이들 현재 독립 국가 중 상당수는 여전히 추출주의적 개발 모델에 갇혀 있다. 그들은 다른 발전 '단계'로 나아감으로써가 아니라 천연자원의 추출과 수출 확대를 통해서만 더 높은 소득을 추구할 수 있다. 일부에서는 중국이 성장을 추구하는 과정에서 '식민지 강대국'이 될 것인지의 여부를 생각하지만, 대부분의 개발도상국에는 이러한 선택권이 없다. 따라서 우리는 오늘날 더 가난한 국가들의 발전 경로를 예측하기 위해 서구의 경험을 이용하는 것에 대해 매우 신중해야 한다.

해설

오늘날의 더 가난한 국가들은 서구 국가들이 발전했던 역사적 맥락과 매우 달라진 맥락에서 발전하고 있으므로, 그들의 발전 경로를 예측하기 위해 서구의 발전 모델을 적용하는 것은 바람직하지 않다는 내용의 글이다. 따라서 글의 제목으로 가장 적절한 것은 ③ '더 가난한 국가들은 서구 국가들이 발전한 대로 발전할 것인가?'이다.
① 무역에서 효율성이 공정성보다 우선되는 이유
② 문화가 국제 무역에 영향을 미치는 시기와 방식
④ 저개발국에 경제 원조를 제공하자!
⑤ 천연자원의 추출 확대: 개발의 열쇠

⊗ 매력적인 오답 주의!

② 글의 요지와 무관하게 상식에 기반하여 서구 국가와 개발도상국의 경제 발전 경로가 달라지는 원인을 문화라고 판단하면 고를 수 있는 오답이다.

TEXT FLOW

도입	서구 국가와 현재 개발도상국 간의 발전 맥락이 다름
전개	발전 맥락의 차이의 여러 사례
결론	개발도상국에 적용되는 서구 발전 모델의 한계

구문

• Increasingly, we recognise [that today's poorer countries are developing in a very different context to the historical context {in which Western countries developed}].

: [ ]는 recognise의 목적어 역할을 하는 명사절이고, 그 안의 { }는 the historical context를 수식하는 관계절이다.

- Trade allows for importing existing technologies rather than developing them domestically, [which could be environmentally beneficial if efficiency is prioritised].
  : [ ]는 importing existing technologies rather than developing them domestically를 부가적으로 설명하는 관계절이다.

03
정답 ④

동기가 무엇이든지 간에, 복지는 현재 어류 양식의 의제에 올라 있으며, 양식 업계의 몇몇 구성원들은 어떤 현행 관행이 양식되는 어류에 부정적인 영향을 미치는지 파악하기 위해 어류 과학자들과 협력을 시작했다. 연구원들은 물고기에게 스트레스를 주는 다양한 일상적인 취급 관행을 이미 확인했고, 어떤 경우에 이것은 관행의 변화를 가져왔다. 예를 들어, 크기에 따른 등급 나누기는 물고기가 그물망에 걸리고 취급되어야 할 필요가 있는 한때 매우 노동 집약적인 과정이었지만, 지금은 계측기 설비가 갖춰진 펌프와 넓은 직경의 호스가 탱크나 연못 사이에서 다른 크기의 물고기를 이동시키는 데 사용된다. 이것은 직접 취급하는 것과 물고기가 물 밖에서 보내는 시간의 양을 증가시킨다(→ 감소시킨다). 그 결과는 물고기에게 분명히 이로운데, 등급 매기기는 이제 스트레스를 덜 받는 과정이고 물고기는 더 빠르게 회복한다. 등급 매기기 절차를 개선하는 긍정적인 경험은 농업의 일상적인 측면을 개선할 수 있는 다른 방법을 찾는 것에 대한 관심으로 이어졌다.

해설
어류 양식에서 물고기의 복지를 위한 관행의 변화에 대한 내용의 글로, 물고기 크기에 따른 등급 나누기는 예전에는 그물망으로 잡아서 다루어야 했지만, 지금은 계측기 설비가 갖춰진 펌프와 넓은 직경의 호스를 사용하여 탱크와 연못 사이에서 다른 크기의 물고기를 이동시킨다고 했으므로, 직접적으로 물고기를 다루거나 물고기가 물 밖에서 보내는 시간이 줄어들 것임을 추론할 수 있다. 따라서 ④ increases(증가시키다)를 decreases(감소시키다)와 같은 단어로 바꿔야 한다.

TEXT FLOW

도입	어류 양식에서 복지가 의제로 올라 있으며 어류 과학자들과 협력하기 시작함
예시	크기에 따른 등급 나누기는 매우 노동 집약적인 과정이었지만, 지금은 계측기 설비가 갖춰진 펌프와 넓은 직경의 호스가 다른 크기의 물고기를 이동시키는 데 사용되어, 물고기의 스트레스를 덜어 줌
결론	이런 개선의 경험은 농업의 개선에 대한 관심으로 이어짐

구문

- Whatever the motivation, welfare is now on the fish farming agenda and several members of the aquaculture community have begun collaborating with fish scientists [to identify {which current practices adversely affect farmed fish}].
  : [ ]는 목적의 의미를 나타내는 부사적 용법의 to부정사구이고, 그 안의 { }는 의문사절로 identify의 목적어 역할을 한다.

- Size-grading, for example, was once a very labour-intensive process [requiring fish to be netted and handled], but now pumps and wide-diameter hoses [fitted with counters] **are**

used to move fish of different size between tanks or ponds.
: 첫 번째 [ ]는 a very labour-intensive process를 수식하는 현재분사구이고, 두 번째 [ ]는 pumps and wide-diameter hoses를 수식하는 과거분사구이다. 「be used+to부정사」는 '~하는 데 사용되다'는 의미를 나타낸다.

04
정답 ③

기후 변화 적응을 연구하기 위한 미시 경제학의 접근 방식은 변화에 대처하는 데 있어서 누가 우위를 가지고 있고 어떻게 이 능력을 구축하는지 탐구한다. 예를 들어, 특정 도시와 그 도시 내의 특정 여가 활동을 좋아하는 사람들은 다른 곳으로 이주하려 하지 않을 것이기 때문에 도시 특유의 기후 충격에 대처하는 데 있어 민첩성이 떨어질 것이다. 스키를 좋아하고 다른 레저 활동으로 대체하고 싶지 않은 사람은 겨울의 지역 기온이 자주 빙점 위로 올라가면 다른 사람들보다 더 많은 것을 잃게 될 것이다. 대체하려는 의사를 보여 주는 바로 그 문제가 기후 변화의 영향을 평가할 때에도 발생한다. 음식을 생각해 보라. 여러분이 딸기와 자두 먹는 것을 똑같이 즐기지만, 기후 변화가 (아마도 그것을 재배하는 데 필요한 물 때문에) 딸기의 가격을 올린다고 가정해 보라. 이 경우, 여러분은 자두로 딸기를 대체할 수 있기 때문에 크게 손해를 보지 않을 것이다. 대용품에 대한 이 중요한 경제 개념은 계속해서 생겨난다. 기후 변화가 과거의 일상적인 일과 소비 습관을 어지럽힐수록 대체하기를 꺼리거나 대체하지 못하는 사람들은 더 손해를 볼 것이다.

해설
미시 경제학적 측면에서의 기후 변화 적응 연구에 관한 글이다. 빈칸 앞부분에서 특정 도시와 그 도시 내의 특정 여가 활동을 좋아하는 사람들은 기후 충격이 오더라도 다른 활동으로 대체하고 싶어 하지 않아 다른 사람들보다 더 많은 것을 잃게 될 것이라고 했고, 빈칸 뒷부분에서도 이와 유사한 예로 대용품에 대한 개념이 소개되므로, 빈칸에 들어갈 말로 가장 적절한 것은 ③ '대체하려는 의사를 보여 주는'이다.
① 그들 자신의 환경을 향상시키는
② 다양한 취미에 적극적으로 참여하는
④ 기후 변화를 지구 온난화 탓으로 돌리는
⑤ 특정한 여가 활동에 대해 열정적인

TEXT FLOW

도입	기후 변화 적응을 연구하기 위한 미시 경제학의 접근 방식의 탐구 방법
예시 1	특정 도시와 그 도시 내의 특정 여가 활동을 좋아하는 사람들의 예
예시 2	대용품에 대한 딸기와 자두의 예
결론	기후 변화의 영향에 대해 대체하기를 꺼리거나 대체하지 못하는 사람들은 더 손해를 볼 것임

구문

- The microeconomic approach for studying climate change adaptation **explores** [who has an edge in coping with change] and [how one builds this capacity].
  : 문장의 동사는 explores이며 목적어 역할을 하는 두 개의 의문사절 [ ]가 and로 연결되었다.

- Those [who are unwilling or unable to substitute] will suffer more [as climate change disrupts past routines and consumption habits].

: 첫 번째 [ ]는 Those를 수식하는 관계절이고, 두 번째 [ ]는 '~할수록'이라는 의미를 나타내는 부사절이다.

05　　　　　　　　　　　　　　　　　　　　　정답 ⑤

원칙적으로 농업 잉여물의 생산은 가능하게 되었지만, 수천 년 동안 이것이 일상적 요구의 충족 외에 인간이 만든 복잡성의 대규모 축적 또는 빠르게 증가하는 사회적 복잡성으로 이어지지는 않았다. 현재의 전통적인 농업 사회가 과거에 일어났을지도 모를 것들에 대한 상당히 좋은 모형을 제공하지만, 생산된 어느 잉여물이든 경쟁적인 연회와 다른 사회적 의무에서 완전히는 아니어도 대부분 소비되었고, 이는 그런 사회 내에서 강력한 경제 평준화 효과를 가져왔을 것이다. 그러한 교류는 사회적 의무 네트워크를 구축하는데, 그것은 더 수확이 적은 시기에 살아남는 데 도움이 된다. 이런 상황의 결과로, 어떠한 실질적인 잉여물도 축적되지 않았을 것이고, 이는 '문명화된' 사회의 보다 더 정교한 형태의 사회적 또는 기술적 복잡성의 출현을 매우 제한했다. 심지어 그런 사람들은 자신들의 사회의 복잡성을 가능한 한 낮게 유지하는 것을 선호했을지도 모른다. 이러한 경향은 아마 근본적인 인간의 특징일 것인데, 이것은 단지 더 많은 복잡성을 생산하려면 더 많은 에너지가 필요하다는 이유만으로 진화했을 것이다.

해설

농업에서 잉여 생산물이 발생하게 되었지만 그것이 복잡성의 축적으로 이어지지 않고 일상적 요구를 충족시키면서 사회 내의 강력한 경제 평준화 효과를 가져왔을 것이라는 내용의 글이다. 빈칸 앞에서 실질적인 잉여물이 축적되지 않았고 사회적·기술적 복잡성의 출현이 제한되었다고 했으므로, 빈칸에 들어갈 말로는 ⑤ '자신들의 사회의 복잡성을 가능한 한 낮게 유지하는 것을 선호했을'이 가장 적절하다.
① 생산된 어떤 잉여물이든 대체 에너지원으로 전환했을
② 사회적 통합과 배제의 복잡성을 통제했을
③ 경쟁에 의해 발생된 복잡한 사회적 문제들을 해결하려고 노력했을
④ 경제적 평등보다는 번영을 위한 환경을 조성했을

TEXT FLOW

주제	농업 잉여물의 생산이 인간이 만든 복잡성의 대규모 축적 또는 사회적 복잡성으로 이어지지는 않았음
전개	어느 잉여물이든 경쟁적인 연회나 다른 사회적 의무에서 대부분 소비되었고, 이는 강력한 경제 평준화 효과를 가져왔을 것임
부연	축적되지 않은 실질적인 잉여물은 보다 정교한 형태의 사회적·기술적 복잡성의 출현을 제한했고, 사람들은 사회의 복잡성을 가능한 한 낮게 유지하는 것을 선호했을 수 있음

구문

• If current traditional agrarian societies provide a reasonably good model of [what may have happened in the past], any produced surplus was mostly, if not entirely, consumed in competitive feasting and other social obligations, [which would have had a strong economic leveling effect within such societies].
: 첫 번째 [ ]는 선행사를 포함한 관계절로 전치사 of의 목적어 역할을 하며, 두 번째 [ ]는 주절의 내용 전체를 부연 설명하는 관계절이다.

• As a result of this situation, no substantial surplus would have accumulated, [which very much limited {the emergence of more elaborate forms of social or technical complexity characteristic of 'civilized' societies}].
: [ ]는 앞 절의 내용 전체를 부연 설명하는 관계절이고, 그 안의 { }는 limited의 목적어 역할을 하는 명사구이다.

06　　　　　　　　　　　　　　　　　　　　　정답 ②

유전자, 상황, 또는 치료가 우리의 성격을 바꿀 때마다, 그것들은 뇌를 변화시킴으로써 그렇게 해야 한다. 그런 의미에서, 모든 성격 차이는 그것이 유전적 특질의 영향을 받든 받지 않든 간에 생물학적인데, 이는 반드시 뇌를 거쳐야 하기 때문이다. (B) 이러한 신경 생물학적 변화는 뇌 내부의 화학적 변화를 동반한다. 예를 들어, 단호함, 경쟁력, 지배, 그리고 호전성은 모두 남녀를 막론하고 테스토스테론의 영향을 받는다. (A) 높은 수치의 테스토스테론은 우리를 공격적인 행동으로 이끌고, 낮은 수준은 공손함으로 이끈다. 테스토스테론 수치는 유전자, 문화, 그리고 기회라는 세 가지 요인에 의해 영향을 받는다. 성공적인 사냥, 빠른 자동차 운전, 대중의 이목을 끌거나 많은 사람을 책임지는 것과 같은 상황은 테스토스테론 수치를 증가시킬 수 있다. (C) 노화의 정상적인 과정은 그것들을 낮추는 경향이 있다. 일반적인 전문적 직업의 경로에서는 나이가 들수록 더 큰 권위를 얻게 해 주는데, 이는 일부 사람들에게서 생물학적으로 낮아진 테스토스테론 수치를 보상해 줄 수 있다.

해설

주어진 글은 성격이 바뀔 때마다 뇌의 변화를 거쳐야 하기 때문에 성격의 차이는 생물학적이라는 내용이다. (B)에서 These neurobiological changes가 주어진 글에 제시된 뇌의 변화를 가리키므로 주어진 글 다음에는 (B)가 이어져야 한다. 그다음으로는 (B)에서 제시된 테스토스테론의 영향이 구체화된 (A)가 이어져야 하고, (C)의 첫 문장에서 them이 가리키는 것이 (A)의 마지막에 언급된 testosterone levels이므로, 노화가 일어나면 테스토스테론의 수치가 낮아지고 이를 보상받기 위해 더 큰 권위를 얻게 된다는 내용의 (C)가 마지막에 오는 것이 글의 흐름상 가장 자연스럽다.

TEXT FLOW

도입	성격은 뇌의 변화를 통해 일어남
주제	성격의 차이는 생물학적이며 뇌 내부의 화학적 변화를 동반함
예시	단호함, 경쟁력, 지배, 그리고 호전성 등은 테스토스테론의 영향을 받음
결론	전문직의 경로에서는 노화로 인해 낮아진 테스토스테론 수치를 보상해 주기 위해 더 큰 권위를 부여함

구문

• [Whenever genes, situations, or therapy changes our personalities], they must do so by changing the brain.
: [ ]는 부사절로 whenever는 '~할 때마다'라는 뜻을 나타낸다. do so는 change our personalities를 대신한다.

• Situations [such as a successful hunt, driving a fast car, being in the public eye, or being in charge of a large number of people] can increase testosterone levels.
: [ ]는 전치사구로 문장의 주어인 Situations를 수식한다.

07　　　　　　　　　　　　　　　　　　　　　정답 ⑤

우리는 흔히 외로운 사람을 수동적이고 조용하고 말이 없다고 생각한다. 실제로, 우리 중 많은 사람들이 인생에서 가장 외로운 시간을 기억할 때, 망치

로 두드리는 듯한 심장, 질주하는 생각들 또는 높은 스트레스 상황의 다른 전형적인 징후들을 즉시 기억하지는 않는다. 대신에 외로움은 고요함이라는 연상을 불러일으킨다. 그러나 체내에 있는 고독의 화학적 존재, 즉 그것이 살고 있는 곳과 그것이 우리의 정맥을 세차게 흐르며 보내는 호르몬은 본질적으로 우리가 공격을 받는다고 느낄 때 우리가 하는 '싸우거나 도망치는' 반응과 동일하다. 가장 서서히 진행되는 외로움의 건강상 영향 중 일부에 연료를 공급하는 것이 바로 이 스트레스 반응이다. 이것들은 광범위한 것일 수 있고, 심지어 최악의 경우 치명적일 수도 있다. <u>그래서 우리가 외로움에 대해 말할 때 우리는 단지 외로운 마음만 말하고 있는 것이 아니라 외로운 육체에 대해서도 말하고 있는 것이다.</u> 그 둘은 물론 서로 얽혀 있다.

해설
주어진 문장은 외로움에 대해 말할 때 외로운 마음과 외로운 육체에 대해 동시에 말하고 있다는 내용으로, ⑤ 다음 문장의 The two는 주어진 문장의 lonely minds와 lonely bodies를 가리킨다. 따라서 주어진 문장이 들어가기에 가장 적절한 곳은 ⑤이다.

TEXT FLOW

도입	외로운 사람에 대한 일반적인 생각
부연	외로움은 고요함이라는 연상
전환	그러나 외로움에 대한 우리 몸의 반응은 '싸우거나 도망치는' 반응과 동일함
결론	외로움은 외로운 마음과 외로운 육체를 포괄하는 것임

구문
• Yet the chemical presence of loneliness in the body — where it lives and the hormones it sends coursing through our veins — is essentially identical to the 'fight or flight' reaction [we have {when we feel under attack}].
: [ ]는 the 'fight or flight' reaction을 수식하는 관계절로, 앞에 목적격 관계대명사가 생략되어 있다. 그 안의 { }는 시간의 부사절이다.

• **It's** this stress response **that** fuels some of the most insidious health effects of loneliness.
: 「It is ~ that ...」 강조구문으로 this stress response를 강조하고 있다.

08
정답 ④

1930년대 Stanford 대학의 사회학자였던 Richard LaPiere는 젊은 중국인 부부와 함께 미국 전역을 여행했다. LaPiere가 연구하던 시절에는 중국인에 대한 광범위한 편견이 아주 흔했고, 많은 식당과 호텔 매니저가 중국인에 대해 부정적인 태도를 보였다. 이런 태도가 행동을 얼마나 잘 예측할지 시험하기 위해, LaPiere는 이 부부를 데리고 미국 전역을 10,000마일 여행했는데, 그것은 251개의 식당, 캠핑장, 호텔에 대한 방문을 포함했다. 무슨 일이 일어났을까? 모든 184곳의 식당에서 그 중국인 부부를 받아 주었고, 그 식당 중 72곳에서 상당한 환대와 함께 그들을 맞이했다. 66개 호텔 방문에서 그들은 단 한 번만 거절당했다. 그 여행을 하고 나서 두 달 후에, LaPiere는 그들이 방문했던 모든 곳에 편지를 보내서 중국인 고객을 받아 줄 것인지 물었다. 응답한 사람들 중 91%는 지난 몇 달 내에 그런 부부가 분명히 서비스를 제공받았는데도 그런 손님을 받아 주지 않을 것이라고 말했다.
➡ LaPiere의 연구에서, 중국인 부부가 여행 중 대부분의 식당과 숙박 시설에서 <u>거절당하지</u> 않았다는 사실은 태도와 행동 사이의 연관성이 생각만큼 <u>강력하지</u> 않다는 것을 보여 준다.

해설
Richard LaPiere의 실험에서 중국인 손님을 받아 주지 않을 것이라는 태도를 보인 대다수의 여행 중 방문지에서 실제로는 중국인 부부가 거절당하지 않았다는 내용의 글이다. 따라서 요약문의 빈칸 (A)에는 rejected(거절당하지)가, (B)에는 strong(강력하지)이 들어가는 것이 가장 적절하다.
① 환영받지 – 밀접하지
② 환영받지 – 직접적이지
③ 서비스를 제공받지 – 흔하지
⑤ 거절당하지 – 간접적이지

⊗ 매력적인 오답 주의!
① 글 내용을 반대로 이해하거나 요약문 속의 not을 고려하지 못하면 고를 수 있는 오답이다.

TEXT FLOW

도입	Richard LaPiere의 연구 배경 소개: 중국인에 대한 편견이 일반적이었던 시대
전개	Richard LaPiere의 연구 세부 내용: 중국인 부부와 함께 미국 전역을 여행함
결론	태도와 행동이 실제로는 일치하지 않은 응답자들

구문
• To test how well these attitudes would predict behavior, LaPiere took this couple on a 10,000-mile trip throughout the United States, [which included visits to 251 restaurants, campgrounds, and hotels].
: [ ]는 a 10,000-mile trip throughout the United States에 대해 부가적으로 설명하는 관계절이다.

• Two months after the trip, LaPiere wrote to all of the places [they had visited] and asked [whether they would accept Chinese patrons].
: 첫 번째 [ ]는 all of the places를 수식하는 관계절이고, 두 번째 [ ]는 asked의 목적어 역할을 하는 명사절이다.

고난도 모의고사 02회

| 01 ② | 02 ③ | 03 ① | 04 ③ |
| 05 ② | 06 ⑤ | 07 ④ | 08 ① |

01
정답 ②

코딩은 항상 그것에 관해 신비로운 마법적 느낌을 가지고 있어 왔다. 물론, 그것은 공학의 한 형태이다. 그러나 기계 공학, 산업 공학, 토목 공학과 같은 다른 모든 종류의 공학에서와는 달리, 우리가 소프트웨어로 만드는 기계는 단어로 짜여져 있다. 코드는 말인데, 인간이 실리콘에게 하는 말이고, 그것이 그 기계가 생명을 얻고 우리의 의지대로 행동하게 한다. 이것은 이상하게도 코드를 문학적인 것으로 만든다. 사실상, 법은 코드의 이러한 본성을 반영한다. 자동차의 엔진이나 깡통 따개 같은 물리적인 기계는 특허법에 의해 적용받는 반면, 소프트웨어는 또한 저작권에 의해 적용받아서, 그것이 시나 소설의 이상한 자매가 되도록 한다. 그렇지만 소프트웨어는 또한 분명히 시나 소설과는 상당히 '다른데', 그것이 우리가 사는 방식에 그러한 직접적인 물리적 영향을 입히기 때문이다. (부분적으로는 이것이 일부 코딩하는 사람들이 코드를 저작권법으로 규제하는 것이 파괴적이라고 생각하는 이유이다.) 코드는 반은 금속의 세계이고 반은 아이디어의 세계에 다리를 걸치고 앉아 있다.

해설
코드는 단어로 쓰인 말이며 시나 소설처럼 저작권에 적용을 받지만, 문학 작품과는 달리 실제로 기계를 작동시키는 역할을 하고 있다는 맥락이므로, 밑줄 친 부분이 글에서 의미하는 바로 가장 적절한 것은 ② '단어들로 구성되었지만 물리적 세계를 통제하며'이다.
① 과학 분야에 있어 가장 시적인 부문이며
③ 인간의 언어로 번역될 수 있는 서면 기호들이며
④ 해석에서는 주관적이지만 표현에서는 객관적이며
⑤ 기계 언어로 기계의 작동 원리를 표현하며

TEXT FLOW
도입	코딩은 공학의 한 형태이지만 신비로운 느낌이 있음
부연	다른 공학과 달리 단어로 짜여져 있으면서 물리적으로 기계를 작동시킴
결론	코드는 물리적 세계와 단어의 세계 사이에 존재함

구문
• [While {physical machines like car engines or can openers} are governed by patent law], software is also governed by copyright, [making it a weird sister of the poem or the novel].
: 첫 번째 [ ]는 접속사 While이 이끄는 부사절이고, 그 안의 { }는 부사절의 주어인 명사구이다. 두 번째 [ ]는 분사구문으로, 능동의 의미이므로 현재분사인 making이 쓰였다.

02
정답 ③

문학의 예술은 아마도 원시 이야기꾼의 예술에서 유래했을 것이다. 그는 단순히 오락을 제공하는 것이 아니라 청중에게 그들이 누구인지, 그들이 어디에서 왔는지, 그리고 그들의 삶이 무엇을 의미하는지에 대한 구전을 전승했다. 그는 청중들의 존재에게서 의미와 질서를 부여함으로써 일이 돌아가는 상황에서의 개인적 가치에 대한 그들의 기분을 향상시키고 그들의 삶을 구성하는 사회적 과제와 관계를 효과적으로 처리할 수 있는 그들의 능력을 키우고 있었다. 한 사회의 신화는 일반적으로 그 사회의 전통적 가치와 도덕규범을 구체적으로 표현한다. 따라서 이런 신화의 반복은 사회의 일관성과 통일성을 강화하고 각 개인에게 의미와 목적의식을 부여한다. 문학은 원래 (사회에) 순응하는 데 있어서 유용했던 활동에서 발전한 것으로 이해될 수 있다.

해설
문학의 예술은 사회 구성원들의 존재에 의미와 질서를 부여함으로써 자기 가치에 자긍심을 가지게 해서 그들이 사회에 잘 순응하게 하는 역할을 해 왔다는 내용의 글이다. 따라서 글의 주제로 가장 적절한 것은 ③ '사회 순응을 위한 문학의 기능적 측면'이다.
① 신화에서 흔히 사용되는 문학적 장치
② 문학 주제의 주된 원천으로서의 일상생활
④ 오락에 대한 인간의 기본 본능
⑤ 도덕규범을 만들어 내는 수단으로서의 신화

❌ 매력적인 오답 주의!
⑤ 도덕규범을 만들어 내는 것이 아니라 전승하는 문학의 사회적 기능을 이해하지 못하면 고를 수 있는 오답이다.

TEXT FLOW
도입	원시 이야기꾼의 예술에서 기원한 문학의 예술
전개	사회 순응을 위한 원시 이야기꾼의 역할
결론	사회 순응에 유용한 활동에서 발전한 문학

구문
• The art of literature probably derived from **that** of the primitive story-teller.
: that은 the art를 대신하는 대명사이다.

• By making sense and order out of his listeners' existence, he was [enhancing their feeling of personal worth in the scheme of things] and [therefore increasing their capacity to deal effectively with the social tasks and relationships {which made up their lives}].
: 두 개의 [ ]가 and로 연결되어 was에 이어진다. 두 번째 [ ] 안의 { }는 the social tasks and relationships를 수식하는 관계절이다.

03
정답 ①

오늘날의 노동 인구에서 관리자들과 감독자들은 다양한 집단의 직원들에게 동기를 부여해야 하는 일에 직면해 있다. 모든 연령대와 문화적 배경을 가진 사람들을 중요하고, 연결되고, 유용하고, 그리고 동기 부여를 받은 것처럼 느끼게 만드는 것이 큰 과제이다. 이토록 경쟁이 매우 심한 줄어든 예산의 시대에, 관습에 얽매이지 않고 비용 효율이 높은 어떤 수단이 직원들의 동기 부여와 잔류(이직 방지)를 증가시키는 데에 필요하다. 잔류는 떠나는 직원을 대체하기 위한 추정액이 그 사람의 연봉의 250%에 이르는 상황에서 기업에 드는 비용의 핵심 변수이다. 이직에 의한 손실은 미국 경제에 매년 5조 달러를 고갈시킨다고 하며, 종종 가장 무시되는 사업 비용이다. 떠나는 노동자들은 당신이 잃고 싶지 않은 바로 그 직원들일 수도 있어서, 그 손실을 훨씬 더 괴롭게 만든다.

해설

① make는 사역동사로 목적어(people ~ backgrounds)와 목적격 보어(feel ~ motivated)를 취하는데, 이 문장에서는 make가 아니라 is가 술어동사로 쓰였으므로, make가 명령문 형태로 쓰일 수 없다. 따라서 문장의 주어 역할을 하도록 To make(to부정사)나 Making(동명사)으로 고쳐야 한다.
② 형용사 competitive를 수식하는 부사 highly는 적절하다.
③ '떠나는'이라는 능동의 의미이므로 명사 employee를 수식하는 현재분사 departing은 적절하다.
④ 주어 Turnover losses와 동사 say는 수동의 관계이므로 수동태(are said)가 쓰인 것은 적절하다.
⑤ 비교급 more painful을 수식하는 비교급 강조 표현 even은 적절하다.

TEXT FLOW

도입	오늘날 관리자들과 감독자들은 다양한 집단의 직원들에게 동기를 부여해야 함
전개	경쟁이 매우 심한 줄어든 예산의 시대에 직원들에게 동기를 부여하고 이직을 방지하는 수단이 필요함
부연	종종 가장 무시되는 사업 비용이지만, 직원의 이직에 의한 손실은 매우 큼

구문

• In these highly competitive times of shrinking budgets, some unconventional and cost-effective means are necessary [to increase staff motivation and retention].
: [ ]는 형용사 necessary를 수식하는 부사적 용법의 to부정사구이다.

04
정답 ③

우리 경험의 많은 측면이 보이는 대로가 아니다. 여러분이 이 단어들을 읽을 때 지금 하고 있는 분명한 경험을 보라. 눈이 페이지를 스쳐 지나갈 때, 여러분의 시각 세계는 계속 이어지고 풍부해 보이지만, 여러분은 사실 그 사이에 있는 모든 글자를 거의 읽지 않고 실제로는 한 번에 텍스트의 일부분만을 본 보기로 살펴보고 있는 것뿐이다. 여러분의 주변 시야는 얼룩지고 무색이지만, 여러분은 그것이 시야의 중심처럼 완벽하게 선명하다고 장담할 수 있다. 어느 정도 거리를 두고 있는 레몬 크기의 두 개의 사각지대가 있는데, 그것은 여러분이 알아차리지도 못하는 시야의 중심에서 바로 벗어나 있다. 여러분의 시각 세계의 모든 것은 끊기지 않지만, 시각 세계는 눈이 움직이는 순식간에 깜깜해진다. 여러분의 뇌가 매우 설득력 있는 꾸며낸 이야기를 제공하기 때문에 이런 결함에 대해 그 어떤 것도 알지 못하게 된다. 우리 인식의 직접성에서부터 내면의 생각에 대한 사색에 이르기까지 똑같은 기만이 모든 인간 경험에도 적용되는데, 그것은 자아도 포함한다.

해설

우리 눈에 존재하는 시야의 중심에서 벗어난 사각지대에 관한 내용의 글이다. 눈을 깜빡이는 동안 우리 시야는 가려지지만, 뇌가 매우 설득력 있는 꾸며낸 이야기를 제공하기 때문에 우리의 경험이 진짜처럼 보인다는 것에서, 자아를 포함한 우리의 모든 경험에 '기만'이 존재한다는 것을 추론할 수 있다. 따라서 빈칸에 들어갈 말로 가장 적절한 것은 ③ '기만'이다.
① 공감   ② 자율성   ④ 가용성   ⑤ 경쟁

TEXT FLOW

도입	경험의 많은 측면이 보이는 것과는 다름
전개	눈이 페이지를 스칠 때 글자들이 이어지고 풍부해 보여도 그 사이의 모든 글자를 읽는 것은 아님
부연	시야에는 사각지대가 있어 결함이 생길 수밖에 없음
주제	뇌가 꾸며내는 설득력 있는 이야기 때문에 그러한 결함을 알지 못하는 것이며 인식의 직접성에서부터 내면의 생각에 대한 사색에 이르기까지 기만이 인간의 모든 경험에 적용됨

구문

• Take the clear experience [that you are having right now {as you read these words}].
: [ ]는 the clear experience를 수식하는 관계절로, 그 안의 { }는 때를 나타내는 부사절이다.

• There are [two blindspots, {the size of lemons at arm's length}], [just off-center from your field of view {that you do not even notice}].
: 첫 번째 [ ] 안의 { }는 two blindspots와 동격 관계를 이루는 명사구이다. 두 번째 [ ]는 첫 번째 [ ]를 수식하는 형용사구로, 그 안의 { }는 your field of view를 수식하는 관계절이다.

05
정답 ②

탄소 저장고 안팎의 흐름을 추정하는 것은 저장고 크기를 추정하는 것보다 훨씬 더 까다로운데, 이는 흔히 이러한 흐름의 원인이 되는 (광합성, 호흡, 분해와 같은) 작용의 속도를 정량화하기 어렵기 때문이다. 실제로 그러한 작용 중 많은 것이 간접적으로 측정된다. 예를 들어, 다양한 유형의 유기 물질이 분해되는 속도는 나뭇잎과 같은 쓰레기를 담고 있는 자루의 일정 기간에 걸친 질량 손실로 현장에서 추정될 수 있을 것인데, 그 자루는 유기체들이 쓰레기를 이산화탄소로 분해하면서 자유롭게 이동할 수 있는 그물 천으로 만들어져 있다. 이와 유사하게 총1차 생산량은 식물이나 나뭇잎을 포함하는 밀봉된 상자 내 이산화탄소 감소 혹은 산소 증가를 추적함으로써 측정될 수 있을 것이고, 순1차 생산량은 성장 기간이 시작될 때 그리고 절정일 때 특정 지역에서 식물 생물량의 무게 변화에 의해 추정될 수 있을 것이다.

해설

탄소 저장고 안팎의 흐름을 추정하는 것이 까다로운 이유는 이러한 흐름의 원인이 되는 (광합성, 호흡, 분해와 같은) 작용의 속도를 정량화하기 어렵기 때문이라고 하며, 빈칸 바로 다음에서 그것을 측정하는 방법의 예, 즉 다양한 유형의 유기 물질이 분해되는 속도가 나뭇잎과 같은 쓰레기를 담고 있는 자루의 일정 기간에 걸친 질량 손실로 현장에서 추정되는 점을 들었다. 이는 탄소 저장고 전체를 대상으로 측정하는 것이 아니라 간접적으로 측정하여 추정하는 방법이므로, 빈칸에 들어갈 말로 가장 적절한 것은 ② '간접적으로 측정된다'이다.
① 비슷한 구조를 갖는다
③ 수동으로 다루어지고 있다
④ 기후 변화와 관련 있다
⑤ 대기에서 이산화탄소를 제거한다

TEXT FLOW

도입	탄소 저장고 안팎의 흐름을 추정하는 것은 까다로움
주제	실제로 그중 많은 것이 간접적으로 측정됨
예시 1	다양한 유형의 유기 물질이 분해되는 속도가 간접적 측정 방식에 의해 이루어짐
예시 2	총1차 생산량과 순1차 생산량의 측정도 간접적으로 이루어짐

구문

- [Estimating fluxes in and out of a carbon reservoir] is even trickier than estimating the reservoir size [because **it** is often difficult {to quantify the rates of the processes (such as photosynthesis, respiration and decomposition) ⟨that contribute to these fluxes⟩}].
: 첫 번째 [ ]는 동명사구로 문장의 주어이다. 두 번째 [ ]는 이유를 나타내는 부사절로, it은 가주어이고 { }가 진주어이다. ⟨ ⟩는 the processes를 수식하는 관계절이다.

- Similarly, [gross primary production may be measured by monitoring the CO_2 decrease or O_2 increase in a sealed box {containing a plant or leaf}], and [net primary productivity may be estimated by the change in the weight of plant biomass over a given area at the beginning of and at the peak of the growing period].
: 두 개의 [ ]는 and로 연결되어 문장을 구성하는 절이다. 첫 번째 [ ] 안의 { }는 a sealed box를 수식하는 분사구이다.

06

정답 ⑤

우리 삶의 많은 부분이 친숙한 상황, 즉 우리 집의 방, 우리 마당, 학교나 직장을 오가는 우리의 길, 우리 사무실, 근린공원, 가게, 식당 등에서 보내진다. (C) 각 유형의 상황에 반복적으로 노출되면 거기서 무엇을 볼 것으로 기대해야 할지에 대해 우리의 마음속에 어떤 패턴이 형성된다. 일부 연구자들이 프레임이라고 부르는 이 지각 패턴은 그 상황에서 보통 우연히 마주치는 대상이나 사건을 포함한다. (B) 예를 들어, 여러분은 모든 세부 사항을 지속적으로 면밀히 조사할 필요가 없을 정도로, 여러분 집에 있는 대부분의 방을 잘 알고 있다. 여러분은 그것들이 어떻게 배치되어 있는지와 대부분의 물건들이 어디에 위치해 있는지 알고 있다. 여러분은 아마 완전한 어둠 속에서도 집의 많은 곳을 걸어 다닐 수 있을 것이다. 그러나 여러분이 집과 하는 경험은 여러분의 특정한 집보다 더 넓다. (A) 여러분의 뇌는 여러분의 집에 대한 패턴을 가지고 있을 뿐만 아니라, 일반적인 집에 대한 패턴도 가지고 있다. 그것은 익숙하고 새로운, 모든 집에 대한 여러분의 인식에 선입견을 갖게 한다. 부엌에서, 여러분은 가스레인지와 싱크대를 볼 것으로 기대한다. 욕실에서, 여러분은 변기, 세면대, 그리고 샤워기나 욕조(혹은 둘 다)를 볼 것으로 기대한다.

해설

주어진 글은 우리 삶의 많은 부분이 친숙한 상황에서 보내진다는 내용이다. 이어서 familiar situations를 each type of situation으로 받아서 그 상황에서 무엇을 볼지에 대한 프레임이라고 불리는 지각 패턴이 생긴다는 내용의 (C)가 와야 하며, 그다음에는 그에 대한 예로 집의 모든 세부 사항을 지속적으로 면밀히 조사할 필요 없이 알고 있다는 내용의 (B)가 오고, (B)의 마지막 문장(But your experience with homes is broader than your specific home.)을 your brain has one for homes in general로 받아 특정한 집뿐만 아니라 일반적인 집에 대한 패턴도 가지고

TEXT FLOW

도입	우리는 삶의 많은 부분을 친숙한 상황에서 보내게 됨
전개	각 상황에 반복적으로 노출되면 거기서 무엇을 볼지에 대한 패턴이 생기고, 그것을 일부 연구자들은 프레임(frames)이라고 부름
예시	집의 모든 세부 사항에 대해 면밀히 조사할 필요가 없을 정도로 대부분의 방에 대해 알고 있음
부연	우리의 뇌는 특정한 집뿐만 아니라 일반적인 집의 패턴도 가지고 있음

구문

- You know [how they are laid out] and [where most objects are located].
: 두 개의 [ ]는 and로 연결되어 know의 목적어 역할을 하는 의문사절이다.

- These perceptual patterns, [which some researchers call frames], include [the objects or events {that are usually encountered in that situation}].
: 첫 번째 [ ]는 These perceptual patterns를 부연 설명하는 관계절이고, 두 번째 [ ]는 include의 목적어 역할을 하는 명사구이며, 그 안의 { }는 the objects or events를 수식하는 관계절이다.

07

정답 ④

자연 선택은 우리 사회를 포함하여, 인간적인 모든 것을 이해하는 데 필수적이다. 신체적 특성과 마찬가지로, 행동적 특성에 있어서도 진화는 '적자생존'에 의해 작동한다. 각 세대에서, 우연한 돌연변이는 한 유기체의 자손이 한 개체가 생존하고 번식할 가능성을 증가시키거나 감소시킬 수 있는 작은 유전적 변화(그 변화는 또한 중립적일 수 있다)를 가질 것이라는 점을 의미한다. 여기서 자연 선택이 등장하는데, 한 유기체가 위치한 환경은 자연스럽게 일부 개체를 선호하겠지만 다른 개체는 선호하지 않을 것이고, 선호되는 개체들은 더 많은 후손을 가질 것이다. 환경은 동물 사육사처럼 행동하여, 누가 번식하게 되는지를 선택함으로써 몇 세대에 걸쳐서 선택된 특성을 수정한다. 하지만 진화는 그것이 어디로 가고 있는지 모르며, 그것에는 궁극적인 목표도 최종 단계도 없다. 유전자, 개체, 그리고 종은 미래에 어떤 특성이 유용할 것인지, 또는 어떤 특성이 이후의 수정을 위한 토대를 마련할 수 있을지를 예측할 방법을 가지고 있지 않다. 유전자는 생물학적 시스템이 정보를 저장하고 전송하는 하나의 방법일 뿐이다.

해설

주어진 문장은 진화는 그것이 어디로 가고 있는지 모르며, 그것에는 궁극적인 목표도 최종 단계도 없다는 내용이다. But으로 시작하여 진화의 부정적인 면을 제시하고 있으므로, 자연 선택을 통한 진화의 특성을 기술하는 문장과 미래에 어떤 특성이 유용할지, 어떤 특성이 이후의 수정을 위한 토대를 마련할 수 있을지를 예측할 방법이 없다는 문장 사이인 ④에 들어가는 것이 가장 적절하다.

③ 충동 – 영향을 미칠
④ 숫자 – 증가시킬
⑤ 기억 – 증가시킬

도입	스탠퍼드 대학 교수가 인지 부하에 관한 실험을 함
전개	기억할 일곱 자리 숫자가 주어진 사람들과 두 자리 숫자가 주어진 사람들을 대상으로 자제력에 관련된 실험을 실시함
결론	인지 부하가 높을수록 충동적인 감정에 의존하게 됨

구문

• The volunteers were then told **to walk** to another room and in so doing **pass** a table [where they had to choose between chocolate cake or fruit salad].
: to walk ~와 (to) pass ~는 and로 연결되어 were told에 이어진다. [ ]는 a table을 수식하는 관계절이다.

• Shiv speculates [**that** remembering seven-digit number required cognitive resources {that **had to come** from somewhere, and in this case **were taken** from our ability to control our urges}]!
: [ ]는 명사절로 speculates의 목적어 역할을 하며 that은 접속사이다. 그 안의 { }는 cognitive resources를 수식하는 관계절로, 동사구 had to come ~과 were taken ~이 and로 연결되어 있다.

• The neurons [that would normally be helping us make healthy food choices] were **otherwise** engaged in remembering a seven-digit number.
: [ ]는 관계절로 문장의 주어 The neurons를 수식하며, otherwise는 '(만약) 그렇지 않으면, 다른 상황에서는'이라는 의미를 나타낸다.

도입	인간적인 모든 것을 이해하는 데 자연 선택은 필수적이며, 진화는 '적자생존'에 의해 작동함
부연	돌연변이가 우연히 생성되기도 하지만, 자연 선택을 통해 선호되는 개체들이 더 많은 후손을 가질 것임
전환	하지만 진화는 그것이 어디로 가고 있는지 모르고, 궁극적인 목표나 최종 단계가 없음
결론	유전자, 개체, 그리고 종은 미래에 어떤 특성이 유용할지, 또는 이후의 수정을 위한 토대가 될지 예측할 수 없음

구문

• In each generation, chance mutations mean [that an organism's progeny will have small genetic changes {that might increase or decrease the likelihood ⟨that an individual will survive and reproduce⟩} (the changes can also be neutral)].
: [ ]는 mean의 목적어 역할을 하는 명사절이다. 그 안의 { }는 small genetic changes를 수식하는 관계절이고, ⟨ ⟩는 the likelihood의 구체적 내용을 설명하는 동격절이다.

• Genes, individuals, and species have no way of predicting [what traits will be useful in the future] or [which traits might set the stage for subsequent modifications].
: 두 개의 [ ]는 or로 연결되어 predicting의 목적어 역할을 하는 의문사절이다.

08
정답 ①

스탠퍼드 대학 교수 Baba Shiv는 멋진 실험을 했다. 그는 지원자의 절반에게는 (낮은 인지 부하를 나타내는) 기억해야 할 두 자리 숫자를 주고 나머지 절반에게는 일곱 자리 숫자(높은 인지 부하)를 주었다. 그런 다음 지원자들은 다른 방으로 걸어가야 하고 그렇게 하는 동안 그들이 초콜릿 케이크나 과일 샐러드 중에서 선택을 해야 하는 테이블을 지나간다는 말을 들었다. 높은 부하를 갖고 있던 사람들 중 59퍼센트가 케이크를 선택한 반면 낮은 부하를 갖고 있었던 사람들 중에서는 37퍼센트만이 그렇게 했다. Shiv는 일곱 개의 숫자를 기억하는 것은 어딘가에서 나와야 하는, 이 경우에는 우리의 충동 조절 능력에서 얻어지는 인지적인 공급원을 요구했다고 추측했다! 해부학적으로 이것은 그럴듯한데, 왜냐하면 (우리가 숫자를 '저장하는') 작동 기억과 자제심은 둘 다 우리의 전두엽 피질에 위치해 있기 때문이다. 다른 상황에서라면 보통 우리가 건강에 좋은 음식 선택을 하도록 도와주고 있을 것 같은 신경 세포들이 일곱 자리의 숫자를 기억하는 데 관여했다. 그러한 경우에 우리는 좀 더 충동적인 우리의 감정에 의존해야만 한다.

➡ 스탠퍼드 대학 교수 Baba Shiv의 인지 부하에 관한 실험은 머릿속에 보유해야 할 많은 것을 갖고 있는 것은 자제심 수준을 낮출 수도 있다는 것을 보여 준다.

해설

기억해야 할 숫자가 일곱 자리인 사람들은 초콜릿 케이크를 선택한 경우가 더 많았고, 기억해야 할 숫자가 두 자리인 사람들은 초콜릿 케이크를 선택한 경우가 더 적었다는 실험 결과로부터, 인지 부하가 높을수록 자제심이 낮았고 인지 부하가 낮을수록 자제심이 높았다는 것을 알 수 있다. 따라서 요약문의 빈칸 (A)에는 plenty(많은 것), (B)에는 lower(낮출)가 들어가는 것이 가장 적절하다.
② 통제 – 낮출

고난도 모의고사 03회

| 01 ④ | 02 ⑤ | 03 ⑤ | 04 ④ |
| 05 ④ | 06 ③ | 07 ⑤ | 08 ① |

01

정답 ④

자기 성찰의 큰 난제가 있다. 관찰이라는 행동 그 자체가 경험이므로, 우리는 경험을 손상시키지 않고 어떻게 우리 자신의 경험을 관찰할 수 있을까? 우리는 이 문제에 상당히 자주 직면한다. 여러분이 컴퓨터 키보드에서 타자를 칠 때 손가락이 하는 일을 관찰하려고 해 보라, 일단 여러분이 여전히 타자를 칠 수 있다면, 여러분은 자신이 천천히 타자를 치고 있고 많은 실수를 하고 있는 것을 빠르게 발견할 것이다. 영화나 게임을 즐기고 있는 자신을 관찰하려 해 보라, 그러면 즐거움이 빠르게 사라져 버릴 수 있다. 몇몇 사람들은 이것을 '관찰에 의한 마비'라고 부르고, 다른 사람들은 그것을 Heisenberg 원리라고 부른다. 양자역학으로부터 나온 Heisenberg '불확정성 원리'와 관련하여 이 원리는 입자의 운동이 관찰될 때마다 그 입자의 동작이 방해를 받는다는 점을 지적한다. 마찬가지로, 하나의 경험의 본질은 그 경험의 본질을 방해하지 않고는 관찰될 수 없다. 이것은 자기 성찰이 가망 없는 것으로 들리게 만든다.

해설

입자의 운동이 관찰될 때면 항상 그 운동이 방해를 받기 마련이라는 Heisenberg '불확정성 원리'에서처럼, 우리의 경험도 관찰에 의해 방해를 받게 된다는 맥락이므로, 밑줄 친 부분이 글에서 의미하는 바로 가장 적절한 것은 ④ '자신에 의해 (면밀히) 관찰되고 있을 때 경험으로부터 덜 풍요로운 느낌을 받는 것'이다.
① 과거의 실수를 기억하고 그것들을 방지하려 노력하는 것
② 행해지고 있는 것에 대해 생각하는 것을 그만두고 속도를 늦추는 것
③ 다른 사람들의 비판에 겁을 먹고 아무것도 시도하지 않는 것
⑤ 관중이 있으면 익숙한 활동에서 열등한 수행을 보이는 것

TEXT FLOW

도입 자기 성찰에는 경험을 손상시키지 않고 어떻게 관찰할 수 있을지에 대한 큰 난제가 있음
예시 컴퓨터 키보드로 타자를 칠 때의 손가락과 영화나 게임을 즐길 때의 자신의 모습 관찰
↓
관찰에 의한 마비 또는 Heisenberg의 '불확정성 원리'
결론 경험은 방해 없이 관찰될 수 없기에 자기 성찰이 어려움

구문

• This principle, in reference to the Heisenberg Uncertainty Principle from quantum mechanics, points out [that the motion of a particle **cannot** be observed **without** disturbing the motion of that particle].
: 주어는 This principle이고 술어 동사는 points out이다. [ ]는 points out의 목적어 역할을 하는 명사절이며 「cannot ~ without ...」 구문이 사용되어 '~할 때마다 (반드시) …하다'의 의미를 나타낸다.

02

정답 ⑤

시간은 변하지 않았다. 한 시간은 여전히 한 시간이고 하루는 하루이다. 달라진 것은 우리의 '시간에 대한 인식'이다. 신경 과학 연구는 뇌가 시간의 흐름을 어떻게 인식하는지가 우리의 하루가 사치스럽게 길게 느껴지거나 짧아서 어찌할 바를 모르게 느껴지는지를 결정한다고 강조했다. 이것 또한 우리가 통제할 수 있는 것이다. '주의를 기울임'으로써 그리고 적극적으로 '새로운 것을 주목함'으로써 우리는 시간을 늦출 수 있다. "날은 길지만 해는 짧다."라는 옛말이 있다. 그리고 그럴 만한 이유가 있다. 아침 출근길과 같이 매우 익숙한 상황과 그런 다음 교통에 갇혀 꼼짝도 못 하는 날에, 우리는 지옥 같은 경험에 대해 불평하고 투덜댄다. 하지만 며칠이 지나면 우리는 그 사건을 거의 기억하지 못한다. David Eagelman이라는 이름의 신경 과학자는 이것이 우리의 뇌가 새로운 정보를 많이 받아들이지 않기 때문이라고 결론을 내린다. 새로운 일이 아무것도 일어나지 않고 되돌아볼 만한 새로운 사건이 전혀 없다면 여러분은 기억할 것이 전혀 없다. 그렇다면, 시간이 빠르게 지나가는 이 문제를 우리는 어떻게 처리하는가? 단지 일을 더 많이 '주목'하려고 애쓰라, 그리고 이것은 '이곳 그리고 지금에 집중된 주의력'을 의미한다.

해설

더 많이 새로운 일을 주목하면 시간을 더 길게 인식하게 된다는 내용의 글이다. 따라서 글의 제목으로 가장 적절한 것은 ⑤ '유념함과 새로움으로 시간을 연장하기'이다.
① 현재에 살기: 행동보다 말하기가 더 쉽다
② 노화가 시간 인식에 미치는 긍정적 영향
③ 과거에 얽매여 현재를 망치지 마라
④ 기억의 발생 방식: 과학자들에게는 여전히 불가사의

⊗ 매력적인 오답 주의!

③ 글의 요지를 파악하지 못하고 마지막 문장의 '이곳 그리고 지금에 집중된 주의력'이라는 표현에만 집중하면 고를 수 있는 오답이다.

TEXT FLOW

도입 시간에 대한 인식의 변화
주제 새로운 것에 대한 적극적 주목이 시간을 늦출 수 있음
부연 시간이 빠르게 지나가는 문제 해결에 대한 시사점

구문

• Neuroscience research has highlighted [that {how the brain perceives time passing} determines {whether our days feel luxuriously long or short and harried}].
: [ ]는 has highlighted의 목적어 역할을 하는 명사절이다. 그 안의 첫 번째 { }는 that절의 주어 역할을 하는 명사절이고, 두 번째 { }는 determines의 목적어 역할을 하는 명사절이다.

• This is also something [we have control over].
: [ ]는 something을 수식하는 관계절이다.

03

정답 ⑤

목표와 즐거움이 합쳐질 때 일은 놀이가 된다. 이런 정신으로 이루어지는 모든 일은 그것을 행하는 사람을 강화시킨다. 그것은 창조적일 뿐만 아니라 기분 전환이 된다. 예술가와 목수는 그림을 그리고 의자를 만들지만, 그들은 훨씬 더 사람들, 즉 그들 자신을 만들어 낸다. 결과보다는 당신이 하고 있는 것

에 관해, 또는 나중에 무엇을 할 것인지에 관해 생각하라. 그러면 당신은 작은 것들의 즐거움을 놓치지 않을 것이다. 나는 펜을 든다. 만약 내가 나 자신이 그것을 경험하도록 허용한다면, 이것에는 순전하고 희석되지 않은 즐거움이 있다. 그것은 자연스럽고 순수하며, 내가 그것과 싸우기를 멈출 때 내 것이다. 그런 작은 것들에서, 생각, 사랑, 그리고 의지가 흐르고 자랄 수 있다. 그리고 그때 평화와 힘, 그리고 적극적인 삶에서 일과 놀이의 분리(→ 결합)가 생겨난다.

해설
목표와 즐거움이 합쳐질 때 창조적이고 기분 전환이 된다고 했으므로, 일과 놀이가 결합할 때 즐거움이 있다는 맥락이 자연스럽다. 따라서 ⑤ separation(분리)을 union(결합)과 같은 단어로 바꿔야 한다.

TEXT FLOW

도입	목표와 즐거움이 합쳐질 때 일은 놀이가 됨
전개	결과보다는 지금 하고 있는 일과 나중에 할 일에 대해 생각한다면 작은 즐거움도 놓치지 않을 것임
결론	작은 즐거움 속에서 생각, 사랑, 의지가 자라고, 그때 평화와 힘, 일과 놀이의 결합이 생겨남

구문
• Think on [what you are doing more than on the result], or [what you are going to do afterwards].
: 두 개의 [ ]는 의문사절로 or에 의해 병렬 구조를 이루면서 전치사 on의 목적어 역할을 한다.

• And then arise [peace and strength and — in active life — the union of work and play].
: [ ]가 문장의 주어이고, 동사는 arise이다.

04   정답 ④

미국에서 대법원은 오로지 국가의 최고 항소 법원으로서만 기능한다. 프랑스나 독일에서 그런 것처럼, 입법부 대표가 발의된 법률이 합헌인지에 대해 미리 판결을 요청하는 것은 가능하지 않으며, 일반 시민이 어떤 법률에 대한 판결을 요청하는 것은 확실히 가능하지 않다. 소송 사건이 대법원에 도달할 수 있는 유일한 방법은 그것이 하급 연방 항소 법원에서 판결이 내려진 후이다. 법률의 합헌성은 그 법률이 의회와 대통령에 의해 통과된 다음, 하급 연방 법원에서 소송 사건에 이의 신청이 제기될 때까지는 대법원에서 그 진위를 판단할 수 없다. 어떤 사람이 연방 항소 법원에서 패소했다면, 그 사람은 그 법률이 합헌인지의 문제에 관해 논하며 그 소송 사건을 대법원에 상고할 수 있다. 대법원은 그것에 제출된 모든 소송 사건을 수용하지는 않지만, 그렇게 한다면 대법원 판사들은 그 법이 헌법에 부합하는지, 그리고 헌법이 의미하는 바에 대한 이전의 모든 대법원 해석과 부합하는지를 고려할 것이다.

해설
프랑스나 독일에서와는 다르게 미국의 대법원은 국가의 최고 항소 법원으로서만 기능한다는 내용의 글이다. 빈칸 뒤에 법률의 합헌성은 하급 연방 법원에서 소송 사건에 이의 신청이 제기될 때까지는 대법원에서 그 진위를 판단할 수 없다고 했으므로, 소송 사건이 대법원에 도달하려면 하급 연방 법원에서 그 소송 사건에 대한 이의 신청이 제기된 후임을 추론할 수 있다. 따라서 빈칸에 들어갈 말로 가장 적절한 것은 ④ '그것이 하급 연방 항소 법원에서 판결이 내려진'이다.
① 그 이면의 이야기가 충분히 전해진

② 대법원이 그것의 진척을 확인하기로 동의한
③ 그것이 어떤 엄청난 국익을 증가시킨
⑤ 하급 연방 법원이 판결에서 변화를 만들어 낸

TEXT FLOW

도입	미국에서 대법원은 오로지 국가의 최고 항소 법원으로서만 기능함
주제	소송 사건이 대법원에 도달할 수 있는 경우는 그것이 하급 연방 항소 법원에서 판결이 내려진 후에만 가능함
예시	연방 항소 법원에서 패소한 사람은 그 법률이 합헌인지의 문제에 관해 논하며 그 소송 사건을 대법원에 상고할 수 있음
부연	대법원은 그 법이 헌법에 부합하는지, 헌법이 의미하는 바에 대한 이전의 모든 대법원 해석과 부합하는지를 고려할 것임

구문
• **It** is not possible, as it is in France or Germany, [for a legislative leader to request a ruling in advance on {whether a proposed law would be constitutional}], and **it** is certainly not possible [for an ordinary citizen to request a ruling on a law].
: It과 it은 가주어이고 첫 번째와 두 번째 [ ]가 각각 진주어로, 두 개의 [ ] 안에서 for a legislative leader와 for an ordinary citizen은 모두 to부정사구의 의미상 주어이다. 첫 번째 [ ] 안의 { }는 on의 목적어 역할을 하는 명사절이다.

• The Court does not accept all cases [that are submitted to it], but if it does so, the Justices of the Court will consider [whether the law is consistent {with the Constitution} and {with all earlier Supreme Court interpretations of what the Constitution means}].
: 첫 번째 [ ]는 all cases를 수식하는 관계절이다. 두 번째 [ ]는 will consider의 목적어 역할을 하는 명사절이고, 그 안의 두 개의 { }는 and로 연결되어 is consistent에 이어진다.

05   정답 ④

권위 있는 양육 모델에서 부모의 보살핌을 자녀에게 전달하는 한 가지 핵심 원칙은 자녀가 위엄과 존중으로 확고하게 대우받는 것이다. 위엄을 갖고 자녀를 대한다는 것은 그들의 입장과 능력을 존중하고 그들을 존중할 가치가 있는 대상으로 여기는 것이다. 자녀를 존중으로 대한다는 것은 표현의 그들의 기본 인권에 대한 배려를 보여 주고 그들이 성공적으로 자신의 삶을 살아갈 능력을 믿는 것이다. 존중은 경청 및 자녀가 말하는 것을 진지하게 고려하는 것을 필요로 한다. 권위 있는 양육에서는 부모가 자녀보다 더 많은 지식과 기술을 갖고, 더 많은 자원을 통제하며, 더 많은 물리적인 힘을 가진 것을 당연하게 여기지만, 부모는 부모와 자녀의 권리가 상호적인 것이라고 믿는다. 상호성이 핵심이다. 자녀들은 능력이 있고 중요하게 여겨지며 정중히 대우받는다. 그들은 상호적인 권리를 가진다.

해설
권위 있는 양육 모델에서 중요한 원칙은 부모가 지식, 기술, 통제력, 우월한 물리적 힘을 가졌지만 자녀의 입장과 능력을 존중하고 그들과 자녀의 권리가 상호적인 것이라는 내용의 글이므로, 빈칸에 들어갈 말로 가장 적절한 것은 ④ '능력이 있고 중요하게 여겨지며 정중히 대우받는다'이다.
① 가족에 더해지는 정보의 원천이 된다

② 그들이 부모에게 응당한 존경심을 보이지 않으면 처벌받는다
③ 여가 시간을 즐기며 보낼 권리를 지닌다
⑤ 가족의 규칙을 만드는 데 참여하고 자발적으로 그것을 따른다

TEXT FLOW

주장	위엄과 존중으로 확고하게 자녀를 대우해야 함
근거	존중으로 자녀를 대하는 것은 기본 인권에 대한 배려이며 그들에 대한 신뢰임
부연	부모와 자녀의 관계
결론	부모 자녀 관계에서는 상호성이 핵심어임

구문

• With authoritative parenting, **it** is taken for granted [that parents **have** more knowledge and skill, **control** more resources, and **have** more physical power than their children], but parents believe that the rights of parents and children are reciprocal.
: it은 가주어이고 [ ]가 진주어이다. [ ] 안의 주어는 parents이며 have, control, have가 술어 동사로 and에 의해 병렬 연결되어 있다.

06
정답 ③

과학자들은 나무와 식물 그리고 화산암과 같은 특정한 물질들이 아주 오랜 세월에 걸쳐 천천히 그러나 규칙적으로 변화한다는 것을 발견했다. (B) 이것은 우리가 언제 그것들이 자랐거나 형성되었는지 산출할 수 있다는 것을 의미한다. 그리고 독일에서의 발굴들 이후, 사람들은 찾고 파내기를 계속 수행했고, 몇 가지 놀라운 발견을 해냈다. (C) 특히 아시아와 아프리카에서 더 많은 뼈들이 발굴되었는데, 일부는 최소한 하이델베르크에서 발견된 턱뼈만큼이나 오래되었다. 이들은 15만 년도 더 전에 이미 돌을 도구로 사용하고 있었을지도 모르는 우리들의 조상이었다. (A) 그들은 약 7만 년 전에 나타난 네안데르탈인들과 달랐고 약 20만 년 동안 지구에 거주했다.

해설
몇몇 특정한 물질이 오랜 세월에 걸쳐 규칙적으로 변화한다는 것을 과학자들이 발견하게 되었다는 내용의 주어진 글 다음에, 이로 인해 그 물질들이 언제 것인지 알 수 있으며, 독일에서의 발굴 말고도 몇 가지 발견이 더 있었다는 내용의 (B)가 이어지고, 그 발견들 중 하나로 아시아와 아프리카에서도 화석 인류의 유골이 발굴되었다는 내용의 (C)가 이어진 다음, 그 화석 인류에 관한 설명이 담겨 있는 내용의 (A)가 마지막에 오는 것이 글의 흐름상 가장 자연스럽다.

TEXT FLOW

도입	나무, 식물, 화산암과 같은 특정한 물질들은 오랜 세월에 걸쳐 규칙적으로 변화한다는 것이 밝혀짐
전개	이 물질들로부터 그것들의 생장 및 형성 연대를 추정할 수 있음
부연	아시아와 아프리카의 원인 화석 발굴과 그에 대한 설명

구문

• They **were** different from the Neanderthal people [who appeared about seventy thousand years earlier] and **inhabited** the earth for about two hundred thousand years.
: were와 inhabited는 They를 주어로 하는 동사로 and에 의해 병렬 구

조로 연결되어 있다. [ ]는 the Neanderthal people을 수식하는 관계절이다.

07
정답 ⑤

어떤 긍정적인 방식으로 성공한 사람들이 다른 사람들에게 그 성취와 자신의 관련성을 알리는 것은 흔히 있고 이해할 수 있는 경향이다. 그러나 사람들이 성공한 '다른 사람'과의 관계를 알리려는, 겉으로는 덜 합리적이지만 어쩌면 더 흥미로운 경향도 또한 있는 것 같다. 이러한 후자의 성향은 반사된 영광을 누리는 경향(BIRG)이라고 불릴지도 모른다. 즉, 사람들은 어떤 방식으로 자신과 연관된 성공한 타인의 영광을 공유할 수 있다고 느끼는 것 같은데, 이런 기분의 한 가지 표현은 그 연관성을 떠벌리는 것이다. 그런 현상은 다른 사람의 성공을 공유하고자 하는 사람이 그 성공에 도움이 된 경우에는 이해하기 어렵지 않다. 그러나 더 흥미로운 형태의 현상은 다른 사람의 영광을 누리는 사람이 상대방의 성공을 유발할 어떤 것도 하지 않았을 때 발생한다. 이 경우에는, 소속이나 회원의 지위라는 단순한 사례만으로도 중요한 관계의 공개적인 발표를 고무하기에 충분하다.

해설
⑤ 뒤의 문장이 언급하는 소속이나 회원의 지위 만으로도 충분한 상황이 주어진 문장에서 언급한, 상대방의 성공을 유발할 어떤 것도 하지 않고 다른 사람의 영광을 누리는 상황이므로, 주어진 문장이 들어가기에 가장 적절한 곳은 ⑤이다.

ⓧ 매력적인 오답 주의!

④ 주어진 문장이 언급하는 경우와 ④ 뒤의 문장이 언급하는 경우가 대조된다는 사실을 파악하지 못하면 고를 수 있는 오답이다.

TEXT FLOW

도입	사람들에게는 성공한 사람과의 관계를 알리려는 경향이 있음
주제	반사된 영광을 누리는 경향: 덜 합리적이고 더 흥미로움
전개	상대방의 성공에 도움이 된 경우와 그렇지 않은 경우로 나눠짐

구문

• **It** is a common and understandable tendency [{for people ⟨who have been successful in some positive way⟩} {to make others aware of their connection with that accomplishment}].
: It은 가주어이고, [ ]는 진주어이다. [ ] 안의 첫 번째 { }는 두 번째 { }인 to부정사구의 의미상의 주어를 나타내며, 첫 번째 { } 안의 ⟨ ⟩는 people을 수식하는 관계절이다.

• That is, people appear to feel [that they can share in the glory of a successful other {with whom they are in some way associated}]; ~.
: [ ]는 feel의 목적어 역할을 하는 명사절이고, 그 안의 { }는 a successful other를 수식하는 관계절이다.

08
정답 ①

인류학자 Joe Henrich에 따르면, 인간은 명망 있는 개인들을 따라함으로써 서로에게서 기술들을 배우고, 또 아주 가끔은 개선된 것들인 실수들을 함

으로써 혁신하는데, 그렇게 해서 문화가 진화한다. 연결된 인구가 크면 클수록, 가르치는 사람은 더 숙련되고, 생산적인 실수의 가능성은 더 커진다. 역으로, 연결된 인구가 적으면 적을수록, 기술의 점진적인 악화는 그것이 전해지면서 더 커진다. 야생의 자원에 의존했기 때문에, 수렵·채집인들은 수백 명 이상의 집단으로는 거의 살 수가 없었고, 현대적인 인구 밀도를 결코 이룰 수 없었다. 이것이 중요한 결과를 초래했다. 그것은 그들이 발명할 수 있었던 것에 한계가 있었음을 의미했다. 백 명으로 이루어진 한 집단은 특정 수의 도구 이상을 유지할 수 없는데, 도구의 생산과 소비 모두 최소 규모의 시장을 필요로 한다는 단순한 이유에서이다. 사람들은 일련의 제한된 기술들만을 배울 뿐이고, 드문 한 가지 기술을 배울 충분한 전문가들이 없다면, 그 기술은 사라질 것이다.
➡ 어떤 특정한 사회의 한 가지 기술이 소실되지 않기 위해서는 다수에 의해 명맥이 유지되어야 한다.

해설

어떤 기술이 사라지지 않고 사람들에게로 계속 전수되기 위해서는 충분한 수의 사람들이 필요하다는 내용이므로, 요약문의 빈칸 (A)에는 numbers(다수)가, (B)에는 lost(소실되지)가 들어가는 것이 가장 적절하다.
② 다수 – 남용되지
③ 장려책 – 금지되지
④ 제도 – 소실되지
⑤ 제도 – 남용되지

TEXT FLOW

도입	인구가 많으면 많을수록 가르치고 배우고 실수하는 사람들이 많아져서 문명이 진화함
전개	수렵·채집인 사회는 인구의 수가 적어서 발명할 수 있는 것에 한계가 있었음
결론	인구의 수가 적으면 제한된 기술들만을 배우게 되어 드문 한 가지 기술은 사라질 것임

구문

• **The bigger** the connected population, **the more skilled** the teacher, and **the bigger** the probability of a productive mistake.
: 「the+비교급 ~, the+비교급 ....」 구문은 '~하면 할수록 더 …하다'라는 뜻이다.

• A band of a hundred people cannot sustain more than a certain number of tools, for the simple reason [that both the production and the consumption of tools require a minimum size of market].
: [ ]는 the simple reason과 동격을 이루는 명사절이다.

고난도 모의고사 04회

01 ⑤	02 ⑤	03 ⑤	04 ①
05 ④	06 ③	07 ③	08 ④

01
정답 ⑤

어떤 부모들은 자녀들의 기본 필수품을 준비하고, 자녀들에게 정중하고 친절하지만, 누군가가 지인들을 위해서 따로 마련해 두었을 법한 방식으로 그렇게 한다. 지인과의 관계는 그 방식에 아무런 깊이가 없다. 그것에는 친밀감이 부족하다. 저명한 관계 전문가인 Gottman은 사람들이 사랑하는 사람들을 위해 가지고 있는 정보의 깊이를 '인지적 애정 지도'라 부른다. 그는 또한 사랑하는 사람들로부터 관심을 끌려는 시도를 받아들이는 것과 꿈을 공유하고 서로의 훌륭한 자질을 칭찬함으로써 서로를 존중하는 것의 중요성을 강조한다. 지도가 더 세밀할수록 서로에게 주어지는 관심은 더 많아지고, 사람들이 서로를 칭찬할수록 사람들은 더 쉽게 자신들의 관계를 처리한다. 친밀도가 떨어지는 부모들의 애정 지도, 유의미한 관심을 주는 그들의 능력과 어린 자녀들과 성인 자녀들에 대한 칭찬을 표현하는 능력은 제대로 발달되지 못한다. 자녀와 그들의 관계는 밤에 지나가는 배에 더 가깝다.

해설

친밀도가 떨어지는 부모들의 애정 지도, 즉 유의미한 관심을 주는 그들의 능력과 어린 자녀와 성인 자녀들에 대한 칭찬을 표현하는 능력이 제대로 발달되지 못한다고 했고 이는 자녀에 대한 정보의 깊이가 부족하다는 의미이다. 따라서 more like ships passing in the night가 의미하는 바로 가장 적절한 것은 ⑤ '친밀하지 않거나 충분히 깊지 않은'이다.
① 서로 이익을 주는
② 노력할 가치가 없는
③ 더 나아질 것 같지 않은
④ 실제보다 더 행복한

TEXT FLOW

도입	일부 부모들은 자녀들에게 친절하지만 친밀감이 부족함
부연	사람들은 사랑하는 사람에 대한 정보가 깊고 서로 관심을 가질수록 자신들의 관계를 더 잘 처리함
결론	친밀도가 떨어지는 부모들은 자녀와의 관계 형성이 제대로 이루어지지 않음

구문

• Gottman, [a renowned relationship expert], **refers to** the depth of information [people have for their loved ones] **as** a "cognitive love map."
: 첫 번째 [ ]는 Gottman과 동격인 명사구이다. 「refer to A as B」는 'A를 B라고 부르다'의 의미이며, 두 번째 [ ]는 information을 수식하는 관계절로 목적격 관계대명사가 생략되었다.

• [**The more detailed** the map, **the more** attention {that is given to one another}], and [**the more** people admire one another, **the more easily** people navigate their relationship].
: 두 개의 [ ]는 모두 「the+비교급 ~, the+비교급 ....」 구문이며, '~할수록 더 …하다'라는 의미를 나타낸다. 첫 번째 [ ] 안의 { }는 the more attention을 수식하는 관계절이다.

02
정답 ⑤

녹색 침입자들이 미국을 접수하고 있다. 그것들은 정원과 마당을 예쁘게 보이게 하기 위해 다른 나라들에서 여기에 들여온 식물들이다. 그러나 이제 이 식물들은 인간 정착민들이 도착하기 전부터 여기에 살아 온 토종 식물들을 죽이고 있다. 그것은 심각한 문제라고 곤충학자인 Doug Tallamy 박사는 말한다. 그는 미국에 있는 거의 모든 초식 곤충들은 오직 특정한 식물들만을 먹는다고 설명한다. 예를 들어, 왕나비 애벌레들은 토종 식물인 아스클레피아스를 먹고 산다. 만약 사람들이 아스클레피아스를 잘라내고 그것을 도입 식물로 대체한다면, 그 애벌레들은 살아남기 위해 필요한 식량원을 가지지 못할 것이다. 그러나 그 문제는 거기서 그치지 않는데, 왜냐하면 그것이 먹이 그물로 바로 건너가기 때문이다. 곤충들이 먹을 수 있는 적절한 식물들을 구하지 못해서 차례로 죽어 간다면, 그다음에는 새들도 역시 식사로 먹을 충분한 벌레들이 없어서 차례로 죽어 간다. 결론은 도입 식물들이 깨지기 쉬운 자연의 먹이 그물을 위협한다는 것이다.

해설
미국 땅에 도입된 외부의 식물들은 인간 정착민들이 도착하기 전부터 그 땅에 살아 온 토종 식물들을 죽이고 있으며, 이것이 곤충들과 새들에게까지 영향을 미쳐 먹이 그물 전체를 위협하고 있다는 내용의 글이므로, 이 글의 주제로는 ⑤ '도입 식물들이 먹이 그물에 끼치는 해로운 영향'이 가장 적절하다.
① 우리가 나무를 많이 심어야 하는 이유들
② 도입 식물들의 좋은 사례들
③ 초식 곤충들을 없애는 방법
④ 잡초의 종류와 그것들의 강력한 생존

TEXT FLOW

도입	다른 나라에서 들여온 도입 식물들이 미국의 토종 식물들을 죽이고 있음
예시	아스클레피아스를 도입 식물로 대체한다면 왕나비 애벌레는 필요한 식량원을 가지지 못해 차례로 죽어 갈 것임
결론	도입 식물들은 토종 식물뿐만 아니라 곤충들과 새들에 이르기까지 먹이 그물 전체를 위협함

구문
• If people cut down milkweed and replace it with an introduced plant, the caterpillars will not have the food source [they need **to survive**].
: [ ]는 목적격 관계대명사가 생략된 관계절로 선행사 the food source를 수식하고, to survive는 to부정사의 부사적 용법으로 쓰여 '~하기 위해'라는 목적의 의미를 나타낸다.

03
정답 ⑤

지엽적으로 코딩된 물건은 소프트웨어가 내장되어 있지만, 소프트웨어는 물건의 주요 기능에 부수적인 것이다. 이러한 물건은 비교적 숫자가 적으며, 그리고 대부분의 경우에 코드는 단지 사용을 증강시킬 뿐이지 그것이 기능하는 데 결코 필수적인 것은 아니다. 종종 코드의 존재는 단지 제품을 전에 있던 것들과 차별화하는, 즉 제품 마케팅의 목표에 기여하거나 또는 부가 가치의 징표 역할을 하는 장식일 뿐이다. 예를 들어, 한 오븐에 디지털 타이머가 내장되어 있을 수 있지만, 만약 이것(타이머)이 기능을 멈추면 그 기기는 계속해서 음식을 조리할 것이다. 마찬가지로 운동용 자전거는 자전거를 타는 사람이 페달을 밟는 속도를 디지털로 표시하는 장치가 있을 수 있지만, 이것이

작동을 멈추더라도, 그 기구는 여전히 운동이 일어날 수 있게끔 한다. 두 경우 모두, 코드는 요리사가 얼마나 오랫동안 요리가 조리되고 있는지를 알게끔, 그리고 자전거를 타는 사람이 주행 속도를 알 수 있도록 해 줌으로써 물건의 사용을 증강시키는 것 이상의 것은 할 수 없다. 둘 다 단지 아날로그 기술에 대한 디지털 대체물이다.

해설
⑤ by 뒤에 「enable+목적어+to부정사」 구문에서 두 개의 「목적어+to부정사(구)」가 and에 의해 병렬 연결된 형태이므로 knows를 to know로 고쳐야 한다.
① 접속사 but 앞에 반복을 피해 주어 the code가 생략된 형태이므로 단수형 동사 is는 적절하다.
② 문맥상 it은 product를 대신하고 있으므로 단수형 대명사 it은 적절하다.
③ a digital timer는 내장의 주체가 아닌 대상이므로 과거분사 embedded는 적절하다.
④ the speed를 수식하는 관계절에서 완전한 문장이 이어지므로 at which는 적절하다.

⊗ 매력적인 오답 주의!
④ the cyclist is pedaling에서 pedal이 목적어가 필요하지 않은 자동사임을 이해하지 못하여 불완전한 구조로 오인하면 고를 수 있는 오답이다.

TEXT FLOW

주제	지엽적으로 코딩된 물건에서 소프트웨어는 물건의 주요 기능에 부수적인 역할을 담당함
부연	코드는 물건의 사용을 증강할 뿐이지 기능하는 데 필수적이지는 않음
예시	오븐의 디지털 타이머와 운동용 자전거의 디지털 속도 표시 장치
부연	둘 다 물건의 사용을 증강시키는 역할만 하며 아날로그 기술에 대한 디지털 대체물에 불과함

구문
• Peripherally coded objects are objects [in which software has been embedded], but [where the software is incidental to the primary function of the object].
: 두 개의 [ ]는 objects를 공통으로 수식하는 관계절이다.

• In both cases, the code does little more than augment the object's use by [enabling {⟨the chef⟩ ⟨to know how long a dish has been cooking⟩} and {⟨the cyclist⟩ ⟨to know the traveling speed⟩}].
: [ ]는 전치사 by의 목적어 역할을 하는 동명사구이다. 그 안의 두 개의 { }는 and로 연결되어 enabling에 이어지며, 그 안에 있는 두 개의 ⟨ ⟩는 각각 enabling의 목적어와 목적격 보어 역할을 한다. enable은 목적격 보어로 to부정사를 취하며 '~가 …을 할 수 있게 하다'의 의미를 나타낸다.

04
정답 ①

십 대가 되는 것이 힘든 한 가지 이유는 여러분이 동시에 청소년이어야 한다는 점이다. 사실 청소년기는 최근에 발명된 것이다. 1800년대에는, 한 사람이 아동기로부터 일과 가족 같은 어른의 책임으로 바로 진입했다. 고작 3세대 후에, 한 사람은 현실 세계에 발을 일체 담그지 않고 13세에서 24세 사이의 여러 해 동안을 고등학교, 그다음에는 대학교, 그다음에는 대학원에 다니며 보낼지도 모른다. 이 길고도 종종 힘든 기간 동안 무슨 일이 일어나야 하

는지에 대해 사회적으로 추적하여 기록한 것이 없다. 우리가 청소년기를 인간 발달의 자연스러운 과정으로 여기기 시작한 지 고작 3세대만이 흘렀기 때문에, 사람들이 이 시기 동안 겪는 증상들과 고통들을 완화하는 검증된 방법들이 거의 없다.

해설
1800년대만 해도 청소년기가 없었고, 그 개념이 만들어진 지 얼마 되지 않았기 때문에 이 시기의 사람들이 겪는 증상들과 고통들을 완화하는 검증된 방법들이 거의 없다는 내용의 글이므로, 빈칸에 들어갈 말로 ① '최근에 발명된 것'이 가장 적절하다.
② 근거 없는 신화　　　　　③ 변화의 시기
④ 정서적 시기　　　　　　⑤ 다른 견해

TEXT FLOW

도입	십 대가 힘든 이유는 동시에 청소년이어야 하기 때문임
요지	사실 청소년기는 최근에 만들어진 개념임
부연	최근의 개념이므로 청소년기의 증상과 고통을 완화할 검증된 방법이 거의 없음

구문
• A mere three generations later, a person **might** spend the years between 13 and 24 going to high school, then college, then graduate school **without dipping** more than a toe into the real world.
: might는 약한 추측을 나타내어 '~할지도 모른다'의 의미로 해석되고, 「without+동명사」는 '~을 하지 않고'의 의미이다.

05
정답 ④

1991년의 소련 붕괴는 그 사건 이후 많은 수의 비전문 역사가들뿐만 아니라 전문 역사가들에게도 불가피해 보이지 않았던 몇 안 되는 역사적 사건들 중 하나일 것이다. 덜 중대한 사건들은 말할 것도 없고, 로마 제국의 몰락, 제3제국의 발흥, 그리고 러시아인들보다 먼저 달에 도착하는 데 있어 미국의 성공은 일상적으로 논평자들에 의해 불가피한 것으로 여겨지는데, 사람들은 그들이 그것들을 예측했을 리가 없다고 강하게 의심한다. 우리는 과거를 '예측'하려 할 때 두 가지 문제를 갖게 되는 경향이 있다. 하나는 최소한 되돌아보면 그렇게 말고는 사건들이 귀결될 수 없었을 것 같다고 믿는 것이다. 다른 하나는 심지어 사실 사건들이 그렇게 귀결될 것이라고 사람들이 미리 쉽게 예측할 수 있었을 것이라고 생각하는 것이다. 많은 증거가 사람들이 자신들이 주어진 사건의 결과를 예측할 수 있었다고 생각하는 범위를 과대평가한다는 것을 보여 준다.

해설
과거를 '예측'하려 할 때 우리가 가지는 두 가지 문제 중 두 번째는, 사람들이 이미 지나간 사건을 놓고 자신들이 그렇게 될 것이라 미리 예측할 수 있었을 것으로 생각한다는 것인데, 많은 증거가 그들이 과대평가하고 있음을 보여 준다고 했으므로, 빈칸에 들어갈 말로는 ④ '주어진 사건의 결과를 예측할'이 가장 적절하다.
① 추측의 결과를 통제할
② 갑작스러운 위협에 대응하여 행동할
③ 위기의 결과를 설명할
⑤ 미래 사건들의 추이에 영향을 미쳤을

TEXT FLOW

도입	불가피한 것으로 여겨지는 과거의 역사적 사건들
전개	사람들은 과거를 '예측'하려 할 때 두 가지 문제를 갖게 되는 경향이 있음
결론	사건들이 그렇게 귀결될 수밖에 없었다고 믿는 문제와 지나간 사건들이 그렇게 귀결될 것이라고 예측할 수 있었을 것이라 생각하는 문제임

구문
• The Soviet Union's demise in 1991 may be one of the few historical events [that has seemed inevitable after **the fact** to large numbers of historians, both lay and professional].
: [ ]는 one of ~ events를 수식하는 관계절이다. the fact는 The Soviet Union's demise in 1991을 가리킨다.

06
정답 ③

기계 학습 알고리즘은 인간이 더 잘할 수 있는 일에서조차 유용하다. 사람들이 인공 지능으로 자동화하고 있는 한 가지 반복적인 과업은 의료용 사진을 분석하는 것이다. (B) 실험실의 기술자들은 혈소판 또는 백혈구나 적혈구의 수를 세거나, 세포 샘플에 비정상적인 세포가 있는지 검사하면서 현미경으로 혈액 샘플을 보면서 매일 여러 시간을 보낸다. 이러한 과업들 각각은 단순하고, 일관되며, 그 자체로 완비되어 있어서, 그런 방식으로 그것들은 자동화의 좋은 후보이다. (C) 그러나 이러한 알고리즘이 연구실을 떠나 병원에서 사용되기 시작하면 위험성이 더 높아지는데, 그곳에서는 실수의 결과가 훨씬 더 심각하다. (A) 자율 주행 자동차에도 비슷한 문제들이 있는데, 운전은 대체로 반복적이고, 절대 지치지 않는 운전자가 있으면 좋겠지만, 아주 작은 결함이라도 시속 60마일로 달리고 있을 때는 심각한 결과를 가져올 수 있다.

해설
주어진 글은 기계 학습 알고리즘이 쓰일 수 있는 의료용 사진 분석 작업을 제시하는 내용이다. 이어서 의료용 사진 분석 작업이 자동화되기에 적절한 이유를 제시하는 내용인 (B)가 오고, 그 알고리즘이 실제로 병원에서 사용될 때 위험성이 있음을 설명하는 내용의 (C)가 와야 한다. 마지막으로 (A)에서 그와 유사한 사례로 자율 주행 자동차가 제시되는 방식으로 이어지는 것이 글의 흐름상 가장 자연스럽다.

TEXT FLOW

도입	기계 학습 알고리즘은 인간이 더 잘할 수 있는 일에서도 유용한데, 일례가 반복적인 의료 사진 분석 업무임
반전	하지만 알고리즘이 연구실을 떠나 병원에서 사용되면 사소한 실수라도 위험성이 커짐
부연	자율 주행 자동차 역시 시속 60마일에서는 알고리즘이 사소한 결함이라도 심각한 결과를 초래할 수 있음

구문
• There are similar problems with self-driving cars — driving is mostly repetitive, and **it** would be nice [to have a driver {who never gets tired}], but even a tiny glitch can have serious consequences at sixty miles per hour.
: and 뒤에 오는 절에서 it은 가주어이고 [ ]가 진주어이다. 그 안의 { }는 a driver를 수식하는 관계절이다.

07   정답 ③

산업적 농업으로 이행하던 초기에, 농부들은 외부의 자원을 거의 이용하지 못했다. 비료는 농장에서 생산된 퇴비와 거름으로 이루어졌다. 그러나 20세기 초반에, 신생 농업 관련 산업 부문에서 일하는 화학자들이 만들어 낸 비료가 농장으로 가기 시작했고, 가축 우리와 밭에서 가축들이 생산했던 것들을 대체했다. 합성 비료는 단순히 토양에 있는 식물의 주요 영양소인 질소, 인, 칼륨의 총량만 증가시키면 생산이 향상될 것이라는 '환원주의적' 전제에 근거해 개발되었다. 그러나, 화학자들은 오랜 기간에 걸쳐 많은 양의 식량을 만들어 내는 것이 직업인 사람들에 의해 요구되는 토양에 대한 깊은 이해가 없었다. 처음에는 합성 비료로부터 나오는 작물의 수확량이 꽤 좋았지만, 그것은 점차 토양을 못쓰게 만들었다. 수확량은 줄어들었고 병과 해충에 대한 민감성은 증가했다.

해설
주어진 문장은 합성 비료가 단순히 토양에 식물의 주요 영양소만 더해 주면 된다는 생각에 근거해 개발되었다는 내용이다. ③ 앞 문장에서는 화학자들이 합성 비료를 만들어 냈다는 내용이 나오고, ③ 뒷문장에서는 당시 화학자들이 고려하지 못했던 점이 언급되고 있으므로, 합성 비료를 어떤 생각으로 만들었는지를 설명하는 주어진 문장은 ③에 들어가는 것이 가장 적절하다.

TEXT FLOW
도입	산업적 농업 이행 초기에는 퇴비와 거름을 사용함
전환	20세기 초반에 생산된 합성 비료가 퇴비와 거름을 대체함
부연	합성 비료 개발자들은 토양에 대한 깊은 이해가 부족했음
결론	결국 화학 비료의 사용이 수확량 감소 및 병충해 민감성 증가를 가져옴

구문
• The chemists, however, lacked the deep appreciation for the soil [that is required by those {whose job **it** is ⟨to produce large quantities of food for extended periods of time⟩}].
: [ ]는 the deep appreciation for the soil을 수식하는 관계절이고, 그 안의 { }는 those를 수식하는 관계절이다. 관계절 { }의 가주어는 it이고 ⟨ ⟩가 진주어이며, whose job은 주격 보어이다.

08   정답 ④

고정 관념의 위협(고정 관념에 의해 행동이 제약받는 것)에 대한 좋은 소식은 그것이 미묘한 개입에 의해 완화될 수 있다는 것이다. 이러한 개입에 관한 가장 흥미로운 사실은 지능의 가변성이라는 질문이 사실상 심리학자들과 신경 과학자들 사이에서 치열하게 논쟁이 되고 있다는 점이다. SAT와 같은 성취도 평가의 점수가 서로 다른 종류의 훈련에 의해 분명 영향을 받을 수 있지만, 가장 순수한 형태의 지능은 전혀 가변적이지 않다. 그러나 Carol Dweck이라는 Stanford의 한 심리학자는 놀라운 점을 한 가지 발견했는데, 지능의 가변성에 관한 사실과 무관하게, 학생들이 지능이 가변적이라고 '믿는'다면 학업 면에서 훨씬 더 잘한다는 점이다. Dweck은 두 부류로 사람들을 나누었는데, 고정된 사고방식을 가졌으며 지능과 다른 기술들이 본질적으로 고정적이고 타고난다고 믿는 사람들과, 성장의 사고방식을 가졌고 지능이 개선될 수 있다고 믿는 사람들이다. 그녀는 학생들의 사고방식은 자신들의 학업의 궤적을 예측한다는 것을 보여 주었는데, 사람들이 지능을 개선할 수 있다고 믿는 학생들은 실제로 자신들의 성적을 향상시킨다.

➡ 지능의 가변성을 믿는 학생들은 <u>우월한</u> 수행을 보였지만, 반면에 순수하게 <u>타고난</u> 지능은 그다지 많이 달라지지 않았으며, 이것은 고정 관념의 위협이 가진 영향력을 반박했다.

해설
지능의 가변성을 믿는 학생들은 성적을 향상시켰다고 했으므로 요약문의 빈칸 (A)에 들어갈 말로 가장 적절한 것은 superior(우월한)이다. 순수하게 타고난 지능은 그다지 많이 달라지지 않아 학자들 사이에서 논쟁의 대상이 되어 왔다는 글의 내용으로 보아 (B)에 들어갈 말로 가장 적절한 것은 inherited(타고난)이다.
① 지속적인 – 사회적인
② 지속적인 – 검사 가능한
③ 우월한 – 사회적인
⑤ 더 나쁜 – 타고난

TEXT FLOW
주제	고정 관념의 위협은 개입에 의해 완화될 수 있음
부연	이런 사실은 지능의 가변성에 대한 논쟁에서 흥미롭게 드러남
예시	한 연구에서 지능의 가변성을 믿는 학생들은 실제로 지능 변화가 없지만 자신들의 성적을 향상시킴

구문
• [Although {scores on achievement tests like the SAT} **can** certainly **be affected** by training of different kinds], the purest kind of intelligence is not very malleable at all.
: [ ]는 양보를 나타내는 부사절이며 그 안의 { }는 부사절의 주어이다. 주어가 '영향을 받은' 수동의 의미이므로 「조동사+be+과거분사」 형태의 수동태 can be affected가 쓰였다.

고난도 모의고사 05회

| 01 ④ | 02 ⑤ | 03 ④ | 04 ④ |
| 05 ③ | 06 ⑤ | 07 ⑤ | 08 ② |

01 정답 ④

성취감을 주는 경력을 만들기 위해서, 여러분은 의식적인 직업 결정을 해야한다. 여러분은 (지도자를 따라가는 것이 아니라) 다른 사람들이 마치 맹목적으로 따라가고 있는 길을 터벅터벅 걸어가며, 단지 추종자들을 따라가는 역할을 해서는 안 된다. 타협하지 말라. 자신의 마음이 내키지 않는 길에 자신이 있다는 것을 발견하면, 가능한 한 빨리 그곳으로부터 벗어나라. 다른 사람들이 크게 항의할 수도 있지만, 몇 년 지나면, 여러분은 꽤 재미있는 일이 일어난다는 것을 알아차릴 것이다. 떠난다고 여러분을 미워했던 바로 그 사람들이 돌아서서 여러분이 했던 일을 자신들이 어떻게 할 수 있는지에 관해 조언을 구할 것이다. 사람들이 그런 상황에서 화를 내는 이유는 여러분이 그들 자신도 피하고 있던 불편한 진실을 그들로 하여금 어쩔 수 없이 대면하게 만들어서이다. 여러분은 여러분의 용기를 가지기를 바라는 사람들을 위해 영감을 주는 사람이 될 것이다. 심지어 여러분 자신의 가족 구성원으로부터 가장 강한 저항이 나올지라도 이것은 진실이다.

해설
단지 다른 사람들이 가는 길을 맹목적으로 따라감으로써 자신이 열정을 느끼지 못하는 일을 하지 말고 진정으로 원하는 일을 찾아 용기 있게 도전하라는 내용의 글이므로, 밑줄 친 부분이 글에서 의미하는 바로 가장 적절한 것은 ④ '여러분이 열정을 느끼지 못하는 일을 구해서는'이다.
① 성공으로 가는 쉬운 지름길을 찾아서는
② 조언과 도움을 여러분의 가족에게 의존해서는
③ 이상적으로 보이는 사회 구성원으로 살아가서는
⑤ 돈이 여러분에게 가장 중요한 것처럼 가장해서는

TEXT FLOW
주제	추종자를 따라가는 역할이 아니라 자신에게 맞는 경력을 선택해야 함
부연	타협하지 말고 자신이 원하는 일이 아니라면 가능한 한 빨리 그곳으로부터 벗어나야 함
결론	반대했던 사람들조차 이후에 조언을 구하고 영감을 얻으려고 할 것임

구문
• [The reason {people get angry in such situations}] is that you force them to face the unpleasant truths [they've been avoiding as well].
: 첫 번째 [ ]는 문장의 주어이고 그 안의 { }는 The reason을 수식하는 관계절로 앞에 관계부사 why가 생략되었다. 두 번째 [ ]는 the unpleasant truths를 수식하는 관계절이다.

02 정답 ⑤

새로운 감미료가 알려진 가장 이상한 방식은 1976년의 어느 날, 런던에 있는 King's 대학의 어느 외국인 연구생이 자신의 교수인 L. Hough의 지시 사항을 잘못 들었을 때였다. Hough는 사탕수수와 사탕무의 공통 당질인 자당의 가능한 인조 산업적 응용을 찾고 있었고, 여러 가지 파생 물질들이 실험실에서 생산되었었다. 이것들 중 하나가 트리클로로수크로오스(세 개의 염소 원자가 넣어진 자당)였다. Hough는 Shashikant Phadnis에게 그 물질을 '검사(test)'해 보라고 했지만, 귀가 그 언어에 불완전하게 적응된 상태였던 Phadnis는 대신 그것을 '맛보았다(tasted)'. 알려진 바와 같이, 수크랄로스는 모든 물질 중에서 가장 단맛이 나는 물질들 중 하나이고, 농도를 1000분의 1보다 적게 해서 자당을 대체할 수 있다.

해설
한 외국인 연구생이 교수가 어떤 물질을 '검사하라(test)'고 말한 것을 '맛보라(taste)'는 말로 잘못 알아듣는 바람에 수크랄로스라는 감미료를 발견하게 되었다는 내용의 글이므로, 이 글의 제목으로는 ⑤ '말을 잘못 들은 실수가 수크랄로스의 발견으로 이어지다'가 가장 적절하다.
① 오늘날 시중에 나와 있는 감미료의 종류들
② 너무 많은 수크랄로스는 기분 변화를 유발한다
③ 수크랄로스와 자당 간의 차이점들
④ 여러분의 의도가 무엇인가를 분명하게 전달하라

TEXT FLOW
도입	새로운 감미료가 알려진 가장 이상한 방식은 한 외국인 연구생이 교수의 지시 사항을 잘못 알아들었을 때였음
전개	교수는 트리클로로수크로오스를 '검사하라(test)'고 했는데, 연구생은 교수의 말을 잘못 알아듣고 그것을 '맛보았음(tasted)'
결론	그 결과, 모든 물질 중 가장 단맛이 나는 물질들 중 하나인 수크랄로스를 발견함

구문
• The oddest manner [in which a new sweetener came to light] was [when, one day in 1976, a foreign research student at King's College in London misheard the instructions of his professor, L. Hough].
: 첫 번째 [ ]는 관계절로 주어인 The oddest manner를 수식한다. 두 번째 [ ]는 동사 was의 보어 역할을 하며 앞에 선행사 the time이 생략된 형태이다.

03 정답 ④

과학이 우리 문화에 매우 중요하다는 사실에도 불구하고, 우리는 흔히 과학을 왠지 문화 너머에 있는 것처럼 여긴다. 과학은 발견에 발견이 누적되어 그 자체의 추진력에 의해 진보한다고 가정된다. 이러한 관점에서 과학은 보통 문화의 힘이라기보다는 자연의 힘처럼 보인다. 과학 자체에 고유한 무언가가 과학을 진보하게 하며 과학의 진보에는 필연적인 무언가가 있다. 따라서 과학은 앞으로 나아가기 위해 문화가 필요하지 않으며, 단지 그 자체의 힘으로 계속 나아갈 뿐이다. 때때로 문화가 방해가 되기도 하지만 결국에는 과학이 항상 승리한다. 이처럼 과학이 문화 외부에 존재한다면, 과학이 어디서 발생했는지는 아마 중요하지 않을 것이다. 이는 과학의 역사 또한 아마 중요하지 않을 것임을 의미한다. 과학의 역사는 기껏해야 누가 언제 무엇을 했는지 우리에게 알려 줄 수는 있지만, 그것은 과거를 단순히 기록할 뿐만 아니라 과거를 해석하려고 애쓰는 역사가 아닌 연대기의 문제이다. 과학에 대한 이러한 관점을 부정하는 사람들(→ 옹호하는 사람들)은 흔히 과학적 방법을 과학의 성공을 이해하는 데 있어 핵심으로 이야기한다. 예를 들어, 일부 전문가들은 동료 검토나 이중 맹검 실험을 과학적 객관성의 특징으로 이야기하는데, 이는 이것이 아주 최근에 유래한 문화적 제도라는 사실에도 불구하고 그렇다.

해설

과학이 문화 외부에 존재하고 과학이 발전하기 위해 문화가 필요하지 않다는 관점을 옹호하는 사람들은 과학 자체에 고유한 무언가가 과학을 진보하게 한다고 믿기 때문에 과학적 방법을 과학의 성공을 이해하는 데 있어 핵심으로 얘기한다는 내용의 글이다. 따라서 ④ Deniers(부정하는 사람들)를 Advocates(옹호하는 사람들)와 같은 단어로 바꿔야 한다.

⊗ 매력적인 오답 주의!

② 과학은 그 자체의 추진력에 의해 진보하며 과학은 자연의 힘처럼 보인다는 내용을 과학의 필연성과 연관시켜 생각하지 못하면 고를 수 있는 오답이다.

TEXT FLOW

주제	과학이 문화에 매우 중요하다는 사실에도 불구하고 우리는 과학을 문화 너머에 있는 것처럼 여김
부연 1	과학의 진보에는 필연적인 무언가가 있으며 과학의 발전에 있어 문화가 필요하지 않음
부연 2	과학의 역사도 중요하지 않으며 과학적 방법이 과학의 성공을 이해하는 데 있어 핵심이라고 생각함
예시	과학적 객관성의 특징으로 제시하는 동료 검토와 이중 맹검 실험도 사실은 문화적 제도임

구문

• [Despite the fact {that science matters so much for our culture}], we often treat it **as if** it **were** somehow beyond culture.
: [ ]는 양보의 의미를 나타내는 부사구이고, 그 안의 { }는 the fact의 구체적인 내용을 설명하는 동격절이다. '마치 ~인 것처럼'의 의미를 나타내는 「as if+주어+과거형 동사」가 사용되어 현재의 사실에 반하는 상황을 나타낸다.

• At best, it can tell us [who did what when], but that is a matter of chronicle rather than history, [which tries to {interpret the past} as well as {simply record it}].
: 첫 번째 [ ]는 tell의 직접목적어 역할을 하는 명사절이다. 두 번째 [ ]는 history를 부가적으로 설명하는 관계절이다. 그 안에 두 개의 { }가 as well as로 연결되어 to에 이어진다.

04 정답 ④

과업을 '함께 묶는 것'은 어떻게 작동되는 것인가? 지금 당장 여러분의 마음에 걸리는 문제가 여러분의 팀이 현재 직면하고 있는 과도한 작업 부하라고 생각해 보자. 모두가 기진맥진한 상태이다. 여러분은 개방된 주방이 있는 와글와글거리는 음식점에서 저녁 식사를 하며 한숨을 돌리고 있는 중인데, 음식을 기다리는 동안 여러분은 그러한 유사성을 찾는 질문들을 곰곰이 생각한다. 먼저, 여러분은 여러분 자신의 팀과 마찬가지로 주방 직원들에게 손님들의 주문이 쇄도하는 것을 알아차린다. 차이점은 음식점의 직원들은 그들이 직면하고 있는 요구에도 불구하고 상당히 평온한 것 같다는 것이다. 그리고 여러분의 팀은 누구에게 유휴 생산 능력이 있는지에 따라 일을 할당하는 반면, 주방의 각 사람은 분명한 할 일이 있는 것 같은데, 어떤 사람들은 샐러드를 만들고, 다른 사람들은 뜨거운 음식이나 디저트를 만든다. 그것이 여러분에게 무엇을 생각하게 만드는가? 여러분은 모두가 항상 한 가지 일에서 다

른 일로 휙 넘어가지 않도록, 각각의 팀원에게 특정 유형의 요청이라는 꼬리표를 붙이기 위해 여러분이 아마도 더 많은 일을 할 수 있을 것이라고 생각한다. 여러분은 이것이 사람들의 스트레스를 줄일 것이라고 생각한다. 한 가지 아이디어가 여러분의 마음속에 형성된다.

해설

각자 할 일이 주어진 음식점의 직원들이 쇄도하는 주문을 차분하게 처리하는 것처럼 과업을 부문별로 나누어 묶어서 부여하면 스트레스를 줄일 수 있을 것이라는 내용의 글이므로, 빈칸에 들어갈 말로는 ④ '각각의 팀원에게 특정 유형의 요청이라는 꼬리표를 붙이기'가 가장 적절하다.
① 팀원들에게 지친 동료의 일을 대신할 것을 요청하기
② 여러분의 팀원들을 음식점으로 초대해 쉬게 하기
③ 여러분의 팀이 문제를 다른 시각으로 보도록 돕기
⑤ 근무 환경을 친근하고 평화롭게 유지하기

TEXT FLOW

도입	과업을 '함께 묶는 것'은 어떻게 작동되는가?
전개 1	팀이 과업의 과부하로 기진맥진한 상태에서 음식점에 감
전개 2	분주한 가운데 각자 주어진 할 일을 차분하게 처리하는 음식점 직원을 보며 통찰을 얻음
결론	각각의 팀원에게 특정 업무를 부여하는 것이 스트레스를 줄일 것이라고 생각함

구문

• And [while your team allocates work depending on {who's got spare capacity}], each person in the kitchen has a clear job to do: **some** make salads, **others** hot food or desserts.
: [ ]는 대조를 나타내는 부사절로, 그 안의 { }는 on의 목적어인 의문사절이다. 「some ~, others ....」 구문은 '몇몇은 ~, 다른 몇몇은 ···'이라는 의미를 나타낸다.

05 정답 ③

감각 입력의 처리라는, 첫 번째 단계 다음의 두 번째 행동 단계를 이루는 반사 작용은 정확히 타고난 것이고, 나중의 기억을 제외하고는 의식적인 생각으로부터 독립되어 있다. 무릎 반사, 무의식적인 눈 깜박임, 얼굴 붉힘, 하품, 타액 분비가 그러하듯이 재채기는 반사 작용이다. 가장 복잡한 반사 작용은 놀람 반응이다. 누군가의 아주 가까운 뒤에서 보이지 않게 거의 닿을 듯이 접근하여, 큰 소리를 낸다고 상상해 보라(실제로 나는 이렇게 해 보는 것을 권장하지는 않는다). 그 사람은 즉시 앞으로 털썩 쓰러지며, 머리를 떨구고, 눈을 감고, 입을 벌릴 것이다. 놀람 반응의 기능은 방어이다. (말하자면 표범 같은) 포식자에 의해 뒤에서 몰래 접근하여 공격당했을 때, 즉시 전반적으로 느슨해진 자세로 앞으로 몸을 구르는 구석기 시대의 사냥꾼을 생각해 보라. 따라서 정확한 결정과 재빠른 행동은 의식적인 생각이 전혀 필요 없이 얻어진다.

해설

감각 입력의 처리 다음에 이어지는 반사 작용은 거의 무의식적으로 이루어지는데 이것은 생존을 위한 진화의 산물이라는 내용의 글이므로, 빈칸에 들어갈 말로는 ③ '의식적인 생각이 전혀 필요 없이 얻어진다'가 가장 적절하다.
① 반사 작용의 개입으로부터 독립되어 있다
② 감각 입력의 제한과 함께 나타난다
④ 정신이 주어진 상황을 평가하는 것을 필요로 한다
⑤ 인간 진화의 산물로 오지 않는다

<table>
<tr><td>주제</td><td>반사 작용은 타고난 것이고 의식적인 생각으로부터 독립되어 있음</td></tr>
<tr><td>부연</td><td>무릎 반사, 무의식적인 눈 깜박임, 얼굴 붉힘, 하품, 타액 분비, 재채기 등이 반사 작용임</td></tr>
<tr><td>예시</td><td>놀람 반응 → 깜짝 놀라는 반응은 방어 기능을 하며 무의식적으로 이루어짐</td></tr>
</table>

구문

• Think of a Paleolithic hunter [who, {when stalked from behind and attacked by a predator (say a leopard)}, instantly rolls forward and away in an overall relaxed posture].
: [ ]는 a Paleolithic hunter를 수식하는 관계절이며 그 안의 { }는 시간을 나타내는 부사절이다.

06　　　　　　　　　　　　　　　정답 ⑤

장소에 대한 애착과 사람에 대한 애착은 진화상의 한 경로를 공유하고, 두 가지 모두에서 하나의 독특한 자질이 핵심이다. (C) 유아에게 젖을 먹이는 것은 그 자체로는 유대 맺기를 촉발하는 데는 충분하지 않은데, 그 이유는 우리가 즐거운 감정뿐 아니라 냄새, 촉감, 소리의 특별함을 통해 애착을 가지도록 생물학적으로 부호화되어 있기 때문이다. 장소도 또한 감정을 불러일으키는데, 자연의 장소는 특히 감각적인 즐거움을 풍부하게 갖추고 있다. (B) 오늘날 우리는 슈퍼마켓과 쇼핑몰처럼 특징과 개성이 결여된 기능적인 장소에 둘러싸여 있다. 그것들이 우리에게 음식과 다른 유용한 물건들을 제공하지만, 우리는 그것들에 대한 애착을 키우지는 않으며, 사실상 자주 그것들은 (마음을) 충분히 회복시키지 않는다. (A) 결과적으로, 현대적인 삶에서 장소라는 관념은 점차 배경으로 축소되어 왔으며, 설령 있다 하더라도 (장소와의) 상호 작용은 지속될 수도 있는 살아 있는 관계라기보다는 일시적으로 머무르는 본성을 가지는 경향이 있다.

해설

주어진 글은 장소와 사람에 대한 애착은 공통적으로 하나의 독특한 자질이 핵심이라는 내용이다. 따라서 장소와 사람에 대한 애착 형성에서 공통적으로 감각이나 감정이 중요한 역할을 한다는 내용의 (C)가 부연 설명으로 이어지는 것이 적절하다. 또한 (C)에서 언급한 자연의 장소와 대비하여 오늘날의 장소가 특징과 개성이 없는 기능적인 곳이라는 내용의 (B)가 온 후, 그런 이유로 장소에 대한 애착이 형성되기 어렵다는 내용의 (A)가 이어지는 것이 글의 흐름상 가장 자연스럽다.

<table>
<tr><td>도입</td><td>장소에 대한 애착과 사람에 대한 애착은 한 가지 독특한 자질을 공유함</td></tr>
<tr><td>부연</td><td>감각의 특별함을 통해 (사람에 대한) 애착이 형성되고 장소에 대한 애착도 감정이 중요함</td></tr>
<tr><td>전환</td><td>오늘날의 장소는 기능적인 곳임</td></tr>
<tr><td>결론</td><td>장소는 배경으로 축소되고 장소와의 상호 작용은 지속되기 어려움</td></tr>
</table>

구문

• As a result, [the notion of place in contemporary life **has** increasingly **been reduced** to a backdrop] and [the interaction, **if there is any**, tends to be of a transient nature,

rather than a living relationship {that might be sustaining}].
: 두 개의 절 [ ]가 and로 연결되어 있다. 첫 번째 [ ]에는 현재완료 수동태인 has been reduced가 사용되어 현재까지 지속되어 오는 상황을 나타낸다. 두 번째 [ ]에서 주어는 the interaction이고 술어 동사는 tends로, 주어와 동사 사이에 if there is any가 삽입된 구조이다. { }는 a living relationship을 수식하는 관계절이다.

07　　　　　　　　　　　　　　　정답 ⑤

내가 아이였을 때, 부모님께서 나에게 장난감 팽이를 사 주셨다. 나는 그것을 돌리는 것을 좋아했고, 그것이 재미있는 패턴으로 마루를 가로질러 움직이는 것을 지켜보았다. 나는 또한 그것의 회전이 느려지기 시작하면 그것이 흔들리기 시작한다는 것을 알아차렸다. 그것을 이해하기에 그때 나는 너무 어렸지만 나는 이제 그 흔들거림이 회전하는 팽이에 작용하는 복잡한 힘의 상호 작용 때문이라는 것을 안다. 만일 팽이의 축이 정확하게 수직이 아니라면, 중력은 중심에서 벗어나 그 팽이를 잡아당기는데, 그것은 '회전력'이라고 불린다. 팽이가 회전하고 있으므로, 여러분은 그 힘이 수평으로 방향을 바꿔 그 팽이가 서서히 흔들리게 한다고 생각할 수 있다. 만일 팽이가 우주에서 돌고 있고 그것을 여러분이 쿡 찔러서 중심에서 약간 벗어나게 하면 같은 일이 일어날 것이다. 그 축은 흔들리면서 작은 원을 그리는데, 찌르는 것이 더 클수록, 그것이 만드는 원은 더 커지기 마련이다.

해설

⑤ 앞에서 팽이의 회전과 팽이에 가해지는 중력의 영향으로 팽이가 흔들거리게 됨을 설명하고 있고, ⑤ 다음에 축으로부터 멀어지면서 흔들리며 원을 그리게 된다는 내용이 이어지므로, 주어진 문장이 ⑤에 들어가야 우주의 물체가 회전하면서 흔들거리게 되는 원인을 설명하게 되어 글의 흐름이 자연스럽게 연결된다.

<table>
<tr><td>도입</td><td>회전 속도에 따른 장난감 팽이의 흔들림</td></tr>
<tr><td>전개</td><td>팽이의 흔들림은 팽이에 작용하는 복잡한 힘의 상호 작용 때문임</td></tr>
<tr><td>전환/요지</td><td>팽이가 우주에서 돌고 있다면 중심에서 벗어난 (천체) 축이 흔들림을 유발할 것임</td></tr>
</table>

구문

• Because the top is spinning, you can think of [that force **being deflected** horizontally], [making the top slowly wobble].
: 첫 번째 [ ]는 of의 목적어인 동명사구이고 that force는 being deflected의 의미상 주어이다. '방향이 바뀌다'라는 수동의 의미이므로 being deflected가 사용되었다. 두 번째 [ ]는 주절에 이어지는 내용을 나타내는 분사구문이다.

08　　　　　　　　　　　　　　　정답 ②

지난 몇 년 동안, 배를 만드는 사람들이 큰 배를 만들려고 계획을 세우고 있었을 때, 그들은 선원들의 생명과 화물의 안전이 그 배의 큰 돛대에 달려 있다는 것을 알고 있었다. 큰 돛대를 만들기 위해서, 그들은 해안 근처의 산꼭대기에 있는 곧고 큰 나무를 찾고 했다. 그다음에 그들은 그것이 바다로부터 불어 닥치는 성난 바람과 강력한 돌풍의 온전한 힘에 노출되도록 그 주위의 다른 모든 나무들을 잘라 내곤 했다. 그런 거친 상태에 수년 동안 노출된 후에, 그 나무는 점점 더 강해지곤 했는데, 그것이 매일같이 경험하고 있던 강렬한 난타에 의해 나무의 바로 그 섬유질이 강화된 것이었다. 마침내, 산꼭대기에서 홀로 힘겨운 많은 폭풍우를 거친 후에, 그 나무는 큰 배의 큰 돛대로 안심하고 맡겨질 준비가 되었다.

➡ 오랫동안 역경에 노출되는 것이 나무를 큰 배의 큰 돛대로 사용될 수 있을 때까지 강하게 만든다.

해설

큰 배의 큰 돛대가 되기 위해서는 곧고 큰 나무가 산꼭대기에서 홀로 성난 바람과 강력한 돌풍에 노출되면서 점점 더 강해져야 한다는 내용의 글이므로, 요약문의 빈칸 (A)에는 adversity(역경)가, (B)에는 strong(강하게)이 들어가는 것이 가장 적절하다.

① 온기 – 유연하게
③ 가혹함 – 부드럽게
④ 풍족함 – 강력하게
⑤ 무관심 – 견딜 수 있게

TEXT FLOW

도입	큰 배의 큰 돛대에 선원들의 생명과 화물의 안전이 달려 있음
전개	큰 돛대를 만들 알맞은 나무를 산꼭대기에서 찾아, 성난 바람과 강풍에 노출되도록 주위 나무를 모두 잘라 냄
결론	산꼭대기에서 오랫동안 많은 폭풍우에 노출된 후에 나무가 강해져서 큰 돛대로 쓰일 준비를 마침

구문

• Then they would cut down all the other trees around it [**so that** it would be exposed to the full force of the angry winds and mighty gusts that blew off the sea].

: [ ]는 '(주어가) ~할 수 있도록'이라는 의미의 「so that+주어+동사」 구문이 쓰인 부사절이다.

하프 모의고사 01회

A

01 확인하다 **02** 차별하다 **03** 원근법; 관점 **04** 영역 **05** 수요가 많은, 인기 있는 **06** 고용하다 **07** 상호 작용 **08** 회의론자 **09** 전통적인 **10** 타당성, 정당성 **11** 농도, 밀도 **12** 변동(성) **13** 견디다, 참다 **14** 권위 있는 **15** 모으다; 편찬하다 **16** 사망자 **17** 조정하다 **18** 악화, 퇴보 **19** 평판 **20** 비참한

B

01 privileges **02** intuitions **03** endure
04 ensure **05** impulsive

하프 모의고사 02회

A

01 조심스러운 **02** 관대한 **03** 행동, 행위 **04** 특성 **05** 저항(력) **06** 노력 **07** 걸작 **08** 흐름, 유동 **09** 변형하다 **10** 사라진, 멸종된 **11** 기만 **12** 납득시키다 **13** 예산 **14** 탐닉하다 **15** 가설 **16** 가늠하다, 평가하다 **17** 하고 싶어 하지 않는, 마지못해서 하는 **18** 오작동하다 **19** 비어 있는 **20** 보살피다

B

01 encircling **02** imprinted **03** cited
04 stimuli **05** procedure

하프 모의고사 03회

A

01 팽창 **02** 수정, 조정 **03** 혁신하다 **04** 번창하다 **05** 선도하다, 개척하다 **06** 억누르기, 억압 **07** 비옥한 **08** 번성하다 **09** 쓰다, 구성하다 **10** 변장한 **11** 정당화하다 **12** 필수적인, 의무적인 **13** ~을 갖추고 있는 **14** 탐색 과정, 탐구 **15** (좌우) 대칭적인 **16** 대단히 중요한 **17** 상업 **18** 선행하다 **19** 비롯되다 **20** ~보다 우월한

B

01 assumes **02** revealed **03** contracted
04 successive **05** alter

하프 모의고사 04회

A

01 나머지 **02** 숨을 내쉬다 **03** 과소평가하다 **04** 축적 **05** 산산조각이 난 **06** 비율 **07** 수용 **08** 주변의, 부근의 **09** 충분한 공간을 제공하다, 수용하다 **10** 기뻐하다 **11** 불신 **12** 인식 **13** 회의적인 **14** 외부의 **15** 갑자기 ~하다 **16** 재개하다 **17** 돌연변이 **18** 왜곡 **19** A로 B를 대신하다 **20** ~에 의존하는

B

01 converted **02** deters **03** ills
04 reciprocal **05** dispersed

하프 모의고사 05회

A

01 현대의, 당대의 **02** 징후, 암시 **03** 논쟁하다; 논쟁 **04** 숭배하다 **05** 전진하다 **06** 전도, 도치 **07** 대화; 교환 **08** 관계, 관련 **09** 명상 **10** 사멸 **11** 바치다 **12** 관련 **13** 공평한 **14** 밀집하여 **15** 간과 **16** 특별히 포함하다, 특징으로 삼다 **17** 별개의 **18** 활성화하다 **19** 생각하다, 존중하다 **20** 결국 ~하게 되다

B

01 statistics **02** static **03** exposure
04 obscure **05** dominant

하프 모의고사 06회

A

01 영역, 영토 **02** ~을 계속하다 **03** (결과 따위를) 내다, 산출하다 **04** 평행의; 평행선, 평행면 **05** 총체의, 전체의 **06** 추구하다 **07** 가설을 세우다 **08** 정당한; 합법적인 **09** 탐구, 연구 **10** 왜곡하다 **11** 침범, 방해, 침입 **12** 중단시키다, 혼란시키다 **13** 전례가 없는 **14** 보급, 확산 **15** 적응의 **16** 위협적인 **17** 유전 **18** 승리를 거둔 **19** ~ 이전에 **20** ~와는 반대로

B

01 incorporated **02** extracted **03** artifact
04 phenomenon **05** paralyze

A

01 회계사 02 협력적인 03 외치다 04 관료제 05 흡수
06 수동으로 07 차원, 치수 08 고갈, 소모 09 (기회를) 붙잡다
10 생겨나다, 나타나다 11 인지적인 12 대체물 13 광범위한
14 국한시키다 15 상당한, 중요한 16 이야기하다, 서술하다 17 강
조하다 18 ~을 위해서 19 ~과 더불어 20 ~을 제외하고

B

01 rational 02 inhibit 03 experimenting
04 Transmission 05 retention

A

01 참담한 02 부족한, 적은 03 배포하다 04 매혹시키다 05 지
위 06 자격을 갖춘 07 독립한, 자율적인 08 기준 09 적응시키
다, 적응하다 10 침입 11 방해하다 12 정의하다 13 지속 가능한
14 은인 15 노출하다 16 파괴 17 발굴자 18 헛된, 소용없는
19 장애물 20 깜짝 놀란

B

01 subscription 02 prescription 03 distress
04 override 05 encoded

A

01 자금 조달, 모금 02 신생 기업 03 조정하다, 변경하다 04 비
유적인 05 정당화하다 06 외교술 07 보증금 08 논란, 논쟁
09 주거지 10 권위 11 혼란 12 실행 13 경쟁의 14 잠재적인
15 결정 요소 16 주제넘은 17 훈육하다 18 계획하다, 고안하다
19 비유 20 갈망하다

B

01 stereotypical 02 balance 03 edible
04 alternative 05 abuse

A

01 여행 일정표 02 관련성; 친밀감 03 분자의 04 착각, 환상
05 복제하다 06 포식자 07 지나친 08 정교함 09 비참한
10 보호, 보존 11 재산 12 간섭, 참견 13 나아지다 14 묘사하다

15 악담을 퍼붓다 16 차별 17 포용적인 18 인과 관계 19 황폐
시키다, 유린하다 20 신체 장애인

B

01 denial 02 counterparts 03 vocation
04 nestled 05 resolving

A

01 후원하다 02 박수를 보내다 03 인지하다, 지각하다 04 개별의
05 비일률적인 06 구성 요소, 재료 07 배출 08 결핍, 궁핍
09 자서전 10 강화하다 11 사라지다 12 혜택, 이득 13 싹이 나
다 14 속박하다, 구속하다 15 감지하다, 간파하다 16 알아차리다,
파악하다 17 기준 18 불필요한, 여분의 19 지속하다 20 숙고

B

01 utter 02 contributed 03 literally
04 bluffer 05 confronted

A

01 (꽉) 움켜잡다 02 성숙하다 03 분해되다 04 냄새 05 신
청자 06 서명 07 인식하다 08 격노 09 ~을 뽐내다[자랑하다]
10 민간의 11 반박하다, 비난하다 12 생물 다양성 13 억울하다고
여기다, 분개하다 14 동일시 15 유대를 형성하다 16 기본이 되는
17 장애물 18 흡수하다 19 위험 20 항체

B

01 mumbled 02 excrement 03 monopolies
04 accumulated 05 hesitate

A

01 난민 02 가혹한, 모진 03 측정하다 04 이루다, 도달하다
05 유발하다 06 분류하다 07 농촌의, 시골의 08 적절한 09 경
시, 무시 10 구축하다, 함양하다 11 애착, 지지 12 구별하다
13 인공의, 인위적인 14 저장 15 입증하다 16 합병 17 통화의,
금전의 18 물러나다 19 A를 B로 보다[칭하다] 20 ~에 굴복하다

B

01 resistant 02 predictable 03 components
04 suburban 05 turmoil

A

01 진단   02 자신감, 확신   03 포기하다, 버리다   04 식물   05 방출, 배출   06 포용하다, 받아들이다   07 똑같은, 동일한   08 존재하다   09 매우 큰, 중요한   10 발언, 언급   11 논란이 되는   12 정제하다   13 행사, 때   14 분쟁   15 (단호하게) 자기 주장을 하다   16 종속적인   17 분명히   18 ~에 대처하다   19 ~을 당연하게 여기다   20 ~을 초과하여

B

01 adversity   02 assessments   03 critical
04 sufficient   05 oblivious

A

01 퇴직, 은퇴   02 요인   03 유전적인   04 결과   05 (사회) 진화론   06 버리다, 포기하다   07 먹이   08 연대기   09 합의   10 상호의   11 객관적인   12 선동, 동요   13 모방   14 결정하다   15 쓸모없는   16 실험실; 실험(실)용의   17 문제가 되지 않는   18 전달하다, 전하다   19 ~을 따라잡다   20 전달하다, 넘겨주다

B

01 appreciation   02 deficient   03 Indigenous
04 deprivation   05 root

A

01 침식시키다   02 고갈시키다   03 마찰   04 우선하다   05 식민지   06 복지   07 의제   08 직경   09 평가하다   10 단호함   11 소비   12 잉여(물)   13 의무   14 정교한   15 치료   16 공격적인   17 말이 없는   18 정맥   19 뒤얽히다, 엮다   20 편견

B

01 acquaintance   02 anticipate   03 dominance
04 evokes   05 hospitality

A

01 짜다, 짜서 만들다   02 특허   03 원시의   04 일관성   05 줄어들다   06 관습에 얽매이지 않는   07 이직(률)   08 부과하다   09 사각지대, 맹점   10 설득력 있는   11 저장고   12 정량화하다   13 분해   14 사육사   15 우연히 마주치다   16 궁극적인   17 가능성   18 중립적인   19 추측하다   20 충동

B

01 regulate   02 embody   03 contemplation
04 scrutinize   05 plausible

A

01 자기 성찰   02 입자   03 강조하다   04 통근(하다)   05 기분 전환이 되는   06 순전한   07 판결   08 합헌의   09 제출하다   10 해석   11 확고하게, 단호하게   12 양육, 가정 교육   13 위엄   14 상호성   15 거주하다   16 연관시키다   17 성향   18 고무하다   19 인류학자   20 명망 있는

B

01 *perception*   02 strengthens   03 startling
04 manifestation   05 deterioration

A

01 장기의; 늘어난   02 위협하다   03 대체하다   04 의심하다   05 친밀감   06 차별화하다, 구별하다   07 중대한   08 민감성   09 필수품   10 청소년기   11 완화하다   12 깨지기 쉬운, 연약한   13 비정상적인   14 전제   15 아주 흥미로운   16 접수하다; 인계받다

17 결코 ~이 아닌   **18** ~을 이용하다, ~에 접근하다   **19** 결론, 최종 결과   **20** ~에 부수적인

B

01 transition   **02** inevitable   **03** stereotype
04 consistent   **05** attributes

고난도 모의고사 05회

A

01 타협하다   **02** 지시 사항   **03** 파생물   **04** 제도, 관례   **05** 방어
06 추진력, 여세   **07** 항의하다   **08** 회전하다, 돌리다; 회전   **09** (쿡) 찌르다; (쿡) 찌름   **10** 복잡한   **11** 의식적인   **12** 타고난, 내장된
13 할당하다   **14** 농도   **15** 일시적으로 머무르는   **16** ~에 적응되다
17 방해하다   **18** (사람들에게) 알려지다[밝혀지다]   **19** (양이) 누적되다, 쌓이다   **20** ~에 노출되다

B

01 intense   **02** substances   **03** vertical
04 progress   **05** flipping

MEMO